The Electronic Publisher

Diane Burns
S. Venit
Rebecca Hansen

Brady
New York

Copyright © 1988 by Diane Burns and S. Venit
All rights reserved,
including the right of reproduction
in whole or in part in any form.

BRADY

Simon & Schuster, Inc.
Gulf + Western Building
One Gulf + Western Plaza
New York, NY 10023

Distributed by Prentice Hall Trade
Manufactured in the United States of America
1   2   3   4   5   6   7   8   9   10

Library of Congress Cataloging-in-Publication Data

Burns, Diane.
    The electronic publisher / Diane Burns and Sharyn
Venit with Rebecca Hansen.
    p. cm.
    Bibliography: p.
    Includes index.
    1. Desktop publishing.   2. Electronic publishing.
 I. Venit, Sharyn.   II. Hansen, Rebecca.   III. Title.
Z286.D47B86   1988
686.2'2—dc19   88-21938
                                                               CIP

ISBN 0-13-251877-5

Table of Contents
The Electronic Publisher

Preface ix

Introduction 1

Significance of Desktop Publishing 2 / Availability of Typefaces 4 / Ability to Merge Text and Graphics 5 / High Resolution Printers 6 / Low-Cost Equipment 8 / **The "Melting Pot" Effect** 8 / Typesetting Traditions 8 / Design Traditions 9 / Printing Traditions 9 / Computer Traditions 10 / **Desktop Publishing Software** 11 / Page-Composition Applications 11 / Page-Composition and Word Processors 12 / Page-Composition and Graphics Programs 13 / Anatomy of a Document 13 / **System Configurations** 14 / Computer and Memory 15 / Hard Disk Storage 15 / Monitors 16 / Scanners 16 / Output Devices 17 / Modems 18 / Workgroup Networks 18 / **Summary** 19

PART 1. The Publisher's Task 21

Chapter 1. The Publishing Cycle 23

Division of Responsibilities 24 / The Publisher 24 / The Managing Editor 25 / The Author(s) 26 / The Designer 27 / The Illustrator and Photographer 28 / The Expert Reader 28 / The Copy Editor 29 / The Production Manager 29 / The Proofreader 30 / The Spec Editor 30 / The Typesetter 31 / The Layout Artist 32 / The Cameraman 32 / The Printer 33 / The Binder 33 / **Steps in the Production Process** 33 / Proposal or Project Definition 36 / Gathering the Team 38 / Writing 39 / First Revision 40 / Copy Editing 42 / Text Processing 42 / Design 43 / Typesetting 44 / Illustration 45 / Page Composition 46 / Printing and Binding 46 / Distribution 47 / Archive Master Files and Boards 47 / **The Battle Between Quality, Economy, and Deadline** 47 / **Summary** 48

Chapter 2. Copyrights, Credits, Permissions, and Contracts   51

Copyright Agreements 51 / Books 53 / Work Made for Hire 54
Periodicals 55 / Reports 55 / Promotional Materials 56
Contributions 56 / Digitized Artwork, Photographs, and Video
Images 57 / **Copyright Waived or Inapplicable** 58 / Public
Domain and Expired Copyrights 58 / Fair Use: Short Excerpts from
Published Works 59 / Paraphrasing 59 / Interviews 59
Publication Design 60 / Images of People and Characters 60
"Influence" vs. Infringment 60 / Ideas and Inventions 62
Permissions and Credits 62 / When and How to Credit 63
Trademarks 63 / **Trade Secrets** 64 / **Contracts** 64
Summary 67

PART 2. Design for Desktop Systems   69

Chapter 3. Typography   71

The Language of Type 72 / What is a Font? 72 / Outline and Bit-mapped Fonts 80 / **Using Fonts in Desktop Publishing** 82
Adding Screen Fonts and Printer Fonts 82 / Printer Fonts 83
Printing a Font 87 / **Design Considerations** 89 / Assemble the
Font List 89 / Follow Basic Principles 92 / Characteristics of
Different Typefaces 97 / Factors in Mixing Typefaces 104 / Line
Length 106 / Alignment 107 / Line Spacing or Leading 108
Expanding or Condensing Type 111 / Kerning Headlines and Titles
111 / Special Treatment of Initial Letters 114 / Special Handling of
Figure Labels and Captions 116 / **Copy Casting** 116 / Using a
Type-Casting Reference Book or Gauge 118 / Preparing Dummy
Pages of Greek Text 119 / A Quick Rough Estimate 121
Summary 122

Chapter 4. Publication Design   123

Principles of Design 124 / Think About What You Want Before You
Do It! 125 / Enforce Consistency 125 / Use A Grid System 127
Pay Attention to the Balance Between Facing Pages 129 / Text On
Each Page Should Bottom Out to Margin 129 / Use White Space to

Give the Eye a Break 130 / Use Graphics in a Meaningful Way 132
Differentiate Figure Captions from Body Text 132 / Use Ruled Lines
or Gray Screens to Differentiate Parts of a Document or Page 133
Use Headers and Footers as Reference Aids 134 / Use Only a Few
Fonts on a Page 135 / Use Larger Point Sizes for Longer Text Line
Lengths 135 / Be Simple 135 / **Using Electronic Aids in Design**
136 / Identify the Capabilities of the System 136 / Identify the
Essential Elements of the Publication 138 / Create Design
Alternatives 140 / Define the Final Specifications for the
Publication 141 / **Creating a Template System** 143 / Benefits of
Using Templates 144 / Components of a Template System 146
Specifications for Programs Other than the Page-Layout Package
162 / Testing the Design and Templates 163 / **Consider the Genre**
164 / Magazines, Tabloids, and Newsletters 164 / Reports and
Proposals 169 / Price Lists, Catalogues, and Directories 171
Brochures, Flyers, and Display Ads 171 / Tables, Charts, and
Overhead Transparencies 174 / **Summary** 177

PART 3. Production   179

Chapter 5. Text Processing   181

Typing Text Directly 182 / List of Standards 182 / Proofreading
Text 184 / Proofreader's Marks 185 / Typesetting Codes 187
Preparing Disk Files 188 / Telecommunication or Conversion 188
Cleanup: Spaces, Tabs, Carriage Returns, Quotemarks, and Dashes
189 / Determine the Minimum Number of Ruler Line Settings 191
Glossaries and Spelling Checkers 193 / Hyphenation 193 / Other
Aids for Editors 194 / Special Handling of Data Formats 194
Typesetting Text: Character and Paragraph Formatting 198
Method 1: Marked Copy 201 / Method 2: Embedded Codes 202
Method 3: Hidden Codes 203 / Method 4: Style Sheets 203
Method 5: Context Coding 204 / Coding for Special Characters 205
Copyfitting Text 208 / **Proofreading Typeset Text** 208
Indentation 209 / Paragraph Spacing 209 / Alignment 209
Hyphenation 210 / Widows and Orphans 210 / Word and Letter
Spacing 210 / Look for Kerning Opportunities 210 /
Summary 211

Chapter 6. Illustrations   213

Graphics Equipment 214 / Graphics Monitors 214 / Mice and Graphics Tablets 214 / Digitizers or Scanners 215 / Graphics Printers 215 / **Sources of Graphics** 216 / Bit-mapped Graphics 217 / Scanned Images 219 / Object-Oriented Graphics 222 / Encapsulated PostScript Formats 224 / **Graphics Design Principles** 225 / Organize the Information 226 / Create Focal Points 226 / Use Contrast and Asymmetry to Create Visual Tension 226 / Maintain Spatial Continuity 226 / Do Not Overannotate 227 / Condense Format 228 / Simplify Titles 228 / Choose Images that Suit the Final Paper Quality 228 / **Graphics Production Techniques** 229 / Enforce Consistency 229 / Use a Grid System 230 / Use Commands to Align Objects 230 / Special Handling of Figure Labels and Captions 231 / Monitor the Complexity of the Illustrations 233 / Tabular Data As Artwork 235 / Keep Artwork Clean 236 / Test Gray Shades Before Finalizing the Design Specifications 236 / Use Photographic Reduction to Improve Images 237 / Allow Time for Image Retouching 237 / Scale Images Proportionally 241 / Establish Naming Conventions 243 / **Graphics Templates** 244 / The Ruler 245 / The Pen 245 / Lettering Guides 246 / Spacing Guides 247 / Repeating Symbols 249 / The Grid Structure 249 / A Scaling System 250 / **Proofing Graphics** 250 / **Summary** 251

Chapter 7. Page Composition   253

Assess Your Needs 255 / Magazines, Tabloids, and Newsletters 255 / Business Reports, Books, and Manuals 259 / Price Lists, Catalogues, and Directories 260 / Brochures, Flyers, and Display Ads 260 / Tables, Charts, and Overhead Transparencies 262 / **Organize Disk Files** 263 / File-Naming Conventions 263 / Hard Disk Directories 263 / Optimum File Size 265 / Backup and Archive System 268 / Font Library 270 / **Create a Template for Page Layout** 270 / Defining the Page Setup 271 / **Building Master Pages** 279 / Create a Master Grid 281 / Headers and Footers 284 / Adding Graphic Elements 285 / **Create Individual Page Layouts** 286 / Methods of Operation 286 / Change Grid As Necessary on Individual Pages 289 / Use the Snap-to Effect 289

TABLE OF CONTENTS

Use Alignment Commands 290 / Force Left and Right Pages 290 / Position Text 291 / Import Graphics 293 / Full Color Page Makeup 299 / **Copy Fitting** 300 / Edit the Copy 301 / Allow a Ragged-Bottom Margin 301 / Add Fillers 301 / Adjust the Leading (Line Spacing) 302 / Hyphenation and Justification 303 / Word and Letter Spacing 304 / **Printing** 305 / Type of Printer 305 / Test Printing a Few Pages 306 / Downloading Fonts Permanently vs. Temporarily 307 / Number of Pages, Reverse Order, and Collated Sets 308 / Thumbnails and Crop Marks 309 / Printing Large or Small Page Sizes 310 / Print Spoolers 312 / **Proofreading** 312 **Summary** 313

PART 4. Beyond the Desktop 315

Chapter 8. Preparing for the Printer 317

Final Pages or "Camera-Ready" Masters 319 / Laser-Printed or Typeset Masters 319 / Mechanicals 323 / What Should a Mechanical Contain? 325 / Decide on the Level of Effort 326 **Line Art and Halftones vs. Continuous Tone Art** 327 / Making Your Own Halftones 331 / Purchasing Halftone Veloxes 336 / Letting Your Printer Create Halftones for You 337 / **Marking an Image for Special Handling** 340 / Scaling and Cropping an Image 340 / Special Effects in Image Placement 344 / Flat-tone Screens 348 / Image Retouching 352 / **Putting It All Together—Complete Mechanicals** 354

Chapter 9. Preparing for Color Printing 357

Spot Color vs. Process Color 358 / **Preparing for Spot-Color Printing** 359 / Marking for Solid Spot Color 359 / Complex Spot Color—Traps and Butts 365 / Spot Tints: Flat-Tone-Screened Spot Color 368 / Duotones: Halftone-Screened Spot Color 368 / Screened Process Color as Match Color 369 / **Preparing Four-Color Process Images** 371 / Color Separation 372 / **Color Correction** 374 / Who Should Make Separations? 375 / Making Your Own Separations 376 / Working with Your Printer to get the Best Possible Separations 379 / Other Alternatives 380 / **Proofing for Color** 381 / Press Proofs 382 / Film-Based Proofs 382

Direct-Digital Proofs 383 / Soft Proofs: On-Screen Color Proofing 384 / How to Judge a Separation Proof 385 / **A Note on Color Transparencies** 386 / Printing on a Color Printer 386 / Adding Color with Ink 387 / Adding Color Overlays 388

Chapter 10. Printing and Binding — 389

How to Select a Printer 390 / How Much Does Printing Cost? 390 Getting Quotes 392 / Judging Bids and Making a Decision 393 **What Does the Printer Do with Your Mechanical?** 395 Stripping 395 / Imposition 396 / Page Proofs 399 / Color Keys 400 / Platemaking 401 / **When You're On-Press** 403 / Checking the Press Sheet 405 / **Printing** 406 / Types of Printing Presses 408 / Inks 413 / Papers 414 / **Postpress Production** 418 Folding 418 / Embossing and Die-Cutting 418 / Binding 420 **Checking the Delivery** 423

Glossary — 425

Index — 451

Preface

Electronic publishing is not a new term. It has been evolving over the past 30 years, as typesetting technology has evolved from pouring hot lead into letter-casting forms to using computer technology to create type as electronic charges on photosensitive paper. What *is* new is that the equipment required for typesetting has dropped in price from over $100,000 to less than $10,000, inaugurating a new age of desktop publishing that brings direct control of production closer to the editorial and design departments.

The full sequence of steps in producing "camera-ready" pages after a manuscript is written has traditionally required the skills of several different people: the designer, the typesetter, the illustrator, the copy editor, the cameraman, and the paste-up artist. Now, desktop publishing makes it possible for the same person to author the words, draw the graphics, and compose the pages directly on the screen using a page layout package. With electronic publishing, the one person responsible for the entire production might be strong in some of these skills, weak in others. For this reason, many desktop publishing departments will divide the tasks of desktop publishing between different people. Even with some division of labor, when the production team is small (as is common in "desktop" environments) there can still be weak spots in the overall expertise of the team. This book will help you by providing the necessary information about all phases of publishing, providing inside tips from areas of expertise that you and your team might lack.

Purpose of This Book

The Electronic Publisher brings together the knowledge and experience that has been accumulated through four disciplines: project management, design, typesetting, and computer processing. This book is intended to help readers who have experience in none or only one of these fields to understand the overall process of electronic publishing. The information here will help designers understand how computers can be used in designing publications, and how to develop designs that make the best use of the computer's capabilities. It will also reveal the mysteries of typography to those who in the past have handled business documents that were not typeset, and it will help typesetters understand the possibilities and limitations of typesetting with a personal computer and laser printer. This book shows what is possible for illustrators using the drawing and painting packages that are supported by most page layout applications, and offers tips for electronic page layout artists in creating master grids and in positioning text and graphics on each page efficiently (as well as aesthetically).

This book will help you identify the different types of programs used in desktop publishing, understand the basic vocabulary associated with desktop publishing applications, identify the possible sources of text and graphics in any document produced using desktop publishing applications, determine your own software needs, and update your current designs and production procedures to take advantage of the capabilities of electronic publishing systems.

How to Use This Book

You can use this book as a text to study all aspects of electronic publishing, or you can use it as a reference to help answer specific questions or to plan your approach to a particular task.

The Electronic Publisher is divided into four sections. Each section concentrates on issues that are usually the concern of one of the four "department" managers in a publishing effort: the project manager, the designer, the *desktop (computer)* production manager, and the *mechanical (paste up)* production manager. In fact, these four functions might be served by the same person, or the functions we have divided into these four groups might actually be shared by more than four people or departments. The following descriptions of each section will help you determine which chapters contain information that relates to your own immediate needs.

INTRODUCTION

The introduction provides an overview of desktop publishing and offers some examples of how it is being used by a wide range of businesses.

PART 1 • THE PUBLISHER'S TASK

The tools now available to desktop publishers make it possible to shorten some of the steps in the production cycle and to eliminate other steps entirely, thereby reducing overall costs.

Chapter 1, The Production Cycle, presents an overview of the steps in the process of producing a document—from inception to final printed matter—including a description of the roles of the players in each step and suggestions for estimating the time and money required per step. Whether you are producing a glossy magazine, a mass-market paperback, a high school textbook, an in-house newsletter, or a project report—whether you are working with a team of two or twenty—your document requires some attention to each of the steps and roles defined here.

Chapter 2, Credits, Contracts, Rights & Permissions, describes the conditions under which credits or permissions to reprint are required, as well as the procedures involved in protecting newly published material from being used by another publisher without the appropriate consent. Examples of Copyright Statements (as printed on the copyright page of published documents), Permission to Reprint, Contract between an Author and a Publisher, and a Contract between a Publisher and an Illustrator are included.

PART 2 • DESIGN FOR DESKTOP SYSTEMS

Traditionally, there has been a distinct break between the writing/editing steps and the design process in producing any publication. The writer had no idea what the final pages would look like, and the designers did not care in what form the text and illustrations were delivered, so long as they were complete and clear. The designer would then set up specifications for the page layout, including type specifications, and mark up the stack of typewritten pages and penciled sketches for the typesetter and illustrator. The stages were distinct because the players and the tools used at each stage were different. Now it is possible for the writer to participate in the design and production if the design function is performed early enough in the cycle.

Chapter 3, Typography, includes a brief history of typography—the design of letters and the methods of composing pages—and describes the differences between low-end laser printers and high-end typesetting equipment. Examples of the most commonly used typefaces are shown, with tips on how they are combined in good design. The pica/point system of measurement is also explained in this section.

Chapter 4, Publication Design, presents an overview of the basic elements of a page, which the designer usually defines, and shows the relationship between the traditional methods and the methods available with computers. If you are familiar with the capabilities of your equipment and software, you can develop designs that are both aesthetically pleasing and conducive to efficient production.

PART 3 • PRODUCTION

Traditionally, production begins after the writing and design steps are complete. When the tools of desktop publishing are used, the production considerations described in part 3 of this book can extend over the whole life of the project.

Chapter 5, Text Processing, outlines the steps involved in preparing text for typesetting and formatting, whether the manuscript is provided as hard copy or on disk. The difference between using WYSIWYG (What-You-See-Is-What-You-Get) typesetting programs vs. typesetting codes is discussed. This section also discusses methods of handling special characters that are not part of the character sets available for standard fonts, and how data can be taken from a spreadsheet or a database and formatted into special documents or forms. For example, membership directories and membership renewal forms; price lists and price tags; exhibit catalogues and display descriptions; corporate phone directories and name tags, etc.

Chapter 6, Illustrations, presents an overview of the different types of programs, printers/plotters and scanning devices available for creating camera-ready graphics such as tables, charts, diagrams, line art, and scanned images. Examples of different computer-generated graphics are shown along with the name of the program used and the estimated time to produce the graphic.

Chapter 7, Page Composition, opens with a general discussion of traditional layout and paste-up procedures vs. electronic page composition. Steps and guidelines for page composition are given for text-and-graphics page composition systems, which are, to some extent, WYSIWYG (i.e., you can see the full page layouts on the screen, including graphics). Tips on using text-only typesetting programs, which produce galleys of text, are offered in Chapter 5.

Chapter 7 also presents general guidelines for the treatment of books, manuals and reports, newsletters and magazines. Key issues that cross all these categories of page composition programs—such as kerning, automatic hyphenation, mock-ups, and thumbnails—are also covered.

PART 4 • BEYOND THE DESKTOP

Chapter 8, Preparing for the Printer, includes a discussion of the different types of hardware—laser printers and phototypesetters—available for producing camera-ready pages or page elements, including consideration of the difference between page proofs and camera-ready copy. The chapter also details the extra steps involved in preparing pages that include photographs, screening for grey shades, hand color separations, and bleeds.

Chapter 9, Preparing for Color Printing, describes the capabilities of graphics and page-composition applications that support color, and it also describes the offset printer's techniques for handling color separations. This chapter includes a description of the types of color printers available, and explains why color printers are used for proofs rather than final copy in most cases.

Chapter 10, Printing and Binding, presents an overview of the steps in the reproduction and binding process along with guidelines for selecting the type of paper and method of binding. Camera work, negatives, and plates are described, and systems that will produce plates directly from disk files are reviewed. Other topics in this chapter include: Signatures, Cover vs. Body, Camera-Work & Plates, Printing Equipment, Paper Quality, Ink Types, and Binding Methods.

APPENDICES

The Glossary includes terms from the design, typesetting, and printing trades as well as terms from the computer industry as they relate to electronic publishing.

Acknowledgements

This book would not have been possible without the help of the following individuals and corporations: Burt Gabriel (Simon & Schuster) for sustained enthusiasm and encouragement; Rosalie Stemer (San Francisco) and Joel Wecksell (Data Recording Systems, Inc.) for reading selected chapters; Wendy Terry (Portfolio, Boston), Gerald M. Rapp, Rob Haimes, and Donna Schenkel for valuable tips; Shana Penn (Schiavo, San Francisco), Edward Boudreau (Scitex America Corp.), Jessica Collett (AGFA-GAVAERT), Mary Codd (coddbarrett, Boston), Wayne Earl (Heidelberg Eastern, Inc.), Eli Barry (Visual Graphics Corporation), and Theresa Marcroft (Networked Picture Systems, Inc.) for slides or photographs used as illustrations; Leticia, Sam, Tony, Ann, Kim, and Denise for computer artwork; Kay and Leigh for word processing support; and Grace and Laura for all the rest.

Special thanks to Brad Bunnin, Attorney at Law (Berkeley, CA) for his contributions to Chapter 2 on copyright law.

This book was produced by TechArt San Francisco using Macintosh computers, a Microtek 300A scanner, LaserWriter printers, and a Linotronic 300 typesetter. Software used to create these pages includes Microsoft Word, PageMaker 3.0, Adobe Illustrator '88, MacDraw and ImageStudio.

Limits of Liability and Disclaimer of Warranty

The author and publisher of this book have used their best efforts in preparing this book and the program contained in it. These efforts include the development, research, and testing of the theories and programs to determine their effectiveness. The author and publisher make no warranty of any kind, expressed or implied, with regard to these programs or the documentation contained in this book. The author and publisher shall not be liable in any event for incidental or consequential damages in connection with or arising out of, the furnishing, performance, or use these programs.

Trademarks

Adobe Illustrator™, Adobe Separator™ and PostScript™ are trademarks of Adobe Systems, Inc. • Apple®, LaserWriter®, and ImageWriter® are registered trademarks of Apple Computer, Inc. • ASCII™ is a trademark of United Software Industries, Inc. • AST TurboLaser™ is a trademark of AST Research. • AutoCAD™ is a trademark of Autodesk, Inc. • Bitstream® is a registered trademark of Bitstream, Inc. • Byline™ is a trademark and Ashton-Tate® is a registered trademark of Ashton-Tate Corp. • Clickart® is a registered trademark of the T/Maker Company. • Epson® is a registered trademark of Epson Corporation. • Freelance™, Lotus™, and 1-2-3™ are trademarks of Lotus Development Corp. • GEM™, GEM Draw™, GEM Graph™, GEM Desktop™ and GEM Paint™ are trademarks of Digital Research, Inc. • Hercules™ Graphics Card is a trademark of Hercules Computing Technology. • HP LaserJet™ and LaserJet™ Plus are trademarks of Hewlett-Packard Corp. • IBM® is a registered trademark and PC/AT™ is a trademark of International Business Machines Corp. • ImageStudio™, LetraStudio™, and Ready, Set, Go!™ are trademarks and Letraset® is a registered trademark of Letraset. • ITC American Typewriter™, ITC Avant Garde Gothic™, ITC Benguiat™, ITC Bookman™, ITC Galliard™, ITC Garamond™, ITC Korinna™, ITC Lubalin Graph™, ITC Machine™, ITC New Baskerville™, ITC Souvenir™, ITC Zapf Chancery™, and ITC Zapf Dingbats™ are trademarks of International Typeface Corporation. • JLaser™ is a trademark of Tall Tree Systems, Inc. • Linotype™ and Linotronic™ are trademarks, and Glypha®, Helvetica®, Melior®, Optima®, Palatino®, Times®, and Trump® are registered trademarks of Allied Corp. • MacDraw® and MacPaint® are registered trademarks of Claris Corporation. • 3M MatchPrint is a registered trademark of 3M Corp. • Mentor Graphics® is a registered trademark of Mentor Graphics Corp. • Microsoft®, Microsoft® Word, Microsoft® Windows, and MS-DOS® are registered trademarks of Microsoft Corp. and Windows Paint™ is a trademark of Microsoft Corp. • Microtek® is a registered trademark of Microtek International Inc. • NEC® is a registered trademark of Nippon Electric Corp. • NPS Image Express™ is a trademark of Networked Picture Systems, Inc. • PageMaker® and Snapshot® are registered trademarks of Aldus Corporation. • PANTONE® is a registered trademark of Pantone, Inc. • PC Paintbrush™ is a trademark of Z-Soft Corp. • QMS® is a registered trademark of QMS, Inc. • Quark™ XPress is a trademark of Quark, Inc. • SuperPaint® is a registered trademark of Silicon Beach Software. • Ventura Publisher™ is a trademark of Ventura Software, Inc.

Introduction

The impact of desktop publishing on professional publishers, corporate publications departments, and self-publishing associations and individuals is best seen through the experiences of those who have made the transition from traditional methods to electronic publishing over the past few years. A few anecdotes will help put this in perspective.

A well-known science fiction writer lives in Sri Lanka and writes his novels using a computer. He then telecommunicates the text to his publisher in New York, where the manuscript is printed out and edited. The author's disk files are edited directly on the publisher's computer and coded for typesetting before being telecommunicated to the typesetter.

Five years ago, a certain designer worked alone in his studio and produced all of the work for his clients using a drawing table, mechanical pens, rulers, triangles, T-squares, and tissue. Today, his growing design firm is staffed by seven desktop publishers and his tools include seven computers, a PostScript printer, a scanner, and a library of software programs.

A research firm commands between $10,000 and $20,000 for their customized reports on the efficiency of their clients' health programs. When the reports were printed in Courier on a letter-quality printer, they tended to be read by one or two representatives from the clients' firms and then summarized verbally in meetings with the rest of the decision-makers. When the research firm switched to desktop publishing for typeset-quality production, the readership more than doubled within each client's staff.

A national law firm was spending over $5,000 each month on typesetting a 16-page monthly newsletter to its corporate clients. More than half of the total typesetting charges were accumulated due to changes that the attorneys made to the text *after* the first version was already typeset. Last year the firm decided to purchase desktop publishing equipment and software in order to bring the typesetting function in-house and increase their control over the content. They cut their monthly expenses in half and extended the deadline for editorial changes by two days.

A regional telephone directory offers the service of designing and typesetting display ads for clients who advertise in the business listings. Sales representatives expected a two- or three-week turnaround on orders for "comps" of the ads using the traditional methods. After the directory company brought production of the ads in-house using desktop publishing equipment, the sales representatives got one-day turnaround on orders for comps and were able to modify the designs directly on the computer when their clients came in to preview the designs.

A single division of one major publishing house estimates a savings of about $250,000 on one series of science books alone. One small-press publisher estimates that her company saves several weeks and thousands of dollars on the production of each title by using desktop publishing. Others support the claim with savings that range from $2,000 to $6,000 for typesetting per title.

The benefits are not solely economic. Editors find that they have more control over content and format, designers can experiment more freely, and the time spent preparing books for printing has been reduced significantly. These stories may sound like the repertoire or anecdotes for a computer sales representative, but they are all actual experiences of using desktop publishing to produce materials that were previously produced using traditional methods.

Significance of Desktop Publishing

Why is desktop publishing so exciting? Because it offers a solution to one of the most critical issues confronting every organization today—namely, the need for more effective communications. Effective communications are critical because, in today's information-intensive economy, a company's performance depends largely on how it handles its most critical assets: people and information. People need timely access to accurate information to make the right decisions. And, to work together effectively, professionals need to communicate their ideas clearly, quickly, and with impact. The primary benefit of desktop publishing is that it affords more control—control over every phase of the process of creating professional documents—at a lower cost, and with greater quality and flexibility than ever before.

We can define desktop publishing as the use of a personal computer to incorporate a wide range of type styles and graphics in a document, make fine adjustments to the size of and spacing between the characters of the text, view and edit pages on a WYSIWYG (pronounced "wizzy-wig") screen display, and print the pages on a high-resolution laser printer or phototypesetter. The term "desktop publishing" did not exist four years ago. It was originally coined by Paul Brainerd, the president of Aldus Corporation and one of the designers of the PageMaker program. The term itself quickly caught on as a shorthand method of describing capabilities that are the combined results of four converging technologies:

INTRODUCTION

- First, the cost of microcomputer equipment has been falling, relative to the graphics processing capabilities of the systems.
- Second, new breakthroughs in laser technology have drastically reduced the price of high-resolution printers and typesetters that are capable of printing text in traditional and new typefaces.
- Third, special computer languages have been developed that give personal computers the ability to produce and manipulate type and graphics for page composition.
- And finally, software developers realized that the three factors just mentioned meant that they could create software applications to merge text and graphics directly on screen.

Due to these four developments, complete "publishing" systems can now be assembled at a revolutionary low price.

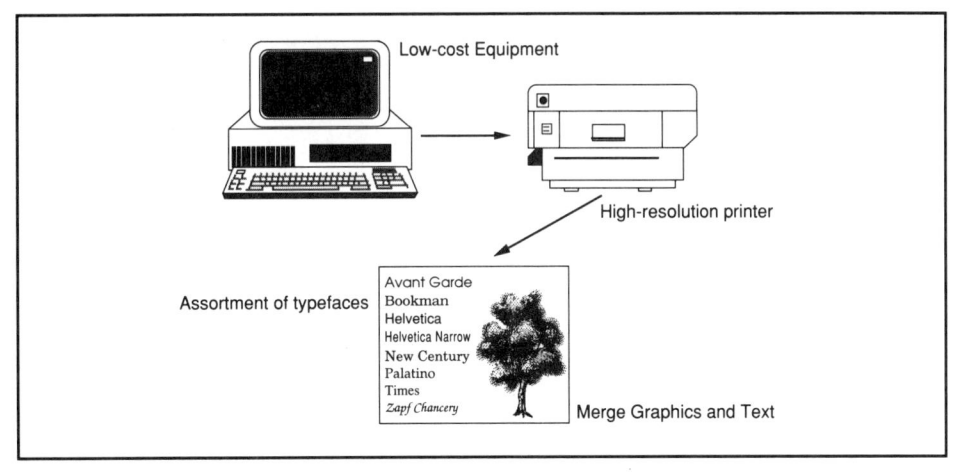

■ **Figure I.1** Essential elements of desktop publishing: Personal computer with graphics capabilities. High-resolution laser printer with a variety of typefaces. New page-layout applications.

This combination of capabilities, now dubbed desktop publishing, has a tremendous impact on typesetters, designers, professional publishers, corporate publications departments, and small businesses, as well as those of us who dream of producing our own great novels. As the interest in this new field has expanded, so has the confusion. If you are new to desktop publishing you will need to learn a new vocabulary of terms from the typesetting industry such as "font," "kerning," "leading," "picas," and "points." before you can distinguish between different desktop publishing products. You need to learn the differences between object-oriented (vector) graphics and bit-maps, and between screen fonts and printer fonts. To understand the significance of desktop publishing capabilities, you need to understand something about the traditions that are the roots of desktop publishing: typesetting, graphic design, printing, and computing.

AVAILABILITY OF TYPEFACES

A typeface is a set of characters (alphanumeric characters, punctuation marks, and symbols) that share the same design. Courier and Helvetica are two different typefaces, for instance. When we say that desktop publishing introduces a new, wide range of typefaces, we are comparing the selection to what was previously available in most office environments. Not so long ago, a typewriter had only one typeface—either pica or elite. More recently, you could change the typeface in your typewriter or your word processor's printer by changing the daisy wheel or type element, but each document tended to use only one typeface throughout—Courier, for example. Depending on the capabilities of your word processor, you could mix bold and normal characters on a page, but you couldn't mix normal and italic unless you could pause the printing and change the type element in the printer. Dot-matrix printers made it possible to mix normal, bold, and italic, and to print different sizes of letters, but the jaggedness of the low-resolution output was considered inferior to "letter quality" printers. (See Figure I.2)

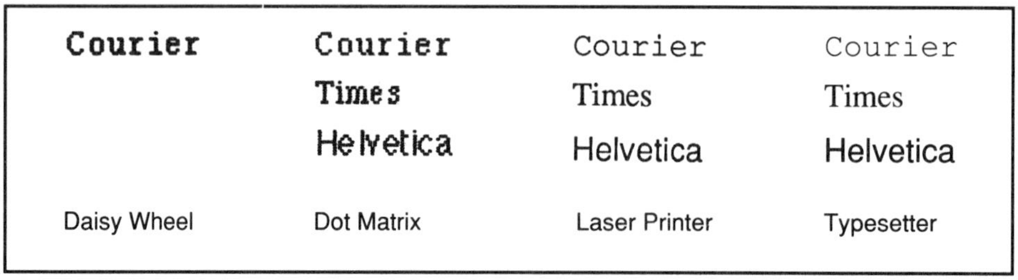

Courier	Courier	Courier	Courier
	Times	Times	Times
	Helvetica	Helvetica	Helvetica
Daisy Wheel	Dot Matrix	Laser Printer	Typesetter

■ **Figure I.2** Typefaces from a character printer, a dot matrix printer, and a laser printer.

Desktop publishing (with all its software and hardware components) makes it possible to print a variety of typefaces, styles, and sizes within a single document. The range of possibilities may vary between printers, but most laser printers offer a selection of more than the two options available with letter-quality printers (i.e., normal and bold text). There are still not as many typefaces available for desktop publishers as there are for professional typesetters, but new typefaces are daily being added to the list.

ABILITY TO MERGE TEXT AND GRAPHICS

The ability to merge text and graphics on a screen is not exactly new. Professional page-composition systems have been doing this for years. *Time* Magazine, for example, started composing its pages on a computer over 20 years ago. Time, Inc. paid over $250,000 for that system, however, while most publishers continued to use X-acto knives and wax to paste up their printed text and line art on boards. (See Figure I.3) (Today it is possible to invest $250,000 in the equipment for a full-service electronic publishing shop, but this investment is still low compared to what the $250,000 spent in 1968 would be in 1988 dollars.)

Meanwhile, microcomputer users have been able to produce text with their word processing programs, and graphics with their spreadsheets or drawing programs, but the output from these various programs was never merged on screen or on paper. Instead, business reports were assembled with all of the graphics in an appendix, for instance, or printed on pages without text and manually collated with the text pages. A few adventurous departments actually left spaces within the text and pasted the graphics in using scissors and glue.

■ **Figure I.3** Manual paste-up: Basic tools include a large clear surface, rulers, knives, pens, a waxer and a burnisher. Boards show blue lines of "grid" layout. Galleys of type are cut up and pasted down on the boards. Line art is sized photographically and pasted down. After all of the pages have been layed out, changes (edits) made to one page can force subsequent pages to be revised as well.

Now, page composition packages are available for microcomputers. These packages let you merge text from a word processor with graphics from a drawing program, and print out fully composed documents in one step, without paste up. (See Figure I.4) Moreover, with some page-composition packages you can actually see what the page will look like on the screen: it is a WYSIWYG system.

WYSIWYG means "what you see is what you get." In other words, you can actually see the graphics and the text on the screen exactly as they will appear on the printed page (with slight variations due to the difference in resolution between the screen and the printer). Only two such packages were available for the IBM PC before 1984, and these were priced over $5,000. Now there are packages available for both the IBM PC and the Macintosh computers for under $1,000.

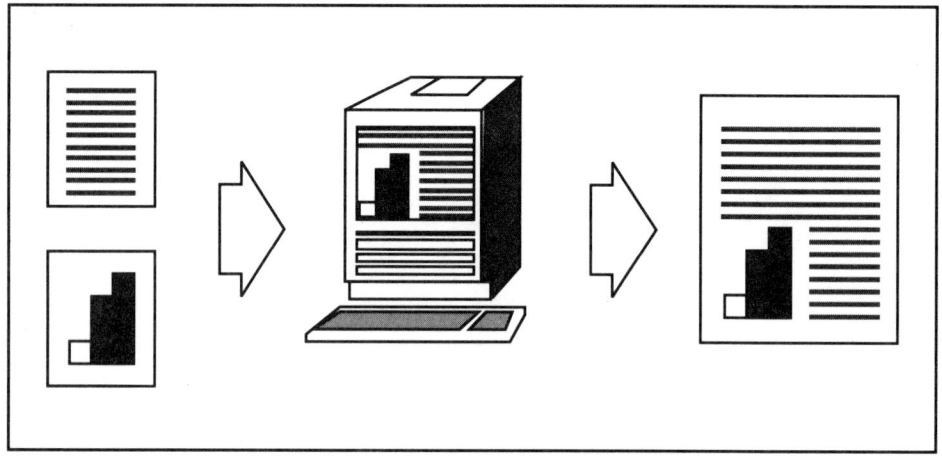

■ **Figure I.4** On-screen paste-up: Basic tool is the computer (with various programs) and a high-resolution printer. A page-layout package incorporates the text and graphics from other programs. Graphics can be copied and scaled directly on the screen. After all of the pages have been layed out, changes (edits) made on one page will cause linked text on subsequent pages to shift automatically.

HIGH-RESOLUTION PRINTERS

"Resolution" is a measure of the sharpness of the edges of printed characters and graphics. It is commonly measured by the number of dots or spots per inch. For example, dot matrix printers print both text and graphics by pushing pins onto the ribbon that strikes the paper. The resolution of the image is limited by the number of thin metal rods the manufacturer puts in the printing head: 120 dots per inch (dpi) is a common resolution for dot matrix printers (such as the one used to print the example shown in Figure I.5). This is considered coarse compared with the resolution of typesetting equipment, which uses a different technology to print images at 1200 or more dots per inch (see Figure I.5)—but typesetting equipment can cost $20,000 to $100,000.

The revolution in resolution came when Canon introduced the 300 dpi laser engine that is used in many of the printers that are now available for under $5,000, such as Apple's LaserWriter (used to print the example shown in Figure I.5) and Hewlett Packard's LaserJet. Other manufacturers have also made laser printers that print 400 or 600 dpi. Linotype Company's Linotronic typesetters use the same laser technology to phototypeset images at 635, 1270, and 2540 dpi.

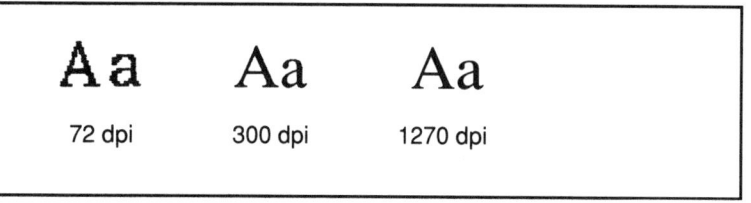

$$\text{Aa} \quad \text{Aa} \quad \text{Aa}$$
$$\text{72 dpi} \quad \text{300 dpi} \quad \text{1270 dpi}$$

■ **Figure I.5**   Characters printed at 72, 300, and 1270 dots per inch.

To the untrained eye, there seems to be little difference between 300, 1270, and 2540 dpi—text looks typeset at all three of these settings (though the differences can be dramatic when printing scanned images). This means that desktop publishers can achieve the same results with a $5,000 printer that previously required an investment of over $20,000—there was nothing in between.

Professional typesetters and others in the graphic industry can see the difference between 300 and 1270, and the difference can affect the appearance of the final document when it is reproduced using offset printing, but with many of the page-layout packages you can print at any of these resolutions—up to 2400 dpi if you have the right equipment. The higher resolutions can make scanned images look like photographically produced halftones.

LOW-COST EQUIPMENT

Finally, not only has the cost of high-resolution printing fallen, but the cost of the computer itself has fallen significantly over the past few years. Whereas "personal computer" once meant a $5,000 investment in a simple computer with no software and very little memory, many PCs that are now priced under $2,000 already include the extra memory, disk storage, and graphics capabilities required for desktop publishing functions.

The "Melting Pot" Effect

Desktop publishing, therefore, merges traditions from four different disciplines—typesetting, graphic design, printing, and computing—each with its own set of technical terms and standards. Professionals from each of these fields are finding that they need to add a few terms to their vocabulary in order to "speak" desktop publishing. They are gradually discovering that terms like *leading* and *line spacing* mean the same thing, and that each area of experience has something to teach the other.

TYPESETTING TRADITIONS

Typesetters are accustomed to working with codes: one code sets the typeface, another sets the style, another the size, and so on. The disadvantage of the code-based systems is that they are difficult to learn. Furthermore, many typesetters do not have the capability of previewing exactly what the text will look like when it prints out; they have to print the text to the photochemical typesetting device in order to find any errors in their coding. Even though it is sometimes slower to work with menu-driven systems, some typesetters welcome desktop publishing's low-cost WYSIWYG screens, short learning curve, and economical printing options.

The advantage of traditional typesetting is precision. Most typesetting systems let you set the spacing between lines and letters in finer increments than are possible with some page-composition packages, for instance. Furthermore, typesetters can set the width or depth of text precisely—in code—rather than using a less precise visual alignment using an on-screen ruler. Typesetters, therefore, may need to adapt their demands and expectations to match the capabilities of desktop publishing systems, rather than reject desktop publishing altogether based on one or two complaints.

At the same time, desktop publishers can learn something from the traditions of typesetting. A typesetter can tell you how many words or characters of a certain typeface and size will fit in a given space, for instance. You'll learn some of the tricks of the typesetter's trade later in this book.

DESIGN TRADITIONS

Professional designers take a lot of pride in their ability to interpret a client's tastes and ideas and translate them into beautiful finished products. The process of putting design ideas down on paper has been painstaking and time-consuming in the past—and this has been reflected in the fees charged for design services.

Page-composition packages make it possible to rough out design ideas quickly and deliver what looks like finished work rather than the traditional penciled sketches in the preliminary stages. In many cases, the efforts that go into producing a design idea with a computer are not lost—the same files can be fine-tuned for the final production. Furthermore, the same files can be duplicated and modified for other documents in the same series, or similar documents in another series.

In the long run, the economies that accrue to the design process with desktop publishing techniques will pass through to the client in the form of lower design fees. In the beginning, however, some professional designers balk at the idea of using a computer for such creative tasks—not to mention the lower billing amounts. In fact, these economies are more likely to result in increased demand for design services at all levels.

The fact that even amateurs can produce nice-looking designs with a computer program seems a bit frightening to the professionals, but the fact is that good design will always require some of the knowledge and skills that are part and parcel of the trade. You'll learn some of these principles in this book, as well as the production methods that will help you blend the designer's tradition of excellence with the business community's demand for expedience.

PRINTING TRADITIONS

Laser printers make it possible to print the entire image of the page—including gray scales—directly on whatever color paper you choose. Instead of reproducing your master copy using xerographic or offset printing equipment, you can print out hundreds of "originals" on a laser printer, ready for immediate distribution. The production of hundreds of originals is not desktop publishing's primary benefit, however, since in most cases you will find that xerographic or offset printing equipment is better-suited for high print runs, special paper, sizes other than 8½-by-11-inch finals, and color reproduction.

Whether you take the master copy of your document, camera-ready mechanicals, to an offset printer or use xerographic equipment, the final result depends on the condition of the original page. Good paste-up artists have the skill of surgeons in meticulously trimming typeset galleys and photostats of line art, painstakingly aligning them (horizontally on the page, vertically with the margins, precise distances from each other), and burnishing down the waxed pieces so they will not fall out of alignment during all the handling they will go through on the way to the camera. This, then, is a primary feature and revolutionary contribution of desktop publishing to the history of publishing: the ability to produce clean, camera-ready master pages, including text and graphics, without the marks and hazards of physically pasted-up boards.

Desktop publishing does not preclude the need for paste-up in all cases, nor does it guarantee perfect reproduction under some conditions. You will find—as designers, typesetters, artists, and printers well know—that the camera (used in making plates for offset printing) does not see the image the same way you do. Black text on a gray background might be easy for your eye to read on the laser-printed master, but the camera that produces the negatives might have trouble keeping the gray tone without over exposing the text.

You'll learn how to prepare your master for offset printing, as well as some of the vocabulary you will need to communicate with your printer, who is accustomed to dealing with graphics professionals. You will also discover that disk file pages can be printed directly to a plate-making output device.

COMPUTER TRADITIONS

The final elements in our "melting pot" derive directly from the computer industry. Pixels and screen fonts, ports and baud rates, icons and menus are all terms that you will quickly become familiar with as you move into the realm of desktop publishing from some of the other trades mentioned here.

You will find throughout this book that we draw clear analogies between the various terms used by different industries to describe the basic concepts underlying desktop publishing: the assembly of finished pages of text and graphics.

Desktop Publishing Software

One characteristic of desktop publishing is that it is not a single-product application. The page composition software packages are just one part of a complete system that requires additional software, powerful hardware, new input devices, and high-resolution output devices for a total solution. The three key application areas are: text processing, artwork and illustration, and page layout. In this book, you'll find tips about making the best use of products from each category. Within each of these areas there is a range of features and capabilities, from simple general-purpose tools to high-end specialized applications. So, you can select from a large library of applications that will help you produce anything from a simple chart to a very complex technical illustration, from a short newsletter to a multi-column newspaper complete with halftone photographs.

PAGE-COMPOSITION APPLICATIONS

We have talked a lot about desktop publishing in general, but what about page composition itself? How is it similar to, or different from, some of the other applications you might be using on your computer? A page-layout program lets you compose complete documents—including text and graphics—and view full pages on the screen before printing them out to a high-resolution printer or typesetter. One of the unique characteristics of page-layout packages is that they can incorporate text and graphics that were originally created in other applications. Page-layout packages incorporate many commands that perform functions once served by the layout artist's tools and resources: pens, pressure-sensitive tapes, knives, wax, blue-line boards, and acetate overlays were, and still are used to lay out typeset galleys of type, photostats of line art, and halftones of photographs. Figure I.6 shows some examples of the types of publications that can be produced using a desktop publishing page-layout package.

You can type text directly into a page-layout package, or you can type text using your word processing program and then bring that text into a page-layout package. You can create simple graphics directly in a page-layout package, and you can bring in graphics that were created using a graphics program. Once the graphics are in a page-layout package, you can move them around on the page, change their size and shape, duplicate them, or delete them easily.

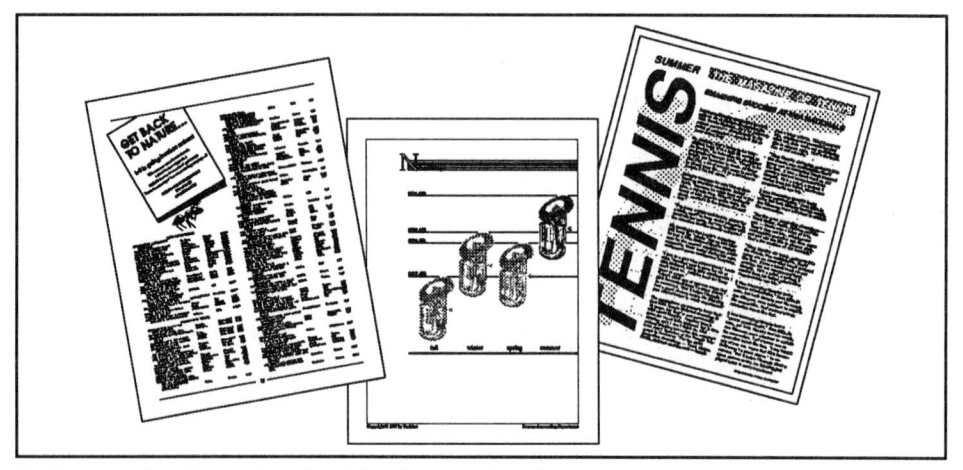

Figure I.6 Examples of publications produced using a page-layout package.

PAGE-COMPOSITION AND WORD PROCESSORS

Most page-composition applications are designed to import text from a word processor. Word processors are basically text-editing programs—they allow you to enter text, change it, print it out, and store it electronically. Word processing programs are evolving into true document processors that combine sophisticated text-handling capabilities like integrated outlining, spell-checking, and style-sheets, with features normally found only in page layout programs, such as multiple columns, and integrated text and graphics. Document processing can be thought of as word processing grown up. That's because document processors assist in the total process of document creation: starting with formulating an idea, creating the document, editing and formatting it, and finally printing it out. True document processors can produce typeset quality work and freely combine graphics and text.

Page-layout packages incorporate some of the basic functions of word processors. You can type text in a page-layout package much the way you type text using your word processor. On the screen, the text looks exactly as it will when you print out the page: you can see the difference between 12-point Times Italic and 14-point Helvetica Bold, for example. Most word processors do not let you make or mix type selections like this, nor do they display different typefaces on the screen.

A page-layout package also lets you arrange text in columns, and jump text from one page to other, nonsequential pages. Most word processing programs do not handle multiple columns very easily, or let you interweave two or more streams of text.

On the other hand, because most page-layout packages are graphics-oriented programs, they tend to be much slower for word processing than a true word processing program that is designed for speed. Furthermore, page-layout packages do not always have some of the functions that most word processing programs incorporate, such as global searches and mail-merge capabilities. For these reasons and others, it is a good idea to prepare long documents using your word processing program, and to go through the initial edit rounds using the word processor before bringing the text into a page-layout package.

PAGE-COMPOSITION AND GRAPHICS PROGRAMS

Page-composition applications and graphics programs work hand in hand, each offering features the other lacks. You can directly draw simple shapes—such as lines, boxes, and circles—in most page-layout packages, but these applications also let you bring in more complicated graphics, or other graphic formats, that were created using other programs. Most drawing programs accommodate some form of text entry, but they do not handle text formatting such as columnar layouts and tabular data the way a page-layout package does. Furthermore, most graphics programs do not handle multiple pages. Page-layout packages offer more flexible text handling than most graphics applications.

Graphic applications usually offer a much wider range of drawing tools and commands than page-layout packages. By working directly with a drawing or painting program you can have access to some of the more sophisticated features such as rotation, air-brush effects, and pixel-by-pixel image manipulation. You can also use a paint program to clean up images that have been digitized through a scanner.

Graphic images that have been brought into a page-layout package can be scaled and cropped to fit the space allowed on individual pages.

ANATOMY OF A DOCUMENT

A complete publication, then, might be composed of text and graphics created in a page-layout package as well as text and graphics brought in from other programs. Figure I.7 shows a typical page created using a page-layout package. All of the body copy (text) was typed in a word processing program, then placed in the page-layout package. Detailed graphics were created in a drawing program and sized and cropped in the page-layout package. Some of the short text elements such as the large banner across the top of the page were typed directly into the page-layout package. Hairline rules and boxes were added using the page-layout package's graphics tools. Running footer and automatic page numbering were set up on the publication's "master page" or "underlying page"—a special page that contains elements that will appear on *every* page of the document.

Examination of Figure I.7 will give you an overview of what's possible with a page-layout package, and the rest of this book will show you how to create such a document.

■ **Figure I.7**   Anatomy of a page that was created using a page-layout package: 1. Banner created in Windows Draw! 2. Footer text, typed onto master pages in PageMaker, appears on every page of the publication. 3. Scanned image cleaned up in PC Paintbrush. 4. Two-column article typed in Microsoft Word. 5. Chart created using Lotus 1-2-3.

System Configurations

Understanding the uses of and differences between the different software applications used in desktop publishing is one half of the process of outfitting a usable desktop publishing system. The other half of the process is to make sure your equipment meets your needs. We have already described the types of printers that can incorporate graphics and text on the printed page, and the typefaces that are required for desktop publishing, but at the root a desktop publishing system is built around a personal computer—an expandable machine that offers access to a range of peripherals that can enhance the typesetting and graphics capabilities of your system.

Higher memory and storage capacities are needed for desktop publishing than for simpler business applications in order to incorporate text and graphics in one document. A graphics monitor is required by most page-composition applications in order to display the icons and menus that are needed for a "friendly" user interface. Most full-featured publishing systems also use a mouse, an input device that makes it possible to draw objects easily on the screen, to move and scale windows on the screen, and to make menu and dialog box selections quickly.

A full-service publications department will also want to add a scanning device for digitizing photographs, logos, and line art that already exists on paper. Other peripherals, such as video digitizers and graphics tablets, add to the flexibility of desktop publishing. The following discussion gives you the background that you'll need in order to make wise hardware decisions for desktop publishing.

COMPUTER AND MEMORY

You can find products that claim to be "for desktop publishing" that run on a single-drive 256K-memory system, but most desktop publishing software requires (or performs faster and handles larger documents if you have) at least 512K memory in your computer. Some programs can require up to four megabytes of memory in order to run. The speed of the processor becomes more important the larger the volume of pages you're working with and the more you deal with graphics. If you are working in an MS-DOS environment, you will appreciate the faster performance of an 80386 system. If you are working in a Macintosh environment, you will find that your natural direction for growth (higher capacity or faster turnaround) will be toward the Macintosh II.

HARD DISK STORAGE

Besides the temporary storage that is built into any computer (i.e., RAM), you need to save programs and documents on disks for permanent storage or transportation. Because desktop publishing often involves the use of several different applications (word processing, graphics, and page composition) and the assembly of files from many sources, it is much more convenient to store all of your applications and your current document files on a hard disk while you are working, and use floppy disks for backups.

The technological breakthroughs that have affected disk storage include higher density disks (so you can store more information in a smaller space), and faster hard disk drives. Hard disks are usually made to store 10, 20, 30, or 40 megabytes of information. A 40-megabyte hard disk can hold as much information as 50 double-sided 3½-inch disks.

MONITORS

One of the keys to desktop publishing, as we define it, is WYSIWYG. It is imperative that the screen offer as close a representation as possible to what will finally print out on a laser printer or other high-resolution device. The higher the resolution of the monitor, the closer the resemblance of the screen to the printed page. For this reason, most desktop publishing applications require a graphics monitor. Word processing applications are not usually affected by the graphics capabilities of the monitor, but graphics and page-composition programs require a system that supports graphics. Some graphics and page-composition applications can run on a system without graphics enhancements, but as you might expect, the higher the resolution of the screen, or the better the graphics capabilities of the monitor, the text and graphics will be easier to read and less jagged.

If you do a lot of desktop publishing, a large-screen monitor can increase your productivity by letting you see a full 8½-by-11-inch page of work. By eliminating scrolling around the screen, it can boost your productivity by 50 percent. Even larger monitors are available now, which let you view two facing pages at once or oversized pages. The downside of these large displays is that you need to make sure your monitor has a driver for your software. While most page composition software will drive the major large displays, your four-year-old word processor might not.

A color monitor lets you display high-resolution color images. Desktop publishing applications that take advantage of color capability let you do spot color separations on the screen and print each color out as a master for the offset printer.

SCANNERS

A scanner or digitizer is an input device that converts a printed image into computer-readable dots. With a scanner you can incorporate halftones or line art of scanned images into your desktop publishing work. Scanners are a good source of graphics if you are not a fine artist and you have a library of logos, line art, and photographs to which you (or your clients) own the rights. The software that accompanies scanners can offer many of the features of paint programs, with eraser and pen tools for touching up scanned images. With the right combination of scanner, page-layout program, and printer, you can produce high-resolution graphics that look like inked line art or halftone photographs.

Most scanners are set up to accept 8 ½-by-11-inch paper. You can also use a video camera to convert printed or three-dimensional images into computer-readable dots. Any scanner requires software in order to set up the specifications for the input image size, the finished image size, the degrees of brightness and contrast, and the resolution of the stored image.

All scanners let you save images in low-resolution paint formats. These images are usually 72 dpi. When printed on a 300 dpi (or higher) printer, each dot is converted to four dots, but the image itself will always appear "jagged" compared with high-resolution scans (unless the image is composed simply of horizontal and vertical lines). Some scanners let you store the image at 300 dpi or more, but a full-page scan can require 500K or more of storage space. High-resolution images can approach the quality of true halftones when printed on a high-resolution printer.

Text-scanning (OCR, or optical character reader) technology has improved over the last few years, getting faster and more accurate. The breakthrough of most relevance for desktop publishers is that some scanners can interpret typeset text in various sizes (whereas in the past OCRs could read only special characters and typewritten text).

OUTPUT DEVICES

In the past, most offices used letter-quality printers like daisy wheel printers that printed one character at a time. These printers are still used to print documents that require only one size of text and no graphics. Desktop publishing, by definition, requires a printer that can produce text in a mixture of different sizes and styles merged with graphics on the same page. In order to do this, a page description language (PDL) is necessary. The most widely used PDL is PostScript. PostScript has been implemented in dozens of laser printers and at least two phototypesetters.

Other breakthroughs in printing technology that affect desktop publishing applications include higher-resolution dot matrix printers (for draft copies) and low-cost laser printers. Dot-matrix printers are impact printers that produce characters and graphics by pushing a combination of pins through an inked film (or ribbon) onto paper. Because the pins must be strong enough to withstand repeated impact, they must be of a certain minimum circumference, and this limits the resolution to 120 dpi or lower. The printed text and graphics have a jagged appearance.

Laser printers also assemble characters and graphics as a pattern of dots, but they use a fine beam of light (a LASER beam) to produce the dots in patterns of 300 dpi or more. The image is layed on the page using either a fine dust-like toner or electromagnetic charges on photosensitive paper—rather than ink that bleeds into the paper. The resulting text and graphics appear very smooth to the naked eye.

Typesetters are available that use the laser technology to set a page image on photosensitive paper or film. Compugraphic, Varityper, Tegra, and other manufacturers offer laser typesetters that image at various high resolutions using PostScript, Interpress, PCL, and proprietary typesetting languages. The resolution can be set to 312, 635, 1270, or 2540 dpi, and the output is much crisper than the output from toner-based laser printers.

MODEMS

Desktop publishing applications accept files from numerous sources, in a variety of formats. Files can be telecommunicated over the phone lines or through a cable from one computer to another. You can also convert files from one application to another type, using communications software that allows you to transfer and translate files. Once the files are transferred, you can edit them using any word processor (if they are ASCII text files), or use the same application that created them to change them, or place them directly on a page using a page-composition application.

Modems can be set to send files at different speeds, measured as BAUD rates (characters per second). The lowest BAUD rate is 300; it can take a long time to send a file at this rate, but it insures a high degree of accuracy in the transmission. A BAUD rate of 1200 is more commonly used to send files over the phone lines. A BAUD rate of 9600 is often used in direct cable connections (rather than over phone lines).

A modem can be used to communicate with any of the electronic information services as well as mailbox services and bulletin boards that are available. When you send your files to an address in an electronic mailbox, the addressee can download the files at their own leisure, rather than be "on line" when you send your files directly to their computer. This exciting solution brings the benefits of desktop publishing to groups of people who need to stay in close communication, but who may be anywhere in the world.

WORKGROUP NETWORKS

Desktop publishing in a workgroup allows people to share information. This is especially important in a production setting where one person is responsible for writing copy, another for designing graphics, and still another for laying out the page, for example. Network users can share printers, files, and information. With a print spooler, network members who share a single printer do not have to wait for others to finish printing. Network users can also send each other electronic memos.

Of course, in many cases workgroups may use various brands of computers. There is an extensive array of products that let different types of computers work together under a network system.

Summary

Electronic publishing systems bring together the features and capabilities that were once dispersed among different professional specialties. The rest of this book will help you identify the different roles and responsibilities associated with a full publishing project, and also update your current designs and production procedures to take advantage of the capabilities of electronic publishing systems. This book will also help you understand the basic vocabulary terms associated with desktop publishing applications, distinguish between the different types of programs used in desktop publishing, identify the possible sources of text and graphics in any document produced using desktop publishing applications, and determine your own software needs.

Part 1: The Publisher's Task

Whether you are producing a glossy magazine, a mass-market paperback, a high school textbook, an in-house newsletter, or a project report—whether you are working with a team of two or twenty—your document requires some attention to each of the steps, roles, and issues defined in Part 1.

Chapter 1
The Publishing Cycle

The tools now available to desktop publishers make it possible to shorten some of the steps in the production cycle, and to eliminate other steps entirely, thereby reducing overall costs.

Electronic publishing in general, and desktop publishing in particular, bring together many functions that were once divided between different people or companies. For example, before desktop publishing, authors and editors typed in the text and sent the file—either on paper or on disk—to a typesetting service (or an internal system that used electronic methods) for formatting. Meanwhile, the graphics department used pen and ink to create the graphic images, and sent them to an outside service to be photostatted to the size needed. Eventually, the galleys of type and the photostats of the figures landed on a drafting table, where a layout artist would use knives to trim the paper and wax to paste it down on boards into final ("camera-ready") pages.

At the other extreme, desktop publishing makes it possible for one person to perform functions that might not previously have been part of the production. If you were accustomed to typing the originals yourself, you probably didn't think to call in a designer to help you set up the pages. The decision to typeset a document usually carries with it the need to involve a designer and a paste-up artist. The difference in costs between these two alternatives were enough to keep many business documents under the category or word processing only.

Desktop publishing makes it possible for the same person to type in the text, draw the graphics, and compose the pages directly on the screen using a page-layout package. The fact that one person can perform the entire sequence of steps in producing "camera-ready" pages does not mean that the list of steps is different from traditional methods. What is more likely is that the one person responsible for the entire production might be strong in some areas and weak in others. For this reason, many desktop publishing departments will still want to divide the tasks of desktop publishing between different people.

Even with some division of labor, when the production team is small there can still be weak spots in the production cycle—areas in which no one on the team has experience. This chapter will help you spot those areas and make adjustments appropriately. Compare the roles and steps described in this chapter with the functions and tasks assigned for your own projects, and adapt the planning aids shown here (budget projections, PERT charts, GANTT charts) to track the progress of each project.

Division of Responsibilities

Even if there is only one person producing the document, the responsibilities involved can be divided conceptually among the following roles:

- The Publisher
- The Managing Editor
- The Author(s)
- The Designer
- The Illustrator and Photographer
- The Expert Reader
- The Copy Editor
- The Production Manager
- The Proofreader
- The Spec Editor
- The Typesetter
- The Layout Artist
- The Cameraman
- The Printer
- The Binder
- The Distributor

All 16 of these roles can be filled by a single individual using desktop publishing techniques, but on a large project it is more likely that many individuals will be involved, and some of these roles will be shared by several people. Here we describe the basic functions of each of these roles and how they are handled during large projects, along with suggestions about their assignment on smaller projects.

THE PUBLISHER

The publisher is the person or company that supplies the money required for the production and distribution of printed media—from books and magazines to business reports. Ultimately, the publisher is the one who defines the content of a publication. In the magazine publishing industry, money for production usually comes through advertising sales and sales of the publication itself. Many private publications are also financed from diverse sources such as corporate profits, personal savings, fundraising, and grants. As the publisher, then, you might be the original source of funds, or the owner of the publishing company, or an individual who has been entrusted with the task of producing the publication for the funding source.

The impact of electronic and desktop publishing techniques for the publisher is made clear by its affordability. As a result, there will be a tremendous increase in the number of people who can legitimately claim the role of publisher in the future. It is worth emphasizing, however, that the role of publisher carries with it the legal responsibility for the debts accumulated by the staff and for the content of the published works. Chapter 2 describes some of the legal issues that concern the publisher directly.

Other than insuring that the funds will be available as needed to pay the bills, your role as publisher can be defined in many ways and is determined by many factors, including personalities and politics. You might take an active part in defining the content and the image of the publication, or simply issue guidelines that can be followed by a professional staff, assigning the responsibility for daily operation to the managing editor. The role of publisher falls on a wide range of shoulders, including corporate officers, department managers, owners of a small press, entrepreneurs, associations, and institutions. In many cases, the publisher will also serve as the managing editor, and in desktop publishing, the publisher can be the whole production team as well.

THE MANAGING EDITOR

The list of responsibilities assigned to the managing editor can vary significantly from one publication to another. Whether the publication is a mass-market paperback, a magazine, or a corporate report, the managing editor is the one person ultimately accountable for the successful execution of all of the roles and tasks described in this chapter. As the managing editor you are responsible for insuring that all deadlines are met by your staff and contractors.

The managing editor might also serve the editorial function of determining the final content of the publication (i.e., executing the wishes of the publisher, or of a review group that represents the publisher's wishes), and this can be a powerful role if the publisher chooses to be passive. Although there are many proofreading tools available through computers, there is still no electronic substitute for the editor's eye in reviewing the author's manuscript.

The editor often recruits the authors, designer, illustrator, and copy editors then monitors the progress of the publication throughout the life of the project. Depending on the size of the effort and the individuals involved, the managing editor can serve primarily as project manager and let subordinate editors monitor the content, or the managing editor can take a very active role in reviewing the content and assign the tasks of project management to a production manager.

The managing editor of a large publication is ultimately responsible for the tone and content of the material, but assigns copy editors to review all of the text and the graphics to be sure that the final document is clear and complete. The managing editor of a corporate publication might be responsible for the project management aspects of the production and serve as the primary copy editor, but have no direct responsibility selecting authors or for determining the content.

Whereas electronic publishing techniques affect the publisher by reducing production costs, they affect the managing editor by condensing the production schedule. This can be an advantage if the result is that you have more time to refine the content of the publication, or it can lead to a heavier burden on the editor if it means that the time allowed for the production is shortened.

THE AUTHOR(S)

The authors are essentially responsible for delivering complete, accurate text. Authors of books and magazine articles are most often professional writers who were assigned, or who solicited an assignment on, a particular topic. Authors of a business report might be experts on a particular topic rather than professional writers. Depending on the size of the project, particularly the number of readers and editors assigned, the author might be asked to revise the manuscript several times before it is finally accepted, or the editors might handle all revisions. As an author, you should always try to get a good idea of how the editors work before you get involved in a project. As an editor, you must be as clear as possible in defining a writing project to an author in order to minimize the amount of rewriting that will be required.

The impact of electronic publishing techniques on the author is twofold: First, there are many author's tools available that automate spelling, outlining, indexing, and simple elements of style. Second, the author has the potential of taking the text through to the typesetting stage using the same equipment that is used in writing the manuscript.

The first category—automated author's tools—offers tremendous advantages for both authors and editors. Some editors now stipulate that the author must run all text through a spelling checker before submitting the manuscript. Many business and professional writers also use software tools that check their style and structure, and rate their writing based on variables such as average word length and sentence length. Some of these programs actually suggest changes to words in the text.

The second category—expanded formatting and typesetting capabilities—can also be an advantage if used to help communicate the author's heading levels and ideas about special formats. This can be a disadvantage, however, if the authors and editors fail to allow additional time for the steps involved in formatting, and the authors trade off by spending less time developing the content itself. Remember that typesetting has traditionally been one of the last steps in the process and can require several days or weeks for a long manuscript. Also, if the author is to participate in the typesetting or formatting process, the designer must determine what the final design specifications will be before the writing is finished, or at least identify the tags to be used in style sheets (through which the specifications themselves can be changed later).

Finally, a major benefit of electronic media in general, for authors and the entire production team, is that the text need not be retyped every time changes are made. Traditionally, manuscripts have been delivered as double-spaced text typed on 8½-by-11-inch paper, and the publisher or typesetter would retype the words to prepare them for typesetting. Electronic publishers prefer that the author's text also be made available on a disk so they can take the text through to final formatting without retyping it.

THE DESIGNER

The designer determines what the finished pages will look like: paper size and orientation, margins, and basic grid structure. The designer also specifies the typefaces, sizes, and styles to be used in the document, and might also specify treatments for all illustrations.

Electronic publishing techniques offer two advantages in particular for designers: One is that the designer can use the computer to generate a series of design ideas quickly. The computer output is often much easier for a client or review team to interpret than the traditional "pencil" sketches that the designer created for each design idea.

The second advantage offered by electronic publishing is the ability to "capture" the design specifications in style sheets and page grids that are stored in the computer and thereby help insure that the design specifications are faithfully followed.

There is no electronic substitute, however, for the designer's "eye" in developing the first design ideas and in evaluating each page layout individually. As the designer, you can cultivate a good sense of design by studying the principles of design (many of which are presented in this book) and by examining well-designed publications. Chapters 3 and 4 describe some of the basic design principles that apply to page design.

THE ILLUSTRATOR AND PHOTOGRAPHER

The illustrator and photographer produce the graphics that will be placed on the page. Most of the page-layout packages that are available now allow you to incorporate graphics and scanned photographs from a variety of sources. Electronic publishers use computer graphics wherever possible rather than traditional pen-and-ink line art, which takes more time and costs more to produce. In the computer, the graphics can easily be scaled to any size and edited quickly without recreating the whole image.

In many instances of desktop publishing, the illustrator will be the author or the designer. Besides making the tools of an artist available to a wider range of people, electronic publishing techniques make it much easier and less costly to incorporate graphics onto a page, and as a result there is an increasing demand for graphics in all types of publications. Although some drawings will still require the skills of an artist or draftsman, you can create many of the types of illustrations required for business and technical documents by using scanned photographs and images from various "clip art" packages that are available for desktop publishers, or by using a drawing program on the computer. Chapter 6 describes some of the sources of graphics for desktop publishers, and offers design guidelines and production tips for illustrations. Chapter 8 describes the mechanical preparation steps for incorporating halftones of photographs in a publication.

THE EXPERT READER

An expert reader is someone who knows enough about a topic to be able to assess whether the author's manuscript is accurate, complete, and clear. Most professional book publishers assign an expert reader to each of their technical publications.

The alternative is to assume that the author is the expert and to trust the author to make sure that the manuscript is accurate, complete, and clear, but this approach has several drawbacks. For one, it is a natural tendency for the "expert" author(s) to believe that they have been perfectly clear, whereas an expert reader might see the possibilities for misinterpretations due to the author's phraseology. Furthermore, asking the author to be sure that the manuscript is accurate and complete can become a conflict of interest as the author nears the end of a long writing project, and the author's interest in completeness competes with the author's interest in finishing.

Electronic publishing offers absolutely no substitute or assistance for the expert reader.

THE COPY EDITOR

The copy editor reads the text and graphics for grammar, typographical errors, treatment of numbers, consistent capitalization (in body copy and figure captions as well as headings), and makes sure that all references to figures or other sections or pages of the document are accurate. The copy editor is not usually expected or authorized to change or rearrange words in sentences, except to correct grammatical errors.

Although some of the electronic author's tools that are available serve some of the functions of a copy reader, they do not eliminate the need for this role on the publication project. Remember that spelling checkers still miss cases where "this" is "thus" in error. Compare the copy editor's role with that of the proofreader and spec editor, described after the production manager.

THE PRODUCTION MANAGER

The production manager oversees the production of the materials once they have passed through all editorial reviews and have been accepted as "final" by the editors. This moment has traditionally been signaled by the delivery of the finished drafts to a typesetter, but in electronic publishing projects the transition from writing to production can be a wide gray area that extends over the life of the project.

The function of the production manager might be served by the managing editor, but when these roles are divided they clearly delineate two "teams"—the managing editor works directly with the authors and editors to develop the content, and the production manager works directly with the production crew and (sometimes) the printer and bindery. The production crew in desktop publishing includes anyone who actually sits down at the computer and uses a page-layout package to assemble the pages and set the text according to the design specifications. Members of the production crew might also format the text using a word processor, if the formatting has not been done by the authors.

The designer and illustrator serve functions that overlap between the editorial and the production functions, and these two roles often fall under yet a third jurisdiction—the art department.

One function of the production manager that is essential in any electronic publishing project is to institute and monitor an efficient system of disk file organization. This includes instituting standards for naming files as well as methods for organizing files in directories on a hard disk and for maintaining a reliable backup system.

THE PROOFREADER

The proofreader might be the same person as the copy editor, but the proofreading stage comes much later than copy editing in the production. Whereas the copy editor might read the manuscript directly, without reference to other documents, the proofreader reads the latest version of a manuscript against edits marked on the previous version, and does not read those parts of the manuscript that were not marked for changes. Proofreading against marked edits should occur every time the manuscript is marked and changed during the production stages. There is no electronic substitute for this function.

THE SPEC EDITOR

The specifications editor marks the final draft of the manuscript (after all editorial reviews and edit rounds) with notes about the type specifications. In traditional publishing, this function might be assigned to the designer who developed the specifications, or to a copy editor who can resolve any questions about the handling of the author's text. The specifications editor's function could be executed by the proofreader or typesetter if the author's clues about heading levels and special formats are clear enough that there is no question about how the designer's type specifications are to be applied to the text. The specifications editor also reviews a printout of the typeset text to verify that all type specifications have been consistently and correctly applied.

Rule of Thumb:

Marking a manuscript for type specifications is usually most efficient when it is performed as a separate step from editing or proofreading the content of the text. If you are responsible for marking the specs as well as marking for content, make these marks on two different passes through the text.

Electronic publishing's biggest contribution to the type specifications editor's task is through the use of style sheets with a word processing program or a page-layout package. Using a style sheet, the selected text is set to the correct font and paragraph format by using a short code such as "heading 1" or "caption." The spec editor can write these short names in the margins in marking the manuscript for the typesetter, instead of writing the longer specifications—such as "14-point Times Roman, 15-point leading, Flush Left" or "14/15 TR FL." Chapters 5 and 7 describe different methods of applying type specifications.

THE TYPESETTER

In traditional terms, the typesetter is a piece of equipment, or the company or person that uses such equipment. In electronic publishing terms, the typesetter might be the word processing program, the page-layout program, the output device, or the person or company that uses such equipment. For the purposes of the division of responsibilities on our publishing project checklist (Figure 1.1), the typesetter is the person who actually uses the computer to format the text according to the designer's type specifications. In some cases, this function might be performed by the author or one of the editors.

Of all of the roles described here, desktop publishing has by far the largest direct impact on the typesetter. Whereas traditional typesetting has required the use of complex codes to identify fonts and formats, desktop publishing applications offer style sheets and menu commands that are easy to remember and apply. Furthermore, laser printers are often used as the final output device in desktop publishing, thereby replacing photochemical equipment with a simpler toner cartridge system.

THE LAYOUT ARTIST

In the days of lead type, the layout artist wielded considerable muscle, literally, to lay out pages in heavy trays of type and metal or wood engravings. More recently, the layout artist or paste-up person used a special razor, called an Xacto knife, to trim the typeset text and photostats of line art, and then uses hot wax to paste the text and graphics in place on a heavy paper *board* for each page of the publication. The manual paste-up process requires patience and attention to detail in carefully aligning pasted-up pieces on the page.

The electronic equivalent of the layout artist's function is served by page-layout packages that let you position text and graphics on a screen view of each page. In electronic publishing, the layout artist is the person who uses a page-layout package to position the text and graphics on each page, and sometimes this function includes the typesetting role. (See Chapters 5 and 7.)

Electronic paste up is much faster than manual paste up, since layout applications offer many tools for aligning objects automatically, and you can re-design a page-layout quickly if necessary when changes are requested. Nevertheless, as the electronic paste-up artist you will still need to pay attention to details and carefully check the printed versions of the page for misalignments that can result if you align objects visually on the screen rather than use the layout application's alignment commands.

THE CAMERAMAN

The cameraman usually falls under the role of *printer*, since every offset printing shop has a person who operates the camera that makes the negatives and the plates required for offset printing. The function is broken out here because some electronic publishing packages offer the option of producing negatives or plates directly from disk files of documents. Settings for scale, brightness, resolution, and color separation—previously the cameraman's responsibility—become the responsibility of the person who operates the negative- or plate-making equipment, and this might be the same person who serves as the electronic typesetter and layout artist.

Sometimes camera work is required in advance of the plate-making steps, to make photostats of line art or halftones of line art or photographs so they can be pasted onto the boards in the size needed. This role can now be handled by many of the graphics applications that are part of desktop publishing, as well as the page-composition packages that let you scale and crop graphics directly on screen. Chapters 6 and 7 describe some of the camera-like functions of graphics and page-layout programs.

THE PRINTER

The term "printer" in this case refers to offset printing equipment or the company or person who operates such equipment (rather than the laser printer that produces the camera-ready master pages). Of all the steps in the publishing process, this step remains the least "electronic" in that the equipment consists primarily of moving parts, and the basic offset printing technology has not changed significantly in 10 years, since the introduction of the fast-printing equipment that launched quick-print shops.

The impact of electronic publishing has been experienced as a growing volume of sales for the printing industry. The growing tendency for print shops to offer some form of typesetting testifies to the direct connection between access to typesetting and the demand for offset printing. As an electronic publisher, you should know something about the offset printer's technology in order to assess how your camera-ready pages will appear when offset printed. Chapters 8, 9, and 10 describe the preparation for and process of printing the final pages.

THE BINDER

Finally, the binder is the person who operates the equipment that binds the pages of the publication together into a finished product. Electronic techniques have had little influence on the binding process, which is described in Chapter 10.

Steps in the Production Process

Whether you are producing a document from start to finish on your own, or working with a team, it will help you to set up an efficient production schedule if you have an overview of all of the steps involved in a typical production cycle. The steps outlined in this section do not necessarily occur in the order shown on the checklist in Figure 1.1. Some steps can take place simultaneously, and the exact sequence of steps may vary. A typical production schedule showing the relationships between the steps is shown in a PERT chart in Figure 1.2. The degree of overlap between tasks is more clearly shown in the GANTT chart in Figure 1.3.

34 THE ELECTRONIC PUBLISHER

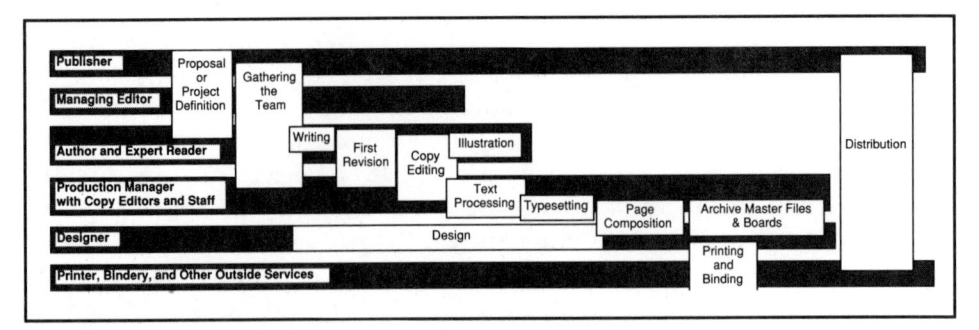

■ **Figure 1.1** Steps involved in a publishing project.

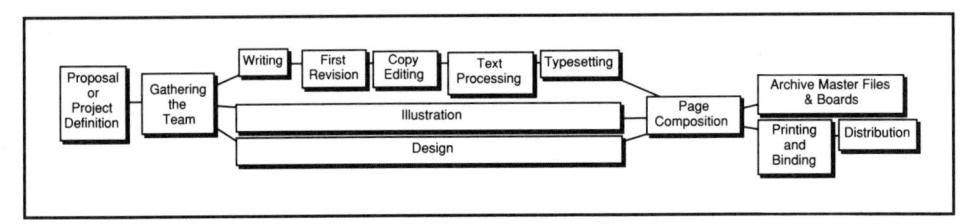

■ **Figure 1.2** A typical production schedule (PERT Chart).

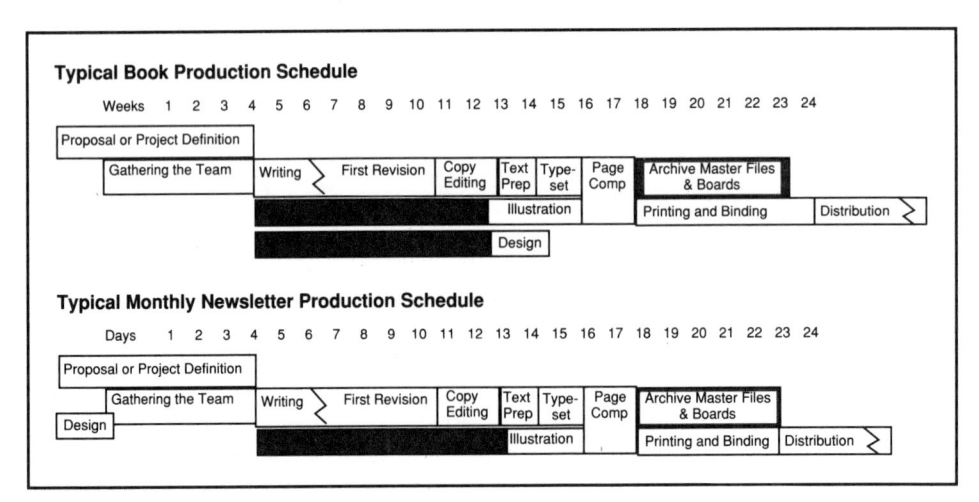

■ **Figure 1.3** A typical production schedule (GANTT Chart).

Steps in the Production Process and Division of Responsibilities

√	Task	Assigned to

Proposal or Project Definition
- ❏ Determine the topic and scope of the project — *Publisher, Managing Editor, Author(s)*
- ❏ Draft written contracts or statement of goals — *Publisher*
- ❏ Determine the preliminary budget and schedule — *Publisher, Managing Editor*

Gathering the Team
- ❏ Recruit personnel as defined in budget — *Managing Editor, Production Manager*
- ❏ Assign responsibilities — *Managing Editor, Production Manager*
- ❏ Update the budget and schedule — *Managing Editor, Production Manager*

Writing
- ❏ Develop authors' guidelines — *Managing Editor, Copy Editor, Production Manager, Spec Editor, Typesetter and Layout Artist*
- ❏ Develop detailed outline — *Managing Editor, Author(s)*
- ❏ Write first draft of text — *Author(s)*
- ❏ Read text and mark edits — *Author(s)*
- ❏ Type changes — *Author(s)*

Design (see below) — *Designer*

First Revision
- ❏ Verify that text incorporates agreed content and tone — *Managing Editor*
- ❏ Read text and mark comments and questions — *Expert Reader*
- ❏ Type changes — *Author(s)*
- ❏ Begin detailed list of standards — *Managing Editor and Production Manager*
- ❏ Update the schedule — *Managing Editor and Production Manager*

Copy Editing
- ❏ Read text for grammar, style, consistency, and completeness — *Copy Editor*
- ❏ Update detailed list of standards and review items — *Copy Editor*
- ❏ Read text and mark comments and questions (see above) — *Expert Reader*

Text Processing
- ❏ Type changes — *Author(s), Copy Editor or Clerical Support*
- ❏ Proofreading — *Proofreader*
- ❏ Update detailed list of standards and review items — *Proofreader*
- ❏ Type changes — *Clerical Support or Typesetter*

Design
- ❏ Create design ideas — *Designer*
- ❏ Review design ideas — *Designer, Managing Editor and Production Manager*
- ❏ Finalize design ideas — *Designer*
- ❏ Incorporate design into specs, style sheets, templates — *Designer, Spec Editor, Typesetter or Layout Artist*
- ❏ Update detailed list of standards and review items — *Spec Editor*
- ❏ Update the budget and schedule — *Managing Editor and Production Manager*

36 THE ELECTRONIC PUBLISHER

| √ | Task | Assigned to |

Typesetting
- ☐ Mark copy for type specifications — *Spec Editor*
- ☐ Typesetting — *Typesetter*
- ☐ Proofreading — *Spec Editor or Proofreader*
- ☐ Revise Typesetting — *Typesetter*
- ☐ Update detailed list of standards and review items — *Typesetter and Proofreader*

Illustration
- ☐ Develop list of illustrations — *Author(s), Designer and Managing Editor*
- ☐ Develop design specifications — *Designer and/or Illustrator*
- ☐ Update detailed list of standards and review items — *Designer and/or Illustrator*
- ☐ Create illustrations — *Illustrator*
- ☐ Review illustrations — *Designer or Spec Editor*
- ☐ Proofreading — *Proofreader*
- ☐ Update detailed list of standards and review items — *Proofreader*
- ☐ Revise illustrations — *Illustrator or Production Crew*

Page Composition
- ☐ Assemble text and graphics files — *Production Manager or Layout Artist*
- ☐ Update detailed list of standards — *Production Manager and/or Layout Artist*
- ☐ Lay out text and graphics on each page — *Layout Artist*
- ☐ Review layout of each page — *Layout Artist, Spec Editor or Designer*
- ☐ Proofreading — *Copy Editor and Proofreader*
- ☐ Update detailed list of standards and review items — *Layout Artist and/or Proofreader*
- ☐ Modify the page layout — *Layout Artist*
- ☐ Update the budget and schedule — *Managing Editor and Production Manager*

Printing & Binding
- ☐ Prep and photograph each page, make negatives and plates — *Cameraman*
- ☐ Run each page through inked press — *Printer*
- ☐ Fold, trim, and bind the publication — *Binder*

Distribution
- ☐ Assemble mailing list/subscription list/buyers — *Marketing Department*
- ☐ Send publication out to mailing list/subscription list/buyers — *Distributor*

Archive master files and boards — *Production Manager*

PROPOSAL OR PROJECT DEFINITION

The first task in any effort is to determine the topic and scope of the project. In the case of a publication, this step might be simply a decision made by the publisher, or the result of a preliminary meeting of the publisher and the managing editor, author(s), and other interested parties, or the result of negotiations between an author and the publisher's agents. The end result of this step is a written proposal or a preliminary contract, along with a preliminary budget and schedule prepared by the publisher and/or the managing editor.

One way of breaking down the budget is to assign a cost to each of the roles or steps described in this chapter. Figure 1.4 shows some of the elements that go into a budget normally associated with publishing projects.

	Rates	Budget 4-page Newsletter	Budget 400-page Book
Writing	Free $.25–.50/word $20–50/hour Royalties	$400	$10,000 (Advance)
Editorial Services	$15–50/hour $1.00/page Bid per ms.	$100	$400
Design	$50–200/hour Bid per ms.	$400	$500
Illustration	$20-200/hour $10-200/piece Bid per ms.	$200	$2,000
Clerical Support	$10-$20/hour	$200	$1,000
Typesetting	$5-$50/page[1] Bid	n/a[2]	n/a[2]
Page Layout	$5-$200/page[1]	$400	$10,000
Printing and binding	$.02-$.10/page	$400	$20,000
Management	Bid or percentage	$300	$5,000
Total **Investment per copy**		$2,400 $2.40	$48,000 $9.60

[1] Typesetting and Page Layout bids vary with complexity of format.
[2] Typesetting charges included in Page Layout bid for these examples.

■ **Figure 1.4** Sample budget: management, writing, editorial services, design, illustration, clerical support, typesetting, page layout, printing.

One element of the budget for electronic publishing projects that was once "hidden" as part of the fees paid to outside service bureaus is the purchase of equipment. The volume and nature of the projects will determine the level of investment required. Table 1.1 provides some rough estimates for equipment used in electronic publishing.

Table 1.1
Equipment Cost Estimates for Three Levels of Publishing

	Type of System		
Item	Low-End	Full Service	High End
Hardware	$1500	$3000	$6000
Page Layout	$300 Byline	$800 PageMaker	$2,500 Interleaf
Printer/Typesetter	$2,000 HP LaserJet	$5,000 LaserWriter	$30,000 Linotronic
Per Font	$200+ Bitmap Additional Sizes	$200+ PostScript $10	$200+ PostScript n/a
Extra Printer Memory	$1,000 2MB	n/a	Hard Disk

GATHERING THE TEAM

Once the topic and scope of the effort are defined, the managing editor and the production manager can recruit personnel as required for the project and as itemized in the preliminary budget. In gathering the team, you should clearly identify the division of responsibilities and update the budget projections and the production schedule based on the demands and skill levels of the assembled team members. The team in this case might be a client who is ordering the work as well as the production group; or, the team might simply consist of all of the talents of one individual, who sits down alone and sketches out his or her own timetable and expense projections.

WRITING

Before the writing actually begins, it's a good idea to develop written guidelines for the author(s) to follow in writing the text. These guidelines usually incorporate recommendations about content, style, vocabulary, and standards. If the project has no written guidelines, it is a good idea to select a published reference book that can be used to resolve all questions raised by the authors and editors throughout the project.

The author is part of the electronic publishing cycle by virtue of using a word processor to create text files that can be converted or telecommunicated to the system used by the production crew for the final stages of the process. In electronic publishing projects, therefore, authors' guidelines can and should also include recommendations about formatting text, with suggestions from the production manager, type specifications editor, typesetter, and layout artist.

Besides the general guidelines that apply to all projects, you (as managing editor) might offer verbal or written guidelines that are specific to each author's assignment. These include stated assumptions about the audience for this particular publication and the level of detail or treatment of the topic. The author develops a detailed outline of the text based on these specific guidelines of the managing editor. In projects that involve many writers, you might opt to prepare the detailed outline in advance of assigning authors, or to review the outlines carefully before letting the authors continue the writing process. In other projects, the outline can be the sole responsibility of the author(s), and you might waive the need to preview the outline before writing begins. Generally it is in the interests of both the editor and the author to agree on the outline before the writing begins.

Rule of Thumb:

Think out (and approve) an outline before the writing begins. The outline is likely to change somewhat as the writing progresses, but the outlining process itself will help the project start out in the right direction. It is often faster to write original text than to reorganize text that has already been written.

After reviewing the authors' guidelines and developing a detailed outline, the author(s) write the text. Part of the writing process can include running the text through a spelling checker or using other author's tools such as automatic outlining and indexing. In most cases, the author reviews and edits the manuscript several times before delivering the first draft to the various readers on the project, who contribute to the next step: the first revision.

FIRST REVISION

After the first draft is completed by the author, it is reviewed and changes are suggested. Usually the original author is responsible for making the changes suggested for this first revision, although in some cases the first revision (and all subsequent revisions) are handled by the editorial staff. The level of effort required for the first revision varies from project to project, but is usually in direct inverse relationship to the effort that was put into developing the authors' guidelines and the outline before the writing began.

Reviewers should include the managing editor (or an assigned support editor) and an expert reader. The managing editor reviews the first draft in order to verify that the author has incorporated the content and tone as agreed. An expert reader reads the text to see that it is clear, complete, and accurate. Readers at this stage should focus on broad issues and those questions that must be resolved by the author; they can ignore details such as misspelled words and formatting issues that can be handled by clerical support staff later in the project. The edits marked at this stage usually call for expanding, condensing, re-arranging, or illustrating the text, and offer global recommendations about style (such as whether to address the reader in the first, second, or third voice).

In reviewing the author's text, you can begin to develop a detailed list of standards and review items that can be handled by the editors, proofreaders, and production crew later in the project. The goals of creating this list include consistency and efficiency: it identifies the standards that need to be applied after the author is finished with the manuscript, and suggests the stage at which the standards are to be applied (see Figure 1.5 and Chapter 5). This list can be a valuable productivity tool for large projects.

Rule of Thumb:
If you can save five minutes per page due to efficient procedures, you save 20 hours in producing a 250-page book.

After reviewing the first draft delivered by the author, it is a good idea for the managing editor and production manager to update the production schedule based on new projections for the delivery of the final manuscript by the author.

THE PUBLISHING CYCLE   41

```
Glossary                                Page 4

    Proofing Checklist                  Page 3

    Proof the page layouts after text has been placed
       to verify:
    ❑ Correct indentation.
    ❑ Correct spacing between paragraphs.
    ❑ Alignment of text and graphics objects.
    ❑ Hyphenation.
    ❑ Widows and orphans should be avoided.
    ❑ Word spacing should be consistent.
    ❑ Look for kerning opportunities.

       Typing Conventions               Page 2

       ❑ Double-space between paragraphs.
       ❑ Do not indent the first line of paragraphs
          using tabs or spaces.
       ❑ Tab after the bullets or numbers in a list.
       ❑ Do not create hanging indents by typing
          carriage returns and tabs within sentences.
       ❑ Use two hyphens for a long dash (Em dash).
       ❑ Do not type headings in all caps unless the
          final typesetting specifications call for all-
          cap headings.
       ❑ Type one space after periods — not two.

          Standard References           Page 1

          To resolve any questions not answered in these
             guidelines, refer to :
          • Chicago Manual of Style

ABC Publishing Group
Guidelines
for Authors and Editors

Standard References                     1
Typing Conventions                      2
Proofing Checklist                      3
Spelling, Capitalization, and Hyphenation
    Glossary                            4
```

■ **Figure 1.5** A detailed list of standards and review items.

COPY EDITING

After the author has revised the text based on readings by the managing editor and expert reader, the manuscript is ready for the first reading by the copy editor for grammar, style, consistency, and completeness. Consistency checks include verification that the correct standards (syntax, capitalization, and punctuation) were applied to section headings, figure labels, and captions. Completeness here refers to the copy editor's verification that all chapters, sections, figures and appendices are supplied as listed in the outline and as cross-referenced in the text.

The copy editor marks the printed manuscript for changes to be made to the disk files, and updates the list of standards and review items that was begun by the managing editor and production editor (see Figure 1.5). In particular, the copy editor looks for consistency issues that can be resolved by global searches (using a word processing program).

The expert reader might also review the manuscript at this stage to verify that suggestions made during earlier readings have been implemented correctly. The expert reader's and copy editor's reviews for accuracy and completeness of the content can occur several times over the life of the project, depending on the volume of changes resulting from each reading.

Often the copy editor is also responsible for marking the type specifications (based on the designer's specifications) and for proofreading for typographical errors (against a marked manuscript). Most professionals find that it is very difficult for one person to read on all these levels in one round. Even if there is only one reader, these readings should be done sequentially rather than concurrently.

TEXT PROCESSING

Text processing at this point is often assigned to clerical support staff or handled directly by the copy editor rather than by the author. The edits made at this stage are based on the detailed checklist of global changes and on the marks made by the copy editor.

After the edits indicated on the detailed list of standards and review items and marked by the copy editor have been entered, the proofreader reviews the revised text against the marked manuscript to verify that all edits have been entered and that no new errors have been introduced. During this reading, the proofreader can accumulate notes about additional global items that can be added to the detailed list of standards and review items to be handled by the production crew.

Edits marked by the proofreader can be entered in the text files by clerical support staff or by the typesetter in an electronic publishing project.

DESIGN

Design specifications can be developed before the text is written, after review of the author's first draft, or after all readings by the copy editor. The earlier the design specifications are known, the sooner they can be incorporated and verified by readers.

> **Rule of Thumb:**
>
> If the "overhead" of editing a file is high (i.e., if a significant amount of time is required simply to open and save a file, regardless of the number of changes) it is most efficient to let the various readers (copy editor, spec editor) mark their changes on one printed manuscript and let the typesetter incorporate all changes in one pass.
>
> If the overhead of opening and saving each file is low, different readers' edits can be incorporated on different printed manuscripts.

Design specifications include:
- Typefaces, sizes, and styles for different elements within the text.
- Basic text format. Will the paragraphs have a first line indent? What will be the space between paragraphs? Will the text be justified? Will headings be flush left or centered?
- Basic page layout or grid, including page size, margins, orientation, number of columns, and positions of other nonprinting guides. This is some of the information required before you start assembling a new document.
- Final (maximum) size of illustrations, as well as typefaces, sizes, and styles to be used within the illustrations and in the captions.
- Final page count, or the range of pages expected to be filled. This will help you decide whether and how to divide a long publication into smaller documents or sections, as well as help estimate the printing costs.

This step has traditionally been performed after the text is written, since the design itself may be affected by the content and structure of the text. If the authors know what the design specifications are before they write the text, however, they can participate in the production by setting tabs and other format requirements as they go along.

Usually the designer on a large project develops several design ideas and reviews them with the managing editor and production manager before the design is finalized. Chapters 3 and 4 offer some tips for experienced designers who are new to electronic publishing as well as basic design tips for new designers. The final design specifications include a list of detailed type specifications to be applied to the text and a sample page layout or list indicating page size, margins, and indents.

In electronic publishing projects, the final design can also be embodied in style sheets and templates that are stored electronically. These electronic aids can help insure a consistent look throughout all the documents produced for a specific project, client, or department. They also help simplify the process of applying the design specifications. The step of creating these master files should be assigned to the most qualified personnel, or carefully reviewed by qualified personnel before the master files are used to generate finished pages. Qualified personnel in this step might include the designer, the production manager, the spec editor, the typesetter, or the layout artist.

Specifications that cannot be incorporated in style sheets or templates should be written in a form that can be easily interpreted into the commands or specifications required by the software applications that are used to produce the final pages, and incorporated into the detailed list of standards and review items and global conditions.

Often the design specifications will affect the budget and schedule for the project, and the design stage should be followed by a review of the budget and schedule by the managing editor and the production manager. In some cases, you can reduce the costs of production by changing the design slightly to simplify the layout process (and thereby save time), to reduce the number of pages required (and save printing costs), or to modify the use of color (and save prep time as well as printing costs).

TYPESETTING

Typesetting here is distinguished from text processing because the two steps are often divided between the production crew and the editorial staff on a large project. With electronic publishing, however, it is often possible to perform both of these processes using the same word processing package.

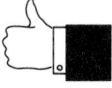

Rule of Thumb:
It's a good idea to do as much of the editing as possible in the word processing program, before placing the text in a page-layout package.

The typesetting stage actually involves several steps or roles: the spec editor marks a printed copy of the manuscript according to the designer's specifications, the typesetter uses a word processor or a page-layout application to format the text according to these specifications, the spec editor or a proofreader then reviews the typeset text against the marked manuscript to verify that all changes were entered and that no new errors were introduced.

As a result of the type specification process, the typesetter, spec editor, and proofreader may have additions to make to the list of standards and review items.

ILLUSTRATION

From the managing editor's and production manager's viewpoint, the illustration process is much more comprehensive than the simple act of drawing. Before the illustration process begins, the author(s) develop a list of illustrations along with pencil sketches of each figure. The designer and managing editor might add to this list.

In an electronic publishing project, the illustrator creates the illustrations using the graphics program best suited for each. The designer's specifications for consistency among the illustrations should be based on a basic knowledge of the capabilities of the drawing programs that will be used.

- Scanners can digitize photographs and line drawings that would be especially difficult to reproduce otherwise.
- Paint-type programs are best suited for working with digitized images and for "fine art" illustrations.
- Drafting-type packages are best suited for line art and technical illustrations.
- Spreadsheets or charting programs are most efficient for charts that are derived from tables of numbers.
- Some illustrations or graphic elements can be added directly in a page-layout package.

The designer's specifications can include updates to the standards and review items list that is used as a reference when the designer or spec editor reviews the author's sketches for the illustrator and reviews the illustrator's first drafts. Besides reviewing the illustrator's work for consistency with the specifications, a proofreader reviews the finished illustrations against the author's sketches to insure that all elements have been incorporated and that all text is correct.

Revisions to the illustrations after the proofreader's review can be made by the illustrator or by members of the production crew who are familiar with the drawing programs used by the illustrator.

PAGE COMPOSITION

Before beginning the page-layout process in an electronic publishing project, it is a good idea to set up a single directory on the hard disk for each document or publication, and move all of the text and graphic files into that directory. The disk organization and file-naming conventions should be determined by the production manager or page-layout artists and announced to all of the production crew. File organization and naming conventions might be incorporated into the list of standards and review items as guidelines for moving or renaming files as they move through the production process.

The layout artist uses an electronic page-layout application to create a master template for the entire publication (if the publication will require more than one document file). The template always includes the elements that appear in the same place on every page, and can include standard elements that will appear on specific numbered pages as well.

The layout artist then uses the page-layout package to build each document, placing the text and graphics files created in other programs, and adding elements using the page-layout package's tools. Chapter 7 includes tips on using electronic page-layout applications.

The step of printing out drafts of pages can occur many times during the production cycle in an electronic publishing project, with readings by copy editors as well as proofreaders.

During or after the page-layout process the managing editor and production manager might need to update the budget and schedule for the last time before sending the final camera-ready pages to the printer.

PRINTING AND BINDING

Using traditional methods, the final camera-ready pages are marked for multicolor printing if necessary and sent to the offset print shop. There, a cameraman photographs each page to create the negatives that are then used to produce the plates that transfer ink from the press to the paper. Some page-layout applications offer the ability to print separate images for each color, or to print directly from the disk files to a negative- or plate-making device. Chapters 8 and 9 describe the steps involved in preparing pages for offset printing.

Finally, the printed pages are collated, folded, trimmed, and bound together to create publications that can be distributed to the readers.

DISTRIBUTION

Under the simplest arrangements, common with many corporate publications, the managing editor or publisher arranges for the copies of the publication to be distributed to a limited number of readers. In the traditional model of professional publishers, the distribution list is the result of the efforts of the marketing department, and the process of actually getting the publication into the hands of the readers is handled by a professional distribution house that has access to a sophisticated distribution network and handles many other publications as well.

In either case, the distribution process involves costs that should be shown on the budget, and requires time that is reflected in the schedule. In many cases, such as periodicals, the date planned for distribution is fixed. Delays and inefficiencies that occur during early parts of the cycle result in extra pressure on the final production team to meet the fixed deadline.

ARCHIVE MASTER FILES AND BOARDS

At the end of most publishing projects, the camera-ready boards and plates are saved in an area where they are protected from dust and moisture. When an electronic publishing project is finished, the files related to that publication are copied onto one or more floppy disks and saved in a temperature-controlled environment. This step may seem obvious, but in many cases you will be so relieved when the publication is finally printed that you omit this last step. The dangers of not archiving your files include the risk of losing the files in a sea of disorganized disks, gradual overload of your active hard disk, losing track of what files go with which project, and confusion about the location of the files if you need to update the publication in the future.

The Battle Between Quality, Economy, and Deadline

When you produced your business reports using a word processor and a letter-quality printer, you probably spent more time editing the content of the document than you spent formatting the pages. With desktop publishing, you might find that the reverse is true: you will spend more time in the formatting stages than in the editing stage per se.

48 THE ELECTRONIC PUBLISHER

This will be especially true if your production group includes professional designers or typesetters, who will not tolerate little inconsistencies and misalignments. It is during the final stages that you will discover how "what you see" on a low-resolution, 72 dot-per-inch (dpi) screen is not exactly "what you get" when you print to a 300 dpi laser printer or a 2400 dpi typesetter. You may have to make fine adjustments to the file to get exactly what you want.

It is almost certain that you will need to print your document out more than once during the final production stages, and it is best to plan for this as part of the production schedule. Remember that printing time can be significant when you are producing a 400-page book with graphics.

More than almost any other business or activity, publishing is ruled by deadlines. You can't send June's news out in July, for example. When the published document is part of a larger product package, it is likely that the marketing or distribution group will want the documents finished as soon as the product itself is ready for shipment, even though you couldn't finish writing the text until the product was complete.

One way or another, the publication department is always pushed to complete everything as quickly as possible. Thus professionals struggle to maintain the highest quality in their productions. In the end, you will find that no document is ever literally perfect in the eyes of those who worked on it.

Summary

Depending on the size of the project, you might serve every role and perform each of the steps described in this chapter yourself, or you might be a part of a large team of people. In either case, if you are new to the publishing process, it is a good idea to start out with small projects that involve mimicking the design of a document that has been printed already. Later, after you have learned how to use a page-layout package's basic features and tried building a few pages, you can tackle more adventurous projects. For this reason, some of the steps defined in this chapter are identified in Figure 1.6 as essential (basic) for any production, while other steps—such as designing a publication from scratch—are considered to be advanced.

THE PUBLISHING CYCLE

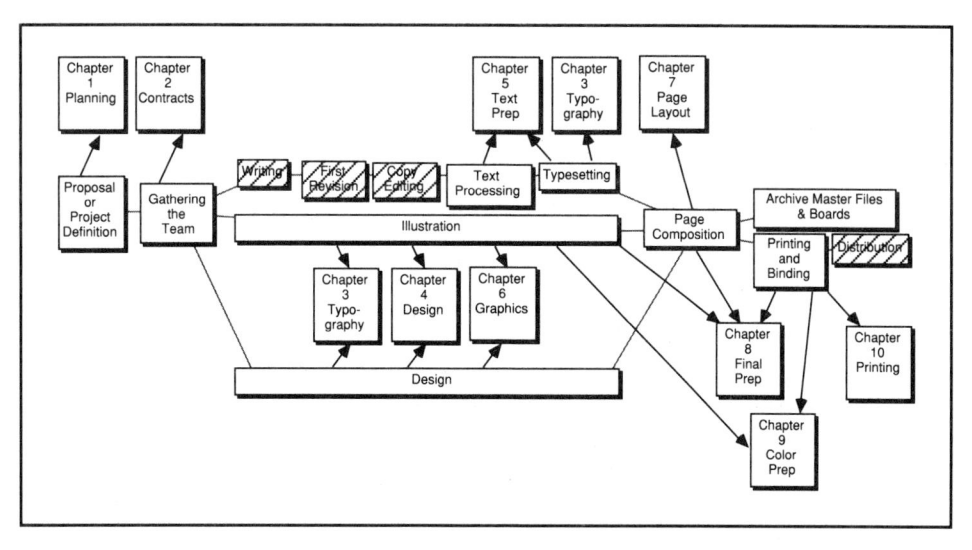

■ **Figure 1.6** Where to find more information in this book about each step in the production process.

Remember that the tools available through electronic publishing can help reduce your costs and shorten your production schedule, but they cannot replace the important functions of planning, designing, and reviewing your publication.

Chapter 2
Copyrights, Credits, Permissions, and Contracts

The opportunity to publish carries with it the responsibility to declare the sources of published information and, in some cases, to obtain permission from those sources and pay fees for the use of that information if so agreed.

Words, artwork, and photographs are *intellectual property* under copyright law. This chapter describes the conditions under which credits or permissions to reprint are required, as well as the procedures involved in protecting newly published material from being used by another publisher without the appropriate consent. A clear distinction is made here between copyrighted material, elements that cannot be copyrighted (ideas, outlines), and materials that are protected by laws other than copyright (trademarks and trade secrets).

There is also a discussion of ownership (of mechanicals, plates, disks, photographs, etc.), the archiving responsibilities of the author vs. the publisher vs. the production group, and the responsibilities to pay for changes or corrections.

Examples of the following documents are included as figures: Copyright Notices (as printed on the copyright page of published documents), Permission to Reprint, Contract between an Author and a Publisher, Contract between a Publisher and an Illustrator.

Copyright Agreements

Copyright laws, like any laws, are constantly evolving, and we can expect to see more changes as a result of the increased volume of published materials made possible by desktop publishing. Between 1909 and 1977 a publisher had to make sure the proper copyright notice appeared on each copy of a published work, fill out an application for copyright for the work, and send an application along with a copy of the manuscript to the U.S. Department of Commerce in order to guarantee full protection. Any failure to meet these requirements was almost always fatal. As of January 1, 1978, the law was changed. Basic copyright protection requires only that the claimant include in the printed publication the copyright symbol (©), the word "copyright," or the abbreviation "copr.," followed by the year and the copyright owner's name, and errors do not necessarily cost the claimant's copyright. But for full protection, including the right to sue infringers, the claimant also has to file an application and send deposit copies to the U.S. Copyright Office.

Many publishers go further to state the nature of the law and their rights, adding a sentence or paragraph about the extent of the copyright, especially international rights and use of the material in other forms (Figure 2.1). For example, if work is to be published in Latin America, the words "All Rights Reserved" must also appear in the copyright notice.

Generally speaking, a copyright protects only the exact words and illustrations used in the publication; copyright does not protect an idea, an outline, or the facts-presented.

The Electronic Publisher
Copyright © 1988 by Simon & Schuster.
All rights reserved. Printed in the United States of America. No part of this book may be used or reproduced in any form or by any means, or stored in a database or retrieval system, without prior written permission of the publisher except in the case of brief quotations embodied in critical artiles and reviews. Making copies of any part of this book for any purpose other than your own personal use is a violation of United States copyright laws.

■ **Figure 2.1** Copyright statement can include explanations of copyright law.

A copyright is property that can be transferred from one party to another. For example, as you will see in the sample contracts included later in this chapter, a book publishing contract might assign the copyright to the publisher, with provisions for paying the author royalties on sales. Magazine publishers might buy all rights to an article or buy only one-time publication rights. Illustrators and photographers might sell one-time publication rights, or forfeit all copyright ownership by doing work for hire.

Under the Copyright Act of 1909, unpublished works were protected by state copyright law, which offered less-than-perfect protection. Until a work was pubished, it was unprotected by federal law. So authors tried to protect their unpublished works by mailing themselves a copy of a manuscript via registered mail, and keeping the dated package, unopened, as proof of date of authorship.

Under current copyright law, however, even unpublished works are fully protected ubder Federal copyright law, if the author follows a few simple steps.

Let's assume an author submits an unsolicited manuscript to a publisher for consideration. Assume further that the author never hears from the publisher—or gets a rejection notice—and the author later discovers that a very similar book or article is published and credited to a *second* author. The burden of proof in any dispute would be on the *first* author to prove that the second author's work was copied from the first author's work. Unless the second work is virtually identical to the first, the usual way to prove copying is by establishing *access* and *substantial similarity.* The best protection is the combination of a copyright notice on the first author's work, coupled with copyright registration.

BOOKS

The copyright for a book is usually found on the so-called copyright page, along with information about the number of printings, and the publisher's name and address (Figure 2.2).

The Electronic Publisher
Copyright © 1988 by Diane Burns and S. Venit.

■ **Figure 2.2** Copyright (as printed on the copyright page of published documents).

Some book publishing contracts assign the copyright to the publisher; in others, the author owns the copyright and licenses to the publisher the control of portions of the copyright. In either case, the contract will provide for the publisher to own the rights it needs and to pay the author royalties on sales. This allows the publisher to negotiate sales of translation and other subsidiary rights freely, and prevents the author from re-using the same material in other works without explicit permission from the publisher.

WORK MADE FOR HIRE

Normally, the person who creates a copyrightable work owns its copyright and, for copyright law purposes, is its "author," a word legally defined to include artists, musicians, and all creative people. The publishing business depends on the author's willingness to sell all or part of the copyright to the publisher. But there is another way for a publisher to obtain copyright from the creator: it's the work-made-for-hire arrangement.

In a work-made-for-hire arrangement, the creator is *not* the author. Instead, the creator's employer, or the person who commissions a freelancer's work, is the author *for copyright ownership purposes* and the automatic owner of the copyright.

An employee's creative work product belongs to his or her employer if it falls within the scope of employment. For example, a technical writer's manuals, done on the job, are works made for hire that belong to the employer. But the novel the technical writer creates at home, on his or her own time, does not.

A freelancer's work becomes work made for hire only if it is specially ordered or commissioned and is the subject of a written work-made-for-hire agreement signed by both parties. And only certain kinds of work may legally be work made for hire. Among them are textbooks and ancillary materials, collective works such as motion pictures or magazines, compilations, and atlases.

The Copyright Revision Act of 1976 allows the author to reclaim rights granted to a publisher during a five-year period that begins 35 years after the grant of rights was executed or, for a grant of rights covering publication, either 35 years after publication or 40 years after execution of the grant, whichever is earlier. But works made for hire aren't subject to the recapture provision. Other than this one difference, a publishing contract can define rights so that a work made for hire is treated exactly the same as any other copyrighted work.

California has tied work made for hire together with employment law so that a freelancer, who is normally an independent contractor, not an employee, becomes an employee by signing a work-made-for-hire agreement that conveys substantially all rights to the client. The consequences were intended to protect the freelancer, by extending coverage for workers' compensation, unemployment insurance, and disability insurance.

PERIODICALS

Magazines and newsletters usually show a general copyright notice in the masthead (Figure 2.3) that globally protects all of the contents, but the actual agreement about copyright for each article or piece of artwork is negotiated in contracts with the contributors. Most periodicals that accept submissions from authors buy only one-time publication rights, thereby freeing the author to use the same material in another form, such as a book, or sell the same story to another publisher who accepts reprints.

> Entire contents copyright © 1988 by ABC Publishing Co. All rights reserved. Authors and advertisers are responsible for the accuracy of their submitted material.

■ **Figure 2.3**   Copyright notice (as printed on the masthead of published periodicals).

> Reprinted from *The Electronic Publisher* by Diane Burns, S. Venit, and Rebecca Hansen, copyright 1988 by Simon & Schuster, reprinted by permission from Simon & Schuster.

■ **Figure 2.4**   Copyright statements (as printed on the credits of reprinted articles).

Magazine publishers that give authors specific assignments (rather than wait for submissions) often describe the relationship in a contract between the publisher and the author, to cover all articles requested by the publisher. When using this method, each future assignment should be the subject of a letter confirming its terms.

REPORTS

You rarely see copyright notices on reports produced by a company for distribution to its own employees and contractors. Usually the content of these reports is too timely and specific to be useful later to other publishers, and the risk of plagiarism by other companies is relatively low. But if the material includes research or commentary that might be of interest to other publishers, a copyright statement similar to the examples shown for books (earlier in this chapter) should be included.

Remember that a copyright does not protect idea or facts. It protects only the expression of those ideas and facts. If the material includes proprietary information, try to protect the information through the trade secret doctrine (see later in this chapter) by severly limiting the distribution to those who sign nondisclosure statements.

PROMOTIONAL MATERIALS

Promotional materials such as brochures and ads rarely show copyright dates or names (although this is changing, and you will see more promotional materials carrying copyright notices in the future). Normally, the assumption is that all contributions to these materials are work-made-for-hire and that the rights remain with the company whose business or service is promoted. Photographers often assign one-time use to their clients and enforce the rule by retaining possession of the film. If promotional material uses original photographs or artwork, and the client may want to use the material for other purposes, a written agreement between the artist and the client regarding future uses of the art is a good idea, but the artist may well charge substantially more.

The buyers interest is usually served by having full rights to re-use the artwork without notifying or paying the artist separately for each future use. The artist's interest is served by requiring the inclusion of the author's "signature" on the art in all uses, and/or additional payments or royalties each time the art is used.

CONTRIBUTIONS

As described in the previous sections, copyrights are usually transferred by explicit agreements between the author and the publisher. The copyright issue is more complicated when a single piece (a book or an article) is a composite of contributions from various sources (several writers, for example, or a writer, an illustrator, and a photographer). Such a composite work may be a joint work, in which case each contributor shares an equal interest in it, or it may be a collection of separate works each of which is owned by its creator. It can happen that all contributors to a work share in the royalties, or it may be that some contributors receive a one-time payment. The payment might buy one-time use of the contributed writing or artwork or photograph, or it might buy all rights to future uses of the contributor's works.

One-time-use rights can be applied by assigning the ownership of the actual mechanicals, plates, disks, negatives, photographs, etc. Sometimes an agreement might include a statement of an option to transfer the ownership of these items for a stated fee. In any case, regardless of the assignment of ownership of the physical components of the publication, the copyright itself is usually assigned to only one entity, who makes contracts with all contributors.

DIGITIZED ARTWORK, PHOTOGRAPHS, AND VIDEO IMAGES

New graphics software and scanning devices make it possible to digitize an image from any printed source. The resulting computer image can be manipulated to create a slightly different image—or one that barely resembles its source. In either case, the "new" image is what the copyright law calls a *derivative work*. That is, the modified work is derived from an exisiting work. If the existing work is protected by copyright, the derivative work infringes the copyright unless the manipulator has permission to use it.

Most professional publishers take copyright law seriously and are meticulous in legally assigning or purchasing rights through contracts. But some desktop publishers, either through unfamiliarity with the law or because they think no one will notice what they do, appear to ignore the obligation to get permission before using someone else's work. One communications manager was quoted as saying that if you alter a graphic "more than 5 per cent" you can call it your own. "It's not copyrightable if you changed it, and so legally you're not bound" to get permission to use it. That statement is, quite simply, as wrong as it can be. Contesting lawyers will insist that anyone using scanning equipment must abide by strict copyright law. Under the Copyright Revision Act of 1976, the author of the creative work—whether the work is words, images, or some other form of intellectual property—has the exclusive right to decide how that work may be used and who may use it. According to section 106(2) of the act, only the owner may "prepare derivative works based upon the copyrighted work."

Rule of Thumb:
Generally speaking, you cannot scan, trace, change the colors of, crop, or combine copyrighted images in any way without getting permission for use from the copyright owner.

You can buy "click art" packages of art that you can use in your publications, and these packages usually include an explicit agreement or statement about the manufacturer's grant of rights to use of the artwork. In some cases you are limited as to the number of times you can use each piece of art; this agreement is intended to restrict the use of the image to individuals and small studios and protect the images from resale through large service bureaus.

Some software packages—word processors, graphics packages, and page layout programs—come with text or graphics files that are used in tutorials or demonstrations of the program's capabilities. If these files include an explicit copyright as part of the text or graphic, you can assume that the file is for use in the tutorial only and cannot be used in your own documents. Unless the manufacturer includes a statement about the allowed uses of these files, it is a good idea to check with the manufacturer before incorporating these demo files into your publications without crediting the source.

If your publications department or service bureau handles a lot of files from other clients, you should assume that all files and images are proprietary to the client. You should also check with the client about the ownership of or permission to use material the client provides that appears to be copyrighted.

There are many sources of "stock photographs" for which one-time or unlimited nonexclusive rights can be purchased. When you purchase a photograph from such a source you can usually assume that the vendor has obtained written releases from all of the people shown in the photograph. When in doubt, you should verify that releases have been obtained.

Copyright Waived or Inapplicable

Copyright law is not so complicated that you have to be a lawyer to understand it, but when you first look into it you might easily be confused about what a copyright covers, when it is waived, and when something other than copyright, such as trademark, patent, or nondisclosure agreement, should be used to protect creative work. The next sections describe some of these situations.

PUBLIC DOMAIN AND EXPIRED COPYRIGHTS

Copyright doesn't last forever. Under the Copyright Act of 1909, copyright lasted for an initial period of 28 years, renewable for another 28 years. Under the Copyright Revision Act of 1976, copyright lasts for the life of the author plus 50 years (or for 75 years from publication or 100 years from creation, in some cases). Works still subject to a valid copyright under the 1909 Act when the new Act took effect are subject to rules that extend the copyright for a maximum of 75 years, if renewal requirement are met.

Copyright protection for millions of works has expired; millions more were never copyrighted. In either case, the work has fallen into the public domain. When this occurs, any publisher can treat the work as its own, editing it, reproducing it, printing it, and selling it.

Some great classics fall into this category; you can find many different published versions of these books, essays, poems, and plays. Other works in the public domain include those that were never copyrighted and the early works that were published before copyright laws were established. One example of a frequently-quoted work that was never copyrighted—and its distribution was encouraged by the author—is the Gettysburg Address. Early works such as Greek and Roman writings are not covered by copyright law in their original form, though specific translations of the works can be protected by copyright.

FAIR USE: SHORT EXCERPTS FROM PUBLISHED WORKS

Although copyright gives its owner a near-monopoly over the use of copyrighted material, exceptions exist that allow use without permission in limited circumstances. The most important for a desktop publisher is the fair use exception found in section 107 of the Copyright Revision Act of 1976.

The fair use exception is an imperfect attempt to set guidelines; it provides no foolproof rules of thumb. Instead, it requires a careful, objective analysis of the purposes, amount, and market effect of the use. If you take too much or what you take is particularly valuable to you or the author of the original work; if your taking will adversely affect the market for the original work; if your purpose is to make money—then in all likelihood your use is not fair use. When in doubt, ask the owner of the work for permission to use it, or ask an experienced copyright lawyer for advice. Do not rely on the rules of thumb developed by publishers over the years, rules that are not soundly based on the law.

PARAPHRASING

A word-for-word copy of an original protected work is plainly an infringment. But even a paraphrased copying may infringe. The legal test is whether the paraphrase is a copy of the original.

INTERVIEWS

A specific interview with an authority or celebrity can be copyrighted, but that doesn't prevent other interviewers from asking the same questions of the same interviewee and printing their version of the interview under their own copyright.

PUBLICATION DESIGN

Copyright does not protect the design of a publication. The selection and placement of design elements is the kind of creative work that can be protected by trademark (see next sections).

IMAGES OF PEOPLE AND CHARACTERS

If you plan to use the image of a person in your work, you may have to deal with the rights of privacy and publicity as well as copyright.

The most common "borrowed" image is the use of a famous personality in promotional material. When you use the image of a current celebrity in a photograph for an ad, you had better be sure that all rights and permissions are covered meticulously in a contract with the celebrity or individual. Both New York and California law specifically prohibit the use of an image for most commercial and promotional purposes without consent.

Even ordinary people have the right to control their images in many cases. Photographers customarily obtain written release statements from the models who appear in their photographs. The release statement can be very simple, whereby the model releases all rights to the photograph and its use, or it can be very elaborate and include clauses that cover payments for future uses.

Using the image of a deceased person will not violate the right of privacy or publicity in most states (although the image may be proteced by copyright). For example, you can thumb through any telephone directory with display ads for businesses and find images of George Washington, Ben Franklin, Venus de Milo, and Jesus Christ. The public domain use of these images does not extend to images of all our dead or fictional heros, however. The use of images of Elvis Presley, Mickey Mouse, Donald Duck, Betty Boop, and many others is heavily and actively guarded by the owners of the rights. The best rule is not to use any images without first seeking permission.

"INFLUENCE" VS. INFRINGMENT

The strong images and designs that are found in promotional materials often inspire "schools" of art or a style that borders on infringment, but is usually claimed to be a part of the creative process. One example is demonstrated by a recent exchange of letters between the president of an advertising agency and a certain magazine. After the image shown in Figure 2.5

COPYRIGHTS, CREDITS, PERMISSIONS AND CONTRACTS 61

appeared in an issue of *ADWEEK's Marketing Week*, the president of Gerald & Cullen Rapp wrote to the editor:

> I call your attention to the two cruise ship images enclosed. ADWEEK's Marketing Week is the last publication I would expect to find guilty of this type of [plagiarism].
>
> Please include your heading and a copy of Michael David Brown's [Kent] ad with a note of apology in an upcoming issue within the next month, or I shall be forced to pursue the matter.

Michael David Brown's Kent ad

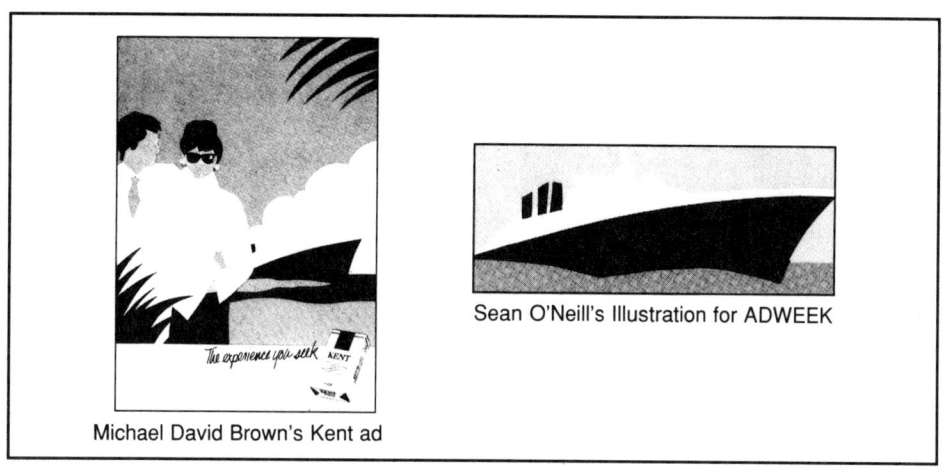

Sean O'Neill's Illustration for ADWEEK

■ **Figure 2.5** Ad and illustration use the same style.

The magazine's reply:

> ADWEEK's Marketing Week pleads not guilty to the visual plagiarism alleged by Rapp. Therefore, we feel no need to apologize. We will admit, though, that our debate with Rapp led to a lively correspondence. And most interesting to us was our artist's distinction between plagiarizing and being directly influenced, particularly as relates to the boat images under discussion.

The artist's reply went on to state that the two images had slightly different shapes and very different colors, and that once shape and color are altered there is no ownership (artistic, legal, or otherwise) of any illustrative image. Further, both the images are most heavily influenced by the paper cuts of Henri Matisse and the travel posters of A.M. Cassandre. No one owns the rights to a style or an observable phenomenon, he concluded.

This example demonstrates one of the possible debates that can and do arise about visual images, and it is neither intended to represent a prevailing attitude nor advocate a point of view. In this case, the advertising agency did get one benefit from the debate—perhaps the only recompense it really wanted: free publicity through the appearance of their client's ad reprinted in *Adweek's* letters to the editor.

IDEAS AND INVENTIONS

A copyright protects the words and images that express an idea. The copyright does not protect the idea. If your article describes a new formula for deciding when to invest in bonds, for instance, a copyright will not prevent another analyst from writing his or her own article describing the same formula. Similarly, a copyright does not protect an invention; if you want to write a book or article about the new mousetrap you invented, you had better apply for a patent before publishing a description of the invention.

Permissions and Credits

Written permission to reprint must be obtained on a case-by-case basis from the owner of the copyright. In many cases the permission to reprint is readily given with the only proviso being that credit be given as well (Figure 2.6). In other cases, the permission might be granted in exchange for a fee or for a favor, such as a free ad in your publication, or a full description of how to order the original work from the publisher.

You are hereby granted permission to reprint the article requested, in the January 1989 issue of your newsletter, *The Red Line*, provided you includes the following statement at the end of the article:

Reprinted from *Bottom Line News*, May 1988. Copyright © 1988 by ABC Publishing Co., reprinted with permission from ABC Publishing Co.

G. Moore
Legal Department
ABC Publishing Co.

■ **Figure 2.6** Written permission to reprint.

Plan to take the time required to trace down the sources of any material you want to reprint or re-use in your own publications. Sometimes it can be hard to locate the person who is authorized to give you permission. Don't let your own tight pressure to meet a deadline be an excuse for printing without permission—counting on the fact that you will be able to get permission after the work is published. Some copyright owners may absolutely refuse to let you use their work, and others might take the belated request for permission as an excuse to charge a higher fee than they might have if you had gotten prior permission.

WHEN AND HOW TO CREDIT

Copyright law states that you must obtain permission for use of copyrighted material. Giving credit for the source of a reprint does not absolve you from the obligation to get permission to reprint.

It's a good idea to credit any outside source of materials you use, whether or not the source (or the law) actually requires that credit. This practice might be considered optional by law, but it is required by convention.

You do *not* need to give credit when you are quoting your own or others' published or unpublished works to which *you* own the copyright (including work-made-for-hire), or when the copyright owner does not specify in the written permission to reprint that credit need be given.

Sometimes, acknowledgement of the permission to reprint is included on the copyright page of the published work, along with a stipulation that any reprints properly credit the source (Figure 2.7).

Reprinted from *Bottom Line News*, May 1988. Copyright © 1988 by ABC Publishing Co., reprinted with permission from ABC Publishing Co.

■ **Figure 2.7** Acknowledgement of permission to reprint.

Trademarks

You cannot copyright single words or short phrases, but you can apply for a trademark that protects the use of a word, phrase, or logo. A trademark can cover the style of type or design of a logo as well as the words themselves.

Trade Secrets

Trade secrets are unlike copyrights, trademarks, or patents in one important respect: a trade secret is something that you do *not* want to publish or disseminate, whereas the other three protections are designed specifically for words or ideas that are intended for general distribution. If you are preparing a limited-distribution report that reveals secrets about your business, it is best protected by obtaining a signed nondisclosure statement from readers—before they read it. In addition to the signed nondisclosure agreement, the printed document itself should include a clear warning statement about violation of the confidentiality that each reader has agreed to. This statement, along with the copyright notice, protects the contents of the report.

Contracts

The rules discussed above are the foundation of property rights in words and images. The actual application of these rules is best expressed in written contracts between the publisher and all contributors. The rest of this chapter shows examples of actual contracts to give you an idea of the types of clauses commonly found in contracts. These examples are not intended to represent the recommended format or content of your contracts, as each situation calls for its own special considerations.

COPYRIGHTS, CREDITS, PERMISSIONS AND CONTRACTS

Agreement

made this <u>DAY</u> day of <u>MONTH</u>, <u>YEAR</u> between <u>AUTHOR</u> of <u>CITY</u> and <u>PUBLISHER, FULL ADDRESS</u>, with respect to a joint Work to be prepared by <u>AUTHOR</u> and tentatively titled <u>TITLE</u>.

AUTHOR and PUBLISHER agree to collaborate in the preparation of the work and to undertake and carry out their respective responsibilities as herein provided.

1.
Publication Rights. Subject to the terms and conditions contained herein, AUTHOR hereby transfers to PUBLISHER the full and exclusive rights comprised in the copyright of the work.

2.
Manuscript. AUTHOR agrees to prepare and submit the final manuscript of the Work, to consist of approximately <u>PAGES</u> printed pages, including illustrative material, not later than <u>DATE DUE,</u> the due date.

3.
Publication. Subject to the terms and conditions herein PUBLISHER at its own expense shall (a) diligently proceed to publish and promote the sale of the Work in the English language in such manner and at such prices as it deems appropriate, and (b) make any and all other arrangements it deems appropriate with respect to the Work and the rights thereto herein granted to it.

4.
Copyright Notice and Registration. PUBLISHER shall print in each copy of the Work published by it a notice of copyright sufficient to meet the requirements of Chapter 4 of the United States Copyright Law and to secure protection under the Universal Copyright Convention.

5.
Royalties. AUTHOR shall receive the following royalties: <u>PERCENTAGE</u> of Publisher's dollar receipts.

6.
Payment and Accounting. Payments to AUTHOR shall be made quarterly.

7.
Arbitration. All differences of disputes arising out of or in conjunction with this agreement or the breach thereof shall be settled by arbitration in accordance with the rules of the American Arbitration Association.

AUTHOR (PRINT)	AUTHOR (SIGNED)	DATE
PUBLISHER (PRINT)	PUBLISHER (SIGNED)	DATE

■ **Figure 2.8** Contract between an author and a publisher.

THE ELECTRONIC PUBLISHER

```
Diane Burns
3915-D 24th Street
San Francisco, CA  94114
(415) 550-1110


CLIENT: _____
        _____
        _____
        _____
        _____


ASSIGNMENT DESCRIPTION:
        _____
        _____
        _____
        _____
        _____
        _____
        _____
        _____
        _____
        _____
        _____
        _____
        _____
        _____
        _____
        _____


DELIVERY DATE:_____ This delivery is predicated upon receipt of all materials to be
supplied by Client no later than_____.

FEE:_____

RIGHTS TRANSFERRED: Designer transfers to the Client the following rights of usage:

Title of Product:       _____
Category of Use:        _____
Medium of Use:          _____
Geographical Area:_____
Time Period:            _____

Any usage rights not expressly transferred are reserved to the Designer. Any usage beyond that
granted to the Client herein shall require the payment of a mutually agreed upon additional fee.
Subject to all terms appearing on reverse.
```

■ **Figure 2.9** Work for Hire agreement, page 1.

COPYRIGHTS, CREDITS, PERMISSIONS AND CONTRACTS 67

```
TERMS

1. TIME FOR PAYMENT:_____

   _____

2. CHANGES: Client shall be responsible for making additional payments for changes in original
   assignment requested by Client. However, no additional payment shall be made for changes
   required to conform to the original assignment.

3. CANCELLATION: In the event of cancellation of this assignment, ownership of all copyrights
   and the original artwork is retained by the Designer and a cancellation fee for work completed,
   based on the contract price and expenses incurred, shall be paid by the Client.

4. RELEASES: Client will indemnify Designer against all claims and expenses, including
   reasonable attorney's fees, due to uses for which no releases were granted in writing.

5. MODIFICATIONS: Modification of the Agreement must be written.

6. ARBITRATION: Any disputes in excess of maximum small claims court limit arising out of this
   Agreement shall be submitted to binding arbitration before the Joint Ethics Committee or
   mutually agreed upon arbitrator pursuant to the rules of the American Arbitration Association.
   The arbitrator's award shall be final and judgement may be entered upon it in any court having
   jurisdiction thereof. The Client shall pay all arbitration and court costs, reasonable attorney's
   fees and legal interest on any award or judgement in favor of the Designer.

ACCEPTED FOR CLIENT:
_____DATE_____

ACCEPTED FOR DESIGNER:
_____DATE_____
Diane K. Burns
```

■ **Figure 2.10** Work for Hire agreement, page 2.

Summary

Copyright law is mostly common sense. If you want to use words or an image from any other source, ask yourself if the author or owner would be annoyed if they found out about your use of their work. Would *you* require permission if the work were yours and someone else wanted to use it? Imagine the worst case: what if the author or owner threatened to sue you: could you defend your use of the work?

If you take publishing seriously, it is a good idea to have a ready reference book on copyright law, and a stock of different contracts at your fingertips to help assure correct practice according to law. That way, the ugly and costly intrusion of the law won't interfere with your creative endeavors.

Part 2: Design for Desktop Systems

Traditionally, there has been a distinct break between the writing/editing steps and the design process in producing any publication—the writer had no idea what the final pages would look like, and the designers didn't care what form the text and illustrations were delivered in, so long as they were complete and clear. The designer would then set up specifications for the page margins and type, and mark up the stack of typed pages and penciled sketches for the typesetter and illustrator. The stages were distinct because the players and the tools used at each stage were different. Now it's possible for the writer to participate in the design and production if the design function is performed early enough in the cycle. Using the tools of electronic publishing, the distinction between the writing, design, and production phases is more of a concept than a matter of fact. If the writers know what the final design requires, they can insert tabs and carriage returns as appropriate while they are writing, and (optionally) perform other formatting operations.

Chapter 3
Typography

> *"We want the ability to take a piece of text and fit a line without any waste at all. Such things as automatic hyphenation and justification with an exceptional dictionary, fractional leading including vertical leading in very small increments, and full control over word spacing, letter spacing, and kerning are all mandatory if desktop systems are going to succeed as design tools or publishing workstations."*
>
> — *Gary Cosimini*
> *art director and book designer*

You see it every day. You just don't realize it. Behind every printed word stand the principles of an art called typography. Invisible to the untrained eye, it is the discipline of typography that can make or break the success of printed communications. The study and practice of good typography is very old—especially if you extend it to include calligraphy. The "modern" period for typography started in the late 18th century!

Until recently, most of us were "sheltered" from this arcane knowledge by the professional designers and typographers who translated our needs into the specifications required by typesetting equipment. In the traditional model, one typesetting system might cost $100,000, be operated by two or three typesetters who serve 100 or more "clients" including designers who in turn serve hundreds of clients. Only those at the top of this hierarchy—closest to the equipment—knew the language of typography.

With the advent of laser printers and desktop publishing, many of us have been catapulted from the straight-laced world of Courier and Elite into the exciting world of publication design and production. In this new model, the same person who writes the text can actually typeset the copy and lay out finished pages with graphics in place. In many respects it is a miracle that so many of us now have access to a wide range of typesetting capabilities that were previously, technologically, reserved for a few professionals.

Unfortunately, the design skills that have supported page layouts in the past are not miraculously endowed on consumers in this expanded marketplace for type. Many desktop publishers are new to the field of typography, and do not realize that graphic designers may invest many hours—over several years—in the study of typography. Fortunately, without such a disciplined background, the conscientious desktop publisher will benefit by studying just a few of the basic rules that govern the usage of type on a page.

The designer and typographer have a unique way of describing the text in a document, expressed in terms of fonts, leading, and kerning. In this chapter you will learn how to look at a publication in these terms and how to set up your design specifications for the fonts and formats to be used in a publication. You will learn how to estimate the amount of text that will fit on each page, and how to make fine adjustments in spacing to fit copy to a defined space.

You will also learn what fonts are available for different types of printers and typesetting equipment, and how new fonts can be added to your system. You will see how important is it to know what font sizes and styles are available for your printer before you start the design process.

Whether you—as the designer/typographer—are writing out the design specifications for a document or actually using a word processor's style sheets or a page-layout package to set up the master template, it will help if you know how the program works before you make your design specifications for a publication. In this chapter you will not only learn something about how professional typesetters and designers determine what fonts to use in a document, you will also learn how to specify them for a production team that will be using common desktop publishing tools.

The Language of Type

The first step in developing a good sense of typography is to become familiar with the terminology associated with traditional publishing and with newer terms that have evolved over the last three years from desktop publishing. Once you know what the variable characteristics of type are, a framework for looking at type can be established. The ability to notice any inconsistencies in the format and spacing of type on a page can be developed once you know what to look for.

WHAT IS A FONT?

The word font is derived from the French word *fondre*, which means to melt or cast. It once referred literally to the trays of cast metal letters that a printer would use to compose a document. Each tray or *font* included all letters of the alphabet for a specific typeface/style/size combination (Figure 3.1). For example, one tray held only 10-point Times italic letters, another tray held only 10-point Times bold, and so on. A font, then, was a particular typeface, style, and size combination.

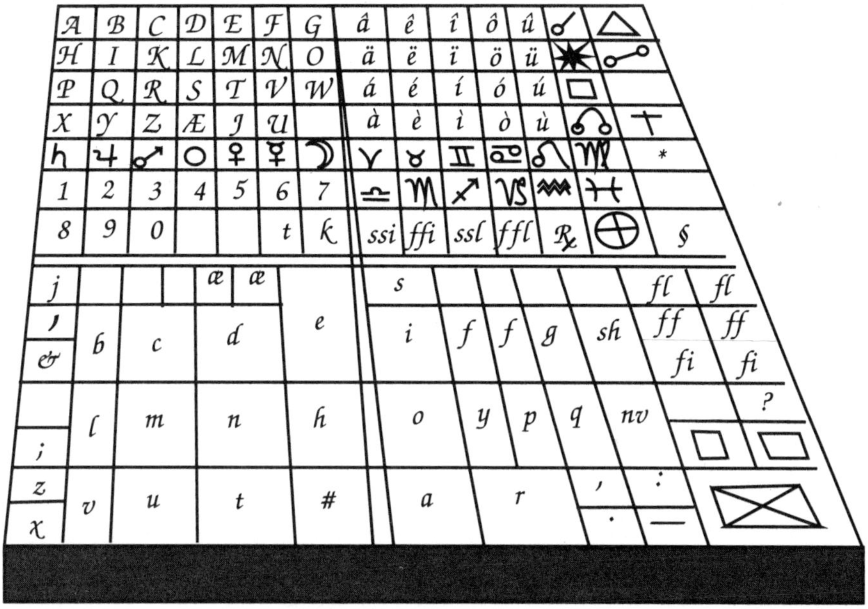

■ **Figure 3.1** A font, or tray of cast metal letters.

More recently, however, the word font has been taken more loosely to mean simply the name of the typeface, such as Times or Helvetica. This definition is rational for the new computer fonts that are based on formulas, such as PostScript fonts. Each letter of the alphabet is "cast" or designed only once, to define the shapes or outlines of the letters. This information is then stored as complex curve-fitting equations. A printer that uses a programming language—such as PostScript—to create text can produce any size of a typeface for which it knows the outline formula of each letter.

When you hear that a certain printer is limited to a certain number of fonts per page or per document, it is important to know which meaning of the word font applies. For printers that use outline fonts, a limit of four fonts usually means four font families or *typefaces*—Times, Helvetica, Courier, and Palatino, for example, each in all sizes and styles. Printers that use bit-mapped fonts are usually limited to a specific number of *fonts* in the more traditional sense—10-point Times Roman, 10-point Times italic, 10-point Times bold, and 10-point Times bold italic, for example.

The designer needs to be specific about the type of printer as well as the fonts (type faces, sizes, and styles) in making the design specifications for the type in a document. The following sections will give you some tips about selecting fonts for a document.

Typeface

In the traditional sense, then, a typeface is a family of type that has the same basic shape for each letter. The typeface Times, for instance, includes all sizes and styles of type that are simply variations on the same basic family of designs for each letter of the alphabet. One way of describing a particular typeface is to identify the relative thickness of the strokes, the slant of the cross bars, the height of the capitals and ascenders, the depth of the descenders, the angle and shape of the serifs, the shape and size of the rounds (Figure 3.2)—all in precise numerical terms.

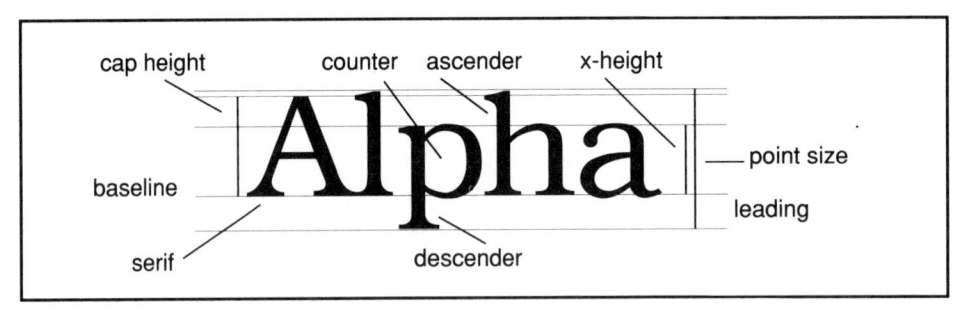

■ **Figure 3.2**   Anatomy of a typeface

An easier way of learning to identify typefaces by name is to group them by similarities. Several ways of grouping typefaces are described in this section.

Typefaces can be distinguished as body copy typefaces (for most text), display typefaces (for headlines or headings, advertising), decorative typefaces (infrequently used), script or cursive typefaces (modelled on handwriting or calligraphy), and special typefaces or character sets such as symbols. *Body copy* typefaces are commonly used for most text, especially the main "body" of a document, and they are designed to be legible in small point sizes. These fonts are usually serif fonts, since serifs actually help carry the eye along and make the text easy to read. Display typefaces, on the other hand, are used primarily in display ads and logos, as headings in documents, and as headlines in newsletters. They are often sans serif faces, and they are commonly used in sizes larger than 12 points. Decorative typefaces can be very ornate, and are used sparingly for eye-catching announcements.

> Body type can be as small as 9 points.
> Body type can be as large as 12 points.
> *Display typefaces*
> *are usually designed for larger sizes.*

■ **Figure 3.3** Display type vs. body copy.

Body copy typefaces are often broadly grouped into two categories: serif and sans serif (Figure 3.4). The word *serif* refers to the fine cross strokes at the top and bottom of the letter "h" (for example). *Sans serif* means without serifs. It is said that the Romans invented the serif as a solution to the technical problem of getting a chisel to cut a neat, clean end to a character. Later it became an emulation of handwriting with flat "pens" that produced thick and thin curves. In general, serif characters help reading by providing a horizontal guideline for the eye to "tie" the letters of a word together.

Rule of Thumb:
Use serif faces when typesetting long stretches of copy such as books. Serif faces cause less fatigue on the eyes than sans serif faces.

> Times is a serifed typeface.
> **Helvetica is a sans serif typeface.**

■ **Figure 3.4** Serif and sans serif typefaces.

Typefaces are also distinguished as being either nonproportional (i.e., monospaced) or proportionally spaced. Nonproportional typefaces like Courier use the exact same width for every character. The spacing between letters may seem to vary because narrow letters (like "i") are given the same amount of space as wide letters (like "w"). Nonproportional typefaces are never kerned (unless you force special spacing between letters).

Proportionally spaced typefaces like Times Roman and Helvetica assign different widths to each character of the alphabet. Narrow letters like "i" and "j" take up less horizontal space than wide letters like "w" and "m," for example. If the text is not kerned, each letter is given a full rectangular area into which adjacent letters will not encroach. The spacing between letters might appear to vary depending on how letters are paired. For example, the space between the letters "AV" will appear to be much wider than the space between the letters "ES" unless the text is kerned. (See "Kerning Headlines and Titles," later in this chapter.)

Typefaces are also distinguished by weight. Weight refers to the lightness or darkness in print of a particular typeface based upon its design and thickness of line. The standard gradations of weight are: extra-light, semi-light, medium, semi-bold (or demi-bold), bold, extra-bold, and ultra-bold. (The last two are also called "heavy" or "black.")

In phototypesetting, differences in weight may be artificially created by adjusting variables such as the density setting on the typesetting machine itself, the condition of the processor chemicals, and the length of time between exposing and processing the galley (fading).

Size

Typesetters measure the size of type in points. The point system was originally developed during the same period that the words font and leading were introduced, and it is derived from the French word *poindre,* to prick. A point was the smallest possible mark that could be made on a page—about 1/72 of an inch. In other words, there are 72 points in an inch.

This is the same system of measure as picas and points. The larger 12-point unit—the pica—is used to measure distances on the page (such as the width of a line of type, the width of a column, the width of the gutter), while points are used to measure small distances (such as type size, distance between lines, height or width of ruled lines, space between text and artwork). A 1.5-inch measure on the page would be measured as 9 picas, for instance, whereas a 1.5-inch high character would be measured as 108 points.

TYPOGRAPHY 77

The size of type was originally measured as the full height of the cast letter or type block. This included some amount of space above and below the letter, so two lines of type would not touch each other. Because the width and exact positioning of the type on the block was determined by the original designer of the typeface, the apparent size of the letters could vary slightly between different typefaces. You can see the differences between the heights of the 36-point letters from an assortment of typefaces in Figure 3.5.

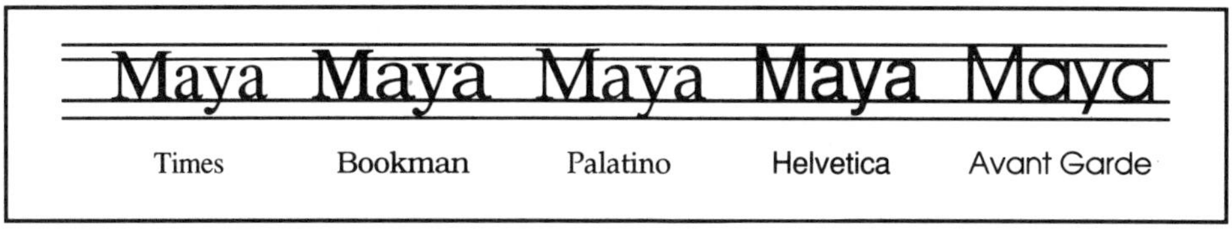

Maya Maya Maya Maya Maya
Times   Bookman   Palatino   Helvetica   Avant Garde

■ **Figure 3.5** Letters with the same nominal size may appear to be very different in different typefaces.

The sizes available for each typeface are shown on a menu or dialog box. You will generally want to stick with those sizes that are supported by your particular printer, however. PostScript printers will be able to handle any size.

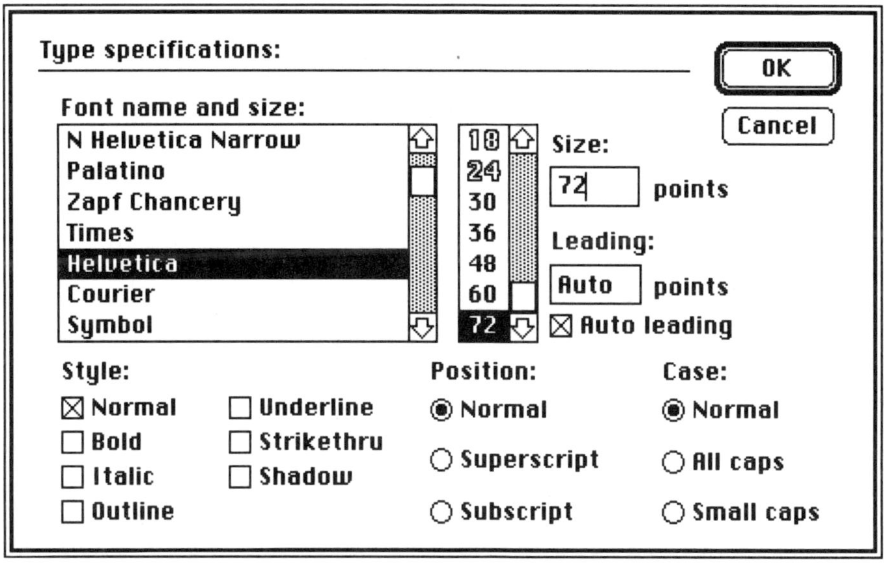

■ **Figure 3.6** PageMaker's type specs dialog box shows the sizes available for each font, or you can type in any size from 4 to 127 points.

Generally, body copy is set between 9 and 12 points in size. Headlines are usually larger. Business cards and classified ads can be smaller—using 7 or 8 point sizes. Text smaller than 6 points is difficult to read in most typefaces, and is infrequently used.

Traditionally, when typefaces were designed for hot-metal casting, slight modifications in the design would be made to make different sizes more legible, especially in small sizes. This does not occur with outline fonts in electronic publishing systems, and it is therefore a good idea to use fonts for the purpose for which they were designed—book fonts in small sizes for body copy, display fonts in larger sizes for headings.

Style

The third basic element of the traditional font is style: different styles listed on the menus and dialog boxes of desktop publishing applications include plain, bold, italic, reverse, and small caps. (Variables such as underscore, superscript, and subscript are not considered styles per se, and their use is usually dependent on the content of the material rather than on the design specifications.)

As with size, not all of the styles shown on the menus are supported by all printers. You will generally want to stick with those styles that are supported by your particular printer.

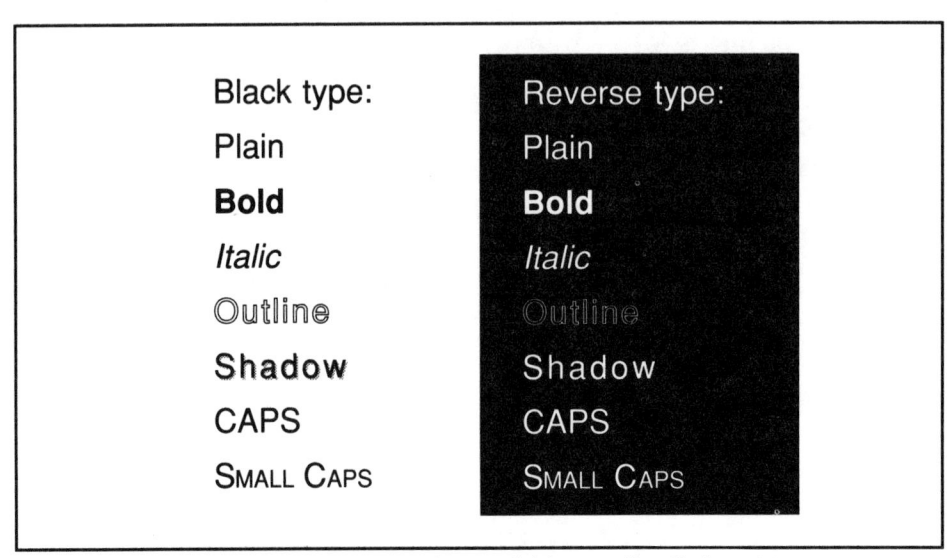

Black type:	Reverse type:
Plain	Plain
Bold	**Bold**
Italic	*Italic*
Outline	Outline
Shadow	Shadow
CAPS	CAPS
SMALL CAPS	SMALL CAPS

■ **Figure 3.7** Examples of the type styles available on a PostScript printer.

Some downloadable typefaces are available in "families" and require the specific installation of each style: you install the bold style of a typeface separately from the italic set, for instance. This usually means that each italic letter has been designed and customized as italic, rather than derived using obliquing formulas. The ability to create an italic form by slanting or obliquing a roman font is an electronic phenomenon, possible with outline fonts only, not bit-mapped fonts (see next subhead). This capability can save a lot of space in the printer's memory (ROM or RAM), but the trade off is that the letter forms may become distorted: curves parallel to the degree of slant tend to become thin or light, while curves perpendicular to the slant become thick. You will get better-looking type by installing Palatino Italic, for example, than by installing only Palatino and letting the application program make it italic through obliquing formulas. Hand-drawn italic letters tend to have more harmonious curves and diagonals, and designed obliques are sometimes referred to as italics to distinguish them from electronically generated obliques. As far as typography is concerned, the terms "italic," "cursive," and "oblique" are all used to mean the same thing: the slanted version of a given typeface.

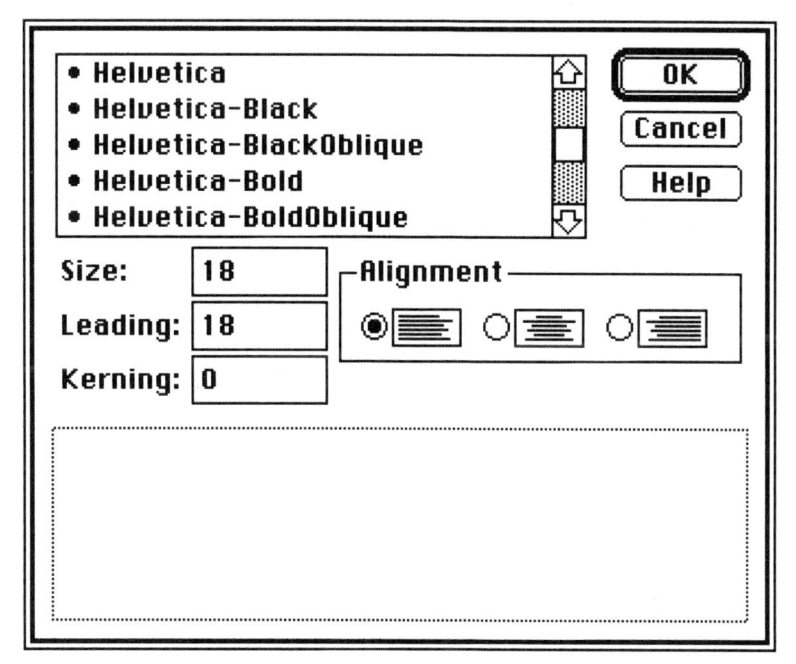

■ **Figure 3.8** Style can be part of the typeface name on the menu.

OUTLINE AND BIT-MAPPED FONTS

In working with computers and laser printers, typefaces are designed as either bit-mapped fonts or outline fonts. Bit-mapped fonts are stored as a pattern of dots, and they usually take up a lot of space in the printer's memory while the page is being printed, but the pages print relatively quickly because there is no "calculation" involved in scaling each character, as required for outline fonts.

Bit-mapped fonts are harder to scale to different sizes, so the font designer usually develops a different set of character designs for each size. This allows the designer the option of following the older tradition of modifying the design of the letters to improve legibility at different sizes. In the electronic age, however, many bit-mapped fonts are actually generated mechanically from outline formulas, with no customization for size.

Typefaces that are defined by curve-fitting mathematical formulas can be scaled to any size, or made bold or italic, by changing a few variables in the formulas that define the shapes of the letters. Fonts that are stored as formulas take up less space in the printer's memory than bit-mapped fonts, so you can download more of these fonts at one time. It can take longer to print these fonts, however, since each character's final form is "computed" at the time of printing. Printers that can handle outline fonts include all PostScript printers and those that use languages similar to PostScript, such as DDL and Interpress.

Outline fonts are sometimes called laser fonts to distinguish them from fonts that were designed for dot-matrix printers, but this is a misnomer since some laser printers use bit-mapped fonts. Outline fonts are said to be device-independent, in that the curves on the letters will be smoother when printed at higher resolutions, whereas bit-mapped fonts that are designed to be printed at 300 dpi do not always improve when printed at higher resolutions.

TYPOGRAPHY

■ Figure 3.9 Bit-mapped font vs. typeface defined by mathematical formula.

As a general rule, outline fonts and the printers that support them cost more than bit-mapped fonts and printers, but the extra expense is easily justified in an environment that calls for a wide variety of type styles and sizes, such as a large corporate publishing department or a typesetting service bureau. For smaller publication departments or support services that always use the same few fonts, bit-mapped fonts and printers may be the best solution.

The list of typefaces or fonts shown on the menu or in a dialog box of a word processing program, graphics package, or a page-layout package will vary depending on which printer drivers you have installed and which fonts you have added (or deleted). The *programs* you are using might support a wide range of typefaces, sizes, and styles that are not supported by all *printers*. You can add a new screen font to the menus, but you cannot print the publication using that font until you also install it on the printer.

You can build documents using fonts that your particular printer does not support, but when you print drafts on a printer that does not support the fonts used, an installed font is substituted, or the characters will be printed as low-resolution bit-mapped fonts. In this way, you can use a low-resolution printer with few installed fonts to print quick drafts of the document, and print the final on a high-resolution printer with all fonts available.

Rule of Thumb:

If you will be printing all drafts of the document on different equipment or with different fonts from the final version, it's a good idea to take a small section of the document through the entire production process early in the project, to assess and adjust for the differences between what you see on the screen, how it looks on the draft printer, and how it looks on the final printer. Sometimes the switch from one printer to another will actually affect the line breaks and page breaks in the text.

By taking a small part of the document through the entire process you can also test the thoroughness and efficiency of the steps you have anticipated and the time allowed for the full production.

Using Fonts in Desktop Publishing

Methods of adding or deleting fonts from a desktop publishing system will vary between systems and between applications. Sometimes the font manufacturer's installation program will be sufficient to make the font available through your applications. Some application programs require their own installation steps in order to display fonts on the menus.

If you are working on a PC under Microsoft Windows, for instance, you can add new fonts to the menu using the Add font command in the Control Panel's Installation menu. You can delete fonts from the menu using the Delete font command under the Installation menu of the Control Panel. (The Control Panel is a Microsoft Windows utility, not a part of the individual application packages.)

Besides adding *screen fonts* to the application menus, you usually need to add the same *printer fonts* to your printer. The difference between adding fonts to the menu of an application and adding them to the printer is described next.

ADDING SCREEN FONTS AND PRINTER FONTS

A screen font is a bit-mapped font that is designed to display letter forms on low-resolution computer monitors. When you add a typeface or font to the list on an application's menu or dialog box, you are actually adding a screen font to the system. This means that the application knows what width table and kerning table to use for that font, and how to display it on the screen.

Some applications will display a generic font on the screen rather than the actual letter forms of the selected font, but the line breaks should be the same as the printed version if the application is truly WYSIWYG.

In order for any font to print out properly, the printer must also know about the font. Printer fonts can be either bit-mapped or outline formulas, but they are specifically designed to be printed at high resolutions (300 dpi or more). A printer font is either built in to the printer, stored on a font cartridge, stored on the printer's fixed disk, or downloaded into the printer's memory. Usually, then, adding a new font to your system is a two-step process: you must install it on the application's menus, and you must install it on the printer.

A font installation program or utility comes with any fonts that you purchase for your system. The process of installing new fonts—screen fonts or printer fonts—is a simple menu selection on some systems and through some applications. In other cases, the installation process can require changes to the system command files and the entry of complex coded font names with little "friendliness" or margin for error. Some of the other factors that might affect your choice of target printer or fonts for a publication design are described next.

PRINTER FONTS

As we have mentioned throughout this chapter, the available fonts vary from printer to printer and from installation to installation. There are, essentially, three types of printer fonts, each with its own method of installation: built-in fonts, cartridge fonts, and downloadable fonts.

Built-in Printer Fonts

Built-in printer fonts, also called resident fonts, or ROM fonts, are installed by the manufacturer. They are always available for any document. They are always high-resolution fonts and are never jagged when printed out. Ideally, every font would be built-in to the printer. Unfortunately, fonts take up space; this is why most printers have few or no built-in fonts.

Apple's LaserWriter is a PostScript printer that comes with four built-in typefaces (13 fonts): Times, Helvetica, Courier, and Symbol (primarily Greek and mathematical symbols). This set is counted as 13 different ROM fonts: Times, Helvetica, and Courier each available in roman, italic, bold, and bold italic, plus Symbol in one style. In fact, many more "fonts" are available through this basic ROM library, because each of the ROM fonts can be printed in any size or style on an applications' menus, and some applications support a wide range of sizes and a few eccentric styles such as "outline" and "shadow." There is almost no limit to how these basic letter forms can be modified through certain graphics applications that can shade, mirror, rotate, and shear text.

> Times **Times** *Times* Times
>
> Helvetica **Helvetica** *Helvetica* Helvetica
>
> Courier **Courier** *Courier* Courier

■ **Figure 3.10** A PostScript printer's built-in typefaces can be printed in any size or style.

Apple's LaserWriter Plus adds seven more typefaces to the LaserWriter's four: Avant Garde, Bookman, New Century Schoolbook, New Helvetica Narrow, Palatino, Zapf Chancery, and Zapf Dingbats (all symbols). Each of these can be printed in any size or style on the menu (except Zapf Chancery), yielding 35 ROM fonts.

> Times
> Helvetica
> Helvetica Narrow
> Courier
> Symbol: Συμβολ
> Avant Garde
>
> Bookman
> New Century Schoolbook
> Palatino
> *Zapf Chancery*
> Zapf Dingbats: ✳❂❑✲

■ **Figure 3.11** LaserWriter Plus's 11 built-in typefaces can be printed in any size or style.

Allied's Linotronic Models 100, 300, and 500 typesetters get their fonts from an interchangeable RIP (raster image processor), the PostScript Interpreter. The basic RIP includes Times, Helvetica, Courier, and Symbol as built-in typefaces. RIP2 includes all of the LaserWriterPlus fonts in ROM. These installed fonts are listed in Figure 3.11.

Cartridge Fonts

Cartridge fonts are similar to built-in fonts: they are built-in to removable cartridges rather than hard-wired into the printer itself. The number of fonts available for a specific document depends on the cartridge that is installed at the time of printing.

The Hewlett-Packard LaserJet is a cartridge printer. If you do not have a cartridge, the default font is 12-point Courier. The LaserJet's memory is too limited to accommodate many downloaded fonts. The Hewlett-Packard LaserJet Plus is a cartridge printer also, but its expanded memory allows you to download fonts to the printer.

Downloadable Fonts

Downloadable fonts, sometimes called soft fonts, differ from built-in and cartridge fonts in this way: they are stored on disk and sent to the printer at the time of printing. Because they are not hard-coded into hardware, downloaded fonts take up memory space (RAM) in the printer. The number of fonts that can be downloaded at one time is limited by the amount of memory in the printer and the size of the fonts.

Figure 3.11 lists some of the fonts that are available for desktop publishing applications. The list of fonts available for your particular system will depend upon your equipment and the capabilities of your application programs. For example, Adobe Systems Inc. offers a wide range of downloadable fonts for PostScript printers, but some applications cannot use downloadable fonts. Bitstream makes downloadable fonts for Hewlett-Packard printers and others. The Fontware installation program from Bitstream can build PostScript outlines based on Bitstream's bit-mapped fonts and download them to memory for PostScript printers. (See Appendix for lists of other sources of typefaces.)

Downloading fonts is not always easy, nor will they always work the way you might expect. For example, many word processing programs have trouble keeping margins aligned when you use proportionally spaced fonts with some printers. You may have to contact the manufacturer (of the software or the printer) to get the appropriate printer driver and font driver for each typeface.

Rule of Thumb:

Make sure the program and fonts will work together before you finalize your design specifications.

Even if your printing equipment supports a particular font, you should check the quality of the type from your printer before finalizing your design specifications. Some fonts will print well at high resolutions, but seem jagged when printed from a 300 dpi printer. Choose these fonts when you will be using the 300 dpi printer for drafts only, and print the final pages on a higher-resolution typesetter.

The number of typefaces that you can download at one time is limited by the amount of memory in the printer or typesetter unless you are using fonts that are permanently downloaded to a hard disk attached to the typesetter. It's a good idea to know the limitations of the printer before finalizing a design. If you are not absolutely certain that the printer can handle the number of fonts in your design, find out by printing a sample page that uses all design elements before finalizing the design specifications.

The number of typefaces you can download for one document might also be limited by the size of your computer disk. In order for any font to be downloaded, it must be available on a disk at the time of downloading. If you are running without a hard disk, you might be limited to a list of fonts that take up less than 400K or 800K (the capacity of your disk drives).

Finally, the number of typefaces downloaded will significantly affect the time it takes to print the document—the more typefaces you use, the longer it will take to print. In the interest of saving time during production, you might deliberately limit the number of downloadable fonts used in a particular publication or in a particular workgroup, or declare different printers on a network to be reserved for special projects or particular downloaded fonts.

The issue of when to download fonts would be moot if the process were fast and easy, but on most systems downloading is slow. It can take a minute or more to download a font, and some fonts may need to be downloaded more than once during the full printing cycle when a lot of fonts compete for printer memory. The efficient procedure is usually to download all of the required fonts at once (if the printer's memory can accommodate them) and then print the document all at once. If you are sharing the printer with others on a network, you can suffer considerable inconvenience and delay if other users' documents keep pushing your downloaded fonts out of the printer, so that they would need to be downloaded repeatedly through the day.

As long as the downloadable font is available on your system, most applications simply download the font at the time of printing, and the fonts are flushed out of the printer's memory when the printing is complete. Some applications require that you run the downloadable fonts through a conversion process (a program supplied by the application manufacturer) that actually incorporates the font specifications (such as character width tables) into the application program.

For some applications, you can send downloadable fonts to the printer before printing the documents. This is sometimes called "permanent" downloading because the fonts are not automatically flushed out of memory after each print job, and this will usually make the printing process faster than if the font is downloaded repeatedly for each document at printing time. In fact, there is no such thing as "permanent" downloading, since downloaded fonts are always flushed out of memory when the printer is turned off and when more printer memory is needed for additional fonts or graphics.

Rule of Thumb:

It is a good idea to download fonts *before* printing if you are printing a long series of documents that all use the same fonts, and it is the recommended procedure if your downloadable fonts cannot fit on one disk along with the document while it is printing. Download fonts at the time of printing if you are only printing one or two drafts of the document that requires the fonts.

PRINTING A FONT

Once a font is available on your applications' menus, you can use it in setting the specifications for type on your pages. When you want to print the publication, the font must be available for the printer. Some applications and PostScript printer processors will search for the font automatically in an orderly sequence:
1. Look in the printer's ROM (i.e., a built-in font).
2. Look in the printer's RAM (i.e., it has been downloaded already).
3. Look on the printer's hard disk (if it has one), and download automatically.
4. Look in the font folder of the computer, and download automatically.
5. Look in the directory of the application that is printing, and download automatically.
6. Search other disks attached to the computer network, and download automatically.

Some applications will stop searching after Step 1 or 2. If the font is not found, some applications will issue a message and terminate printing or wait for the operator to supply the font disk. Other applications might proceed to print the publication, using a substitute font or using the low-resolution screen font.

Fonts stored in ROM are available instantly. Fonts that have already been downloaded to RAM are available instantly, but it can take 30 seconds or more per font to download the first time, and automatically downloaded fonts can loose their place in RAM if more fonts are downloaded during the process of printing different publications.

Whether design as a bit-mapped font or as an outline, all laser typefaces are printed as a pattern of dots. Typefaces that use line segments, or "vectors," to outline a character still use dots as the basic building blocks. All digital typesetters (sometimes called "third generation" devices) use the very basic principle of turning some light source on and off to create an image. That light source can be a cathode ray tube (CRT) or a laser or it may not be a light source at all as newer technologies apply electro erosion, magnetography and light emitting diodes. The placement of the dots for an individual character is stored in memory. Because every character is made up of dots, the diagonals and curves may not be as smooth and sharp in their edge resolution as straight lines. At 1,000 dots per inch, a measurement of resolution, acceptable quality is produced. At 5,000 dots per inch, there is no visible difference between digital type and other photographic type.

Rule of Thumb:

The best place to check quality levels is the dot on the lowercase i or the entire typeface Optima.

Outline fonts, therefore, must go through an additional process after downloading, and that is to build the font in each size used on the page. This makes printing with outline fonts somewhat slower than printing with ready-made bit-mapped fonts. Once each size is built, however, it stays in the *font cache* for easy access throughout the printing process for that publication—the *font cache* is often erased and replaced by subsequent printings of other documents.

Design Considerations

Design specifications for a publication usually include:
- Typefaces, sizes, and styles for different elements within the text.
- Basic text format. Will the paragraphs have a first line indent? What will be the space between paragraphs? Will the text be justified? Will headings be flush left or centered?
- Basic page layout or grid, including page size, margins, orientation, and number of columns.
- Typefaces, sizes, and styles to be used within the illustrations and in the captions.
- Final page count, or the range of pages expected to be filled.

Type specifications that cannot be incorporated in style sheets or templates should be written in a form that can be easily interpreted into the commands or specifications required by the software applications that are used to produce the final pages, and incorporated into the detailed list of review items and global conditions.

ASSEMBLE THE FONT LIST

The first decision in the design process is the determination of the type of printer that will be used for the final production of the document. What printers and typefaces are already installed in your organization? What typefaces are available by expanding your font library or by using an outside printing service bureau? The danger of developing design specifications without full knowledge of the final production resources include:
- The possibility that the budget for the project will increase if additional typefaces must be purchased to accommodate the design. In the best case, you simply add a typeface to the system, or exercise the option to choose a different typesetting service bureau. In the worst case, you end up purchasing many new fonts, and perhaps a new printer, rather than change the design specifications to match your current system. The cost charged to the project can justifiably be shared with other projects that will make use of the expanded capabilities required by your design.
- The possibility that the design must be changed in order to accommodate the current equipment configuration and type library. In the best case, any conflict between the design specifications and the equipment capabilities is discovered early in the project, before elements of the

design specifications are incorporated into any style sheets or templates for the project and applied to any of the text or graphics. In the worst case, the design change requires many hours to go throughout the files that have already been prepared using the old specifications. Remember that the original design usually considers the choice of typefaces and fonts in light of other design elements, such as page size and column width. A forced change in the fonts might also require some adjustments to these other elements of the design (Chapter 4). In what some designers would consider the very worst case, the type specifications are changed without changing any other element of the design and the resulting pages lose something on the aesthetic scale.

The first step in the design process, then, is to list all of the different fonts that are available for use in your design specifications, based on the current font library. This step was less important in traditional typesetting environments, where literally hundreds of fonts are available through commercial typesetting services. When so many fonts are available, experienced designers often sketch out their rough ideas for the design first, and then check their specifications against the typesetter's catalogue of fonts. In a desktop publishing environment, however, it is more likely that the number of typefaces and fonts available will be limited (unless you are a service bureau that supports a wide range of clients).

The second step is to list the fonts that you will actually use in a particular publication. One reason for limiting the number of fonts used is based on design considerations: "winning" designs use only a few fonts on each page. Another reason for limiting the number of fonts is a practical one: some printers cannot handle more than a few fonts per page or per cartridge. Be sure to find out what your system's limits are before choosing combinations of fonts.

A third factor in limiting the number of fonts is the number of text elements used in the document. Elements that require differentiation can include:
- Chapter Titles, section openings, or feature article headlines
- Different levels of headings or headlines
- Body copy
- Figure captions
- Labels within figures
- Footnotes
- Special sections such as sidebars, summaries, tables, etc.
- Table data
- Running headers and footers

Each of these elements might be further broken down and distinguished by type specifications. In the running footer, for example, you might want the page number to be bold and the section name italic. It's a common tendency to want to use a different font for each element—and this is a good idea within limits. If you study other published works, you'll see that most books use only one or two different typefaces, and that variations in size and style are used very sparingly. One reason is the guiding principle of simplicity in design. Another reason is that some laser printers are limited to only eight fonts per page or per publication.

The type specification process, then, involves merging the two lists: a list of the fonts that are available, or that you wish to use, and a list of the different type elements within the document. Complete specifications include alignment (left, right, centered, or justified) and leading (spacing between lines). Additional specifications can include identifying when to use all uppercase letters (all caps), upper and lowercase (initial caps), large initial caps (i.e., a larger point size than the characters that follow), drop caps, small caps, inverse or negative leading, and other special effects.

Available fonts:	Document elements:
8-point Times Roman	Figure labels
10-point Times Roman	Body copy
10-point Times Bold	Subhead
10-point Times Italic	Figure captions
14-point Helvetica Bold	Headlines

■ **Figure 3.12** The type specification process begins by listing the available fonts and the different type elements used in the document.

If you are not familiar with the different typefaces named on the type specs dialog box, or if you don't know which ones are supported by your printer, make up and print out a dummy copy using each of the options on the menu. In other words, type the name and size of each font on your menu, set the line in that font, then print out the list as a "type-sample" sheet. A complete type-sample book would show all of the characters of the set: uppercase, lowercase, numbers, and symbols.

> We offer...
>
> Times
>
> ₈ ₉ 10 11 12 14 18 24
>
> **Bold**
> *Italic*
> ***Bold Italic***
>
> Helvetica
>
> ₈ ₉ 10 11 12 14 18 24
>
> **Bold**
> *Italic*
> ***Bold Italic***
>
> Reverse type (all fonts)

■ **Figure 3.13** Example of a type-sample sheet.

FOLLOW BASIC PRINCIPLES

One approach to creating type specifications is to study the characteristics of different typefaces and the underlying principles that designers and typographers follow. Some of these guidelines and characteristics are listed here, but few documents can follow all of these guidelines without making exceptions to the rules. The mark of a good designer is that he or she knows when and how to break the rules.

Don't Use More Than Two Typefaces in a Document

Most published works use a greater variety of fonts than the traditional business report, which was usually plain Courier and Courier bold—all in one size. When you switch from using a letter-quality printer for business reports to using a laser printer, the wide selection of fonts may seem confusing at first. Magazines and newsletters often include many more fonts than business reports, books, and manuals, especially when you count all of the fonts used in display ads. However, the basic principle of simplicity remains the best guide if you are unsure about what fonts to use.

You will find that most publications use only one or two different typefaces. Use different *fonts*—variations in size and style—to distinguish between different elements. The body text for most books can be set using one typeface with the five conventional alphabets (upper and lower case roman and italic, and small capitals) at one point size. Footnotes are generally two points smaller in size but in the same face as the body copy. Boldface and size variations are used to set headings and figure captions and labels.

> **Rule of Thumb:**
> When two typefaces are used, one typeface is usually seriffed (for body copy) and the other sans serif (for headings and/or figure labels and captions).

Brochures often use decorative or unusual typefaces for the headings, and sometimes for the body copy as well. The typeface can convey a sense of seriousness, elegance, or frivolity. If you are not clear in your own mind how different faces affect the reader, it's best to stay with traditional book faces rather than experiment with more decorative faces.

> **Rule of Thumb:**
> In brochures, the choice of font sets the tone of the piece.

This guideline—to use only one or two typefaces—can be difficult to follow when graphic images are derived from a variety of different programs. The number of different fonts available with a spreadsheet charting program might be more limited than the number of fonts available in a drawing program, and both types of programs are likely to be more limited than the page-layout program in setting fonts. You should be familiar with the font options in all of the programs you will be using before deciding the final specifications.

Use Variations in Size and Style of One Typeface to Distinguish Different Heading Levels

Typography provides more opportunities for emphasizing information than typewriters or line printers. Consider using some of these variations instead of relying on size alone to distinguish headings:

- ALL CAPITALS
- SMALL CAPITALS
- CAPS AND SMALL CAPITALS
- Underlined
- *Italic*
- *ITALIC CAPS*
- *ITALIC CAPS AND SMALL CAPS*
- *ITALIC CAPS & SMALL CAPS*
- *ITALIC SMALL CAPS*
- **Bold**
- **BOLD CAPS**
- **BOLD CAPS & SMALL CAPS**
- **BOLD CAPS & SMALL CAPS**
- **BOLD SMALL CAPS**
- ***Bold Italic***
- ***ITALIC BOLD CAPS***
- ***ITALIC BOLD CAPS & SMALL CAPS***
- ***ITALIC BOLD SMALL CAPS***

Use Italics Rather Than Underscores for Emphasis Within Body Copy

Underscored text was a convention used for emphasis in documents printed on letter-quality printers, and is generally not appropriate in typeset publications.

If you are going to be printing on a textured paper stock, you will probably want to avoid very light italic faces in your design. The thin diagonal strokes of such faces may not print clearly on a textured stock.

Rule of Thumb:

The color of the paper and the ink as well should be considered in relation to typeface readability and how they will enhance or detract from illustrations.

TYPOGRAPHY 95

> NEW WAVE DISCO
> SETS PACE
>
> Heading set with default leading and kerning
>
> NEW WAVE DISCO
> SETS PACE
>
> Heading set with reduced leading and tighter kerning

■ **Figure 3.14** All-cap heads are usually set with minimum leading and kerned letter spacing.

Use ALL CAPS as a Deliberate Design Strategy, Rather Than as a Method for Showing Emphasis or Differentiating Heading Levels

If you are coming from the tradition of using letter-quality printers, then you might be accustomed to using uppercase type to add emphasis or to distinguish headings. This can still be a useful method in cases where other variations in size or style are not possible, and it can still be a part of your deliberate design strategy. Don't let it happen, however, just because "that's the way the author typed it."

Consider changing all-cap headings to bold or italics, for instance. Use variations in size rather than all-caps text to differentiate headings. One common exception to this rule occurs when the list of available fonts is too limited to accommodate all heading levels; in this case, all caps can be used to distinguish between two heading levels that are otherwise the same font. Text set in all caps usually requires kerning (see "Kerning," later in this chapter). Consider setting all-cap words or acronyms in text to be small caps.

All-cap heads are usually set with minimum word spacing and kerned letterspaces. The space between words should not be greater than the space between lines.

Rule of Thumb:

Mechanical line-up of caps on the left usually results in uneven alignment: visual alignment may require kerning.

For Images That Will Be Projected as Slides or Overhead Transparencies, Use Large Point Sizes for the Text

For overhead transparencies, one rule of thumb is that the image on the paper (not the projected image) should be easy to read from approximately 10 feet away (Figure 3.15). For most audiences, this means that important words should be no smaller than 36 or 24 points in size.

For slides, an image on 8½-by-11-inch paper should be easy to read from seven feet away (Figure 3.15). This means that the text can be 18 or 24 points in size, slightly smaller than that used on overhead transparencies.

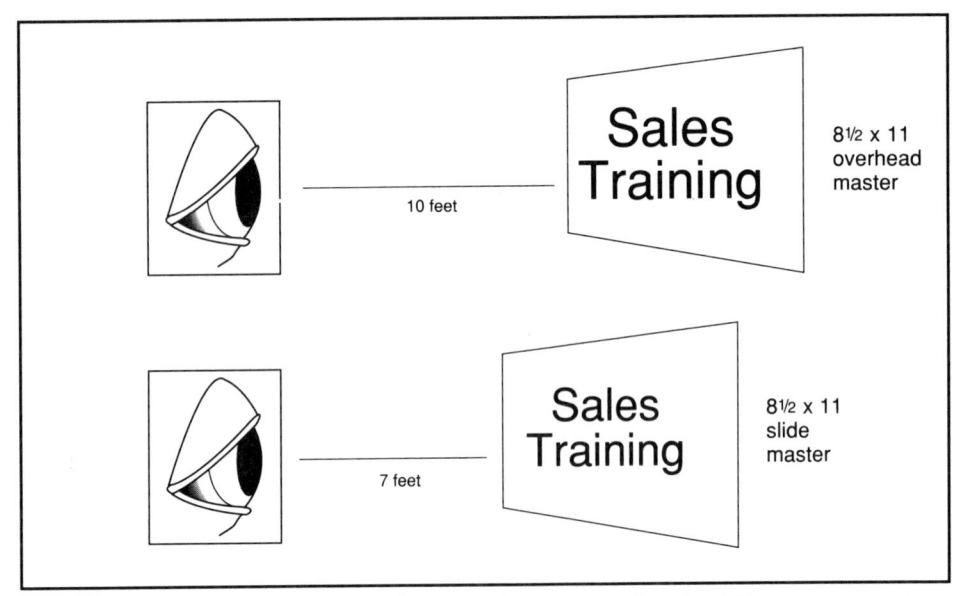

Rule of Thumb:
The paper printout of overhead transparencies should be easy to read from 10 feet away, slides from 7 feet away.

■ **Figure 3.15** The paper printout of overhead transparencies should be easy to read from 10 feet away, slides from 7 feet away.

CHARACTERISTICS OF DIFFERENT TYPEFACES

The use of fonts in the design of a document plays a very subtle role in determining how the reader receives the content of the message. In choosing between different typefaces, some designers can get a good idea of the effect a typeface will have on the reader simply by looking at the typeface. Like a connoisseur of good wines, the typographer can describe the characteristics of different typefaces in eloquent terms that the average reader experiences on the subliminal level only. If you are coming from an office environment in which all publications were previously printed on a letter-quality printer, then you may find it hard to distinguish the different typefaces available through desktop publishing and know their effects on the reader. If so, there are two ways of approaching the type specifications for a document.

The fastest way to acquire a sense of design and develop good design specifications is to study and imitate published works that are similar in structure to your document. Match your design specifications as closely as possible to the published documents; in other words, select fonts that are similar to those used for headings, body copy, and captions in the published document. You need not match the typefaces exactly, but try to substitute typefaces that are in the same category (seriffed or sans serif, roman, italic, or bold, etc.).

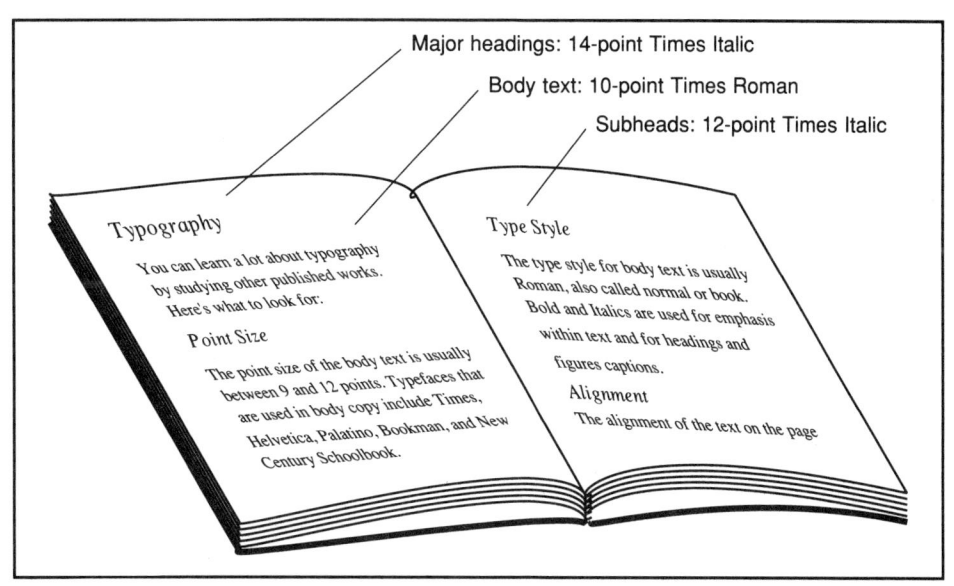

■ **Figure 3.16** Study other published works similar to the one you are producing to get ideas about type specifications for your document.

Gradually, as you gain experience using different typefaces, you will be able to distinguish between typefaces and the effects they can have on the reader. Descriptions of a few typefaces are included here, and you can extend these descriptions to many other typefaces that are similar to these basic forms. Table 3.1 shows some of the typefaces commonly used in various types of documents.

Warning:
Don't be surprised if you find different typeface vendors offering very similar or identical typefaces with different names. Some typeface names are actually copyrighted to the original designer whereas the design itself is not protected from imitation (with minor modifications).

Also, you might find that a typeface offered under one name can have different character width and stroke definitions, as a result of different designers' renditions under the same noncopyrighted typeface name.

Table 3.1
Typefaces Available for Desktop Publishing Applications

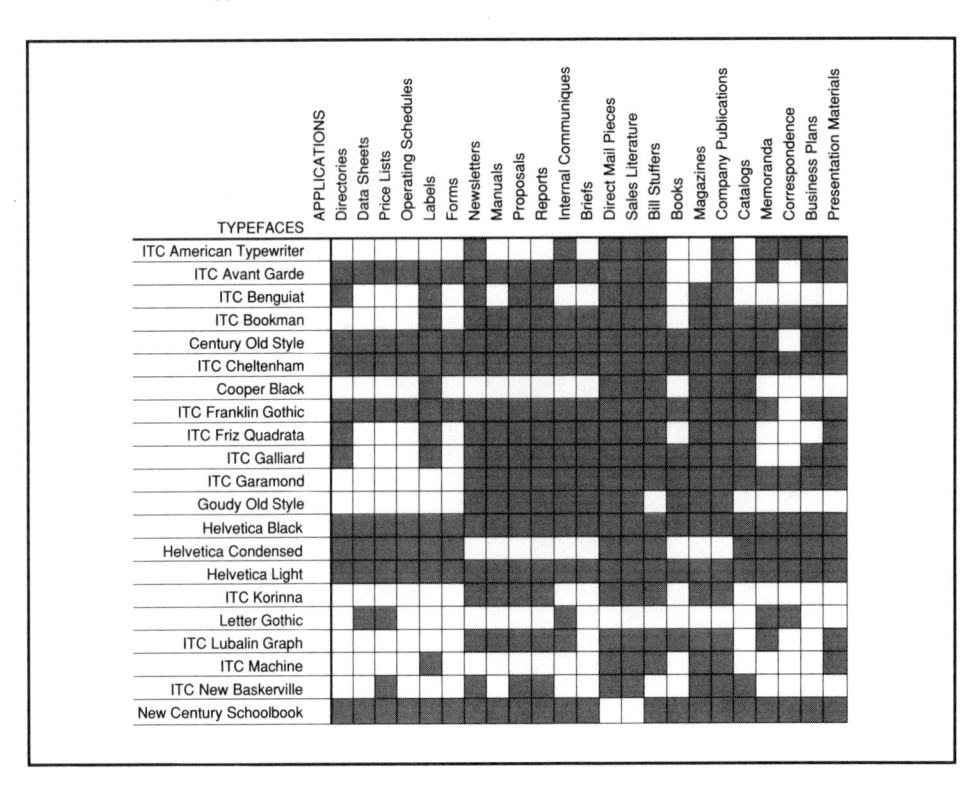

Courier and Other Typewriter Faces

Courier is a typewriter face designed in 1952 by Howard G. Kettler for IBM, based on constructions of circles (or ellipses) and straight lines. Kessler used a large x-height and very open ellipses so the typeface would resist accumulation of ink and debris from the ribbons. Most readers recognize it as *the* typewriter face, and due to this association it is rarely recognized as a typeset font.

Because Courier seems less formal than typeset fonts, it is often chosen in situations where friendliness or familiarity is an important part of the message. It is also used in special cases that require a monospaced font rather than a proportionally spaced font like Times or Helvetica. By design, Courier's "narrow" letters like "i" have been expanded and wide letters like "m" have been condensed to fit the same width of space as the "n." This makes it suitable for representing any monospaced text (such as representations of some computer screen images) and for aligning tabular material that was originally aligned by typing spaces (rather than the tab key).

	Set Using Tabs			*Set Using Spaces*		
	Month	IN	OUT	Month	IN	OUT
Courier	JAN	100	120	JAN	100	120
Font	FEB	110	110	FEB	110	110
	MAR	120	100	MAR	120	100
	Month	IN	OUT	Month	IN	OUT
Helvetica	JAN	100	120	JAN	100	120
Font	FEB	110	110	FEB	110	110
	MAR	120	100	MAR	120	100

■ **Figure 3.17** Tabular material created using the tab key vs. same material aligned using spaces.

ITC American Typewriter, designed specifically for typesetting text to look like typewritten text, combines the comfortable feeling of a traditional typewriter face with modern typographic techniques that enhance readability and use of space, including proportional spacing. Other typewriter faces that are available as laser fonts include Prestige or Prestige Elite, Letter

Gothic (a sans serif face), and Orator (all uppercase letters designed to be used by lecturers reading notes at a distance). All of these are monospaced fonts that offer the same advantages as Courier, though Letter Gothic and Orator are unsuitable for long stretches of body copy in small point sizes.

Times and Other Serif Book Faces

Originally designed by Stanley Morrison for the Times newspaper of London in 1931, Times New Roman evolved from Plantin (designed by F.H. Pierpont in 1913 for Monotype) and Gros Cicero (designed by Robert Granjon in 1568 and used by the printer Christophe Plantin in Antwerp). Times is scientifically engineered to save space in newspaper printing, and it became popular during WWII because it helped save paper. It was later adopted by Henry Luce for his publishing empire in the United States, and has been used by newspapers and magazines ever since.

The typeface family has been extended to include nonroman styles such as italic, and typographers usually shorten the name to Times Roman or simply Times (though you will still find oxymorons like Times Roman Italic). The typeface name Times Roman is licensed through Allied Linotype for use on many popular printers such as the Apple LaserWriter and Linotronic typesetters. Imitations, with some slight variations in quality, have been issued under other names such as Tms Rmn, Tempora, English, London, Dutch, and Press Roman.

Original versions of Times Roman were designed for hot-metal composition, and the basic character designs and spacing were modified slightly in each point size to maximize legibility: small sizes had looser letter spacing and thicker strokes, while larger sizes had relatively narrower strokes, tighter spacing, and longer ascenders and descenders. These fine adjustments are lost when Times is scaled from an outline font for electronic typesetting, and the characters lose their elegance when printed at low resolutions.

Times is a bookish face that connotes tradition and elegance. Characterized by narrowed shapes and tight letter spacing, Times works best in narrow columns of text, no more than 60 characters wide. Add leading between lines if you must use Times in wider columns, to make it easier for the eye to follow. Sizes smaller than 9 points may need added letter spacing to prevent the serifs of letters from actually touching each other.

For wider blocks of text, use some other serif font that is designed primarily for legibility, such as Century Old Style (designed by Morris Fuller Benton in 1906 for the American Type Founders) or its cousin, New Century Schoolbook (available from many sources as it is not copyrighted). ITC

Bookman is a sturdy, readable face that has become more widely used since Apple built it in to the LaserWriter Plus.

ITC Garamond originated in Renaissance France during printing's golden age, and remains a graceful, readable serif face with thin strokes that add elegance and conserve space on the page. ITC Cheltenham (designed by Tony Stan in 1975) is a robust typeface suitable to many typographic applications and is able to survive poor printing conditions: though the letters are slightly condensed for economy, the interior spaces of the characters are open and full, increasing the face's legibility and minimizing the filling-in effects of heavy inking on porous paper. In direct contrast to Cheltanham, Bodoni (designed by Morris Benton but based on the 17th-century master Giambattista Bodoni) is characterized by thick vertical lines and very closed interiors, making it less suitable for body text but excellent for headlines and short blocks of text requiring an elegant, graceful look. ITC Korinna is marked by short serifs and swelling curves, reminiscent of *Art Nouveau.*

Rule of Thumb:

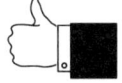

Use a serif face, rather than sans serif, for better legibility of body copy.

The calligraphic serif faces such as Souvenir, Palatino, ITC Galliard, and Zapf Calligraphic have strokes that swell and recede, as if drawn by a brush, culminating in distinctive serifs. These faces can serve for body copy as well as display type. The italic in these faces is especially calligraphic and serves well for formal invitations and announcements.

Newer text fonts that have been developed specifically for electronic typesetting include Lucida (designed by Charles Bigelow and Kris Holmes in both a serif and a sans serif set), Computer Modern (designed by Donald Knuth of Stanford University, including many symbols used in scientific books and treatises, also available as serif and sans serif), and Bitstream Chart (designed for Bitstream by Matthew Carter to perform well on 300 dpi printers).

Helvetica and Other Sans Serif Faces

Helvetica was designed by Max Miedinger for Edward Hoffman of the Haas type foundry near Basel, Switzerland, and was named Haas New Grotesque when first produced in 1957. (*Grotesque* was an early name for sans serif typefaces.) In 1965 Linotype Company issued it under the name Helvetica (the Roman name for Switzerland). Helvetica became the most available and most favored sans serif typeface in all countries where Linotype dominated the typesetting market, whereas markets dominated by Monotype equipment made Univers the sans serif of choice.

The name Helvetica is actually licensed from Allied, so imitators come under a wide assortment of names, including Swiss, Helios, Geneva, Megaron, and Triumvirate. Some imitation Helvetica fonts bear little resemblance to the original letters designed by Miedinger, but Helvetica's popularity has insured its availability—in one form or another—on virtually every typesetting or desktop publishing system.

Helvetica is considered modern, clean, orderly, and serious.

> **Rule of Thumb:**
>
> "The worst possible use of Helvetica is in all caps in a centered composition; the text looks too boring to read. The best use is in caps and lowercase, in more than one weight and size, in an asymmetric composition that uses white space and unequal margins to create action and dynamic tension on the page."
>
> — *Charles Bigelow*

Sans serif typefaces are often used for headings and captions in publications that use a serif face for the body copy. Sans serif faces are also commonly used in forms, price lists, and catalogues where economy of space and maximum legibility are important. If Helvetica seems overworked, use another sans serif typeface in its place. ITC Avant Garde and ITC Avant Garde Gothic, based on the logo of *Avant Garde* magazine in 1970, is a graceful, open sans serif face that is composed of perfect circles and triangles and is available for most printers. ITC Franklin Gothic was refined by Victor Caruso in 1980 to have a slightly enlarged lowercase x-height and somewhat condensed character proportions compared with the original Franklin Gothic, giving it increased readability and economy of space. Futura typifies Bauhaus experiments in geometric form in the early 20th century.

Calligraphic sans serif faces are very readable as body copy as well as display type, such as ITC Friz Quadrata, Optima, and Zapf Humanist. The brush-like strokes of these faces make them more elegant than most sans serifs.

TYPOGRAPHY   **103**

| Avant Garde | Helvetica | Helvetica Light |
| **Helvetica Bold** | Helvetica Condensed | Optima |

■ **Figure 3.18** Examples of sans serif typefaces.

Display and Decorative Typefaces

Cooper Black was designed by Oswald Cooper in 1921 for "far-sighted printers with near-sighted customers," and its heavy strokes with rounded corners make this a very readable display type.

Benguiat is related to Friz Quadrata in that it is calligraphic, but its thicker cross stokes and more slanted diagonal lines make it more suitable as a display type, or for short blocks of text in large point sizes. Other decorative faces include Cloister Black and Old English (as used by Gutenberg in body copy but now rarely used, and only as display type).

Script Typefaces

Script typefaces imitate handwriting or calligraphy, and tend to require more space per letter than the other typefaces described here. In most cases the letters do not actually connect (as they would in true handwritten script) but they seem to flow together. These faces are often used in announcements, invitations, event programs, and certificates, and may be found in advertising or promotional material as well.

Rule of Thumb:
Never use all caps in text set in a script font.

All script fonts are calligraphic in nature—though some nonscript fonts that vary the stroke width are also called calligraphic. Zapf Chancery is a calligraphic face built-in to all Apple LaserWriter Plus models and available from Adobe for all PostScript printers. Park Avenue is a light-hearted script in the American tradition designed by Robert E. Smith in 1933, and available in PostScript from Adobe Systems.

Symbol Typefaces

Symbol typefaces are composed primarily of symbols, such as those used in physics and mathematics, special punctuation marks (such as square bullets and arrows), and various "dingbats" (a term used to refer to a typesetter's collection of flowers, hearts, stars, and other decorative markers and border elements).

Two of the most common symbol fonts for PostScript printers are Adobe's Symbol and ITC Zapf Dingbats PostScript fonts, built-in to all Apple LaserWriter Plus models and supported by all PostScript printers and typesetters. Adobe also offers a font for maps, Carta, which includes symbols, and a Sonata typeface composed of musical notes and note components (clefs, staffs, rests, etc.).

The two most common noncharacter characters used in typography are boxes and bullets. These symbols are included as part of some font sets, or you can set them by using one of the symbol fonts mentioned here. More often than not, if you use boxes and bullets from a font that is different from the body copy, you will have to change point size so that the box or bullet will optically match the x-height.

Rule of Thumb:

Boxes and bullets should be as close to the x-height as possible if used full size, or centered on it if not.

FACTORS IN MIXING TYPEFACES

As mentioned in the guidelines above, it's a good idea to stick to one or two different typefaces—usually a seriffed and a sans serif typeface—and use variations in size and style to differentiate elements. You will find that there are many production efficiencies involved in using only one typeface whenever possible.

One convenience of using all one typeface (with different sizes and styles) is that you can globally change to any other typeface without affecting the different sizes and styles set up in the text. Most desktop publishing applications let you select a whole story or article and change it from Times to Helvetica, for example, but few applications let you globally change only Times to Helvetica in a block of text that mixes typefaces. Starting with one typeface can be handy if you want to quickly generate several variations on a basic design, or when you want to use one printer or cartridge for all drafts, then switch to a different printer, cartridge, or downloadable font for the final printing. Another pragmatic reason for using one typeface is that it can save time spent formatting (i.e., specifying different typefaces and fonts) in the page-layout package or in the word processing program itself.

TYPOGRAPHY 105

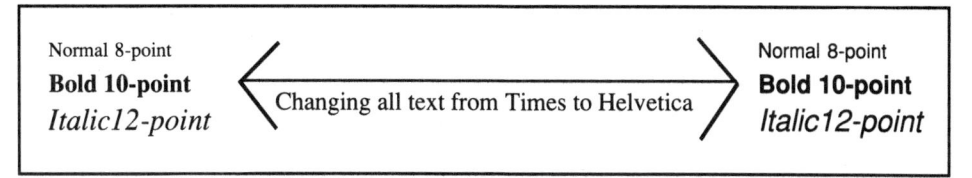

| Normal 8-point
Bold 10-point
Italic12-point | ⟨ Changing all text from Times to Helvetica ⟩ | Normal 8-point
Bold 10-point
Italic12-point |

■ **Figure 3.19** You can globally change the typeface for selected text without affecting the sizes and styles.

At the other extreme, there may be good reasons for using more than two typefaces. For example, you may be forced to use all of the fonts on an eight-font cartridge in order to achieve the required differentiation between text elements. Or documents that incorporate many changing formats—such as magazines and newsletters—might use more than four typefaces throughout the document, though each page or feature or ad uses only one or two typefaces.

■ **Figure 3.20** Example of a document that uses all four typefaces (eight fonts) on a Hewlett-Packard cartridge.

Special considerations also arise when you are using downloaded fonts. Downloaded fonts are not stored in the permanent memory (ROM) of the printer or in the printer cartridge, so they take up space in the printer's temporary memory (RAM). This usually means that you cannot download more than a few fonts at one time, and on some printers it can also mean that you cannot print high-resolution graphics when the downloaded typeface is required.

LINE LENGTH

Line length is the measure of the area between two margins. The optimum width of a column of text is a function of the typeface and point size. Sometimes the formula font size x 2 is used to determine the maximum line length. Lowercase alphabet x 1.5 is also used. Another common rule of thumb is that a line should be about 55 to 60 characters (or 9 to 10 words) wide for optimum readability. The corollary to this rule is that wider line lengths call for larger sizes of body copy. Wider faces look best with wider line lengths; condensed faces look best with narrow line lengths.

Rule of Thumb:
Instead of wide line lengths, double or multiple columns of smaller line lengths should be used. Multiple, narrow columns are preferable to single, wide columns.

Besides specifying the width of pages or columns for electronic systems, the designer should verify that the first pages that are produced yield the desired results; minor differences between the original specifications and the final pages can result when the designer's specifications are converted into the terms required by the layout program. For example, if the column width is specified in picas by the designer, but the page-layout program calculates the column widths based on entry of the full page width and the gutter measurements, the final column width might not match the original specifications exactly.

Paragraphs, the basic units of English composition, are often defined by an indent at the beginning of the first line and may be delineated by a short line of characters at the end. An alternative format involves additional line spacing (twice the visual line spacing) between paragraphs instead of the indent, or running all paragraphs together, separated by a special character, such as the paragraph symbol.

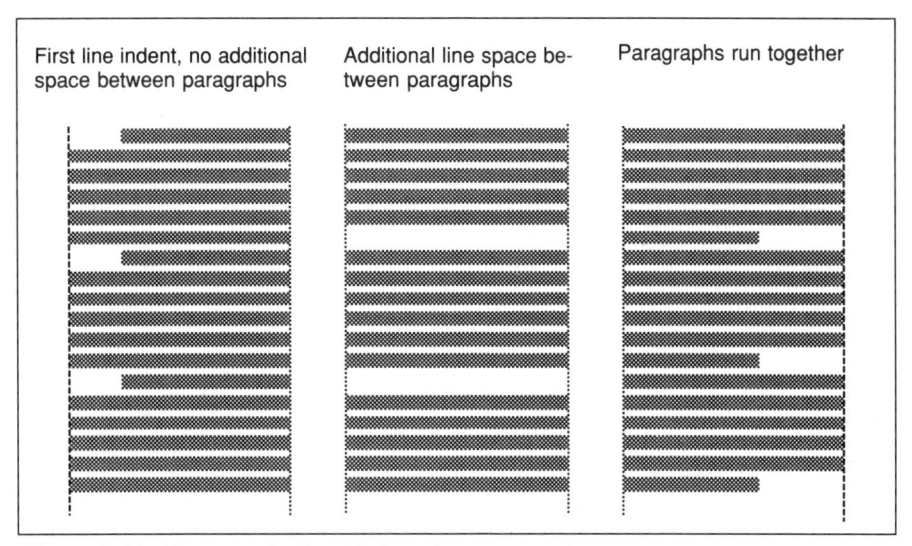

■ **Figure 3.21** Three methods of delineating paragraphs.

Rule of Thumb:
Paragraph indents should be at least one EM. As a line length increases, paragraph indentions should increase.

ALIGNMENT

The two standard alternatives for aligning body copy are ragged right and justified. Justification forces text lines to be the same length so that they line up on the left and the right. The practice originated with mediaeval scribes who ruled margins and text lines to speed writing and fit as many characters on a line as possible. Later, metal type required even copy blocks to allow "lock up" into page form. The opposite of justified text is ragged text.

There is continuing argument about whether text should be justified or ragged, how "ragged" ragged should be, and whether or not hyphenation should be allowed. Legibility studies have found that there is no noticeable difference in legibility (reading speed and comprehension) between justified and ragged-right text, and the average reader does not even notice whether text is justified or not. Alignment therefore becomes a purely aesthetic variable, and as such there are no strict rules about when to justify text.

Rule of Thumb:

Short line lengths (less than 60 characters) should not be justified.

There is a direct relationship between hyphenation, justification, and the width of the text column: Text in wide columns will tend to require less hyphenation, and unjustified text will appear less ragged, than text in narrow columns. Justified text is likely to have more "rivers" of white space in narrow columns than in wide columns. Flush left (ragged-right) text that is not hyphenated will usually appear more ragged than hyphenated text.

Ragged-right text is easier to edit than justified text if you are making corrections to individual lines that have already been typeset and pasted onto boards, as often happens when traditional typesetting is used, but this consideration is not so important when you are using electronic full-page-layout methods and can reprint the entire page easily. Ragged text creates more white space on the page, and can take up more room (i.e., require more pages) than the same text set justified.

Hyphenated text will extend over fewer lines than text that is not hyphenated, and justified text will take up less space than text that is not justified. Besides using the hyphenation and justification settings to fit copy to a page, you can achieve unusual affects by changing the hyphenation zone on unjustified text (if the application offers this feature). A large hyphenation zone can be used to deliberately exaggerate the ragged right margin, or to minimize hyphenation without turning it off entirely.

(Chapter 7 includes more discussion about how justification, hyphenation, and letter-spacing variables can be adjusted during the page-layout process to make copy fit or improve line breaks.)

LINE SPACING OR LEADING

Line spacing—the space between lines of type—is called leading (pronounced "ledding") or vertical spacing. If you are coming from a traditional typesetting environment, then you are probably accustomed to specifying the exact leading for type (the space between lines) as well as the type size. Desktop publishing applications usually have an automatic leading feature, which means that the leading will be determined automatically based on the point size of the type if you do not specify otherwise. In most cases, the automatic-leading formula yields results that are consistent with good typography.

TYPOGRAPHY　109

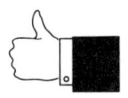

Rule of Thumb:
The space between lines should be at least 20% of the point size of the type, and should never be less than the the word spacing.

Automatic leading for 10-point Times
is 12 points, or 10/12.

Automatic leading for 12-point Times
is 14.4 points, or 12/14.5.

Automatic leading for 14-point Times
is 16.8 points, or 14/17.

■ **Figure 3.22** In some applications, automatic base-to-base leading is roughly 120% of the point size (rounded to the nearest half point).

The correct formula for setting the space between lines should be affected by the other considerations besides type size, and for this reason you might want to specify the leading precisely throughout a publication. For example, sans serif faces merit wider spacing between lines than serif faces in the same point size. Faces with small x-heights can be set in tighter leading than faces with large x-heights. Long line widths are easier to read when the leading is increased beyond the normal formula.

Generally speaking, it's a production convenience rather than a design principle to use automatic leading unless you have a reason to override it. This way, if you change the point size of all or part of the text, the leading will change automatically to match the new size. You can deliberately manipulate the leading to achieve a custom look or to make the copy fit the column or a certain number of pages (see Copy Casting, in this chapter, and Copy Fitting, in Chapter 7).

Usually, the leading for any line will be determined by the largest characters in that line. If you want to create large initial caps, for instance, you may need to adjust the leading for the large letter. One of the capabilities that modern typesetting techniques makes available is called minus leading. This means that the type is set with a leading value *less* than the point size, such as 9 on 8½. Usually, this can only be done with faces that are small on body or have short ascenders/descenders, or for all caps as in heads.

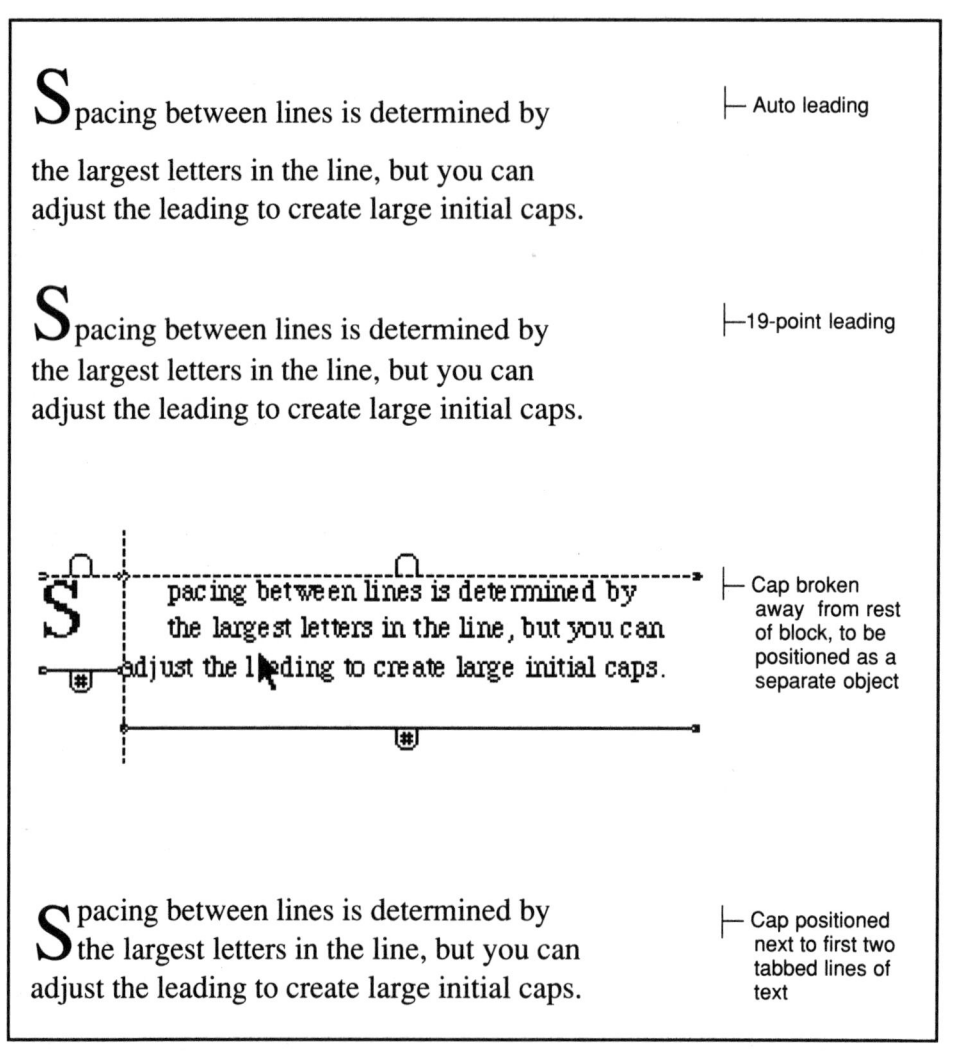

S pacing between lines is determined by the largest letters in the line, but you can adjust the leading to create large initial caps. ⊢ Auto leading

S pacing between lines is determined by the largest letters in the line, but you can adjust the leading to create large initial caps. ⊢ 19-point leading

S   pacing between lines is determined by
     the largest letters in the line, but you can
     adjust the leading to create large initial caps.
⊢ Cap broken away from rest of block, to be positioned as a separate object

S pacing between lines is determined by the largest letters in the line, but you can adjust the leading to create large initial caps. ⊢ Cap positioned next to first two tabbed lines of text

■ **Figure 3.23** Spacing between lines is determined by the largest letters in the line, but you can adjust the leading to create large initial caps.

EXPANDING OR CONDENSING TYPE

The terms expanding and condensing have been used in two different ways in desktop applications. Expanding usually refers to the width or wideness of all characters in a particular type style, but it can sometimes be used to mean expanded *letter spacing*. Expanded faces are often used for heads, subheads, and small blocks of ad copy. Expanded or condensed letter spacing, on the other hand, is used for special effects, such as forcing a subtitle to match the line length of a title (Figure 3.24). Some desktop applications can modify character "set width" electronically to create wider characters, or you can purchase expanded typefaces as separate fonts from some manufacturers.

> Helvetica normal
> Helvetica Condensed Typeface
> Helvetica normal, kerned tighter

■ **Figure 3.24** Condensed typeface vs. tighter letter spacing.

Rule of Thumb:
Never use expanded typefaces with a short line length.

KERNING HEADLINES AND TITLES

Kerning refers to the fine adjustments made to the spacing between certain pairs of letters to give the overall text an even appearance. With kerning, the spacing between letters is variable. Rather than assigning the same width to each character (as in nonproportional type) or assigning different widths to each character (as in proportional type that is not kerned), kerning gives each letter a different width depending on what letters are adjacent—sometimes to the extent that one letter actually encroaches into another's rectangular space, so the two letters touch each other.

Headlines and titles such as figure titles, newsletter banners, and advertising copy should stand out from the body copy of the document. As mentioned in the guidelines listed earlier in this chapter, you can use size rather than bold style to differentiate and emphasize these elements. Large-size text is usually kerned. Text set in all uppercase letters or set in small caps (i.e., capital letters the size of the x-height of the font to which they belong) can also require kerning for improved letter spacing and legibility.

"To kern or not to kern" is a decision appropriate to the typographer or designer. The design specifications can include a general recommendation to expand or condense certain elements of the text, but the final decisions about kerning are usually made during the production phase rather than the design phase, after an examination of the first drafts of typeset text. Candidate "kerning pairs" are well known to professional typesetters, but one way of assessing the space between pairs is shown in Figure 3.25.

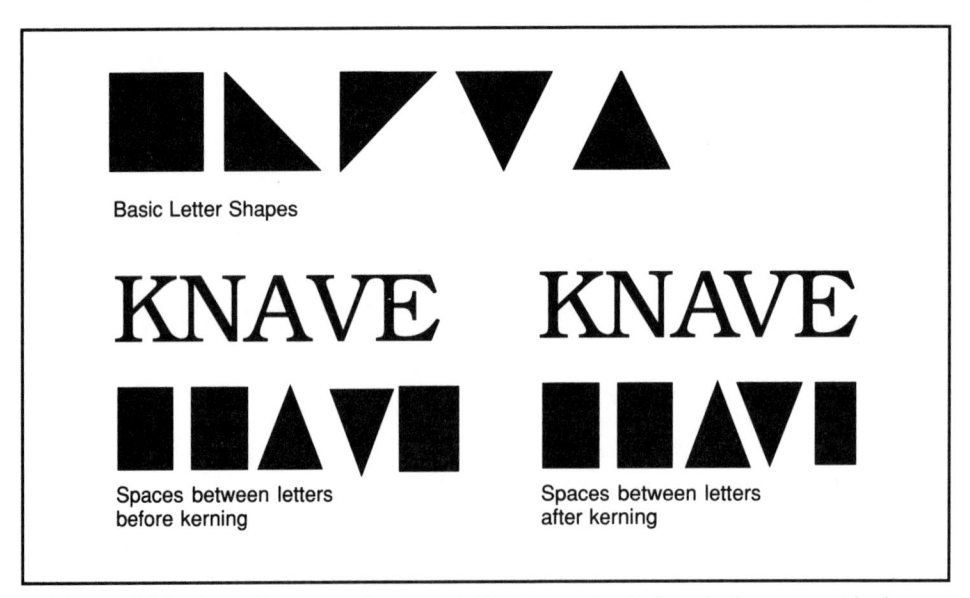

■ **Figure 3.25** The white space between letters is made obvious in the geometrical representation of each letter.

There are three basic methods of kerning. The first method is automatic: in this case, the application program uses an internal table of kerning pairs to determine the adjustments to be made between letters. Some programs let you select the text to be kerned (and thereby leave some of the text unkerned), or let you select the relative degree of kerning (to produce condensed or expanded text). Some programs also let you adjust the values in the kerning table directly for each pair listed.

A second method, offered by some programs as a supplement to using automatic kerning, is to individually adjust the spacing between any two letters—usually by pressing a key to move the letters closer together or further apart, or by entering a numeric kerning factor.

The third method is actually a "workaround" when neither of the other two methods is available. That is, to manually position characters beside each other, either on the screen (by moving each character as a separate object on the screen) or on paper (by cutting a whole word into pieces and manually positioning and pasting down each character).

In applications that let you manually adjust the space between any two letters, this procedure is applied on a case-by-case basis, and cannot be handled with global type specifications. The designer prints the document and examines the headlines, looking for pairs of letters that appear to have extra space between them.

The apparent space is something of an optical illusion caused by the angles of the two adjacent letters. For example, the edges of the capital A have the opposite slope of the letter V. When the letters A and V are adjacent in a word like KNAVE, the space between the A and V will appear to be much wider than the spaces between any of the other letters.

Don't confuse kerning with letter spacing—another variable that can be adjusted in some programs. Letter spacing is automatically adjusted during the process of justifying a line of text. Some programs let you specify the limits for these adjustments (to eliminate the creation of wide gaps during justification), or specify the "normal" space between letters (as a percentage of an En space), but these adjustments do not require a kerning pair reference table.

Also, don't confuse kerning with ligatures: two or more characters designed as a unit. There are five f-ligatures plus the dipthongs ae and oe, æ and œ. The traditional ligatures are included as part of some font sets. Although book production most often finds them mandatory, advertising typography rarely finds them useful—in fact, they cannot be used in copy set tighter than normal spacing. They should be used in headlines sparingly.

SPECIAL TREATMENT OF INITIAL LETTERS

One design option that has always presented a problem during production is a larger-than-body-copy initial letter. Some desktop publishing applications offer this feature as an automatic option, but most still require some judgment and adjustment on the part of the designer or page-layout artist. The two basic positions for a large initial letters are sunken (or drop cap), or raised (Figure 3.26).

> L ast year, the largest growth was seen in three areas: deciduous plants, irrigation systems, and lawn furniture. This year we expect to see a major shift
>
> L ast year, the largest growth was seen in three areas: deciduous plants, irrigation systems, and lawn furniture. This year we expect to see a major shift

■ **Figure 3.26** Large initial letters can have sunken or raised positions.

Rule of Thumb:
Generally speaking, the initial letter should be the same typeface as the copy; or from the same group, either serif or sans serif.

A sunken initial letter is normally set flush left with the margin of the text, with the top of the letter aligned with the top of the first line of text. The lines of text beside the initial cap are normally set flush left with respect to each other, at a distance from the initial that equals the distance below the initial. (Sometimes the first line of copy is brought closer to the initial, to give a stronger link spatially between the cap and the word of which it is a part.)

Rule of Thumb:
It is a good idea to set the entire first word in all caps when an initial cap is used, and bring it closer to the initial if it is part of the word.

TYPOGRAPHY 115

> Last year, the largest growth was seen in three areas: deciduous plants, irrigation systems, and lawn furniture. This year we expect to see a major shift
>
> A major shift in the primary areas of growth is expected over the next five years. Last year, the largest growth was seen in three areas: deciduous plants,

■ **Figure 3.27** First line is brought closer when initial cap is part of the first word, not otherwise.

The base line of the initial should align with the base of the last line of copy beside the initial. This usually means that you want to pick a cap height that equals the height of the lines of text beside it, rather than change the leading to make the base lines align.

Rule of Thumb:

If you cannot or do not wish to change the leading of the copy or the size of the initial, it is better to keep the base lines aligned and let the initial raise slightly above the top line of copy.

One trick in this situation is to make the first word of the copy small caps rather than all large caps, and thereby drop the apparent height of the top line of copy.

> LAST year, the largest growth was seen in three areas: deciduous plants, irrigation systems, and lawn furniture. This year we expect to see a major shift
>
> LAST year, the largest growth was seen in three areas: deciduous plants, irrigation systems, and lawn furniture. This year we expect to see a major shift

■ **Figure 3.28** First word in all caps and in small caps.

A raised letter should be set with the base line of the initial aligned with the baseline of the first line of copy. The raised initial may be indented, and the word following it need not be set in caps.

Rule of Thumb:

If the design calls for a large initial, avoid starting with opening quote marks. Omit the opening quote (and let the closing quote suffice) or set the quote smaller than the initial cap (but larger than the body copy).

SPECIAL HANDLING OF FIGURE LABELS AND CAPTIONS

One of the characteristics of any designed document is consistency of treatment, and this includes the labels within figures as well as the figure titles or captions. This can be difficult when you are bringing figures from several different programs into a page-layout application for final composition. The designer needs to specify how captions, figure titles, and figure labels will be handled in each different program that may be the source of illustrations for the document. Will the charting program be able to match the fonts used in figures from other drawing packages? Will the figure be scaled larger or smaller after it is in the page-layout application?

You might decide that all figure titles and captions will be entered directly in the page-layout application to insure consistency, but you will still need to specify the preferred font for labels that fall within the figures. Furthermore, you may need to account for changes in the size of type that will result when you shrink or enlarge a figure. When you change the size of a graphic imported from another program, you also change the size of the type used in that graphic. If you know that you will be shrinking a figure by 50 percent, for instance, then the illustrator might need to make the type twice as large in the drawing program as it will be in the final document.

Copy Casting

Copy casting is the process of predicting the number of words or characters required to fill an allotted amount of space, or the process of determining how much space the finished text will require. In both cases, copy casting takes place before the pages are actually laid out. Once you go through the process of actually laying out the pages, using a word processing or page-layout application, you can force copy to fit a given area by adjusting variables such as leading (line spacing), hyphenation zone, justification, word spacing, and letter spacing. Because changes to the leading and spacing within the text amount to changes in the design specifications, many designers prefer to predict the amount of space required (or allowed) for the text before going through the page-layout process, and to let the editors cut or expand the text itself to make it fit rather than change the type specifications.

> **Rule of Thumb:**
>
> It is a good idea to provide character-count estimates per column to contributors/editors.
>
> This is something that professional editors do as a matter of course when making an assignment, and it helps eliminate the many problems that arise when you go to lay out the pages. It involves estimating the number of characters per page in a book design, or planning the amount of space that will be allocated for the text of each article in a magazine of newsletter, and letting the type specifications for the article determine the number of words that will fit in the space.

It's a good idea to estimate the amount of text that will fit—and compare that with the actual text provided by the authors—before beginning to lay out a whole document using a page-layout application. This way, if the amount of text provided is very different from the amount required, you can force the copy to fit by adjusting the margins before you place the text, or you can edit the copy in the word processing program to make it the desired length before placing the text on the pages.

The basic variables in any formula relating character count to vertical space requirements include:

Count	=	Number of characters in manuscript
C/Pica	=	Number of characters per pica
Width	=	Width of column in picas
Lines	=	Number of lines of typeset text
Depth	=	Vertical measure of typeset text

The expression of the formula will change depending on whether you are trying to estimate the number of characters that will fit a given space, or trying to estimate the amount of space that a given number of characters will require:

$$\text{Count} = \frac{\text{depth} \times \text{width} \times \text{C/pica} \times 12 \text{ points/pica}}{\text{point size w/ leading}}$$

$$\text{Depth} = \frac{\text{count/(width} \times \text{C/pica)} \times \text{(point size w/ leading)}}{12 \text{ points/pica}}$$

Although these formulas accurately represent the relationship between character count and space, the results of the formulas are estimates only—actual copy fitting will need adjustments during the page-layout process (as described in Chapter 7). Nevertheless, traditional typesetters consider copyfitting an important part of the prepage-layout process, including making fine adjustments to the formulas to account for special characters such as quotation marks and fractions (if the manuscript includes many of these). If the delivered manuscript will not fit the space allowed, the designer might opt to change the type specifications (font, size, etc.) *before* going through the steps of typesetting and page layout.

Three practical methods used by typesetters to cast type are described next.

USING A TYPE-CASTING REFERENCE BOOK OR GAUGE

One traditional method used in both of these cases is the type-casting reference book. This type of book provides examples of text in various sizes, with various leading, from which you can choose the look you want for your body copy. They also give the average number of characters per pica for each font. The designer gets the character count from the word processing program, or by estimating the number of characters per page or per line of printed copy, or uses a measuring guide to cast the type against a specific column width and length to estimate the number of lines of final copy. Finally, the designer uses another measuring guide or gauge to determine how many lines per inch there will be at various leadings. The sequence of calculations would go something like this:

- Select a font to be used for the text.
- Look up the average number of characters per pica.
- Count the number of characters in the word processing file (if the text has already been written).
- Divide the TOTAL NUMBER OF CHARACTERS by the AVERAGE NUMBER OF CHARACTERS PER PICA to estimate the TOTAL NUMBER OF PICAS that will be required by the text.
- Divide the TOTAL NUMBER OF PICAS by the COLUMN WIDTH IN PICAS to estimate the TOTAL NUMBER OF LINES of final copy.
- Look up the number of lines per inch for the leading you will be using.

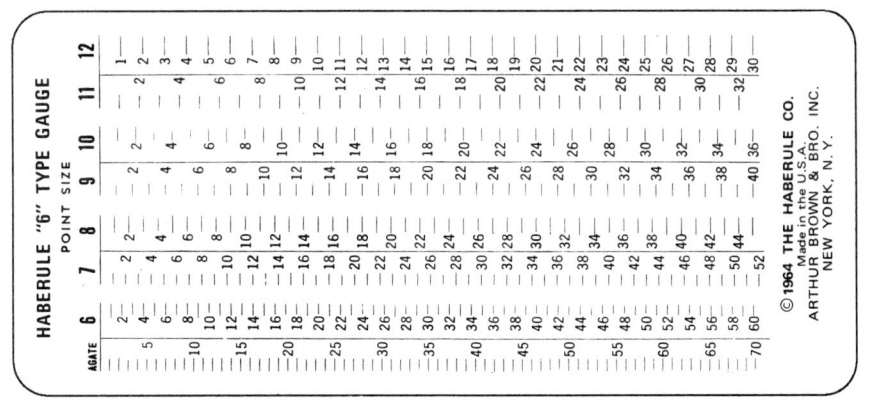

Figure 3.29 A type gauge shows the number of lines per inch at various leading settings.

- Divide the TOTAL NUMBER OF LINES by the NUMBER OF LINES PER INCH to estimate the NUMBER OF INCHES OF FINAL COPY.
  If you cannot look up the number of lines per inch, simply multiply the body text size (point size plus leading) times the total number of lines to get the total depth in points, then divide this value by 12 to get the depth in picas, or divide by 72 to get the depth in inches.
- Divide the NUMBER OF INCHES OF FINAL COPY by the NUMBER OF INCHES PER PAGE to estimate the total number of pages.

Altogether, this method of casting copy or estimating length is a tedious process with a wide margin for error. The process is complicated by the fact that the same typeface might actually have a different number of characters per pica from different manufacturers.

PREPARING DUMMY PAGES OF GREEK TEXT

A second method used by many typesetters is to lay out one or two sample pages using stock type samples and estimate the number of characters that will fit on a page. Often, the character count is converted to an estimated number of words to be assigned to the author. You can use this technique with any word processor, graphics package, or page-layout package that lets you specify the full range of typefaces you will be using, as shown in Figure 3.30.

- First, type one paragraph of exactly 100 characters (or words).
- Set the type in the specified font.
- Duplicate the paragraph as many times as necessary to fill the column or page.
- Count the paragraphs required to fill the column or page, and multiply by 100 to get an estimated character count per page.
- Multiply by the number of pages to determine the maximum character count.
- Use the word processing program to count the number of characters in the document.

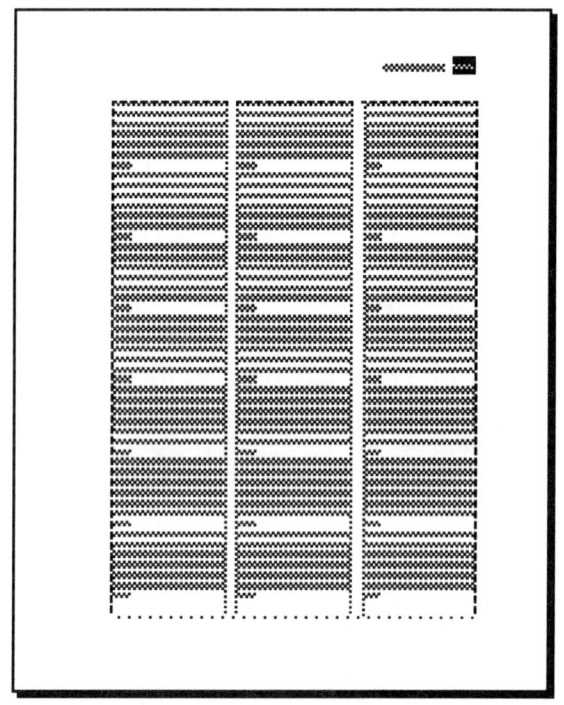

■ **Figure 3.30** Using a page-layout package to estimate the character (or word) count for a document. Type in one paragraph of exactly 100 characters (or words). Set the type in the specified font. Duplicate the same paragraph as many times as necessary to fill the column or page. Count the paragraphs required to fill the column or page, and multiply by 100 to get an estimated character (or word) count per page. Multiply by the number of pages to determine the maximum character (or word) count to be assigned to the author, or use the word processing program to count the number of characters in the document and divide that by the number of characters per final page to estimate the number of pages.

A QUICK ROUGH ESTIMATE

A third quick method of fitting copy is to take a 100-character paragraph of text and set it in the exact width that will be used throughout the document. Set copies of the same paragraph in different sizes or with different leading, and measure the depth of each variation. The total number of column inches for the document can be roughly estimated using the following formula:

Total number of column inches for the document = inches required per 100 characters x (Total number of characters in text files/100).

This paragraph is exactly 100 characters long. This paragraph is exactly 100 characters long. 12/12 Times	This paragraph is exactly 100 characters long. This paragraph is exactly 100 characters long. 12/auto Times	This paragraph is exactly 100 characters long. This paragraph is exactly 100 characters long. 12/14 Times	This paragraph is exactly 100 characters long. This paragraph is exactly 100 characters long. 12/15 Times

■ **Figure 3.31** Measuring lengths of text in different leading settings.

Because none of these copy-casting techniques can absolutely guarantee that copy will fit the space allowed, you will still need to do final copy fitting directly in the page-layout application by adjusting one or more of the variables described in Chapter 7—leading, hyphenation zone, and word and letter spacing (for justified text).

By the way, if you are accustomed to traditional typesetting techniques you have probably specified text in terms of the width of each column. Some desktop publishing applications, on the other hand, define a page in terms of the number of columns and the space between columns. Because you cannot enter the column widths directly, your design specifications should be defined in terms of the number of columns and space between, rather than the width of the text.

> **Rule of Thumb:**
>
> One rule of thumb for determining the optimum width of text is: Equivalent to 60 characters of the specified font, style, and size. Columns that are too narrow will have awkward line breaks and hyphenation; lines that are too long will be hard for the reader to follow.

Summary

This chapter has provided information about fonts and copy casting that will help you design your publications with the features of your application programs in mind. You have examined some of the issues involved in choosing fonts for a publication, and in working with built-in vs. downloadable fonts. You have also learned how to fit copy to a defined space, and to estimate the amount of space that will be required before you place the text in the final page layout.

> **Rule of Thumb:**
>
> Ideally, you want the ability to fit text to a specific line width with a minimum of extra space.
>
> For maximum flexibility, choose applications that offer good typographic controls, letting you adjust all spacing in fractional units.

The next chapter offers more tips on the overall design of a publication, including developing an underlying grid structure and setting up template files that will make large projects go efficiently. Chapter 5 describes methods of actually typesetting the text to match the typographer's specifications, and offers tips on what the typographer should look for in reviewing the typeset text.

Chapter 4
Publication Design

"If you are familiar with the capabilities of your equipment and software, you can develop designs that are both aesthetically pleasing and conducive to efficient production."

This chapter presents an overview of the basic elements of a page, which the designer usually defines, and shows the relationship between the traditional methods and the methods available with computers. Instead of printing blue lines on boards to hold the "grid" of the design, for instance, you can specify exact page margins and tab settings through the software. Some software lets you draw columns and other blue lines directly on the screen. Text and blue lines specified on a master grid will appear on all pages of the document. You can build template files, which can be reused for different chapters of a book or issues of a periodical. Using a computer, the designer can easily generate several alternative designs for review with the publisher.

A computer equipped for desktop publishing is a tremendous design tool in at least three respects:

- A drawing program or page-layout program can be used directly to sketch out rough ideas for designs that can be reviewed with the rest of the team or the client.
- The application menus and options provide a structure for organizing the specifications.
- Different applications can be used to create template systems that help insure that all parts of a publication will follow the same specifications.

This chapter will present an overview of the considerations that go into any design, with tips about using desktop publishing applications directly as design tools. You will first see how you can use a drawing or page-layout application to develop a series of different design ideas for a project. Then you will learn what goes into a template system to create a series of publications with the same design.

In practice, some of the steps described here might be done first on paper rather than while sitting at the computer. In fact, the designers on some teams might never actually touch the computer. Whether you—as the designer—are simply writing out the design specifications or actually setting up the master template yourself, it will help if you know the capabilities of the applications work before you make your specifications.

For example, many desktop publishing applications—word processors and page-layout packages—define a page in terms of the margins, the number of columns, and the space between columns. You cannot enter the column widths directly. Your design specifications, therefore, should be in terms of the number of columns and space between, rather than the width. You can compute the column width based on the width of the image area and gutters, or you can compute the margins and gutters based on your desired column widths. In either case, it is a good idea to prepare your design specifications in terms of a computer's commands and capabilities.

Traditionally, the designer does not get involved in a production until the writing is complete or well under way. If the project team is small, however, and the authors are willing, you can begin incorporating some of the design specifications in the text during the writing stage. If you think about the design ahead of time, you can let the authors know whether they should type two carriage returns between paragraphs, for instance, and whether to indent the first line of each paragraph. Other design details, such as the page size and margins, can be decided later—after the writing, but before placing the text in the page-composition application. In other words, some of the design specifications can be developed during the project-planning stage alluded to in Chapter 1, during which the text and graphics required for the publication are identified.

Principles of Design

One of the criticisms leveled at desktop publishing by graphics professionals and others is that desktop publishing puts powerful tools for the creation of page layout in the hands of people who don't know the first thing about good design and page layout. This is true; desktop publishing represents a merging of two disciplines that in the past have been almost at opposite ends of the spectrum: computers and the graphic arts.

Even the best software will not turn desktop publishers into professional designers, yet many people who have previously been responsible for word processing are suddenly expected to produce beautiful pages on their new desktop publishing system. Is this demand unfair? We don't think so. You do not have to be a graduate from Pratt Institute or the Rhode Island School of Design (two of the nation's leading graphic arts schools) to use desktop publishing tools to produce pages that are well designed and that communicate the message clearly. By understanding and implementing a few basic principles, you should be able to produce documents you can be proud of. Remember, the primary goal is clear communication.

If you are a new desktop publisher with no experience in traditional design, it's a good idea to study the habits and principles of professional designers. In spite of the popular myth that a good sense of design is bestowed upon the chosen ones at birth, good designers have inevitably invested years in the study of the history and principles of good design. No matter how diverse the designs of award-winning publications may appear to be, you will find that they all generally adhere to a few basic principles that can be studied and applied by anyone. You don't have to reinvent the wheel every time you begin a new document.

THINK ABOUT WHAT YOU WANT TO DO BEFORE YOU DO IT!

The first tip is one that applies to many things we do, and page layout is no exception. Never sit down at your computer to produce a report or newsletter without thinking about what you are going to do.

ENFORCE CONSISTENCY

It goes without saying that a good designer always applies the rule of consistency. The principle itself becomes a much harder taskmaster when put in these stronger terms—*Enforce consistency.* This indicates that part of the designer's *responsibility* is to make sure that all elements have been considered, and that no one on the production team will need to invent design specifications for details that were not covered by the designer's original specifications.

Besides the type specifications (which insure consistent treatment of heading levels, body copy, figure captions, etc.), areas that call for consistency include specific use of different ruled line lengths and weights, fill patterns, tab settings, paragraph alignment (left, justified, etc.), indentations, bullet sizes and styles, and in-figure labels. In the past, this last principle would have been followed naturally from the fact that all of the figures came from one source: one spreadsheet program and letter-quality printer (in the case of business reports), or one illustrator and one typesetter. This general principle takes on a new importance when you start using a desktop publishing system to assemble graphics from many different sources. With a page-layout program, some graphics might come from a spreadsheet program, some from a draw program, and some from the page-layout program's built-in graphics tools. Some of the figures might be full-size in the final document, while others might need to be reduced or enlarged in the final page-layout.

You want to be sure that all of the final Figures have consistency in their type specifications. You can enforce your standards for captions by making the captions a part of the word processing text files, rather than a part of the graphics files. You may need to derive your standards for in-figure labels based on the capabilities of the drawing programs you are using. For example, if your report includes a lot of charts and the spreadsheet program has a more limited number of fonts available than you have in the other graphics programs or the page-layout program, you might want to match the fonts used in your all images to the spreadsheet graphics.

The designer also needs to specify standard spacing between figures and text, as well as the spacing between headings and body copy. You can create a spacing guide using tools within the page-layout program (Figure 4.1) to position adjacent graphics and text blocks. Even if you do not want strict rules for positioning graphics—rules that might slow down the production schedule considerably by requiring meticulous adjustments—it's a good idea to know and declare your ideal positioning rules and your limits of tolerance. Your specification might be as simple as "roughly center the graphic between the adjacent text blocks," but even this simple guideline is worth stating explicitly. Don't just assume that graphics will fall into place naturally.

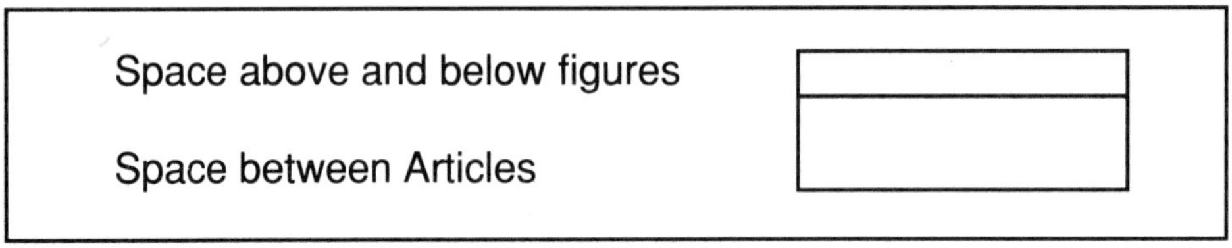

■ **Figure 4.1** Use a spacing guide to position graphics and text.

Another area that calls for consistency is the page-layout. It seem axiomatic that the margins and columns should be consistent throughout the document. This means that headers and footers should align with each other or with the text vertically on the page. In addition, there may be elements that merit consistent placement horizontally on every page.

In traditional systems, the design enforces consistency by issuing lists of standards and having blue lines printed as grid guides on the final page-layout boards. In electronic publishing, you can enforce consistency by working with electronic templates to enforce a grid system, as described later in this chapter.

USE A GRID SYSTEM

A grid refers to the underlying structure of a page-layout. In traditional terms, a grid system is a series of vertical and horizontal lines drawn in light blue ink on the layout boards used to paste-up galleys of typeset text and inked line art. The "non-repro" blue lines are not picked up by the camera during the process of making plates for printing the final pages. The practical function of the blue lines is to help ensure that the galleys of type are laid straight on each page and that all pages have the same margins. Because every page is pasted up using the same grid of blue lines, the entire publication has a fundamental consistency.

We normally think of a grid as simply the page margins and column guides for a publication. A grid structure, in its simplest form, insures consistent alignment of margins, headers, footers, and columns. Of course, these are the basic elements of any publication design. Professional designers often use grid systems that are much more elaborate than that, however. Designers have used very complex grid structures for well-known books, magazines, and newspapers.

The design and production of books has the oldest tradition of any type of document described in this book. Gutenberg's bible shows traces of the grid system he used to lay out his pages. A few decades later a book named De Divina Proportione, written by Fra Luca Pacioli and illustrated by Leonardo da Vinci, applied the rules of classic proportion to book design. Contemporary designers still study this master work and apply the same principles in new book designs. One such method of defining the margins for a book is shown in Figure 4.2.

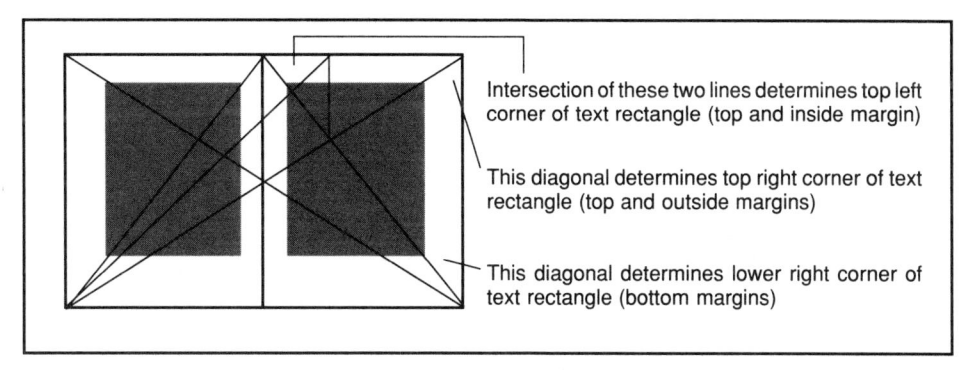

■ **Figure 4.2** One method of determining the classic proportions for a book design.

The basic grid is specified during the design phase, but variations to the grid may be introduced during the page-layout steps. Some common grid structures are shown in Figure 4.3.

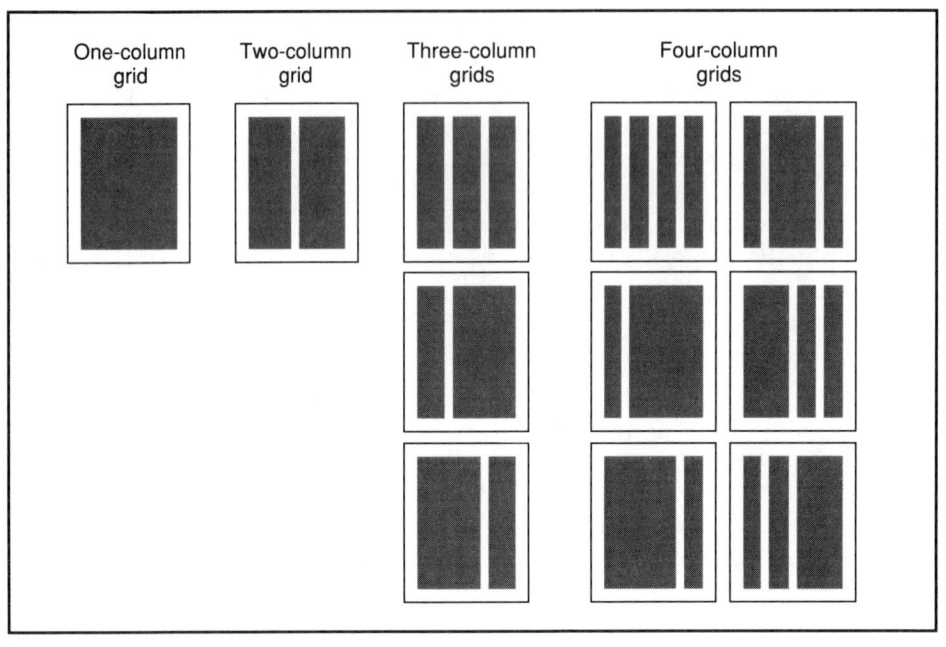

■ **Figure 4.3** Some common grid structures.

Rule of Thumb:

For materials that will be made into slides, set all images within an area of approximately 2:3 proportions; 35mm slide frames usually have a 35mm by 24mm clear window. It's a good idea to design your graphics in this proportion, especially slide images that have a ruled border around them.

Simple grid structures that involve one, two, or three columns are relatively easy to work with, but complex grids usually offer more design possibilities. For example, a one-column grid structure can have only as much variety in the layout as can be achieved by varying the type specifications and paragraph indentations. A two-column grid structure offers the added possibility of making graphics and text expand to the full page width on selected pages if necessary or desired.

In desktop publishing systems, you can set up a simple vertical grid by defining the page size, margins, and columns in electronic terms, using the commands of the word processor or page-layout package. Use your word processor's or page-layout package's built-in tools for establishing a grid using margin settings, column guides, and ruler measures. Most page-layout applications offer vertical rulers on the screen to help you position text and graphics, and some packages let you add additional horizontal guides that appear on the screen but do not print out. For example, the text might start at a lower position on pages that start new sections or new articles than it does on pages containing continuations of articles.

Within the grid, use menu commands to align text and graphics rather than align objects visually. If, for example, you want a title on the left side of a running head, and a page number of the right side, use a right tab, if available, to align the page number where you want it rather than use spaces or move a left-aligned block to the right. These last two techniques may get it right on the screen, but it will probably not print out the way you'd expect.

Besides using nonprinting guides to help you lay out your pages, you can use ruled lines to enhance the appearance of the pages. Designers often drop hairline rules between columns of text, for example. You'll see this technique applied in many published works.

PAY ATTENTION TO THE BALANCE BETWEEN FACING PAGES

In reading any publication that is printed on both sides of the paper, the reader will always see two pages at a time—the left and right facing pages. Only the front and back pages, or cover pages, stand alone. Many page composition applications now let you view facing pages on the screen. Pay attention to the balance between facing pages, or you may find that two pages with individually balanced layouts yield an imbalanced effect when they face each other.

Do not confuse balance with symmetry. While symmetry is a property of many beautiful designs, perfect symmetry in page layout lacks drama. Use white space and position graphics in asymmetric arrangements to invite the reader's interest.

TEXT ON EACH PAGE SHOULD BOTTOM OUT TO MARGIN

Book, magazine, and newspaper designers have traditionally applied the principle that every page should bottom out at exactly the same point. This is easy for books that were primarily body copy without graphics or subheadings—like the traditional Victorian novel. The principle becomes increasingly difficult to apply the more your document incorporates complicating factors such as:

- Subheadings within each chapter or section
- Figures
- Footnotes
- Tables that cannot be broken across pages
- Limitations for widows and orphans

This rule is much more strictly applied in magazines than in most newsletters—or any other type of document described in this book. In many documents you will find it impossible to bottom out all pages to the same point, and in some documents you might plan extremely ragged bottom margins as a deliberate design strategy, but in general you want to let the bottom margin that is set in the page-layout program define the maximum length of the text.

USE WHITE SPACE TO GIVE THE EYE A BREAK

This is one of the most basic principles of good design, though it is violated on the most regular basis. White space is the term used to identify areas of a page that are not printed with text, graphics, or design elements (ruled lines and shades). White space can also refer to the spacing between words and letters on the page.

The natural tendency is to fill each page from margin to margin and condense the spacing between words and letters in order to minimize the total number of pages and thereby save printing costs. Pages that are crammed full with text and graphics are simply not inviting; the eye needs a rest.

This principle is applicable to any document, but is worth special mention as applied to books and business reports. Traditionally, business reports have been produced using the same margin settings as used for letters, memos, minutes, and agendas. Books also have a tradition of minimizing white space—leaving only enough room at the edges for the thumbs to hold the book open without covering the text. Contemporary books tend to have smaller margins (less white space) than the classic proportions shown in Figure 4.2, perhaps in the interest of cutting printing costs. More white space in the design usually means more pages.

Depending on the content of the book and how it will be used, you can increase the apparent white space in a book design without increasing the total number of pages by using a smaller size of type, a different typeface, or tighter leading. Figure 4.4 shows the relative amount of space required by the same text layed out in different grids and fonts.

Rule of Thumb:
One of the simplest ways to bring white space into a design is to specify ragged right margins rather than justified text.

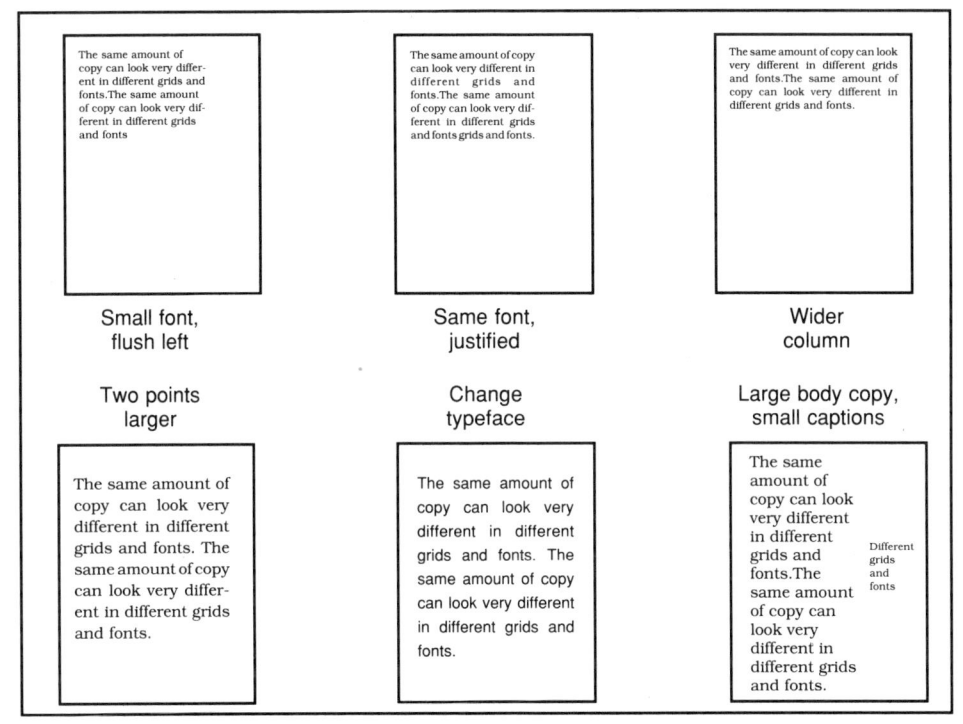

Small font, flush left	Same font, justified	Wider column
Two points larger	Change typeface	Large body copy, small captions

■ **Figure 4.4** The same amount of copy can look very different in different grids and fonts.

As you can see by studying examples of well-designed books and reports, you can often have the effect of producing more white space on a page without actually reducing the amount of text or increasing the number of pages, for instance, by using a smaller point size. If you are unsure about how to create white space in the design, the simplest approach is to specify wide margins: leave an inch-wide margin all the way around the edge of a page, and, if economizing on the final number of pages isn't an issue, leave more space on one side than on the other. For example, offset the left margin of text by two to three inches.

Magazines fall into a wide range in applying this principle. Some magazines—the *New Yorker*, for instance—fill every column completely with galleys of small type, and this type of design can be attractive as well as functional (maximizing verbal content, minimizing the number of pages). Good designers can make designs like this work, but for those who are just beginning to learn the ins and outs of page layout, the better rule to follow is to allow some white space on the pages.

Newspapers and tabloids commonly waive this principle in the interest of minimizing the number of pages, since the headlines on each page are designed to attract or maintain the readers' attention. Newsletters may imitate newspaper layouts when there is a lot of information to convey in a restricted amount of space, but newsletters can be more inviting to the reader if they imitate the open designs that are more common in magazine layouts.

If you are writing your own copy, try to put yourself in the frame of mind of a professional copy writer as you formulate your message. Professional copy writers can get the point across in as many or few words as specified by the designer.

In any case, your publication design might benefit from the addition of pages without significantly increasing the printing or production costs. If you start out with a specific number of pages in mind as a goal, and this limit dictates a crowded design, it would be worth researching the cost of adding pages.

USE GRAPHICS IN A MEANINGFUL WAY

Another way of stating this principle is: Avoid clutter. With the availability of click-art packages (diskettes of predrawn art) on the market today, there is a tendency for beginners to randomly add these graphics to a page, just because they're excited about the ability to add graphics. Use only graphics that bear some meaning to the text, or, if your goal is decorative, keep the graphics simple and small. Other techniques, such as using white space, may break up the page better than adding decorative graphics.

DIFFERENTIATE FIGURE CAPTIONS FROM BODY TEXT

The term caption means different things to different people. Here we use it to describe the lines of text that run below, beside, or above a photo or illustration and describe it. Some layout men use the term cutline instead of caption, reserving the term caption (or lead-in or catchline or kicker) to describe only the bold-faced words that lead in to the rest of the descriptive text. Whatever you call it, the caption is usually differentiated from the rest of the text by making it bold or by using a different typeface.

Besides specifying the font to be used in captions, you should also specify the positioning of the caption text. The most natural position is below the illustration or photo, extending the same width as the graphic. Other variations include: indenting a pica or more on each side, centering the catchline above justified text. Some variations are shown in Figure 4.5.

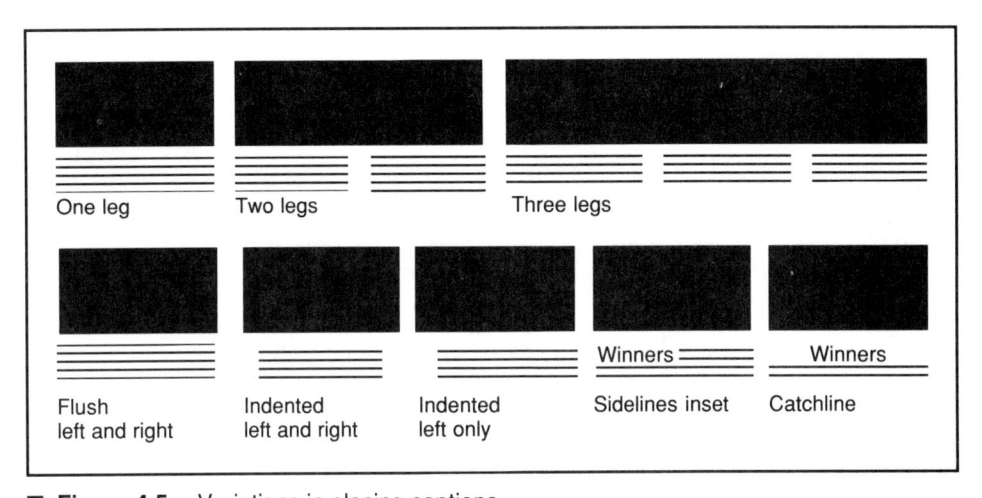

■ **Figure 4.5**   Variations in placing captions.

USE RULED LINES OR GRAY SCREENS TO DIFFERENTIATE PARTS OF A DOCUMENT OR PAGE

Remember that one of the goals of good design is to help highlight important information and organize the material for the reader, clearly distinguishing between different levels of information. If you are producing a document with a variety of different topics, such as a newsletter, differentiate between stories by surrounding text with a thin rule, or by dropping a screen fill behind special short features to highlight them and separate them from the rest of the articles. Ruled lines between columns can often make a page easier to read and more inviting at the same time.

Boxes or borders can be used to set off stories or graphics. You can add interest to the layout by breaking the border with a kicker—text inset over a broken edge of the border. Figure 4.6 shows some variations in bordered elements.

Rule of Thumb:

The white space between the border and adjacent text or graphics should be uniform.

■ **Figure 4.6** Variations in the use of borders.

If you are boxing text within a column, the borders of the box should align with the margins of the column, and the text inside the box must be set at a narrower width than the rest of the column (Figure 4.7).

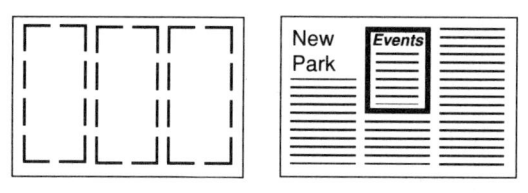

■ **Figure 4.7** Boxed text is set narrower than the rest of the text on the page, with box borders matching column margin width.

USE HEADERS AND FOOTERS AS REFERENCE AIDS

This principle is applicable to any long document, including magazines, but it is a mandate in the case of reference books and manuals. Besides the page number, the name of the section or chapter should be included in the running header or footer and positioned at the outer edges of the pages for easy reference.

The most readily referenced part of any book is the outer edges of the pages. Figure 4.8 shows some examples of how these four positions can be used to make page numbers and section names easy to find.

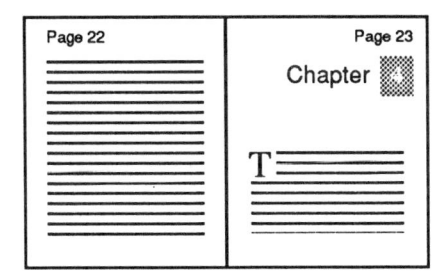

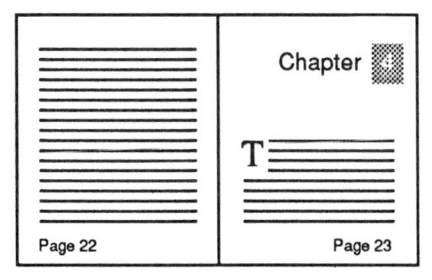

■ **Figure 4.8** Four common page number settings and their effects on the document. Top left of even-numbered pages; Top right of odd-numbered pages; Bottom left of even-numbered pages; Bottom right of odd-numbered pages.

USE ONLY A FEW FONTS ON A PAGE

This principle is covered more thoroughly in Chapter 3, but it is worth repeating here. Just as graphics are too often used simply because they are available, so too are fonts—simply because they're there. Most designers will mix two different type faces at most, such as a sans-serif face for headlines and a serif face for body copy. Too many different fonts tend not to clarify, but to make the page uninviting.

USE LARGER POINT SIZES FOR LONGER TEXT LINE LENGTHS

There is a good reason why the pages of a magazine run the text in two, and often three columns. It is very difficult for the eye to follow text, especially in small point sizes, from one edge of an 8½-inch-wide page to the other. If you must use a small point size to fit more text on a page, be sure to break the page into at least two columns. Even regular text, i.e., 12 point, is easier to read if it runs in columns no wider than 4 to 5 inches. Above all, the text should be easy to read. If the copy doesn't fit the space allowed, think about editing out some of the text rather than reducing the point size or the space between lines.

BE SIMPLE

This last principle is sometimes the hardest to apply. What it means is this: don't try to do too much in one design. In applying the other principles suggested here, don't go overboard trying to incorporate every guideline in one document. There are exceptions to every rule. A page with very little white space (in violation of one principle) can still be pleasing if the other principles are followed, for example. Similarly, the use of ruled lines and gray screens to differentiate parts of a page or a document work well with documents that have only a few different elements, but a document with many different elements will become cluttered if every element is differentiated by lines and shades.

Using Electronic Aids in Design

You can use a drawing program or a page-layout package to create a series of quick roughs of different designs for a publication before deciding on the final design. The advantage of using the computer rather than pencil and ruler to sketch out your ideas is three-fold:

- It is easy to copy and move elements on the screen as you work on one design.
- It is efficient to make copies of the first design and modify it to create alternative designs.
- It is effective to show clients crisp text and graphic elements printed on a high-resolution printer. (We'll use the term "client" throughout this chapter to include managing editors, publication department managers, end-user groups, or whoever else the designer must share decisions with.)

IDENTIFY THE CAPABILITIES OF THE SYSTEM

Just as the typographer needs to know what fonts are available before recommending type specifications, the designer needs to know something about the final production environment before "imagining" a design. If you, as the designer, do not know the production environment very well, then it is a good idea to review your design ideas with the production manager before finalizing the design.

Besides knowing what fonts are available, the designer should know the resolution of the final printer or typesetter, the line weights and fill patterns that are available through the various applications, the maximum image area accommodated by the system, and the capabilities or limitations of the applications as related to text formatting.

For example, you should know the final printing resolution of the system, and have a good idea of what the text and graphics from various sources will look like when printed. Your design specifications might call for a lot of bit-maps and scanned images if the final printer has 300 dpi resolution, but conventional halftones (to be produced photographically and pasted in manually) might be the better choice if the printer's graphics resolution is low, or if the final resolution is high but it takes too long to print scans and bit-maps. (See Chapters 6 and 7.)

Similarly, you should know the graphics capabilities of the system. Confirm that the applications support hairline rules before specifying hairlines as part of the design, for example, and that the printer can handle all of the variations allowed in the applications. Be sure that the hairlines will have the appearance you intend when printed on the final target printer (this might not be the same width as printed from draft printers). Know what fill patterns or percentage screens are available, what they will look like on the final printer, and how they will be seen by the camera that might be used to create the final plates for offset printing. It's a good idea to know how much time will be added to the printing process by the types of graphics you choose for the design, so the decision to use designs that print slowly is made deliberately rather than out of ignorance. (See Chapters 6 and 7.)

Don't assume that the final printer can handle the full image area that your application programs might allow. For example, the LaserWriter prints on 8½-by-11-inch paper, but the image area is limited by the printer's 1.5 MB memory to about 87 square inches per page. This translates into an 8-by-10.92-inch area, or a 6.72-by-13-inch area. Many laser printers have much less memory than the LaserWriter. In addition, most laser printers (like offset printers) reserve about one quarter of an inch on one or more sides of the paper for the grippers that pull the paper through the drum or the ink rollers. Many page-layout packages let you specify page sizes up to tabloid size (11-by-17-inches) or larger, but your printer might require that you print these pages out in tiles—different sheets of paper that will need to be pasted together. If your final typesetter uses 12-inch wide rolls of photosensitive paper, then the final master copy will not need to be pasted together, but otherwise you might want to adapt your basic grid to simplify the paste-up process.

Table 4.1
Maximum Image Areas (in Inches)
on Various PostScript Printers and Typesetters

Device	Width	Length
LaserWriter		
Letter Paper	8	10.92
Legal Paper	6.72	13
Linotronic 100		
1270 dpi	11.7	45.5
312 dpi	11.7	48
Linotronic 300	12	25.8
Linotronic 500	18	25.8

Finally, know the text formatting capabilities of the system. For example, most desktop publishing applications can easily handle page layouts that call for using graphics and more than one font in the header or footer, but it is a good idea to confirm that this is possible in your environment before designing pages with complex header or footer formats. Also, most word processing applications and page-layout packages offer automatic hyphenation, but if your system does *not* offer this feature you might want to avoid using justified text (which generally requires hyphenation unless the column is very wide). If your design forces the production team to repeatedly work around the limitations of the system, you could be losing the advantages offered by an electronic system.

IDENTIFY THE ESSENTIAL ELEMENTS OF THE PUBLICATION

The first step in the design process is to identify the essential elements of the publication. Whereas the overall production manager views the elements in terms of stories that must be written by various authors, the designer views the elements from a different perspective, and might list them this way:

- Page size and margins
- Underlying grid structure
- Running headers and footers
- Two different page formats
- Three heading levels
- Four types of graphics

PUBLICATION DESIGN 139

In addition, a particular publication might include one or more of the following special considerations or constraints that affect the design:
- Chapter openings always on right-facing pages
- Feature articles require special placement
- Sidebars must be distinct from the rest of the text on a page

Traditionally, designers render rough sketches in pencil of their ideas for handling these elements on paper. If you know how to use the applications, you can use the computer as a design tool, using its built-in text and graphics features to create representations of the basic elements in a publication. For example, you can use dummy text to show the position and size of text on a page. You can use shaded boxes to show where graphics will be placed. You can use ruled lines to enhance the design. Figure 4.9 shows how design ideas can be handled in the computer's terms.

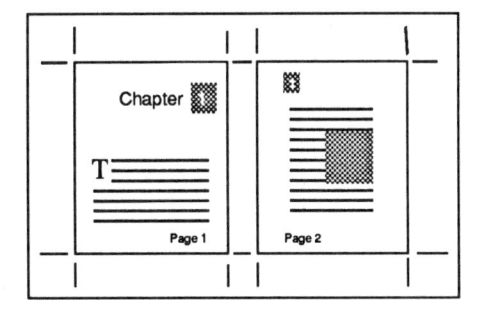

■ **Figure 4.9**   Rough page comps can be done by hand or using the computer. Dummy text to show size and position; Shaded boxes to show graphics; Crop marks or ruled border to show page size.

Once you create the basic elements that will compose the publication, you can modify them or rearrange them on the page to develop variations. Rather than start from scratch each time you want to represent each design idea, you can use one design file to create many design variations, as shown in Figure 4.11:
- Create representations of all the basic design elements once, and store them as the first design.
- Rearrange individual design elements into different page layouts and change the type specs of selected text as needed to represent the new designs, and save each design idea under new file name.
- Add a new file for each new design idea.

140 THE ELECTRONIC PUBLISHER

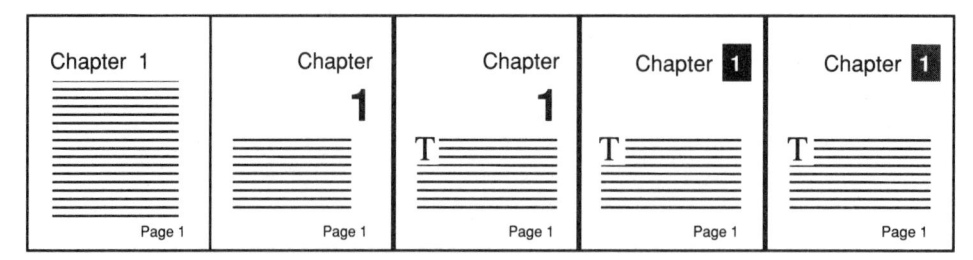

■ **Figure 4.10** Example of consecutive pages in a design publication.

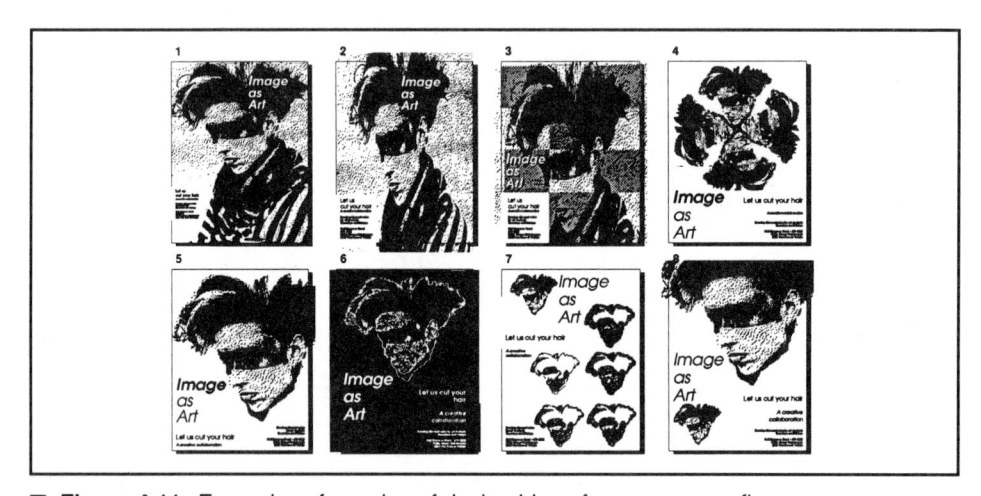

■ **Figure 4.11** Examples of a series of design ideas for a one-page flyer.

CREATE DESIGN ALTERNATIVES

Whereas in final production you place the actual text and graphics that compose the work, in a design cycle you can use the computer to create *representations* of the basic elements. You need not know the exact text or contents of the publication in order to rough out a design idea. Use dummy text for headlines or headings, boxes filled with horizontal lines for body copy, and black or gray boxes for Figures.

If the trim size of the publication will be smaller than 8½-by-11-inches, you can use a solid border to represent the edges of the pages in the design publication. This can make it easier to see how the final pages will look when trimmed (Figure 4.12). In the final publication, however, you would use crop marks rather than solid lines to indicate the edges of the paper. Otherwise, the solid lines might show in the final publication—especially if the pages will be folded into signatures before being trimmed.

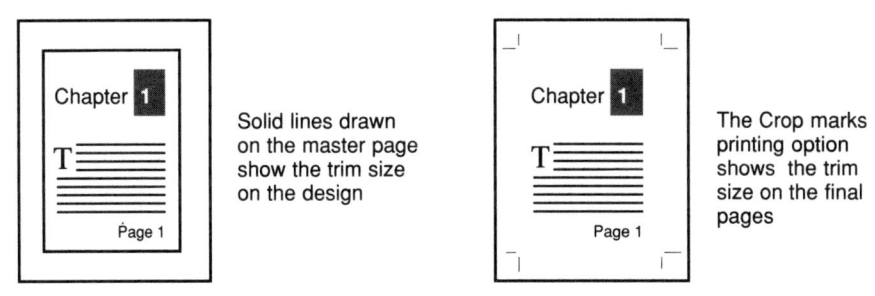

Figure 4.12 Use solid lines to show the trim size in a design publication; use crop marks in the final publication.

After reviewing different design ideas and settling on one of them, the designer can translate those ideas into the specifications that will be applied in the page composition application and the other programs used to construct the pieces of the publication.

DEFINE THE FINAL SPECIFICATIONS FOR THE PUBLICATION

Once the final design is selected, the designer usually needs to define the basic defaults and standards that will be used throughout the publication in specific terms that can be interpreted by the production team. Besides the type specifications (described in Chapter 3) the final design specifications include the page size and orientation, the page margins, the target printer, and the positioning of text and graphics within a grid of column guides and measurements from a common reference point (a zero point).

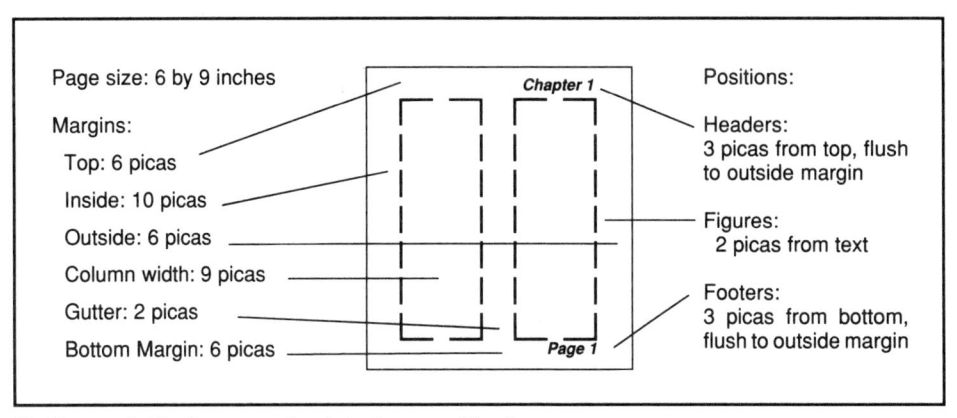

Page size: 6 by 9 inches

Margins:
 Top: 6 picas
 Inside: 10 picas
 Outside: 6 picas
 Column width: 9 picas
 Gutter: 2 picas
 Bottom Margin: 6 picas

Positions:
 Headers: 3 picas from top, flush to outside margin
 Figures: 2 picas from text
 Footers: 3 picas from bottom, flush to outside margin

Figure 4.13 An example of design specifications.

142 THE ELECTRONIC PUBLISHER

In specifying line widths and gray screen percentages, be sure to take into account the differences between the printers and typesetters that will be used throughout the production cycle, and differences between different applications' handling of these specifications. For example, hairlines created in most applications will nearly match traditional hairline widths regardless of the final printer's resolution, but some applications see hairlines as simply "one pixel wide," so the line will print as 1/300 of an inch from a laser printer, but 1/1200 or 1/2400 of an inch from a typesetter. Similarly, 10 percent gray screen will seem darker when printed on a 300 dpi printer than on a 1200 dpi typesetter, and at 2400 dpi the 10 percent screen will nearly disappear.

Rule of Thumb:

Screens that are below 50% gray will tend to print lighter on a high-resolution typesetter than on a low-resolution printer; screens that are above 50% gray will tend to print darker on a high-resolution typesetter than on a low-resolution printer.

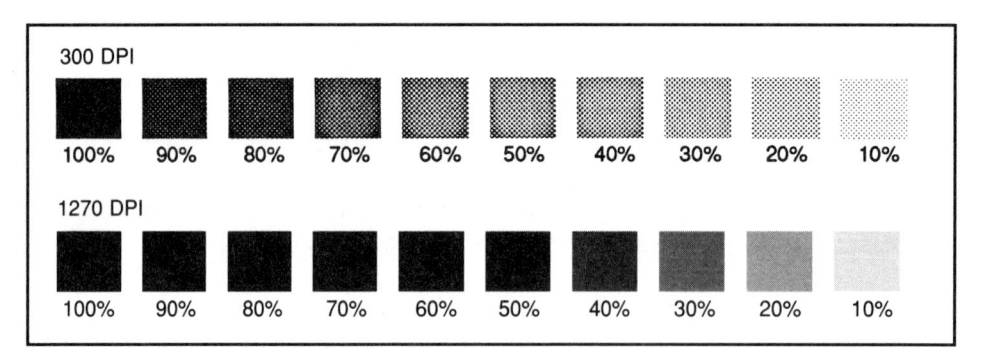

■ **Figure 4.14** Screens printed from a 300 dpi laser printer and from a 1270 dpi typesetter.

Traditionally, these design specifications have been typed as lists or marked with measurements on a dummy representation of a page layout. Ideally, in electronic publishing projects the designer knows enough about the production process to express the design specifications in terms that are expected by the various applications that will be used. Finally, after the design is finalized and before the production cycle begins, the designer (or a member of the production team working closely with the designer) sits down at the computer and builds a template system that will be used to produce the final publication.

Creating a Template System

A template is a computer file that embodies the basic features of the design specifications, as shown in Figure 4.15. A template is simply a dummy publication that is already set up with the basic elements of a page layout that will be shared by several publications. There are packaged template systems available for some page-layout applications that provide an assortment of page-layouts that you can start with to create your own documents. By our definition the term template includes these packaged designs within the broader category that incorporates custom templates that you create for your own projects.

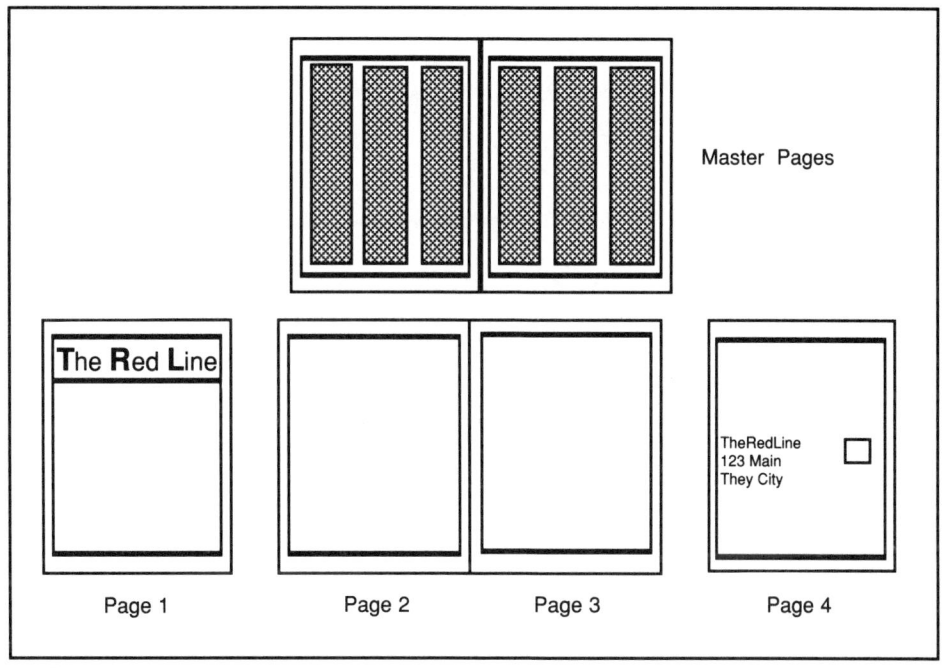

■ **Figure 4.15** A template publication.

A template might consist of no more than a simple grid (i.e., page size, margin specifications, and column guides). For example, whenever you start a new document in any page-layout program, you specify the basic parameters such as the size of the sheets of paper, the orientation of the printed image, and the text margins before adding any text or graphics to the pages.

A template is set up with all defaults tailored to match the design specifications for the publication. By setting these up in the template, you can be sure that all files cloned from it have the same page size and orientation settings.

The template for the word processing files might include the margin settings, standard footers that show the chapter number or text file name, and a style sheet that incorporates all of the design specifications that apply to the text. The template for the illustrations might include dummy text for captions and callouts that will be used in the same type specifications in every illustration, as well as default settings for line weights and fill patterns. The template for the page-layout package shows the basic grid system to be followed on all pages.

A more complex template might include common text and graphics elements such as dummy headers and footers, dummy headlines or text labels, ruled lines, and other repeating symbols and graphic elements. A template can include a style sheet for applying type specifications used throughout the publication. A template can also incorporate productivity tools such as guides for aligning objects across facing pages and spacing guides for positioning text and graphics. It can include common elements that will appear within the publication in specific locations or at repeated intervals.

Once a template is created, it can be cloned to create a series of files that follow the same design specifications. For instance, a long publication might have one template publication that is cloned to create a series of sections or chapters that all follow the same design specifications. A short publication that is produced on a regular basis—such as a newsletter—would have one template from which each issue is cloned. Some publications might be composed of sections that follow different design specifications, and these would require a series of template publications—one for each different section layout.

BENEFITS OF USING TEMPLATES

The essential benefits of using a template system are that it saves repeated set-up steps, forces you to think ahead, embodies design, enforces consistency, and simplifies the page-layout process.

Saves Repeating Set-up Steps

One major benefit of using a template system is that the decisions and actions described in the next sections are executed only once during the production cycle, rather than once for every new file that will compose the full publication. Whenever you start a new publication, there are a certain number of steps and commands you must go through in order to set up the pages before you begin typing text or drawing illustrations or placing text and graphics from other programs into a page-layout package. In the computer's terms, you define the margins, the page size, the number of columns, and the default settings (for font, line weight, paragraph alignment, etc.).

Templates save time in large production projects by capturing a few of the steps required to set up a new document once, so the same steps do not have to be repeated every time a similar document is started. You can save hours or days over the life of a project by using a template system for large publications.

It is a good idea to develop a template system for any publication project that will require more than one page-layout file. Books, reports, manuals, newsletters, and magazines are candidates for template systems whereby a single template is used to create a separate page-layout file for each chapter, section, or issue of the publication. Even if the number of pages required for a document is less than the maximum allowed by the page-layout program, there are good reasons for dividing these documents into several files, all cloned from the same template. Shorter documents such as price lists, menus, ads, and brochures are candidates for template systems if you will be producing more than one document with the same or similar layout.

Forces You to Think Ahead!

It's a good idea to think out the design of your document before making your initial page set-up. Never sit down at your computer to produce a report or newsletter without thinking about what you are going to do. The first step in thinking out a production plan is to list the design specifications that will be applied throughout a publication. Wherever possible, design specifications should be captured in the template system. Even if the design specifications are already clearly written out on paper, the page-layout application menus and options can provide a structure for organizing the design specifications.

Embodies Design

Aside from the practical considerations of saving time and having a disciplined approach to producing a document, a template system can serve the function of preserving a design on an aesthetic level. By incorporating as many of the design specifications as possible into an electronic template, the production group is aided in preserving the look intended by the designer.

Enforces Consistency

It goes without saying that a good designer always applies the rule of consistency. In the past, the designer enforced consistency by issuing lists of standards and having blue lines printed as grid guides on the final page-layout boards. In electronic publishing, you can enforce consistency by working with electronic templates to enforce a grid system, apply type specifications, and set up specific ruled line lengths and weights, fill patterns, tab settings, paragraph alignment (flush left, justified, etc.), indentations, bullet sizes and styles, and in-Figure labels.

Simplifies Page-Layout Process

A good template system can help simplify the page-layout process by providing guides that help the layout artists arrange elements on each page. Some software programs let you see column guides and other blue lines directly on the screen. Text and blue lines specified on a master grid will appear on all pages of the document.

COMPONENTS OF A TEMPLATE SYSTEM

A template usually includes some sort of grid system for laying out the pages (beginning with page size and margins), an assumption about the type of laser printer or typesetter that will be used, aids for aligning objects (a common unit of measurement, with spacing guides), a system for applying type specifications (via dummy text or using style sheets), a source of standard symbols and graphics used in the document (stored in a work area or as import files), and standing items that are always printed in the same location on certain pages (such as a newsletter banner). Some templates also include instructions for using the template.

Define the Page Size and Margins

Initial setup includes defining the paper size and orientation and measure of the margins. By setting these up in the template, you can be sure that all files cloned from it have the same page size and orientation settings.

Although the page size is usually the same size the final publication will be once it is mass produced, bound and trimmed, you can deliberately specify larger page sizes for special layouts. For example, in a page-layout package you might specify that you are printing on 8½-by-11-inch paper, and use that as the board size for designing a 6 by 9 booklet, as in Figure 4.16. You can use nonprinting guides, margins, and columns to define the 6 by 9 layout area, and use the area beyond that to print project-control information, registration marks, and instructions to the printer. The printed pages can also show crop marks that you draw on the master pages. Similarly, if you are printing galleys or finished pages from a word processing program, you can put project-control information in the headers and footers, as in Figure 4.16.

6x9 page size printed on 8½x11 paper with automatic crop marks.

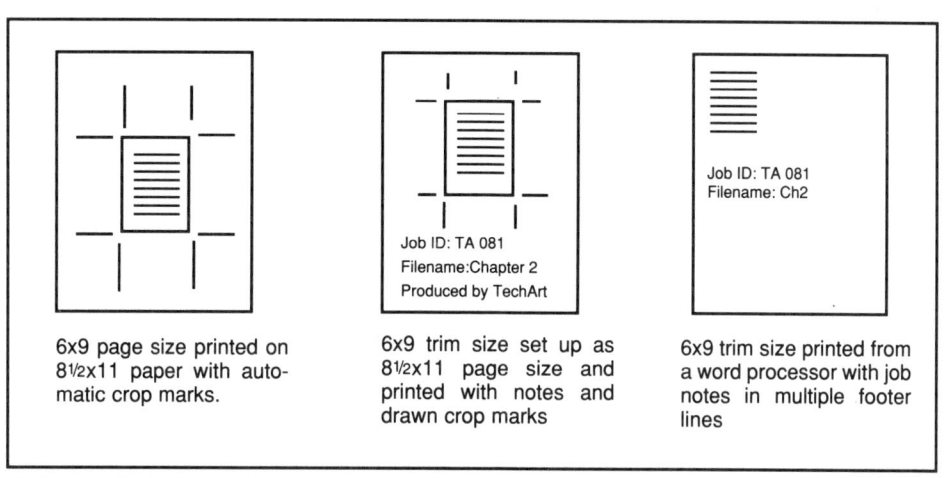

6x9 trim size set up as 8½x11 page size and printed with notes and drawn crop marks

6x9 trim size printed from a word processor with job notes in multiple footer lines

■ **Figure 4.16** Page size is not always the same as the paper in your printer tray, and not the same as the final publication pages. 6 by 9 booklet pages, defined as 8½ by 11 and printed on 8½ by 11 paper with crop marks and project-control information entered on the master pages of a page-layout package. 6 by 9 booklet pages, defined as 6 by 9 on the page setup and printed on 8½ by 11 paper with automatic crop marks printed by the page-composition application. 6 by 9 booklet pages, defined as 8½ by 11 in a word processing program and printed on 8½ by 11 paper with multiple-line footers that include project-control information beyond the page trim size.

Most publications will have the same page size for all sections, but the orientation of the pages may vary from section to section. For instance, you might have a set of appendices that need to be printed wide in order accommodate many columns of numbers in a financial report. In this case, you can set up two templates—one for tall pages, and one for wide pages.

The page margins set up in the template will hold for all pages of the document, and they usually cannot be changed for individual pages within a file. (You can change the effective margins on individual pages by moving column guides or adjusting indentation settings for the text, but you cannot change the page margins themselves.) Each section of the publication that requires different margins should have a separate template (Figure 4.18).

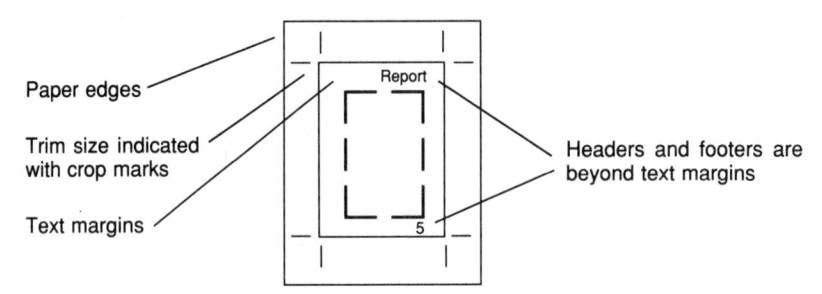

■ **Figure 4.17** Page size and margins.

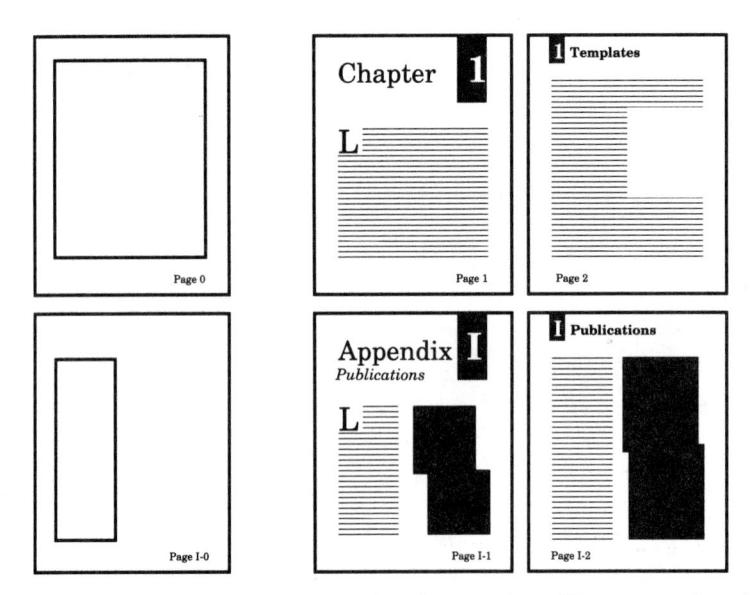

■ **Figure 4.18** Each section of the publication that requires different margins should have a different template.

Depending on the application, the margins are not necessarily the same as the limits of the text and graphics that appear on a page: text and graphics can be positioned beyond the margins in most page-layout packages, for instance. The side margins usually determine the width of the column guides, however, and the bottom margin determines where automatic page breaks will occur. Other elements may fall outside of these margins, such as ruled lines around pages, vertical and horizontal rules that are part of the design, and headers and footers (Figure 4.19).

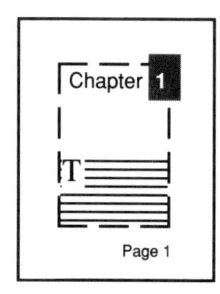

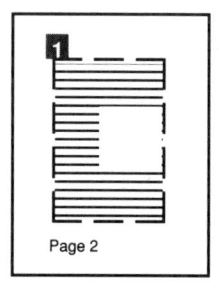

■ **Figure 4.19** Margins help define column guides, and are not necessarily the limits of all text and graphics.

If you are accustomed to defining page layouts in terms of the width of the text, rather than the width of the margins, you will need to convert your specifications to the terms used by the production team. Or the production group will need to convert your specifications into the application's terms, and this might require slight modifications to the design specifications if the application cannot match your terms. For example, if you know you want the text to be 6 inches wide on an 8½-inch wide page, then the total amount of space available for both the inside and the outside margins is 2½ inches (i.e., 8½ minus 6).

In other words, if you know what the margins are and what the page size is, as specified using the application's commands, you can calculate the width of the text using this formula:

text width = (page width)-(inside margin measure + outside margin measure)

On the other hand, if you know the page size and the text width, you can calculate the margin allowance using this formula:

total space available for inside and outside margins = page width - text width.

Variations on these formulas can be used to determine the top and bottom margins, or to calculate the measured depth allowed for text on each page. The exact measurements entered for the top and bottom margin will depend on whether the application program puts headers and footers within or outside these measures. The design specifications should identify clearly the margins for the text to differentiate from the margins of the headers and footers, but translate the specifications into terms used by the application programs.

You can use an expanded version of the formula to calculate the widths of columns that will be set up automatically by an application that calls for entry of the number of columns and the space between each column: column width = [page width - (inside + outside margin measures) - (space between columns x (number of columns - 1)]/number of columns.

If the column guides differ between pages or between sections, you may need to set up a different template for each column grid as needed, though most word processors and page-layout packages let you change the column settings within a single file.

Select a Unit of Measure and Display Rulers

If all of your design specifications are given in the same unit of measure, then you can set your preferences in the template files and the same unit of measure will apply to all files cloned from the templates.

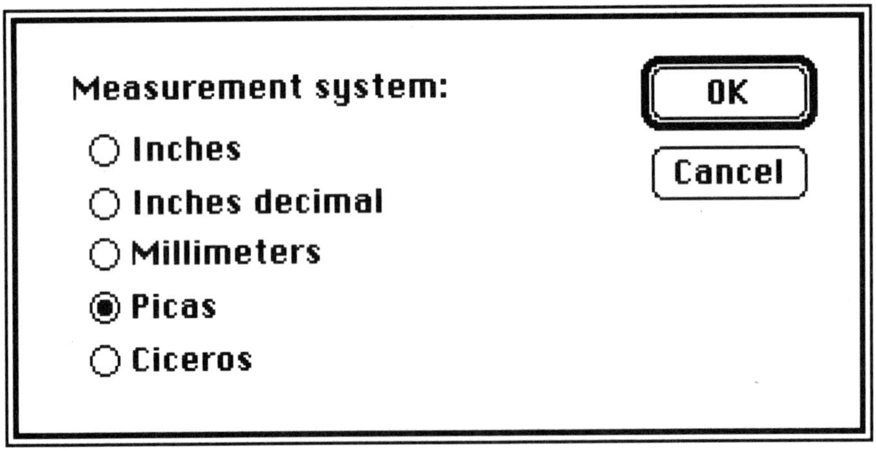

■ **Figure 4.20** Set the preferred unit of measure in the template publication.

If your specifications are given in two or more different measures—inches for margins and points for type, for instance—then select that unit of measure in which you prefer to view the ruler line.

You need to turn the rulers ON during the design phase in order to lay out your grid precisely. With some applications, if you leave the rulers ON in the template, they will be displayed automatically in all files that are cloned from the template. This will be a convenience during the production phase if the rulers will be used for scaling or cropping graphics.

Design specifications should be stated as a measure from a specified zero point on the ruler line whenever possible. This reference point may be the top left corner of the page, or the inside edge of double-sided publications (Figure 4.21), or the top left corner of the text margins. Ideally, the design specifications are given in terms of the zero points that are set up in the templates. Otherwise, if a changing zero point is required or implied by your designs, its position should be given as a part of the design specifications.

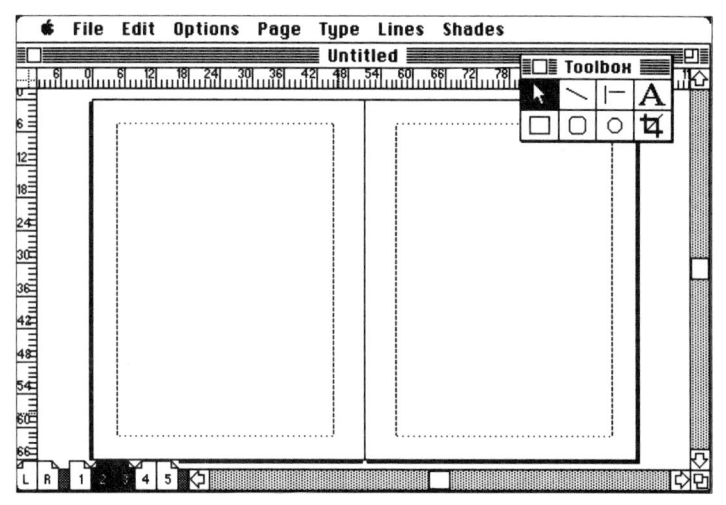

■ **Figure 4.21** Design specifications are given in reference to a zero point.

Create a Grid System

The best publication designs are based on an underlying grid structure that is used to position elements throughout the publication. Using a page-layout package, the grid can be defined on master pages, along with other printing elements such as ruled lines and folios. Nonprinting grid lines displayed in most page-layout packages include page margins, column guides, and ruler guides.

The grid structure can be set up automatically using an application's column guide command for even spacing, but most page-layout packages let you set up or move the column guides independently for unequal column settings.

152 THE ELECTRONIC PUBLISHER

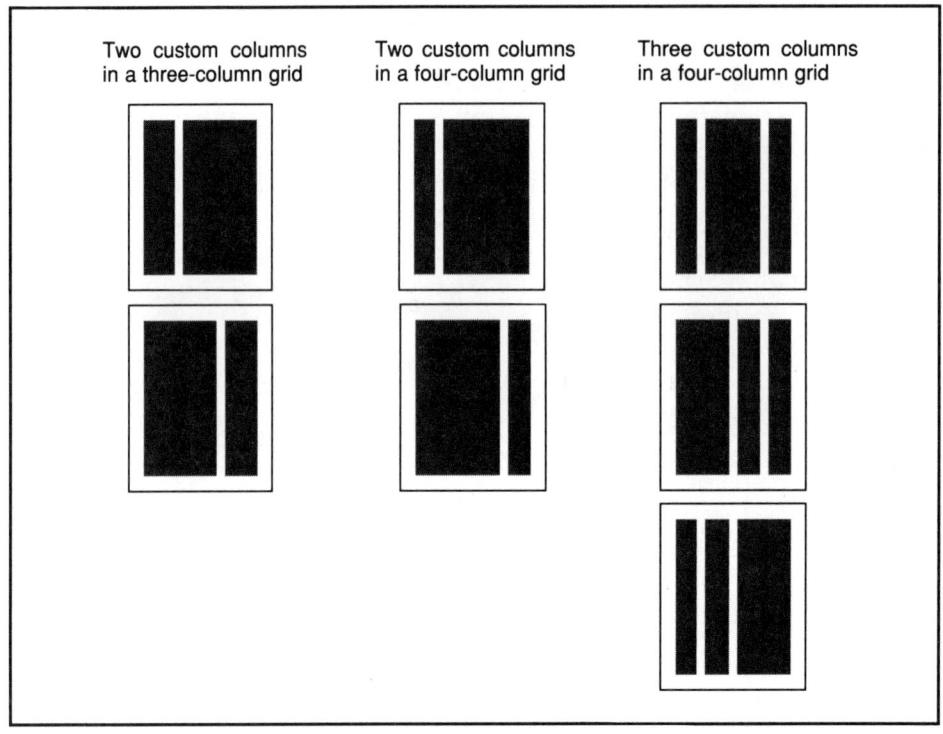

■ **Figure 4.22** In some page-composition applications, you can move the column guides to create custom grid settings.

Normally, the default width for spacing between the columns set by the page-layout package or the word processing program can be changed to any value specified by the designer. You can make this space wide if you will be dropping hairline rules between each column, but a good rule is to keep the space between columns under two picas.

Documents that use the same grid on every page will be much easier to produce than documents that switch between several variations on the grid. One common variation that is particularly hard to work with is the mirror image page-layout, such as the one shown in Figure 4.23. What makes this layout difficult is not the layout of individual pages, it is the chaos that ensues if you insert or delete one page after the publication has been layed out. The best rule of thumb in working with mirror-image designs is to always insert or delete an even number of pages, so you don't upset all of the subsequent page layouts.

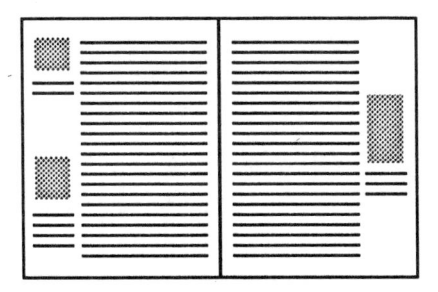

Figure 4.23 The mirror-image page design is particularly tricky to produce.

If you must create mirror-image grid designs, develop all measurements starting from the inside edges of the facing pages to insure symmetry. If the final page-layout package lets you display rulers with these two different zero points, all the better—in double-sided, facing-page publications, on the left page the zero point is set at the top-right corner; the right page has the zero point set at the top-left corner. If you are working with a program that lets you set only one zero point throughout the publication (as many word processing programs require) you will need to convert your initial measurements for left pages, as shown in Figure 4.24.

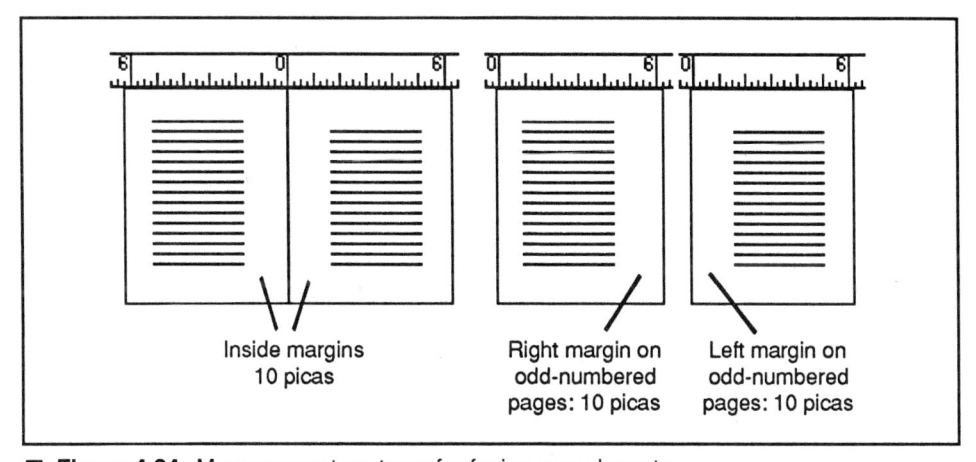

Figure 4.24 Measurement systems for facing page layouts.

THE ELECTRONIC PUBLISHER

Identify the Target Printer

As already emphasized in Chapter 3, one decision that must be made from the beginning is what target printer will be used. It's a good idea to become familiar with the capabilities of your particular printer before designing publications. Not all printers can take advantage of all of the features supported by page-composition applications. You will generally want to design your publications with your specific final-copy printer in mind.

Ideally, if there is more than one printer or cartridge available on your system, you can make this selection once for each application by defining the target printer in the template file. Thereafter, all files that are cloned from the template will have the same printer specifications. The target printer selection will dictate certain font selections for the rest of the design (see Chapter 3).

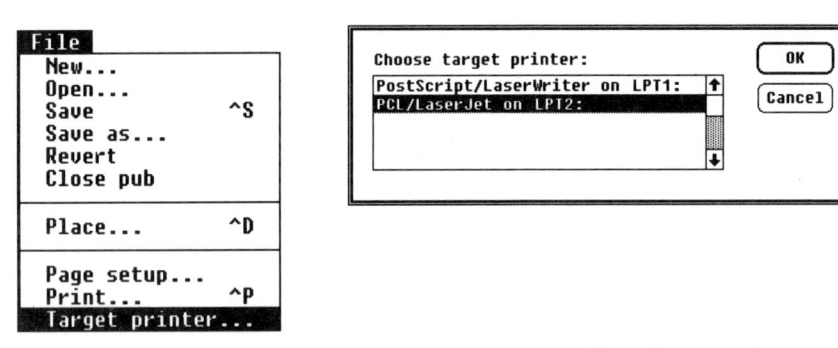

■ **Figure 4.25** In some applications, the target printer specified in the template publication will hold for all cloned versions of the template.

Set Defaults for Type Specifications

Most word processors and page-layout packages let you set the defaults for the font and alignment (flush left, right, centered, justified) of the body copy in the template file. All files that are cloned from the template will retain these settings. This way, any new text will automatically take on the template's default settings.

The process of inserting codes or using menu commands to format characters and paragraphs other than the body copy (default) might take place in either the word processor or in the page-layout program, depending on the features and capabilities of the programs in your system. Ideally, the template system incorporates some type specifications through dummy text or a style sheet feature, as well as through custom default settings.

The term dummy text here refers to standing lines of text that have already been set to the appropriate type specifications in the template, to be copied or edited as needed for each cloned document. For example, the template for a series of graphics might include dummy text for the title line (already centered) or the caption line (fixed in place) and in-Figure labels (to be copied, edited, and repositioned on different parts of each illustration). A newsletter template might include dummy text for headlines and Figure captions, as well as dummy text for the volume/issue number and date under the banner on the first page.

Some word processors and some page-layout packages offer a style sheet feature—the ideal system for handling formats. A style sheet system lets you define the character and paragraph format for each type of text element in a document, such as major headings, subheadings, captions, and body text. With a style sheet, you can format the text using short keystroke commands instead of opening different dialog boxes for character and paragraph formats. Text-formatting features supported by a style sheet can include:

Character-specific Formatting—
- Character styles like bold, underscore, strikethrough, italic
- Letter spacing (normal, condensed, expanded)

Paragraph-specific Formatting—
- Tabs
- Paragraph indentation
- Paragraph alignment (flush left, right, center)
- Line spacing, or leading

The style sheet is set up in the template, for use in all documents cloned from the same template. To format the text of a manuscript using the style sheet, you select the text to be formatted and then choose from a list of style names, such as "heading level 1" and "caption." You can then change the font or paragraph formats for each item simply by changing the settings for one style name. You can change the formatting of all of the level-1 headings, for instance, by changing the style sheet only.

Identify Common Text and Graphic Elements

Most of the contents of the publication will probably be placed from various programs in a final page-layout package. There will be some elements, however, that are repeated throughout the publication. In a page-layout template, these repeated elements appear on the master pages, on the pasteboard or scratch page, and on some numbered pages as described in this section.

Any elements that appear on every page in the same position belong on the master pages. This includes headers and footers as well as graphics elements that are part of the basic page design. The headers and footers on the master pages of the template are set up as place holders only: they are set up in position with the correct type specs and alignment, but the text is likely to change for each publication or part of a publication that is cloned from the template. One of the first steps in cloning the template will always be to change the text of the header and/or footer (Figure 4.26).

■ **Figure 4.26** The headers and footers on the template publication are place holders only, and will be updated each time the template is cloned.

In addition to the elements that belong on the master pages, there might be other elements that will be repeated throughout the publication in an irregular pattern. These can be created once and stored on the pasteboard, scratch page, or scrapbook, for copy/paste duplication wherever they are needed, if your application supports these handy work areas (Figure 4.27).

For example, if every story in a newsletter or magazine ends with a graphic symbol or a dingbat from a symbol font, you can store it in the work area and copy it whenever you reach the end of a story. Just as you created textual place holders for the header and footer, you can create standard dummy text blocks for headlines or captions within the publication and store them in the work area. If the publication will include display ads in predetermined sizes, you can store boxes drawn to those sizes in the work area, for duplication and positioning as the pages are layed out.

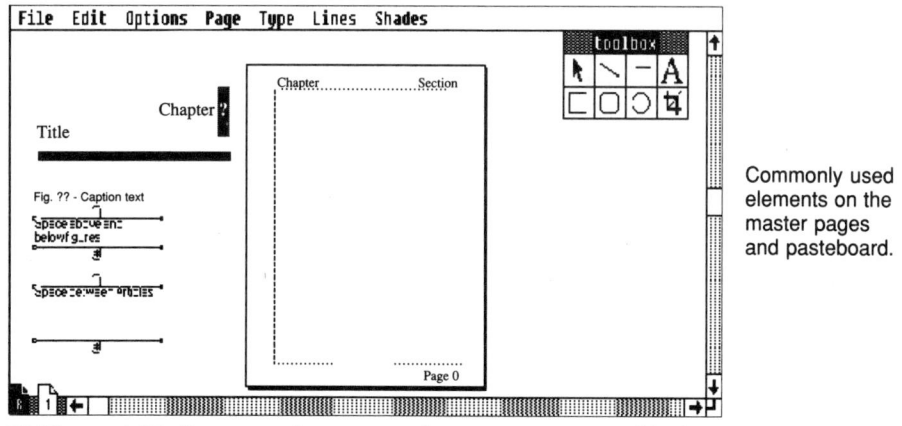

■ **Figure 4.27** Common elements on the master pages and in the work area, if your application supports this feature.

The template can contain a complete set of the symbols to be used throughout the illustrations, or the template system might include many different graphics files that are imported every time a symbol is required. Scale the repeating symbols to the size(s) that will be used before incorporating them into the template system. Unless the repeating symbols can be stored in a nonprinting work area, they should be deleted from the file before the final printing.

Besides the elements that are positioned on the master pages or stored in the work area, there may be elements that appear on the numbered pages in predictable locations. For example, the template for a newsletter should include the banner on page 1 (Figure 4.28). If each issue of the newsletter is always the same number of pages, you might also be able to predict the positions of the subscription information and other standing features. You can also add place holders for the text of headlines for feature articles that start on page 1.

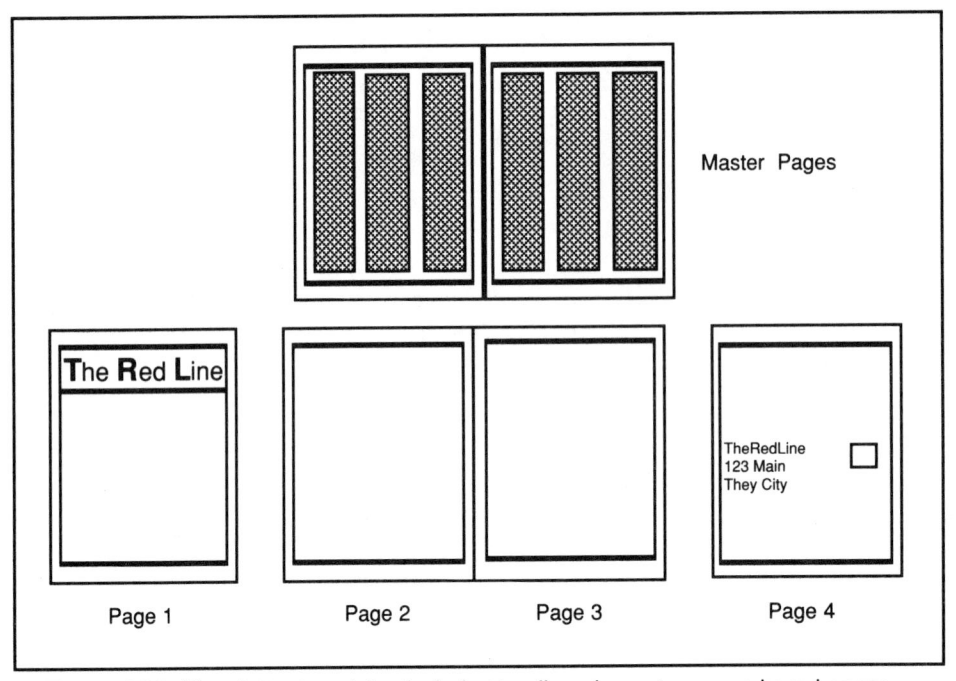

Figure 4.28 Newsletter templates include standing elements on numbered pages.

Add Spacing Guides

Normally, the spacing within the text will be determined by the type specifications and set up in the word processing program. The designer also needs to create specifications for the spacing between Figures and text, between text and ruled lines, and between text blocks (such as the spacing between headings and body copy, between paragraphs in a section, or between articles in a newsletter). In word processing applications and full-featured page-layout packages, you can set the space between paragraphs through a menu command for paragraph formatting. In graphics programs and some page-layout packages, rather than express the spacing in numbers only, you can help the production process by setting up physical spacing guides and storing them as part of the template.

A physical spacing guide can be created in either of two ways. The simplest way is to use the application's drawing tools to draw a box the height of the space called for in the design specifications. Give the box a hairline border and no fill pattern. You will need to draw one such box for each spacing specification, and label it with text as shown in Figure 4.29.

PUBLICATION DESIGN   159

Space above and below figures

Space between articles

■ **Figure 4.29** Draw boxes with a hairline border to represent spacing requirements, and label them in the template.

When you need to check the spacing between two objects on the page, move the appropriate spacing guide into position on the page and use it to align the objects.

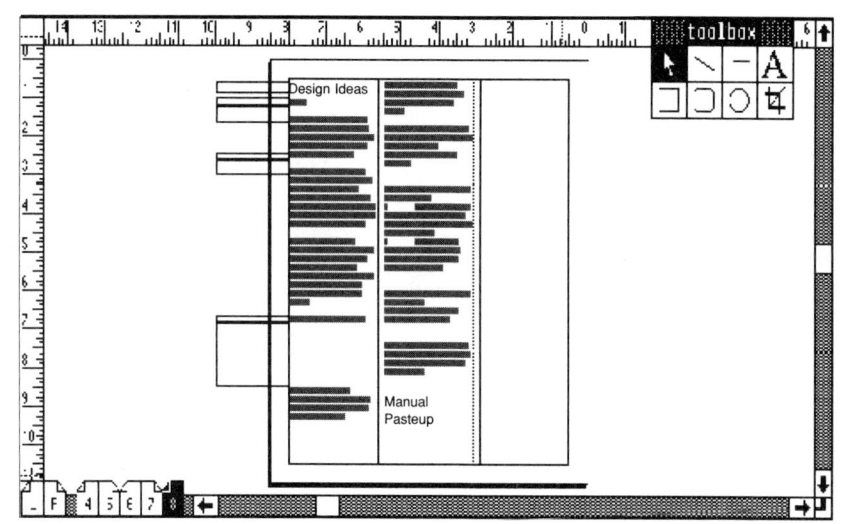

■ **Figure 4.30** Move the spacing guide to the page and use it to align the objects.

The second method of creating spacing guides is applicable to WYSIWYG page-layout packages that can import graphics from a drawing program. By this method, you can create a single spacing guide to encompass all specifications, and place it in the page-layout package as a single object, including the labels (Figure 4.31).

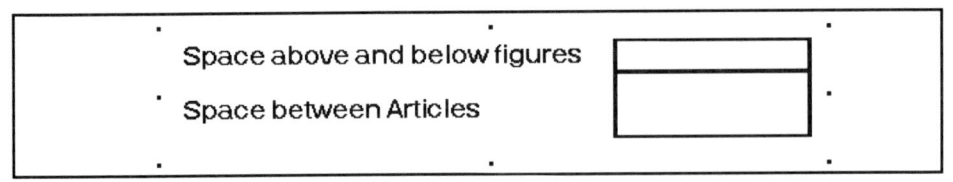

Figure 4.31 A spacing guide created in Windows Draw! and placed as one object in the page-composition application.

Identify the Number of Templates Required

We have already suggested that a different template file will be required for each unique page size, orientation, and margin settings. In addition, there may be other essential differences between sections of the publication that can be efficiently handled through a template system. For example, when the overall format for the headers and footers change between major sections of a publication, then multiple templates are called for (Figure 4.32). On the other hand, if the only difference between sections is the number of columns, then one template may suffice.

Rule of Thumb:

Create separate templates if any of these conditions apply: The page size varies. The page orientation varies. The master page elements change (except the text of headers and footers). The basic grid varies.

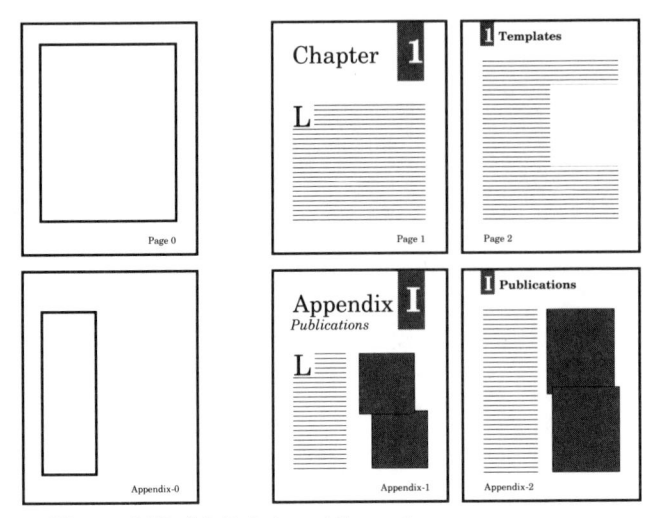

Figure 4.32 Multiple template systems.

Add Instructions for Working with Each Template

In a large publishing production project, it is a good idea to list the steps that will be repeated throughout the production cycle, regardless of how simple the steps may seem.

1. Type and format the text files in the word processing program, and store them in the subdirectory for this document.
2. Open the page-layout template document for this document, and modify the headers and footers to reflect the issue number (for periodicals) or chapter or section name (for books and reports). Save the modified template under the new section name.
3. Place the text on consecutive pages in the document, working in full-page view until all text is placed.
4. Go back to the beginning of the document, and work in 50 percent view, making formatting corrections as necessary, and opening up spaces for figures. Place the figures, scaling, and cropping as needed.
5. Print and proof drafts.
6. Edit page-layout file, print and proof finals.
7. Back up and archive the disk files.

If the person who designs the template is not the same person who will be using it for production, it's a good idea to list the steps that will be involved in working with the template. The steps can be very simple; they serve primarily as reminders so that no step is overlooked. For example:

1. Open the template and immediately save it under a new name.
2. Change the headers and footers on the master pages.
3. Change the volume/date information on page 1, below the newsletter banner.
4. Place the table of contents on page 1 before placing the feature article.
5. Delete these instructions.
6. Continue placing text and graphics as specified for the current issue.

These can be typed directly onto the first page of the template so they will catch the attention of the production staff (Figure 4.33). The production person can move them or delete the instructions after they read them.

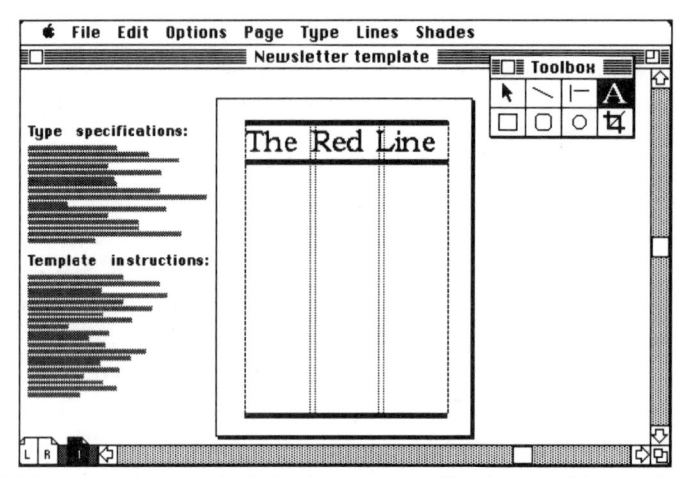

■ **Figure 4.33** A template can include the type specifications and instructions for using the template.

SPECIFICATIONS FOR PROGRAMS OTHER THAN THE PAGE-LAYOUT PACKAGE

In Chapter 3, Typography, we discussed most of the considerations that go into the selection of fonts for different text elements. Some of these specifications—such as the specifications for the position and format of headers and footers—can go directly into the page-layout template. Other specifications—type specifications, for example—might be implemented through the word processing program. Line widths and fill patterns can be set up as default values in the templates, or stored as pre-defined elements in the work area, or applied in the graphics programs that are used to create the content of the publication.

The designer should have a good idea of the number and source of graphic elements that will go into the publication. Knowing the capabilities and limitations of the programs available, it is the designer's responsibility to specify the treatment of each illustration. What are the size limitations or preferences for the figures? If you are following a grid system, you will want to make each figure's width match the increments allowed by the grid: a two-column grid allows two figure widths (one-column wide or the full page width); a three-column grid allows only three different figure widths; a four-column grid allows four widths; and so on.

What fonts/styles/sizes will be used in illustrations and their captions? Will the figures be enlarged/reduced during page composition? Will photographs and other special illustrations be pasted up by hand or scanned into the computer? These specifications can be written down, or the programs that will be used to create the illustrations can be used to create figure templates just as the page-layout package is used to create publication templates.

The design specifications should also include directions for paragraph alignment (flush left, right, justified, centered) and spacing between paragraphs (Figure 4.34), for the body copy, the captions, and the figure titles. See Chapters 3, 5, and 7 for more examples and discussion of different alignment settings (ragged-right vs. justified).

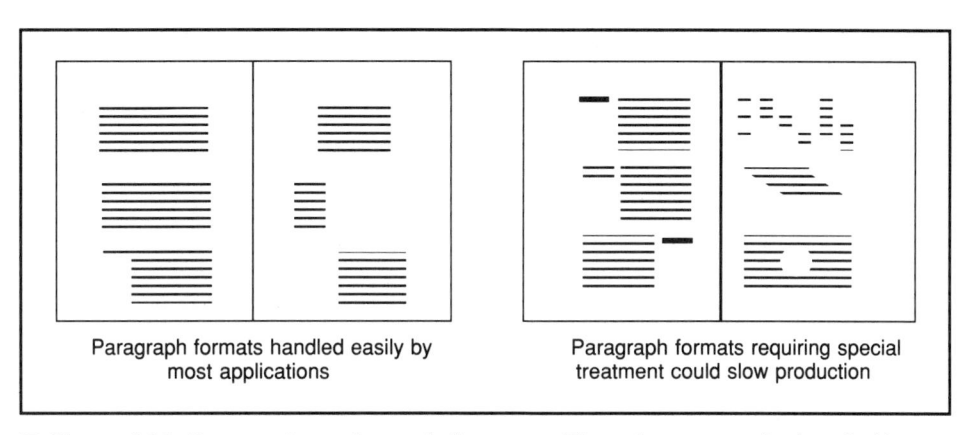

| Paragraph formats handled easily by most applications | Paragraph formats requiring special treatment could slow production |

■ **Figure 4.34** Paragraph spacing and alignments. These formats can be handled by menu selections in most page composition applications and word processors. These formats require special treatment, and could slow down the production process.

TESTING THE DESIGN AND TEMPLATES

Finally, it is a good idea to run a few sample pages of the publication through the various application programs that will be used to test all of the specifications before finalizing the design and the templates. This dry run is much more effective than any other review procedure in offering these benefits:

- Flush out any mismatches between the design specifications and the system capabilities.
- Fine tune the templates as needed.
- Identify the detailed list of steps that should be followed for efficient production.

Unfortunately, we often skip this final test: it may seem like a luxury when you are working under the pressures of a short deadline, and we tend to trust that our own knowledge of the system is sufficient to anticipate any problems that might develop. In fact, the test run can end up saving time on a project by developing efficient procedures and thereby shortening the production cycle, and you can add many hours to a project by failing to anticipate major problems (such as discovering that your printer cannot handle the graphics from the sources specified in the design).

Consider the Genre

Large projects or long documents may benefit more from using a template system than short, one-time documents. Assess your needs and adapt your approach to file management and page layout based on the characteristics of the documents you are producing. Some of the characteristics shared by different types of publications are discussed in the following sections.

MAGAZINES, TABLOIDS, AND NEWSLETTERS

The template systems for newsletters and magazines can be very elaborate compared with most other types of documents. Three of the most distinguishing characteristics of this category of documents are that:
- The document is often multicolumnar, and the number of columns can change on a single page.
- The text can skip from one page to a point several pages later.
- The documents are usually produced as a series: a document of the same basic format and length is produced at regular intervals.
- The documents often call for special layouts that may involve kerning headlines, wrapping text around graphics, or pasting display ads from one page-layout document into another.

These and other characteristics of these documents present their own special design and production problems and practices. The template for a complex document is a key production aid for each issue. The template can require many hours to build the first time (including time for test building one page, printing it out, and writing up procedures that can be followed by the authors and editors as well as by the production staff). But by putting extra care into the development of a good template system, you can save many hours over the life of a periodical publication.

Use Variations in the Grid to Distinguish between Sections of a Magazine

You have probably seen how some newsletters and magazines separate sections by giving them different grid structures. For example, the main feature might begin on several two-column pages before it continues to the back of the magazine in three columns; or the "letters to the editor" section might be three columns while all of the articles are two columns.

Sketch Page Layouts

Publications with very complex grid systems may require the designer's attention throughout the production cycle. This is especially true for magazines and newsletters that incorporate display ads of various sizes throughout the publication. The designer can work ahead of the production team to specify where ads are to be placed and how articles will jump from one page to another.

Traditionally, this procedure would be done by hand as pencil roughs of each page, or "thumbnail" sketches. The term originally derived from the fact that the sketches could be literally as small as a person's thumbnail, as they were intended to be very quick to produce. Some page-layout packages offer a thumbnails option that prints out miniature versions of the pages of the publication (if your printer can support this option). If the template for the publication is rather complex, thumbnails of the template can be printed out and marked up with instructions to the production team.

Thumbnail printouts of blank pages from the template for a magazine or tabloid newspaper can be used by the editors to mark positioning of articles. Alternatively, the designer can make rough page layouts using shaded boxes and article titles on every page of a magazine or newsletter, for example, and print out thumbnails as a guide for building the publication (Figure 4.35). This same "rough" file can be used as the starting point in placing the finished text and graphics files on each page when they are ready.

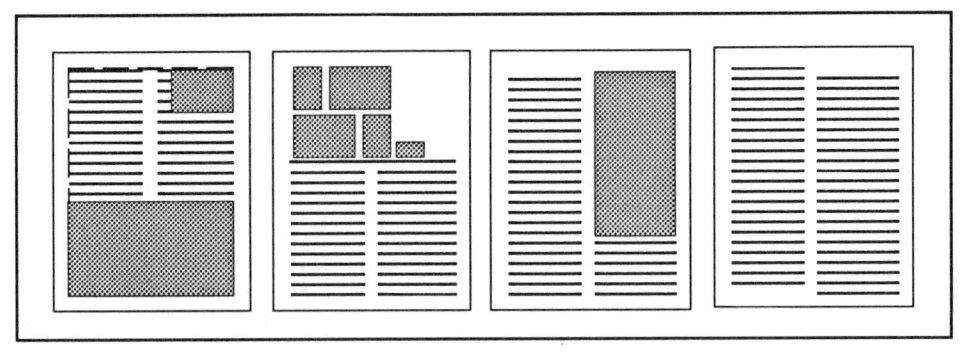

Figure 4.35 Shaded boxes and dummy text represent rough layout.

If tabloid pages are too small to be practical using a thumbnails feature, a printout with a percentage reduction can be used to print quick miniatures of each finished page. These reductions can be used by the editors to mark positioning of ads and articles. Reductions can also be used for control and review purposes after pages are built—to proof for positioning of ads and articles and review overall page layout.

Change Grid as Necessary on Individual Pages

Usually the initial template settings can be changed on individual pages as needed, i.e., you can move column guides, or suppress headers and footers as needed for exceptional page layouts. Some page-layout programs let you suppress or hide all of the master guides, text, and graphics from an individual page. You can use the program's command to eliminate all of the master elements, then use the program's text and graphics tools to add back only those elements you wish to use on a selected page.

If you want to suppress only a part of the master page elements, you can hide them in some page-layout programs by covering them with white boxes—rectangles created with a box tool and given a Shade of White and a Line style of None. This trick won't work with all printers. (Some printers cannot print reverse type or white boxes.)

A newsletter template can be designed specifically for ease in coordinating the production process among a group of volunteers who have many other—perhaps more pressing—responsibilities in their lives. One useful trick in cases like this is to decide that the newsletter always contains the exact same set of features, each of which are always the same size and fall into the same position on the pages. Furthermore, you can create standing back-up copy or artwork—sized to match each feature's space—for use in a month when a particular feature is missing.

Predict the Placement of Ads in Newsletter, Magazine, and Newspaper Layouts

Any publication that includes advertising is a challenge for the page designer. One problem is that ads tend to trickle in up to the last minute, and the general rule is that the customer is king. It is the editor's responsibility and the designer's chore to include all paid advertising—to redesign page layouts if necessary to make room for last-minute additions. The second problem is one of aesthetics: the addition of a single ad may upset the balance of an already-planned page-layout. The third problem is emphasis: the upper horizontal half and the left vertical half of a page are natural focal points, so when stories take these positions they may distract the reader's attention from ads in the lower or right half of the pages, and vice versa.

Magazine and newspaper designers have developed a few standard layouts or "ad profiles" for these types of pages. For example, one common layout is the *blocked* or *ganged* ad format, which puts all of the ads in a rectangle on the bottom portion of the page (Figure 4.36). A *panel* format is a vertical cluster of ads that take a third or half of a page (Figure 4.36).

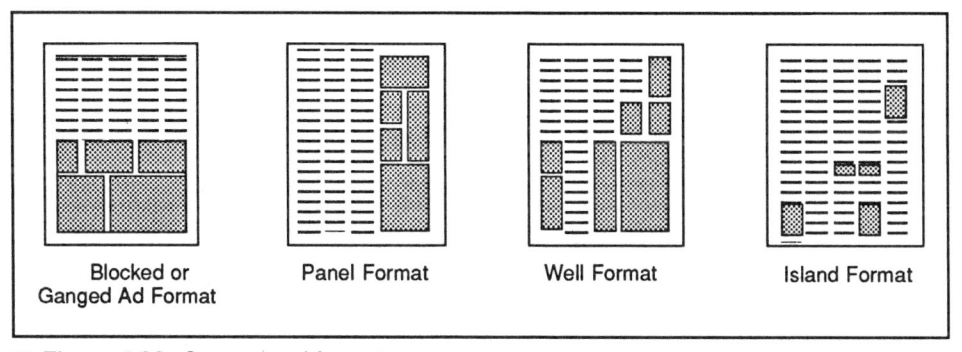

■ **Figure 4.36** Common ad formats.

The *half-pyramid* ad layout is based on a stepped pattern, usually with the lowest step at the outside margin of the page (Figure 4.37). Two facing pages layed out this way would create a *full pyramid*, but this effect is not so commonly used since (as mentioned earlier) perfect symmetry lacks drama.

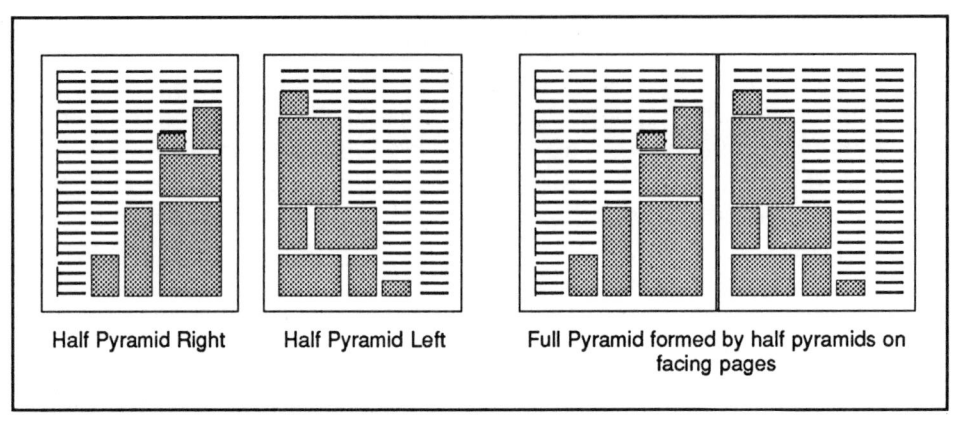

| Half Pyramid Right | Half Pyramid Left | Full Pyramid formed by half pyramids on facing pages |

■ **Figure 4.37** Pyramid ad formats.

Two other common formats are the *well* format, in which a column or more of type extends down between clusters of ads on both sides of the page, and the *island* format, in which individual blocks of ads can be surrounded by text. These last two formats are more difficult to master without a strong sense of design.

Avoid "Dutch Wraps" in Newsletter, Magazine, and Newspaper Layouts

If you are jumping a story from one column to another, be sure to include a jumper line (continued to/from page *x*) and a short headline at the top of the text in the new column. The only exception to this rule is when the story continues at the top of the next adjacent column—whether on the same page or on another page of the publication. Otherwise, by separating text from a headline, you are creating what is called a Dutch wrap (Figure 4.38) which forces the reader to hunt for the continuation.

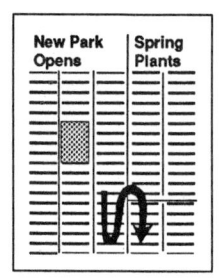

■ **Figure 4.38** By separating part of a story from a headline, you create a "Dutch wrap" that forces the reader to hunt for the continuation.

Special Considerations for Web Presses

If you're going to print your newsletter on a web offset press, you should also be aware before designing your piece that this type of press, while faster and less expensive for some jobs, cannot provide the accuracy and color consistency of a sheet-fed press. You'll want to avoid design elements that could draw attention to discrepancies, such as colored bars at the tops of pages, and rules or other graphic elements that cross over facing page boundaries.

REPORTS AND PROPOSALS

Business reports, books, and manuals share many characteristics and the same design principles and production tips can be applied to all projects in this category. For example, these documents are usually longer than the documents in the other categories that are described in this chapter. The full document is usually composed of several files, making these types of documents good candidates for a template system.

Most business reports and many manuals happen to be published in 8½-by-11 format, whereas books frequently have smaller dimensions. In the past, most business reports have been produced as single-sided documents, whereas manuals and books are usually double-sided documents. The single-sided vs. double-sided options can also be used as production aids, regardless of how the final document will be produced.

Page layouts for documents in this category are usually not as complex as for the other categories described here. The documents in this category most frequently use a one-column grid, or they might have a second column reserved for Figures, captions, callouts, or section titles. It is not uncommon to use two different page grids, as shown in Figure 4.39. The document shown there switches back and forth between a two-column format (in which one column is wider than the other) and a three-column format (in which all columns are the same width. Most page-layout packages allow only one grid for the master pages—or two grids if the left and right master pages are different.

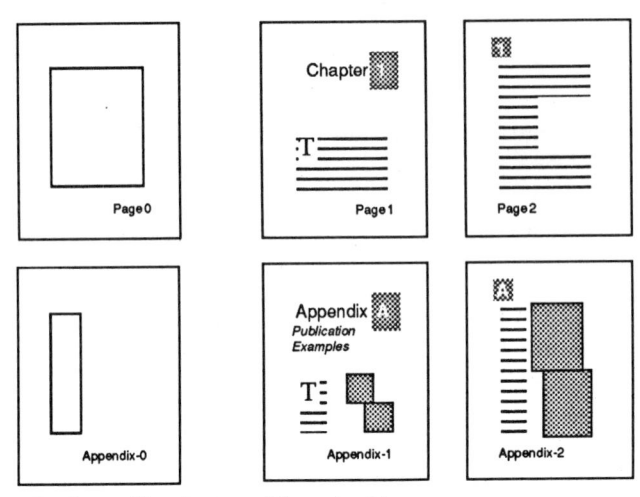

■ **Figure 4.39** Design calling for two different grids.

Documents that use the same grid on every page will be much easier to produce than documents that switch between several variations in the grid. One common variation that is particularly hard to work with is the mirror-image page layout, such as the one shown in Figure 4.40. What makes this layout difficult is not the layout of individual pages, it is the chaos that ensues if you insert or delete one page after the publication has been layed out.

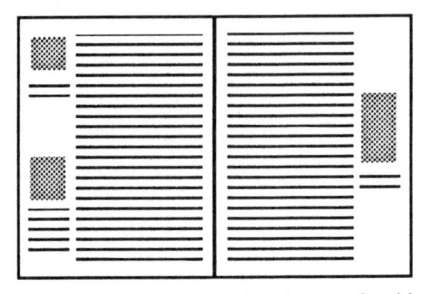

■ **Figure 4.40** A mirror-image page design is hard to work with.

The trick to alternating between two grids that are *not* tied to left or right orientation is to use the master pages for the more complex or customized grid, and use the program's automatic grid features for the simpler grid (in this case, the three-column grid). In the alternating design shown in Figure 4.40, the three-column width can be set up automatically by a column-guides command if the first column's right margin and gutter in the customized format is designed to fall in the exact same position as the first column of the automatic three-column grid.

Most publications will have the same page size for all sections, but the orientation of the pages may vary from section to section. For instance, you might have a set of appendices that need to be printed wide in order to accommodate many columns of numbers in a financial report. In this case, you can set up two templates: one for all tall pages, and one for all wide pages.

PRICE LISTS, CATALOGUES, AND DIRECTORIES

Price lists, catalogues, and directories are all promotional material. Their similarity is more in their use than in their format, since materials in any of these categories come in a wide variety of forms. Price lists can be any number of pages long, for example, and this format includes menus. Long price lists of inventoried products can, like member lists, be derived from spreadsheet data or database files.

The publications in this category are often a nonstandard size—the final pages might be trimmed and/or folded, and if they are more than eight pages long the booklet might be stapled or bound.

BROCHURES, FLYERS, AND DISPLAY ADS

Brochures, flyers, and display ads all share these characteristics:
- They are usually only one or two pages long in the page-layout file, though they might be folded into four or more panels.
- They are often a nonstandard size—the final pages must be trimmed and/or folded.

Brochures are usually only one or two pages long in the page-layout file, though they might be folded into four or more panels. Some of the tips in this chapter can also be applied to brochures that are longer—like booklets.

A one-time brochure can use a template system that can be adapted to other similar formats. Several brochure templates are shown in Figure 4.41.

172 THE ELECTRONIC PUBLISHER

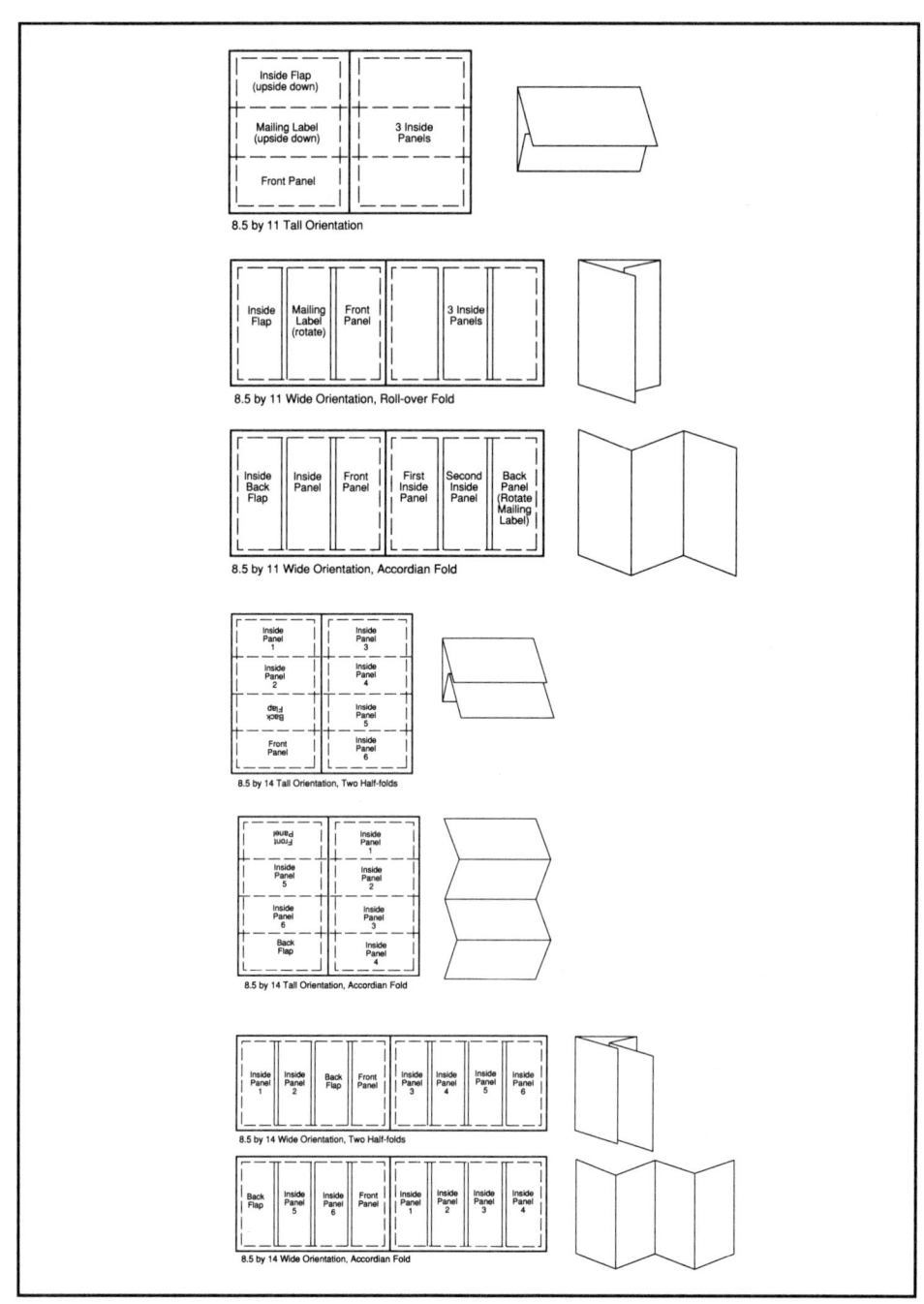

■ **Figure 4.41** Templates for three-fold and four-fold brochures.

For most publication designs, white space—areas of the page that will not have text or graphics—is used to help invite the reader into the page layout. This guideline is often relaxed when you are designing a functional reference listing, like a telephone book for an association, a company, or a department. If there is a lot of information in a repeated format, like a price list for a large store or warehouse, it can be be easier for the reader to find a specific product if the information is compact. Since the audience is usually looking for one reference at a time and rarely reads full pages of these materials, the eye doesn't require as much rest, and the reader need not be invited into each page by the design.

On the other hand, white space is especially important if the publication is intended to represent your product or service to your clients and the general public. For example, if a price list is also a catalogue that describes your product in detail and includes illustrations to attract the readers' interest or clarify the value of a special offer, then white space can help the overall effect of the publication as a sales tool. If you are working with a small format, as many brochures are, this might translate into writing less copy or using fewer illustrations in order to open up white space.

If you are creating a brochure for your own small business, it's a natural tendency to want to give the readers as much information as possible about your product or service, and at the same time to save printing and postage costs by minimizing the number of pages. In fact, the reverse effect can occur when you put too many words into a brochure or listing of members or services—the final document is uninviting, and readers might not read any of the text if it is in a small point size. By choosing your words carefully, you can get a few important points across and draw the reader toward taking action—calling to receive a service or coming to the store.

You can plan your publication for most economical use of color if you know on what kind of printing press it's going to be run and how your printer will run it. For example, if you have an eight-page four-color brochure, on some presses it will be printed so that four pages are on one side of the sheet and the other four pages on the reverse. First one side ill be printed, then the plates will be changed and the other side will be printed. This means that you can save money by printing four-color only on one side. Your printer can tell you which pages these will be (they will not be consecutive), and you can plan your design so that only those pages have four-color images.

You can take the same brochure, however, and print it on a different press using a different method, and it will cost you no more to print *all pages* in color. If the job is being printed on a large-enough press "work and turn" or "work and tumble," all eight pages will print on one side of the sheet, and then print in reversed order on the other side. This means that the same plates are used for both runs—and there is no extra charge for running color throughout.

TABLES, CHARTS, AND OVERHEAD TRANSPARENCIES

We tend to associate the term desktop publishing with books, reports, newsletters, and magazines, but a page-layout package can be an excellent tool for creating presentation materials. You can create charts and graphs using other programs and place them in the page-layout, and you can add captions and topic summaries using the page-layout program's tools directly. You can print the images directly on clear acetate using a laser printer, or you can print the images on paper and then photograph the printed sheets to make slides.

Some of the documents in this category might be designed specifically for use as overhead transparencies or slides, while others are designed as printed handouts, but they all share the following characteristics:

- They are part of a series of materials.
- They are primarily graphics. The word charts among them have very few words, usually in a large font.
- They each require some extra touches in a page-layout program that might not be possible in the graphics programs that are used to create the charts and diagrams.

One editorial guideline that applies to materials in this category is *be concise.* Try to keep the text on each overhead down to 25 words or less. The number 25 is only slightly arbitrary. Billboard designers follow a rule of not exceeding seven words if possible—and you have probably experienced what a strong impact a billboard can have. At the other extreme, you have also seen how much effort you must put into reading and understanding slides and overhead transparencies that have a lot of words in small type.

You might decide that your limit is 50 words per page or more—especially if the text is the caption on a page to be handed out rather than projected onto a screen. The important point is to recognize that this genre of materials requires a special attention to word count and point size.

If you are designing slides or overhead transparencies for a presentation, design all of the images in a series to use the same perspective—either tall or wide. This level of consistency is not only a design goal, it is a convenience that will make the production steps much easier than if you mix tall and wide pages in a series. If the material being presented is such that this rule cannot be followed, then the presentation materials themselves must be developed using two or more different template publications.

Another one of the underlying principles for these designs is that graphic images generally benefit by being surrounded with white space. For overhead transparencies, fit all images to a 7 inch by 9 inch area. This rule applies particularly to overhead transparencies that will be framed, since the frames for overhead transparencies usually have a 7½ by 9½ inch window (Figure 4.42).

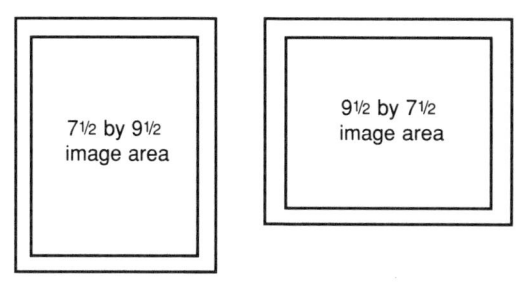

■ **Figure 4.42** Overhead transparencies with a 7½-by-9½-inch "window" frame.

This is a good guide to follow even if the images will not be framed. The viewing conditions in many cases will restrict some people in the audience from seeing the extreme edges of the overhead, but the center of the image should be visible to all. These measurements also approximate the proportions used in slides: 24 by 35 mm. For materials that will be made into slides, set all images within an area of approximately 2:3 proportions. Generally, 35mm slide frames have a 35mm by 24mm clear window. It's a good idea to design your graphics in this proportion, especially slide images that have a ruled border around them.

You can use the page-layout program's automatic page-numbering feature to number the images used in a presentation. This way, you can easily find the images in the page-layout document when you want to update them selectively. If you do not want the numbers to show when you are projecting the images, use a small point size and place the page numbers at the bottom of the image area.

If the sequence of the images will change for particular presentations, or if some presentations will be shortened by omitting selected images, you can still use the automatic page numbering feature to number the master set, and identify alternate positioning on each page in the same small font (Figure 4.43).

```
┌─────────────────────┐
│                     │┐
│   Sales Training    ││┐
│      Seminar        ││││┐
│                     │││││┐
│         Overhead #1 │││││
└─────────────────────┘││││
    └──Overhead #2─────┘│││
       └──Overhead #3───┘││
          └──Overhead #4─┘│
             └──Overhead #5┘
```

■ **Figure 4.43** Page-number feature can be used to sequence overheads.

If the final output will be on a laser printer, use gray screen rather than solid black areas for the best projection image. If your printer's toner cartridge is at its peak performance, you can get solid black areas to print solid on paper. Even with a good cartridge, however, there may be some unevenness in the black areas when printing directly to transparency sheets (acetate), and this unevenness will be exaggerated when the image is projected. You can reduce the effects of uneven toner by using gray fill patterns instead of black.

Use Alignment Commands

WYSIWYG (what you see is what you get) refers to what you see on the screen as compared with what prints out. Highly accurate WYSIWYG systems produce 100 percent fidelity between the screen and the printer. Most desktop publishing systems and applications are not 100 percent WYSIWYG. Discrepancies occur because fonts displayed on the low-resolution screen are shown as bit-maps, while high-resolution printers refine the letters during the printing process.

One way to work with the discrepancies is to always use the applications commands for aligning text, rather than visually positioning text on the screen display. For example, if you want two lines of text to be centered, use the centering command for both lines, rather than insert space at the beginning of each line until the two lines appear to be centered. Always use tabs rather than spaces to align tabular columns.

Summary

In Chapters 1 through 4 you learned about the planning and design issues involved in producing a publication. The following chapters of the book describe the actual production process, from typesetting and illustration through page layout and printing.

Part 3
Production

Traditionally, production begins after the writing and design steps are complete. When the writer or designer are using the tools of desktop publishing, the production considerations described in the following chapters can extend over the whole life of the project. Because the author and/or designer may have the tools to take the document through to final camera-ready copy, they need to pick up the skills of production specialists—attention to detail, organizing their work to facilitate teamwork, and working quickly under pressure.

When the project schedule slips at the writing or editing stage, the burden of meeting the deadline often falls on the production group. Whereas the writer and designer may be valued most for their creativity, the production staff (or function) is most valued for its efficiency—it is at this stage, more than any other, that a thorough knowledge of the tools is essential.

Chapter 5
Text Processing

One of electronic publishing's distinguishing features is its ability to import text from word processing programs into page-layout programs and, in many cases, preserve the formatting (type specifications, tabs, and paragraph alignment) that was started at the word processing stage. The primary goal of this chapter is to help you prepare text using your word processor. In most publication projects, the word processing step must come first, and the step of actually bringing the text into a page layout comes much later—Chapter 7 in this book.

Some page-layout programs retain the text formatting that is set up in the word processor, and you can add or change the formatting directly in the page-layout program. Text editing and formatting is often a slower process in a page-composition program than it is in a word processing program, however, so it is a good idea to do as much editing and formatting as possible using the word processor, before importing the text into a page-layout package. This chapter outlines the steps involved in preparing text for typesetting and formatting—*before* the final page-layout process—with attention to the following issues:

- If the manuscript is provided as hard copy only, it can be typed into the computer from scratch or it can be scanned in through an optical character reader. Guidelines for typing text in from scratch will be provided, as well as a discussion of the types of character readers that are available.
- If the manuscript is provided on disk, it may need to be telecommunicated from one system to another, converted from one word processing program to another, or cleaned up using the text processor in which it originated. Here, methods and programs for telecommunications or conversion will be reviewed, and a list of the steps involved in cleaning up files will be given.

Rule of Thumb:

In general, it is a good idea to get the text files as clean as possible while still in the word processing program—before taking the text into a page-composition program.

Special techniques for handling data files (from spreadsheets and databases) will also be discussed.
- As a separate step from cleaning the files, the printed copy of the manuscript may need to be marked for typesetting according to the designer's specifications. The difference between using WYSIWYG typesetting programs vs. typesetting codes will be discussed.

There are several different ways of handling special characters that are not part of the character sets available for standard fonts. Font-design programs will be discussed, as well as handling special characters as artwork (to be pasted up on screen or by hand).
- Final formatting of the text to fit the page margins specified by the designer may be done through the word processing program or saved for the page-composition step.

Typing Text Directly

If the manuscript is provided as hard copy only, it can be typed into the computer from scratch or it can be scanned in through an optical character reader. In typing text from a manuscript, it is usually most efficient to type the text first without inserting cumbersome typesetting codes, so the typed text can be easily proofread against the author's original manuscript, but clear, consistent conventions should be established in advance for distinguishing between different elements in the text.

LIST OF STANDARDS

A detailed list of standards and review items can be evolved throughout the project, as described in Chapter 1. Sometimes this list is called an author's or editor's style sheet, but this is not to be confused with the style sheet feature that some word processors and page-layout programs offer for formatting paragraphs.

An example of a list of standards and review items is shown in Figure 5.1, and these recommendations and other good typing practices are summarized in the following more general descriptions:
- Name the preferred reference books or sources to be used in resolving all questions of style and usage, punctuation, capitalization, abbreviations, spelling, treatment of numbers, and other special matter (footnotes, bibliography, etc.).
- Provide a list of terms that require capitalization, acceptable abbreviations, preferred spellings, special characters (and the codes used to

indicate them), and other special requirements for the publication—not covered in the preferred reference books or sources.
- Establish clear word processing guidelines for typing the text. Should paragraphs be indented with the tab key or with spaces or through paragraph formatting commands? Should a tab character always follow the bullets or numbers in a numbered list? Should an extra carriage return be added between paragraphs?

```
ABC Publishing Group
Guidelines
for Authors and Editors

Standard References            1
Typing Conventions             2
Proofing Checklist             3
Spelling, capitalization,
    and hyphenation Glossary   4
```

■ **Figure 5.1**   Table of Contents from a list of standards and review items.

- Use automatic word wrap for text (i.e., soft carriage returns at the end of lines within a paragraph, hard carriage returns at the end of paragraphs). Use the word processor's commands to indent text—do not create hanging indents by typing carriage returns and tabs within sentences (Figures 5.2 and 5.3).

```
Note:→ This.paragraph.has.been.typed.         Note:→ This.paragraph.has.been.typed.¶
       with.automatic.indentation.and.              →   with.hard.carriage.returns.at.the.¶
       soft.carriage.returns.at.the.end.            →   end.of.each.line.and.¶
       of.each.line.¶                               →   indentation.forced.with.tabs.¶
¶                                                   ¶
```

■ **Figure 5.2**   Arrows and ¶ symbols show where tabs and carriage returns were inserted in two paragraphs to yield the same printed result.

> **Original Margins**
> **Note:** This paragraph has been typed with automatic indentation and soft carriage returns at the end of each line.
>
> **Margins Changed**
> **Note:** This paragraph has been typed with automatic indentation and soft carriage returns at the end of each line.
>
> **Note:** This paragraph has been typed with hard carriage returns at the end of each line and indentation forced with tabs.
>
> **Note:** This paragraph has been typed
> with hard carriage returns
> at the
> end of each line and indentation forced with tabs.

■ **Figure 5.3** When the text margins are changed, the automatic paragraph indentation holds, but the forced indentation does not.

- Distinguish between numbers and letters by using the appropriate keys for "1" and "l" and "0" and "O."
- Use two hyphens to indicate a long dash (an Em dash). Establish clear conventions for indicating other special characters such as bullets and trademark symbols (see Special Characters, later in this chapter).
- Divide long documents into separate word processing files—one for each chapter or section or article.
- Do not insert hyphens to break words at the end of lines (unless the word processor offers automatic hyphenation that is compatible with the page-layout program).
- Do not type headings in all caps unless the final typesetting specifications call for all-cap headings. Develop clear conventions for distinguishing between heading levels. (See Typesetting Text, later in this chapter.)

PROOFREADING TEXT

Whether the text is typed directly or scanned in through an optical character reader, a thorough proofreading is required. An electronic spelling checker can help eliminate some of the most obvious typographical errors, but a visual reading is also required to find words that may be in the dictionary but out of context, such as when "that" should be "than."

Electronic media can progressively reduce the time spent proofing after each round of changes to the files. Whereas a copy editor's readings may result in changes to the author's words (long before the production team handles the text), the proofreader's task is to make sure that the latest printout of the manuscript conforms exactly to the previous version plus the edits based on the author's and copy editor's marks. The proofreader usually reads the new manuscript against the old one with its marked edits. A typical production cycle will include only one copy edit, but will include several proofreading rounds.

In general, it is a good idea to proofread the processed text against the author's original manuscript, and to perform all copy edits in the word processor. The visual proofreading should include cross-checking the original manuscript against the electronic version to verify that no lines of text have been skipped. This will be easier for one person to verify if the electronic manuscript is set at the same line length as the original manuscript. Otherwise, this kind of proofing is often done with a pair of readers—one reading aloud (including the punctuation, and very quickly) from the original manuscript while the other reader follows the words of the retyped manuscript.

Rule of Thumb:
It will be easier to proofread the electronic manuscript against the original manuscript if the two documents have the same line lengths.

For text that is input through an optical character reader, proofreading should include searches for cases where tabs or special paragraph formats are required, since most optical character readers will interpret white space within a line of text as spaces rather than tabs or indentation settings.

Proofreading for *font* and *format* is usually more efficient after the full pages have been composed in the page-layout program, and it requires a printer that accurately displays each font used. See Proofreading Typeset Text later in this chapter.

PROOFREADER'S MARKS

In mark-up, there are many symbols commonly used by copy editors to indicate changes to the text and to the format of the text, and you will find that conventions vary. For example, bold is usually indicated by a wavy line

186 THE ELECTRONIC PUBLISHER

Mark	Meaning	Example	Results
ℓ	Take out	Exxperience	Experience
∧	Insert	Experice	Experience
⌒	No space	E xperience	Experience
⌣	Less space	Experience ⌣ is a	Experience is a
∼	Transpose	Epxerience	Experience
/	Lower case	ExpErience	Experience
≡	Capitalize	experience	Experience
≡	All caps	experience	EXPERIENCE
sm caps	Small caps	sm caps experience	EXPERIENCE
C+sc	Caps and small caps	experience	EXPERIENCE
rom	Roman	rom (Experience)	Experience
ital.	Italic	ital. Experience	*Experience*
bf	Bold	bf Experience	**Experience**
stet	No change (ignore marks)	Experience stet	Experience
¶	New parargraph	and now. ¶ Experience	and now. Experience
No ¶	No paragraph (run in)	and now. No ¶ Experience	and now. Experience
∥	Align left	∥Experience ∥ Experience	Experience Experience
∥	Align right	Experience ∥ Experience∥	Experience Experience
⊙	Period	Experience⊙	Experience.
✸	Comma	Experience✸	Experience,
✌	Apostrophe	Experiences ✌	Experience's
∨	Superscript	Experience ∨	Experience[1]
❝ ❞	Quotes	❝Experience❞	"Experience"
(/)	Parentheses	(Experience)	(Experience)

■ **Figure 5.4** Common proofreading symbols.

drawn under the word(s) to be made bold, but some editors might use two straight lines to indicate bold. It doesn't matter what conventions you follow, so long as everyone on the project understands the meaning of the marks. Some common marks are shown in Figure 5.4.

TYPESETTING CODES

The type specifications set up by the designer must be entered into the text as typesetting codes—whether typed, selected from menus, or embodied in style sheet tags. Type specifications include:
- Typefaces, sizes, and styles for different elements within the text.
- Basic text format. Will the paragraphs have a first line indent? What will be the space between paragraphs? Will the text be justified? Will headings be flush left or centered?

In this chapter, discussion of text composition will include three different types of applications:
- Text-only typesetting programs that produce galleys of text.
- Text-only typesetting programs that produce composed pages, leaving space for graphics to be pasted in.
- Text-and-graphics page-composition systems that are not WYSIWYG.

Key issues that cross all these categories of page-composition programs—such as kerning and automatic hyphenation—will also be discussed.

Traditionally, typesetters are accustomed to entering typesetting codes at the same time as they are typing the text of the manuscript. This can be efficient, but there are several reasons for making the typesetting codes a separate step from typing the manuscript itself. First, if the typesetting codes are typed as ASCII characters directly into the text, they can diminish the efficiency of using an electronic spelling checker (unless the typesetting codes have been added to the electronic dictionary) and they will make it much more difficult to find typos during the visual reading (if the codes appear as ASCII characters in the draft printouts. Second, entering typesetting codes may slow down the text entry process; it might be more efficient to let a fast typist enter the text first, then let a formatting expert enter the typesetting codes later, after the proofreading steps.

This last consideration—when to enter the typesetting codes—falls into new light when the author is working directly with the disk files that will eventually be used in typesetting the text. The author needs to have some method of indicating heading levels for the designer and copy editor. If the author uses a style sheet or inserts codes that can be easily converted for use in the final typesetting and page composition, then the typesetter's task might simply be to adjust the style sheet tags as necessary to match final design specifications, or perform global search-and-replace operations to change the author's codes to the correct codes required for the final production.

Otherwise, if the author's manuscript is completely unformatted (i.e., ASCII), or if the author's coding conventions cannot be easily converted (i.e., they will be stripped out in preparation for typesetting), then the question of when to enter typesetting codes might be affected by the type of coding required, the division of responsibilities between the production group, or the number of edit rounds expected on the text itself.

> **Rule of Thumb:**
>
> Working in small point sizes.
>
> If the final document will be printed in a small point size—for instance for a phone directory—work in large type size through initial text edit rounds, so production staff and proofreaders can see text easily. Convert to small typeface for the last edit rounds and page-layout process.

Preparing Disk Files

Whereas authors and editors once had to retype edited pages completely, most writers now use word processors, which let them enter changes and reprint the document easily. These same files can be further transformed by the editors and finally prepared as direct input into the typesetter or laser printer. Two of the great advantages of using the same disk files from start to finish in a publishing effort are: 1) the tremendous economy of keystrokes and 2) progressively shortened proofreading rounds.

TELECOMMUNICATION OR CONVERSION

If the manuscript is provided on disk, it may need to be telecommunicated from one system to another, or converted from one word processing program to another. Not so long ago, word processing programs were incompatible with each other: you could not take the text from one word processor and convert it for use on a different manufacturer's word processor. Similarly, you could not take the text from a word processor and read it into a typesetting system. Over the past few years, however, many conversion programs have become available, and text from virtually any word processing system can be converted into a form that can be handled by any other word processing system.

CLEANUP: SPACES, TABS, CARRIAGE RETURNS, QUOTEMARKS, AND DASHES

The level of effort required to clean up the author's text files will depend on the results of the conversion process and the degree to which the author's conventions for using tabs and carriage returns are consistent with the production group's standards. In most cases, the cleanup steps described here can be executed as global searches if your word processing program lets you search for nonprinting characters such as spaces, tabs, and carriage returns. In the worst case, you may need to perform one or more of the following steps manually, i.e., by visually scanning the text on screen and making each change individually. In either case, it is a tremendous help if your word processing program offers the option of displaying nonprinting characters on the screen.

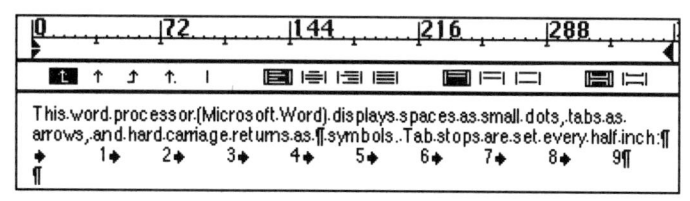

■ **Figure 5.5** Spaces, tabs, and carriage returns are displayed on the screen as small dots, arrows, and paragraph symbols by this word processor.

If the conversion process from the author's word processor to the production group's word processor results in a hard carriage return at the end of each line of the manuscript, you will need to change these to soft carriage returns within paragraphs in order to enable automatic word wrap. In this case, it is preferable that the author entered two hard carriage returns (i.e., double-spaced) between each paragraph and after each heading, so you can clean up the text in three global searches:

1. Change all occurrences of two carriage returns to some unique code such as "ZZZ."
2. Next, replace all remaining carriage returns with a space or with nothing.
3. Then, replace all "ZZZ" with one or two carriage returns (depending on whether you want single or double spacing between paragraphs).

Rule of Thumb:

Whenever you are performing global searches/replacements, it is a good idea to save the file before each search, and to verify the results of the search before saving the file again.

When performing a long series of global searches on a large volume of text, it is a good idea to test the series of steps on a small portion of the text before searching the complete text.

If the author typed two spaces after each period, most typesetting systems will handle justified text better if these are converted to only one space:

4. Replace all occurrences of two spaces with one space.

If the conversion process converted tabs to spaces, or if the author typed spaces instead of using the tab character to align tabular data, you can replace the spaces with tabs through a series of global searches:

5. Replace all occurrences of three spaces with two spaces. Repeat this search as many times as necessary until no more occurrences of three spaces are found.
6. Finally, replace all occurrences of two spaces with the tab character.

If the author used straight quotation marks (", '), you can change these to open and closed quotes using the following global searches:

Change all occurrences of space" to space".
Change all occurrences of space' to space'.
Change all occurrences of "space to "space.
Change all occurrences of space' to space'.

Then selectively change any remaining occurrences of " and '.

If these cleanup steps can be taken care of using global search-and-replace commands, and the content of the author's edited text is not altered, the proofreading step here is abbreviated to checking for format only—the text should be visually scanned to find any obvious formatting errors that might have resulted from the blind global searches. If these changes could not be accomplished through global searches, then the proofreading step should include a more detailed comparison of the processed files against the original manuscript to verify that no lines or paragraphs were erroneously deleted.

DETERMINE THE MINIMUM NUMBER OF RULER LINE SETTINGS

In general, it is a good idea to define as few ruler line variations (or style sheet tags) as needed for the entire document. One variable that requires a different ruler line or tag for each change is the indentation setting, for instance. If you are using a style sheet, you will also need a different tag for each font used in headings and body copy. On the other hand, the same tab settings can be shared by several different text formats. For example, the three formats shown in Figure 5.6 all share the same paragraph format and ruler line settings: flush left text with no indentation, tabs set at intervals of ½ inches. Paragraphs here are indented using the tab character.

| This paragraph is flush left with no indentation, tabs set at intervals of 1/2-inch. | This paragraph is indented by typing the Tab key at the beginning of the first line. | The same ruler line accomodates this list:
•   Item 1
•   Item 2
or this table:
Item 1   String
Item 2   Paper |

■ **Figure 5.6**   Three formats that share the same paragraph format and tab settings.

As a more complex example, the document shown in Figure 5.7 looks at first glance as though three or more ruler line settings were used. In fact, all of the text in this example uses the same ruler line (Figure 5.8). All body copy is formatted with a hanging indent. From there, the first tab is the flush-right tab used by section subheads. The second tab is used to position major section headings and all body copy, and the hanging indent point corresponds to this tab. A third tab is set up for tabbing after bullets in short lists.

192 THE ELECTRONIC PUBLISHER

Title

Heading Lorem ipsum dolor sit amet, con sectetuer adipicising elit, sed diam nonnumy nibh euismod tempor inci dunt ut labore et dolore magna ali quam erat volupat.

Subhead
Ut wisi enim as minim veniam, quis nostrud exerci tation ullamcorper suscipit laboris nisl ut aliquip ex ea commodo con sequat.
- Duis autem vel eum irure
- Dolor in henderit in vulputate velit
- Esse consequat.

■ **Figure 5.7** Text looks like it was formatted with three or more different ruler line settings.

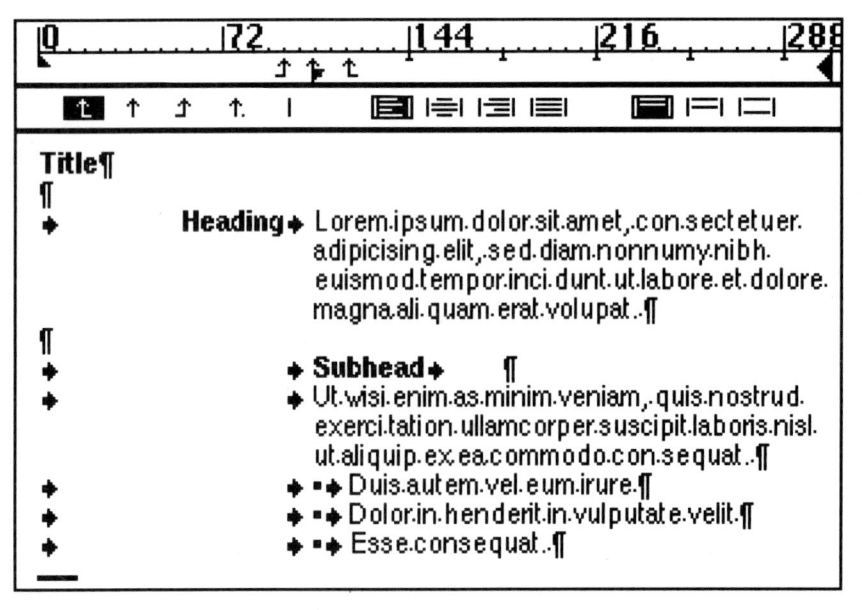

■ **Figure 5.8** Same ruler line is used for all text.

See Chapters 3 and 7 for more examples and discussion of different alignment settings (ragged-right vs. justified).

GLOSSARIES AND SPELLING CHECKERS

A glossary feature lets you enter long phrases, such as your company name, into a glossary of terms that are linked to short keystroke commands. You could type "DTP," for instance, and press one or two keys to expand it to "Desktop Publishing."

Some word processors come with electronic dictionaries that they use for automatic hyphenation and spelling checks. If your word processor does not support hyphenation or have a spelling checker, you can buy utility programs that are designed to handle these functions for any text file.

Most spelling checkers let you:
- Correct the spelling of words manually (rather than presume what the word is supposed to be)
- Ignore words that are found to be misspelled (but are actually proper names or technical terms that aren't in the dictionary)
- Add words to the dictionary, or to a supplemental dictionary

Additional features might include:
- Offer suggestions for words to replace misspelled terms
- Ignore words in ALL CAPS

HYPHENATION

If your page-layout program supports automatic hyphenation, you might want to turn hyphenation off in the word processor. In any event, be sure to verify that hyphenated text from the word processor is handled appropriately in the page-layout program when the line endings change.

You can insert discretionary hyphens manually within words in some word processors and page-layout programs. Discretionary hyphens behave exactly the same way that automatic hyphens do: they only appear on the screen and the printed pages when they fall at the end of a line. (See additional notes about hyphenation in Proofreading Typeset Text later in this chapter.)

Rule of Thumb:
Never use normal hyphens (the hyphen key on the keyboard) to break words across lines in the word processor. Use normal hyphens only if you want them to print within lines on the final page layout.

OTHER AIDS FOR EDITORS

Some word processors offer additional features that can aid in the writing and editing process such as:
- Automatic outlining
- Automatic table of contents generation
- Automatic footnoting
- Automatic indexing

Sometimes these additional features can be a good reason for producing a finished document using the word processor alone, without taking the text into a page-composition package that does not support these features.

SPECIAL HANDLING OF DATA FORMATS

If your data is prepared using a database or a spreadsheet, you may be able to set up a form for printing out formatted listings directly, or you might be forced to take the data through a series of conversions in order to produce a clean text file.

Data from a spreadsheet or a database can be formatted into special documents or forms such as membership directories and membership renewal forms, price lists and price tags, exhibit catalogues and display descriptions, corporate phone directories and name tags, etc. In the ideal system, you can use the report-writing feature of the data program, or the mail-merge feature of some word processing programs, to define the format for printing the data out directly from the spreadsheet or database. By this method, all character and paragraph formatting is specified in the report form or mail-merge form, not in the data files. This is usually faster than converting the data files to text (described next), even if the printed listings are simply galleys that must be pasted up onto boards with the folios.

```
                    Mail-merge Form
        «number»
   «itemname»
   «description»
   Value:         «value» Minimum bid:   «minimum»
   Donor:         «fname» «lname»
          «company»
          «street»
          «city», «state» «ZIP»
          «phone»

                    Resulting Printout
        001
   Your Next Brochure
   Typeset copy and graphics for ads, brochures, fliers, booklets,
   reports, and presentations. Good for 2-sided flier.
   Value:         $50      Minimum bid:   $15
   Donor:         Grace Moore
          TechArt
          3915 24th Street
          San Francisco, CA 94114
          (415) 550-1110
```

■ **Figure 5.9**   A mail-merge form and the resulting printout.

If you cannot use a report format or a mail-merge program to print the data, you must convert the data into a text file and perform all formatting using the word processor or typesetting program. This process might involve one or more of the following steps:

1. While the data is still in the spreadsheet or database, arrange the items within each record or row in the order you will be printing them out. For instance, the data file might initially show the last name before the first name, but most data programs let you reverse this order easily. Reversing the order using a word processing program would be extremely time-consuming.

Rule of Thumb:

Sort all data (rows and columns) before converting the data into a text file.

2. Save the data file as "text only." Most spreadsheets and database programs offer this option under the Save command. Some data programs offer this option under the Print command, letting you print the data as text only to a disk file.
3. The text-only version of the data is usually delimited by some special character, i.e., each item is separated by a comma or a tab character. Commas will need to be converted to tab characters if you will be printing the data in tabular format. Commas and tabs will need to be converted to carriage returns if you are printing the data in mailing-list format (with each item on a separate line).

Comma-delimited format

001,Your Next Brochure,"We prepare typeset copy and graphics for ads, brochures, fliers, booklets, reports, and presentations. We can incorporate your photographs as half-tones, or as computer-digitized images. Good for 2-sided flier, or $50 off any order.",50,15,Grace,Moore,TechArt,3915 24th Street,San Francisco,CA,94114,(415) 550-1110

■ **Figure 5.10** Text-only data file before global searches.

You can use global searches to begin the cleanup of these files, but in most cases you will need to perform additional clean-up steps manually. For example, the data file might show the first name and last name as two different items, but you want them to appear in one column or on one line in the final text document.

> 001
> Your Next Brochure
> We prepare typeset copy and graphics for ads
> brochures
> fliers
> booklets
> reports
> and presentations. We can incorporate your photographs as half-tones
> or as computer-digitized images. Good for 2-sided flier
> or $50 off any order.
> 50
> 15
> Grace
> Moore
> TechArt
> 3915 24th Street
> San Francisco
> CA
> 94114
> (415) 550-1110

■ **Figure 5.11** Text-only data file after global searches.

If the data is delimited by commas, the text-only files might include additional characters such as quotation marks around items that include commas. The quotation marks will need to be stripped out globally, and a visual search performed for commas that were erroneously replaced by tabs or carriage returns.

001

Your Next Brochure

We prepare typeset copy and graphics for ads, brochures, fliers, booklets, reports, and presentations. We can incorporate your photographs as halftones, or as computer-digitized images. Good for 2-sided flier, or $50 off any order.

    Value: $50   Minimum bid: $15
    Donor: Grace Moore
    TechArt
    3915 24th Street
    San Francisco, CA 94114
    (415) 550-1110

■ **Figure 5.12** Text-only data file after final cleanup.

Rule of Thumb:

If you are working with large files that originate as a data format, it's a good idea to take a small amount of data from a spreadsheet or database through a test run of the complete production cycle—word processing, typesetting, and page layout—before finalizing the specifications for a large listing. This way, you can develop a list of the specific steps that will be required, and make an assessment as to how much of the design specifications can or must be handled in the database or spreadsheet directly.

Typesetting Text: Character and Paragraph Formatting

The process of inserting codes or using menu commands to format characters and paragraphs might take place in either the word processor or in the page-layout program, depending on the features and capabilities of the programs in your system. We describe these steps here, since the text processing steps offer the first opportunity to format characters and paragraphs.

  The process of specifying different fonts in a manuscript varies from one system or program to the next. What one system uses to indicate a type size command will be different on another system, even though both systems generate identical printouts of the typeset text. Such coding variations are true for virtually every aspect of composition, including typeface, line measures, column depth, indentations, outlines, and horizontal and vertical positioning.

You will need to assess the degree to which your page-layout program retains formatting from the word processor before deciding how much formatting to perform at the word processing stage. When text is imported into most page-layout programs, the right margin is changed to match the page-layout column width, with right margin indents preserved from some word processors. Most page-layout programs also ignore specialized formatting commands such as headers and footers and footnotes. The degree to which page-layout programs retain other formats from the word processor varies greatly between programs.

Generally speaking, you should do all formatting in the word processing program only if the formats will be retained in the page-composition application as a result of importing the text. Otherwise, if the page-composition application strips out all paragraph formats, then do not format the word processed text (unless you need to show different heading levels for the first proofreaders). Some page-composition applications will accept style sheet tags that are coded in the word processing application, but if the same page-composition program offers an easier method of applying tags—through a menu or checklist, for instance—you could save all formatting for the page-layout steps rather than type codes in the text file.

Rule of Thumb:

If your page-layout package will preserve all formatting done in the word processing program, use the word processor to format the text, *except* the right-margin setting.

If your page-layout package preserves only bold and italic settings and not the fonts, then use the word processor to format only those words that are bold or italic within paragraphs.

If your page-layout package accepts unformatted ASCII text files only, do all formatting in the page-layout package.

Text-formatting features supported by most word processing packages include:
Document-wide Formatting—
- Page margins
- Paper size and orientation

Character-specific Formatting—
- Character styles like bold, underscore, strikethrough, italic
- Positions like superscripts and subscripts
- Letter spacing (normal, condensed, expanded)

Paragraph-specific Formatting—
- Tabs
- Paragraph indentation
- Paragraph alignment (flush left, right, center)
- Line spacing, or leading

Rule of Thumb:

Never use the tab key to indent every line of indented paragraphs. Always use the ruler line or paragraph formatting commands to set indentation.

Wherever possible, use paragraph formatting commands rather than carriage returns to adjust spacing between paragraphs. In general, it is better to specify spacing *after* each paragraph rather than spacing *before* (if both options are available).

Some word processors also let you select different typefaces and sizes, but most do not offer these options. In any case, you should know how formats will be handled in taking text from your word processor into your page-composition application before doing any formatting in the word processor.

Even if your word processor is not supported directly by your page-layout program, you can still place your text files in the page-layout program if they have been saved under the text-only option that most word processors offer. At minimum, the authors will need to have a method for indicating the different heading levels and special formats within the text.

The level of effort required for character and paragraph formatting will depend on the degree to which the author has entered formatting codes, the degree to which those formatting codes are maintained when the text is converted from the author's system into a different system for typesetting, and the nature of the entered codes. In the ideal system, the author uses the exact same system as the production group, and any formatting codes entered by the author are accurate, thereby saving the production group some of the following formatting steps. Therefore, some publishers request that the authors enter the typesetting codes. However, most publishers still prefer that the authors deliver the unformatted text only, leaving the formatting steps to the professional production team.

METHOD 1: MARKED COPY

This first method is what most traditional typesetters are accustomed to—the electronic text files are completely unformatted, and a printed copy of the manuscript is marked by hand with type specifications by a designer or copy editor. Traditionally, the designer would mark the printed manuscript with abbreviated expressions for common typesetting terms such as 12/13 Times Roman and Demi 20/22 ctr. The typesetter would then mark the manuscript with the codes required by the typesetting equipment, such as <f52p12l13><224>.

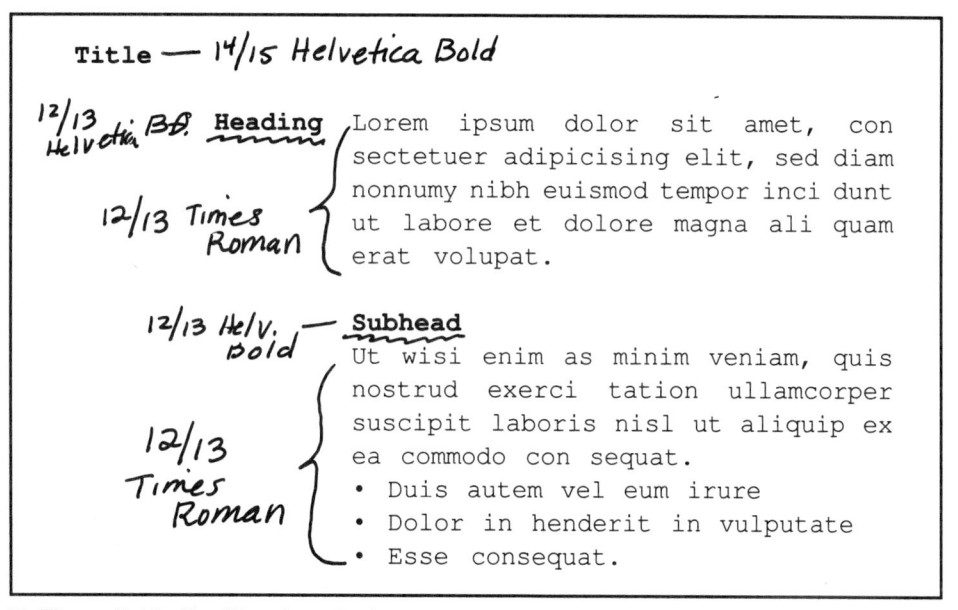

■ **Figure 5.13** Traditional marked copy.

Unless the author has entered typesetting codes during development of the manuscript, the copy editor or designer will need to mark the printed manuscript by hand to indicate type specifications in terms that can be understood by the person responsible for coding the disk files. Ultimately, the person who actually codes the electronic text files is the one who will use one of the following methods to typeset the manuscript.

METHOD 2: EMBEDDED CODES

By this method, codes that can be interpreted by the typesetter are typed directly into the text. The codes usually include some special character such as a semicolon, ampersand, or a bracket to distinguish them from normal text, as well as abbreviated commands that represent type specifications. A traditional typesetter's codes are usually long and cumbersome, with commands and numeric values that indicate the typeface, size, style, line width, leading, alignment (flush left, justified, centered, flush right), and other values. Because these codes are complicated, they are best left to the professional typesetting staff.

```
<cp20><c120><cc45><cfhkc><rr><xh><sw-5>
Title<EP>
<e112><cp8><c18><cc21><cfcos><t1><xr><ah><xr>
<sf50><it0,11><pm><dl$40><rm><it11,0><dl$40><el48><ef><uf50>
  Lorem ipsum dolor sit amet, con sectetuer adipicising
elit, sed diam nonnumy nibh euismod tempor inci dunt ut
labore et dolore magna ali quam erat volupat.<ep>
  <em>Ut wisi enim as minim veniam, quis nostrud exerci
tation ullamcorper suscipit laboris nisl ut aliquip ex ea
commodo con sequat.<ep>
  <ma><ql><cfcos><qc>
  <ma><ql>[bu]<ql>Suis autem vel eum irure<qc>
  <ma><ql>[bu]<ql>Dolor in henderit in vulputate<qc>
  <ma><ql>[bu]<ql>Esse  consequat.<qc>
```

■ **Figure 5.14** Embedded codes.

Some typesetting systems will accept short formatting codes that are defined for each document and set up in a "translation table" that converts the short codes into the longer typesetting codes. Many electronic publishing systems now use style sheets (described later in this section) that can interpret short codes typed directly into the manuscript. Even if the programs cannot interpret short codes, a system of short codes can be developed for easy entry, then replaced with the long codes by global searches.

Short codes reduce the chance for errors and invite the participation of the authors and editors in the typesetting process: the author or word processing group types a short code in front of each new text format, such as ";H1," ";H2, and ";H3" to indicate headings levels, ";FIG" to indicate a Figure caption, ";IL" to identify an indented list, etc. Using a special character such as a semicolon in the code helps distinguish embedded codes from actual text. The production group can then perform global searches to find these codes and change them to the appropriate full-blown typesetting specifications.

The main disadvantage of embedded codes—short or long—is that they appear in printouts of early drafts of the manuscript and make proofreading much more difficult. Furthermore, errors in the codes themselves are not evident until the text has been typeset.

METHOD 3: HIDDEN CODES

Under this method, typesetting specifications entered by the author or the production group result in a WYSIWYG display on the screen. This can be convenient for verifying the accuracy of the coding immediately.

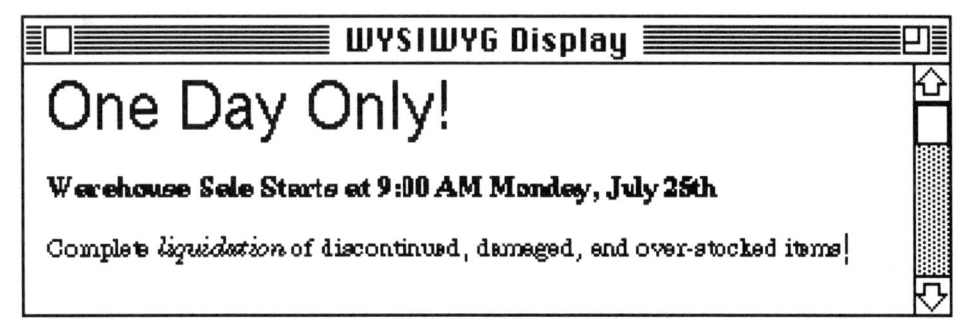

■ **Figure 5.15** WYSIWYG display of hidden codes.

The main disadvantage of hidden codes is that most systems that accommodate WYSIWYG coding do not allow global searches for formatting codes (unless they are entered through style sheets), so the codes cannot easily be changed by global searches.

METHOD 4: STYLE SHEETS

Some word processors and some page-layout packages offer a style sheet feature—the ideal system for handling formats. A style sheet system lets you define the character and paragraph format for each type of text element in a document, such as major headings, subheadings, captions, and body text. With a style sheet, you can format the text using short keystroke commands instead of opening different dialog boxes for character and paragraph formats.

You can then change the font or paragraph formats for each item simply by changing the settings for one style name. You can change the formatting of all of the level-1 headings, for instance, by changing the style sheet only. Ideally, the author uses the appropriate style sheet names to mark the text.

Rule of Thumb:

If a style sheet feature is available, the design specifications need not be finalized during the writing stage, since the production group can change the format of the entire manuscript by changing the style sheet only.

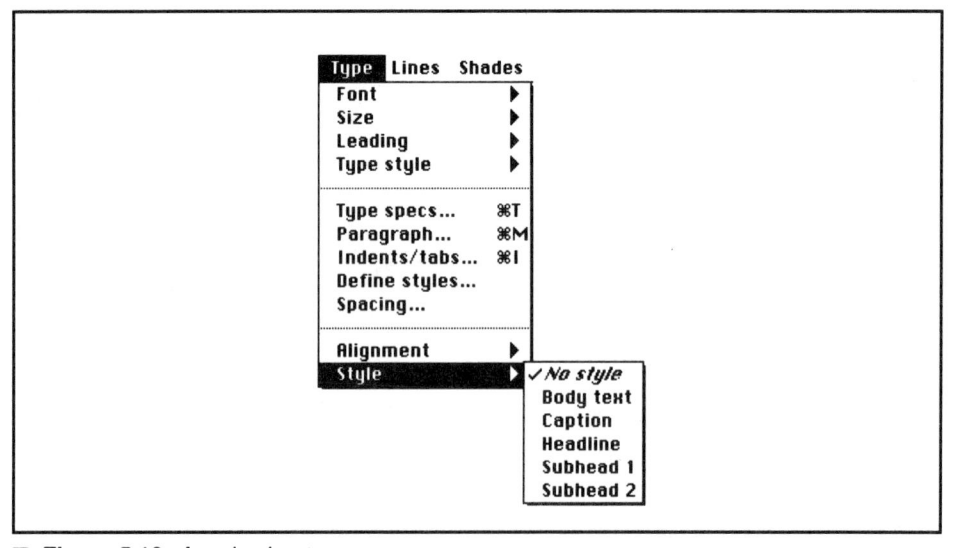

■ **Figure 5.16** A style sheet menu.

METHOD 5: CONTEXT CODING

Context coding is an automated method of inserting typesetting codes into material that has regular patterns of text elements that can be interpreted by the computer. When the electronic manuscript is perfectly consistent—as in text generated from a database—the typographic formats for each text element can be calculated by software from its position in the line or its relationship to other elements.

For example, in a computer-generated price list the first eight characters on each line might be the part number, the next six characters might be the base price, the next twenty-four characters the part name, and the last characters the description. A context coding program could automatically code a consistent file quickly and with relatively few errors—once the program is written.

In the simplest context coding, the author inserts a specific number of carriage returns in front of each new text element, so the typesetter can set up a context-coding program that correctly formats each heading level based on the number of carriage returns.

Some word processors offer a mail-merge feature that lets you print the fields from a data file as formatted text. In this case, a mail-merge file could be set up to make the product number and name print bold, the price print roman, and the product description print italic. Ideally, the merged data could be "printed" to disk as a text document that can be further processed through the word processor or page-layout program.

CODING FOR SPECIAL CHARACTERS

Virtually all word processing programs offer the basic set of characters that was developed for typewriters: the upper and lowercase alphabet, numbers, basic punctuation, and common symbols such as the dollar sign. Available symbols often vary between word processors and between character sets or typefaces, and typesetting systems generally offer a much wider range of symbols than most word processors. For example, hyphens entered through the word processor may be more appropriately changed to En or Em dashes or minus signs. Similarly, typeset text normally distinguishes between opening and closing quotes, whereas some word processors use the same symbol for both.

Most electronic publishing systems make use of special function keys (Option key, Command key, Control key, Alt key, Esc key, etc.) to offer a wider variety of special characters than found on an ordinary typewriter keyboard. The list of special characters can vary between fonts, so manufacturers usually provide a list of special characters for each program or each font. The most widely supported special characters include the copyright symbol (©) and the trademark symbol (™).

If the word processing program can handle a wide variety of symbols, be sure that these symbols will be converted correctly as the text goes from the word processing program to the typesetter or to the page-layout program. If the word processor's special characters are not correctly interpreted by the other programs that will be used to produce the final document, use codes in the word processing stages of text preparation.

If the word processor cannot handle all of the symbols required for the publication, but the final typesetting system *does* accommodate all symbols, the symbols can be represented by unique character combinations in the word processing files and then replaced in the final typesetting stages. For example, the copyright symbol might by typed as "(co)"—enclosing the characters within parentheses will help distinguish between the intended symbol from words that include the same character combination (such as "cost"). Some other special characters that are commonly used to distinguish coded symbols from normal text include square bracket ([co]), plus sign (+co), and semi-colon (;co) as shown in Table 5.1

Table 5.1
An Example of Abbreviations Used to Represent Special Characters That Will Be Substituted in the Final Typesetting Program

Typed Code	Description	Final Typeset Text
;aa	accent acute	´
;ab	accent breve	˘
;af	accent circumflex	î
;ag	accent grave	`
;al	accent cedilla	ç
;am	accent macron	ā
;an	angstrom	å
;as	at sign	@
;at	accent tilde	~
;au	accent umlaut	¨
;bc	close brace	}
;bo	open brace	{
;bu	bullet	•
;ck	check mark	✔
;co	copyright symbol	©
;ct	cents	¢
;da or ;dr	dagger	†
;de or ;dg	degree	°
;dv	division sign	÷
;eq	equal sign	=
;ft	feet	'
;ge	greater than/equal to	≥
;gt	greater than	>
;in	inches	"

(Continued)

Table 5.1 (Continued)

;lt	less than	<
;md	Em dash	—
;mi or ;ms	minus sign	–
;nd	En dash	–
;no	number sign	#
;pa	paragraph sign	¶
;pc	percent sign	%
;pl	plus sign	+
;pm	plus or minus	±
;rg or ;rm	registered trademark	®
;se	section symbol	§
;ti	times (multiply)	x
;tm	trademark	™

Some typesetting systems need only an initial code to make a font change (typeface, size, or style), and the original font is resumed after one word (such as the codes shown in Table 5.1. Other systems need an additional code in order to return to the original font—in some cases this can be a delimiter on *both* sides of the code. For example, the accent circumflex (^) in the word *tête* might be coded as:

t;afete, or

tête, or

t<cir>ete.

If your application supports WYSIWYG fonts, you might type the following characters, using the control key and the letter i to yield the accent:

t *option-i* e t e.

There are several different ways of handling special characters that are not part of the character sets available for standard fonts. Traditionally, typesetters could order custom fonts from their manufacturers, but this was usually a costly procedure (which is why few documents used special characters in the past). More recently, font-design programs are available for many desktop publishing systems, whereby the production group can design their own special fonts and characters.

If a font design program is not available, you can create special characters as artwork (to be pasted up on-screen in the page-layout program, or by hand on the final boards). This solution is the most time-consuming since 1) the same characters will need to be pasted up manually every time the final pages are edited or reprinted, or 2) the graphic objects will need to be moved on the screen every time the text is edited, and the WYSIWYG display might not accurately show the alignment that results on the final printouts.

Copyfitting Text

In general, it is a good idea to estimate the maximum number of characters or words that will fit on the final page layouts, or to estimate the final number of pages based on the number of characters written by the author. Methods of estimating the number of characters that will fit on a page are given in Chapter 3. An actual count of the number of characters in a text file can be made through any word processing program that offers the feature of providing a character count. If the word processor does not offer this feature, you can roughly estimate the number of characters by checking the size of the file: a 6K file holds about 6,000 characters, for example.

If you cannot use your word processing program to count the number of characters in a text file, you can quickly count the characters on printed pages using this technique: If the text is justified, count the characters in one representative line of text and multiply that number by the total number of lines. If the text is not justified, draw a vertical line down the page, roughly in the middle of the ragged-right margin area, count the characters on one line up to the vertical line, then multiply that number by the number of lines. Characters that extend beyond the vertical line should be counted and added to the total, and character space on short lines should be estimated and deducted from the total. This method of counting characters works best with nonproportional (monospaced) type that is produced by most typewriters, such as Courier or Elite.

If the writer is given no guidelines about the number of words initially, but the number of pages is limited, the designer and editor may need to work closely with the writer to expand or reduce the number of words to better fit the space and leave enough white space on each page. If a large amount of editing is required to make the copy fit, it is usually better to anticipate this ahead of the page-layout steps and perform the edits in the word processing program. Minor edits for copy fitting can still be expected at the page-layout stage.

See Chapter 7 for other suggestions on making copy fit a given space.

Proofreading Typeset Text

We have described several methods of typesetting the text to match the typographer's specifications,

This section offers tips on what the typographer and proofreader should look for in reviewing the typeset text—and this step can occur either before or after you have positioned the text on pages in a page-composition application. The important point is that this review procedure should take place after all of the text has been printed in its typeset form, whether as galleys or as finished page layouts.

INDENTATION

There are three possible indentation settings for any paragraph: left indent, first-line indent, and right indent. Proof the page layouts after text has been placed to confirm that all indentation has been retained from the word processing program or corrected in the page-layout package.

PARAGRAPH SPACING

The spacing between paragraphs can be defined through the paragraph specifications commands of the word processor or the page-layout program. The value you enter for spacing between paragraphs will be added wherever there is a hard carriage return in the text.

This method of defining breaks between paragraphs yields more flexible results than using extra carriage returns (empty lines) or changes in leading in order to add space between paragraphs. Where there are two or more hard carriage returns in a row, the spacing value will be added twice or more. If you are accustomed to double-spacing between paragraphs, you might want to play with the spacing setting on small documents before you decide to globally strip out all double carriage returns in your text.

ALIGNMENT

Word processors, illustrators, and page-layout artists should specify the alignment of text and graphics objects using the commands of the programs. If instead they use spaces to align text, or otherwise visually position graphics or text on the screen, the final printed pages will show misalignments.

Also, the fonts that are shown on the screen are refined when they are sent to the printer, the text on the screen can be slightly condensed or expanded from what you see on the screen. This is another reason why it is a good idea to use the application's menu commands for aligning text and graphics, rather than the "eyeball" method (i.e., positioning the text visually on the screen).

HYPHENATION

Another area that usually requires proofing is the hyphenation in the publication. An incorrect word division is called a bad break. Most applications that offer hyphenation are designed to follow the rules for breaking words, but you should still check the typeset copy visually. The basic rules for hyphenation are:
- There must be at least two characters on either side of the hyphen point.
- Numerals should not be hyphenated (but they could be in an "emergency" at a comma point).
- It is not good practice to hyphenate in a headline.
- Never hyphenate a one-syllable word.
- Divide on a double consonant, unless the word root ends with a double consonant (e.g., miss-ing).
- Not more than two (some allow three) hyphens in a row.

A discretionary hyphen can be inserted in a word during input (see Hyphenation earlier in this chapter) to give the system a specific point to hyphenate, and that point will take precedence over any logic-generated point.

WIDOWS AND ORPHANS

Widows and orphans should be avoided if possible. The short line at the end of a paragraph, if less than one-third the line length, is called a widow. Sometimes a widow is considered the carryover letters of a hyphenated word (if there are no other characters on the line). If a widow is carried to the top of a column or page, it is called an orphan.

WORD AND LETTER SPACING

You should also review the type after setting to find and correct problems with typographic color (see glossary) such as rivers. Rivers are patterns of white that result from the random positioning of word spaces in adjacent lines. Word spacing should be as consistent as possible.

LOOK FOR KERNING OPPORTUNITIES

The term kerning refers to the spacing between letters. When kerning is not active, each character is assigned a specific width that is determined by the font selection and the character itself. All 10-point Times Italic "A's" will have the same width allowance, for instance, regardless of what other characters are adjacent.

When kerning is turned on, the spacing between two letters will be adjusted slightly in accordance with the values stored in a table of kerning pairs. For example, the space between the characters "AV" can be tighter than the space between the characters "AX." In fact, if the spacing between the different pairs is not adjusted, then it will appear to the eye that the A and V are actually further apart than the A and X are. For this reason, kerned text generally looks better than text that is not kerned.

Not all page-layout programs and printers can handle kerning, but if you do have this capability, review all headlines and section titles to find pairs of letters that should be kerned.

For more information about the pros and cons of kerning, and to see how to manually kern the space between letters, see Chapter 3, Typography.

Summary

Build a test file using your own word processor to see how your page-layout package handles the text when you place it on a page. Try placing the same test file under each of two options (if both are available)—"retain format" and "text-only"—to see how they differ.

Once you are familiar with how your page-layout program will handle your files, do as much preparation as you can in the word processing program, before placing the text in the page-layout.

Chapter 6
Illustrations

> *"Some traditional artists dismiss computer graphics as inferior to hand-drawn art—claiming that the hand work is just as fast to produce and not as 'jaggy.' While it may be true that a computer-generated graphic is no faster to produce in the first round, tremendous economies are realized as soon as the artwork must be changed. Furthermore, laser printers and typesetters can eliminate the 'jaggies,' which are associated with dot-matrix printers."*

One of the characteristics of page-composition programs is the ability to incorporate graphics with text on a page. By *graphics* we mean drawings, scanned images, charts, graphs, diagrams, shaded areas, boxes, borders, and ruled lines—literally anything that is not straight text (though in some cases text can be handled as a graphic object, as described later in this chapter). Many of the page-layout programs offer some graphics tools of their own, as well as your import graphics that were created in other programs, including scanned images.

The advantage of having all of the graphics on-line is that they can be scaled and cropped to fit the page on-screen (thereby saving photostatting charges) and they become permanently integrated with the rest of the page layout—that is, they don't have to be pasted up every time you print a new version of the page. In spite of these advantages, there may still be cases in which you will choose to paste up the artwork rather than use electronic sources, or to paste up electronic art manually rather than on screen. (For a discussion of manual paste-up techniques, see Chapters 8 and 9.)

There are many different graphics applications available for desktop publishing systems, but the graphics themselves can be broken down into four distinct categories:
- Bit-mapped graphics
- Scanned images
- Object-oriented graphics
- Encapsulated PostScript formats

All of these categories can encompass both types of artwork required for publishing: line art (composed of solid lines or shapes) and halftones (composed of shades of gray). In this chapter you'll learn the differences between graphics from various sources. This chapter will help you decide how to prepare graphics, using other programs, before the page-layout stage begins.

Graphics Equipment

Not so long ago, computers that could handle high-resolution graphics cost $20,000 or more. The desktop publishing revolution itself has been spurred by the more recent availability of low-cost personal computers with sophisticated graphics programs. Not every computer can support a complete desktop publishing system with graphics, however. You will need a graphics monitor, a mouse, and peripherals that add flexibility to your graphics handling.

GRAPHICS MONITORS

A truly WYSIWYG system is able to display different typefaces, sizes, and styles on the screen. It also gives you the confidence that the image you see on the screen is the same one that will print out. Not all monitors are designed to handle graphics, however. If your screen cannot display graphics, you can use a graphics programming language to create an illustration, but you have to print it out every time you make changes, to see how it will look.

A full-featured graphics system allows you a variety of video display options, such as a larger display area, higher resolution, or color, as well as access to peripherals such as a scanner.

MICE AND GRAPHICS TABLETS

Some graphics applications let you work entirely through a keyboard, but most graphics packages and page-composition programs now require a movable input device like a mouse—a hand-held object that moves a pointer on the screen as you drag the mouse on a flat surface. Some artists prefer alternative input devices like joy sticks or fixed objects that you can roll your palm over in order to move the pointer on the screen. All of these devices have one or more buttons that you click or hold down in order to communicate commands to the computer.

Graphics tablets generally offer improved drawing capability over a mouse, and they can add to the flexibility of a desktop publishing system by making it easy to trace over images that are already on paper. Graphics tablets are sometimes referred to as digitizing devices, but for our purposes we will always use the term digitizing to describe the transformation of an image from paper or a video camera into a pattern of dots that can be stored electronically (as described in the next section).

DIGITIZERS OR SCANNERS

Digitizers are input devices that convert a continuous-tone image into computer-readable dots. Most sheet-fed and flat-bed scanners are set up to accept 8½-by-11-inch paper. You can also use a video camera to convert printed or three-dimensional images into a digitized image.

Most digitizers perceive each dot as either on or off (black or white). Gray shades are *simulated* by creating patterns of dots. All of the dots are solid black, and the image appears solid black where the dots are dense and appears gray where the dots are scattered.

The simplest scanning systems store one bit per pixel. This is considered two shades of gray: black and white. Sophisticated gray scale systems can assign a numerical value for the gray scale of each dot by storing four or eight bits per pixel, to yield 16 or 256 shades of gray per pixel (respectively). Images stored as one bit per pixel tend to distort when they are scaled larger or smaller than the original scanned input, and they do not improve significantly when printed at higher resolutions. Images that are stored as true gray scales can be scaled without compromising the quality of the image, and they can be manipulated for brightness and contrast with far more precision than one-bit-per-pixel patterns. Furthermore, gray scale images are usually improved—to look more like halftones—when printed at higher resolutions.

The drawback is that complex images stored in gray scales can require a lot of disk storage space, take a long time to process (i.e., edit or change brightness), and take a long time to print. Both of these disadvantages are compounded if the image is stored with color information as well. A scanned color image can require up to 10 megabytes of storage.

GRAPHICS PRINTERS

Breakthroughs in printing technology that affect graphics applications include higher-resolution dot matrix printers (for draft copies) and low-cost laser printers. Dot-matrix printers are impact printers that produce characters and graphics by pushing a combination of pins through an inked film (or ribbon) onto paper. Because the pins must be strong enough to withstand repeated impact, they must be of a certain minimum circumference, and the printed text and graphics have a jagged appearance.

Laser printers also assemble characters and graphics as a pattern of dots, but they use a fine beam of light (a LASER beam) to produce the dots in patterns of 300 dots per inch or more. The image is layed on the page using a fine dust-like toner or electromagnetic charges on photosensitive paper—rather than ink that bleeds into the paper. The resulting text and graphics appear very smooth to the naked eye.

Finally, phototypesetters that can print graphics have become available. The photochemical process accommodates resolutions greater than 2000 dots per inch (much higher than possible with toner systems), and can print halftone images from high-end scanners.

Plotters and ink-jet printers are available for producing color images from many graphics programs, but these are not usually applicable for publishing applications for three reasons. First, and most serious, the text printed by these types of printers is usually below standard for publishing purposes—the characters are clear enough for slides, overhead transparencies, or video projection, but they are too jagged at the edges for publishing applications. Second, the nature and expense of color offset printing is such that full color originals are rarely used for artwork unless it is fine art or a color photograph. More often, color graphics are delivered as a series of overlays—one for each color to be used in the offset printing process—each printed in black and white (see Chapter 9). Third, one of the advantages of electronic publishing is the ability to paste up the text with the graphics directly on the screen and print full pages on a high-resolution printer, rather than use different printers for the text and graphics and paste them up manually on boards.

Sources of Graphics

Broadly, there are three sources of graphics in electronic publishing: bit-mapped graphics that are created in paint-type programs, artwork on paper that is scanned into the computer as digitized images (which are also bit-mapped), object-oriented graphics that are created in drawing or drafting programs, and Encapsulated PostScript code. Each of these sources is discussed in turn below. (Adding graphics in manual paste-up and dropping in photographic halftones are discussed in Chapters 8 and 9.)

We should add that there are many sources of graphics in these four categories we have named. You can purchase packages of clip art (also called click-art when in electronic form) from many sources, and you can download art via modem if you subscribe to one of the graphics networks that are becoming available. Whether you purchase the artwork or create it yourself, you should be familiar with the differences between and capabilities of the different types of graphics applications, and apply the basic design principles described in this chapter.

BIT-MAPPED GRAPHICS

Bit-mapped graphics are composed of a pattern of dots or pixels, rather than being stored as mathematical formulas (see Object-Oriented Graphics). There is a one-to-one relationship between the pixel and the bit in computer memory. Thus blocks of 1s and 0s create a sort of map of the image, so we speak of a bit-mapped image.

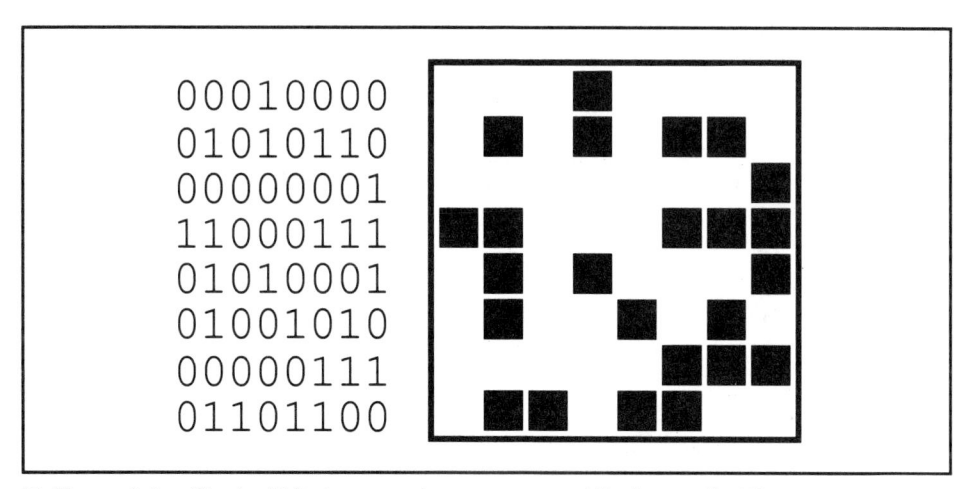

■ **Figure 6.1** Block of bits in computer memory, and the image that they map.

To understand the difference between a bit-mapped and object-oriented graphic, think about drawing a circle overlapping a square. In an object-oriented system, you can select and move the circle and square separately. In a bit-mapped system, however, the computer sees only a pattern of pixels, each of which is either on or off (black or transparent). You cannot separate the two objects once they are drawn, except by erasing part of the image. This type of graphic comes from a paint-type program such as Windows Paint (Figure 6.2), PC Paintbrush, or Publisher's Paintbrush.

Because bit-mapped images are composed of dots, they are not smoothed like object-oriented graphics are when printed, and they are generally considered inferior to object-oriented graphics for most line art. They are superior, however, for scanned images and for fine art images that call for air-brush effects.

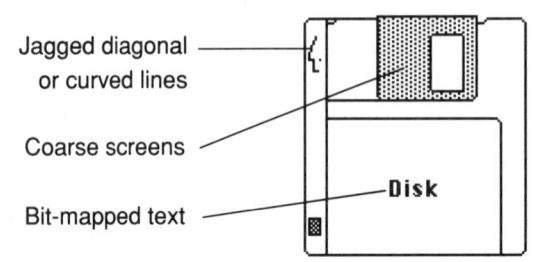

■ **Figure 6.2** A bit-mapped image drawn using a paint package. (Approximate time to create: 5 min.)

Rule of Thumb:

Use object-oriented graphics rather than bit-mapped graphics whenever possible. Bit-mapped graphics have a jagged appearance and take much longer to print.

When bit-mapped graphics are required, do not include text in the file in the paint program. Place the graphic portion in the page-layout program, and use page-layout program's text tools to add captions and labels.

Rule of Thumb:

Some bit-mapped graphics may seem distorted on the screen, but they should print well if the original graphic was not distorted. In general, graphics look best on the same equipment used to create them. A graphic created on equipment using a Hercules graphics card may look distorted when displayed on equipment with an EGA graphics card, for instance, or a different monitor.

Bit-mapped graphics can be either high-resolution and low-resolution images. Low resolution images are stored at 72 dots per inch. This is considered to be relatively low-resolution, which is why the image usually appears jagged at the edges, especially the edges of curved or diagonal lines.

When you print these images on a high-resolution printer, each dot from the 72-dot-per-inch version is multiplied by the number that brings it closest to the printer's resolution. For example, one dot would become 4 dots when printed to a 300-dot-per-inch printer. To the naked eye, the image would look the same regardless of how high the resolution of the printer is.

Some programs offer the option of smoothing bitmaps as they are printed. In the smoothing process, the computer fills in the large steps created when the dots are multiplied for higher resolutions, as shown in Figure 6.3.

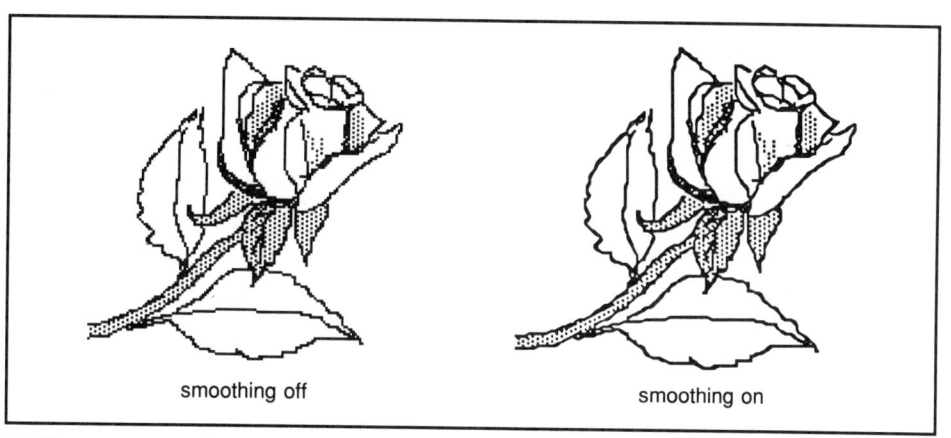

■ **Figure 6.3** A low-resolution bitmap image printed with smoothing on and off.

Some paint programs can handle high-resolution images of 300-dpi (dots per inch) or more, letting you create these high-resolution images with the program's graphics tools, or edit scanned images.

SCANNED IMAGES

Scanned images are bit-mapped images, and they share most of the features and disadvantages described in the previous section, but they are usually stored at higher resolutions than allowed by most paint-type programs—300 dpi or more. Some scanning software creates paint-type bit maps based on one stored bit per pixel (in which each dot or pixel is stored as either black or white—on or off), while others offer gray-scale capabilities that give you the potential to output a higher-quality image by storing four or eight bits per pixel. Based on the amount of light intensity reflected from the original at each location sampled during the scan, up to 256 different levels of gray between pure black and pure white can be recorded for each pixel.

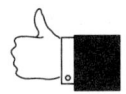

Rule of Thumb:

High-contrast images, or images with a wide range of evenly distributed grays, will generally yield better scanned images than low contrast images with a narrow range of shades.

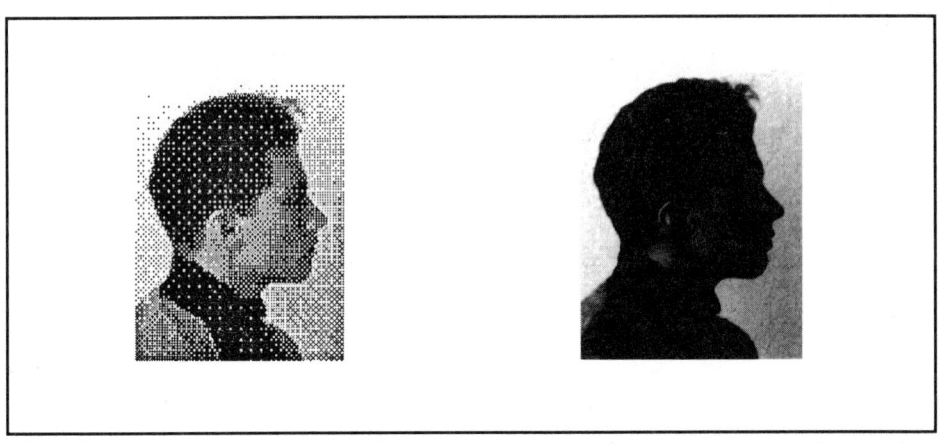

■ **Figure 6.4**   Scanned images: one-bit-per-pixel bit-map image at 1270 dpi (left) and gray scale image at 1270 dpi (right).

If you do not have a scanner that has the ability to record gray-scale information, then continuous tones must be translated upon input into one-bit-per-pixel patterns of black and white. Depending on the amount of light reflected from the continuous-tone original at each location (the picture elements or pixels—sampled during the scan) the image is converted into bits that are either on or off (black or white).

If you do have a scanner capable of recording gray-scale information, you can maintain images in this format until output. At output, all images are automatically converted to black-and-white-only patterns of dots to create halftones (see Chapter 8). Retaining gray-scale information until output, however, gives you more information for editing images, adjusting contrast, and scaling. It also gives you greater flexibility at output to create halftones of various screen fineness at the specific resolution of a particular output device.

Because scanned images are stored at higher resolutions than most paint images, files can be quite large—sometimes larger than 256K—and take a longer time to print. Images stored with gray-scale information can require several megabytes of storage, and may require several megabytes of memory if you want to edit the image (though you can still position the image, scale

ILLUSTRATIONS 221

it, and crop it in a page-composition application). The same image stored with color information can require as much as 10 megabytes of storage.

Because of the depth of the information recorded in gray-scale images, they can usually be sampled at fewer pixels per inch (see Chapter 8). Similarly, in color images, spacial resoluton (number of samples per inch) is only one factor affecting image quality. Data depth and other factors affecting the range of colors that can be reproduced are equally important.

Rule of Thumb:

Scanning Resolution

If your scanner offers a choice of resolutions, choose the one that matches your printer's resolution. The image may seem rough on low-resolution screens, but it should look better when printed.

Saved at 72, printed at 72   Saved at 300, printed at 72

Saved at 72, printed at 300   Saved at 300, printed at 300

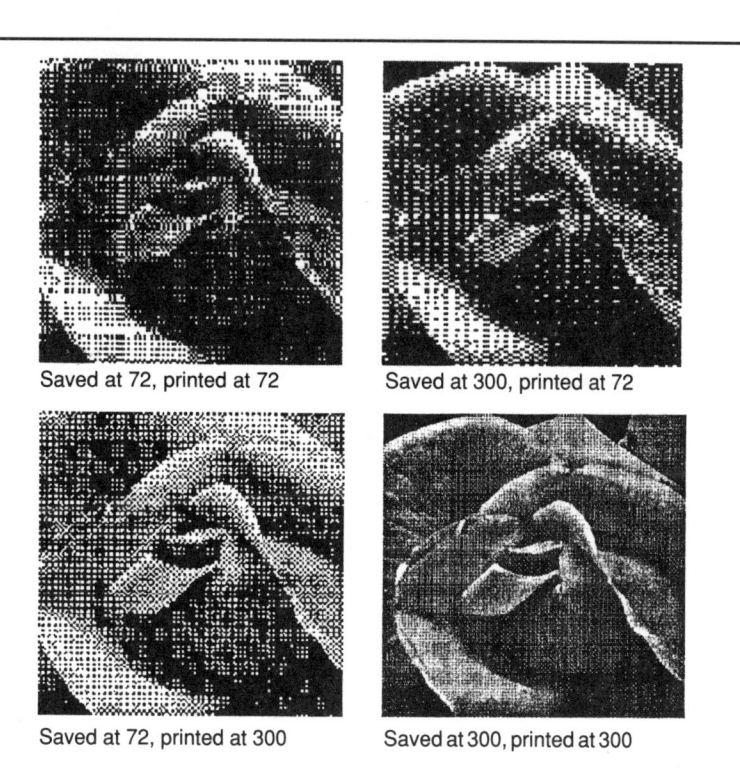

■ **Figure 6.5** Scanned images saved at 72 and 300 dots per inch, printed at 72 and 300 dpi.

High space requirements—in storage and in memory—is one area that is likely to improve significantly over the next few years, however, as file formats (such as TIFF and compressed TIFF color PostScript) improve and become standardized. For now, however, this is a disadvantage compared to object-oriented graphics.

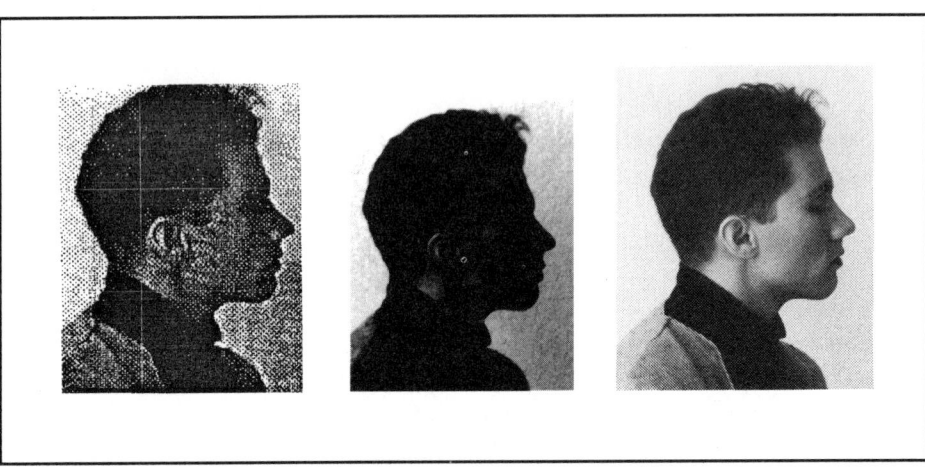

■ **Figure 6.6**   A 300 dpi scan (left), 1270 dpi gray-scale image (middle), and photographic halftone (right).

OBJECT-ORIENTED GRAPHICS

Object-oriented graphics (also called vector graphics) are those that are created using drafting programs or draw-type programs, and files created by spreadsheet graphics. They are called vector graphics because the lines and patterns that you see are actually stored as mathematical formulas for the vectors that compose the image. (A vector is a line defined by a starting point, a directional angle, and a length—see Figure 6.7)

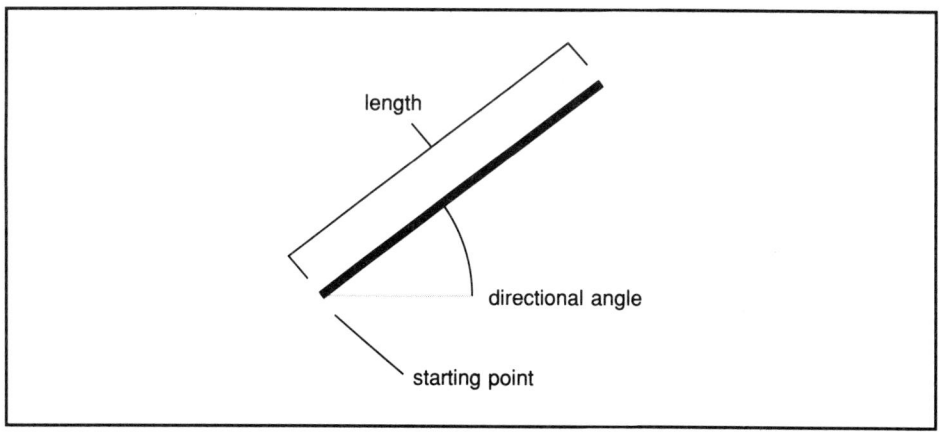

■ **Figure 6.7** A vector is a line defined by a starting point, a directional angle, and a length.

Object-oriented graphics come in many different formats (graphics languages), but one that is supported by most page-layout programs is the PIC or PICT format. The PICT format is simply a mathematical language for defining objects like circles, squares, and lines.

Unlike bit-mapped graphics, which consist of one layer of black and white pixels, object-oriented graphics are composed of separate objects that can be layered on top of each other. If you draw a circle overlapping a square, for example, your eye sees two objects and the computer sees two mathematical formulas that define the shape and position of each object. You can easily move the two objects separately once they are drawn, but you cannot erase part of an object or manipulate individual dots on the screen.

Because object-oriented graphics are defined mathematically, they take up much less disk space and memory than bit-mapped images or scans, and they can be smoothed during the printing process to create crisp line art and precise fill patterns. Object-oriented graphics are considered better-quality images, therefore, than bit-mapped graphics.

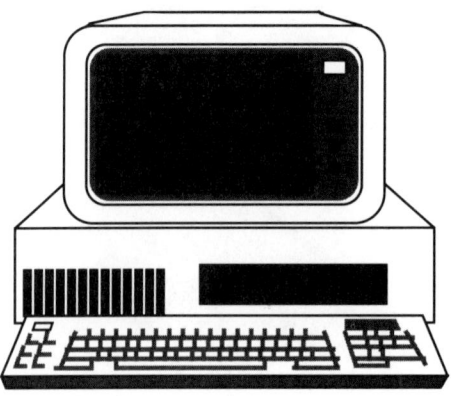

Figure 6.8 A graphic created in a drawing package (Approximate time to create: 90 min.)

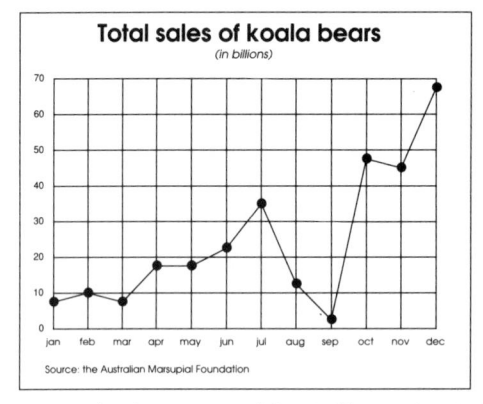

Figure 6.9 A chart created using a spreadsheet. (Approximate time to create: 30 min.)

ENCAPSULATED POSTSCRIPT FORMATS

Encapsulated PostScript files can be created using some drawing programs (such as Adobe's Illustrator program on the Macintosh) or by coding directly in the PostScript programming language.

The PostScript language is more flexible in defining curved lines (for graphics and text) than the other drawing languages that are available, and as a result you can create fine illustrations and special effects with both text and graphics using Adobe Illustrator or PostScript code directly.

■ **Figure 6.10** Graphics drawn with Adobe's Illustrator program to create Encapsulated PostScript (EPS) code. (Approximate time to create: 15 min.)

PostScript code is also more transportable than the PICT format, since you can print PostScript files to any PostScript printer from any type of computer. Since the PostScript code itself is simply text, you can telecommunicate it and edit the code on any type of computer easily.

Graphics Design Principles

A graph designed by an artist might be more visually pleasing than the same information presented by the scientist, but in either case the design and the accuracy of the data are only two elements that affect the clarity of the information. A major consideration is the right view of the information being presented. Just as a grammatically correct paragraph of text can confuse the reader with obscure terminology or incomplete description, an illustration can be both visually pleasing and technically accurate without conveying the underlying message clearly.

No rules can insure that graphical representations will be clear, but basic design principles can be applied once the concept for an illustration is developed. The limiting factor is no longer the hardware or software as much as the illustrator's imagination and understanding of the information.

Having said this, there are still many basic principles of design that can be applied to illustrations. Ideally, the graphics programs you are using allow enough flexibility for manipulating the illustration to meet the needs of the intended message. If you are using a spreadsheet program to generate charts from data, consider using a full-featured graphics package to enhance the generated charts and highlight information that would otherwise be lost in the layout that is dictated by the charting program.

Most of the design principles described in Chapters 3 and 4 apply to illustrations as well as to text and to full page layouts. The principles listed here apply specifically to graphics, though they can also be applied to the design of full page layouts.

ORGANIZE THE INFORMATION

Before releasing your creative energies on an illustration, think about the content of the message. Remember that the purpose of most illustrations is to communicate information. The message should not be obscured by the design. Normally, important information is made prominent by its position and size in a design.

CREATE FOCAL POINTS

This is related to the first principle in that you can highlight important parts of an illustration by creating visual focal points—elements to which the eye is naturally drawn. Sometimes the focal points can help the reader determine the sequencing of the information in an illustration. Even when all of the information shares the same level of importance, with no implied sequence, visual focal points can help maintain the interest in examining the illustration. Illustrations without focal points can lead to a subtle form of boredom for the reader and make the eye want to move away from the figure before all of the information is assimilated.

USE CONTRAST AND ASYMMETRY TO CREATE VISUAL TENSION

In addition to creating focal points in a design, use contrast in shades and line weights, and use asymmetry in the arrangement of the elements to create a dynamic tension. Again, this helps maintain the eye's interest in examining an illustration. Perfectly symmetrical, balanced arrangements that show no contrast in elements can fatigue the eye before the information is assimilated.

MAINTAIN SPATIAL CONTINUITY

The eye naturally tends to associate elements that are grouped by proximity in an illustration. Whenever possible, group labels that are related, and use more white space to separate different groups than to separate elements within a group.

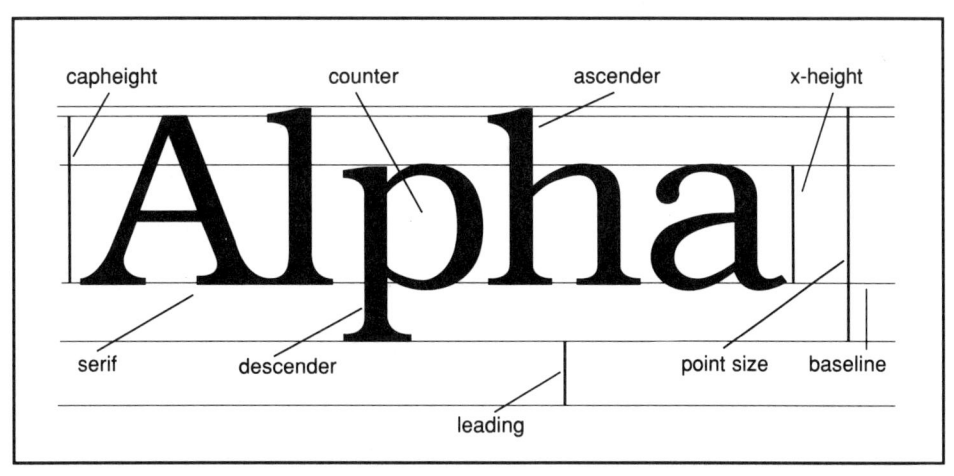

■ **Figure 6.11** Spacing used in this illustration leads the reader to see nine distinct elements.

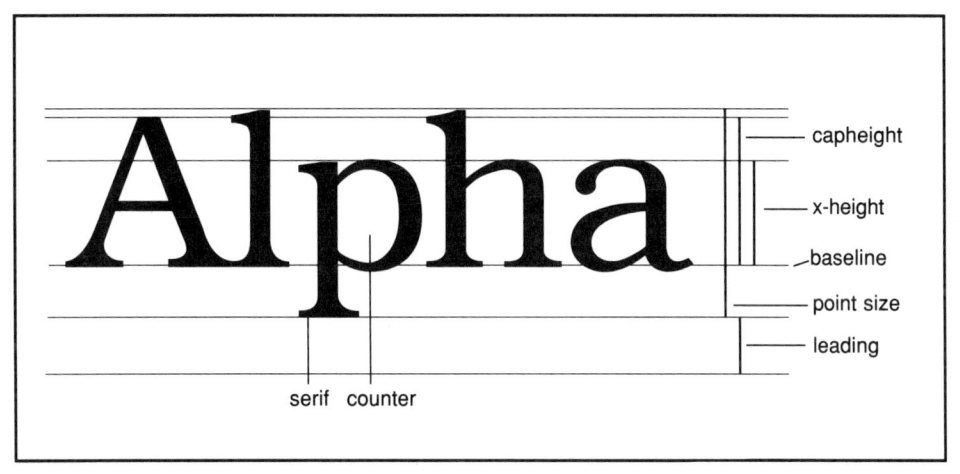

■ **Figure 6.12** Grouping related elements improves readability.

DO NOT OVERANNOTATE

Another way of saying this is do not include all of the known information. This may seem unfair to the reader at first, but the fact is that an overannotated, busy graphic can end up confusing the reader or concealing the information in a sea of words. Generally speaking, illustrations are simple representations of concepts that are more fully explained in the manuscript text—not in the illustration itself.

CONDENSE FORMAT

Generally speaking, the overall composition of an illustration should be tight without crowding. Columns of tabular material should be positioned close together, for example. Boxes in an organization chart can be close together and still read well—adjust spacing to create an aesthetic balance.

SIMPLIFY TITLES

For graphics that include a title and a caption, the title should be short and specific. Use the title to summarize the contents of the illustration, and to distinguish the contents from similar contents or related illustrations. Let the caption and labels explain the content in more detail.

CHOOSE IMAGES THAT SUIT THE FINAL PAPER QUALITY

We have already mentioned some of the decisions that might be affected by the choice of paper stock for the final reproduction in Chapters 3 and 4. Avoid small italic fonts if you are printing on textured stock, for instance. Use typeset output (rather than a toner-based laser printer) for your final pages if you will be printing on a high-grade glossy stock.

Care should also be used in applying hairlines, and the printing requirement should be considered. A hairline is the thinnest possible line that can be printed. Reverses (white hairlines on black backgrounds) or overprints (black hairlines on gray backgrounds) could present problems unless you are typesetting the final pages at a high resolution, using metal plates for offset printing (as opposed to plastic or paper), and printing on a coated stock of paper.

If you're publishing a newsletter and you are going to print it on a fairly low-grade paper, such as newsprint or even vellum, you'll want to avoid using photographs or scanned images that have lot of detail. Since the rough surface of such papers tends to absorb and spread ink, printed images will lack crisp definition and cannot hold detail.

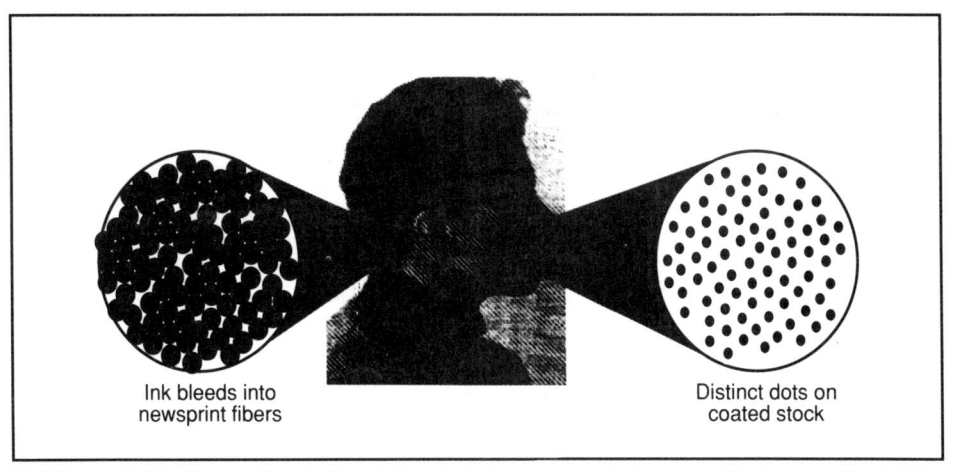

■ **Figure 6.13** Comparison of a photo printed on newsprint vs. an offset paper like LOE.

See Chapters 8 through 10 for additional considerations that are affected by the choice of reproduction methods.

Graphics Production Techniques

A few of the guidelines described in Chapters 3 and 4 are repeated here, with their specific application to graphics production techniques, as well as some additional techniques that apply to graphics only.

ENFORCE CONSISTENCY

The principle of consistency is worth repeating (from Chapter 4). Part of the designer's responsibility is to make sure that no one on the production team will need to invent design specifications for details that were not covered by the designer's original specifications.

Besides the type specifications (which insure consistent treatment of figure labels and captions), areas that call for consistency include specific use of different ruled line lengths and weights, fill patterns, and text alignment (flush left, centered, etc.). In the past, this principle would have been followed naturally from the fact that all of the figures came from one source: one spreadsheet program and letter-quality printer (in the case of business reports), or one illustrator and one typesetter (in traditional publishing).

This rule of consistency takes on a new importance when you assemble graphics from many different sources. With a page-layout program, some graphics might come from a spreadsheet program, some from a draw program, and some from the page-layout program's built-in graphics tools. Some of the figures might be used full-size in the final document, while others might need to be reduced or enlarged in the final page layout.

You want to be sure that all of the final figures have consistency in their type specifications. You can enforce your standards for captions by making the captions a part of the word processing text files rather than a part of the graphics files. You may need to derive your standards for in-figure labels based on the capabilities of the drawing programs you are using. For example, if your report includes a lot of charts and the spreadsheet program has a more limited number of fonts available than you have in the other graphics programs or the page-layout program, you might want to match the fonts used in *all* your images to the spreadsheet graphics.

The designer also needs to specify standard spacing between the text and the graphic elements. Even if you do not want strict rules for positioning graphics—rules that might slow down the production schedule considerably by requiring meticulous adjustments—it's a good idea to know and declare the basic guidelines.

In electronic publishing, you can enforce consistency by creating electronic templates to enforce consistency.

USE A GRID SYSTEM

As explained in Chapter 4, the term *grid* refers to the underlying structure of a page layout. A grid structure, in its simplest form, insures consistent alignment of figure titles and captions. You can set up a simple grid by defining the page size and margins in electronic terms, using the commands of the graphics package. Most graphics applications offer horizontal and vertical rulers on the screen to help you position text and graphics.

USE COMMANDS TO ALIGN OBJECTS

Because the fonts that are shown on the screen are refined when they are sent to the printer, the text on the screen can be slightly condensed or expanded from what you see on the screen. This is why it is a good idea to use the application's menu commands for aligning text and graphics, rather than the eyeball method (i.e., positioning the text visually on the screen). You should also test printing a few pages on a laser printer before you print a long document.

SPECIAL HANDLING OF FIGURE LABELS AND CAPTIONS

When you change the size of a graphic imported from another program, you also change the size of the type used in that graphic. Unless you decide that all figure titles and captions will be entered directly in the page-layout application to insure consistency, you need to account for changes in the size of type that will result when you shrink or enlarge a figure. If you know that you will be shrinking a figure by 50 percent, for instance, then the illustrator will need to make the type twice as large in the drawing program as it will be in the final document.

In-figure labels should be positioned consistently throughout a series of illustrations. Decide in advance whether in-figure labels will share a common alignment (flush left, flush right, or centered) or be positioned a standard distance from the elements within the illustration (see Spacing Guides, later in this chapter). If lines (or leaders) are used to link labels with elements of the illustration, all lines should be draw at the same angle.

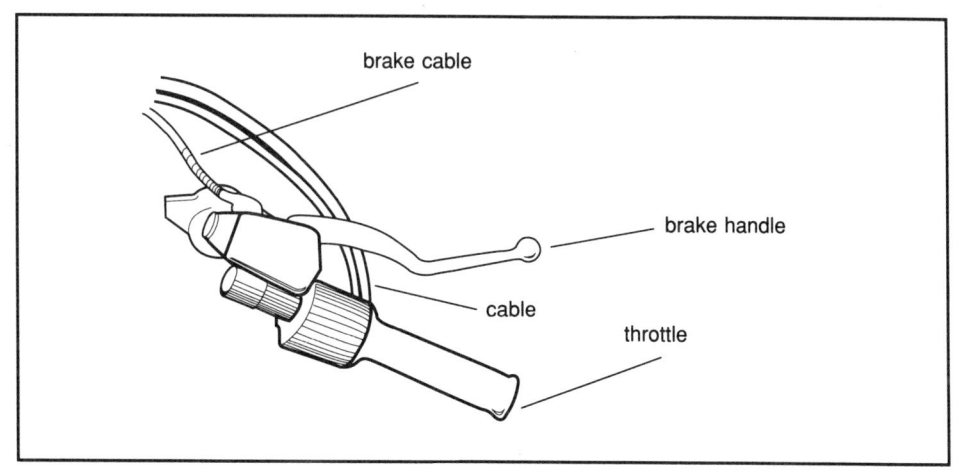

■ **Figure 6.14** Labels placed randomly with lines at all angles.

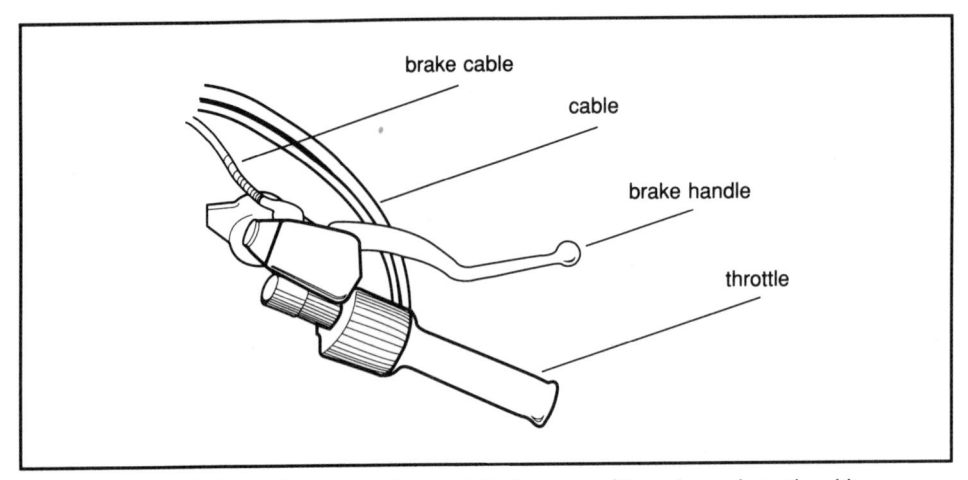

Figure 6.15 Balance is improved when labels are positioned consistently with a spacing guide and leaders are all drawn at the same angle.

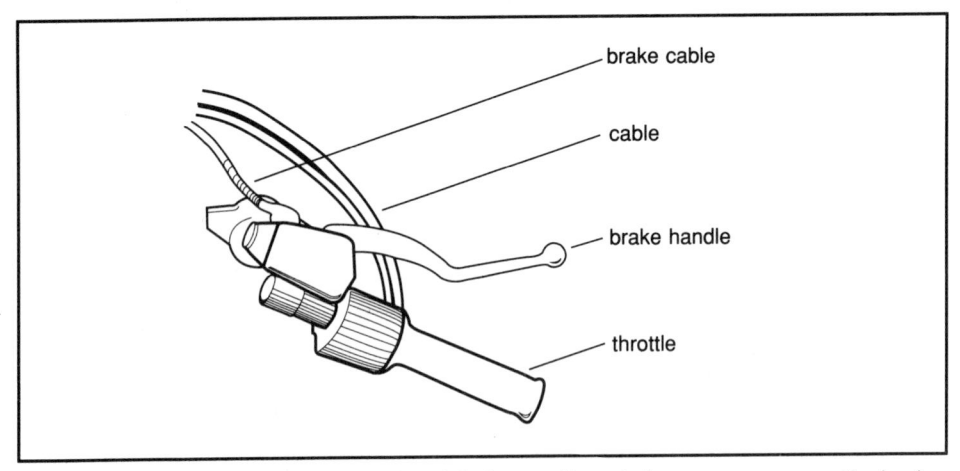

Figure 6.16 Readability is best when labels are aligned along a common vertical axis.

Figure titles and captions can be added in most graphics programs, but you can instead add these in the page-composition application as text. One reason for doing this is to maintain consistency in type specifications and positioning (as mentioned earlier in this chapter). Another good reason for adding text in the page-layout program is that most graphics applications do not offer the typographic controls provided by page-composition programs, such as kerning and justification. There is one exception to this bias:

most word processors and page-layout programs do *not* offer the ability to rotate text, or to stretch or condense text *as a graphic object*—and this is one instance where graphics applications have the edge in text. (Even if you cannot stretch or condense the text in the graphics application itself, you can do so in the page-composition application if you *import* the text from a graphics package.)

Chapter 4 offers specific design tips on developing type specifications and positioning for figure captions.

MONITOR THE COMPLEXITY OF THE ILLUSTRATIONS

This guideline has special significance for electronic images, separate from the be simple principle described in Chapter 4. Here we are not referring so much to the design or appearance of the illustration to the eye, but to the electronic complexity of the graphic. For example, a graphic that looks like a drop-shadowed box can be created in either of two ways: 1) draw a black box, then lay a white box on top of it, or 2) draw a white box, and add two nonoverlapping black rectangles on two sides (Figure 6.19). The first method yields a more complex graphic than the second, which can mean higher storage requirements and longer printing times.

Similarly, a bit-map image composed of many dots is technically more complex than an object-oriented image composed of a few geometrical objects. If you specify the preferred methods of creating graphics in advance, you can save a lot of disk space and printing time in the long run.

Rule of Thumb:

Bit-map graphics take longer to print than object-oriented graphics.

High-resolution scans take longer to print than low-resolution paint images.

Layered graphics take longer to print than nonlayered forms.

234 THE ELECTRONIC PUBLISHER

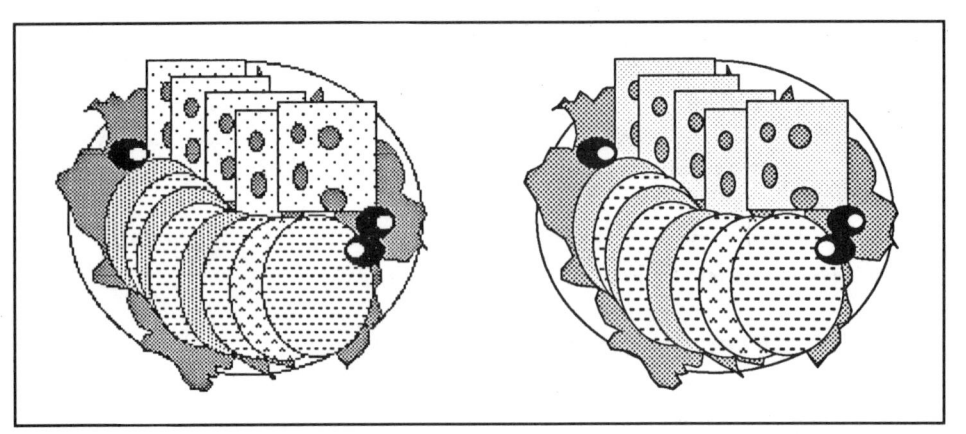

■ **Figure 6.17** Bit-map graphics (left) take longer to print than object-oriented graphics (right). (Approximate time to print bitmap: 1.5 min., object-oriented: 30 sec.)

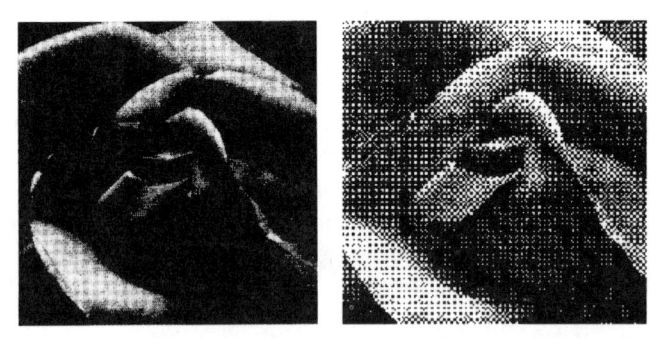

■ **Figure 6.18** High-resolution scans (left) take longer to print than low-resolution paint images (right). (Approximate time to print scan: 1 min., paint image: 10 sec.)

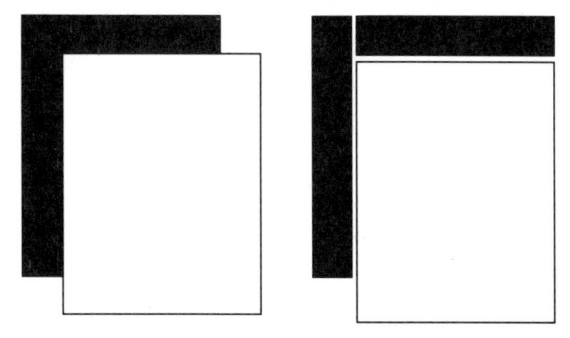

■ **Figure 6.19** Layered graphics (left) take longer to print than nonlayered forms (right). (Approximate time to print layered: 10 sec., not layered: 5 sec.) You can save printing time by creating shadow effects out of three nonlayered rectangles, rather than two overlapping rectangles.

TABULAR DATA AS ARTWORK

Depending on the features of your word processor and page-layout program, you might handle tabular data as artwork rather than as text out of necessity or by personal choice. In particular, if the tabular data requires horizontal and vertical rules to separate rows and columns, you might have one or more of the following options for creating the table:

- Create the table as text and use the word processor's or page-layout program's commands for including ruled lines as part of the text.
- Create the table as text, and add ruled lines as artwork in the page-layout program.
- Create the table entirely in a graphics package.

In the case of the third solution, you may need to consider special handling of text in a graphics program that does not support tabs. You cannot use spaces between columns to align entries unless you are using a nonproportional font. With most graphics programs, you will need to type each column's entries as a separate block of text, and use the graphics program's commands to align each column's text left (for normal text) or right (for numbers). Aligning decimal numbers can be difficult if the program does not support decimal tabs: for perfect alignment, you can type the numbers to the left of the decimal as a single column, aligned right; then type the numbers to the right of the decimal as a single column, aligned left.

KEEP ARTWORK CLEAN

Clean artwork is the hallmark of any professional illustrator. Traditionally, this meant that the final artwork didn't have smudges of ink and glue from sloppy production techniques. In electronic publishing, the issue of clean art is slightly different. Here we use the word clean to refer to two aspects of electronic artwork:

- The graphics file should not have extra elements, other than what is required for the artwork. For example, production aids that are included in the template (explained later in this chapter) should be removed when the artwork is finished. Similarly, don't leave unused graphic elements hidden in the layers below the final image.
- For scanned images, be sure that the original is clean (in the traditional sense) before you digitize it, adjust the contrast and brightness controls to get the best image, and clean up the final scan by removing stray dots that are not part of the main image. This last step can be achieved by using a pixel-editing tool in the graphics program, or by cropping parts of the image away during the page-layout process.

TEST GRAY SHADES BEFORE FINALIZING THE DESIGN SPECIFICATIONS

Gray-fill patterns are available through most graphics programs, but they should be used cautiously in any design. The quality of the final product will depend upon the type of printer used to produce the camera-ready master pages, the method of reproduction, and the range of contrast on the page.

For example, the apparent darkness of gray-fill patterns will vary depending on the resolution of the printer (a 30 percent screen will appear darker when printed at 300 dpi than when printed at 2400 dpi). It is a good idea to test print the patterns you will be using on the final printer before using the patterns in all of the illustrations.

Rule of Thumb:

Gray screens of 50% or less will appear lighter when printed at higher resolution, and screens of 50% or more will appear darker, than when printed on a low-resolution printer.

Problems with gray screens can also arise when you reproduce pages with text on a gray background. The camera used to produce negatives for offset printing are usually set to photograph high-contrast, black-and-white images. Light-gray screens tend to wash out under normal settings, so the camera needs to be adjusted to pick up 10 percent gray screens, for example. This adjustment can result in darker text, and text in small point sizes will fill in when photographed on the same page with light-gray screens. Similarly, text might be perfectly readable when overlayed on a dark-gray screen and printed on a laser printer, but the camera used to prepare the plates for offset printing will not be able to distinguish the text clearly from the background, resulting in a dark, muddy image.

USE PHOTOGRAPHIC REDUCTION TO IMPROVE IMAGES

For example, most Publishing programs let you output complete pages with text and line art in place. If your output device is fairly low-resolution, however, you may want to enhance the line art by outputting it separately at 150 times the final size, making a glossy photostat of it, and pasting the stat in place. Shooting the art down will not only increase the resolution and reduce jaggies in diagonal lines, but through the photostat process, you can also eliminate any toner dust (artifacts) from your laser printer.

ALLOW TIME FOR IMAGE RETOUCHING

Retouching involves changing scanned images—color or black and white—in a much more specific way than in color *correction* (described in Chapter 9). The original art might have a scratch that needs to be removed, or your design may call for part of an image to be altered or removed (the color of a woman's dress must be changed, for example, or the watch on her wrist must be removed).

■ **Figure 6.20** Before and after retouched image from Superset, Inc.

Image composition is another form of retouching in which one or more images are combined to look as if they are one image.

■ **Figure 6.21** An example of image combination: a ship on an island.

Image retouching has traditionally been a labor-intensive manual task performed by highly trained retouching artists. Original color transparencies or prints are retouched using special dyes. Films are generally retouched through photomasking or chemical retouching. Once halftones have been generated, the only way to retouch is through dot etching (changing the image by reducing the size of the halftone dots in specific areas of one or more separation films). All of these are painstaking, expensive processes. Retouched images can also be very delicate and require special handling during production. Dyes used in retouching originals, for example, don't always photograph the same way as the rest of the image and can cause unexpected problems and extra work during the separation process.

Retouching, however, is one of the areas that has been most affected by electronic technology. Not only can you perform many retouching techniques faster and less expensively on a computer than you can by traditional methods, you can also create effects that are simply not practical, or even possible, with traditional methods.

Images that have been retouched electronically have some additional advantages over photographically and chemically retouched images. For one thing, you don't lose quality as you manipulate the image. In photographic processes, each manipulation usually involves a new generation of film. With each generation removed from the original, you lose some image quality. Also, with traditional methods, the original image is altered irretrievably. With electronic methods, you can make any number of copies and try any number of effects, and still go back to where you started.

Retouched images are not delicate, since the changes are made digitally. Other important advantages, of course, are that you can create any number of variations without altering the original. While the big, expensive color prepress workstations that printers use are impressive in their capabilities, it is amazing how much retouching and special effects work you can do on a desktop computer today. Quite a few desktop illustration packages include common retouching functions such as masking, cut and paste, cloning, air brushing, scaling, flipping, rotating, and image assembly and compositing.

Desktop systems have some pluses of their own: You can usually integrate other graphics software, such as 3-D modeling and charting/graphing programs. Desktop systems tend to have more flexible paint than color prepress systems. And they may offer functions unavailable in color prepress, such as texture mapping (the ability to capture surface textures through video cameras or scanners, and then paint with them or wrap them around three-dimensional objects).

■ **Figure 6.22** An example of texture mapping; wood grain texture scanned into computer and texture mapped to computer-generated 3D model. (© 1988 Coddbarrett Associates, Inc.).

At the low end, any paint program that lets you zoom in and edit at the pixel- or near-pixel level can be used to retouch images. Some of the full-featured programs in this category can handle gray scale information, and produce results that approach the quality of the high-end systems when you output to a high-resolution typesetter. If your system cannot handle gray-scale information, however, your editing capabilities will be limited. You'll be able to turn bits off and on, and thus erase or add to your image. What you won't be able to do is blend one area gradually into another or make overall adjustments in tone and contrast.

240 THE ELECTRONIC PUBLISHER

Another plus that some desktop software has is that color images can be converted after retouching into PostScript or TIFF files and thus inserted as black-and-white images into publishing software. This is a fast way of inserting position-only indications of where color images should eventually be—and it saves you the cost of photostats.

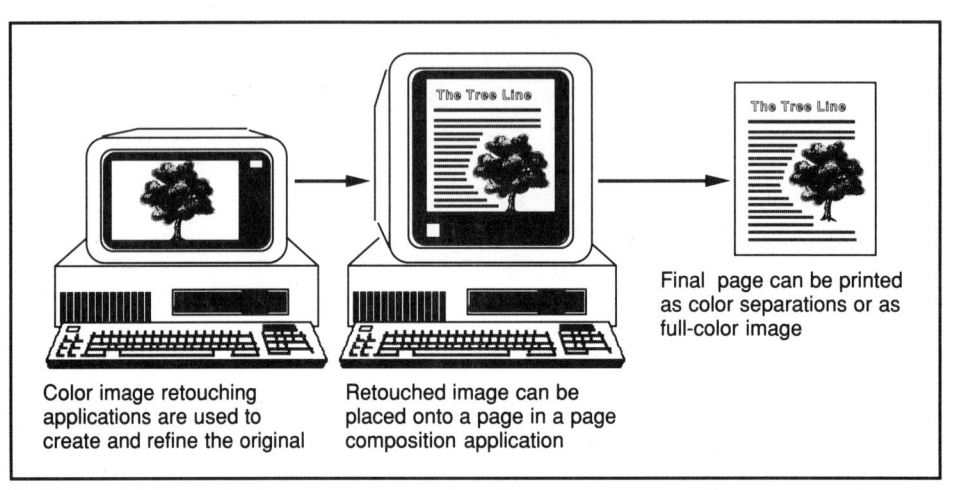

■ **Figure 6.23** A color image on-screen; then the on-screen imposition in a page-layout application.

The disadvantage of desktop systems is that pictures must be kept small if they are to meet print standards for image quality. Desktop paint systems typically provide only a fraction of the resolution available on expensive color prepress systems. (Prepress systems typically offer the capability of working with images at resolution levels of 300 pixels-per-inch or more, with 32-bit color data depth: 256 levels each of yellow, cyan, magenta, and black. Screen resolutions are much less, usually under 100 pixels per inch, and thus users must window into virtual data space, just as on most desktop systems.)

Some desktop systems offer interfaces that enable you to pass electronic image files to color prepress systems, where they can be further enhanced and output to high-resolution film plotters. During the translation, the files can sometimes be interpolated to higher resolution levels, but the results are mixed (you can't really make up for image data that isn't there). Interpolated images generally lack detail and crispness. For high quality, you are better off restricting yourself to passing resolution-independent page information line art (at least one color prepress manufacturer has announced support for Display PostScript).

Figure 6.24 The image on Scitex.

SCALE IMAGES PROPORTIONALLY

Applications that offer scaling options can work in one of two ways: some applications let you scale an image by specifying a percentage reduction or enlargement. Depending on the application, you can either scale the entire image, or a selected portion of the image. Other applications let you scale images visually, usually by moving a corner of the image on the screen. In either case, you normally want to scale the image proportionally (unless you intend to create a special effect by disproportionate scaling).

There are several methods of figuring scaling percentages. One way is to measure your original *cropped* image area and then to measure one or more dimensions of the reproduction image area on your final page mock-up. Take one set of dimensions and divide the reproduction dimension by the original dimension. For example, if your original image is 8 inches by 10 inches, and you want to print it at 5 inches wide, it needs to be shot down to 62½ percent (5 divided by 8). If you don't have the other reproduction dimension, you can figure it easily by multiplying the corresponding original dimension by the same percentage. In this case, multiplying 10 by .625 gives us 6¼ inches. You can also use a scaling wheel (as described in Chapter 8).

Figure 6.25 An example of figuring scaling by percentages.

If your application does not let you enter precise percentages, or if you prefer to scale visually, there are a couple of visual methods for scaling art that work just as well. Most applications let you control visual scaling to force it to be proportional. Otherwise, you can draw a diagonal line from the lower left-hand corner of the original image to its upper right-hand corner. Measure off the reproduction width at the bottom of the image, drawing a perpendicular line up from the mark until it intersects the diagonal line. Drag the corner of the image until it meets the intersection of these two lines, then delete the lines.

Figure 6.26 Diagonal line scaling.

When selecting scaling factors, try to avoid anything over 200 percent. If possible, your original art should be larger than the image area it will occupy in the finished piece.

ILLUSTRATIONS   243

Rule of Thumb:

Image quality is improved by shooting art down to size, and lost by enlarging it.

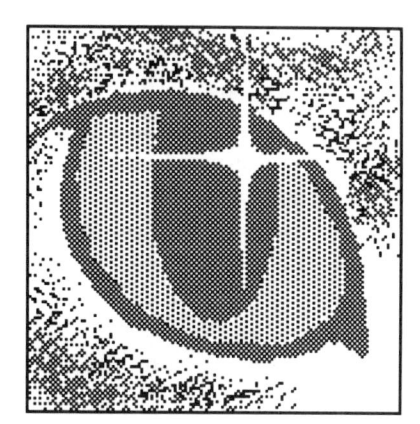

■ **Figure 6.27**   Image quality at 50%, 100%, and 250%.

ESTABLISH NAMING CONVENTIONS

Traditionally, the publisher would receive the completed manuscript from the author before assigning the illustration process to an artist. The figure numbers would be known and finalized before the artists started, so each illustration board would be easily labeled and the paste-up process would be straightforward.

Rule of Thumb:

Use the word processing package's footnoting feature to automatically number figures: each figure caption is a footnote, and the footnote reference appears in the text where the graphic should be inserted.

With electronic publishing, it is possible for the author to participate in the illustration process by using a graphics program, scanner, or screen shot utility to create illustrations. When some illustrations are started before the writing process is completed, it can happen that new figures get inserted and the numbering sequence will change. It is important to establish procedures for naming files so that the final figure numbers in the manuscript can be

matched against the graphics files' names. There are three approaches to handling this problem:
- Include the figure number in the name of the graphics file, and remember to change all of the file names whenever a figure is deleted or moved or a new figure is inserted. If the figure number is also typed within the graphics file, you will need to *open* each graphics file and change the figure number. This works well if you have the time and the discipline to rename all of the files every time the figure numbers change, but it is time-consuming and prone to error.
- Give each graphics file a descriptive name, and include the file name in the text file near the spot where the figure should be inserted. By this technique, the graphics files retain the same name throughout the project until the final page-layout stage begins. When the final sequence of figures is known, the descriptive names in the text are changed to reflect the final figure numbers, and the graphics file names are also changed to include the figure number. This technique can save time in the long run if the figure numbers change frequently during the editorial stages.

Some page-layout programs can automatically number the figures for you. In this case, it can be especially important to develop a procedure for matching the figure numbers in the text—which will automatically change when figures are added—to the graphics files whose names will not change automatically.

Graphics Templates

You can help enforce consistency and provide a common grid for all of the graphics that will be used in a publication by using the computer graphics programs to create templates. Besides enforcing consistency, a template system can significantly reduce the time required to produce a large number of illustrations. A template is a dummy file that contains all of the basic default settings and some of the graphic elements that will be used in all of the illustrations in a series. To create a new illustration, the artist opens the template file, creates the illustration out of the building blocks provided on the template, and saves the file under a new name (thereby preserving the original template for future use).

A template for graphics might include a common ruler line, predrawn lines and boxes that show the line weights and fill patterns to be used in all illustrations, lettering guides, spacing guides, a common grid structure, and a system for scaling the illustrations to their final size.

THE RULER

Most graphics programs can display horizontal and vertical rulers and offer a choice between various units of measure. Normally, the same unit of measure will be used for all of the illustrations for one publication. If the template is set up to automatically display the rulers with the common unit of measure, the artist need not repeat the command to display rulers and specify the unit of measure each time a new illustration is started.

In some cases, it may be efficient to create a custom ruler that reflects the scale of drawings that represent physical objects. For example, if a series of illustrations uses miles or kilometers as the common unit of measure—a unit not available through the automatic rulers of most drawing programs—you can create a moveable ruler as artwork.

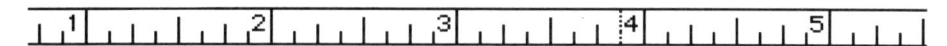

■ **Figure 6.28** A custom ruler created in a paint program.

THE PEN

The design specifications for a document should include guidelines for the line weights to be used in illustrations. The graphics templates can be set up with the most commonly used line weight selected as the default. A template could also include a key to correct line weights: use the graphics program's line tool to draw a short line in each of the weights to be used, and add text next to each line specifying when to use that weight (Figure 6.29).

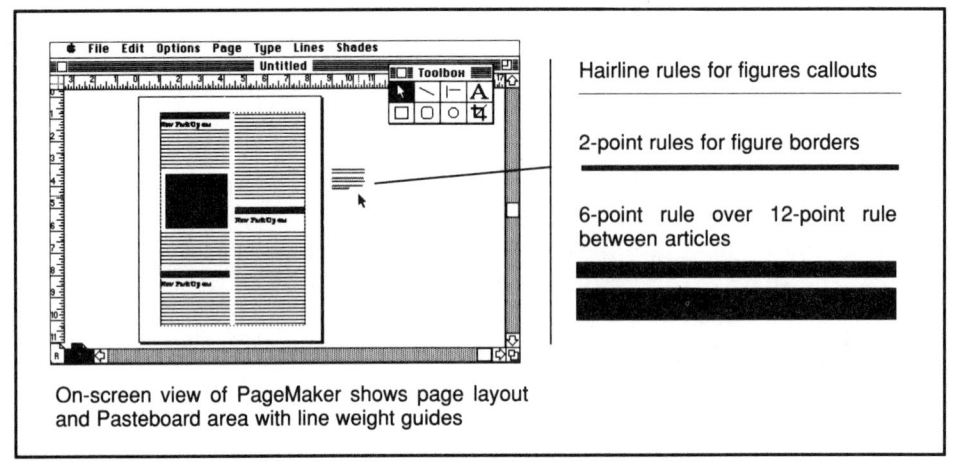

Figure 6.29 A guide to line weights can be part of the template used during production, then deleted from the file before the final version is printed.

The guide to line weights can be used as a reference during production, then deleted from the file before the final version is printed. Depending on the program's procedures for changing line weights while working on an illustration, production time might be further reduced by *copying* the lines from the guide (using the program's copy command) and *pasting* the copy as part of the illustration. Careful positioning and scaling of these copied objects might still be required, but the artist can save the time it would take to change the selected line weight and draw the object from scratch.

LETTERING GUIDES

Electronic lettering guides are simply dummy blocks of text that are already set in the font to be used for each element of an illustration. Some lettering guides might already be positioned and aligned exactly where they will appear in the final illustration—the title, caption, and legend dummy text, for instance. Other lettering guides can be copied and moved into position on each illustration, such as the axis labels or item labels. Figure 6.30 shows one system of lettering guides.

ILLUSTRATIONS 247

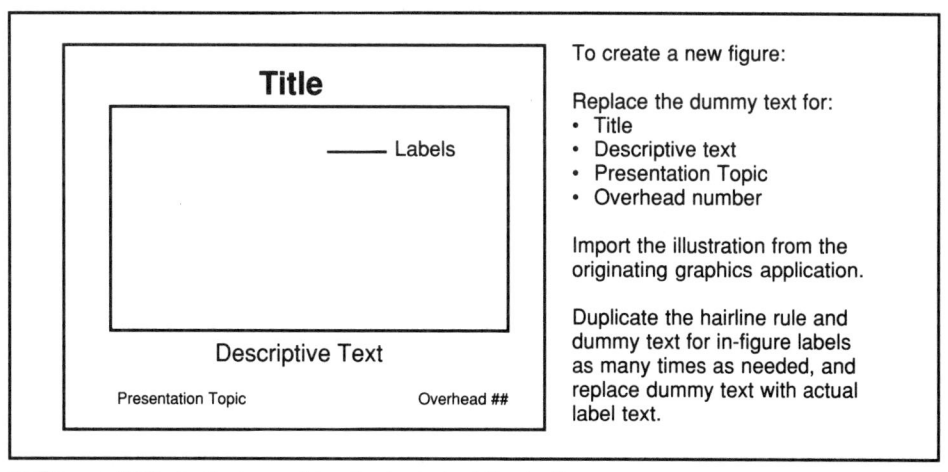

■ **Figure 6.30** Lettering guides for technical illustrations.

Unless the guides for line weights can be stored in a nonprinting work area, they should be deleted from the file before the final printing.

SPACING GUIDES

Spacing guides help position text next to the objects in the illustrations. A spacing guide is an object of a fixed size that can be moved around on the screen and used as a guide in positioning text and graphics.

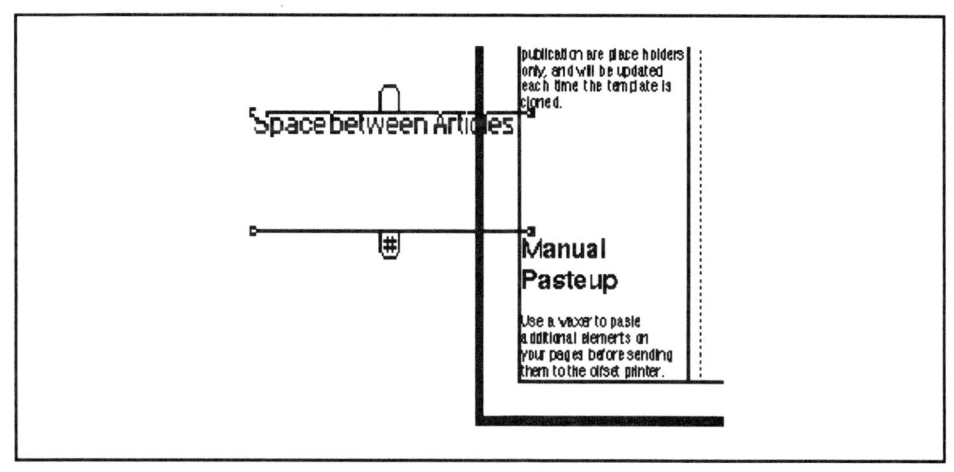

■ **Figure 6.31** A spacing guide helps align text and graphic elements.

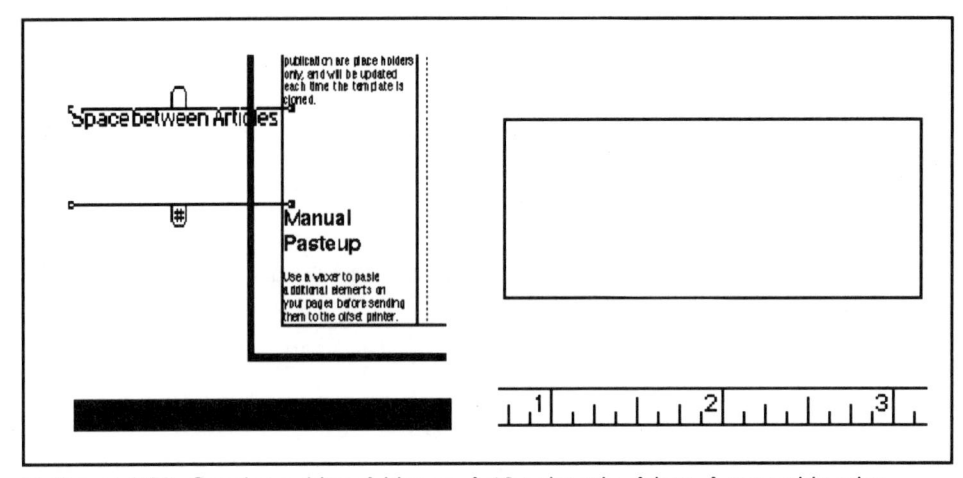

Figure 6.32 Spacing guides: A bitmap. A 12-point rule. A box. A moveable ruler.

It goes without saying that all of the labels *within* an illustration should be positioned the same measured distance from the objects they refer to. Violation of this principle is demonstrated in Figure 6.33.

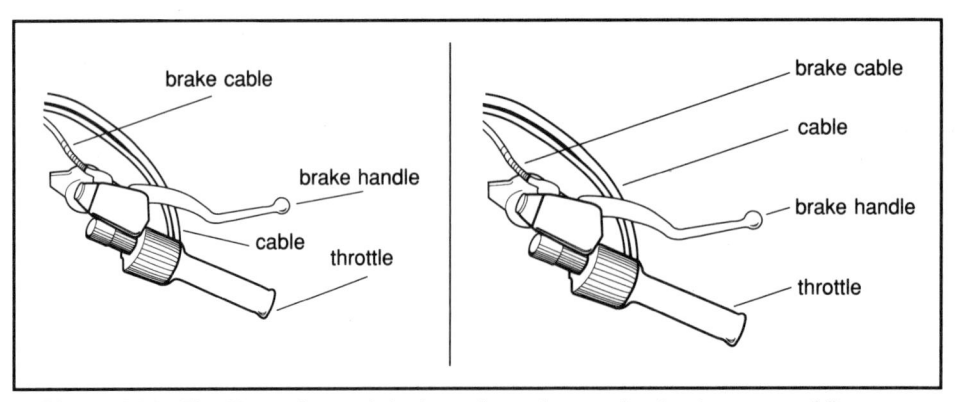

Figure 6.33 The illustration on left shows irregular spacing in placement of figure labels. The illustration is improved by consistent spacing shown on right.

A spacing guide can be useful for a single illustration, but it is critical for a series of illustrations. By creating spacing guides in the template, the same consistent positioning can be attained throughout the series of illustrations cloned from the template.

How the spacing guides are created will vary from program to program. Unless the spacing guide is designed as a moveable ruler that can show several measures, one spacing guide is required for each measurement called for in the design specifications. For example, the distance of the axis labels from the axes might be smaller than the distance of the title from the top of the graphic.

If more than two spacing guides are required, they should be set up on the template with text describing the appropriate uses. Unless the spacing guides can be stored in a nonprinting work area, they should be deleted from the file before the final printing.

REPEATING SYMBOLS

Many series of illustrations make use of repeating symbols—elements that appear throughout the series. For example, many of the illustrations in a textbook for student drivers will use the same basic drawing of the overhead view of a car, though in each illustration the car might be pointed in a different direction. The car is a repeated symbol that can be created once and then copied and pasted for use in many places.

The template can contain a complete set of the symbols to be used throughout the illustrations, or the template system might include many different graphics files that are opened and copied every time a symbol is required. Unless the repeating symbols can be stored in a nonprinting work area, they should be deleted from the file before the final printing.

Rule of Thumb:
Scale repeating symbols to the size(s) that will be used before incorporating them into the template system.

THE GRID STRUCTURE

Most drawing programs incorporate a grid feature whereby you can specify the increments by which objects can be moved. For example, a ¼-inch grid would let you move objects in increments of ¼-inch along the horizontal or vertical; the objects will snap to these incremental grid lines unless you turn the grid off.

A template can go further than simply setting up the automatic grid. You can define the grid to be used in a series of illustrations by setting up a template with a specified paper size, define margin widths by drawing a box in the template (that might be deleted when the illustration is complete), and mark standard positions (for figure titles or axis lines).

A SCALING SYSTEM

The final ingredient of a graphics template is a scaling system. Here we are not referring to the ruler described at the beginning of this section, but to a method of determining the size of type and width of lines to be used in creating illustrations that will eventually be scaled down during page layout.

Simply stated, the question that a good scaling system answers is: What size(s) type and line weight(s) should be used in illustrations that will be reduced by some percentage in the final page layout in order to maintain consistency with illustrations that will *not* be reduced? Inconsistencies arise when all of the original figures use the same type specifications, the originals are created in varying sizes without regard to the final page layout, and then each is reduced by a different percentage in order to fit the page. This might be the only solution if the final size is not known in advance and the illustrations cannot be modified directly once the final size *is* known.

For example, if the design specifications call for 14-point figure titles, then the titles should be set at 28 points in the original versions of figures that will eventually be reduced 50 percent.

The easiest solution is to draw all figures to the same scale, using the same type specifications. When the originals cannot be drawn to fit the page (due to the complexity of the illustrations) make sure that the final size is known (*before* the illustration process begins) and accounted for by adjustments to the type sizes used in the originals.

Proofing Graphics

The art of proofing graphics calls for the same concerns as in proofreading text, and it adds a few dimensions that are often overlooked by the untrained eye. Most proofreaders and copy editors are on the lookout for misspelled words. In later stages of production, the proofreader also verifies that the correct fonts are used throughout.

When proofing graphics images, you also need to verify that elements are aligned correctly—flush left, right, or centered—and that the spacing between elements is consistent throughout a series of illustrations. Sometimes this means that you must proofread with a ruler in your hand, to measure the distances between elements or to confirm that elements are centered correctly. The graphics proofreader might also look for titles that call for tighter kerning between letters, especially if the figure titles are typed in all caps.

Finally, the graphics proofreader needs to verify that the figure numbers correspond correctly to the references within the manuscript.

Summary

Now that you see what alternatives are available for creating graphics using electronic tools, you are equipped to make decisions about what type of graphics program to use to create various graphics for your publication. The next chapter takes you through all of the steps of laying out a publication, incorporating the principles offered in Chapters 4 through 6 and offering tips about using a page-layout program's tools during the layout process, including guidelines for cropping and scaling graphics.

Chapter 7
Page Composition

"When most people think of desktop publishing, they think of WYSIWYG page-composition packages. In fact, these 'sexy' programs are often not as flexible as their code-oriented, workhorse counterparts. We can expect this difference to narrow in the future."

After the text and graphics files have been prepared using word processing and graphics programs, the actual page-layout process begins. The difference between word processing and page-layout is becoming increasingly blurred as packages in the two categories share many capabilities. Since the process of formatting text (fonts, tabs, and paragraph alignment) was already described in Chapter 5, we will not repeat that information here, even though the formatting function is often performed in the page-layout application and not at the word processing stage.

Let's remember that desktop publishing is simply a subset of the larger and older category of electronic publishing. Desktop publishing as we define it is the ability to edit a page that is displayed on the screen exactly as it will appear when printed. Packages in this category are a fairly new addition to the desktop software library. Meanwhile, there have been and continue to be many packages in the market that use codes embedded in ASCII text to indicate to a code-driven output device what format the document should take. While these packages are not what desktop publishing is all about, the high-end programs in this category are still preferred for certain applications. For example, there has been a trend over the last five to six years toward making desktop computers compatible with phototypesetting terminals. Some of these code-based packages have evolved specifically for use by departments and service companies that already have an investment in a particular brand or model of typesetting equipment, and want to add personal computers to their system as low-cost alternatives to expensive typesetting terminals. These packages can also be used on personal computers at remote sites to prepare text that can be telecommunicated to the typesetter. Some of these packages offer a WYSIWYG interface rather than using codes, and as a general rule they provide more extensive typographic controls than the lower-priced desktop systems that are more specifically addressed in this chapter.

At the other end of the spectrum, some of the products that are being marketed under the desktop publishing umbrella are print utilities that help word processing programs print to laser printers, code interpreters that help you merge text with graphics files during the printing process, or display type packages that offer bit-mapped type styles for dot-matrix printers or low-resolution printing on a laser printer. These packages often use codes for typesetting as described in Chapter 5. Some of these packages may offer features that are similar to the full-page-layout packages that are more specifically addressed in this chapter, offering a WYSIWYG interface rather than using codes, but as a general rule they provide limited typographic controls, and support only bit-mapped graphics.

Our comments in this chapter specifically address the use of page-layout packages that let you assemble text and graphics files from many different programs and lay them out with a full view of the pages on the monitor, as well as those word processing programs that offer some of these page-layout features. There are a few basic features that all these packages have in common, but there is a wide range of features that are not shared by all or implemented as well in every package. Each package has its own area of specialty that makes it well-suited for certain types of documents but ill-suited for others.

Basic features offered by page-composition packages described in this chapter include:
- A WYSIWYG interface. Some WYSIWYG packages show "greeked" text in the full-page view, but every package shows text characters in closer views of the page. Screen displays may differ from final output because some packages show text in the font in which it will be printed while others display only generic fonts.
- Master pages can be set up with elements that repeat on every page, including headers and footers with automatic page numbering.
- Simple graphics like lines, boxes, and ovals can be added.
- Column guides and other guides can be set up to help you work with complex grid designs.
- Rulers can be used to measure horizontal and vertical distances on a page.
- Custom page sizes and document formats that are not possible with most other programs can be set up.

In Chapters 3 through 6 you learned basic principles of design and how you can prepare text and graphics in other programs. In Chapter 4 you learned how the designer can work ahead of the production team, sketching the layout of each page of the publication before the text and graphics from other programs are placed on the pages. In this chapter, you will learn certain production techniques that can be applied using a page-layout package, including how to set up margins and column guides, and how to layer, arrange, and edit the text and graphics once they are placed on the pages.

Table 7.1
Summary of Steps in Creating a Document

Develop Design Specifications	(Chapters 3, 4)
Prepare Text and Graphics	(Chapters 5, 6)
Create a Page-layout Template	(This Chapter)
Change Grid on Individual Pages	(This Chapter)
Place Text and Graphics	(This Chapter)
Format Text	(Chapter 5)
Prepare Boards for Reproduction	(Chapters 8, 9)
Print and Bind the Document	(Chapter 10)

Assess Your Needs

The procedures best suited to your project may vary depending on the type of document you are producing. Large projects or long documents carry a greater imperative for efficient disk file organization than short documents, for instance, though all projects will benefit by following the guidelines for disk organization presented in this chapter.

Similarly, large projects or long documents may benefit more from using a template system than short, one-time documents. Assess your needs and adapt your approach to file management and page layout based on the characteristics of the documents you are producing.

MAGAZINES, TABLOIDS, AND NEWSLETTERS

The template systems for newsletters and magazines can be very elaborate compared with most other types of documents. Three of the most distinguishing characteristics are that:
- The document is often multicolumnar, and the number of columns can change on a single page.
- The text can skip from one page to a point several pages later.

- The documents are usually produced as a series: a document of the same basic format and length is produced at regular intervals.
- The documents often call for special layouts that may involve kerning headlines, wrapping text around graphics, or pasting display ads from one page-layout document into another.

These and other characteristics of these documents present their own special design and production problems that are explained in Chapter 4.

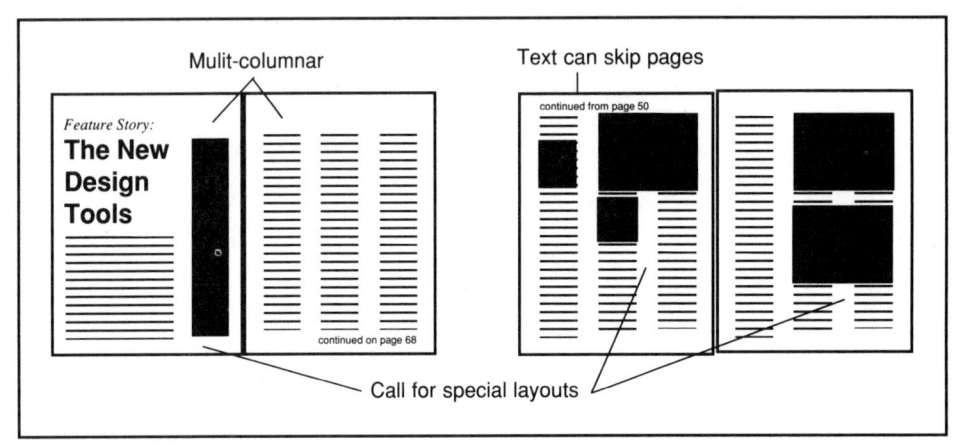

■ **Figure 7.1** Common characteristics of newsletters, newspapers, and magazines.

EFFICIENCY TIP:

The template for a complex magazine or tabloid can be set up as a one- or two-page document. Each page or series of consecutive pages starts from this template, but a single issue is stored as three or more different page-layout files. This way, the production and editing tasks can be shared by a group of people, and individual pages can move at their own pace through the production cycle.

The template for a complex document is a key production aid for each issue. The template can require many hours to build the first time (including time for test-building one page, printing it out, and writing up procedures that can be followed by the authors and editors as well as by the production staff).

PAGE COMPOSITION

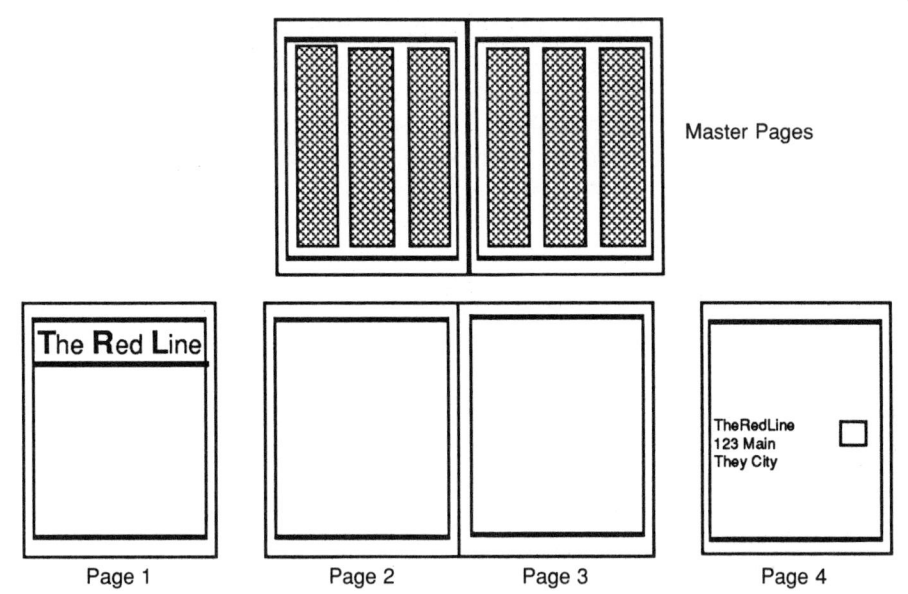

■ **Figure 7.2** The template for a complex tabloid. The master pages are set up as three-column formats with running headers. Standard elements are stored on the pasteboard. Page 1 of the template includes the banner and a ruler guide for starting articles on this page.

The thumbnail printouts of blank pages from the template for a magazine or tabloid newspaper can be used by the editors to mark positioning of articles.

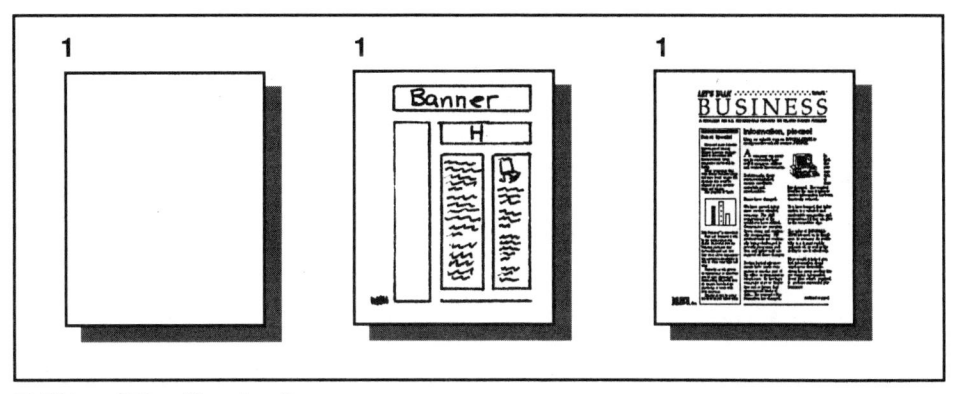

■ **Figure 7.3** Thumbnails.

If tabloid pages are too small to be usable using a thumbnails feature, a printout with a percentage reduction can be used to print quick miniatures of each finished page. These reductions can be used by the editors to mark positioning of ads and articles. Reductions can also be used for control and review purposes after pages are built—to proof for positioning of ads and articles and review overall page layout.

■ **Figure 7.4**   Pages are printed at 45% reduction to fit on one sheet of 8½ x11 paper, instead of using thumbnails to make snapshots of finished pages.

A list of steps like the one shown in Figure 7.5 might appear directly in the template for a newsletter, to be used as an aid to the production team and deleted from the finished document.

1. Type and format all text in the word processing program. Save each story as a separate text file, or type all text into one file in the order it will appear in the newsletter. Total number of characters for all stories should not exceed ??. (check)
2. Place text in sequence, starting in column one on page one and continuing to column 3 on page 3, working in Fit in Window. If there is more text still to be placed after you have filled page 3, place it on the Pasteboard.
3. Select the one-point rule on the Pasteboard and Copy it into the Clipboard.
4. Go back to page one and, working in Actual size, scroll down each column, making fine adjustments between stories as necessary, and Pasting the one-point rule from the Clipboard into position between each story. If making the spaces between stories wider or smaller will help make room for the text overflow, make that adjustment during this sweep.
   Add the black box for one photograph during this sweep. (Only one halftone is permitted per issue, to keep down production costs.)
5. If the final text still does not fit within the 3 pages allowed, select all of the body copy on the most crowded page and change the leading to shrink or stretch the text. You may need to sweep through in Actual size again to check for widows and orphans and to move the one-point rules between articles.
6. If the text still does not fit the number of pages allowed, sweep through in actual size and change the figure size (black box for photo) or selectively change the spacing between each article.
7. On page 4, change the issue identification and "Inside. . . " tag.
8. Print out on Apple LaserWriter and send camer-ready pages to ABC Printers. Use ink color: PMS 282. Paper stock: White laid 60 lb. 1,000 copies.
9. Copy the archive page layout file for this issue onto the disk named ALUMNI NEWS, and delete all text files from the disk.

■ **Figure 7.5**   List of steps in producing a newsletter.

BUSINESS REPORTS, BOOKS, AND MANUALS

Business reports, books, and manuals share many characteristics. Because these documents are usually longer than the documents in other categories, the full document is usually composed of several files, making these types of documents good candidates for a template system—and making a good system of file management imperative. Even if the number of pages required for a document is less than the maximum allowed by the page-layout program, there are good reasons for dividing these documents into several files. Tips on when and why to divide a document into several publication files are given in Chapter 4.

In the past, most business reports have been produced as single-sided documents, whereas manuals and books are usually double-sided documents. In this chapter, you will learn that the single-sided vs. double-sided options can also be used as production aids, regardless of how the final document will be produced.

As mentioned in Chapter 4, documents that use the same grid on every page will be much easier to produce than documents that switch between several variations in the grid. The trick to the alternation shown in Figure 7.6 is that the three-column width can be set up automatically by a column-guides command *if* the first column's right margin and gutter in the customized format is designed to fall in the exact same position as the first column of the automatic three-column grid.

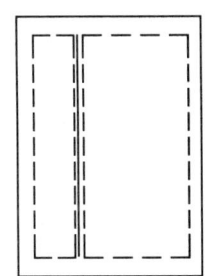

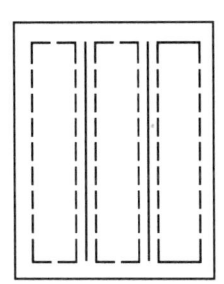

■ **Figure 7.6** Alternating between two grids: When you need a page in format one—two unequal columns—keep the master page elements. When you need a page in three-column format, use the column-guides command to set up three columns.

One common variation that is particularly hard to work with is the mirror-image page layout, such as the one shown in Figure 7.7. What makes this layout difficult is not the layout of individual pages—it is the chaos that ensues if you insert or delete one page after the publication has been layed out. The best rule of thumb in working with mirror-image designs is to always insert or delete an even number of pages, so you don't upset all of the subsequent page layouts.

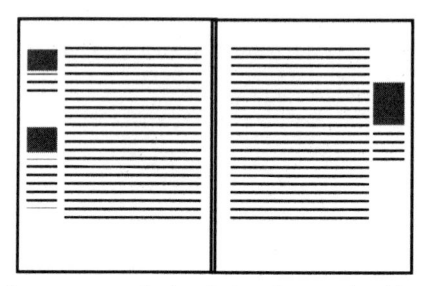

■ **Figure 7.7**   A mirror-image page design is hard to work with.

Chapter 4 describes some of the design principles and production tips that can be applied to all projects in this category.

PRICE LISTS, CATALOGUES, AND DIRECTORIES

Price lists can be any number of pages long, and this format includes menus. Long price lists of inventoried products can, like member lists, be derived from spreadsheet data or database files. Chapter 5 explains the importance of using tabs and carriage returns correctly in tabular formats, and it describes some of the issues and tricks in converting a database file into text.

BROCHURES, FLYERS, AND DISPLAY ADS

Brochures, flyers, and display ads all have these characteristics in common:
- They are usually only one or two pages long in the page-layout file, though they might be folded into four or more panels.
- They are often a nonstandard size—but the final pages must be trimmed and/or folded.

Some of the tips in this chapter can also be applied to brochures that are longer, like booklets.

A one-time brochure can use a template system that can be adapted to other similar formats. Several brochure templates are shown in Figure 7.8.

PAGE COMPOSITION   261

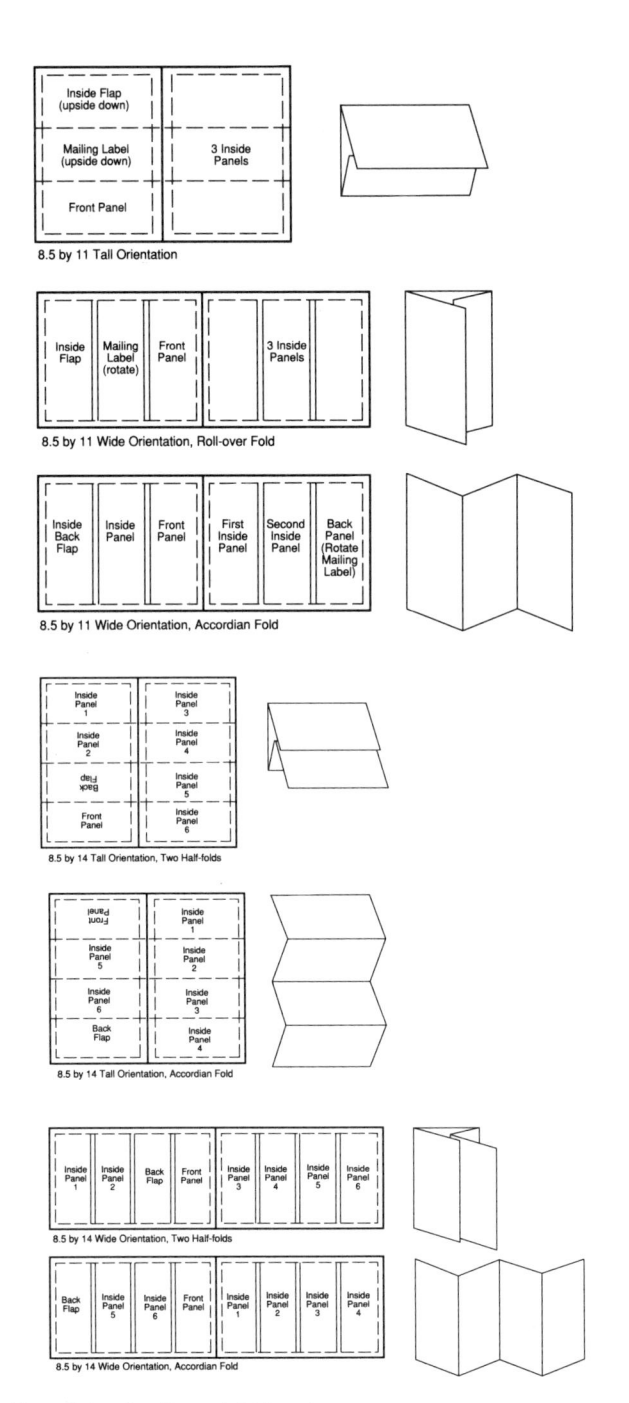

■ **Figure 7.8**   Templates for three-fold brochures.

TABLES, CHARTS, AND OVERHEAD TRANSPARENCIES

Some of the documents in this category might be designed specifically for use as overhead transparencies or slides, while others are designed as printed handouts, but they all share the following characteristics:

- They are part of a series of materials.
- They are primarily graphics. The word-charts among them have very few words, usually in a large font.
- They each require some extra touches in a page-layout program that might not be possible in the graphics programs that are used to create the charts and diagrams.

Rule of Thumb:

Black or Gray?

If the final output will be on a laser printer, use gray screen rather than solid black areas for the best projection image.

If the final output will be offset printed, you can use solid black boxes and let the offset printer's cameraman make the screens.

To create a set of overhead transparencies that will be overlaid, create the whole image first on one page. Copy the whole image onto subsequent pages—once for each overlay. Then go back to the first page and delete those parts of the image that will be overlaid. On the subsequent pages, delete all parts of the image except those that will appear on the overlay. One example of a set of overlaid images is shown in Figure 7.9.

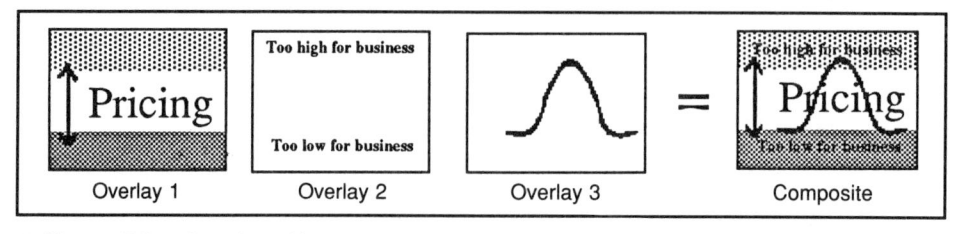

■ **Figure 7.9**   A series of images designed as overlays.

You can achieve a similar effect in preparing slides. Build the full image first, then copy the full image to subsequent pages. Keep the full version on the *last* page in the series, and delete selected elements from each page that precedes the full image. (Each page in a series of slides repeats elements from the previous page and adds new elements, whereas pages in a series for overlays of overhead transparencies do not repeat the same elements.)

Organize Disk Files

An effective method of organizing disk files is important throughout the development and production process. Chapter 6 addressed the issue of controlling file names for illustrations. We have chosen to make our main arguments in favor of organized files here, in the chapter about page layout, because it is at this point that text and graphics files from a (potentially) wide range of sources are brought together in a marriage that yields one or more page-layout files.

FILE-NAMING CONVENTIONS

It is important to gain the consensus of the production team to follow certain conventions in naming files. For example, here are some simple standards that might be applied in a magazine or newsletter project:
- All names begin with the chapter number or issue number.
- Signed articles are identified with the author's initials (three initials are preferable).
- Text and graphics files will be distinguished from each other by suffix only.
- The page-layout file names include issue number and page number(s).

HARD DISK DIRECTORIES

Each time a new document is to be produced, create a new subdirectory on the hard disk to store all of the files related to that document. The master template for the document is stored in this directory, along with all of the text and graphics files required for the document.

If the document is very large (such as a book), and composed of many different text and graphics files, create a subdirectory to store all of the files related to that chapter or section. If the same or a similar document is produced periodically, create a subdirectory for each issue or volume.

264 THE ELECTRONIC PUBLISHER

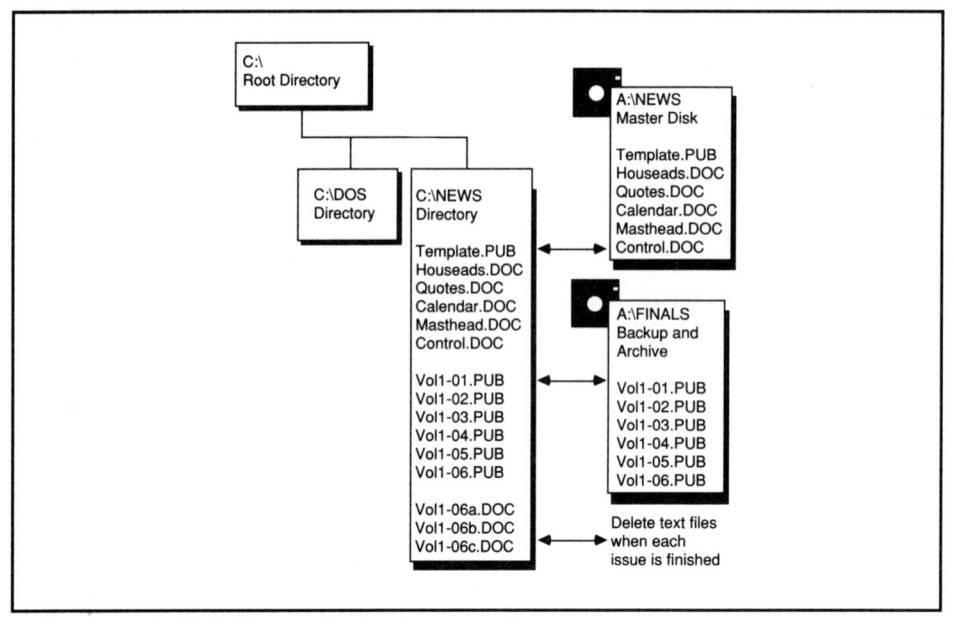

■ **Figure 7.10** Disk file organization for a newsletter.

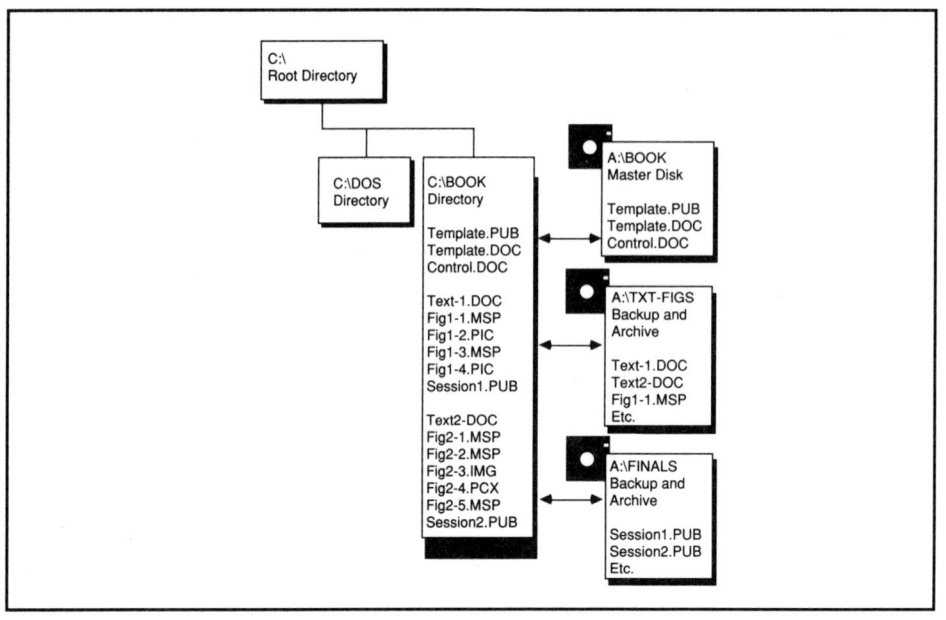

■ **Figure 7.11** Disk file organization for a book.

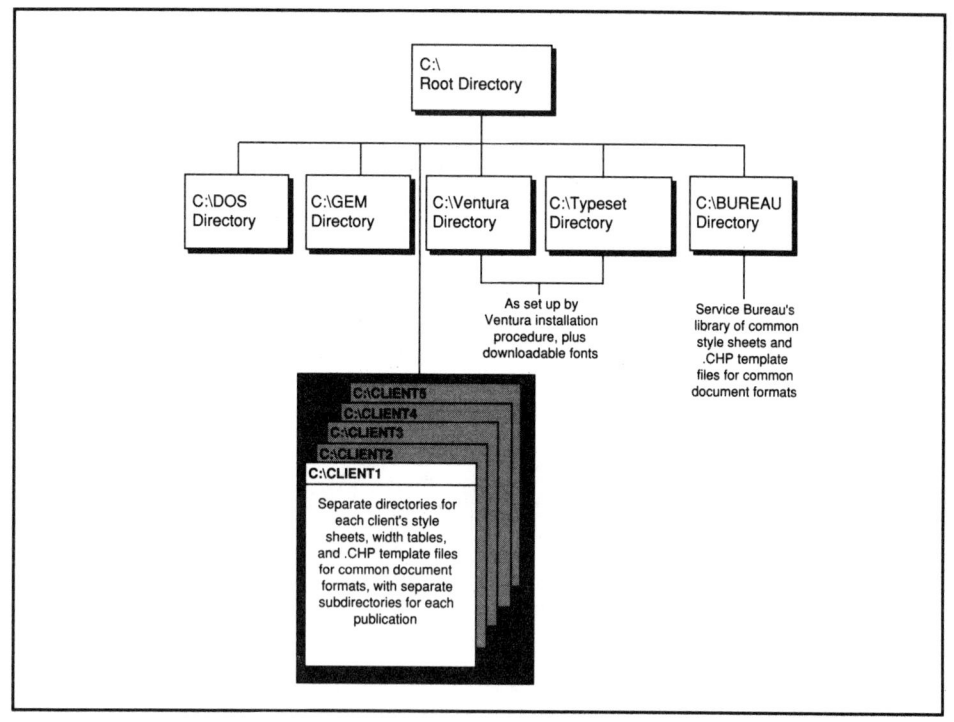

■ **Figure 7.12** Disk file organization for a service bureau.

OPTIMUM FILE SIZE

Most page-layout programs let you create documents of 50 or 100 pages or more (and some have no limits), but you will find in practice that it is more efficient to work with smaller files.

- Small files are faster to work with: faster to save, and faster to print. Long files will have slower response time when turning pages or making text edits that carry over to subsequent pages.
- Another important consideration in deciding how many pages a single file will have is the size of the final publication in bytes. If your document is very long or includes a lot of graphics, you may need to break it into sections in order to keep file sizes small enough to fit a backup on one floppy disk. You want to be able to back your publications off onto floppy disks for storage and for transport. This means that you need to keep your files under 360K or 400K for single-sided, low-density disks, or under 800K or 1.2 megabytes for double-sided, high-density disks.

THE ELECTRONIC PUBLISHER

Rule of Thumb:

Check the File Size as You Work

In creating large publications, save your file frequently while you work, and check periodically to see how large your publication is. Don't build a publication file larger than a floppy disk can hold. Break large documents into sections or chapters.

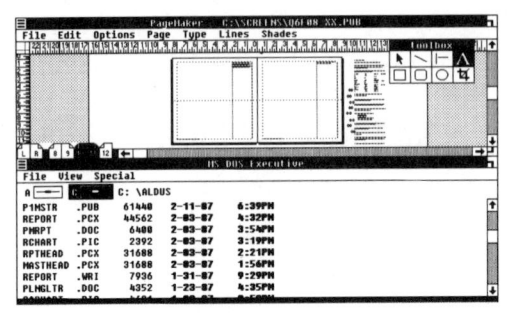

■ **Figure 7.13** If you are running Microsoft Windows, you can view the list of files in the MS-DOS Executive window while you are working in the page-layout application.

- If different sections of the document will be completed at different times—not necessarily sequential sections—then you can begin each new section when it is ready, and have different sections of the publication at different stages of the production process.
- You can divide the production tasks between several people on the production team.
- You can set up a different running header and footer for each chapter (Figure 7.14). (With most page-layout programs, headers and footers cannot be changed in the middle of a file.)

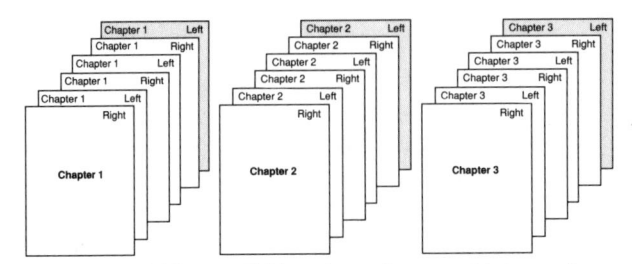

■ **Figure 7.14** It's a good idea to divide a long document into sections or chapters, so that each file can have a different header or footer and start on a right page.

- You must make separate files of any sections that require a different page setup. For example, an appendix might require wide format for presenting tables of figures, whereas the rest of the document is printed in tall format. You cannot mix tall and wide pages in one document file.
- You might want to start with a different master page grid for different sections.

This production practice—of dividing a document into parts—is most often required for long documents such as books and manuals, and is more rarely used in smaller publications.

Page Numbers

When a publication is stored as several different files, you can usually specify the page number that should start each new file. For example, if you fill one file with 50 pages, then you could continue building a second file that starts with page 51. You can change the starting page number of the document at any time, and all of the pages of the document will shift to match the new sequencing. This may cause left pages to become right pages in double-sided documents.

> **Rule of Thumb:**
>
> Controlling Left-Right Page Positions
>
> In preparing a document for double-sided printing, be sure to account for and print every page—including blank "left" pages that will be needed to force new sections or chapters to start on a right page. Having a numbered sheet for every page of the document will help whoever is printing or copying the document before binding.
>
> If you change the starting page number of a document that is set up for double-sided printing, it may happen that pages that formerly printed as right pages will shift to print on the left.

If you expect to be updating sections within the document periodically—without reprinting the entire book—include section numbers in the page numbers and let each section start with page 1. This useful production trick may conflict with design ideas and the offset printers' preferences, but it's the best way to handle living documents like procedures manuals that are constantly changing. The alternative of adding a suffix to pages that are inserted into a book—23a, 23b, 23d, for instance, or 23.1, 23.2, 23.3—cannot be handled using most page-layout programs' automatic page-numbering feature.

THE ELECTRONIC PUBLISHER

Workgroup Environments

In a network environment, current files can be stored on the shared hard disk. In a multistation production environment that is not on a network or common file server, the template can be stored on a floppy diskette that is declared the authorized source for any new chapters or documents in this series. In this way, enhancements made to the template from any station can be saved for use by all of the production staff.

BACKUP AND ARCHIVE SYSTEM

Floppy disks are used as backup throughout the production cycle, and the same floppy disks become the final archived version of the document.

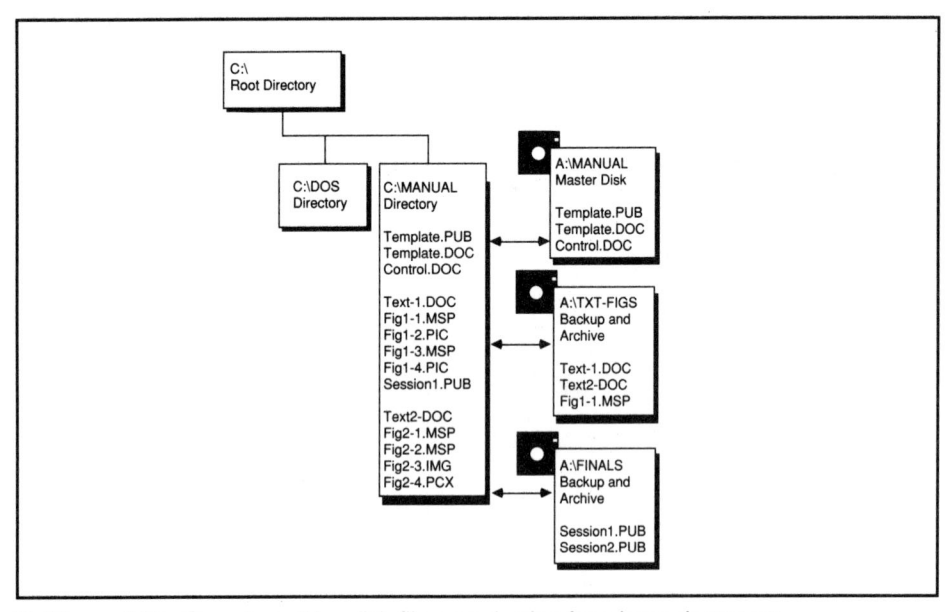

■ **Figure 7.15** Sample archive disk-file organization for a large document.

Decide how frequently you will back up all current files (by copying them from the hard disk onto floppy disks, or by duplicating the floppy disks that are used during production). For example, you might decide to keep current versions of files on the hard disk in a subdirectory set up for each issue, and remove the file from the hard disk (making a backup of it on a floppy disk that is reserved for this issue) whenever the file is sent to another computer for further changes.

If the text, graphics, and publication files are too large to fit on one floppy, all of the text files can be copied onto one floppy disk, all graphics files onto another, and all page-layout files onto another. Another way of dividing files is to copy all of the text, graphics, and page-layout files related to a single chapter or section onto each backup disk.

The backup and archive process is simplified if the files that fit on one disk are grouped in separate directories, or grouped by sharing the same characters at the beginning of the file name (or in the suffix of the name). For example, if all of the text files end in the suffix ".doc," and all of the page-layout files end with the suffix ".pub," you can copy these sets onto two different disks in an MS-DOS system using the following commands:

1. Insert floppy for text files into the A drive, then, from the subdirectory on the hard disk, type:
   c>copy •.doc a:
2. Remove text floppy, insert page-layout file floppy and type:
   c>copy •.pub a:

(Caution: Don't use MS-DOS commands to copy files that are created using applications that maintain their own directory of elements, such as Ventura Publisher. Use the application's copy commands instead.)

Each document's text and graphics files and page-layout file are copied onto floppy diskettes when the document is complete. In archiving the files when a project is finished, you can discard the unformatted text-only files, but save any formatted text files and spreadsheet data if you expect to change the figures extensively for next year's presentation. It will make it easier to make new entries down each column, so long as the row and column headings remain the same. If you expect minor changes, you can update the page-layout file directly. If you expect to change many entries in scattered rows and columns, save the formatted text file and make the changes there.

Not only must the production team be able to distinguish the text file for one article from another within an issue (by file name), but they must also be able to distinguish between the latest version of an article and earlier versions that might have been left on disks or archived.

Rule of Thumb:

Make sure that the date and time stored in their systems is kept current, so that questions about the most recent version of a file could be resolved by looking at the date of the file.

FONT LIBRARY

In most systems you will need to copy those fonts that you wish to use into a special folder or directory, such as the system directory—refer to specific font manufacturer's and application manuals for the procedures required in your case. Some font installation programs create their own directories. Unless your system requires that you store all fonts in one directory, it is a good idea to store different families of type in different directories or folders. This helps to shorten the list of fonts viewed at one time (if you have a very large font library), and can be helpful in distinguishing between fonts with cryptic coded file names like "??."

Create special folders that contain all of the fonts used by a particular project so they can be easily loaded as a group and transported to other directories or to other workstations involved in the project.

If you are working under Microsoft Windows, create and save different versions of WIN.INI and let the suffix of the file name indicate the name of the font that would be downloaded when you boot the system—such as WIN.GAR for Garamond. When you want to download Garamond, copy (do not rename) WIN.GAR to WIN.INI and reboot to download.

Create a Template for Page Layout

Besides the carefully controlled organization of disk files, the second important factor in making each document's production run smoothly is a template system. As already defined in Chapters 4, 5, and 6, a template is simply a dummy publication that is already set up with the basic design elements called for by the design specifications. There are packaged template systems available for some page-layout packages, but our use of the word template indicates template systems that you create for your own publication projects.

It is a good idea to develop a template system for any publication project that will require more than one page-layout file. Books, reports, manuals, newsletters, and magazines are candidates for template systems whereby a single template is used to create a separate page-layout file for each chapter, section, or issue of the publication. Shorter documents such as price lists, menus, ads and brochures are candidates for template systems if you will be producing more than one document with the same or similar layout.

Templates save time in large production projects by capturing a few of the steps required to set up a new document once, so the same steps do not have to be repeated every time a similar document is started. A template might consist of no more than page size, margin specifications, and dummy headers and footers for a simple document. A more complex template might include ruled lines, guides for aligning objects across facing pages, dummy headlines or text labels, and repeating graphic elements. The template systems for newsletters and magazines can be very elaborate compared with most types of documents.

DEFINING THE PAGE SETUP

Whenever you start a new document in any page-layout program, you should specify the size of the sheets of paper you will be using, the orientation of the printed image, and the text margins before adding any elements to the pages. Figure 7.16 shows how the margin settings affect a page.

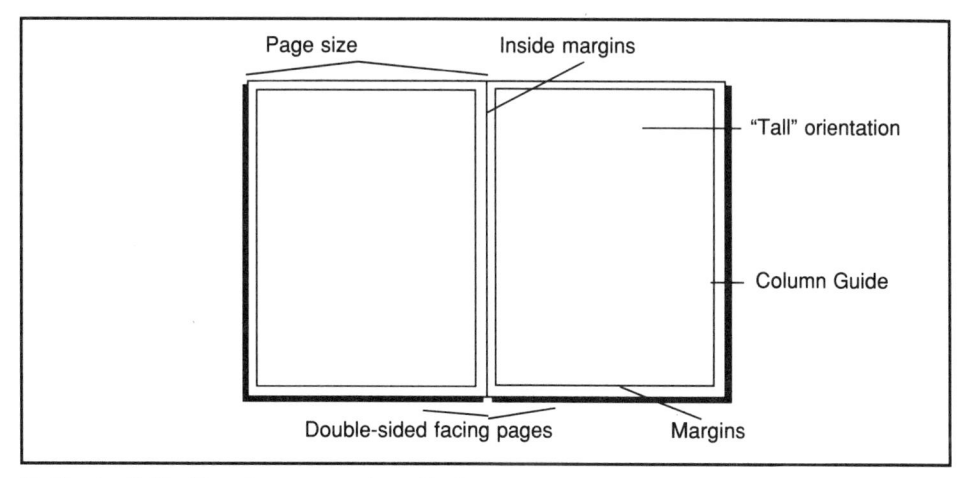

■ **Figure 7.16** How the page setup affects a page.

Other options such as double-sided printing, the number of pages, and the starting page number can be changed at any time during document production. Some of the reasons for changing or not changing these settings after you have started building the document are given under each of the headings below.

Page Size

Most page-layout programs offer several predefined page sizes that match the standard paper sizes available, and some let you specify any size up to 17 by 22 inches. There are three standard American paper sizes and four European standards:

Letter	8½ by 11 inches
Legal	8½ by 14 inches
Tabloid	11 by 17 inches
A4	210 by 297 millimeters
A3	297 by 420 millimeters
A5	148 by 210 millimeters
B5	250 by 176 millimeters

The page size specified in the page-layout program is not necessarily the exact size of the paper that you will be feeding into a laser printer. Most precisely, the size you specify will dictate the measurements of the page border on the screen. You can specify tabloid size in some programs, for example, and print it out in pieces on 8½ by 11 sheets.

Although the page size is usually the same size the final publication will be once it is mass-produced, bound and trimmed, you can deliberately specify larger page sizes for special layouts. For example, Figure 7.17, shows one publication that specified an 8½ by 11 inch page size for a document that would eventually be trimmed to 6 by 9 inches. Nonprinting guides, margins, and columns were used to define the 6 by 9 layout area, and the area beyond that was used to print project-control information, crop marks, registration marks, and instructions to the printer. The printed pages show crop marks that were created with the line tool on the master pages.

PAGE COMPOSITION **273**

PRINT OPTIONS

☐ Paper Size [8 1/2] X [11]
☐ Page Size   [6]   X [9]
■ Crop Marks
☐ Tiling

6 by 9 booklet pages printed on 8½ by 11 paper with automatic crop marks.

☐ Paper Size [8 1/2] X [11]
☐ Page Size   [8 1/2] X [11]
☐ Crop Marks
☐ Tiling

6 by 9 booklet pages printed on 8½ by 11 paper with crop marks and other elements entered on the master pages.

☐ Paper Size [8 1/2] X [11]
☐ Page Size   [11]   X [17]
■ Crop Marks
■ Tiling

Tabloid pages print "Tiled" on 8½ by 11 paper.

☐ Paper Size [12] X [20]
☐ Page Size   [11] X [17]
■ Crop Marks
☐ Tiling

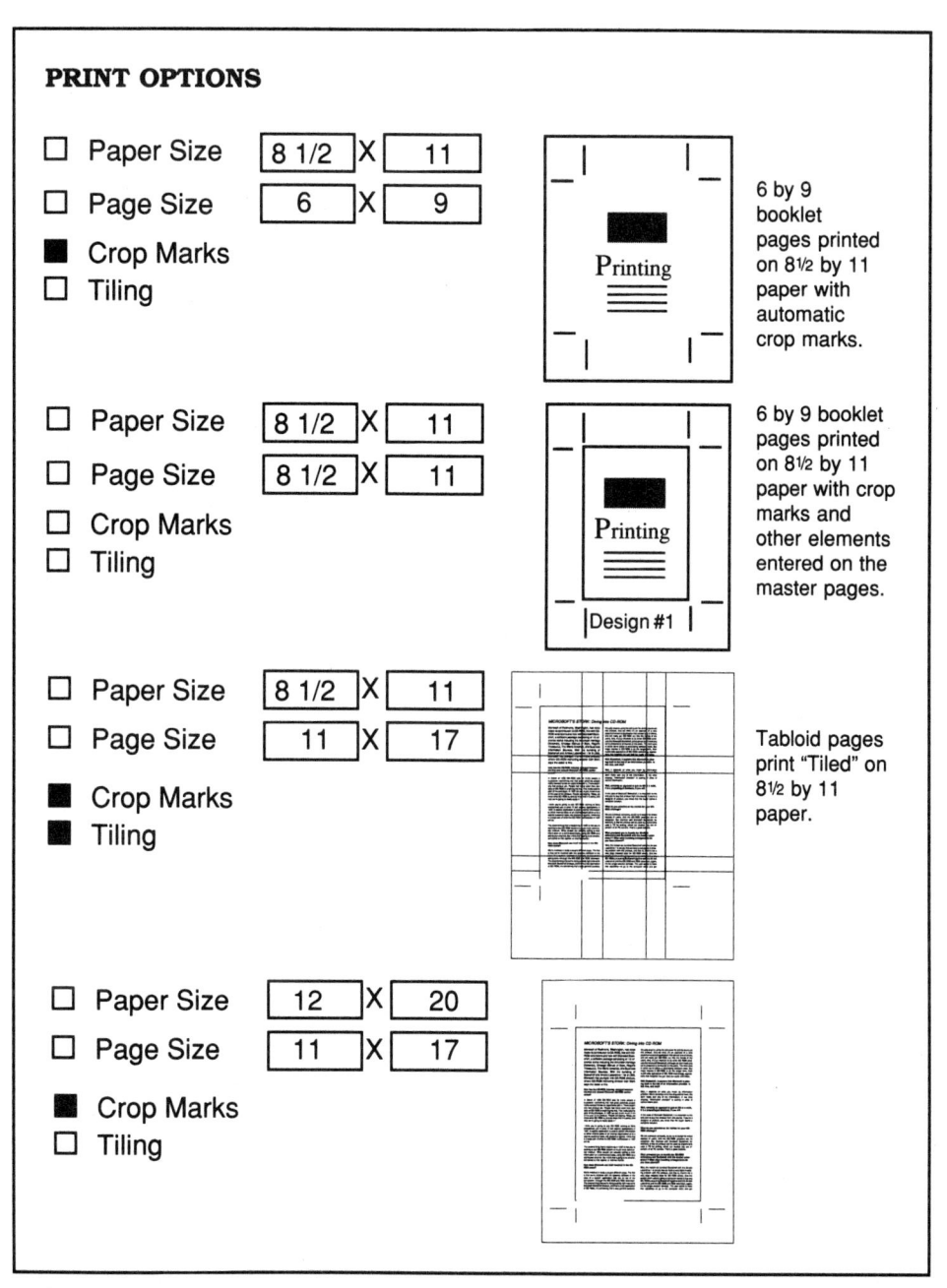

■ **Figure 7.17** Page size is not always the same as the paper in your printer tray, and not the same as the final publication pages.

Besides the size of paper you choose, the exact width and length of each page will also be determined by the next option—orientation.

Orientation

With most page-layout programs you can orient your pages to print either tall or wide. The most common page size and orientation for business documents is tall 8½ by 11. Other variations are shown in Figure 7.18.

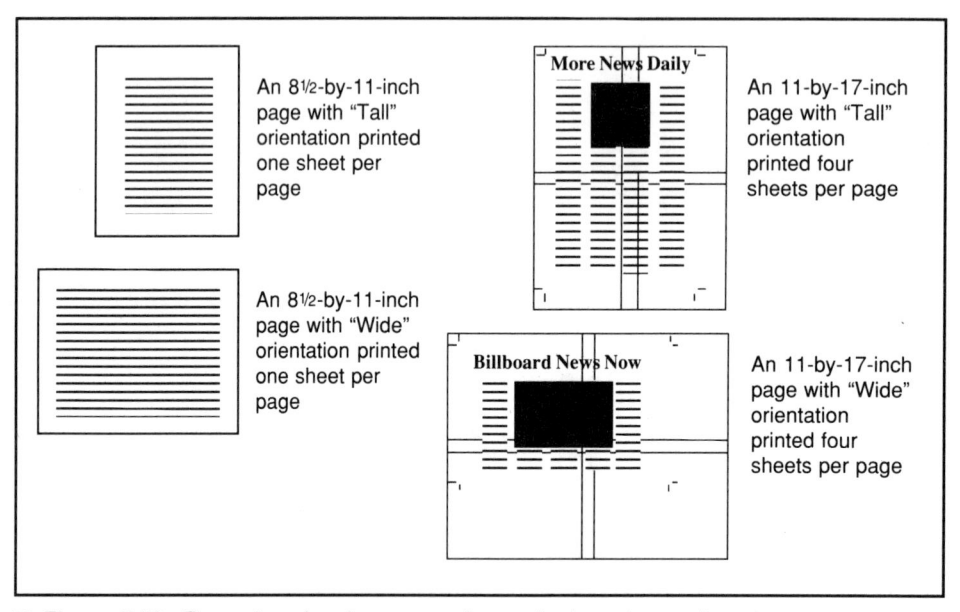

■ **Figure 7.18** Examples of various page size and orientation settings.

Margins

The page margins set up in the template will hold for all pages of the document, and they usually cannot be changed for individual pages within a file. (You can change the effective margins on individual pages by moving column guides, but you cannot change the page margins themselves.)

Margins are normally measured from the edges of the page. That is, margins are measured from the page size, which is not necessarily the paper size, as explained earlier in this chapter. With page-layout applications that allow you to position text and graphics objects outside of the margins, the margins should reflect the limits to be used for text and column settings on numbered pages (Figure 7.19) rather than the limits allowed for graphics and for master page elements.

Figure 7.19 Margins should define the limits of the text area.

Rule of Thumb:

Use Margins to Control Placed Text

Position the headers and footers outside of the page margins. Use the top and bottom margins to define the length of the columns in placing text on other pages.

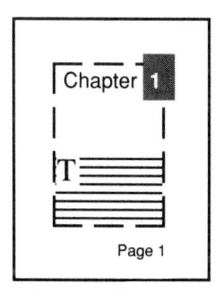

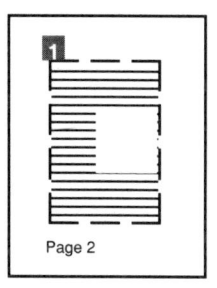

Figure 7.20 The headers and footers are normally positioned outside the page margins.

The margins are displayed in the measure specified, and most page-layout programs offer a choice between several units of measure (Table 7.2).

Table 7.2
Equivalent Measures: Inches, Millimeters, Picas and Points, and Ciceros (with Common Measures in Bold)

Paper	Inches	MM	Picas	Ciceros
	.04	**1**		
	.167		**1p0**	
	.177			**1c0**
	.25	6.36	**1p6**	1c4.9
	.5	12.7	**3p0**	2c9.9
	.75	19.06	**4p6**	4c2.8
	1	25.4	**6p0**	5c7.8
A5	5.827	**148**	34p11.6	32c10.7
B5	6.929	**250**	41p6.9	39c1.4
A4, A5	8.268	**210**	49p7.3	46c8
Letter, Legal	**8.5**	215.9	51p0	47c11.7
B5	9.842	**176**	59p.07	55c6.7
Letter, Tabloid	**11**	279.4	66p0	62c1.1
A4	11.693	**297**	70p1.9	66c0
Legal	**14**	355.6	84p0	79c0.3
A3	16.535	**420**	99p2.6	93c4
Tabloid	**17**	431.8	102p0	95c11.5

With some layout programs, if you change the margins after you start building a document, the text and graphics that have already been positioned in the document will shift to match the new upper left-hand corner specifications on every page. Generally speaking, however, it's a good idea to stick with the margins you first set up on the template, rather than change them after beginning any page layouts.

Double-sided Documents and Facing Pages

The double-sided document option of a page-layout program does not mean that pages will be printed on both sides of the paper as it comes out of the laser printer or whatever printer you are using. It means that you *intend* to have the final pages reproduced as a two-sided document, using either xerographic or offset printing equipment, like the examples shown in Figure 7.21.

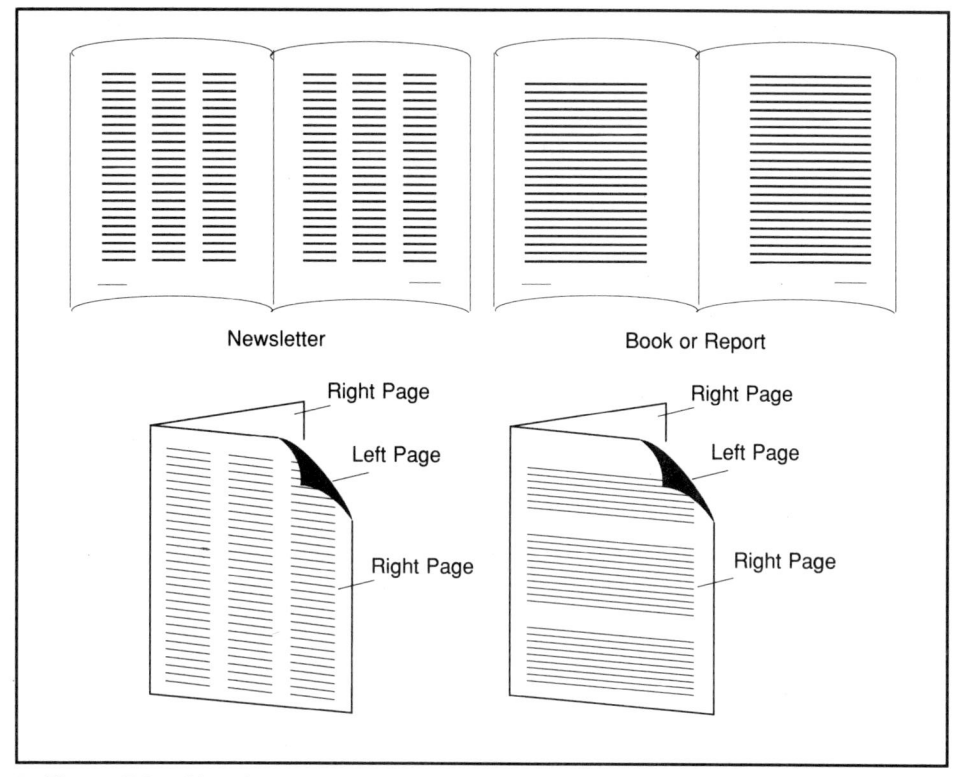

■ **Figure 7.21** Newsletters, magazines, books, and some business reports are created as double-sided publications, then offset-printed and bound.

When you choose the double-sided option, the measure specified for the inside margin will be applied to the left margin of odd-numbered pages, and to the right margin of even-numbered pages. The inside margin is often wider than the outside margin, to accommodate the binding (Figure 7.22). With double-sided documents you also have two master pages—one for even-numbered left pages and one for odd-numbered right pages. You can set up different running headers and footers for left- and right-side pages.

278 THE ELECTRONIC PUBLISHER

Single-sided publication: Displays one page on the screen at a time. One master page or grid for all pages of the document. Same header and footer on every page. Left margin is wide enough to accommodate binding.

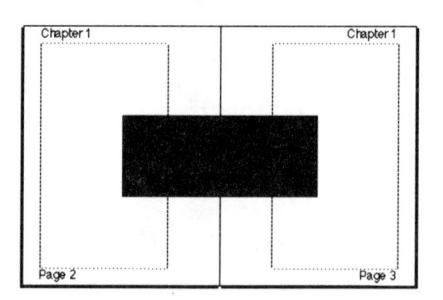

Double-sided publication: Option of viewing one page on the screen at a time or two facing pages. Option of bleeding an illustration across two pages. Two master pages, one for left (even-numbered) pages and one for right pages. Header and footer can differ between left and right pages. Inside margins are wide enough to accommodate binding.

■ **Figure 7.22** Single- vs. double-sided documents.

The *facing-pages* option available with some layout programs lets you view pages that will face each other in double-sided printing. This can be useful when you are designing pages with graphics that bleed across the inside margin, or when you want to be sure that the overall two-page layout is balanced.

The facing-pages option can also be used as an efficiency tool: it is much quicker to layout pages and change pages when you can see two pages at once.

Rule of Thumb:

Using the Double-sided Option for Single-sided Publications

In building long single-sided documents, set them up as double-sided documents and view facing pages as you are working. If the right and left margins are the same measure, you can print the publication as a double-sided publication with identical left and right master pages. Otherwise, if the left and right margins are not equal, you will need to turn the double-sided option off before printing the final pages.

Of course, a double-sided document can be set up as a single-sided publication if the inside and outside margins are the same measure and the master pages are identical. In most cases however, it is a good idea to use the double-sided option for any document that will be reproduced double-sided, and turn the facing-pages option off if you want to work on one page at a time.

Number of Pages in the Template

With some page-layout programs you can define the number of pages before you start building the document, or, if the program does not offer this feature or you don't know how many pages it will be, you can add or delete pages as you work.

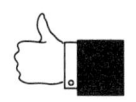

> **Rule of Thumb:**
>
> Always Enter a Page Estimate or Limit
>
> If you don't know exactly how many pages you will need, enter a rough estimate whenever possible. If you don't use all of the pages, delete the extra pages before printing.

Target Printer

The target printer is part of the template specifications for most page-layout programs. If your installation has more than one type of printer, or if you are using a font cartridge system and you have more than one cartridge, then it is important to define the target printer that you will be using for the *final* printouts before you start a new document, and stick with that setting throughout the production cycle.

For the full discussion of the differences between printers, how to install and select them, and how they can affect your document design and production, see Chapter 3, Typography, and Chapter 8, Preparing Mechanicals.

Building Master Pages

Most page-layout programs offer a feature whereby you can set up repeating elements on master pages for the publication. Any text, graphics, or guides set on the master page will appear on every page in the document; any text, graphics, or guides set on a numbered page will apply to that page only.

Settings that are normally made on the master pages are shown in Figure 7.23, and these include column guides, running headers and footers, and non-printing guides that define the basic grid system that underlies the document's design. Usually the settings made on the master pages can be changed on individual pages as needed—you can move column guides, or suppress headers and footers.

280 THE ELECTRONIC PUBLISHER

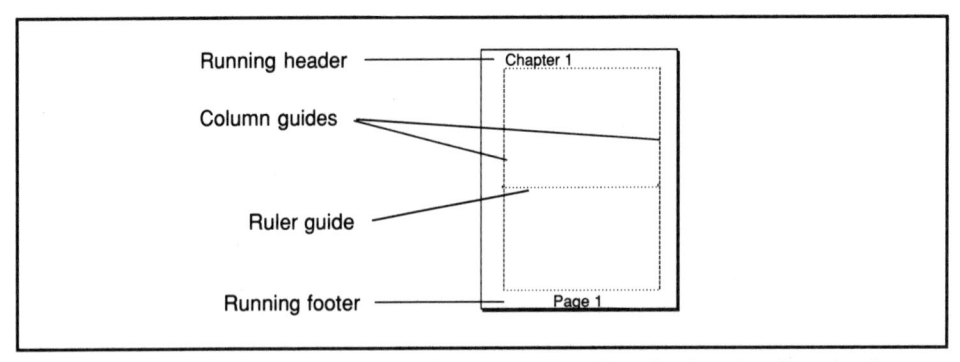

■ **Figure 7.23** Master page elements: Column guides. Running header. Running footer. Ruler guides that define grid. Other repeating elements.

Figure 7.24 shows how left and right master pages affect numbered pages. Those elements that are set up on the right master page will appear on every page of a single-sided document, but only on odd-numbered pages of double-sided documents. Elements that are set up on the left master page will appear on all even-numbered pages of double-sided documents. If you have selected the double-sided and facing-pages options, you will be able to work on both master pages at once. (Elements defined for one master page usually do not affect the other; you must build two master pages for double-sided documents).

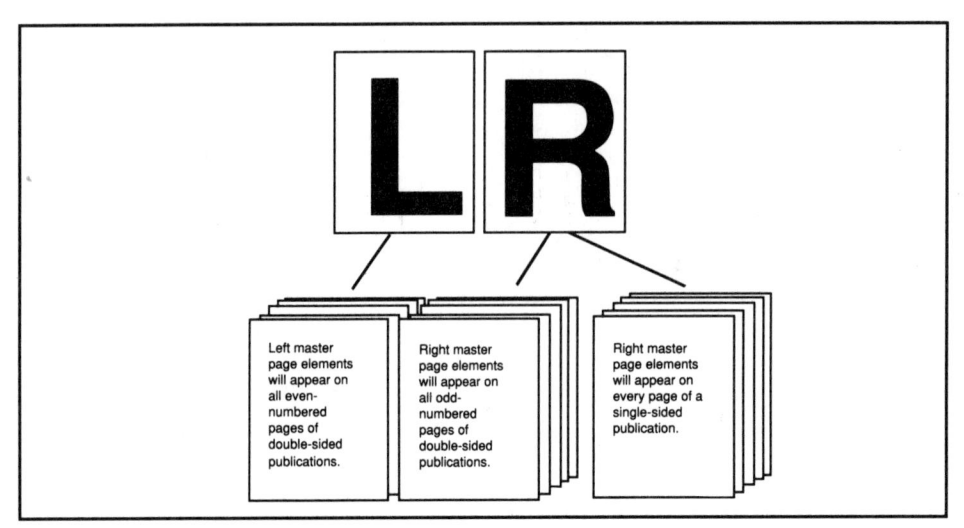

■ **Figure 7.24** How left and right master page settings affect numbered pages.

CREATE A MASTER GRID

We normally think of a grid as simply the page margins and column guides for a publication. Of course these are the basic elements of any grid system. Professional designers often use grid systems that are much more elaborate than that, however, as described in Chapter 4, Page Design. The grid can include ruler guides as well as graphic elements such as hairline rules between columns. The principle in designing a grid for the master pages is to identify the relative position of all the basic elements that will appear throughout the document.

Some examples of grid systems are shown in Figure 7.25. For a more complete discussion of using the grid system in design, see Chapter 4.

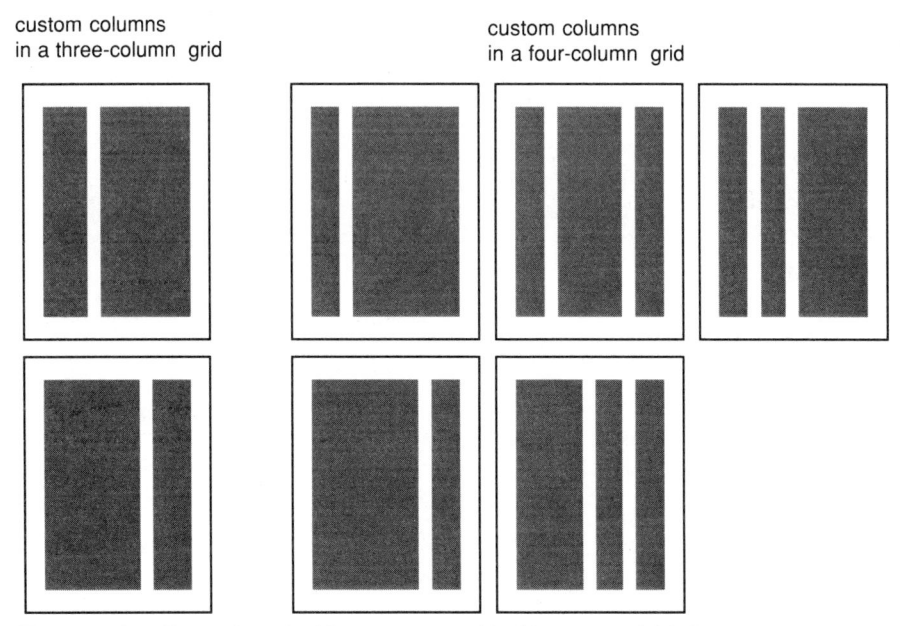

■ **Figure 7.25** Examples of grid systems used in Chapter 4 of this book.

The grid for left pages may differ from that for right pages. More likely, however, the grid itself will be the same on all pages; only the text of the headers and footers will differ between pages.

Setting Column Guides

Most page-layout programs' normal default setting is one column. You can specify the number of column guides, up to the limits defined by the program. In practice, you should rarely run into this limit, since most publications have no more than five columns on a page.

In most page-layout programs you select a number of columns and specify the amount of space you want between each column. The page-layout program takes these figures and divides the page into equal columns between the page margins (Figure 7.26). In most cases you can also specify unequal columns and customize the layout to meet your needs. Column guides will automatically define the width of text that is placed or pasted in the column.

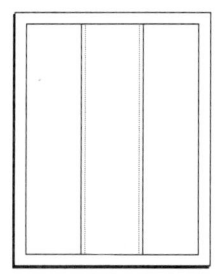

■ **Figure 7.26** The page-layout program divides the page into columns of equal width.

Using the Ruler Line to Position Objects

The ruler line is used to display or hide the horizontal and vertical ruler lines at the top and left edges of the screen (Figure 7.27). Ruler lines can be used to help position guides, text, and graphics on the page; to measure distances or to draw or scale graphics to fit an area.

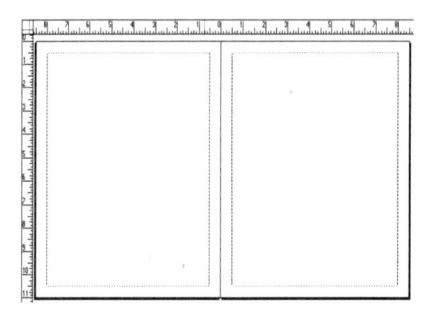

■ **Figure 7.27** The ruler command displays or hides the ruler line.

Choosing the Unit of Measure

As mentioned earlier, you can change the preferred unit of measure at any time without affecting the document—only the ruler line and other displays that show measurements will change. You may choose to work with one unit of measure throughout the production, or to switch between the different measures (using points for measuring type and vertical spaces between elements; picas for margins, columns, gutters and alleys; and inches for column lengths and for scaling figures, for example).

In most page-layout programs, the number of increments displayed along the ruler line will vary depending on the size in which you are currently viewing the page (Figure 7.28). The ruler line will show finer increments of measure in enlarged views, such as 200 percent, than it will show in reduced views.

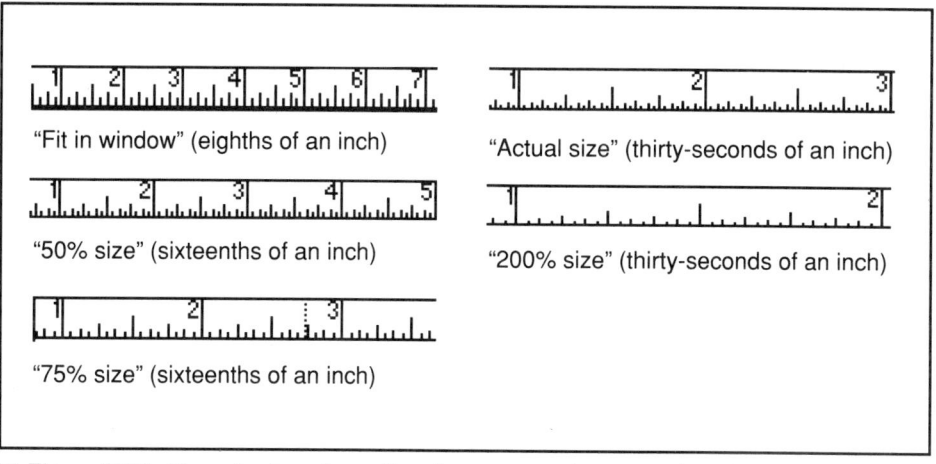

"Fit in window" (eighths of an inch)

"Actual size" (thirty-seconds of an inch)

"50% size" (sixteenths of an inch)

"200% size" (thirty-seconds of an inch)

"75% size" (sixteenths of an inch)

■ **Figure 7.28** The ruler line shows finer increments of measure in enlarged views than in reduced views of the page.

Working with Nonprinting Guides

Nonprinting guides include any of the various dotted and dashed lines that might be displayed on the screen in a page-layout package but they do not print out. These include the page margins, column guides, and ruler guides (Figure 7.29), and some programs offer the option of positioning additional guides manually or displaying a square grid all over the page.

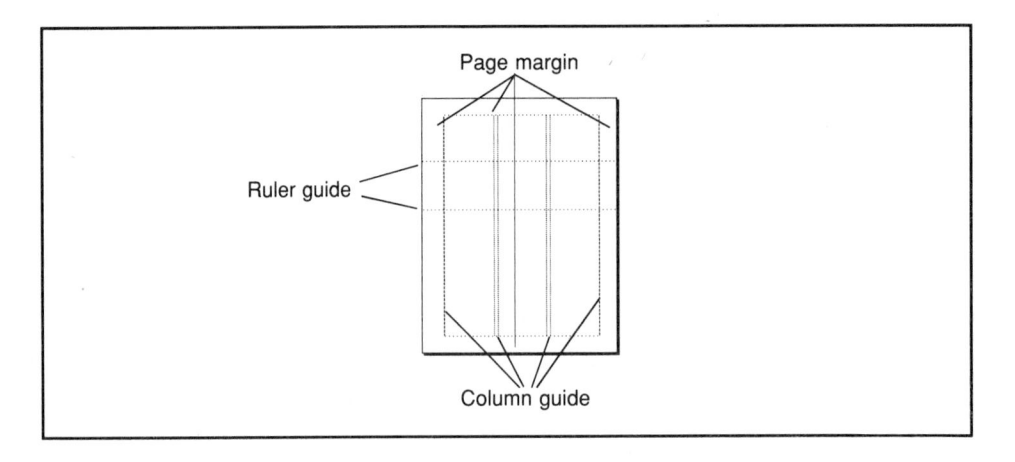

Figure 7.29 Nonprinting guides include page margins, column guides, and ruler guides.

The Zero Point

The zero point is the point of reference used in the design specifications when indicating position. Normally, the zero point falls at the top left-hand corner of the page. For double-sided publications viewed under the facing pages option, the zero point can fall at the top right-hand corner of left pages.

Some programs let you move the zero point to any location. You can select a custom zero point in the template for a document, or you can move the zero point many times while you are building pages.

Rule of Thumb:

When to Move the Zero Point

Move the zero point whenever you want to measure the size of an object, or scale a graphic or a column to match a specific size. Keep the zero point at the top left-hand corner of the page when you want to position an object relative to other objects on the page.

HEADERS AND FOOTERS

The template for a document should include running headers and footers as well as automatic page numbering.

PAGE COMPOSITION 285

ADDING GRAPHIC ELEMENTS

Besides text and guides, master pages can include graphics that have been created in the page-layout program or placed from other programs. We have already mentioned that the grid system might include hairline rules between each column, for instance. Figure 7.31 shows some examples of documents that incorporate graphics on the master pages.

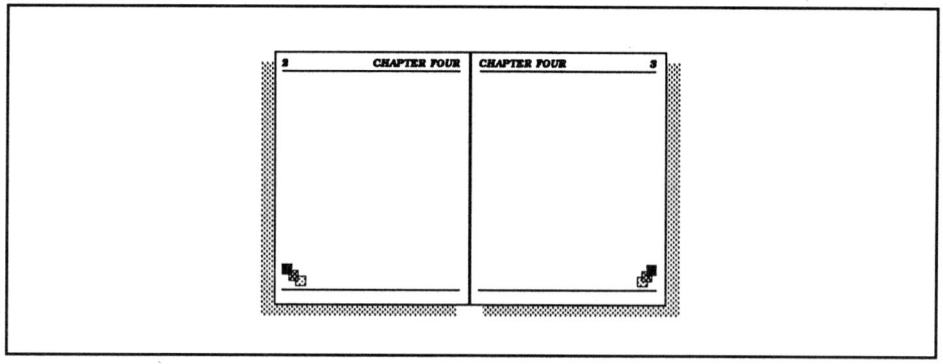

■ **Figure 7.30** Examples of master pages that include hairline rules and other graphics drawn in the page-layout program.

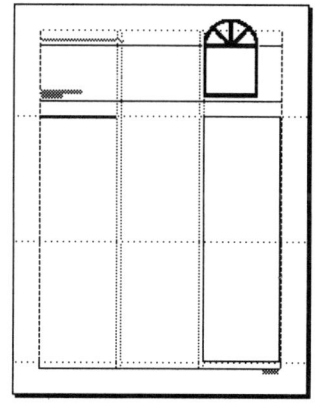

■ **Figure 7.31** The master pages can also include graphics from other programs, such as logos or section icons.

Remember that the guiding principle behind putting something on a master page is that it appears on all or most of the pages of the document. Once you are on a numbered page of the document, you can suppress all or parts of the master page elements using one of the techniques described later in this chapter.

Once the master pages are set up, you are ready to begin on page 1, using the page-layout program's commands to bring in graphics and text from other programs, or using the page-layout program's built-in text and graphics tools.

Create Individual Page Layouts

The process of building finished page layouts consists of designing each individual page layout (to the extent that variations are allowed by the design specifications), determining the most efficient approach to the page-layout process (graphics or text first?), importing or typing the text, importing or drawing the graphics, and fitting the text and graphics to the page.

METHODS OF OPERATION

Up to this point you have learned that it is best to build the master pages before going on to build individual pages, and that you can easily add or remove pages or hide master items on selected pages. In actually building a document, however, it will help you to study various methods or sequences of operations before deciding on the one that suits you best.

Sketching Page Layouts

Publications with very complex grid systems may require the designer's attention throughout the production cycle. This is especially true for magazines and newsletters that incorporate display ads of various sizes throughout the publication. The designer can work ahead of the production team to specify where ads are to be placed and how articles will jump from one page to another, using one of the techniques described in Chapter 4.

If the designer made rough page layouts using the page-layout application, this same rough file can be used as the starting point in placing the finished text and graphics files on each page when they are ready.

PAGE COMPOSITION   **287**

Rule of Thumb:

Build up a Page Layout like a Painting

An electronic publication need not be built linearly—front to back, page by page. A publication can be constructed in layers, just as painters work on canvas: first they draw the rough outline on the canvas in pencil, then they gradually add layers of paint.

In electronic page layout, the pencil sketch is the basic grid system. Shaded boxes can be used to reserve certain areas for planned graphics and particular articles. The gradually layers of paint are the text and graphics that are brought in from other programs to replace the place holders.

If the template for the publication is rather complex, thumbnails of the template can be printed out and marked up with instructions to the production team (Figure 7.32).

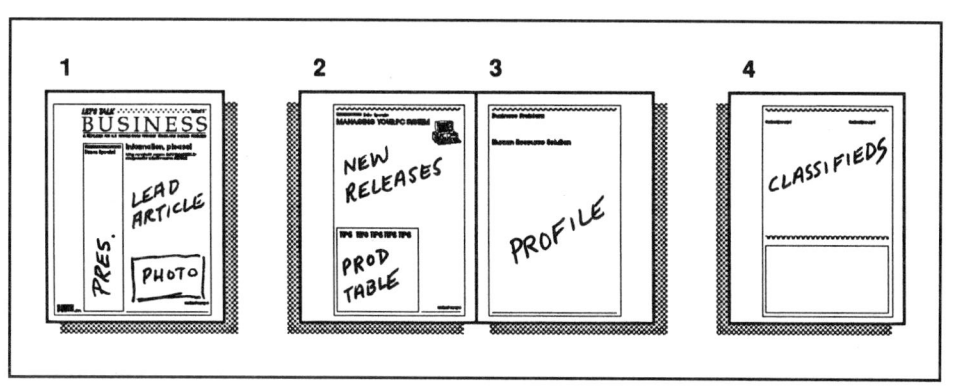

■ **Figure 7.32** Thumbnails of the template can be printed out, marked up, and distributed to the production team for reference.

Working on Facing Pages

With most page-layout packages and some word processing programs, you can work on views of facing pages for double-sided publications. This can be an advantage during both the design and production phases when, in designing each page layout, you want to consider the overall impact of the open publication on the reader, or you want to create graphics images that bleed from one page to the other.

Determine the Length of Each Page-layout File

Keep each text file (from the word processing program) confined to a single page-layout file if possible. Otherwise, the text blocks will not be linked between documents, and you might want to break the text file into parts for convenience during production. In either case, problems can arise when the text is edited later if the blocks are not linked to each other.

For example, don't let articles or chapters jump to more than one page-layout file. The size of each file is limited by the page-layout package or by your own decisions on how to divide a large document into separate files. Remember that you don't want to build a document that is too large to be backed up onto floppy disks.

List Repeated Steps

In a large production project, it is a good idea to list the steps that will be repeated throughout the production cycle, regardless of how simple the steps may seem.

1. Type and format the text files in the word processing program and store them in the subdirectory for this document.
2. Open the page-layout template document for this document, and modify the headers and footers to reflect the issue number (for periodicals) or chapter or section name (for books and reports). Save the modified template under the new section name.
3. Place the text on consecutive pages in the document, working in Fit-in-Window view until all text is placed.

> **Rule of Thumb:**
>
> Start a Page in Fit-in-Window View
>
> Start building each page by working in Fit-in-Window view, letting the snap-to effect of the guides help you place text and graphics from other programs. Change to actual size or closer views to type or edit text or to draw graphics. Change to 200 percent to work with small type (eight points or less) and to align graphics and text precisely without guides.

4. Go back to the beginning of the document, and work in 50 percent view, making formatting corrections as necessary, and opening up spaces for figures. Place the figures, scaling, and cropping as needed.
5. Print and proof drafts.
6. Edit page-layout file, print and proof finals.
7. Back up and archive the disk files.

CHANGE GRID AS NECESSARY ON INDIVIDUAL PAGES

Once you have built your master pages, some page-layout programs let you suppress or hide all of the master guides, text, and graphics from an individual page. You can use the program's command to eliminate all of the master elements, then use the program's text and graphics tools to add only those elements you wish to use on a selected page.

If you want to suppress only a part of the master-page elements, you can hide them in some page-layout programs by covering them with white boxes—rectangles created with a box tool and given a shade of white and a line style of none. This trick won't work with all printers. (Some printers cannot print reverse type or white boxes.)

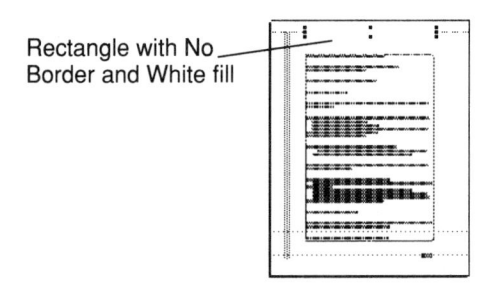

■ **Figure 7.33** Hiding parts of the master-page elements with white boxes.

USE THE SNAP-TO EFFECT

With most page-layout programs, all guides—page margins, column guides, and ruler guides—have a snap-to effect: they will pull the pointer or the edges of a graphic or a block of text into position when you bring the object close to the guide (Figure 7.34). This is extremely useful when you want to align objects quickly and precisely, especially when you are working in reduced views.

290 THE ELECTRONIC PUBLISHER

Text and graphics automatically snap to nearby margins or to an invisible grid of crossed lines

Turn the snap-to effect OFF if you want more flexibility in positioning text and graphics

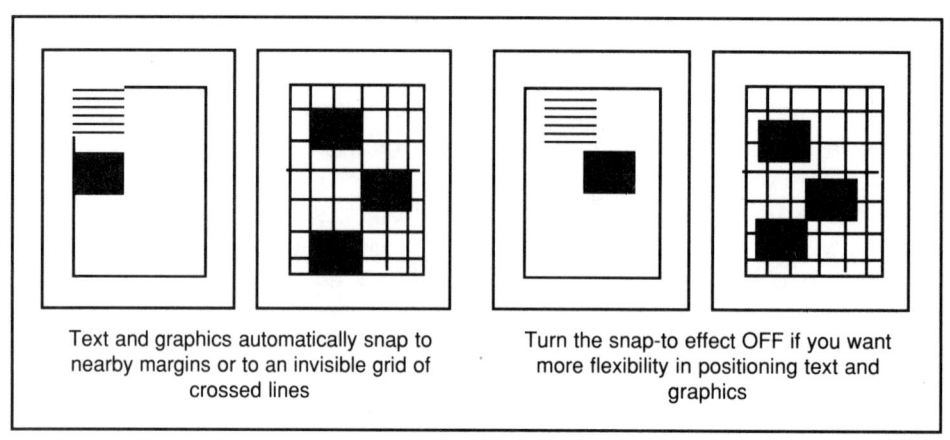

■ **Figure 7.34** The snap-to effect.

Sometimes you may prefer to work with the snap-to effect turned off—as when you are forcing something into a position outside of the basic grid structure. For example, when you are drawing a hairline rule between two columns, you do not want the crossbar or the rule to "snap to" either column guide.

USE ALIGNMENT COMMANDS

WYSIWYG (what you see is what you get) refers to what you see on the screen as compared with what prints out. Highly accurate WYSIWYG systems produce 100 percent fidelity between the screen and the printer. Most desktop publishing systems and applications are not 100 percent WYSIWYG. Discrepancies occur because fonts displayed on the low-resolution screen are shown as bit maps, while high-resolution printers refine the letters during the printing process.

One way to work with the discrepancies is to always use the application commands for aligning text, rather than visually positioning text on the screen display. For example, if you want two lines of text to be centered, use the Centering command for both lines, rather than insert spaces at the beginning of each line until the two lines appear to be centered. Always use tabs rather than spaces to align tabular columns.

FORCE LEFT AND RIGHT PAGES

You can force a left (even-numbered) page to fall on the right (odd-numbered) by inserting a blank page in front of it. In publications that are composed of many sections, each section might be created as a separate file, with each file always starting with an odd page number (Figure 7.35).

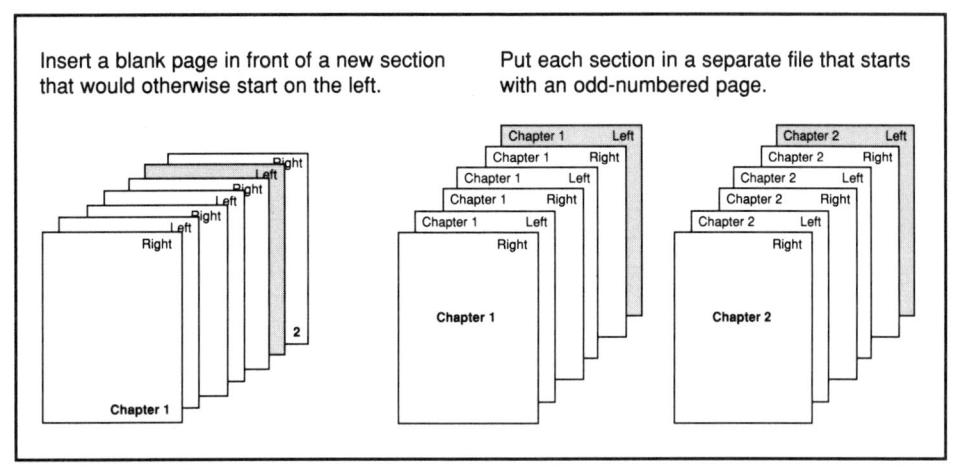

■ **Figure 7.35** Two ways of forcing new sections to start on a right page

POSITION TEXT

There are three ways of entering text on a page in most page-layout programs: you can type text directly using the program's text tool, you can use the program's import command to bring in text that has been typed using a word processing program (or other programs that can save data as text), or you can use the Paste command to pull in text from the clipboard. You'll see the pros and cons of each of these methods in the sections below.

Typing Text

A page-layout program's text tool is used primarily for editing text, rather than typing it in from the keyboard. Nevertheless, there will be many occasions when you will use the text tool to type in short segments of text. The format and position of the typed text will vary depending on where you position the text insertion point. For instance, if you position the text insertion point on an empty part of the page between two column guides, the typed text will be in the default character format and fall between the two column guides, snapping to the left column guide and automatically wrapping at the right column guide.

If you position the text insertion point within an existing block of text, the typed text will be inserted within the text block and it will have the same format as the text immediately to the left of the insertion point.

Changing the Default Settings for Text

Most text typed directly into a page layout will take on the default characteristics unless you specify otherwise. For example, if you want to change the typeface for the next text typed, first position the text insertion point, then use the page-layout program's commands to specify the font and alignment, then type the text. In this case, you will be setting new specifications for the current insertion point only.

Importing Text

Most publications that are longer than one page (and many one-page publications) will be composed of text that has been typed in a word processing program and placed in the page layout. Use the page-layout program's Import command to import text that has been typed in a word processor, or to import any data that has been saved as "text-only" from a spreadsheet or database program.

In most cases, it is better to place all of the text in the document before you go back and do any detailed text editing. It is a good idea to finish placing one whole text file before you start placing another. This is not a requirement of most page-layout programs—you can work with as many loose ends of unplaced text as you like. In practice, however, you may find that it becomes confusing to work with more than two text files in process at a time.

If the text has been formatted in a word processing program that is supported by the page-layout program, the import process will usually retain some of that formatting such as bold and italic words within paragraphs of normal body copy. If the placed text has not already been formatted in a word processing program, or if the page-layout program does not support the word processor and therefore cannot preserve the formatting, the text will take on the default format and type specifications. For example, placed text will take on the width of the column in which it is placed, and stop flowing when it reaches the bottom of the column, or when it runs into another object on the page.

Text editing and formatting is often a slower process in a page-composition program than it is in a word processing program, so it is a good idea to do as much editing and formatting as possible using the word processor, before importing the text into a page-layout package.

Efficiency Tip:

Working with Reverse Type

When working with reverse type on a separate black-box background (i.e., the black box is not simply part of the type specifications), put a nonreverse character at the end of the text. This way, if the reverse text falls on a white background you can still see where it is relative to other text and graphics.

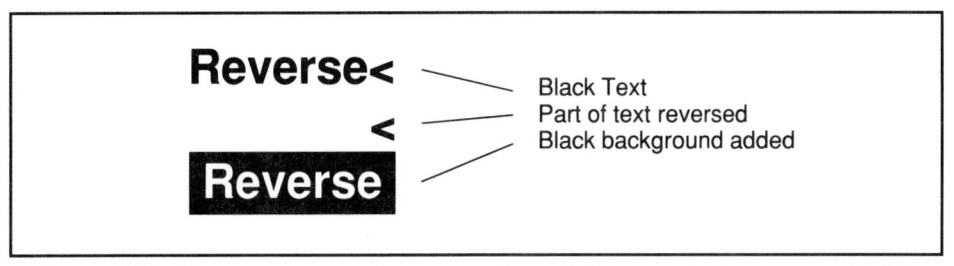

■ **Figure 7.36** Put a nonreverse character at the end of reverse text so you can find it no matter what the background; or use outline instead of reverse.

Formatting procedures for text—whether performed in the word processing program or the page-layout program—are described in Chapter 5.

IMPORT GRAPHICS

Page-layout programs let you import graphics that were created in other programs, adjust the size of graphics that were imported from other programs, and trim the edges from imported graphics—but you cannot edit imported graphics directly in the word processor.

It is usually a good idea to place graphics as you go along, and fit the text around them on each page before going on to a new page. Ideally, each page is complete before you go on to the next. In practice, however, there will be many cases where this guideline does not apply. For example, you might want to place all of the text first, leaving space for graphics to be positioned later, to be sure that the text will fit the number of pages allowed. In another case, such as a brochure that uses graphics as the primary communicators, you might want to position all of the graphics first and make the text wrap around them afterward.

Selecting, Moving, and Scaling Graphics

You can select, move, or scale graphics after they have been drawn or placed on the screen in most page-layout programs. Two-dimensional objects can have eight or more handles (guides used in scaling and cropping): one at each corner and one in the middle of each side, for example. When you drag one of the handles that falls in the middle of a side, you stretch the graphic along one axis only—in other words, you stretch the graphic out of proportion. When you drag one of the corner handles, you can stretch the graphic in two directions at once.

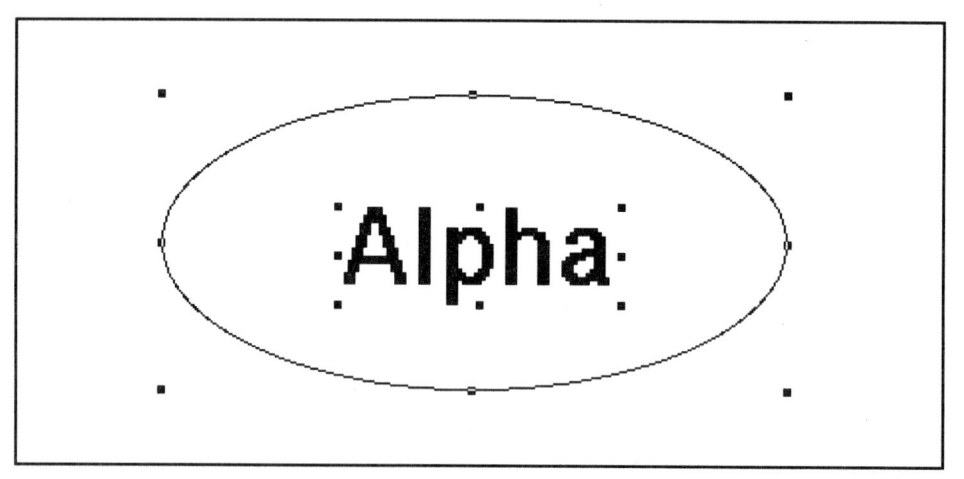

■ **Figure 7.37** Graphic objects that are selected usually display "handles"—small black squares that are used in scaling or cropping.

Rule of Thumb:

Handling Text Logos as Graphics

Although it is possible to create text logos by manually kerning letters in the page-layout package, you can also create them in a drawing program and kern the letters by making each one a separate object and positioning them as close together as you like. The advantage of importing a text logo from a drawing program is that you can change the size of the kerned logo the way you would change the size of any graphic object—by dragging a handle.

Cropping Graphics

Many page-layout packages let you crop (trim the edges from) graphic objects that are brought in from other programs. Cropping trims the edges from a graphic without changing the size of the remaining portion of the graphic.

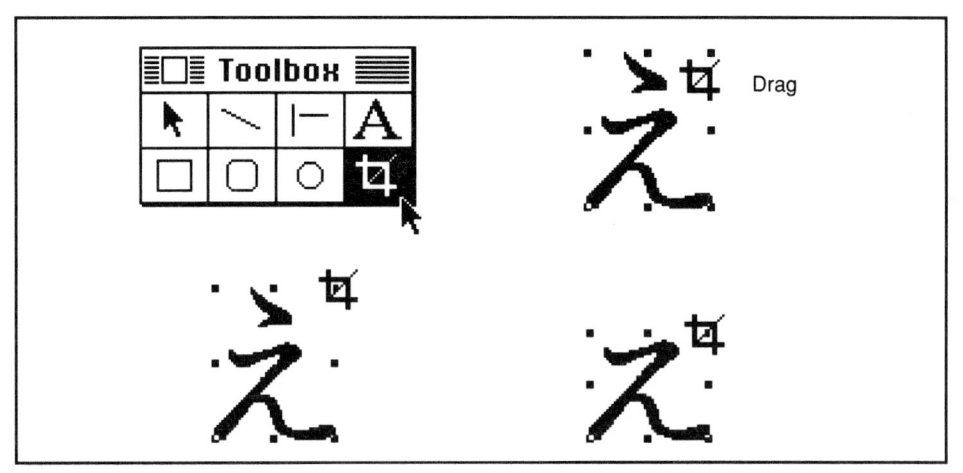

■ **Figure 7.38** Cropping graphics placed into PageMaker from other programs.

Rule of Thumb:

Crop images down to the essential elements, eliminating excess background and other superfluous elements.

Bleeding Graphics Across Pages

Be careful when producing page layouts that bleed off the edges of the paper or across facing pages. Figure 7.39 shows how part of an image that bleeds across two pages may be lost in the nonprinting edges of the paper, depending on the type of printer you are using. You can determine the limits of the margins for printing on your printer by printing out a page that is covered by a solid black box.

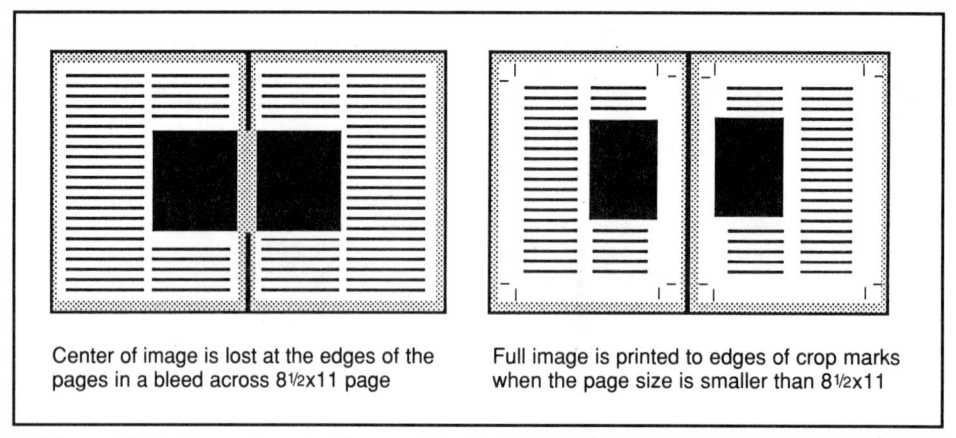

Center of image is lost at the edges of the pages in a bleed across 8½x11 page

Full image is printed to edges of crop marks when the page size is smaller than 8½x11

■ **Figure 7.39** Page size must be smaller than paper size in order to print true bleeds on most printers.

Wrapping Text Around Graphics

Some programs will automatically wrap text around graphics, while others let you wrap text around graphics by dividing the text into blocks of different widths. Remember that one suggested approach is to build each page completely before going on to the next, but you will find that the best approach to laying out a page can vary between documents or designs.

Special Handling of Captions

In most cases, you want text blocks to be linked continuously throughout a document or throughout an article or story, so that edits made to one part of the text will cause adjustments to all the line breaks and column breaks that follow. One exception to this rule is the treatment of figure captions (Figure 7.40). Once a caption is positioned next to a graphic, you do not want that text to be moved out of position when you later make edits to the text that precedes it. Some page-layout programs provide ways of automatically linking captions to illustrations, and these programs can actually move graphics from one page to another automatically when the text is edited. Most programs do not offer this feature, however, so careful planning is required in order to keep figures and captions together.

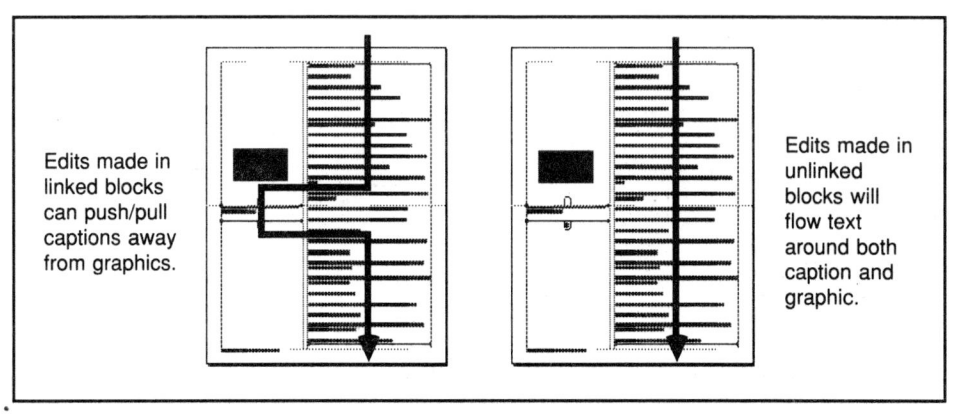

Figure 7.40 Make captions separate text blocks, unlinked to the body of the text.

There are four methods of making captions appear as separate blocks from the rest of the text:
- You can include the caption as part of the graphics file. The drawback is that text attached to graphics placed in page-layout programs cannot be edited directly. A second drawback is that the width and point size of the captions may vary between illustrations that are scaled to fit the page, unless this problem is anticipated in advance and accounted for in the graphics program.
- You can type each caption individually in the page-layout program. The drawback here is that the page-layout artist will be typing new text that has missed all of the copy edit rounds and proofreading that has taken place for the main body of the manuscript, with the risk of introducing new errors.
- You can type all of the captions into a separate caption file using a word processor, then place that file as a separate stream from the rest of the text. This is a good alternative when you don't know exactly where each figure will be placed in the final document. The drawback here is that the layout artist may need to determine where each figure should go by reading the text, thereby slowing down the production process tremendously.
- You can type the captions into the main text file, roughly where the graphics should fall. When you place the text, use the Cut and Paste commands (available in most page-layout programs) to separate them from the body of the text and to make them individual, unlinked blocks of text. This is the best solution in that the page-layout artist does not have to type new text or guess where the graphics should be placed.

THE ELECTRONIC PUBLISHER

Reserving Space for Manual Paste-up

Use black boxes to reserve space for photographs that need halftones dropped in by the printer. When printers prepare plates for pages that require halftones, they usually black out the space for the camera to create a window in the negative. You can save your printer the extra step of blacking out the area by using black boxes to reserve space for halftones.

Use white boxes to reserve space for line art that will be pasted in before it's sent to the printer. While the printer wants to lay halftones on transparent windows in the negative, the paste-up artist usually wants to paste figures down on a white background. Chapters 8 and 9 discuss manual paste-up techniques in more detail.

Rule of Thumb:
Whether you reserve an area with a black box or a white box, you can use small type to identify the figure to be hand-placed.

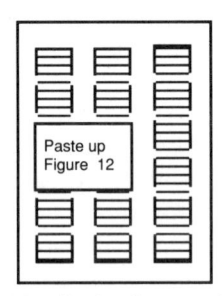

■ **Figure 7.41** Use small type to identify the figure to be hand-placed.

Use the Clipboard

Most page-layout programs have a Paste command to bring in text or graphics from the clipboard, provided that you have already put something into the clipboard using the Cut or Copy command (Figure 7.42). If the clipboard is a feature of the operating system, you can put text or a graphic into the clipboard while you are working in another program, then open the page-layout document and paste the text onto the page. You can also use the clipboard to paste from one page-layout file to another, or from one part of a publication to another.

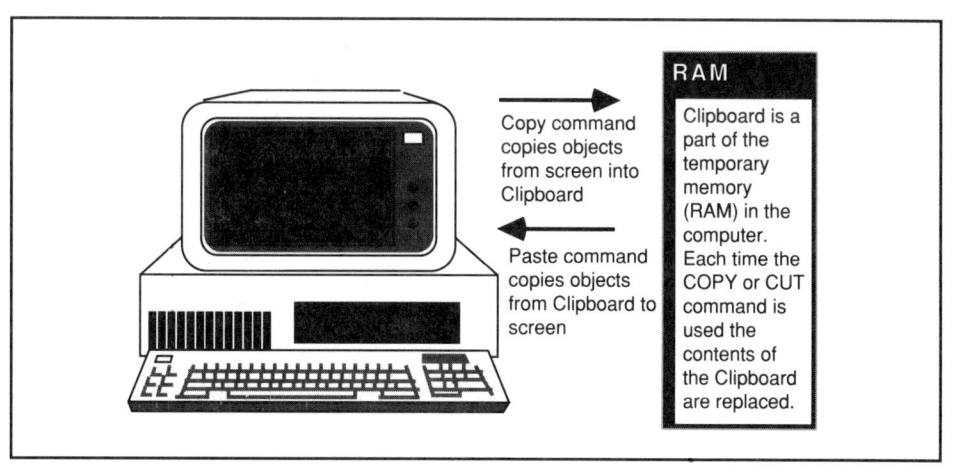

■ **Figure 7.42** Pasting text from the clipboard.

FULL-COLOR PAGE MAKEUP

Many of the expensive color prepress systems also have the ability to do full-page makeup: to position color images with type, rules, and all other page elements, and output complete-page or even multi-page (in imposition sequence) negatives that require little or no stripping. This sort of capability is also beginning to appear on desktop systems, again, in a rudimentary way.

Today, there are a handful of systems on the market (and more under development) that combine the features of a black-and-white page-composition system with color illustration (line art and continuous tone), separation, correction, and retouching.

While they still provide only "pleasing-color" quality, and while their price/performance levels are still impractical for most users, they indicate a major direction for development of electronic publishing technology. In fact, by providing text composition and pagination, they have leap-frogged color prepress systems (which merge text files with graphics, but do not allow users to compose and edit text on-screen).

As in monochrome electronic publishing, we are likely to see system functions at the low-end of the market begin to influence high-end systems. We are also likely to see cross-pull, with low-end systems gaining increased performance, and high-end systems tumbling in price. Eventually, we may reach price/performance levels that are practical for a wide segment of users.

As this happens, electronic publishers are going to face some critical decisions. Monochrome electronic publishing has made the tools, though not necessarily the skills, of the typographer and designer accessible to a wide range of users. Color publishing systems will open the gates to another once-highly specialized, esoteric part of the publishing process. As an electronic publisher, you'll have to make decisions about how much of the process you want to take over—how much control you want to exercise, and how much responsibility you're willing to accept.

Chapter 9 describes the issues involved in color processing in more detail.

Copy Fitting

Copy fitting is the process of making text fit into a predefined area—a column, a page, or a specific number of pages. Professional designers have traditionally approached the problems of copy fitting from two angles. First, based on the design specifications, they can estimate how many words (or characters) will fill the space allotted. This is how magazine editors operate when they assign authors articles of a specific word length. Second, the designer can take the text from the author and either estimate how much space that text will fill, or make up design specifications that will force the text to fit a specified area.

For suggestions on how to *cast* copy *before* the page-layout stage, see Chapter 3, Typography. Chapter 3 describes several methods of copy casting before the text is written—determining how many characters will fit on a page based on the type specifications—as well as estimating the amount of space that will be required to accommodate a delivered number of words.

It is during the page-layout process that the issue of copy fitting can be a major problem. What do you do when the text for a four-page newsletter runs to four and a half pages? How do you make a table of numbers fit a predefined area on the page? How can you force two columns to bottom out at the same measure when they are composed of mixed sizes of text? You can change the length of the text in a column using any of the techniques described here for generally fitting copy to a column or to a predefined number of pages.

One way of changing the overall amount of space taken up by the text is to change the width of the text. Another way is to change the point size. These methods are fine for copy fitting if you are literally designing the document as you go along, or designing the text deliberately to fit the space allowed. Additional methods of fitting copy *after* it has been written, without changing the design, are described under the following subheadings.

EDIT THE COPY

It is common for magazine and newspaper editors to add or delete words in the text in order to make copy fit a predefined space. This is usually the best approach to copy fitting, but when this approach is impractical, one of the other alternatives suggested here must be used.

ALLOW A RAGGED-BOTTOM MARGIN

Some publications—like most magazines and newspapers—enforce the rule that the text in each column throughout the publication must meet the same bottom margin. By relaxing this rule, you have greater flexibility in forcing text to fill the space allowed for it. For example, you can decide to vertically align adjoining columns on the same page or across facing pages, but let the bottom margin vary slightly from page to page.

In other words, if the text is only slightly too long or too short to fill the pages, and if the designer allows such flexibility, go through the document looking for widows and orphans, adjusting the bottom margin on each page to add or subtract lines.

ADD FILLERS

In newsletter and magazine format, you can expand the text to fit by extracting pull-quotes—short excerpts from the text that are printed in a larger type size than the body copy and framed in ruled lines (or otherwise separated from the flow of body text). You can develop simple formulas for adding space, such as those shown in Figure 7.43. Besides expanding text to fit the space, pull-quotes help break up the simple columnar grid of the pages. The design should include guidelines for setting and positioning fillers if this solution is allowed.

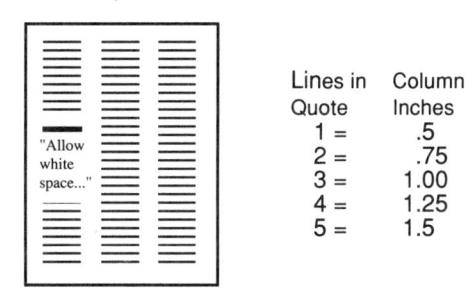

Lines in Quote	Column Inches
1 =	.5
2 =	.75
3 =	1.00
4 =	1.25
5 =	1.5

■ **Figure 7.43** Column inches required by the number of lines in quote = number of inches added.

ADJUST THE LEADING (LINE SPACING)

Changing the leading is a common method of fitting copy, and preferred over changing the specifications for typeface, size, or style once the design specifications are finalized. Whether you initially use the application's auto leading feature or specify the exact leading yourself, you can usually make fine adjustments in the leading (spacing between lines) in order to fit copy into a defined space. You can change the leading for the entire document, for selected text elements, or for selected pages only in order to make copy fit, but whichever approach you take in adjusting the leading, be consistent: change the leading on *all* of the body copy rather than on individual paragraphs. If you cannot or do not want to change the leading for an entire article or publication, change it for whole pages and keep the leading the same across columns on a single page.

This paragraph is exactly 100 characters long. This paragraph is exactly 100 characters long. 12/12 Times	This paragraph is exactly 100 characters long. This paragraph is exactly 100 characters long. 12/14 Times	This paragraph is exactly 100 characters long. This paragraph is exactly 100 characters long. 12/auto Times	This paragraph is exactly 100 characters long. This paragraph is exactly 100 characters long. 12/15 Times

■ **Figure 7.44** 12-point Times with 12, 14, 15, and auto leading.

If you are trying to fit a table of tabbed entries into a particular width of space, you can change the tabs and, if necessary, change the size of the type used. To fit a tabbed table to a particular length, you can adjust the leading as described above, or you can adjust the inter-paragraph spacing (Figure 7.45).

Table 1	Table 2
Item Price	Item Price
Shoes $5.00	Shoes $5.00
Taps $7.00	Taps $7.00
Bolts $10.00	Bolts $10.00
Table too short for space allowed.	Table extended by changing the leading to fill the frame.

■ **Figure 7.45** You can adjust tables to fill space available by changing the leading, or by changing the inter-paragraph spacing.

HYPHENATION AND JUSTIFICATION

Text is said to be justified when both the left and right margins are flush to the column edges. Because the process of justification is accomplished by adjusting the normal spacing between words and between letters, whereas text that is not justified has standard spacing between words and letters, the justification process can *reduce* the space between words and between characters within words. For this reason, justified text usually takes up less space than text that is not justified. Similarly, hyphenated text takes up less space than text that is not hyphenated.

The designer should be called in on any decisions to change the alignment or hyphenation settings in order to make copy fit. Justified text usually calls for hyphenation, especially when the columns are narrow. Otherwise, justified text that is not hyphenated tends to have more "rivers"—wide areas of white space within the text caused by forced spacing between words.

> Justified text requires less space than text which is not justified. Justified text requires less space than text which is not justified. Justified text requires less space than text which is not justified. Justified text requires less space than text which is not justified.
>
> Justified text requires less space than text which is not justified. Justified text requires less space than text which is not justified. Justified text requires less space than text which is not justified. Justified text requires less space than text which is not justified.

■ **Figure 7.46** Justified text requires less space than text that is not justified.

Justified text can also be fit to a given space by adjusting the spacing between words and letters, described next.

WORD AND LETTER SPACING

Some applications let you specify the ranges for adjusting the spaces between words and letters during the justification process. Most publishers are likely to accept the defaults for these settings rather than change them. You can change these settings to force copy to fit a given space, however, and you might want to change these settings as a deliberate design strategy for special publications such as ads and brochures.

If you think you can fit copy by making the spacing between words smaller, consider the tradeoffs: with a wide allowance for spacing between words and letters, the rivers of white space may seem wide in justified text, but fewer words will be hyphenated. Text with a narrow allowance for space between characters and words is likely to be highly hyphenated.

Spacing attributes:		OK	Tradeoff between tightening the spacing between words: wider rivers vs. more hyphenation. Tradeoff between tightening the spacing between words: wider rivers vs. more hyphenation.
Word space:	Letter space:	Cancel	
Minimum: 25 %	Minimum: 0 %		
Desired: 50 %	Maximum: 10 %		
Maximum: 100 %			
Hyphenation zone: 0.5 inches			

Normal (default) word spacing

Spacing attributes:		OK	Tradeoff between tightening the spacing between words: wider rivers vs. more hyphenation. Tradeoff between tightening the spacing between words: wider rivers vs. more hyphenation.
Word space:	Letter space:	Cancel	
Minimum: 100 %	Minimum: 0 %		
Desired: 200 %	Maximum: 50 %		
Maximum: 300 %			
Hyphenation zone: 0.5 inches			

Tighter word spacing to decrease rivers

■ **Figure 7.47** Tradeoff between tightening the spacing between words: wider rivers vs. more hyphenation.

It's a good idea to keep the defaults for word and letter spacing, unless you have some special effects in mind. Generally speaking, changing the word and letter spacing should be the last resort in copy fitting.

Printing

The ultimate goal of the production process is to print the publication on a high-resolution printer. Sometimes this output becomes the distribution copy or copies. More often, this output will become the camera-ready pages from which the document is reproduced using xerographic or offset printing equipment.

Rule of Thumb:

Save Your Publication Often

It's a good idea to save your publication immediately before using the Print command.

TYPE OF PRINTER

Publications that have been created using desktop applications can be printed on certain dot-matrix and laser printers and typesetters. It's a good idea to become familiar with the capabilities of your particular printer before producing publications. One difference between printers is the resolution in which they print (as discussed in Chapter 4). Some printers have a range of settings for resolution. Most printers can print pages of text at the higher resolutions, but pages with graphics might overload some printers' processing capabilities unless they are set to lower resolution.

Another major difference between printers is the number of built-in fonts that they have (as discussed in detail in Chapter 3). When a font is built into the printer, it is always available for any publication. Sometimes the fonts are available in replaceable cartridges that can be inserted into the printer. Fonts that are neither built into the printer nor built into the printer's cartridges can be downloaded to some printers.

Efficiency Tip:

Printing at Lower Resolutions

Use lower-resolution printing during the early stages of a project for faster printing of draft copies.

If you run into memory-overload problems printing a publication at 300 dots per inch, try printing it at 150 or 75 dots per inch.

In many cases you will go through the entire production sequence using the same printer for early proofs as for final masters. If you change the output printer for a publication from one type of printer to another, the new printer may substitute fonts automatically (in other words, replace fonts it doesn't have with those it does have), and the printed results may differ from what you see on the screen.

Warning:

Switching a publication from one printer to another—from a PostScript printer to a nonPostScript printer, for example—may cause unexpected changes to the page layouts.

TEST PRINTING A FEW PAGES

You should test print a few pages on a laser printer before you print a long document. Anticipate events that might slow down your production process or that call for special handling. For instance, if the document calls for a downloadable font that is not stored on the system at the time of printing, the application might pause the printing process automatically and wait for you to supply the font on disk, or the document might print out with a bit-mapped version of the font.

By printing a few sample pages you can predict the time required to print the entire publication. For example, if it takes 30 minutes to print a page—as it can when you use high-resolution scanned images—and you have only one printer, you will only be able to print 16 pages during one 8-hour day.

Another good reason for testing a few pages on the final printer is that there may be major differences between draft printer and final printer. Test a small sample on both printers early in the project to assess and adjust for differences, and develop a list of proofreading considerations that should be deferred until the document is printed on the final target printer.

For instance, some applications calculate line breaks based on the screen font rather than the width tables that will be used in the printer. This is especially true of word processors that do not offer WYSIWYG capabilities. In this case, you can expect to print several versions of the "final" on the target printer, making adjustments each time for bad breaks that you could not anticipate on the screen.

DOWNLOADING FONTS PERMANENTLY VS. TEMPORARILY

The first step in using a soft font is to follow the manufacturer's instructions and a utility program for downloading the fonts to your printer. In this step, the downloaded fonts are assigned numbers by which the printer will identify them. This is also the step in which you specify whether the fonts are to be permanently or temporarily downloaded.

To say that a font is permanently downloaded is slightly misleading. To be more accurate, the only truly "permanent" fonts are hard-coded into the chips, and these are by definition not downloadable. In reference to downloadable fonts, the term permanent refers to downloading a font into the printer's memory at the beginning of a session, where it remains until the printer is turned off.

Temporarily downloaded fonts are sent to the printer's memory as the publication is printing. When the publication has finished printing, the temporarily downloaded font is flushed out of the printer's memory. Printing tends to be slower with temporarily downloaded fonts, since the fonts are downloaded each time the publication is printed.

Because permanently downloaded fonts remain in the printer's memory, you can print publications more quickly, but the amount of memory remaining for processing each page will be limited by the number of fonts downloaded. In particular, you might experience problems printing pages with graphics.

Efficiency Tip:

Erase "Permanent" Fonts

If you have permanently downloaded any fonts at the beginning of the day, and you run into memory problems when printing pages with graphics that do not use those fonts, you can flush the fonts out of the printer's memory by turning it off. When you turn it back on, print the pages with graphics first, before you permanently download the fonts again.

Most printers can handle no more than 16 soft fonts per page and 32 soft fonts per publication. These limits are considerably smaller for printers with limited memory available. A 512K printer might be able to hold only 10 different text-size fonts that are 9 or 10 points in size.

Remember (as you learned in Chapter 3) that a font is a particular combination of typeface and style (and sometimes point size). You need to download four different fonts in order to use the entire family in the Garamond typeface, for example—normal, bold, italic, and bold italic. Chapters 3 and 4 offer some design suggestions along with other production considerations in choosing fonts for a publication.

Remember that different typefaces, styles, and sizes take up different amounts of memory, and different types of graphics make different demands on memory as well. Before you produce a long publication that calls for downloadable fonts, try printing one or two sample pages with representative graphics as well as text that uses all of the fonts called for in the design.

NUMBER OF PAGES, REVERSE ORDER, AND COLLATED SETS

You can select a range of pages to be printed if you do not want to print the entire publication. This option is useful when you make changes that affect just a few pages, or when you want to print the finished parts of a publication that is still in process.

Usually you can specify the number of copies that you want printed of each page, and whether they should be printed collated or in reverse order. Reverse order may take longer to print than the natural order, and you might prefer to reorder the pages manually.

If you are printing more than one copy and choose the Collate option, then one full copy will print out completely before the next copy is printed. This can be handy if you want the first copy to be available for review while the other copies are printing, and it definitely saves you the time it would take to sort the copies manually, but it can often require significantly longer printing time than when multiple copies are not collated (Figure 7.48). When copies are not collated, the printer can process each page only once and print multiple copies immediately from the same drum image. Collated copies require that the printer process each page for each copy, i.e., the drum image is reprocessed for each sheet of paper printed.

PAGE COMPOSITION 309

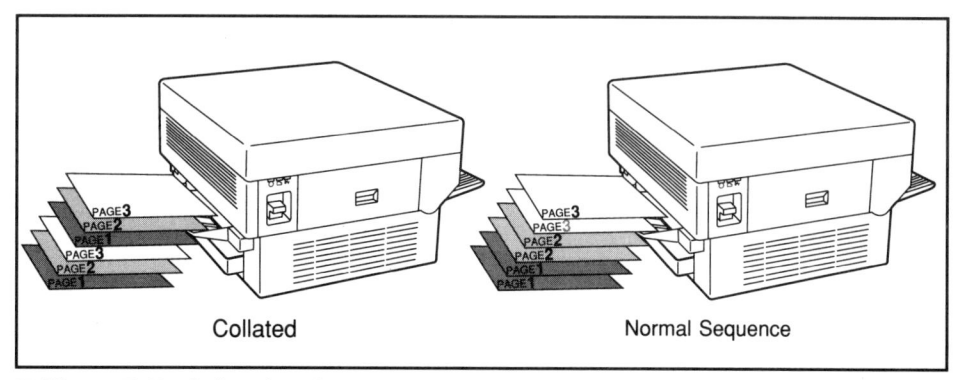

■ **Figure 7.48** Collated copies require that the printer process each page for each copy. When copies are not collated, the printer can process each page once and print multiple copies immediately from the same drum image.

THUMBNAILS AND CROP MARKS

The Thumbnail option available with some applications prints miniature pictures of each page (Figure 7.49). This option is not available for all printers, even if your *application* supports it. Thumbnails can be useful during the design stage (as described in Chapter 4), and they can also be used for assessing the overall layout of each finished page, or as miniature records of a completed document.

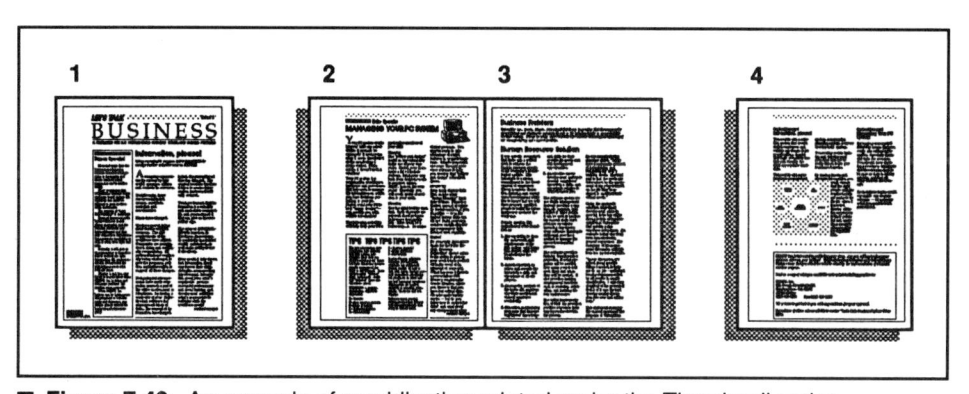

■ **Figure 7.49** An example of a publication printed under the Thumbnail option.

You can use the Crop marks feature to automatically generate the marks traditionally used to indicate where the pages would be cut when trimmed to their final size (Figure 7.50). This option works when you are printing on a paper size larger than the page size specified for the publication. You can also use this option when you are printing a reduced page size using the scaling option, if available.

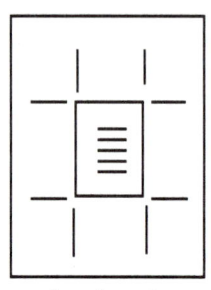

■ **Figure 7.50** You can print crop marks when the page size is smaller than the paper size.

PRINTING LARGE OR SMALL PAGE SIZES

You can use a Tiling option in some applications to print large pages in pieces on smaller paper. A common application of the Tiling feature is to print out tabloid-size (11-by-17) pages on 8½-by-11 paper (Figure 7.51). The tiled papers can be assembled into one piece for reproduction, or they can be used as proof sheets only: you can print the final version of a tabloid page directly to a Linotronic typesetter's 12-inch wide roll of photosensitive paper without using the Tiling option.

PAGE COMPOSITION 311

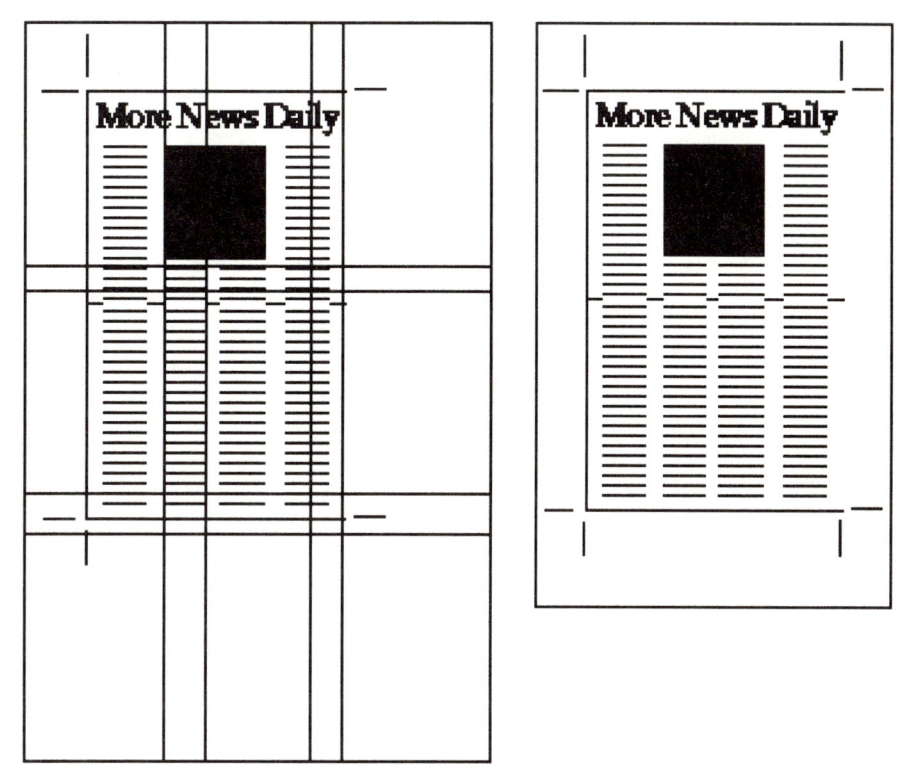

■ **Figure 7.51** Printing a tabloid size page on 8½ by 11 paper using the Tiling feature vs. printing the full page on a Linotronic typesetter with crop marks.

In tiling, you can usually select an Auto option and specify by how much you want the images on each tile to overlap, or you can also select the Manual option and define the limits of each tile piece by moving the zero point on the ruler line. For example, under the Manual Tiling option you would first print one "tile" with the zero point at the top left-hand corner of the page, then you would move the zero point to mark the top left-hand corner of the next tile and print again.

With some printers, you can print the publication in percentage reductions or enlargements between 25 percent and 1000 percent. The top left-hand corner of each page as shown on the screen remains the top left-hand corner of the printed pages, and all enlarging or reducing is done to the right and down the page.

> **Efficiency Tip:**
> When creating a document that uses very small point sizes throughout or calls for more columns than will fit on an 8½-inch width, you can work on a large, tabloid-size page on the screen in larger point sizes, and print the publication out at 50% to fit on an 8½ by 11 page.

PRINT SPOOLERS

A print spooler utility lets a program perform all of its print processing quickly and store the results in the computer's memory. This way, you can resume working with the program while the printing is in progress. While you go on working, the spooler manages all of the jobs that wait to be printed.

Proofreading

Ideally, the *content* of the text and graphics have been thoroughly proofed before the page-layout stages. If any editing takes place during the page-layout stage, you must proof the draft printouts against the marked copy that shows the editor's changes. In proofing the text and graphics individually, take into consideration the proofreading issues described in Chapters 5 and 6. These include:
- indentation
- paragraph spacing
- alignment
- hyphenation
- widows and orphans
- word and letter spacing
- kerning opportunities
- consistent spacing between elements

Additional considerations that apply specifically to proofing a final page layout include:
- print quality
- correct page numbering
- figures and figure captions adjacent to each other—not pushed out of alignment by edits made to other parts of the text
- page breaks correct, new sections start on a right-facing page (for books, manuals, and reports)
- registration (for overlays or color separations)

Rule of Thumb:

Some people leave their computers turned on all of the time, and there is no clear winner in the debate about whether this is a good practice. There is one very good reason why you should turn your laser printer off overnight: whereas a computer might draw as little electricity as a light bulb or television, laser printers draw up to 760 watts during use—as much as a small room heater—(less when on but idle).

Summary

For some publications, the final pages will be printed on the laser printer for distribution. In most cases, however, you will be making multiple copies using a photocopier or an offset printer. After the publication has been assembled by the production team, the final pages may still require the designer's finishing touches in the steps described in Chapters 8, 9, and 10.

Part 4
Beyond
the
Desktop

No matter how sophisticated your computer system, some designs still require traditional graphic arts skills in the final stages of production. Even if your publication requires no special handling, the more familiar you are with the final reproduction process, the more efficient you can be in the design and production phases.

Chapter 8
Preparing for the Printer

In the last three chapters of this book, you will learn how to go from a composed page on the screen of your publishing system to a final product—the finished piece you hold in your hand (unless you are distributing your publication via electronic media). The final product you want to achieve should drive the entire publishing process.

How do you want the document to look and feel—casual, formal, luxurious, fun (see Figure 8.1)? How will you distribute it—by mail, by hand, from a literature stand? What do you want the reader to do with it—file it, display it, circulate it, return it? The answers to these questions, along with document content, are the fundamental criteria for publication design (see Part Two, Design for Desktop Systems). They also affect what is done at every step of production.

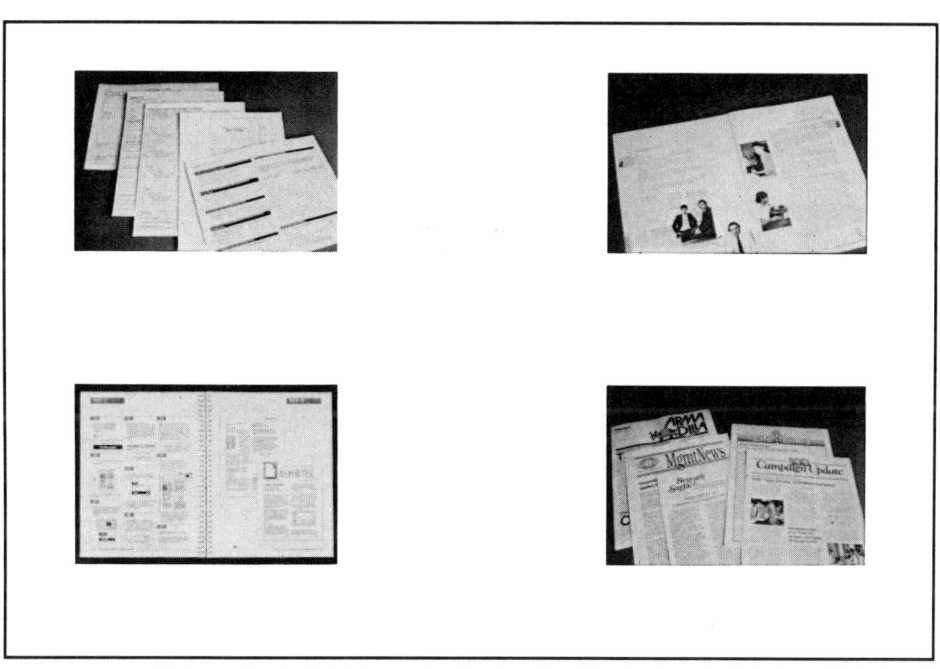

■ **Figure 8.1** Different types of publications requiring different degrees of preparation, contrast style, purpose, etc.

Depending on the results you want to achieve, you will make decisions about method of printing, paper, and ink. These decisions will affect how you compose your document and create your art.

For example, if you are going to be printing on a textured paper stock, you will probably want to avoid very light italic faces in your design (as mentioned in Chapters 3 and 10). If you're publishing a newsletter and you're going to print it on a fairly low-grade paper, such as newsprint or even vellum, you'll want to avoid using photographs that have a lot of detail (as mentioned in Chapters 6 and 10).

If you're going to print your newsletter on a web offset press, you should also be aware before designing your piece that this type of press, while faster and less expensive for some jobs, cannot provide the accuracy and color consistency of a sheet-fed press (see Chapters 7 and 10). You'll want to avoid design elements that could draw attention to discrepancies, such as colored bars at the tops of pages, and rules or other graphics elements that cross over facing-page boundaries.

Similarly, you can plan your publication for most economical use of color if you know on what kind of printing press it's going to be run and how your printer will run it. For example, if you have an eight-page four-color brochure, on some presses it will be printed so that four pages are on one side of the sheet and the other four pages on the reverse. This means that you can save money by printing four-color only on one side (see Chapters 7 and 10). In other cases, with the right combination of trim size (final publication dimensions), paper size, and press, you may be able to print color on *all* pages at no additional cost.

For some publications, you will distribute pages that are output from your laser printer directly. Or you may use laser output (or higher-resolution typeset output) as the master for xerographic reproduction or offset printing. In many cases, however, camera-ready master pages may require some additional preparation. Depending on the capabilities of your publishing software, your design, and the final results you are trying to achieve, there may be a few elements that must be added to the output page to make it a camera-ready master. Certain types of ruled lines may need to be created using traditional paste-up techniques. In addition, you may need to mark up photographs and other continuous-tone art for halftone processing; mark up or separate elements that are to be printed in color; and indicate bleeds, folds, and other aspects of the final assembly (if you don't know what these are, don't worry—keep reading and you'll learn).

These are the kinds of considerations you will learn more about in the next three chapters.

Final Pages or "Camera-Ready" Masters

Desktop printing is a practical way of printing a document that requires only medium-resolution output quality and only small quantities are to be printed. If you need a large number of copies, desktop printing becomes less efficient and less economical. Instead, you could output your document on a high-volume-on-demand printer if your system has that capability. More often for high quantity reproduction, you will output a single copy on a printer or typesetter and use it as an original for offset printing or xerographic duplication. In this case, the output pages are *masters*.

Masters must be camera-ready—i.e., ready to be photographed by the electromechanical device in the photocopier, or by the graphic arts process camera used by the offset printer to make film negatives (which are, in turn, used to make printing plates). You want to provide the best possible camera-ready master, as it will determine the quality of your final pages. You will need to select an output device that will give you the quality of master suitable for your purposes.

LASER-PRINTED OR TYPESET MASTERS

Laser printers and some typesetters use a laser technology to transfer an image to a page, and we describe both types of output in this section. The quality of the master pages they produce varies considerably, however.

Up until this point let us assume that you have only printed draft versions of your pages, and you might have been using a draft printer that is different from the final printer that will be used for the final master pages. The first decision you need to make—and this should take place long before final production begins—is what type of printer will be used for final output.

One of the variables that is most evident in comparing output from different printers and typesetters is resolution. Resolution is a measure of the density in which text and graphics are printed, and it is usually given in dots-per-inch (dpi). Laser printers like the LaserWriter and LaserJet print at 300 dots-per-inch. This is considered high-resolution compared with dot-matrix printers that print at 120 dots-per-inch, but it is low-resolution compared with typesetting equipment that prints at 1200 or 2400 dots-per-inch.

Some printers have a range of settings for resolution (Figure 8.2). Most printers can print pages of text at the higher resolutions, but pages with graphics can overload some printers' processing capabilities unless they are set to lower resolutions.

320 THE ELECTRONIC PUBLISHER

The resolution in dots-per-inch can be translated into a density in dots-per-square-inch (dpsi). An average dot-matrix printer can print between 72 and 120 dpi, or 5184 to 14,400 dots-per-square-inch. Laser printers range between 300 and 600 dpi, or 90,000 to 360,000 dpsi. Typesetters leap to 1200 to 2540 dpi or more, or 1,440,000 to 6,250,000 dpsi. As you can see, the dpsi increases tremendously with typesetting, and this translates into much sharper lines, finer detail, and better halftones. The higher the resolution, the smoother the appearance of the edges of text and graphics; the lower the resolution, the greater the jaggedness of the edges.

AppleLaserWriter 300 dpi

Hewlett-Packard LaserJet: 75,150, or 300 dpi

Linotronic 100: 300, 600, 900, or 1270 dpi

Linotronic 300: 1270 or 2540 dpi

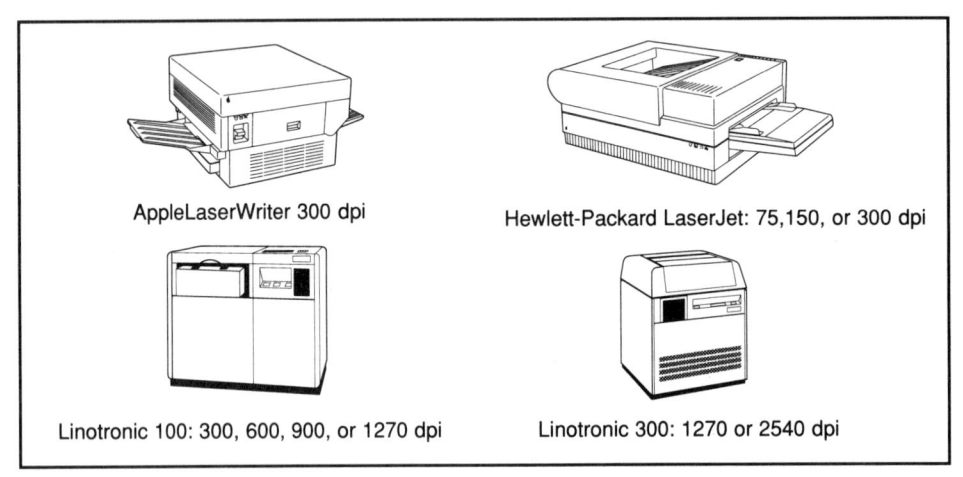

■ **Figure 8.2** Resolutions of some of the printers that are compatible with desktop systems.

If you are printing the final publication on glossy stock (like a magazine) it is a good idea to use a high-resolution typesetter such as the Linotronic 100 or 300 for final masters. If you will be printing on newsprint, on the other hand, the ink will tend to be absorbed more and the fine dots will bleed together, and the output from a 300 dpi laser printer may be fine for a master. In between these two extreme cases there is a wide range of variables—availability, cost, time allowed, final form, distribution method, etc.—that should affect your decision on what type of laser printer to use.

The advantages of typeset output include resolution, output size (up to 14 inches wide, height limited only by the application used to print), and paper quality (the output will be on photosensitive paper or film that will hold wax well if you are pasting additional elements onto the pages or pasting the pages onto boards). The three drawbacks of typeset output are: additional cost, additional time (if your pages include scans and other bit-mapped images), and output size (i.e., since the photosensitive paper comes on a roll, the final output always has to be trimmed on at least two sides).

> **Rule of Thumb:**
>
> Ads that are to be sent to other publications for insertion should be printed on the Linotronic typesetter, or photostatted. If this isn't possible, you might want to include a note about the fact that the camera-ready copy you are delivering is actually on normal bond paper. Otherwise, production department staff who are not familiar with laser printing might think that you are delivering a photocopy copy, and that you forgot to include the original. (This common misunderstanding should occur less frequently in the future, as more production departments start using laser printers.)

The advantages of desktop laser printers are: lower cost (compared with typesetting), faster turnaround (in most cases), paper variety, and output size (i.e., the standard letter-size paper of the master matches the final trim size of many newsletters and business publications, and now trimming is required). You can get the best quality by making sure your toner cartridge is fresh and by using one of the special laser papers that are available. Some of these papers come with finishes that accept wax for manual paste-up. You can also get special adhesive stock—opaque or transparent—that can be used for printing graphics that will be pasted onto other masters manually. The disadvantages of desktop laser printers are: lower resolution (compared with typesetting), difficulty with solid black areas (due to uneven toner distribution), and output size limitations (most laser printers handle only 8½-inch-wide papers).

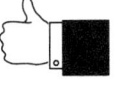

> **Rule of Thumb:**
>
> When printing masters to a laser printer, you can use special laser papers that are designed to hold the best image from a toner cartridge.

Make sure the large areas of black or gray are as dark and even as possible on your final pages. For best results, use a typesetter to print pages with grays or solid black areas. You can darken the image printed on the laser printer by using a special laser paper or coated stock, or by spraying the page with a matte finish (available in any art supply shop), after laser printing on noncoated paper stock. If your laser printer cartridge is printing black areas poorly—unevenly gray—the image might blacken (i.e., improve) when made into plates by an offset printer, but never count on getting printed quantities that look better than the original.

If your final page size is larger than the maximum paper size handled by your laser printer, you will need to print the pages out in fragments or tiles and paste them together before sending the full-size page layouts to the print shop. Sometimes you will need to tile images that come close to (or bleed off) the margins of the paper. You have probably already noticed that laser printers do not print to the very edges of the paper. One edge of the paper is used by the grippers inside the printer. Offset printers also need to allow ¼ inch at the edge of the paper for the printer's grippers, so the fact that laser printers force this same edge is not usually a problem.

The other three edges of the paper are defined by the code inside the printer: the larger the image area, the more printer memory required. Therefore, the maximum image area for most desktop printers would be slightly larger than 8 by 10½ inches, taking about one pica away from the top and bottom of a page, and about 1.5 picas away from the sides. In a 300-dpi printer's terms, this yields a maximum number of pixels per page—printed at 300 pixels per inch, or 90,000 pixels per square inch. When this same limit is applied to 8½ inches by 14 pages, the margins around the edge become even wider. You can easily test the limits for any printer by drawing a black box to cover an entire page (in an *application* that allows full 8½-by-11-inch image areas), then printing it out.

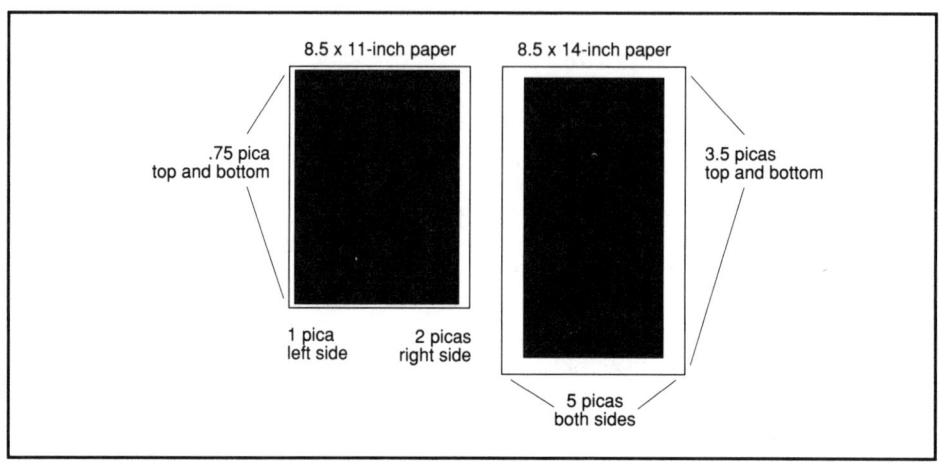

■ **Figure 8.3** You can see the limits imposed by your printer by printing out a page of solid black. In this example, different paper sizes force different margin limits.

These limitations are not a problem for most documents, but when you are designing a small-format brochure you want the freedom to come within ¼ inch of all sides—the same limit that would be imposed by the offset printer unless you want to pay the extra charges for printing bleeds. The problem is eliminated entirely with the Linotronic typesetter, which has no limits and uses 12-inch wide film.

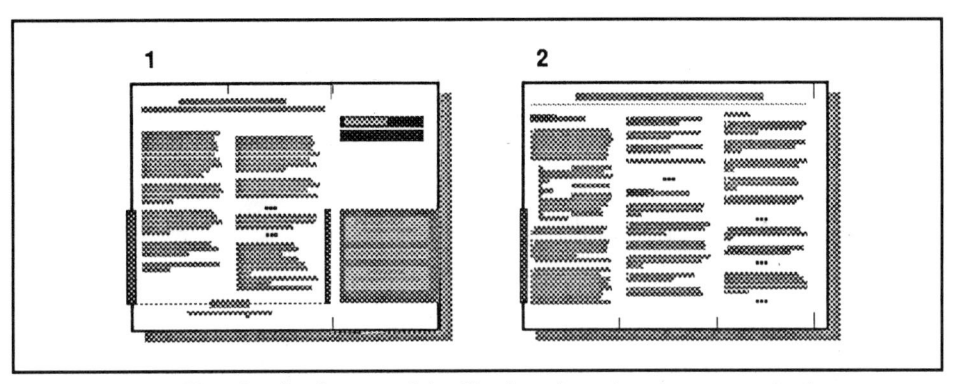

■ **Figure 8.4** Thumbnail printouts of the file show how the pages were broken up.

Rule of Thumb:

When designing pages that will be pasted together for final reproduction, do not cross seamed edges with gray fill patterns; use solid white or black only. Otherwise, when you paste the pages together, you will be able to see the seam where two edges of a gray pattern meet.

It should be noted that the term typesetting is sometimes used to indicate laser-printer output as well as phototypeset output, and in the not-too-distant future there may be less need for making a distinction between typesetters and laser printers—only the resolution will be specified. Imaging technologies are similar and the resolution gap between high-end and low-end systems is narrowing. Already there are 1000-dot-per-inch printers that are called plain paper typesetters.

MECHANICALS

In graphic arts terminology, camera-ready masters are called mechanicals. The word mechanical is a traditional graphic arts term. It derives from mechanical artist, an infrequently used term today, but one that once distinguished the graphic designer or paste-up artist from the fine artist. Mechanicals are also sometimes called boards, in reference to the stiff illustration board or art board on which type and other elements of the page were pasted. Prior to electronic page composition, every element of the page—columns of type, heads, header and footer information, line art, footnotes, tables, etc.—was literally pasted down on these boards. This is a very labor-intensive, time-consuming process requiring skill and precision by a paste-up artist.

■ **Figure 8.5** Traditional mechanical partly pasted up.

■ **Figure 8.6** Today's mechanical, an electronically composed page.

Today, your composition program handles much of this work automatically for you (see Chapter 7, Page Composition). Instead of outputing text in long columns (galleys), cutting them to page length, and pasting them down in position, you can output fully composed pages. You can also output graphics in position on those pages. Nevertheless, some publications will still call for some additional treatment before they are ready for reproduction. You can do this additional work yourself using traditional paste-up techniques or you can instruct the print shop to do it (usually through photographic or electronic techniques).

WHAT SHOULD A MECHANICAL CONTAIN?

A mechanical should contain all the elements of your page. If these elements are not camera-ready, they should be in the form of instructions to the printer. Instructions can be written on tissue overlays or in nonrepro blue ink to indicate elements that the printer should add to the camera-ready copy.

Rule of Thumb:
If you are going to be pasting up very many elements, you might want to lay all of the pages down on boards—white index paper that will keep the pages flat and prevent pasted-down elements from peeling up.

By simply writing instructions in red ink or grease pencil on the edges beyond the crop marks of your mechanical, or on a tissue overlay, you can tell your printer to add rules, spot color, and photographs. You can tell him to put heads and rules in color, or to create a block of gray and reverse type out of it (called a dropout, the type prints white on the gray field). This sort of mechanical is called a keyline, and it leaves all of the tricky work of precise alignment, known as registration, to the printer.

■ **Figure 8.7** Keyline mechanical.

You could also add these elements to your mechanical yourself. You'd need to use a variety of paste-up techniques working with materials such as mylar overlays and positive and negative photostats.

DECIDE ON THE LEVEL OF EFFORT

What's the best way to prepare a mechanical? How much work should you do yourself and how much should you leave to the printer? It really depends on you. Consider these essential variables: cost, quality, and responsibility.

Cost

The more elements the printer has to photograph separately and piece together, the more he or she will charge you. If budget is the determining factor in the job, you'll want to do as much of the mechanical as you can yourself. The simpler you can make the printer's job, the less expensive it will be.

But unless you have graphic arts training, or have access to someone who does, you should restrict your pasteup work to a minimum. If the printer has to redo a lot of the work on the mechanical, it will cost you more time and more money than paying for professional services from the beginning.

Rule of Thumb:
If you haven't dealt with the offset printing process before, it's a good idea to find out what form your printing service prefers for camera-ready pages, and how the printing charges might change if you do more of the preparation at your end.

Quality

How exact are your quality requirements? Can you produce a good enough result with your equipment and your own abilities?

Sometimes if you're working with a new printer, or one who is very inexpensive and/or less-skilled, you may not have the confidence that he or she will be able to create the effects you want. If you don't want to take chances, you'll want to provide him or her with completely camera-ready mechanicals.

At the same time, most high-quality printers today are using such sophisticated computer-based technology that they can perform many tasks faster and better than even an experienced graphic artist. Computers are more precise than human beings. No matter how good you are with an Xacto knife, there are some things that you can't do as well because you simply can't see with the human eye what the computer can see.

How much you can do yourself will depend not only on your equipment and skills, but on the complexity of the job.

Responsibility

When you mark up your mechanical with instructions for the printer, the printer is responsible for achieving the result you've specified. You are responsible for the quality of the mechanical you deliver.

If two color elements that must meet exactly are not precisely in register, you may overlook it in your mechanical. All of a sudden in the proof, or on press, you'll notice either an overlap (which will show as a colored line) or a thin gap (which will show as a white line). Similarly, if a rule that crosses over two pages is off just a fraction of a point in your mechanical, that fault too is likely to be accentuated during final production. When these kinds of problems show up in the proof or on press, the first thing the printer will do is to look at your mechanical to see if it was correct as delivered. If not, he has no responsibility to correct the mistake free of charge. If it was the printer's job to add the rule, however, there is no question where responsibility lies.

It comes down to whether you're comfortable assuming that kind of responsibility. If you are, you may be able to stretch a tight budget. If you're not, the reassurance that it's someone else's headache may be worth the extra dollars.

As we talk about preparing publications for the printer, we'll give you both options and a variety of compromise techniques in between.

Line Art and Halftones vs. Continuous Tone Art

Printers often refer to mechanicals as artwork. There's good reason for this, since to the printer, everything on the mechanical is considered line art. Whether it's a column of type, a rule, or a drawing, it's the same thing—a solid black form with no gradations of tone (no grays).

A mechanical that is completely camera-ready—containing nothing but line art—can be photographed all at once as a single piece of art.

Figure 8.8 Mechanical with different kinds of line art.

This is the main thing to keep in mind about mechanicals: Every element on the page must be transformed into line art, either by you or by the printer. The reason that everything on the page must eventually be converted into line art has to do with the nature of the offset printing press.

Offset lithography, and most other printing processes (gravure printing is an exception, see Chapter 10, Printing and Binding) lay ink down in a single density, or tone. They print solid black (or solid colors).

Yet many types of illustrations, such as photographs and shaded pencil drawings, contain an almost infinite variety of tones between 100% black and 100% white. The printing press can't print these mid-tones by varying ink density.

While it is not possible to actually reproduce these tones, it is possible to fool the eye into believing they are there by converting a continuous tone to a fine pattern of dots—called a halftone. The optical illusion of an infinite range of tones is created by laying the ink down in an intricate pattern of dots of varying size and shape. The eye doesn't perceive the dots (unless you look through a magnifying glass). The brain mixes them into a gradual progression of tones. An area with a low percentage of dots appears lighter; an area with a high percentage of dots appears darker. The shapes of dots also affect what we see in terms of image shape and contour.

PREPARING FOR THE PRINTER   329

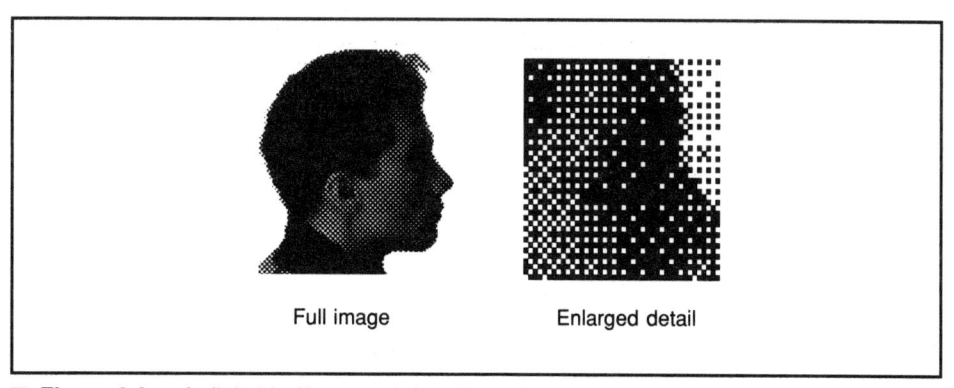

■ Figure 8.9 A digital halftone and the close-up dot pattern.

The number and size of dots needed to create a good halftone depends on the original image (amount of detail, tonal range) and the combination of press, paper, and ink with which it is printed. Newspapers, for example, are printed with high-speed web presses (not capable of fine registration), rough-surfaced and absorbent paper, and watery inks. Under these conditions, an 85-line halftone screen (85 halftone dots-per-inch) usually provides the best image reproduction. A finer screen would actually print a poorer image since closely spaced dots would tend to fill in and lose definition. Magazines, on the other hand, which are printed on smoother stock with different inks, generally use 133-line to 150-line screens.

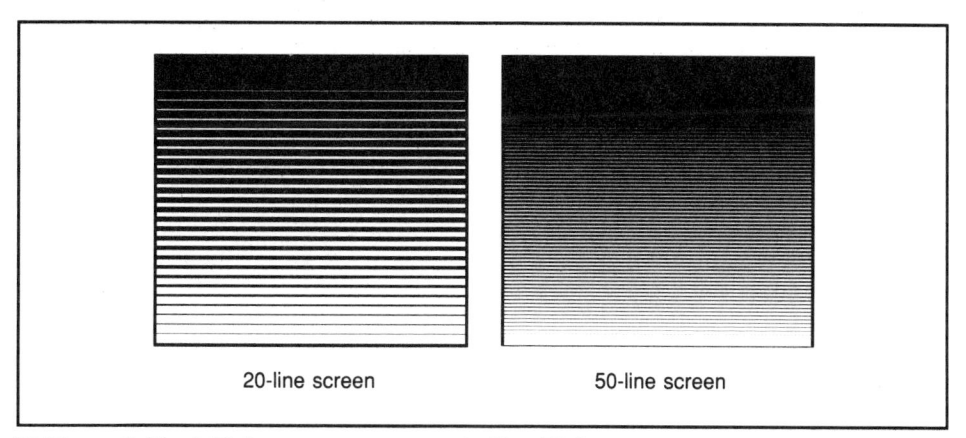

■ Figure 8.10 A 20-line screen compared with a 50-line screen.

330 THE ELECTRONIC PUBLISHER

In addition to normal halftone screens of varying degrees of fineness, there are also a variety of other types of screens used to create special effects. There are screens with square dots and screens such as mezzotint, circular, pebble, wood grain, linen, and crosshatch that impart unusual texture to images in the process of converting them to line art. The use of this type of screen is called *line conversion*.

CUT-LINES **MEZZOTINT**

■ **Figure 8.11** Examples of textured halftone screens from Visual Graphics Corporation.

How do you create a halftone? Traditionally halftones have been created photographically, using a halftone screen in the form of a film mask applied either to the process camera back or placed directly in contact with the original (Figure 8.12). Today you can also generate halftones by scanning original art and outputting it in the form of an already-screened image (the dot pattern is generated electronically) along with other page elements on a laser printer or typesetter.

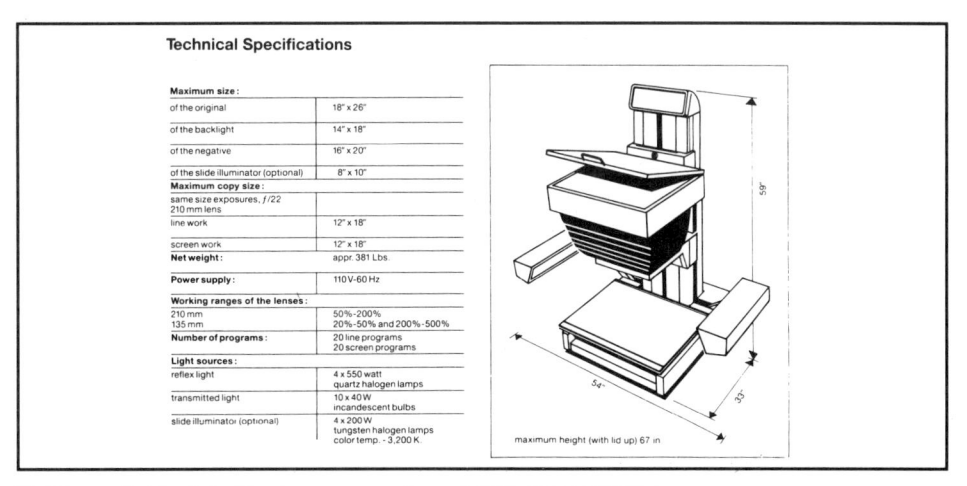

Figure 8.12 A halftoning camera from AGFA-GAVAERT, Inc.

In other words, if you are using photographs or other continuous-tone artwork, you have the option of scanning them into the computer and placing them on the page in a page-layout package (see Chapters 6 and 7), or the print shop can use a camera or scanner to create halftones for you.

MAKING YOUR OWN HALFTONES

To create your own digitized halftones, you will need a scanner, publishing or illustration software that can work with bit-mapped or continuous-tone images, and an output device that can output halftone-screened images.

PostScript and several other page-description languages have the ability to create halftones. Postscript, in particular, is extremely versatile in its ability to generate halftone screens of various degrees of fineness, and also screens that produce special effects through textures or patterns.

In early desktop publishing programs, these capabilities were resident in the underlying PostScript. If you knew how to program in PostScript, you could create a wide variety of halftone effects. Today, most desktop publishing programs give you a number of menu options for halftoning, as well as tools for scaling and cropping images.

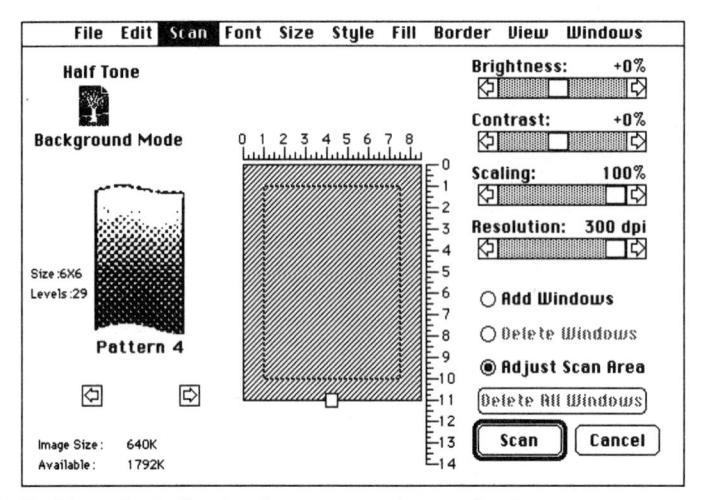

Figure 8.13 Menu for halftoning from a scanning application.

Depending on the capabilities of your system, halftoning can be performed at various stages. It can be performed by the scanner; it can be performed (at input or at output) by the application software; or it can be performed by an external raster image processor (RIP) in your output device.

The PostScript Interpreter in a laser printer is an example of this type of RIP. It tells the laser printer how to create patterns of output pixels (bitmaps). Output pixels are similar to screen pixels except that they are created by putting a spot of toner on a piece of paper instead of by exciting a dot of phosphor on a CRT tube. The halftone is created by grouping several output pixels together to form each halftone dot. By printing or not printing individual output pixels within each group, different size and shape halftone dots can be created, affecting the amount of gray the eye perceives.

Output resolution is not the same thing as halftone screen resolution, and halftone screen resolution is not the same as on-screen resolution (the resolution of the monitor). If you create a 75-line screen halftone with 300 dots-per-inch output resolution, a matrix of 16 pixels (four in each direction) will make up each halftone dot. If you create a 150-line screen with 300 dots-per-inch, a matrix of 4 pixels (two in each direction) will make up the halftone dot. The *output resolution* in both cases is 300 dpi, but the 75-line screen will appear coarser than the 150-line screen when printed out, because the smallest halftone dot is larger. On a 72 dpi monitor, both images will look the same.

PREPARING FOR THE PRINTER   333

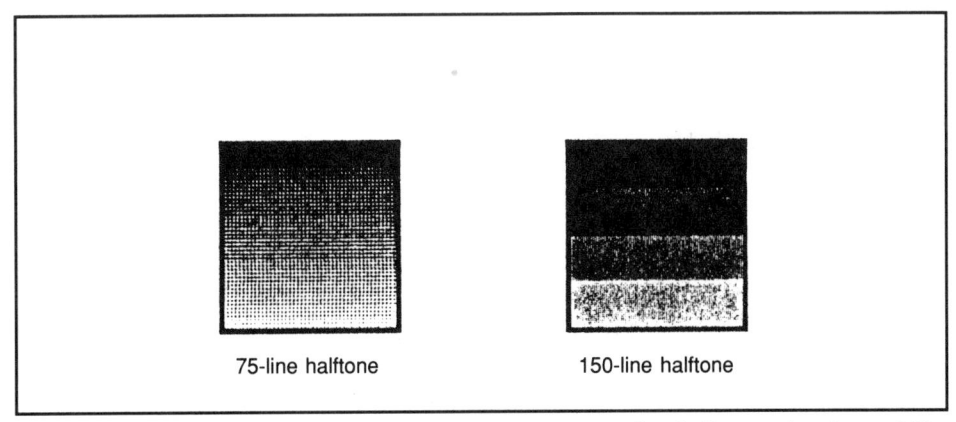

Figure 8.14 Magnified view of 75-line halftone and 150-line halftone printed on a 300 dpi printer.

Good-quality scanned images can look nearly as good as photographic half-tones when printed out, even though they may look coarse on your low-resolution screen. A 150-line screen printed on a laser printer or typesetter will usually look coarser than a 150-line screen created photographically, however. This is because a photographic halftone yields rounded (or variously shaped) dots of different sizes, whereas the laser-printed image *simulates* dots of different sizes by printing clusters of output pixels that are all the same size.

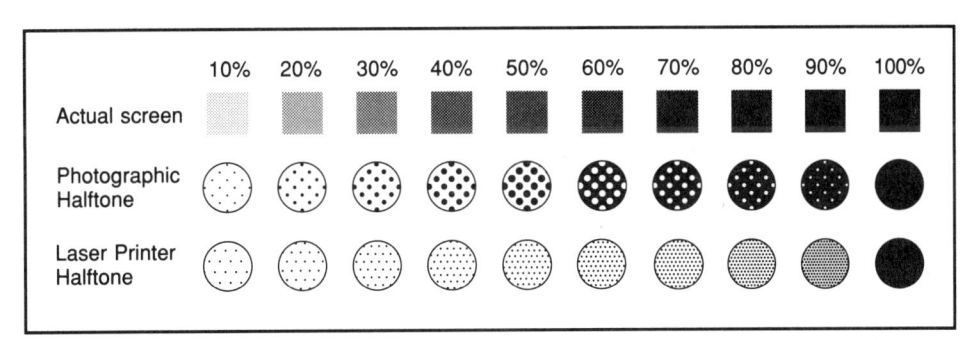

Figure 8.15 Closeup of output pixels forming a halftone dot from a photographic process and from a laser printer.

A PostScript Interpreter can create optimal halftones specifically for the size, screen fineness, and resolution you require. Whether you can take advantage of this capability, however, depends on what type of scanner you are using. Many scanners can record only bilevel (black or white, on or off) information; so they convert continuous-tone images to halftones during the scan. That limits you to the resolution of the scan and the bit-level information in that halftone. If you print the image at a higher resolution, each dot will be multiplied, and the result will be a coarse, fat dot look.

The other problem is that you will not be able to take advantage of software available for altering scanned images. The only editing that's possible is at a pixel level (turning bits on or off). You can not alter contrast or tonal progression. Also, when you scale a bit-map image, unless you pick a set of dimensions into which the original number of dots convert evenly, you can end up with unwanted moiré patterns.

If you have a scanner that can capture gray-scale information (the percentage of black at each location), however, you'll have much more information and flexibility for editing images, and the PostScript Interpreter will have more information and flexibility for creating good output halftones.

Remember (we are going to repeat this several times), a black and white scanner records one bit of information for each pixel sampled. This translates directly into output pixels that are either black or white (i.e., either printed or not). A group of these pixels together forms the halftone dot. With gray-level scanners, however, for each pixel sampled during the scan, several bits of information are recorded. *Each pixel* thus contains enough gray-level information to generate a complete halftone dot. At output, the PostScript Interpreter uses the gray-level information in each pixel to decide how to turn on or off a matrix of output pixels that form the halftone dot. Unlike the image stored as a black-and-white bitmap, the conversion of gray-scale bit-level data into output pixels is not a direct one-to-one translation. The decision about which output pixels to print is based on sophisticated averaging algorithms and adjustments to provide the optimal screen resolution and gray levels possible at the output resolution of the device.

We say optimal because you can't have maximum screen fineness and maximum gray levels at the same time—there is always a tradeoff. That's because the more pixels you devote to creating each halftone dot (to portraying levels of gray), the fewer halftone dots you can print (the coarser the halftone screen).

Consider 300 dot-per-inch output. The minimum level of quality is generally considered to be 64 shades of gray and a 65-line screen. You need at least this many shades of gray to represent the original photograph with an acceptable degree of accuracy; below that, too much information is lost.

With fewer than 64 gray levels there is also too large a gap between gray tones to simulate a continuous tone original.

On the other hand, with a coarser than 65-line screen, the eye begins to discern the individual halftone dots, and the brain does not mix what it sees into gray tones. To get 64 levels of gray from 300 dpi output, however, you need to devote eight pixels to each halftone dot. (Actually you get 65 gray levels: eight times eight plus one for no pixels or white). Then you can have 37½ pixels (300 divided by eight) across and down your page. A 37½-line halftone screen is too coarse, even for newspaper printing.

You could achieve a 65-line screen on a 300 dot-per-inch output device, but then you could devote only 4 bits or less to each pixel (divide 300 by 65). On output, that would give you a 4 by 4 matrix of pixels and 17 different possible halftone dots, or gray levels.

■ **Figure 8.16** Examples of images showing the tradeoff between gray-scale and screen fineness.

Rule of Thumb:

The Ten-Times Rule

In general, you'll need an output resolution that is ten times the halftone screen resolution. In other words, to output a 65-line screen and still retain 65 possible gray levels, you would need to go to a 600 dpi output device (multiply 65 halftone dots times eight pixels per dot).

Note also that while gray-scale images require more memory and storage to accommodate the extra bits of information, you can often achieve a better quality image scanning at lower resolutions. Let's say you are going to output an image on a 1250-dot-per-inch typesetter with a 150-line screen. If you were to scan the image on a black-and-white scanner at 300 dots per inch, you would have 300 times 300 pixels per square inch, each with a bit of information. An 8½ by 11 inch image would require about a megabyte of storage. On output, these would convert directly to output pixels, and you would need to use several output pixels to create each halftone dot. At a 150-line screen, you would have only a 2 by 2 matrix of output pixels for each dot, which would not give you a very good capability for simulating the wide range of grays in the original image.

If, however, you were to scan the image on a gray-scale scanner, you could scan at only 150 samples per inch. Since each pixel sampled with 8 bits of data would contain 256 possible levels of gray, each pixel would contain enough information to create a complete halftone dot. The PostScript Interpreter could then determine how to turn on or off the output pixels in a matrix of 8 by 8 dots to create each halftone cell. This would give you a much improved capability to reproduce the grays from the original image. An 8½-by-11 inch image scanned at 150 dots per inch times 8 bits would require only a little more than a megabyte of storage. (See Chapter 6 for more information about creating your own digitized images.)

PURCHASING HALFTONE VELOXES

If you don't have halftoning capabilities in your publishing or illustration software, yet you don't want to leave the halftoning to the printer, you have another option. You can send your photographs out to a graphic arts service and have them produce veloxes for you.

Veloxes are screened photostats, i.e., line art. They can be ordered in any standard screen ruling. You can leave blank spaces for veloxes on your pages, and just paste them in. Your page can then be shot as one piece of art, and you'll save the cost of stripping (see Chapter 10).

PREPARING FOR THE PRINTER

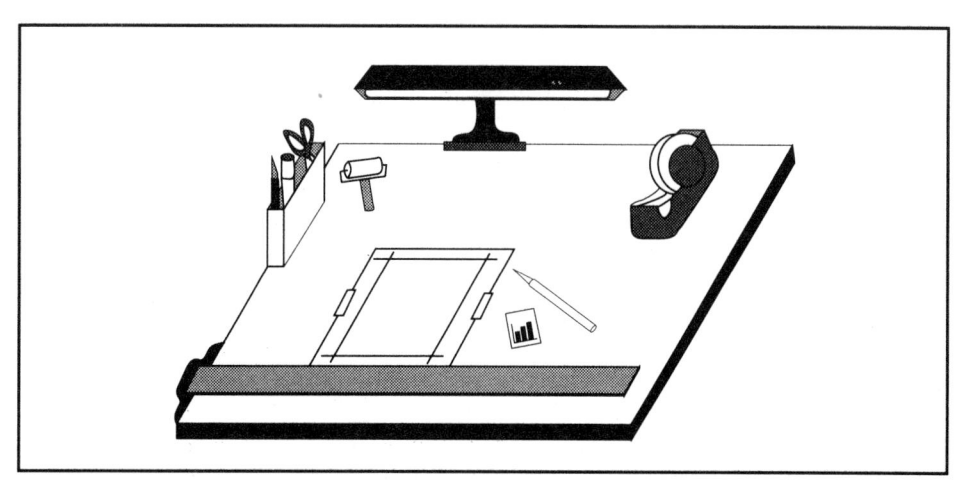

■ **Figure 8.17** Velox of a chart to be pasted onto mechanical.

Using veloxes, you'll be able to see your entire page with all art in place, which is an advantage with complex designs. Veloxes are also useful if you want to alter the image in some way. You can draw directly on veloxes with opaque white or black ink. The quality of the velox, and the cost, will depend on the quality of the camera used (you can buy a photostat camera with halftoning capability for under $500) and the skill of the cameraman. For a low-budget job, a quick, fast velox may be an efficient and appropriate solution.

LETTING YOUR PRINTER CREATE HALFTONES FOR YOU

For higher-quality results, you'll probably be better off giving the original continuous-tone art to your printer along with the mechanicals. You must mark the position and size of each illustration clearly on your mechanical. The photographs supplied to the printer may need to be marked for cropping. One method is leave space on the page for the printer to drop in the artwork, and simply to write instructions on a tissue overlay.

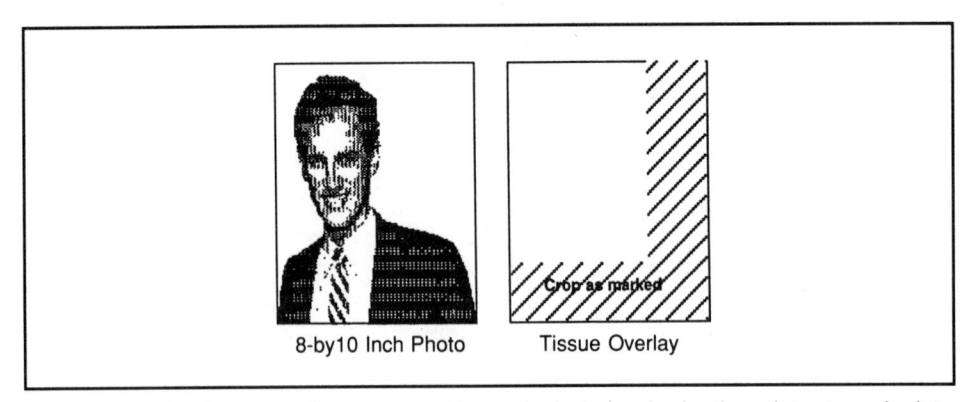

Figure 8.18 Tissue overlays are used to mark photographs for the printer to make into halftones.

Another way to mark position and size is to create a black box (dropout) with your publishing or illustration software (see Figure 8.19). Or you can draw an outline, and then paste down a photomasking film, such as rubylith on the mechanical. The films used in the process camera will photograph red as black, so there will be a clear area in the film negative. The printer will use this window to strip the halftone film in.

Figure 8.19 An electronic page with a dropout next to a mechanical with a rubylith.

Another way of marking position is to have a photocopy or photostat made of the original art and paste it into position on the mechanical. (Photocopies are perfectly acceptable now, but photostats have often been used for cleaner pasted-up pages. You should order a matte photostat, rather than the glossy photostats you would use for camera-ready line art. Matte photostats are used for indicating location only—they are not of high enough quality to be used as camera-ready art.) To make sure that there is no confusion, print "For position only" directly on the stat (see Figure 8.20). Alternatively, you can output a low-resolution halftone from your printer as part of your camera-ready page, mark it "for position only," and give the original to your printer for rescanning or shooting at a higher resolution.

■ **Figure 8.20** Using a scanned image to hold the place where a halftone will be used in the final production; mechanical with image marked "for position only."

Rule of Thumb:

It's a good idea to check with your print shop before you set up pages for halftones. It might help them if you use solid black boxes to reserve space for photographs on the pages. Otherwise, you could use a scanned image of the photograph to indicate the exact size and cropping required.

When you submit an original image, it should be as high-quality a print as possible. Try to use images with good detail in the brightest and lightest areas. Try to avoid high-contrast images, since contrast is generally increased during the printing process. An image a little on the flat side will reproduce better.

Marking an Image for Special Handling

SCALING AND CROPPING AN IMAGE

In many cases you will want the original photograph or image to be reduced or enlarged for the final page. Chapter 6 describes how some graphics programs can handle scaling, and Chapter 7 describes the scaling process during page layout. Otherwise, if you are giving the printer or cameraman artwork that needs to be scaled and stripped into the page layout, you can use some of the tips provided here.

Mount the image on an art board and indicate scale (how much you want the printer to increase or decrease the image) and cropping (what part of the image you want to preserve). Mark it with letters or numbers that correspond to positions on the mechanical.

Figure 8.21 Image with cropping and scaling information.

You can make a handy tool to help yourself visualize cropping by cutting two right angles out of the art board. By moving them around over the image, you can previsualize different croppings (see Figure 8.22). Once you've decided on one, mark the crop lines on the margins of the mounting board or on a tissue overlay. (If you write on the overlay, be sure to protect the image underneath, as any slight impression will show in reproduction.) You can also indicate cropping by pasting a paper frame over the original, with an opening that displays what you want the image area to be.

■ Figure 8.22 Cropping aids.

Scaling should always be done *after* cropping because you only want to measure the image area (not the parts of the photo that are going to be cropped out). You should mark the percentage by which the art should be scaled along with the cropping information on the mounting board or overlay.

There are several methods of figuring scaling percentages. One way is to measure your original *cropped* image area and then to measure one or more dimensions of the reproduction image area on your mechanical. Take one set of dimensions and divide the reproduction dimension by the original dimension. For example, if your original image is 8 inches by 10 inches, and you want to print it at 5 inches wide, it needs to be shot down to 62.5 percent (5 divided by 8). If you don't have the other reproduction dimension, you can figure it easily by multiplying the corresponding original dimension by the same percentage. In this case, multiplying 10 by .625 gives us 6¼ inches. The window in the mechanical should be 5 inches by 6¼ inches, and the original art should be marked "shoot at 62.5 percent." (Unless your cropping must be absolutely precise, you may round it out to 63 percent. This will give the printer a little room to make sure the image completely fills the space allotted for it. Always round *up*, never down.) These same techniques can be applied when scaling electronically (Figure 8.23), but the advantage of on-screen scaling is that it can also be done visually, without numeric entries.

342 THE ELECTRONIC PUBLISHER

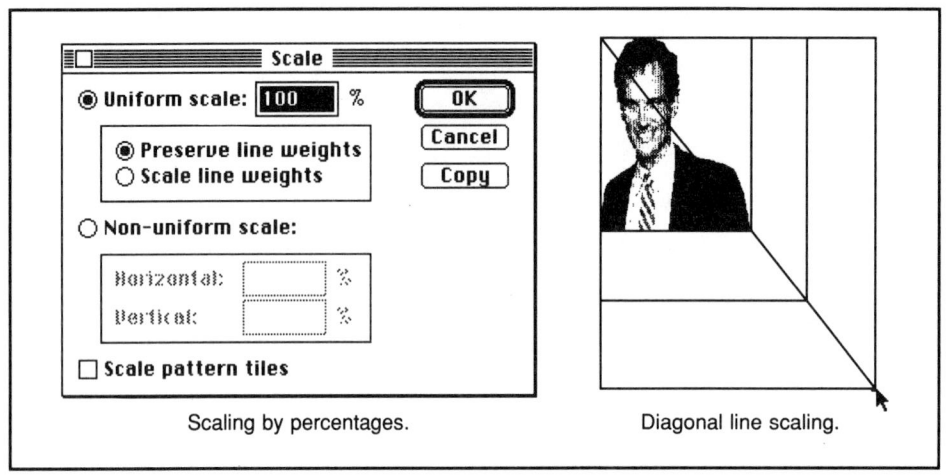

Figure 8.23 Two methods of scaling.

If you prefer to avoid calculators, there are a couple of visual methods for scaling art that work just as well. Using a tracing paper overlay, you can draw a diagonal line from the lower left-hand corner of the original image to its upper right-hand corner. Measure off the reproduction width at the bottom of the image and mark that width, drawing a perpendicular line up from the mark until it intersects the diagonal line. The length of the perpendicular line is the reproduction height of your image.

You can also purchase a scaling wheel (Figure 8.24) at any graphic arts store. The wheel does the calculations for you. The scaling wheel actually has two wheels: an inner one for original size and an outer one for reproduction size. You simply take one set of corresponding dimensions and line them up—the little window in the center of the wheel displays the scaling percentage reduction or enlargement. Leave that percentage in the window, and find the point on the original wheel for the other dimension, and you will see the corresponding reproduction dimension lined up next to it.

PREPARING FOR THE PRINTER 343

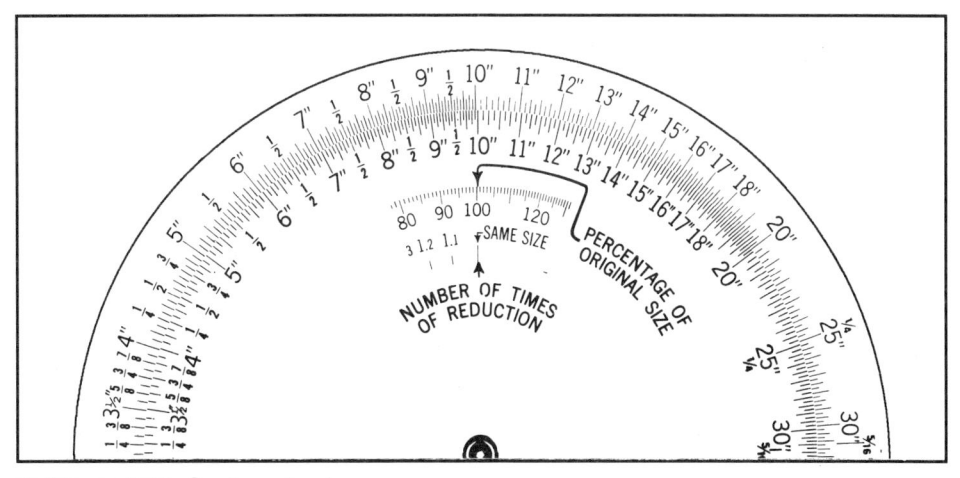

Figure 8.24 Scaling wheel.

When selecting scaling factors, try to avoid anything over 200 percent. If possible, your original art should be larger than the image area it will occupy in the finished piece. Image quality is improved by shooting art down to size, and lost by enlarging it.

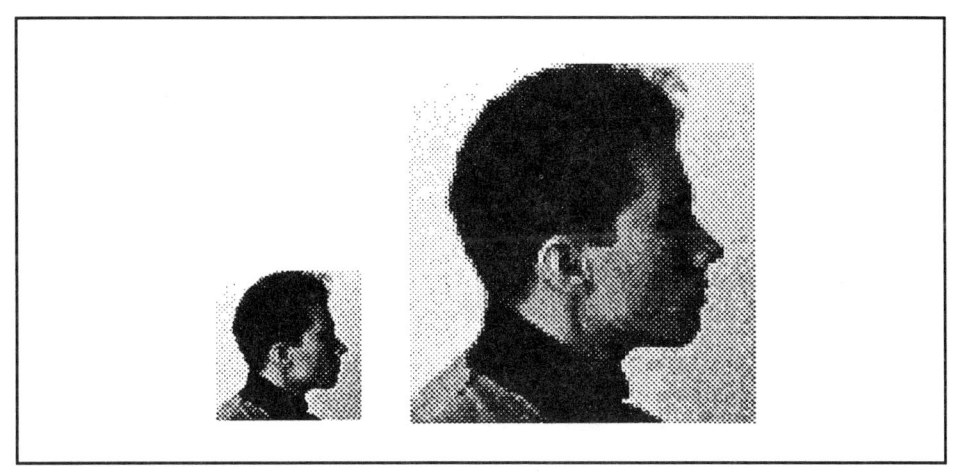

Figure 8.25 Show image quality lost at 250%.

As in other parts of your mechanical, you can save money by saving the printer a few steps. By having all of your prints made to scale and, if possible, pasting them into your mechanical, you enable the printer to shoot them all at one time—this is called ganging (see Figure 8.26). The printer can then shoot the mechanical one time for line art, and one time (using a halftone screen) for photographs. Another option is to submit prints each sized in such a way that they can all be scaled by the same percentage. Again, the advantage is that the printer can gang the art. Before you do this, find out the maximum image area of your printer's process camera—that will determine how many prints of what size you can gang at a time.

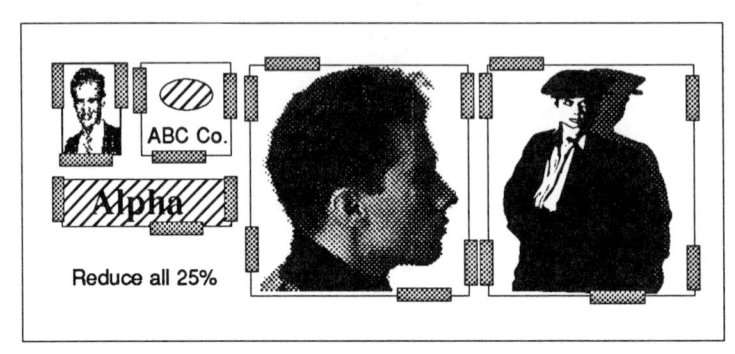

■ **Figure 8.26** Prints sized to scale for ganging.

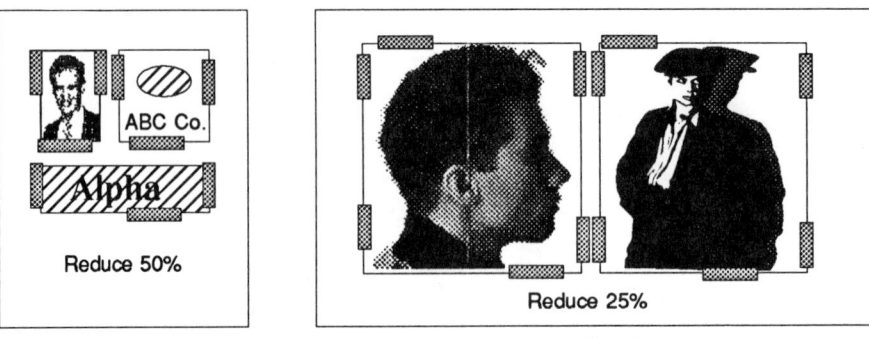

■ **Figure 8.27** Prints sized for reproduction at the same scaling factor.

SPECIAL EFFECTS IN IMAGE PLACEMENT

What if you want to crop the image into something other than a rectangle? (Printers' reps will generally ask you when quoting on your job how many squared up or rectangular images you have and how many other images.) If the shape is irregular—for example a triangle—you simply create a triangular hole on your mechanical using the same methods as described for a rectangular image (being very careful to mark your original with cropping dimensions that correspond precisely). If you want to do it electronically, you'll have to have a program that lets you fill shapes with bit-mapped images.

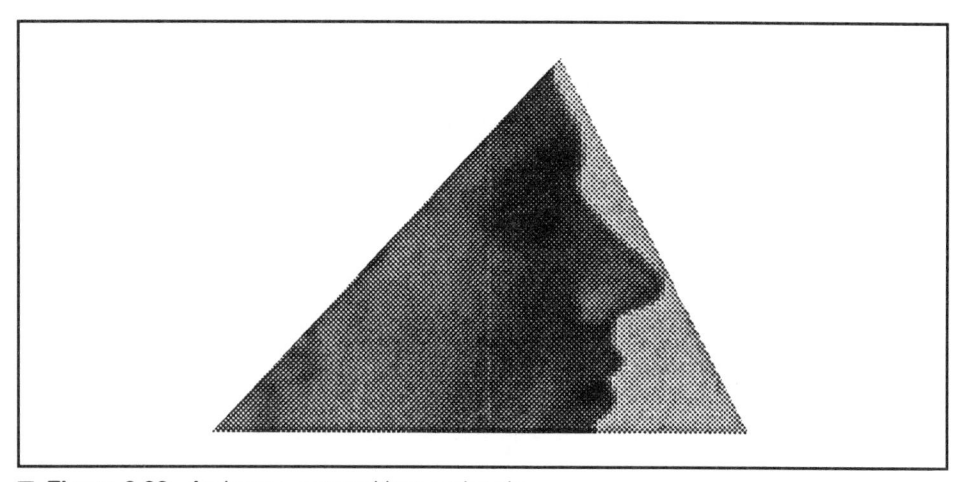

■ **Figure 8.28** An image cropped into a triangle.

Many times, however, designs call for pictures to be silhouetted, which means that they have an irregular outline. Silhouetted images are often placed on the page so that there is no background other than the page, and thus they appear to be floating directly on it.

346 THE ELECTRONIC PUBLISHER

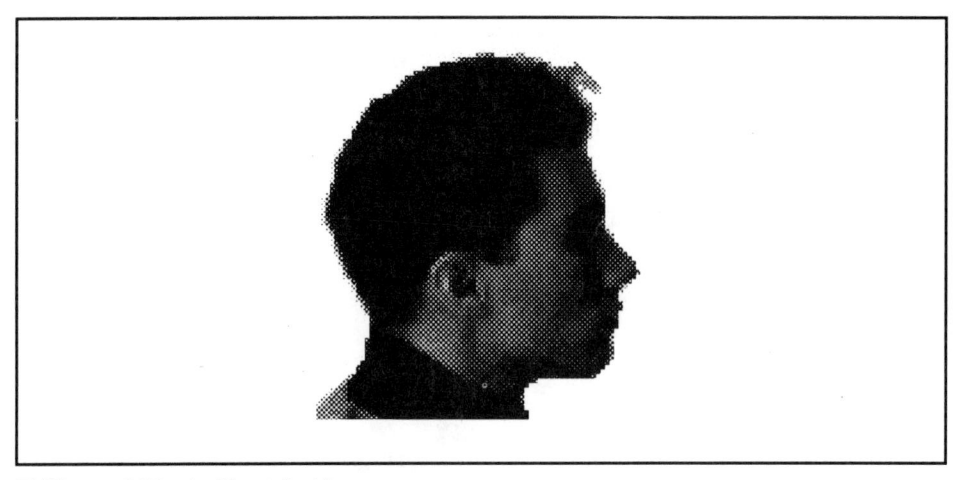

■ **Figure 8.29** A silhouetted image.

How do you create a silhouette? Again, your options for silhouetting are to do it yourself or to leave it to the printer. Some graphics applications, such as Adobe Illustrator 88, have an automatic masking feature. Otherwise, you can simply mark the tissue overlay where you want the outline to fall (Figure 8.30). The printer will create a mask, which will block out all other elements. You can do that yourself using rubylith or some other material and an Xacto knife (Figure 8.31). You can also paint an opaquing solution around the outline of the image area and cover the unwanted parts of the image with a paper matte.

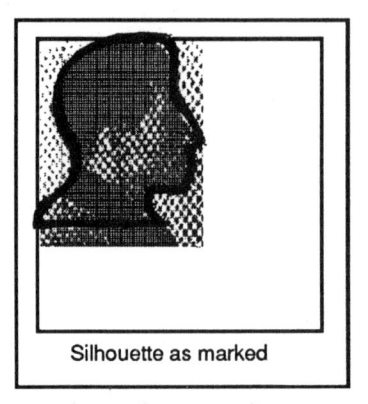

■ **Figure 8.30** A silhouette traced on a tissue overlay.

PREPARING FOR THE PRINTER   347

Figure 8.31 A rubied silhouette.

Another special effect is an image that runs beyond the margin of the page, all the way to the trim. This is called a bleed because the image appears to be bleeding right off the edge of the page (Figure 8.32). Usually this means that the color or image must be printed beyond the trim area. These pages are often handled separately at the print shop, since larger paper and more cuts are required than for nonbleed pages.

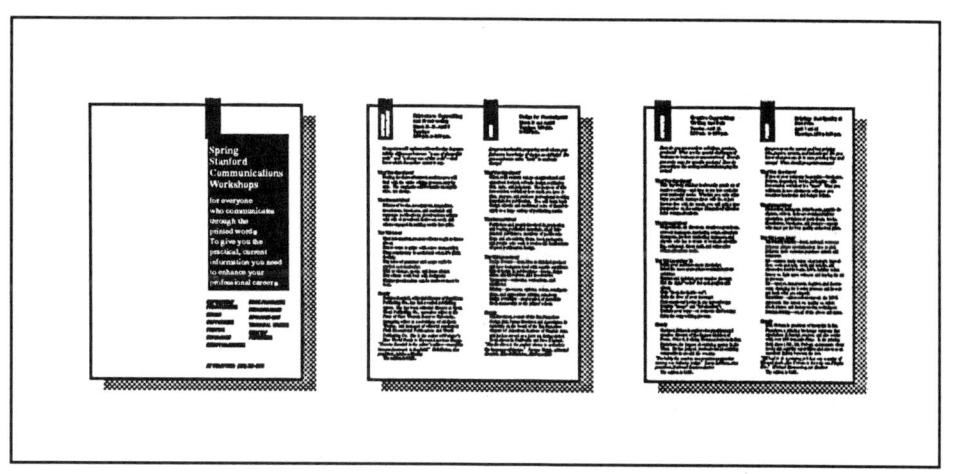

Figure 8.32 A finished piece showing a bleeding top border element.

To indicate a bleed on your mechanical, the image rectangle (other shape or silhouette) should extend at least ⅛ inches beyond the trim dimensions. Print image bleeds on the mechanical or its overlay, and also mark the original art with the word bleed. In contrast, an image that continues from one consecutive page to another, called a crossover, should be lined up directly with the trim line. Crossovers in center spreads are fairly easy to accomplish, but are very tricky on other pages (see Figure 8.33 and Putting it All Together later in this chapter).

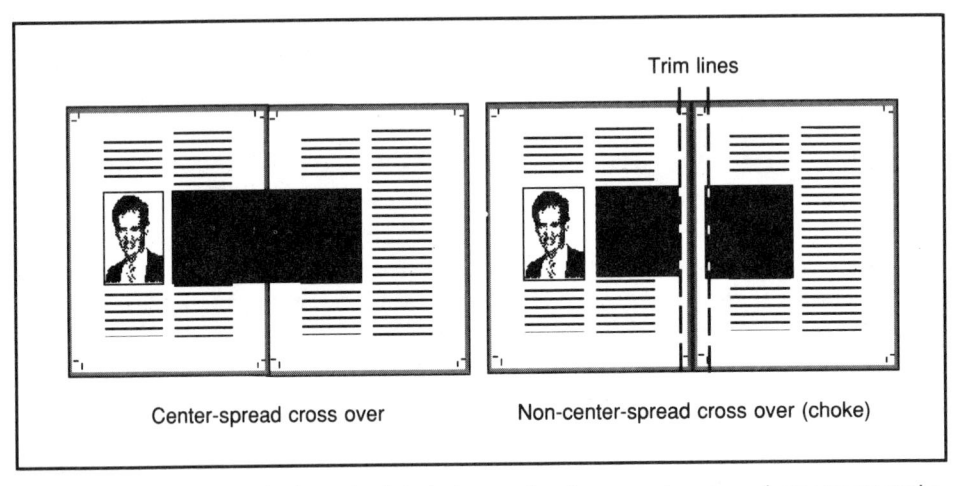

■ **Figure 8.33** Mechanicals and printed pieces showing a center spread crossover and a noncenter-spread crossover (choke).

Pages that call for bleeds at the edges should be delivered to the offset printer as a separate set from the rest of the document, with a note that they call for bleeding. Page numbers beyond the bleed area indicate where each page will be inserted into the finished document.

FLAT-TONE SCREENS

You can use screens not only to convert continuous-tone elements into line art, but to create solid tonal areas, called tints, as well. A screen of white dots applied over type or a rectangle, for example, will break up solid ink into a pattern of dots and create the illusion of a gray headline or gray block (Figure 8.34). Unlike the halftone dots, which simulate a range of tones by varying in size and shape, tint-screen-dots are usually uniform (Figure 8.35). This is an easy way to add a variety of tones and create some visual liveliness in a black-and-white piece.

PREPARING FOR THE PRINTER 349

■ **Figure 8.34** Tinted type and bar.

■ **Figure 8.35** Close-up flat-tone-screen dots.

Many electronic publishing programs give you menu options for creating screen tints. (You can think of them as fill patterns that happen to be patterns of dots; see Figure 8.36.) You can also purchase contact screens (black-on-clear or white-on-clear for reversals) and mount these on your mechanical (Figure 8.37). Or you can simply instruct the printer to fill a certain shape or area with a particular screen tint. Screen tints are commonly specified (and sold, if you go the contact route) by percentages. A 10 percent screen is a very light gray, while a 90 percent screen is almost black. A 50 percent screen will give you an even gray (Figure 8.38).

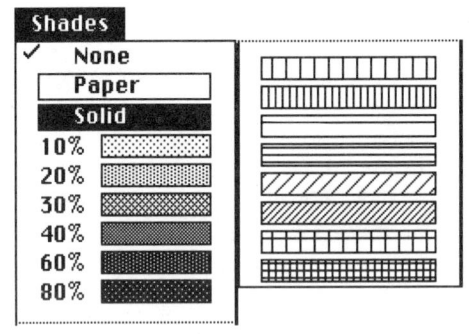

Figure 8.36 Screen tint menu.

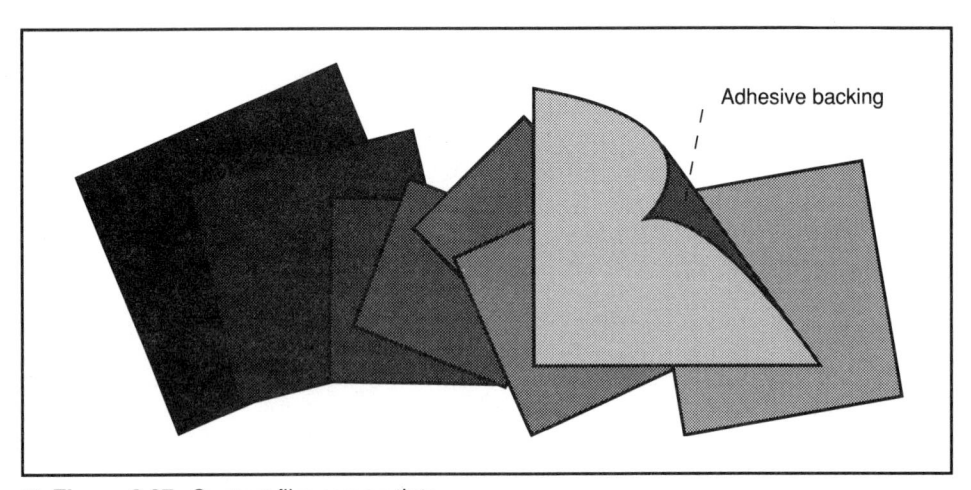

Figure 8.37 Contact film screen tints.

Figure 8.38 10 percent to 90 percent screens.

Be careful when you're using tints for type, rules, and other thin or small elements, because tints are made up of dots, and thin lines can break up and characters can lose definition. You want to be especially careful of dropping type out of a tint block—make sure that the characters are big enough and the tint dark enough to be legible, but be careful that the tint is not so dark it obscures the text.

■ **Figure 8.39** Close-ups of type dropped out of a tint block next to type dropped out of a solid.

Be careful, too, in setting up screens and tints behind type using your page-composition program. Sometimes it is better to let the printer set up screened backgrounds for you. The offset print shop uses a photographic process to produce the plate that will pick up the ink and lay it on the paper. When the camera is set to pick up a fine screen—a 10 percent fill pattern, for example—it will tend to darken each character of text and make the edges of the characters seem less sharp. When the camera is set to make the text sharp, the 10 percent screen tends to disappear in the camera's view of the page. In other words, if the image includes a wide range of gray tones, it can be difficult to find a camera setting that can pick up 10 percent screens without making the text too dark. If the final output will be offset printed, you can use solid black (or rubylith) boxes to marked screened areas on overlays, and let the offset printer's cameraman make the screens, as was done in the case of this brochure (Figure 8.40).

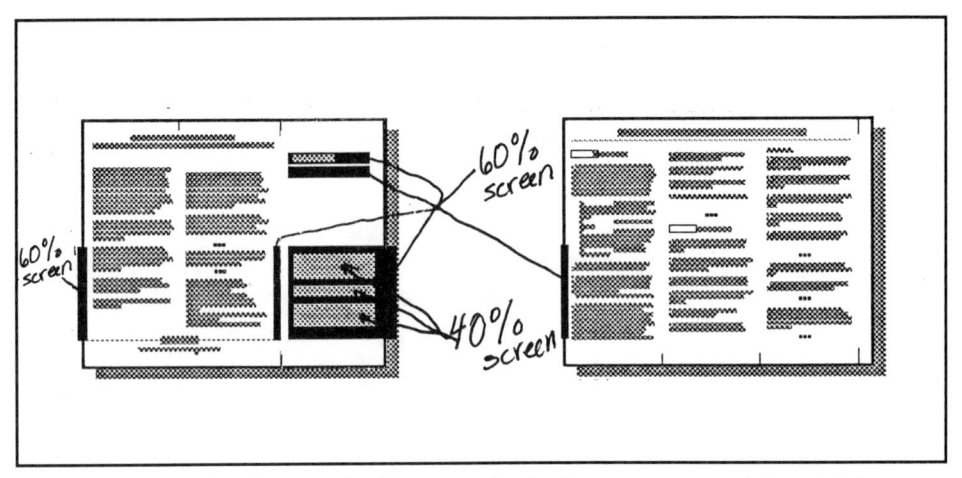

Figure 8.40 A brochure marked for screening by the cameraman at the print shop.

IMAGE RETOUCHING

Occasionally images need to be retouched before reproduction. Perhaps there is a flaw in the original (dirt, a scratch, an imperfection in the film emulsion, etc.) or perhaps a part of the image needs to be removed (a mole on the subject's face, a logo from a product) or changed.

Figure 8.41 Before and after retouched original art from Superset, Inc.

Picture retouching has traditionally been the realm of highly skilled craftsmen, who work with paints called retouching grays and tools such as airbrushes. With an airbrush, for example, a skilled retoucher can create an effect called a vignette in which an image seems to softly dissolve onto the page.

Certain kinds of retouching can also be done during the filmmaking process using photographic masks. Prior to halftoning, the films can be retouched using dyes and chemicals. After halftoning, the only way to retouch is through dot etching (lightening or eliminating images by chemically reducing the size of the halftone dots in that area). For example, even in areas that appear white in a printed image, there are usually a small number of tiny halftone dots. By removing these through etching, the highlights in the printed halftone can be made more vivid. This is called a dropout halftone.

All of these methods of retouching are labor-intensive and expensive. The closer you are to the printing press, the more difficult and expensive they become.

Today retouching can also be done electronically. Some printers have sophisticated computer-based systems that enable them to retouch both black-and-white and color images. The high-end equipment used by professional services offer high-quality results, but require investments of $100,000 or more. There are also less expensive professional tools available, such as Interleaf publishing software, LetraSet's Image Studio, and Aldus' Snapshot, which have well-developed continuous-tone image editing functions. Some of the full-featured programs in this category can handle gray-scale information, and produce results that approach the quality of the high-end systems when you output to a high-resolution typesetter.

At the low end, any paint program that lets you zoom in and edit at the pixel- or near-pixel-level can be used to retouch images (see Chapter 6). If your system cannot handle gray-scale information, however, your editing capabilities will be limited. You'll be able to turn bits off and on, and thus erase or add to your image. What you won't be able to do is blend one area gradually into another or make overall adjustments in tone and contrast.

354 THE ELECTRONIC PUBLISHER

Images that have been retouched electronically have some important advantages over photographically and chemically retouched images. For one thing, you don't lose quality as you manipulate the image. In photographic processes, each manipulation usually involves a new generation of film. With each generation removed from the original, you lose some image quality. Also, with traditional methods, the original image is altered irretrievably. With electronic methods, you can make any number of copies and try any number of effects, and still go back to where you started.

Putting It All Together—Complete Mechanicals

We've been focusing on how to add photographs and other elements to individual pages. Your mechanicals, however, should include not only clear instructions for how to put together pages, but also instructions for how those pages should be put together to form the publication. If your printed pages do not show page numbers, the mechanicals should indicate the correct sequence of pages, either written on overlays or in nonrepro blue on the boards.

In printing, pages are organized into signatures. A signature is a sheet of pages laid out in such a way that when the sheet is folded, the pages are consecutive (Figure 8.42). The printer assembles page films into signatures in the process of making final negatives. This process is called imposition (see Chapter 10, Printing and Binding).

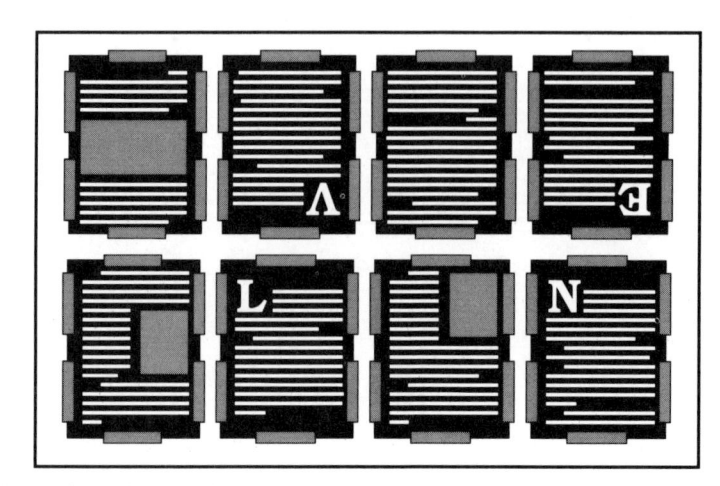

■ **Figure 8.42** An eight-page flat.

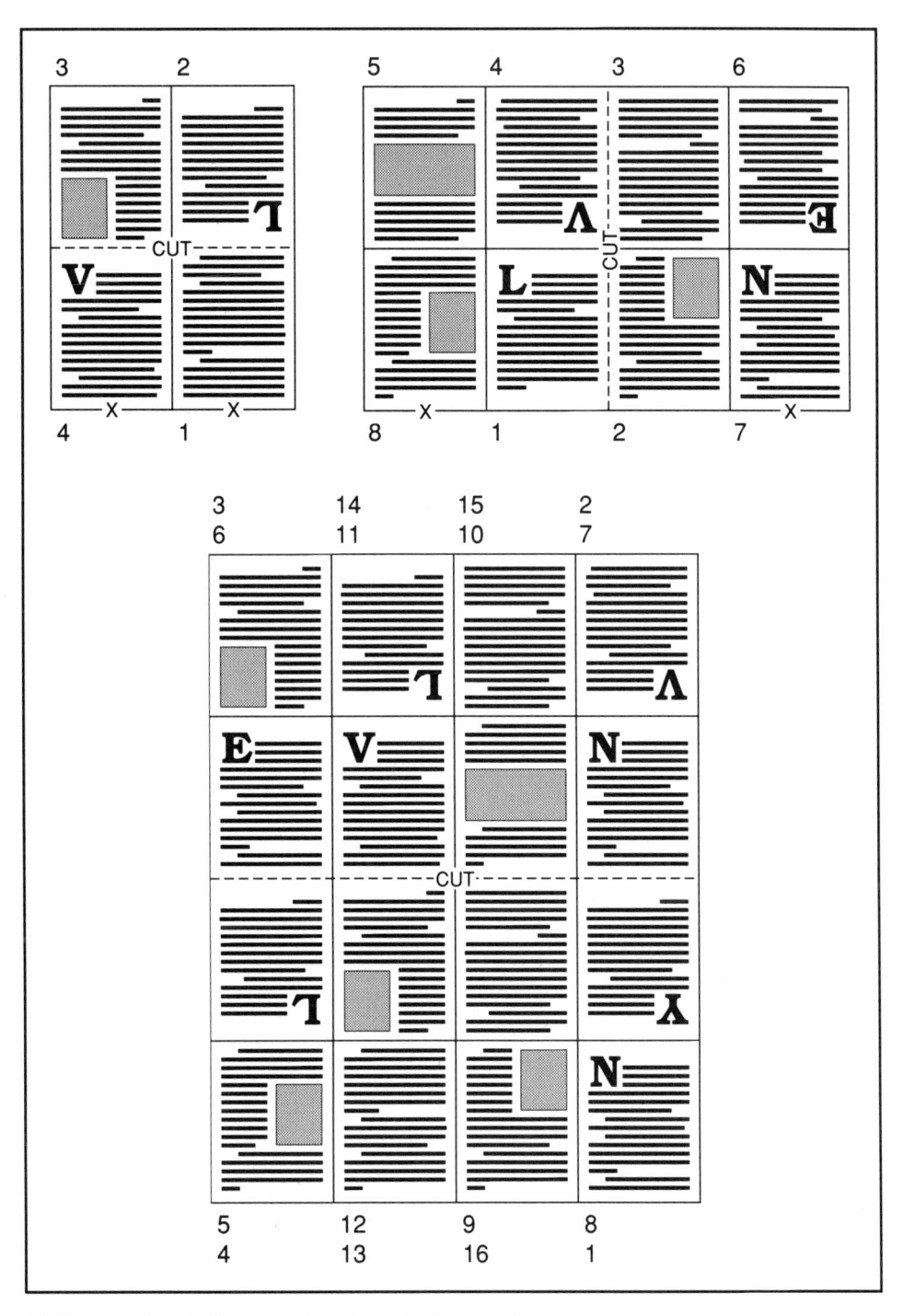

■ **Figure 8.43** A diagram of 4-, 8-, and 16-page signatures.

The smallest-possible signature is four pages. Thus, unless the design calls for a folder (e.g., a six-page barrel fold), publications are always printed in multiples of four pages. Since order of pages is based on where they will be after folding, it is not consecutive.

Here again the choice is yours in terms of how to prepare your mechanical. You can lay out camera-ready pages in consecutive order or in imposed order (a common four-page signature would be laid out with pages 1 and 4, and 2 and 3 side by side; an eight-page signature would run 1 and 8, 4 and 5, 2 and 7, 6 and 3).

By submitting your mechanicals in imposed order, you enable the printer to shoot them as a unit in correct position and you avoid some of the stripping charges. The drawback is that in a complex design, you won't be able to see how spreads (side by side pages in the final piece) look. Especially if you have elements—such as photographs or blocks of color—that extend across spreads, consecutive order will probably be preferable.

All pages should be numbered and marked clearly with trim lines (intersecting lines that show the final outer dimensions of the piece; see Figure 8.44) or crop marks. Gatefolds (full or partial pages that fold out from another page) and other kinds of folds should be marked with a dotted line. The page that folds is usually about ⅛ inch smaller than the others, since it must fit within a bound signature. Be aware that since gatefolds require special treatment in imposition, folding, and binding, they involve extra charges.

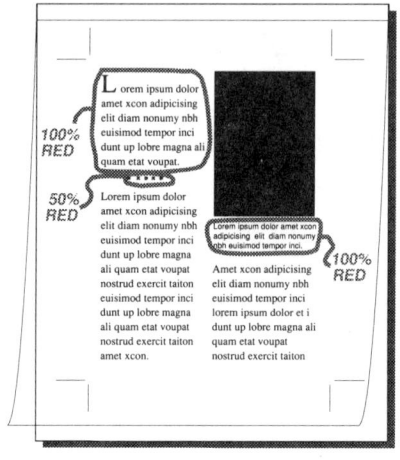

■ **Figure 8.44** The final mechanical showing trim marks.

Chapter 9
Preparing for Color Printing

Mechanicals are black-on-white. So what do you do when you want color in your publication? Of course, you can print your publication in any color ink you choose. As long as there is only one color, it's the same as a black-and-white job. With multicolor publications, however, you enter a new level of complexity. They are more complex to print, and they require more complex mechanicals.

In the discussion of continuous-tone images in Chapter 8, we gave you a basic principle to keep in mind: All elements on the page must eventually be made into line art. For color printing, the underlying principle is: Elements that are to be printed in different colors must be separated from each other. This is because each color is printed with a different printing plate.

If the publication is to be printed in more than one color, there are two methods used to prepare the pages for the print shop. If the areas printed in each color do not overlap, you can overlay tissue paper on the page and mark the colors to be used for each element as shown in this chapter. If the colors overlap, then the process is more complicated. Like halftoning, separating color elements is a task that is frequently left to the printer. And also like halftoning, there are many things you can do in preparing your mechanical to save steps for the printer, and thus save money. There are also an increasing number of tools for working with color on desktop publishing systems.

We should mention that you don't necessarily have to make mechanicals for color printing at all. Today there are an increasing number of color printers available for electronic publishing. There are electrophotographic, ink jet, thermal, and thermojet color printers which offer a range of resolutions (200 dots per inch and up) and color quality. Very often, they are used as proofing devices for color graphics systems, but they also offer opportunities for printing short-run color publications. There used to be no economical means of producing short-run color publications. If you wanted 50 copies of, say, a poster or a program for a conference, you quickly found that color printing was prohibitively expensive. Your only choice was color xerographic reproduction (that, too, is improving in quality) or to order a Cibachrome print and mount it on a black-and-white page.

Today you can print short-run color publications on an electronic printer. While most of these printers do not currently have the resolution to do a good job with type, we're likely to see significant advances in this area in the near future. We will discuss color printers as proofing devices later in this chapter, and otherwise assume that you will use offset printing for your final color print run. See Chapter 7 for additional discussion of full-color page-makeup applications.

Spot Color vs. Process Color

There are two major ways of printing color on a printing press: spot color (usually used for line art) and process color (used for both line art and continuous-tone art). Each spot color is printed with a single, solid color of ink (or several solid inks if you are using more than one spot color in the final piece). Process color, on the other hand, is made up of up to four inks—the three *subtractive* primaries, yellow, cyan, magenta, plus black—printed one on top of the other in a pattern of halftone dots (Figure 9.1). Both spot color and process color require separation of color elements.

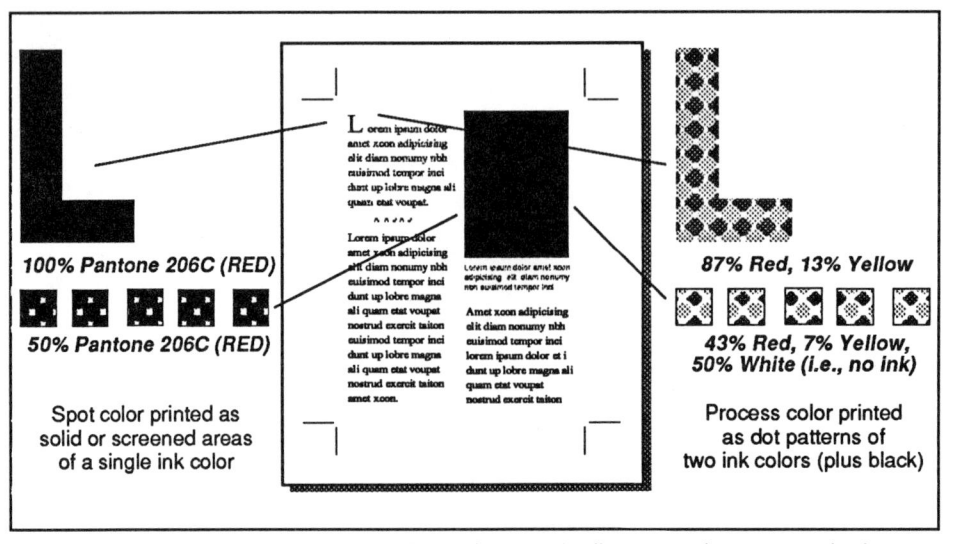

■ **Figure 9.1**   A side-by-side comparison of spot-color line art and process-color line art.

To understand spot color, think about a pen plotter. A plotter might have four pens, each with a different color of ink. The pen plotter can print each element in a different color, but you cannot have one element composed of two different pen colors (because the resulting color would be muddy). Offset printing presses produce spot color the same way: the ink well(s) of the press are each filled with one color, and the spot colors never overlap on the final page. If the press has only one ink well, the job would be run through once with one color, then the pages would be allowed to dry, the press would be cleaned and filled with a second color, and the dry pages would be run through a second time for the second color. Many print shops have presses that can print two or more colors in one run, but in any case each color would require a separate plate, or color separation.

To understand process color, think about a pointillist painting. The painting actually consists of many minute dots of paint, but the eye blends the dots into solid tones. Similarly in four-color process printing, adjacent dots of ink printed in different colors will be interpreted as a single color by the eye. For example, in areas where yellow and cyan are printed together, the eye will perceive green. The fine pattern of nonoverlapping dots keeps the colors distinct. Otherwise, if both colors were printed solid (as in spot color) the final effect would be muddy. As with spot color, each of the four colors requires a different plate, or color separation.

Some graphics programs and page-composition programs offer color options, but they must also offer color separation options if they are to be useful (i.e., economical) for producing camera-ready masters for offset printing.

Preparing for Spot-Color Printing

Using just a few ink colors, you can print solid spot color, more complex spot colors (with traps and butts), spot tints (flat-toned-screen spot color), or duotones (halftone-screened spot color). These four techniques are described in the following sections. A fifth section describes the advantages and drawbacks of using screened process color as match color, i.e., using process color to produce the same effects as spot color.

MARKING MECHANICALS FOR SOLID SPOT COLOR

If you decide to let the printer separate spot color, then you simply have to mark your black-and-white mechanical with instructions about which elements are to be in which colors. These instructions can be written in red directly on the mechanical (which is, in this case, a keyline mechanical, Figure 9.2) or on a tissue overlay (Figure 9.3). The printer will shoot the mechanical twice—once for each color—and mask out or opaque the unwanted image from each set of films.

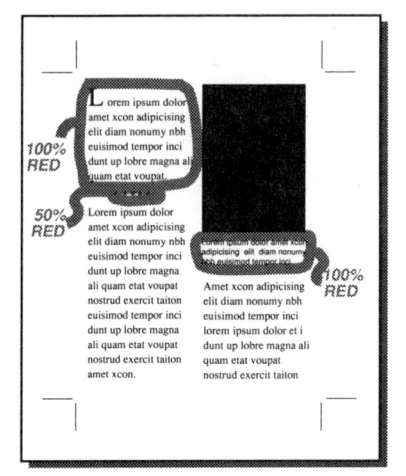

■ **Figure 9.2** A keyline mechanical marked for spot color.

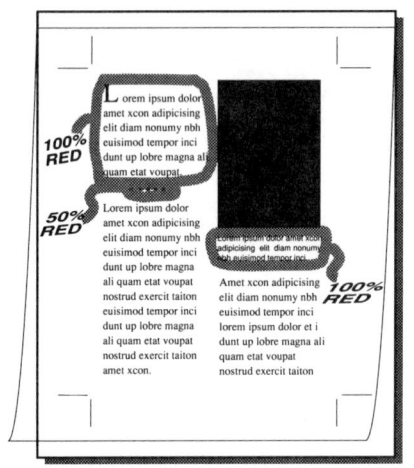

■ **Figure 9.3** Tissue overlays indicate the colors to be used.

If you decide to separate the spot color yourself, there are a number of options, depending on what kind of electronic publishing software you have. An increasing number of desktop publishing programs make it easy by giving you menu options for spot color.

One program, for example, has a "Make Separations" option in the dialog box. It lets you assign any one of up to nine different colors to text elements or borders, and also lets you select a tint (see below) of those colors (Figure 9.4). When you output a page with spot color, you get two pages (or up to 10 if you've used all your options, Figure 9.5). All are black-and-white of course, but one contains all elements that will print black, and the other(s) contain all elements that will print in specified colors. Registration marks on each output page indicate how they should overlay. If you output pages with spot-color elements on mylar (or another type of clear polyester film overlay), you can mount them over your mechanical and check the registration yourself. (Figure 9.6)

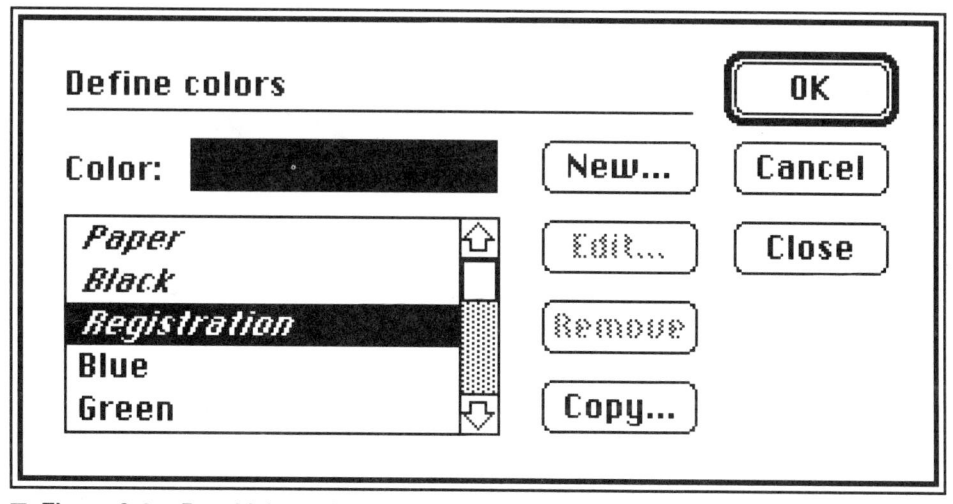

■ **Figure 9.4** PageMaker's dialog box for spot color.

362 THE ELECTRONIC PUBLISHER

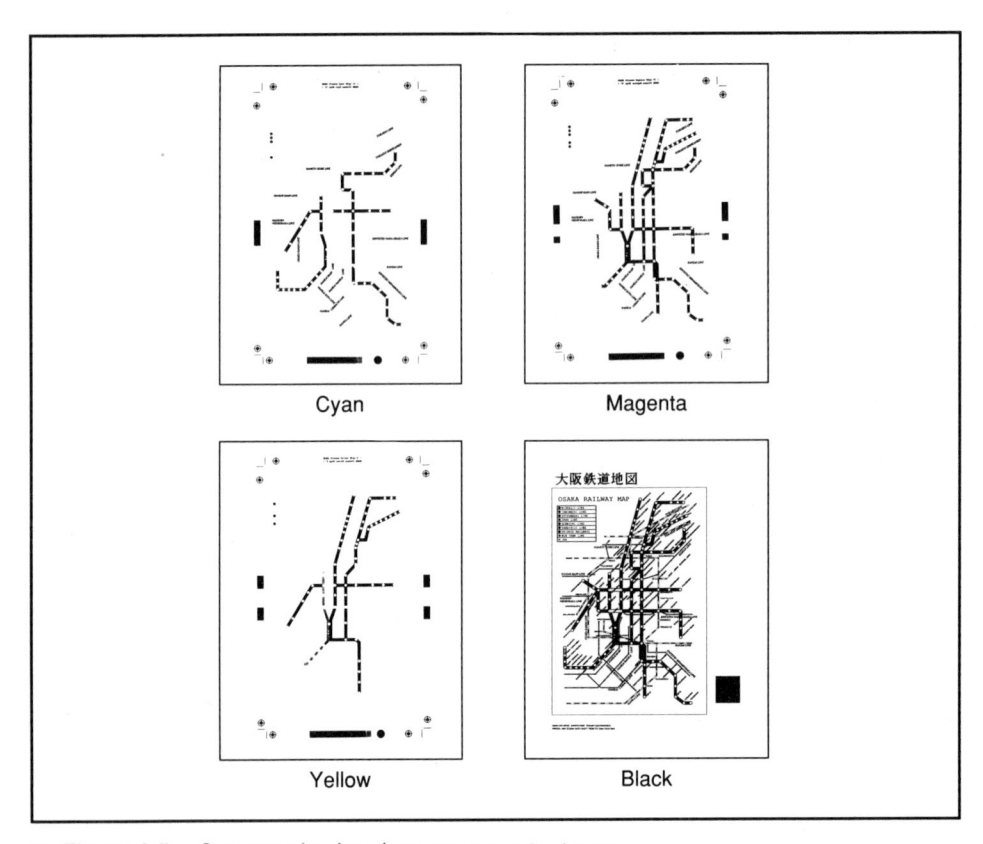

■ **Figure 9.5**   Separated color elements on output pages.

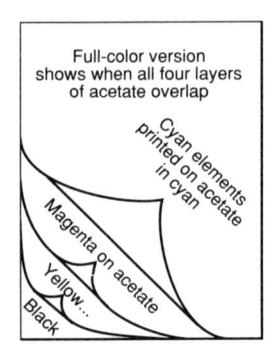

■ **Figure 9.6**   A mylar overlay of color elements.

PREPARING FOR COLOR PRINTING

If your publishing program does not have spot color capability, you can still arrive at the same result, but with a little more effort. You can manually separate the elements by cutting them out of your page and pasting them onto mylar. This would not be advisable unless your paste-up skills are strong enough to achieve proper registration.

A better alternative, if the different color elements are separate objects on your electronic page layout, is to cut up the elements electronically: After building the publication in one file, make as many copies of it as there are colors. Then open each copy and delete all of the elements that are not to be printed for each color (Figure 9.7). For instance, of you are using two colors you would make two copies of the publication file. Open one copy and delete all elements except those that will be printed in color number one. Open the second copy and delete all elements except those that will be printed in color two. Print out each of these files, with registration marks as well as crop marks (if possible).

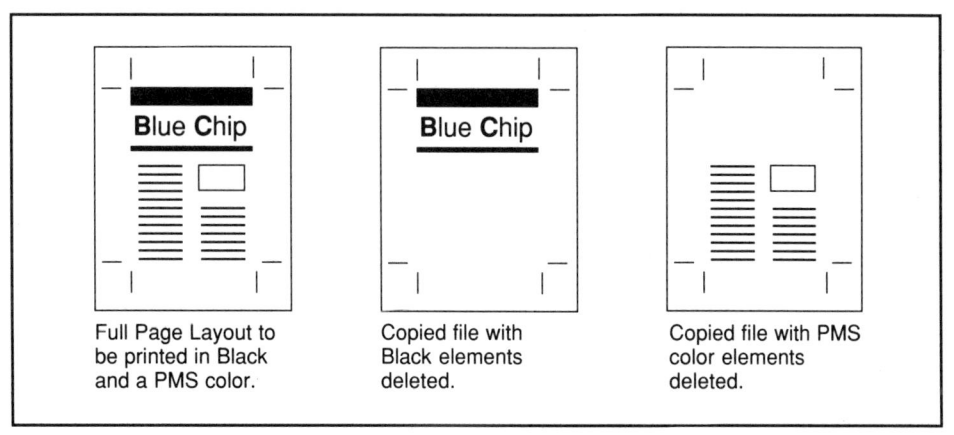

■ **Figure 9.7** Color separations created by deleting portions from the electronic artwork.

In addition to indicating which elements should be in color—or physically separating them yourself—you must also specify on your mechanical precisely what color you want. There are a number of different ways of doing this. You can, for example, give the printer a sample of the color you want—it can be a piece of paper, a piece of material, anything—and asking him to duplicate it as closely as possible.

A more precise way of specifying color is to use a color matching system, such as the Pantone Matching System (PMS). PMS ink swatchbooks (the most commonly used, Figure 9.8), as well as Toyo and occasionally other brands, can be purchased at any graphic arts supply store. Printers can usually get most of these types of inks, or they will mix the inks they have to match your swatch.

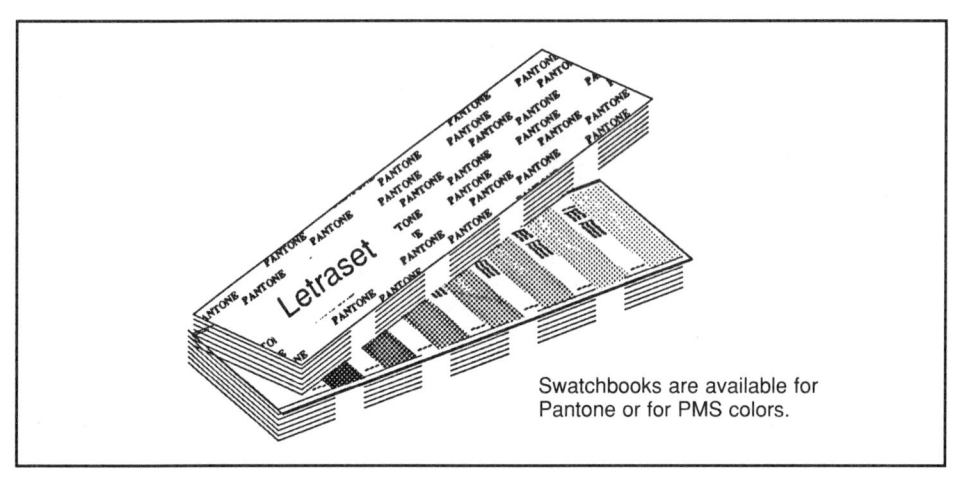

Swatchbooks are available for Pantone or for PMS colors.

■ **Figure 9.8**   A Pantone ink swatchbook.

Ink swatchbooks generally give you a sample of a wide range of different inks, printed on both coated and uncoated paper (for information about paper types, see Chapter 10, Printing and Binding). This is very important because the appearance of the ink varies a great deal depending on the type of paper on which it is printed. In general, inks appear more brilliant on coated papers, softer and duller on uncoated papers.

Swatchbooks usually present inks grouped according to hue (part of the color spectrum, as in red vs. blue), progressively in saturation (amount of color, as in red vs. pink) and luminance (amount of brightness, as in dull brick red vs. fire-engine red). Thus you will often see two colors side by side that have the same hue, but one is denser than the other. Near each color sample there will usually be information about how the color is created—that is, what base color inks in what proportion equal this color (Figure 9.9). By taking some time to understand and use a color specifier, you can actually learn a great deal about color. For example, you may be surprised to find that the difference between two apparently very dissimilar colors can be as little as 10 percent more green and 5 percent black.

PREPARING FOR COLOR PRINTING 365

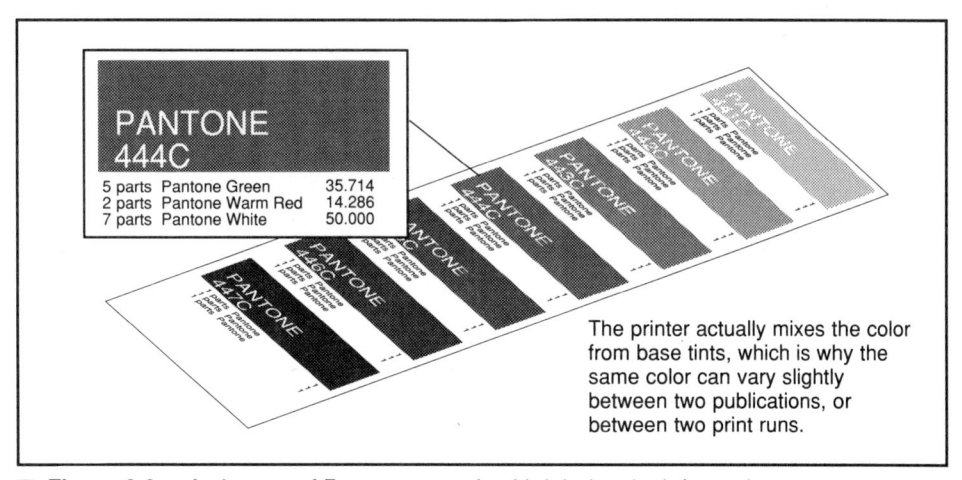

PANTONE
444C
5 parts Pantone Green   35.714
2 parts Pantone Warm Red   14.286
7 parts Pantone White   50.000

The printer actually mixes the color from base tints, which is why the same color can vary slightly between two publications, or between two print runs.

■ **Figure 9.9** A closeup of Pantone swatch with ink density information.

Rule of Thumb:

A word of caution when specifying colors for type or thin graphic elements such as rules: swatches are usually printed in 1 inch strips or squares. When you print color as a headline or a 2-point rule, it is going to look very different. Bright colors will look duller. Dark colors, such as a deep blue, may look black. Light colors, such as pastels, may nearly disappear. To visualize how your printed color will look, use a piece of white paper to cover up all but a small piece of the swatch.

COMPLEX SPOT COLOR—TRAPS AND BUTTS

If you're using more than one color, but elements of different colors do not directly touch each other, then printing is fairly simple. But if elements do touch—for example, if you have purple type in the middle of a red circle—then special care must be taken to ensure that these elements meet precisely (see Figure 9.10). If they are even a hairline out of register, you will see it in the printed piece (either as a dark line where they overlap or as a white line where they gap).

366 THE ELECTRONIC PUBLISHER

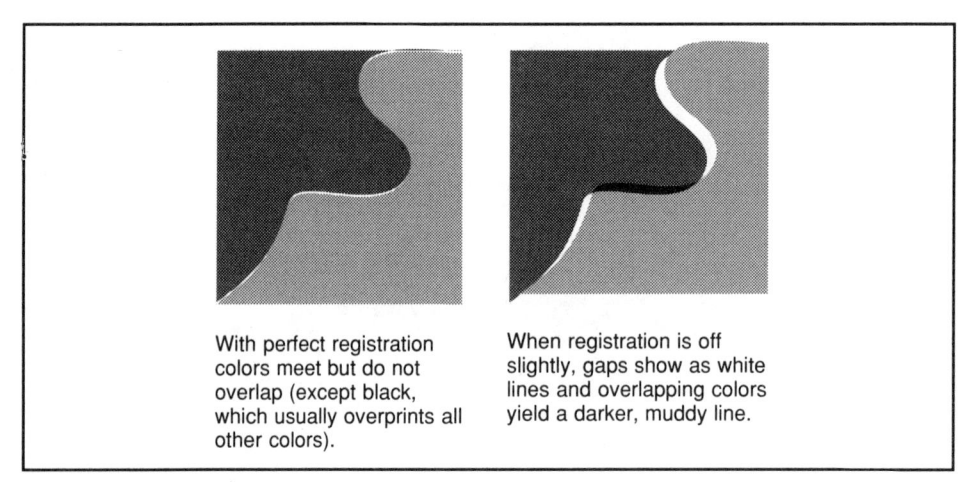

With perfect registration colors meet but do not overlap (except black, which usually overprints all other colors).

When registration is off slightly, gaps show as white lines and overlapping colors yield a darker, muddy line.

■ **Figure 9.10** Adjacent spot colors must meet exactly, without a gap or overlap between them.

If you don't want to take the responsibility for registration, then prepare your mechanical as a keyline. Using the above example, you would place both the circle (as a red outline or a black solid circle) and the type on your mechanical and write something like: "Circle prints PMS 282. Type prints PMS 141 and traps in circle."

Artwork delivered to printer as one black-and-white image marked: "CIRCLE PRINTS PMS 282 TYPE PRINTS PMS 141"

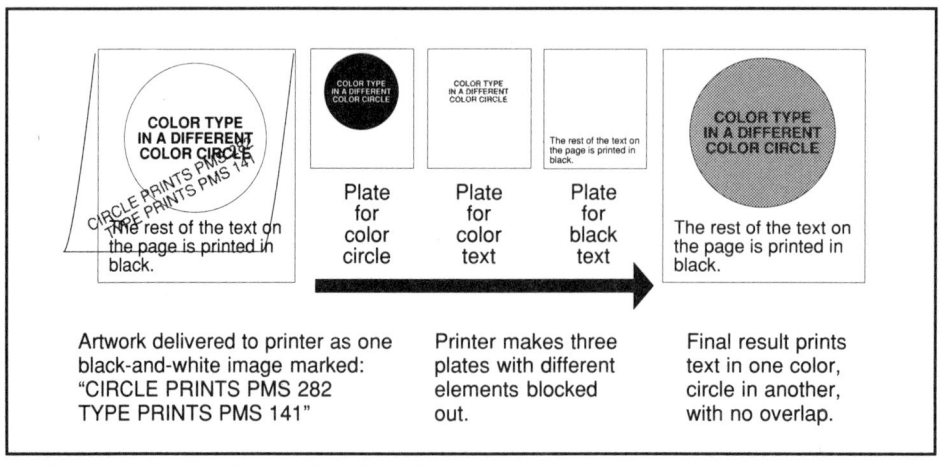

Printer makes three plates with different elements blocked out.

Final result prints text in one color, circle in another, with no overlap.

■ **Figure 9.11** A keyline marked for color trap.

If you wanted to save the printer the job of shooting twice, you could output the circle and the type on two different pieces of mylar and instruct the printer to trap.

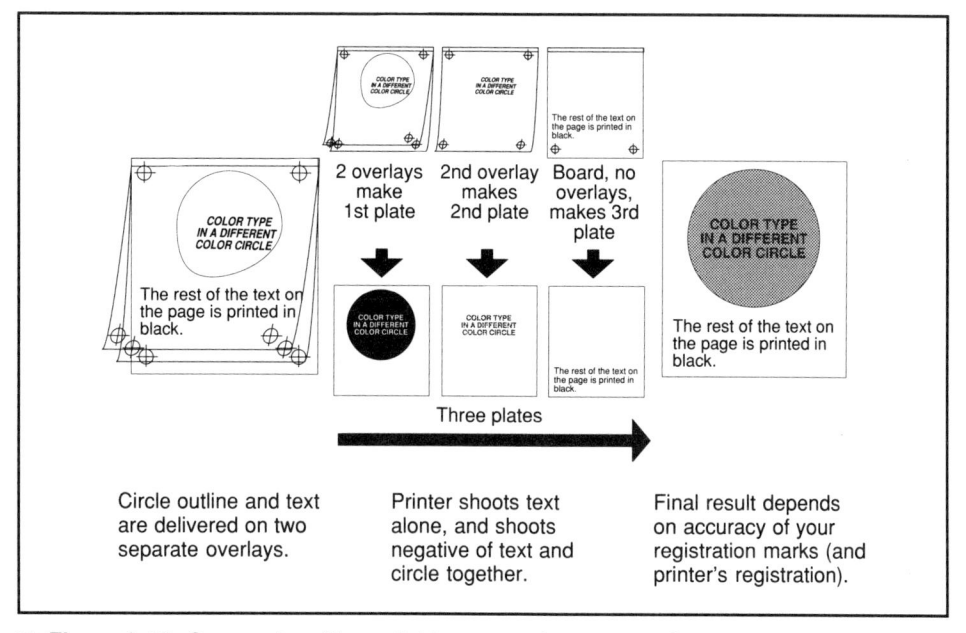

■ **Figure 9.12** Same art as Figure 9.11, prepared as two overlays.

You could also produce the trap yourself by shooting two photostats of the type in position with the circle, one a negative and one a positive. On a mylar overlay, you would then place the stat with a black circle and white type. On another mylar overlay you would place the white circle with black type, matching registration marks. The printer would shoot the first for the red printing plate, and the second for the purple printing plate. With some applications, you can print reverse images directly instead of making photostats.

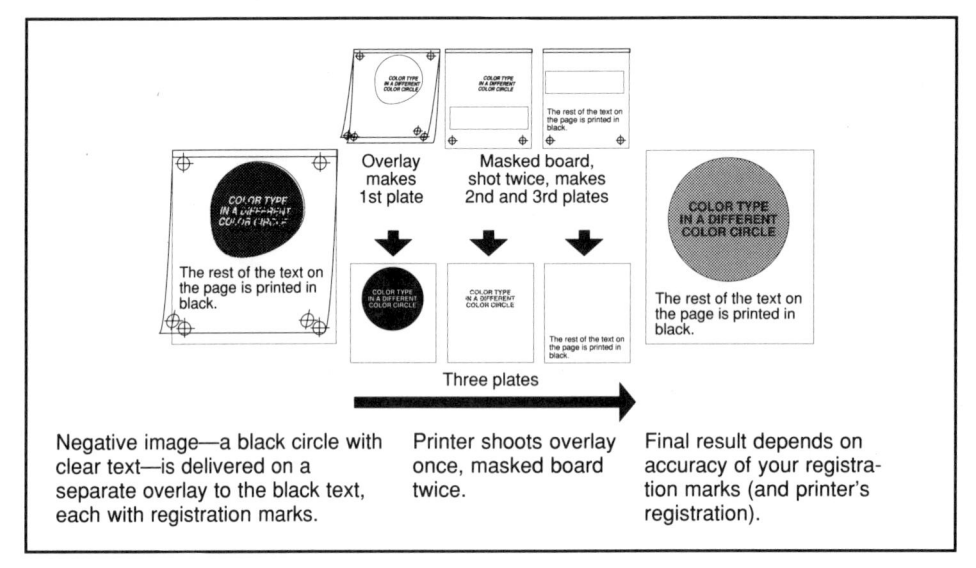

■ **Figure 9.13** Same art as in Figures 9.11 and 9.12, prepared as a negative overlay.

Similarly, if you had two solid shapes of color that met on one edge, you could output them on different layers from your computer. You could also cut pieces of rubylith and position them on different mylar layers. In either case, you would want to make sure that the two elements overlapped at the butting edge by a point or so (about the width of an Xacto blade).

SPOT TINTS: FLAT-TONE-SCREENED SPOT COLOR

If you're working with only a limited number of colors, such as black and one accent color, you can create additional visual interest, and the feeling of a multicolor piece by using screens with spot color. A 30 percent screen of PMS 200 (a deep red), will give you a pink shade.

Color tints can be very attractive printed in large blocks or across a whole page. With a light tint, you can overprint type in black or most other colors. Be careful about dropping out type from a color tint, however. Color tints like gray tints may not provide enough character definition.

DUOTONES: HALFTONE-SCREENED SPOT COLOR

You can print a color or flat-screen tint behind a photograph to give it an unusual appearance. A more subtle technique to enrich black-and-white images combines two halftone screens, one usually in black and the other

PREPARING FOR COLOR PRINTING 369

in a gray or other color (the best colors are ones that do not overpower the black). The second color can be at full density, or it can be a percentage screen. This is a good technique when you want to achieve as high-quality a look as possible in a brochure with black-and-white pictures.

To create a duotone, the original image is shot twice using halftone screens at slightly different angles. The black plate is shot for maximum definition in darks tones, and the color plate for maximum definition in light and midtones. The result, if a fairly subtle second color is chosen, is an image with richer blacks and a greater range of midtones. Of course, depending on the colors you use, you can also get some very striking special effects.

Rule of Thumb:

A word of caution: Some people mistakenly think that duotoning will improve poor originals by giving them better tonal progression. Remember that the quality of your original always determines the quality of your reproduction, unless of course you improve the original through retouching. The added time and expense of duotones is justifiable only when you have excellent black-and-white originals that contain a full range of gray tones, from black to white.

SCREENED PROCESS COLOR AS MATCH COLOR

Screens can also be used with the four process colors to create a wide range of other colors. These colors can look very much like spot colors, but they're not actually solid—they're combinations of screen dots.

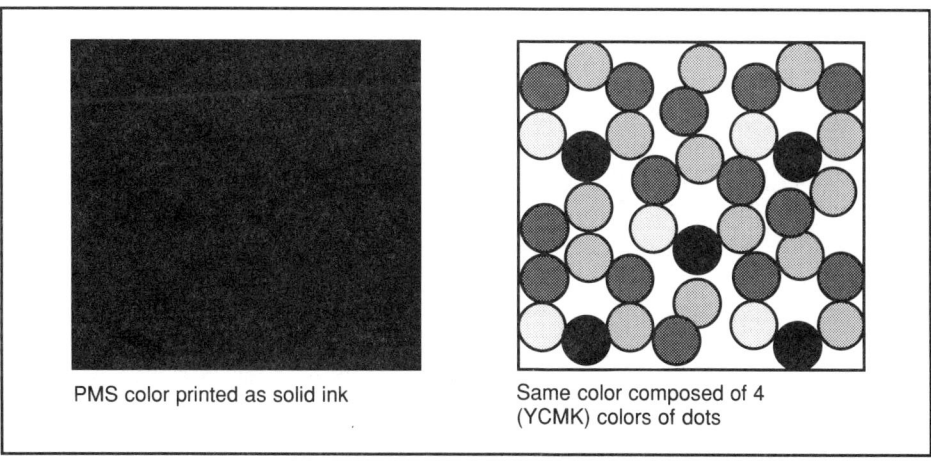

PMS color printed as solid ink

Same color composed of 4 (YCMK) colors of dots

■ **Figure 9.14** A close-up of the same color produced as spot color and produced as process match.

For example, you can create what appears to be a solid block of standard process blue by printing screens of cyan and magenta in equal proportions (i.e., a 50 percent screen of cyan and a 50 percent screen of magenta). By varying the density of these screens, you can also create many other colors. By reducing the proportion of cyan ink (i.e., a 70 percent screen of magenta and a 30 percent screen of cyan), you can produce a purple, and by reducing the proportion of magenta ink, you can produce teals and turquoises. (Percentage screens can actually equal as much as 200 percent or more—after about 240 percent, there is too much ink on the press, and colors become muddy.)

This means that instead of paying for 10 different plates for 10 different PMS inks, you could print all 10 inks with the 4 process-color plates only. You would simply tell your printer to match the PMS colors. For example, PMS 147 (an olive color) can be created by printing a 100 percent screen of yellow, a 30 percent screen of magenta, and 0 percent screen of cyan, and a 65 percent screen of black.

If you want to specify the percentages exactly, you can use a process-match swatchbook, also available in graphic arts stores (Figure 9.15). With some illustration and publishing software, however, you don't even need that, since the programs automatically calculate process ink screen percentages when you specify a PMS color.

The process-match method is especially economical if you're printing color photographs anyway, since you can get additional accent colors by simply adding a few screens—which are generally a great deal less expensive than adding colors. By using process-match techniques, you could, for example, have color photographs and two or three accent colors for heads, rules, and other elements—and still actually only print four colors.

Rule of Thumb:

Use spot color rather than process color if the difference in price is not significant, or if you need to match colors precisely (as when a specific PMS color is identified with the logo). Solid spot colors tend to look more saturated (full of color) and have more punch. Also, a drawback of using process color instead of spot color is that process-match colors are more difficult to print accurately than single-color inks. Printing four inks makes color fidelity harder to hold across an entire publication. You also have a lot more registration problems; so this method is not a good one when your design calls for dropped-out type, traps, or butts.

Preparing Four-Color Process Images

Four-color process printing is the method used to print continuous-tone color images. It is basically a multiplication of the halftone method: each color is printed as a pattern of dots. This is because, just as the printing press cannot reproduce an infinite variety of gray tones, it cannot reproduce the infinite number of colors that you perceive in the real world and that are reproduced in a continuous-tone color photograph. To do so, the press would require literally thousands of ink wells, whereas most presses have one, two, four, six, or eight ink wells for different colors.

You can fool the eye, however, into seeing both a wide range of tones (light and shadow) and of colors (hue and saturation) by printing four separate layers of halftone dots in each of the subtractive colors plus black. The brain does not perceive the dots, unless you look through a magnification device such as a loop (checking dot density in films or proofs happens to be one of the ways printers and astute customers ensure quality control). The brain blends the dots into overall tones just as it does when viewing a pointillist painting. You think you're seeing the full range of colors in the original image, but you're actually seeing only minute dots of yellow, magenta, cyan, and black.

Each of the four halftone screens is shot at a slightly different angle, so the dots do not overprint or create *moiré* patterns (a pattern of lines such as a plaid pattern that can appear where dots overlap if the screens are not rotated, instead of the illusion of a smooth continuous tone). Common screen angles are black—45 degrees; magenta—75 degrees; yellow—90 degrees; and cyan—105 degrees (Figure 9.15).

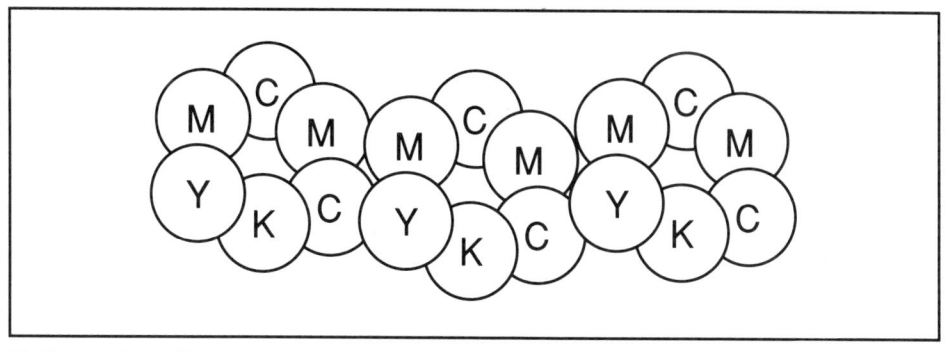

■ **Figure 9.15** Four-color process prints adjacent dots in four colors: cyan, magenta, yellow and black.

COLOR SEPARATION

The first step in four-color process printing is to separate the color in a photograph or other element into its *additive* primary components: red, green, and blue.

Why separate color into the additive primaries when you need to print the subtractive primaries—yellow, magenta, and cyan? Remember that printed color is *reflective* and that the subtractive primaries are each formed by subtracting one of the additive primaries from white light.

Yellow is the result of subtracting blue from the color spectrum of white light. The yellow separation film is thus created by photographing the original through a blue filter. When printed, yellow ink acts as a light filter, absorbing blue and reflecting (or allowing you to perceive) red and green.

Magenta results when green is removed from the spectrum. When printed, magenta absorbs green and reflects blue and red.

Cyan results when the red part of the spectrum is removed. When printed, cyan absorbs red and reflects blue and green.

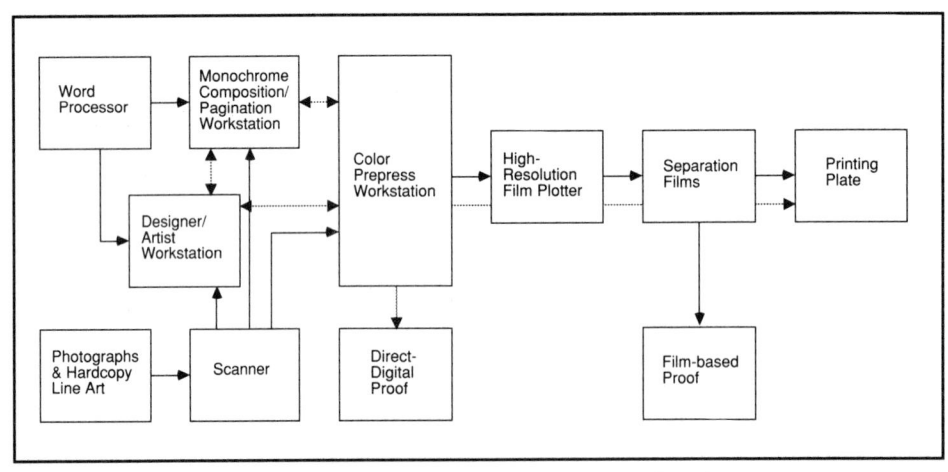

■ **Figure 9.16** A single desktop workstation can serve many functions.

So if you want to print an image that closely resembles your original photograph, *you must print each of the subtractive primaries in those areas where their complementary additive primary*—yellow/blue, magenta/green, cyan/red—*does not appear in the original.* Thus, you print yellow in all those areas where blue does not appear in the original. You print magenta in all those areas where green does not appear in the original. You print cyan in all those areas where red does not appear in the original.

In areas where you print only one subtractive primary, one additive primary will be blocked and two additive primaries will be reflected. For example, where only cyan prints, red will be absorbed, and blue and green will be reflected. As a result, the eye will perceive blue and green—cyan. But if both cyan and yellow are printed in a certain area, both red and blue will be absorbed, and only green will be reflected and perceived. Where all three inks print, they will absorb red, green, and blue, and the eye will perceive no color—black. Where no ink is printed, the entire spectrum will be reflected, and the eye will perceive all colors—white.

This is the theory. Because of the physical imperfections of papers and inks, however, colors aren't absorbed and reflected precisely. Cyan ink, for example, reflects a small percentage of red and does not absorb all of the blue and green portions of the light spectrum. When all the subtractive primaries are printed together, the results should be black, but it is actually brown. To correct for these imperfections and increase image sharpness a fourth process ink, black, is printed.

Different colors are achieved by varying the density of YMCK halftones. This is done by varying the sizes of the halftone dots (and thus the relative amounts of inks printed in the subtractive primaries). By printing equal proportions of yellow and magenta, for example, you can produce a red. By reducing the amount of magenta, you can shift the color toward orange. Magenta and cyan printed together produce blue. By reducing the amount of cyan, you can shift the color toward purple.

How Are Color Separations Made?

Original color art can be separated into its red, blue, and green components in one of three ways. For simple pieces of continuous-tone art, such as a painted illustration, it can be mechanically separated just like spot color. Elements that are to print in each of the four process colors are positioned on four separate layers of the mechanical. This method is time-consuming and requires extreme precision.

Art can also be separated by photographing it successively with three different filters. The result is three separation negatives—black-and-white film maps of where the red, green, and blue components of the picture lie. These are used to expose the positive printing plates for cyan, magenta, and yellow respectively. This is the traditional method employed by printers and color trade shops (businesses that specialize in making color separations, and that usually work in conjunction with printers).

Most continuous-tone artwork today, however, is separated automatically by electronic scanners. Scanners are devices that use lasers or charge-coupled devices (CCDs) to read the amount of light in each part of the color spectrum from the original. Most scanners can output the four separation films directly or convert the information into digital form so that a computer-based color workstation can receive electronic image files for color correction, retouching, and other kinds of manipulation (see below; see also Chapter 6 for more details about creating your own scanned images in desktop publishing).

Color Correction

Color correction goes hand in hand with color separation. It is usually performed as an automated second step in four-color process printing. (Note that color correction is not the same as color retouching. Retouching involves changing specific areas of the original art *before* separations are made, as described in Chapter 6. Color correction, on the other hand, applies generally to the entire image and is part of the color-separation process.) There are three basic categories of color corrections:

- The first is when you are correcting for a problem in the original art, such as an overall color cast. This is usually done in the process of making the separation films.
- Another category is corrections to problems in the separation (i.e., flesh tones being too red). Depending on how close the separation is to being acceptable, the printer will adjust the separation or may elect to redo it altogether.
- The third category of corrections is performed pretty much as standard operating procedure on all images. These are adjustments to compensate for imperfections in the physical nature of printing inks as well as press and paper characteristics. Unfortunately, the four-color process works more neatly in theory than it does on press. Paper doesn't perfectly reflect white light; inks don't always perfectly reflect and absorb colors; mechanical processes tend to drift gradually out of calibration. Separations are thus adjusted as much as possible to compensate for specific combinations of presses, paper, and ink.

Printers traditionally performed all of these color correction tasks using masques and other photomechanical methods. Today, most printers continue to use these methods along with electronic ones. Many corrections can be made during scanning (or rescanning) of the original image. Film masks can be created by computer and merged with separation films photographically, or they can be merged electronically by sending masking data to a color prepress workstation. A wide range of other fine corrections can be made on these powerful color workstations.

■ **Figure 9.17** A Scitex color workstation.

Common corrections include adjustments to improve gray balance and tonal progression (highlight to shadow), increase image sharpness (unsharp masking), and reduce the amount of color inks printed in neutral (gray) areas. This standard technique is called under color removal (UCR) or gray component replacement. It improves color saturation, color balance in neutral and black areas, and gives the printer better control on-press. It also reduces cost since less color ink—more expensive than black ink—has to be printed.

WHO SHOULD MAKE SEPARATIONS?

As you no doubt noted in the above discussion, making good color separations is a difficult, exacting process. There are highly trained craftsmen who have specialized in color separation all their lives.

Yet today, as with other graphic arts processes, color separation is no longer exclusively the domain of the specialist. Basic capabilities are now available on inexpensive standard desktop platforms for separating digitized art (hardcopy art captured electronically) as well as art created on computers and for performing both color correction and retouching. While these methods are not going to enable you to produce separations that rival those produced by printers and color trade houses, they can be reasonable alternatives for some types of publications (primarily those with very tight budgets and fairly low-quality requirements).

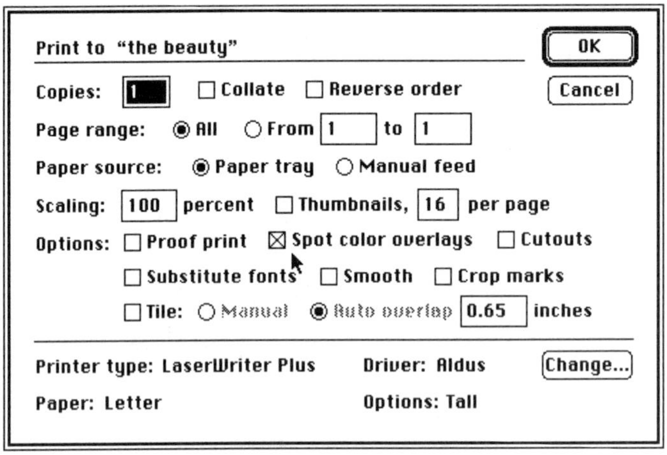

376 THE ELECTRONIC PUBLISHER

```
Print to "the beauty"                              [ OK ]

Copies:  [1]    ☐ Collate  ☐ Reverse order       [ Cancel ]
Page range:   ⦿ All  ○ From [1]  to [1]
Paper source:  ⦿ Paper tray   ○ Manual feed
Scaling: [100] percent  ☐ Thumbnails, [16] per page
Options:  ☐ Proof print  ☒ Spot color overlays  ☐ Cutouts
          ☐ Substitute fonts  ☐ Smooth  ☐ Crop marks
          ☐ Tile:  ○ Manual  ⦿ Auto overlap [0.65] inches

Printer type: LaserWriter Plus    Driver: Aldus    [ Change... ]
Paper: Letter                      Options: Tall
```

■ **Figure 9.18** Menu from a desktop color separation package.

The goal is usually pleasing color (color the client approves) as compared with match color (the ability to match a particular color precisely) or original reproduction color (the ability to closely imitate the original art). We'll discuss your options, and the trade-offs, if you decide to do some part of the color work yourself.

Your decision about which method to use should be based not only on the equipment you have, but on the same factors we mentioned before in relation to mechanicals in general. How large is your budget? What level of quality do you need? How much responsibility do you want to take?

MAKING YOUR OWN SEPARATIONS

Like the professional, you can produce separations in three ways: mechanically, by camera, or automatically.

Mechanical Separations

We've already described using an Xacto knife to physically separate picture elements for simple continuous-tone art (see above, How Are Color Separations Made?). Let's look at some of the ways you can use your desktop computer to separate process-color elements on your mechanical.

You don't necessarily need to have a color computer to do this, but you do need publishing or illustration software that has spot-color and halftoning features. The process is very similar to that of separating spot-color elements by computer, except that you output four different halftones, and you must be able to set a different screen angle for each one.

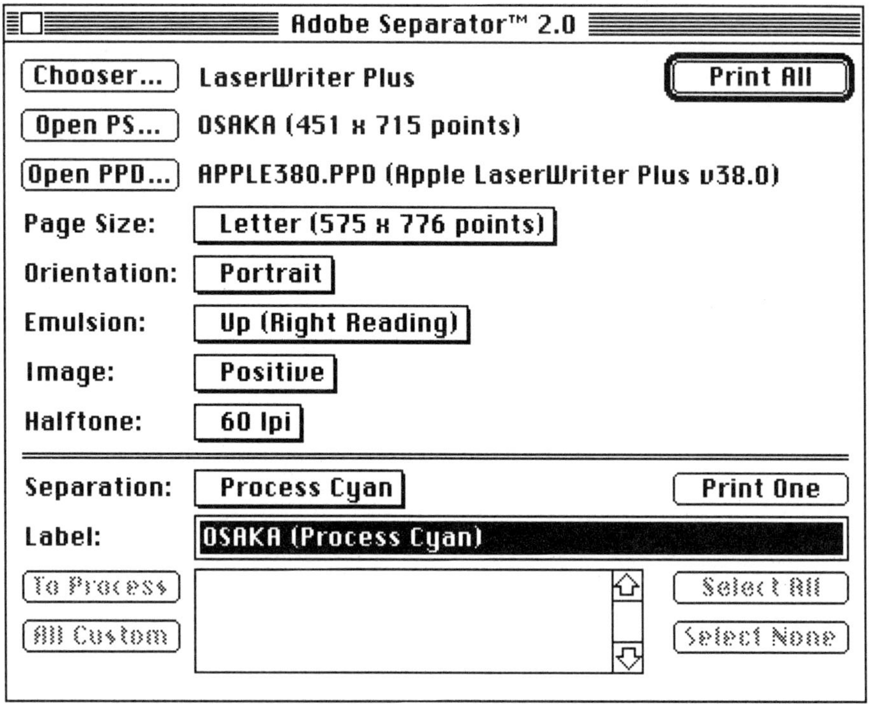

PREPARING FOR COLOR PRINTING   377

■ **Figure 9.19** Menu from a DTP program that lets you output four-color process separations.

The software that accomplishes this can be fairly rudimentary. For example, one program requires you to actually copy parts of your illustration into four separate files in order to achieve four different output layers. Another program is more streamlined, not only automatically outputting four different pages, but also automatically setting screen resolution depending on the output device (e.g., a 72-line screen for a laser printer and a 120-line screen for a typesetter).

Like the Xacto blade method, however, even the most sophisticated of these types of systems are only appropriate for simple artwork. That's because although you're not physically cutting and pasting elements, you must still be able to isolate them visually (obviously, that's not possible to do with a photograph) and then previsualize the result.

Making Separations with a Camera
While printers use expensive graphic arts cameras, today there are video camera systems that enable desktop publishers to create their own separations. Video has the advantage of allowing you not only to capture hardcopy

images, but three-dimensional real-world images as well—and input them directly into your publishing system. The disadvantage of video, however, is that affordable cameras offer low resolution levels compared with print resolutions. Thus the best results are achieved when the final reproduction image area is kept fairly small (4 inches by 5 inches or under).

You don't actually even have to have a color video camera. There are several desktop video subsystems that allow you to make separations using a black-and-white video camera and color filters. These work in much the same way as traditional graphic arts process cameras: you shoot the scene or original art four times using red, green, and blue filters, plus once for black. The four separate black-and-white images are then input into a personal computer, converted into YMCK, and output to a laser printer or typesetter.

If you have a color video camera or color scanner (basically a high-resolution digitizer in a box—see Chapter 6, Illustrations), then you don't need filters. Images are separated into RGB during the digitizing process. RGB information must then be converted to YMCK.

Converting RGB into YMCK—Color Separation/Correction Software

There are a growing number of software products for personal computers and workstations that perform basic RGB to YMCK conversion. Some are integrated with color illustration, design, and retouching systems, and some are independent software packages that work with a variety of other applications. For PC-ATs and compatibles, for example, you can purchase a color separation/correction product that will work with any image created or stored using popular graphics boards or frame-grabbing boards. There are also several products, with many more on the way, for creating and separating color PostScript images on Macintoshes and ATs.

You should be aware, however, that a good color-separation program must do more than simply translate red, green, and blue to cyan, magenta, and yellow. Determining how much black to print, for example, is a sophisticated task and one that is crucial to producing good-quality printed color. Undercolor removal is an important quality-control feature that is standard on expensive color prepress systems, which is not available with most desktop products.

Other color-correction functions are far less developed and less precise in desktop products. In general, desktop products offer basic features such as the ability to make global color adjustments (e.g., removing a yellow overall cast). This is a different process than making a local change (e.g., changing

PREPARING FOR COLOR PRINTING   379

a model's dress from yellow to green), which can usually be accomplished using a good paint program (see Chapter 6), but may not be integrated into a desktop color corrections program. Other common features include tools for the user to adjust image contrast, tonal gradation, and sharpness. The better products also attempt to emulate expensive color prepress systems by providing tools for adjusting separations to accommodate different output devices (laser printer, typesetter, film recorder), and specific press/paper/ink combinations (compensating for dot gain on press for example).

WORKING WITH YOUR PRINTER TO GET THE BEST POSSIBLE SEPARATIONS

If you decide to let your printer handle color separations, what will he or she expect from you, and what should you expect in return?

Basically, *you* are responsible for the quality of the original photographs or other artwork you submit. While printers can provide color correction and retouching services to improve poor originals, in general, the better the image looks in the original, the better it's going to look in the printed piece.

You can submit color prints or transparencies (if shots have been bracketed, select the ones that are darker—lighter images tend to wash out). In either case, you should prepare the artwork with cropping and scaling information just as you would a black-and-white print (see Chapter 8).

Rule of Thumb:
Be careful if you're using 35mm slides—as a general rule, you don't want to scale them up more than 100 percent or they'll be grainy. Also, 35mm slides originally shot for audio-visual purposes may have been shot with high speed film, which is faster and thus good for capturing images outside of a controlled studio environment, but also has a more pronounced grain than lower speed films.

Color separations usually cost about $200 each. If your budget is tight, and you're willing to give up a little quality, you can save money by letting the printer separate more than one image at a time. This is called ganging. Ganging works best when all of the images you need to separate are more or less in the same color range, since the printer cannot make the fine adjustments for color correction and balance that he can when doing individual separations. Originals must all be to scale, or at a size such that they are all going to be scaled at the same percentage. Check with your printer as to how large an image-area he can separate at one time—in general, you'll be able to gang more images if you submit 35 mm transparencies.

What should you expect from your printer? Generally, you should expect him to reproduce as closely as possible your original art. You will receive separation proofs back from your printer, and you should compare these side-by-side with the original art, which will also be returned to you for review. You should try to view these under neutral light (fluorescent lights for example, will give the proof a cool, or blue, cast). If possible, it's always better to view separations at your printer's shop, where there are specially constructed viewing rooms.

How closely is it possible to reproduce images? That depends partly on the type of original you provide. It is not possible to reproduce the vibrant colors in a transparency, for example. Light is passing through a transparency, while it is being reflected off of the proof.

You can come closer when the original is a print, but remember that the proof and the photographic print are created with entirely different processes and materials.

OTHER ALTERNATIVES

Fortunately, you have a wider range of choices than simply to let the printer do it, or to try to do it yourself. Opportunities created by computer-based color technology have led to the emergence of a new class of production services. A plethora of small companies are now nosing up between client and printer to offer a wide range of graphics services. They can help you prepare your publications for printing in a number of flexible and innovative ways.

Buying Separations from an Electronic Processing Lab

If you don't have the capability of producing separations yourself, but you don't want to give original art to the printer, you can buy separations from a conversion service. These services will take your image files on a floppy disk, and return to you separation films produced on a high-quality color prepress scanner. This would be an appropriate thing to do if you've created or modified your art by computer, but don't have an appropriate output device (one that would give you high-quality enough output to be treated as an original for the printer to rescan and separate). Some of these services have also developed proprietary techniques for enhancing low-resolution images during the transfer to the color prepress system.

PREPARING FOR COLOR PRINTING

Working with One of the New Electronic Studios

There's still another alternative that goes beyond color separation. There are new electronic studios or print boutiques, which will not only perform color separation, but design layout, comprehensives, illustration, special effects graphics, image retouching compositing, and sometimes even complete color page makeup. They tend to use an eclectic mix of tools—page-composition software, paint, vector art, video, 3D graphics, animation—enhanced with their own proprietary software, to achieve effects that go beyond off-the-shelf capabilities.

Most of these services can take input from your system via modem, and can thus offer a valuable service just in providing access to a wider range of input and output devices, software, and techniques than those to which you may have access. If you don't have a color scanner, for example, they can input your images for you. They can also supplement your technical and artistic capabilities by performing the more demanding retouching and color correction tasks. They can work with you to create unusual special effects, which you may not have the experience to even visualize.

Equally valuable, these shops can serve as a liaison to printers and color trade shops. While they may have the equipment to do desktop-color page makeup for appropriate jobs, most also work closely with traditional suppliers. They are knowledgeable about the most effective ways of mixing the capabilities of desktop systems and other equipment, and they can help you make the best decisions for your budget and the final results you want to achieve.

Proofing for Color

To proof for color is basically to check on whether the separation has been performed correctly. Has the image been taken apart in such a way that it can be put back together on press and come out looking reasonably close to the original? The proof will not show you exactly how the printed image will look, but it should reliably predict how it will look. The key requirements of any proofing system is that it be predictable and repeatable. The next sections describe four methods for proofing for color—traditional press proofs (rarely used because of the expense), common film-based proofs, new direct digital (pre-film) proofs, and soft proofs (on-screen color proofing)—with comments on the accuracy of each.

In the future, there is likely to be even more variety in proofing methods. The whole area of proofing is undergoing tremendous change because of computers, just as is every other area of publishing.

PRESS PROOFS

A press proof is run on press (a small proofing press or the actual press) with the actual printing plates, paper, and ink. This is very expensive and is done only for the most elaborate, high-ticket jobs. Even if you do print the proof on the actual press that will be used to run the job, it's still not a 100 percent accurate proofing method since the actual conditions—weather, paper inconsistencies, ink batch variations—may be different.

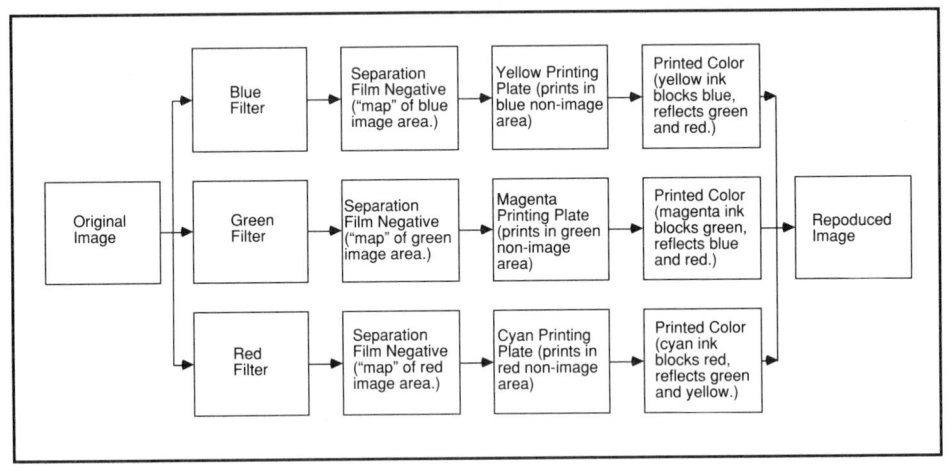

Figure 9.20 Diagram of the color printing process.

FILM-BASED PROOFS

Today, the proof you're more likely to receive from your printer is a film-based proof—a proof imaged directly from the separation negatives. DuPont Cromalin and 3M Matchprint are two of the most common brands of film-based proof materials. They are made by laminating layers (one for each process color) of toner-treated polyester or mylar.

The production of this kind of proof usually takes about 45 minutes and costs the printer about $30 in materials. Proofs may actually have to be made, however, several times. Even with today's computer-based separation systems, the first set of films are rarely exactly right. It is not uncommon for jobs to go through numerous rounds of separation, correction, and proofing. As a client, you don't see all the proofs—only the ones that the printer thinks are close enough. If you ask for changes, another round of separation and proofing begins. You're usually charged a flat average fee, which is included in the cost of separations.

There are a lot of improvements being made in film-based proofing methods today, so it's increasingly likely that you'll receive something other than the standard Cromalin or Matchprint. Manufacturers are trying to find ways of creating proofs that are closer to final printed results. New proofing methods include electrophotographic processes, which lay down toners for each separation successively (like a printing press) on the actual paper that is going to be printed. Several new systems also use the toners colored with the same pigments used in offset printing inks. And a few are even able to imitate the way paper and ink behave on press by imitating phenomena such as dot gain (the increase in halftone dot size caused by ink spreading under the force of the press).

DIRECT-DIGITAL PROOFS

Some of the scanners and color workstations that printers use now have the ability to output digital information directly to proofing devices. These direct-digital proofers vary a great deal. Some use electrophotography to create continuous-tone proofs. While these proofs often look extremely close to the original (which is also continuous-tone), there are people who object to them because they don't reproduce the halftone dot patterns that will print on press, and thus do not predict press results accurately enough.

Ink-jet proofing devices, on the other hand, create images by spraying minute droplets of ink. The spots formed by the droplets do not correspond to halftone dots, and thus ink-jet proofs are often objected to on the same grounds.

Currently, ink-jet and continuous-tone proofing devices are being used primarily as position-proofs (for judging the position and general color of page elements). Continuous-tone proofers are also being used to generate electronically retouched pictures, called second originals, which can be separated and printed just like originals.

Most of these new proofing methods are also being used to generate preliminary proofs. By using direct-digital proofs to judge the initial results of separations, printers can save the cost of outputting several sets of films. When the results are close to the original, they can then output films and create a Cromalin or Matchprint. As the client, you may or may not see these preliminary proofs. Even if you don't see them, they will probably have saved you time and money.

Eventually, however, direct-digital proofing is expected to reach acceptable levels for final color proofing as well. The key requirement for a proof is not that it look exactly like the printed piece, but that it accurately, and repeatably, predict it. Improvements in the technology should bring direct-digital proofs well within that criteria. Systems now under development will also be able to simulate the dot patterns of separation films. Some new systems, in fact, will apparently use a single method to image proofs, films, and plates with identical dot patterns.

SOFT PROOFS: ON-SCREEN COLOR PROOFING

On-screen color proofing, or soft proofing, is also a new method currently being used only for preliminary and position proofing. You can review the results of YMCK color separations and correction on a desktop color monitor, provided you have the appropriate software. There are some more expensive and highly calibrated systems for color proofing, which are used by many professional color shops and printers, however. There are also remote proofing systems that enable printers to send softproofs to their clients's personal computers. The client can veiw the proof simultaneously with the printer and either discuss it by phone or annotate it with comments directly on screen and return it to the printer electronically.

Soft proofing is another controversial area, however, because it is extremely difficult to simulate the color of ink on paper with the color viewed on monitors. Most monitors are based on a CRT (cathode ray tube), which displays colors by electrically stimulating phosphors on the surface of the tube. The color is *transmitted*, and it is made up of dots of the *additive primaries*, red, green, and blue, which make up white light. These dots, or screen pixels, are fixed in size and position. CRT displays create different colors by varying the intensity of pixels. If red and green pixels are stimulated at the same intensity, for example, the result will be a yellow hue. If the intensity of green is reduced, the result will be an orange hue.

Printed color, you recall, is reflected and made up of dots of the *subtractive* primaries—yellow, cyan, and magenta, plus black. Different colors are created by varying the size of the dots (and thus the density of the printed ink).

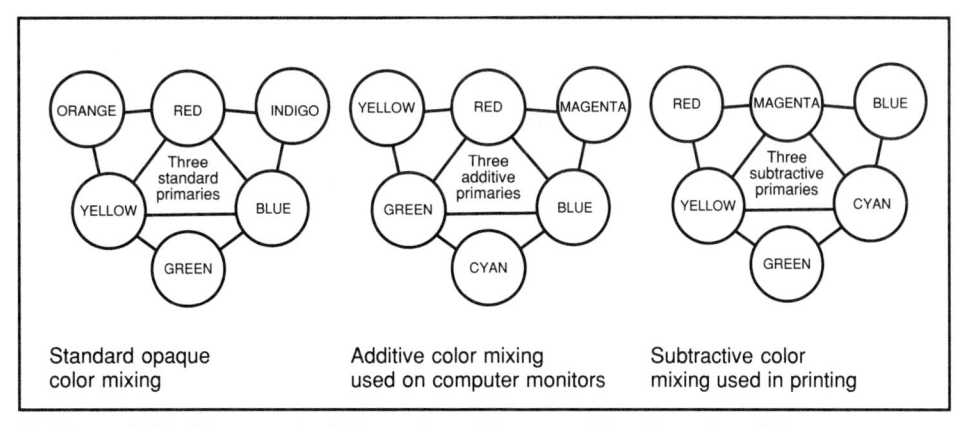

Figure 9.21 Diagram of additive color mixing vs. subtractive color mixing.

Matching screen colors to printed colors is less of a problem with spot color, since the system can use a color matching system to calibrate the two. A color lookup table, for example, can be set up so that when you select PMS 235 you get a color on-screen that looks as close as possible to PMS 235 when printed. (The color can also be adjusted to the kind of paper that will be used.) The actual color values may be quite different however. With process color it becomes much more complicated, since screening, dot gain, and all kinds of other complications of the four-color process must be taken into account. Vendors of expensive color prepress systems have done a lot of work in the area of calibration (particularly those working in the area of soft proofing). Desktop systems have a way to go. Continued improvements in software and in display color controllability may someday make soft proofing a viable alternative to press proofs or film-based proofs. For the time being, they are good partners. Use soft proofs for preliminary checking, but always follow up with one or more of the other proofing methods described here.

HOW TO JUDGE A SEPARATION PROOF

As you can see from the foregoing discussions, proofing, which was for a long time fairly standardized, is now undergoing so much change and development that it can be very confusing to know what you're getting and how to judge it. One thing is for certain: there will be more variety in the future. It's a good idea, therefore, to discuss your options, and the tradeoffs of each, with your printer in advance. Remember that every proofing method is an approximation, and requires a leap of faith of some distance. The important thing is that you must have confidence that the method you and your printer select will anticipate the final result in a way that is acceptable and comfortable to you.

What should you be looking for as you compare your original image with the proof? Most graphic designers have their own special methods, but in general, it's important to make sure that flesh tones look natural (often they come out too warm—people should look healthy, not sunburned). Also, look at objects and areas of the background that should be white or neutral and make sure that they do not have a color cast. Check shadows, highlights, and details against the original to make sure you're getting proper image definition (clouds, for example, should probably be white, but not flat white).

Respond to the printer in simple language without trying to be too technical. If flesh tones are off, say something like, "This person's face looks too red." Discuss the options for correcting the problem. Make sure the corrections are written directly on the proof.

Remember that there is an intricate relationship between the four process printing colors. If a person's face looks too red, then red can be reduced by increasing the relative proportion of cyan in the proof (actually by reducing the density of the yellow and magenta separations). But that change will also affect other parts of the image (reducing the magenta separation may make another part of the image too green for example). Additional steps may have to be taken, such as photographically or electronically masking some areas—and that can cost time and money (whether you end up paying for it depends on whether the color problem began with your original or with the separation).

A Note on Color Transparencies

Throughout this chapter we have assumed that you are preparing your pages to be printed in color using offset printing. One common exception is worth a few comments: color on overhead transparencies and slides. These materials are never offset printed because they are required in very low quantities. There are three common methods of creating color images for presentations: printing on a color printer or plotter, coloring a black-and-white image by hand with inks, and overlaying color acetates.

PRINTING ON A COLOR PRINTER

Color printers were mentioned as proofing devices earlier in this chapter. They can also be used as the final output device for overhead transparencies and slides. You can print the image directly on clear film to produce overheads. You can also print the images on paper (which often yields a crisper image) and have them reproduced using color photocopiers or color photoprocessors, or photograph them to make slides.

ADDING COLOR WITH INK

You can color a black-and-white image by hand using color inks with a brush, or color pens. You need to be sure that the inks you are using will adhere to the transparent film, or will not bleed across boundaries on paper. Coloring by hand this way requires skill and patience in order to get even coverage and avoid streaking.

ADDING COLOR OVERLAYS

You can also add color to printed images using traditional paste-up techniques. Unless you are especially skilled with special pens, or brushes and inks, you'll get the best results by overlaying printed images with the adhesive color acetates that are available from art supply shops. You can lay a sheet of color over the printed image and trace over the area to be colored using a cutting edge, then pull the color away from those parts of the image that are not to be colored (Figure 9.25).

Rule of Thumb:
Use color acetate rather than color pens to add colors to a printed image.

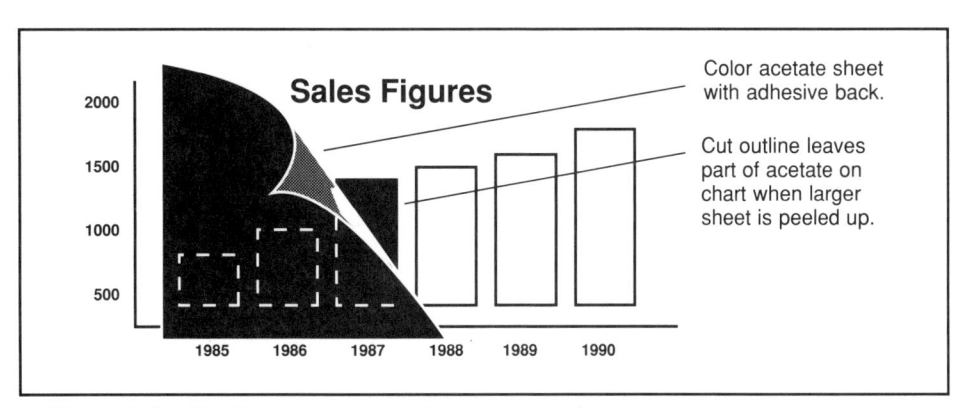

■ **Figure 9.22** Tracing over an area with a cutting edge.

The publishing process is changing today, across the entire spectrum of production, under the impact of electronic technology. Methods are changing and so are roles and relationships. To understand what is happening, and to work effectively with other participants, you must understand the entire process. In the next chapter, you will learn about the final steps: printing and binding.

Chapter 10
Printing and Binding

Here you are at last. It's time to go to press with the project you've put weeks, maybe months, of time and effort into. All of the work you've done suddenly comes together, and all of the things you've done—right and wrong—become physically evident.

This final stage of production should be exhilarating and rewarding, but to many people it is mysterious and, in the end, extremely frustrating. The piece didn't turn out exactly as you'd hoped. Every little thing seemed to go wrong. Why didn't the printer understand what you wanted?

In this chapter you will learn what happens after you submit your camera-ready mechanicals to the printer. You will learn about different printing and binding processes, materials, and techniques. Most important, you'll learn how to work with vendors effectively to achieve the final product you've envisioned.

A couple of general things to keep in mind:

One cause of problems is that people often mistakenly think their job is done when they turn over mechanicals to the printer. Actually, you've probably entered the most critical phase of your job, because if it doesn't turn out right, all of the time and effort spent so far won't matter much. You have to stay involved. If you just sit back and expect the publication to arrive on your doorstep on the scheduled day and be exactly as you've imagined it, you're likely to receive a disappointing surprise.

Nor should you regard printing and binding (because they take place somewhere else) as being totally separate from everything that has gone on before. In fact, all stages of production—from concept to delivery—are intimately entwined. It's kind of like an engineer designing an automobile. He can create a great design, but is it manufacturable? Somehow all of the parts have to come together on the assembly line into an automobile, that runs. The more you know about printing and binding—and the better job you do in preparing your publications for manufacture—the more pleased you will be with the final product.

The other important thing to remember is that printing is a little bit science and a little bit art. Computers are affecting printing too, bringing more precise control and quality assurance. Yet printing is still a mechanical process that depends on the skills of expert craftsmen. It's also a process that involves a wide range of variables. Small imperfections in paper or ink, weather conditions such as humidity, the number and type of jobs in the print shop, and the kind of day the foreman's had can combine to create problems at any point.

You can avoid as many problems as possible, and be prepared to cope with them if they occur, by being as knowledgeable as possible about the process and by not expecting perfection. Expect excellence, and work to develop *a good business relationship* with your printer. Know enough about the printing and binding processes to be able to work with your printer to find solutions.

How to Select a Printer

Even if you do have a good ongoing relationship with a printer, it is wise to get competitive bids on every job. It will not only keep your printer on his toes, but it's also a good idea because printing prices can vary so widely.

Differences between bids often surprise even experienced print buyers. This is because the price a printer offers you is partly based on formulas (which take into account the cost of his equipment, labor, materials, overhead, etc.) and partly on a complex interaction of factors such as how busy he currently is, how complex the job is, how flexible the schedule is, whether he's really set up to handle that particular kind of job efficiently, whether he's using an older press or amortizing expensive new equipment, and how much he wants the job. Printers will bid low when work is slack or when you're a desirable new client. If they're very busy, if the job is likely to be the only one they ever get from you, if it appears to be a small but difficult job, or if you've been a troublesome client in past jobs, they'll bid high.

HOW MUCH DOES PRINTING COST?

The cost of your job will depend on your design, the number of copies you are going to print, the kind of paper and ink you've chosen, the amount of prepress work required, and the type of press and method of printing.

Printing offers significant economies of scale as quantities increase. This is because so much of the labor involved in printing takes place in prepress (shooting, stripping, platemaking, etc.) and in makeready (all of the tasks that have to be performed to set up the press). Once the press is finally ready and sheets are being printed correctly, there's very little difference on today's high-speed presses between printing slightly different quantities—for example, 5,000 copies and 7,000 copies. The only major difference is paper, and that too is less expensive in quantity.

One-color printing is least expensive, of course. Is two-color print twice as expensive, and three-color printing three-times as expensive? Not exactly.

Rule of Thumb:

Two-color printing usually runs about 1½ times more than one-color, and sometimes even less. This is because most printers today have presses that run at least two colors in one pass. Additional cost for adding the second color is incurred only in terms of the cost of the ink, any stripping required, and the labor and materials required to make an additional set of films and printing plate.

Three-color printing, on the other hand, usually jumps considerably. This is because a three-color job either has to be run twice through a two-color press (which means plates have to be changed and press makeready has to be performed twice) or it has to be run on a larger, more expensive four-color press.

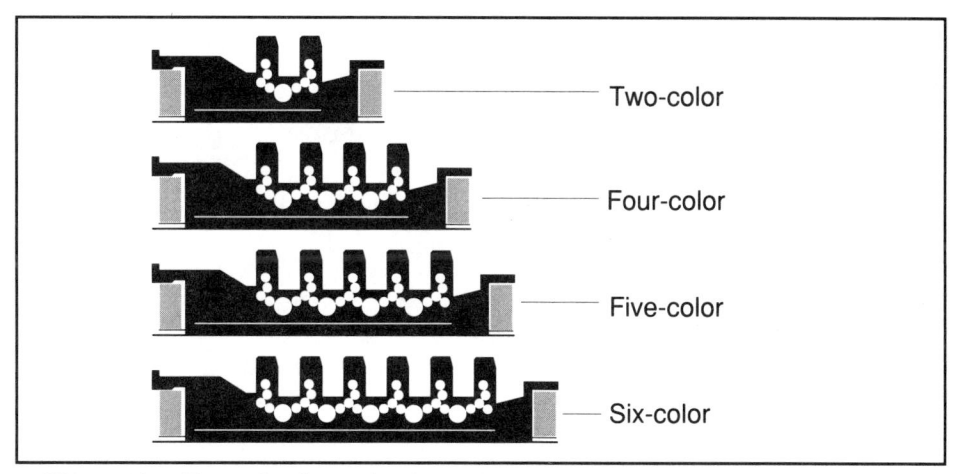

■ **Figure 10.1** Two-color, four-color, five-color, and six-color Heidelberg presses.

Not surprisingly, the cost of a four-color, spot-color job is only slightly higher. A four-color process job, however, will cost significantly more because of the cost of making, proofing, correcting, and printing color separations.

The complexity of the job is thus a major cost determinant and so is the size of the press—although not always predictably so. For example, let's say you're printing a six-color job with process-color photographs. One printer may be able to give you a better price running the job three times through a two-color press than another printer can give you running it once through a six-color press. This may be because the second printer has to amortize the cost of his expensive new press over your job. On the other hand, the second printer might actually give you a lower quote because his press is so fast and efficient, and with one six-color run, he can minimize makeready labor.

It could go either way—quotes are impossible to predict. Just remember when you're reviewing quotes and options that you may not be comparing apples and apples: Even if the six-color press quote is more expensive, you are going to have fewer registration problems, and you are going to be able to judge the results more accurately on-press than if you run the job three times on a two-color press. While you might decide to take a chance with a six spot-color job, the savings may not be worth it when you have process-color images.

GETTING QUOTES

How do you initiate the quote process? First, make sure you have complete specifications. Printers take quoting very seriously, both because it takes time to quote and because it's a commitment. They tend to get a bit annoyed when they're asked to quote on theoretical jobs.

Of course, this can be a Catch-22 situation. At the beginning of a project, you want to know about how much it's going to cost you and whether your budget can afford certain design alternatives. If you've developed a good relationship with a printer, and he knows you're not just "tire kicking," you can usually get him to give you an unbinding estimate or a range of what a certain project might cost. Even to get a general estimate, however, you'll have to develop a set of specifications.

What specifications does the printer need in order to give you a quote or estimate? These are the basics:

- Trim size (The exterior dimensions of cut and bound pages, e.g., 8½ inches by 11 inches or 4 inches by 9 inches)
- Number of pages, type of paper
- Number and type of colors (black only, black plus one or more PMS colors, four-color process plus one or more PMS colors, process match colors, etc.)
- Number of screens (tints etc.)

- Number and type of halftones (black-and-white, duotone, or four-color process; squared up, silhouetted, inset)
- Number and type of other illustrations that require special treatment (complex line art that needs to be assembled, rules that need to be added)
- Number and type of special treatments (bleeds, crossovers, dropouts, traps, butts)
- Schedule (when will mechanical be ready; when do you need delivery)
- Proof requirements (will you want to see page proofs or a press proof)
- Finishing requirements (trimming, folding, binding, etc.)

In addition, especially if your job is complex, it's a good idea to give the printer a copy of either your mechanical or, depending on how early you have to get your bids, your design comprehensive. On an extremely complex job, printers will often be willing to give you only an unbinding estimate, or "preliminary quote" until they can actually see the mechanical. This is because they know from experience that verbal or even written descriptions often fail to communicate adequately all of the potential problems. Also, they know that the cost of the job for them, and the price and schedule by which they can deliver it to you, depend very much on how well you prepare your mechanicals. If they haven't worked with you before, they may be reticent about committing to a price.

One thing you can do that is very useful, both in keeping the price down and in developing mutual confidence in your relationship with a printer, is to ask the printer *how to put together your mechanicals* in order to make his job easier. As you learned in Chapters 8 and 9, there are many different options for preparing camera-ready pages. Depending on the kind of press and binding equipment the job is going to be run on, some options will be better than others.

JUDGING BIDS AND MAKING A DECISION

Once you have all the quotes, compare them. Who can do the job less expensively? And, if schedule is your determining factor, who can do the job for the least amount of money in the least amount of time?

Be careful that you are comparing apples and apples as much as possible. Make sure that you gave each printer *exactly* the same specifications, and that you know how they're going to print the job (see How Much Does Printing Cost above).

THE ELECTRONIC PUBLISHER

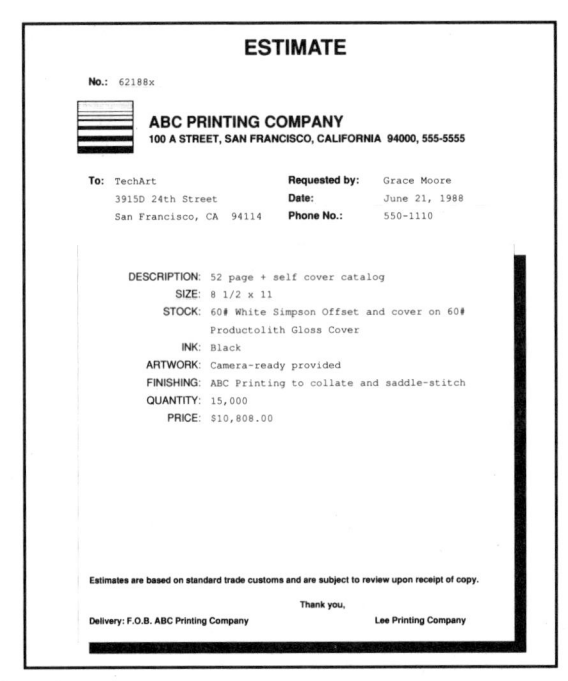

```
                          ESTIMATE
        No.: 62188x

        ABC PRINTING COMPANY
        100 A STREET, SAN FRANCISCO, CALIFORNIA 94000, 555-5555

        To:  TechArt                  Requested by:  Grace Moore
             3915D 24th Street        Date:          June 21, 1988
             San Francisco, CA 94114  Phone No.:     550-1110

        DESCRIPTION: 52 page + self cover catalog
               SIZE: 8 1/2 x 11
              STOCK: 60# White Simpson Offset and cover on 60#
                     Productolith Gloss Cover
                INK: Black
            ARTWORK: Camera-ready provided
          FINISHING: ABC Printing to collate and saddle-stitch
           QUANTITY: 15,000
              PRICE: $10,808.00

        Estimates are based on standard trade customs and are subject to review upon receipt of copy.
                              Thank you,
        Delivery: F.O.B. ABC Printing Company              Lee Printing Company
```

■ **Figure 10.2** Sample quote.

The other factor that you should consider is your confidence level with the printer, and how you feel about the printer's rep who is handling your account. If you've never worked with a printer, make sure you ask to see samples, and get references. This will help you to judge their competency to do your job. Still, sometimes the only way to make a decision between two equally competent printers is to go with your subjective reaction to the printer's rep. Do you feel comfortable working with this individual? Is he willing to answer your questions fully? Is he willing to put in a little extra effort to track down information or find solutions? It's very important to ask yourself these questions, because on a complex, tightly scheduled job, this is the person you're liable to end up with at 2 a.m. on-press. And this is the person with whom you are going to have to negotiate when a problem occurs or a critical decision has to be made.

If there is a printer with whom you would really prefer to do business, but their bid is high, don't be embarrassed to call them and give them an opportunity either to lower their bid or to explain why it is high. Sometimes there may be a single factor that you can change—such as a few additional days in the schedule—which can enable the printer to quote substantially less. You can also try to work together to find creative ways to bring the cost of the job down.

Once you've made a decision, don't forget to call the other bidders, tell them the outcome, and thank them for their quotes. This is common business courtesy, and will ensure that you receive a courteous reception the next time you need a quote.

A final note: remember that the price is based on the specifications. If the job requirements change—which they have a way of doing as you get further into the process—don't assume that the quote is constant. If problems arise in production that require solutions outside of the original quote, make sure you ask how much they're going to cost. Ask for a new quote.

What Does the Printer Do with Your Mechanical?

In order to print your job, the printer must make printing plates (various types of presses are described below). Printing plates are usually exposed from film negatives. These negatives can be created photographically with traditional graphic arts cameras, or today, they may be created electronically. Depending on the kind of equipment the printer has and what kind of work remains to be done on the pages, your mechanicals may be scanned into a computer system, manipulated in some way, and then output from the scanner or other type of film recorder in the form of positive or negative film.

As you may have gathered from the discussion elsewhere in this book, the entire publishing process is moving from film-based methods to electronic methods. There are some computer prepress systems available already that can output directly to printing plates, leaving film out altogether. These systems are still under development, but they are being used in some large newspapers, and they certainly demonstrate the direction in which publishing is likely to go. For today, however, film is still the key medium in the final steps of production.

The films that are used to create printing plates must contain all elements of the publication. So the printer's job at this point depends on how much work you've left him.

STRIPPING

If you've provided a keyline mechanical, the printer has a lot of camera (or electronic page makeup) work to do before he can even get to the point of generating negative films and making plates.

All elements that are not black-and-white line art must be photographed onto separate pieces of film. For example, photographs must be screened and perhaps a silhouette mask will need to be cut. Headlines that are to be in color must be shot and perhaps some rules added. If the job is not being done electronically, then each of these pieces of film must actually be taped together—thus, the term stripping.

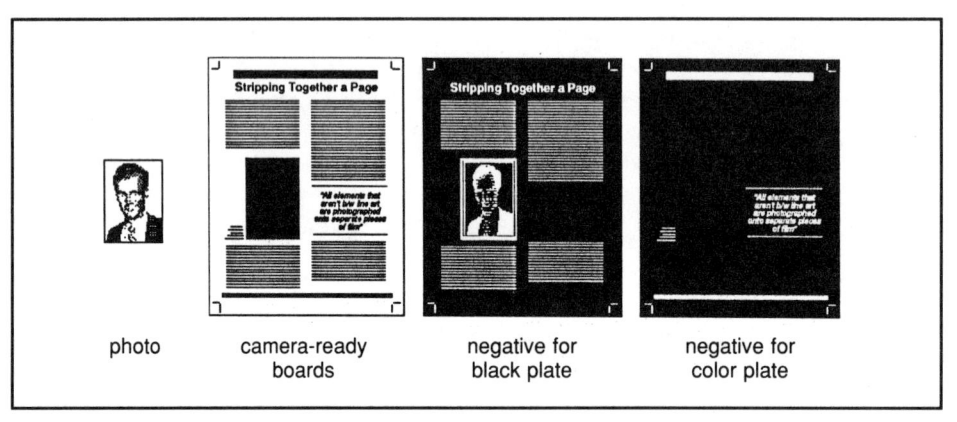

■ **Figure 10.3** Stripped together page.

IMPOSITION

Once all page elements have been stripped together, pages must be assembled in the order in which they are going to be printed (Figure 10.4). *This is not the order in which they will appear in the final printed, bound piece.* Rather, pages are arranged within flats so that after printing and folding, all pages will be in correct order. The process is called imposition, and the result is called a printing flat.

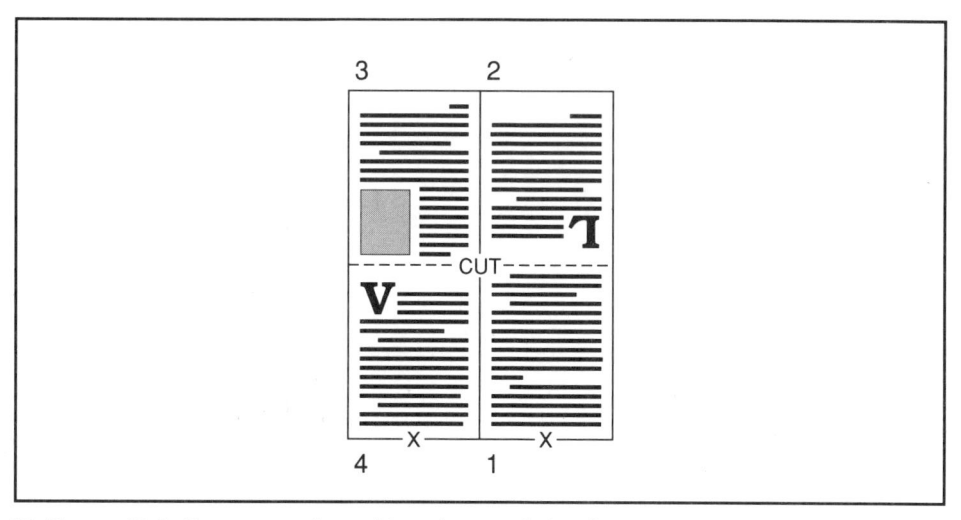

■ **Figure 10.4** Four pages, impositioned onto printing flat.

    The actual number and position of pages that can fit in a flat depend on the size of the trim, the number of pages in the publications, the size of the sheet of paper that will be printed and cut to trim, and specific characteristics of the press, and folding and binding equipment.

    The easiest way to get a sense of how imposition works is to fold a piece of paper into a mock eight-page brochure. Cut it so that you can open it like a book. Then number the pages. Now unfold the piece of paper and look at the order in which the pages fall.

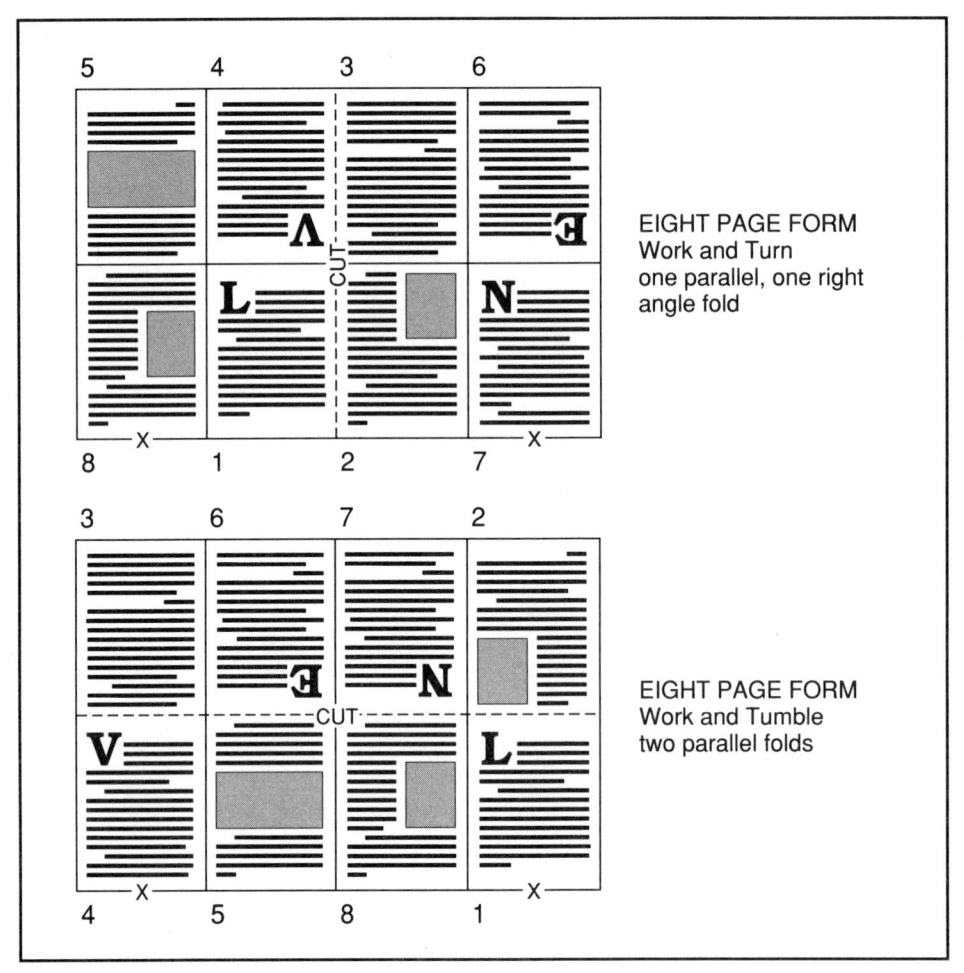

Figure 10.5 Diagram of flats for folded, cut 8-page "brochure."

If you have prepared your mechanicals in consecutive order, the printer will have to photograph, cut, and strip them into imposition order. There are several ways of doing this. The traditional way is to tape films together on goldenrod paper. He can also output very large pieces of film on a plotter from a prepress system in imposed order. There are also projection systems that position multiple pages onto film in proper sequence.

Whatever method is used, it is absolutely critical that pages not only be in correct order but in precisely correct register. If you have a rule or an image that crosses over two pages, those elements must meet exactly *after the flat has been printed, folded, cut, and bound.* This is what we meant in Chapter 8 when we discussed how much responsibility you want to take. When there is a really tricky element, such as a crossover, many experienced graphics designers will want to ensure accuracy by doing the crossover themselves on the mechanical unless they have absolute confidence in a particular printer. If you're not experienced, you may want to leave tricky elements to the pros.

PAGE PROOFS

For large runs and jobs that require a lot of stripping and other preparation by the printer, the printer often produces page proofs or imposition proofs for you to preview before the job is actually run on the press. Proofs are crude photocopies of film negatives. They are referred to as "salts," "browns," "blues," or "blue lines," depending on the particular chemistry used to develop them. Proofs are often folded, cut, and bound to look like the final piece. They show you all elements in position, including halftone photographs. They don't show you color.

■ **Figure 10.6** Proof marked up and approved "with changes."

The proof is where you can see if all elements are positioned correctly. This is your chance to catch any mistakes made by the printer or any problems you missed in your mechanical. While changes are relatively expensive at this point—new films must be generated—they are much less expensive than trying to make a change on press. Of course, the printer will correct his own mistakes free of charge.

Check page proofs carefully to make sure, first of all, that all elements are there. Occasionally, things fall off of mechanicals. You need to check the proof with special care if you've left a lot of the page assembly to your printer. Make sure that all elements are in proper position and alignment (the best way to do this is to measure it against your mechanical). Make sure that halftones were properly cropped and were not accidentally flopped. If you see anything wrong, mark it clearly directly on the proof with a pen or grease pencil.

> **Rule of Thumb:**
> It is a good idea to make a photocopy of the mechanical for each page before sending the masters to the printer. The photocopies can help resolve questions if parts of the pasted-up mechanicals literally become unglued and fall out of position during handling.

Other things to look for include imperfections in the film, which can appear as white dots or scratches. Circle anything that looks wrong to you. (Some things that might appear to be imperfections in the films are really only in the proof—but circle them anyway. Better to be safe than sorry.)

When you are finished, indicate the status of the proof in the little box that is usually stamped on the front. Sign it and date it.

When you sign-off on a proof, whether "as is" or with corrections noted, you take a certain amount of responsibility. If you fail to notice a missing element or to call the printer's attention to a slightly askew photograph, he will not be liable for that mistake on-press (i.e., he will not be required to correct it free-of-charge). When you sign-off on a proof, the printer is responsible only for delivering a final piece that meets the standard of quality represented in the proof. For this reason, when corrections are fairly extensive it is a good idea to request a second proof for review and approval.

COLOR KEYS

To see color in position on the page, you will need to order an additional proof, called a color key. Color keys are similar to separation proofs in that they are made up of laminated layers of mylar. But don't mistake them for separation proofs, because they are for checking color position only, and the colors are not accurate.

Color keys will show you both the position of spot color and four-color process. Because they are not folded, trimmed, and bound, however, you can't judge the positioning of adjacent pages. For that, you'll still need your imposition proof.

PRINTING AND BINDING 401

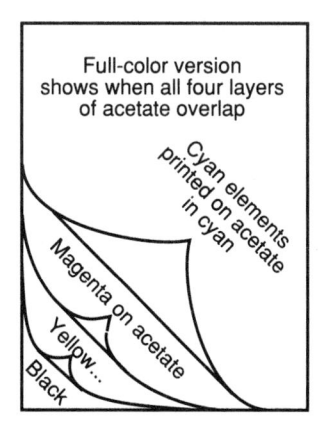

■ **Figure 10.7** Color key.

PLATEMAKING

Today, printing plates are generally made through photographic processes. Basically, negative films are used to expose a light-sensitive surface of some kind, which is then chemically treated. The plates may be made of metal, plastic, or paper. Metal plates last well through long print runs and can be archived for reuse if the publication is ever reprinted, but the cost is more than plastic or paper plates. Paper plates gradually deteriorate, so they do not work well for long print runs and they cannot be reused, but these are the least expensive plates and are often used in quick-print shops. Plastic plates last well through long print runs but are not usually saved for future runs.

■ **Figure 10.8** Steps in making plates.

A key feature of a printing plate is that the image and nonimage areas are separated. How this is accomplished differs between platemaking for different kinds of presses. Letterpress plates, for example, raise the image area above the nonimage area—something like a rubber stamp. Gravure plates depress the image area below the nonimage area. Offset plates—used in offset lithography, the most common printing method today—are flat, but are chemically treated so that image areas accept ink and nonimage areas repel it.

Letterpress plates raise the image area above the non-image area.

Gravure plates depress the image area below the non-image area.

Offset plates are flat, but are chemically treated so that image areas accept ink and non-image areas repel it.

■ **Figure 10.9** Drawing of letterpress, gravure, and offset plates (side view).

Recently, some desktop system manufacturers have announced equipment that can produce negatives or plates electronically, directly from your disk files. This avenue is worth exploring if your pages are completely composed on the screen and do not require additional paste-up or special handling, but until the equipment becomes more generally available you may have trouble finding a service bureau or printer that offers this type of platemaking service.

When You're On-Press

The best way to ensure that everything goes well during the print run is to be there. Despite the expense of correcting the occasional serious problems that do occur on press, it is much better to make a hard decision at that point than to be disappointed when the job arrives. It is much easier to negotiate with the printer before 5,000 copies have been printed, folded, bound, trimmed, and delivered to your doorstep.

No matter how precise your mechanical and specifications are, there are just too many variables in printing to predict exactly what will happen. For example, you may have correctly specified a 30 percent blue screen—which turns out looking like a 50 percent screen on-press. This could be caused by ink being run heavy (in order to achieve a good fill in adjacent solid areas of color or because of your paper choice), or it could be that you're printing with a different screen ruling than was used to print the swatchbook (133-line, for example, instead of 150-line). The possibilities are endless—and if you're not at the press run, you won't know until it's too late.

Going to a press run is also the best way to learn. Most printers will welcome you at the press run (it takes some of the responsibility off their shoulders) provided that you know what to expect (if you don't, ask them in advance) and know how to behave (common courtesy and patience count for a lot at a difficult run).

Going to a press run is a lot like going to a photo shoot—there's a lot of hurry up and wait. Usually, the printer will ask you to arrive at a time when he expects to have most of the preliminary problems solved and the pages are just about "up to color." This means that the printing plates have run sufficiently to be "inked up" and are giving a pretty close impression of the ultimate page. Normally, he'll confirm the time in advance, giving you an hour's notice or so.

It's critical that you arrive when you are requested. It is extremely expensive to have presses and printing crews sitting around idle—and being late can not only cost you money and a good relationship with your printer, it can endanger the delivery of your job.

When you get to the printing house, you will be taken into a waiting area with a special viewing booth. The printer will bring you a sheet to view. If your job is one or two colors, you will probably see it all at one time. If it combines a number of colors and varnishes, you may see only part of it.

For example, if you are on a four-color press and you are printing a four-color process job with two matched spot colors and a varnish, you will see the four-color process (including all black type, of course) on the first run. Then you will probably have to come back later in the day to see the complete piece, since it will normally take several hours or more to complete the first run, change the plates, wash the blankets, etc.

You also may or may not see all of your pages at one time. For example, if you are printing an eight-page brochure "work and turn" (the entire brochure is printed on one side of the sheet, then turned and printed in opposite order on the back of the sheet), you can see your entire brochure after a single run. With other methods, however, you may see only half of your publication after printing one side, then the other half when the reverse side is printed. Before they can print the other side, they have to give the first side time to dry (or your job could be smeared), and if it's raining or humidity levels are high, that could mean waiting even an extra day before you see your entire job.

■ **Figure 10.10**   Printed flat, marked-up with corrections.

Rule of Thumb:

Allow time for press checks. If you are checking a four-color process 256-page book, for example, it can take between one and two weeks for a 25,000-copy run.

CHECKING THE PRESS SHEET

Whatever part of the job you're given, check the press sheet just as carefully as you did the proof. Don't be intimidated by the printer standing at your elbow. Take as much time as you need to check it, but concentrate and work efficiently. Most printers will leave you alone for fifteen minutes or so—they want you to check the sheet carefully and catch any problems before they've printed thousands of sheets. If you OK'd the prepress proofs, the printer is not responsible for any problems you find at the press-sheet stage except those associated with printing quality, but the printer would still rather fix any other problems (and charge you for the fix) *before* running the whole job.

Just as with the proof, circle mistakes or flaws directly on the sheet. Check to see that all elements are printing clearly. Check to see that all spot color elements are in the correct color. Check printed versions of color images against the separation proofs. The mechanical and approved salt proofs will also be in the room to check alignment and registration if necessary.

What do you do if you see something wrong? First, you bring it to the attention of the printer. Find out what caused the problem and discuss possible solutions. If it is not the printer's mistake, then you can expect an additional charge for making the correction. The printer should be able to tell you how much more it is going to cost, not only in charges but in time; so you can make an informed decision, balancing budget, schedule, and quality concerns.

There are a lot of common problems which are relatively easy to correct. White spots, called hickies, are caused by loose fibers in the ink or paper and can often be corrected by washing the blanket.

A wide range of color adjustments can also be made on-press. For example, photographs that are printing too cool (bluish) can be warmed up (more red). It's even possible to make color adjustments to small areas, depending on the type of press and the intricacy of the design. For example, the printer can increase the amount of cyan coming from a particular inkwell, but it will also affect any other elements being printed with cyan nearby—or in the same position further down on the sheet. Thus, sometimes, the only solution will be to stop the press and remake the films and plates.

Fine registration problems (butting lines that don't meet exactly, or elements that are overprinting instead of trapping) may be adjustable on-press, but more likely will also require remaking the plate. If you have (heaven forbid!) found a typo at this late date, it will require going all the way back to the mechanical, correcting it, reshooting the films, and remaking the plates. With press charges running between $250–500 per hour, it's an expensive time to find that kind of a mistake.

How long it takes to make corrections such as these can range from 20 minutes to half a day or more. Be prepared to wait at the printer's, or to come back later.

In order to understand better what is happening when your job is on-press, and to make better decisions when they have to be made, you should have some knowledge of printing presses, papers, inks, and folding and binding techniques.

Printing

The essential feature of printing that has not changed since the first press was invented is simply stated: ink is picked up on a "plate" or drum of some kind, and transferred to sheets of paper. This requires making a mirror-image version of your mechanicals, and separating parts of the image by etching, casting, carving, or electronically charging the surface of the plate.

PRINTING AND BINDING   407

Pagemaker Printout

Photograph   Halftone   Negative

Negative Page Image
with Photo stripped in   Plate   Final Printed Page

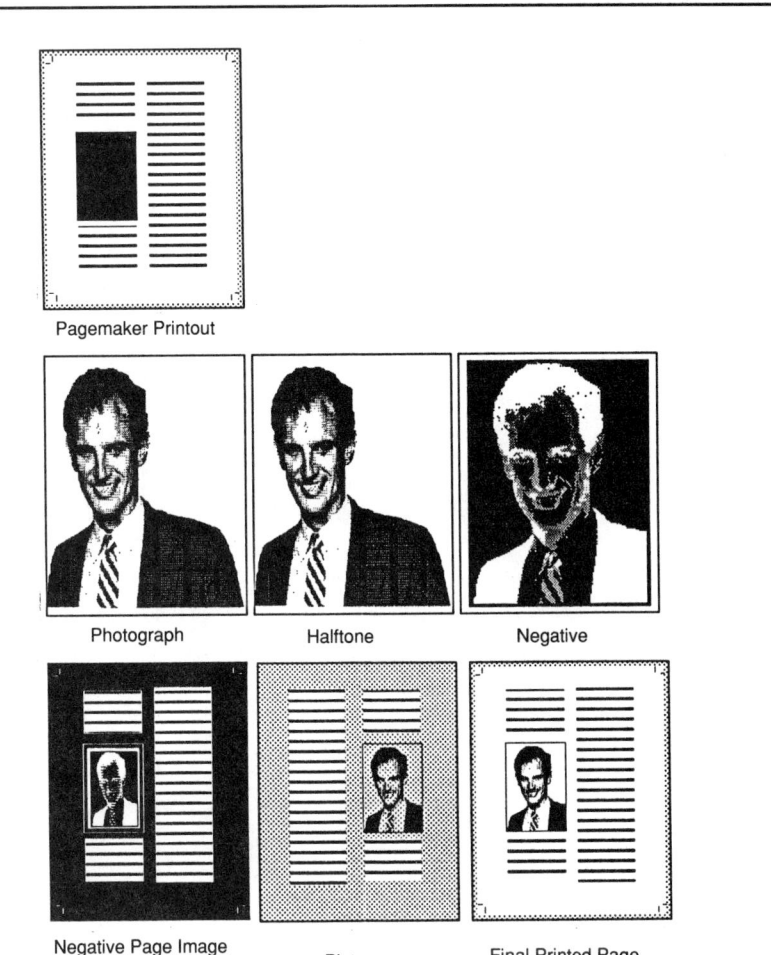

Camera-ready master pages—black images on white paper—printed directly from a page-composition application. Photographic negative is prepared by the offset printer—the print image is transparent on a black background. The plate made from the negative has a raised surface that picks up ink from the roller and lays it on the paper—the plate is a mirror-image of the final page.

■ **Figure 10.11**   The offset printing process.

TYPES OF PRINTING PRESSES

The oldest form of printing, called letterpress, has been replaced by offset lithography and gravure as the most commonly used printing press technology, but it is perhaps the easiest method to understand, and serves as a good example through which to compare the two other printing methods. Letterpress, as its name indicates, derives from hot-metal typesetting (before phototypesetting and electronic publishing).

In letterpress, graphic images are engraved onto metal (usually zinc, magnesium, or copper). After being exposed with the printing flat, they are etched in acid so that the nonimage areas are lowered beneath the printing surface. These etchings may be combined with cast-metal type in some cases to form the final printing surface. In letterpress, the plate when inked, directly imprints the paper.

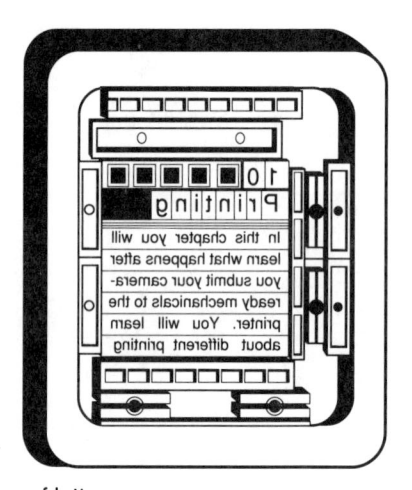

■ **Figure 10.12** Diagram of letterpress process.

Letterpress is generally only used today for stationery, business cards, and other specialized applications such as wine bottle labels and limited-edition books of archival quality.

Offset Lithography

Offset lithography printing is the most common type of printing today. As in artistic lithographic techniques, lithographic printing is based on the principle that "oil and water don't mix." The offset printing plate (it may be made of aluminum, stainless steel, or even paper) is chemically treated so that parts of it (the image area) will reject water and other parts (the nonimage area) will accept water and reject ink.

The printing plate, which is wrapped around a cylinder, never actually comes in contact with the paper. The offset plate is very delicate and the abrasiveness of the paper's surface would cause damage. Instead it imprints a rubber blanket, also mounted on a cylinder, which in turn imprints the paper.

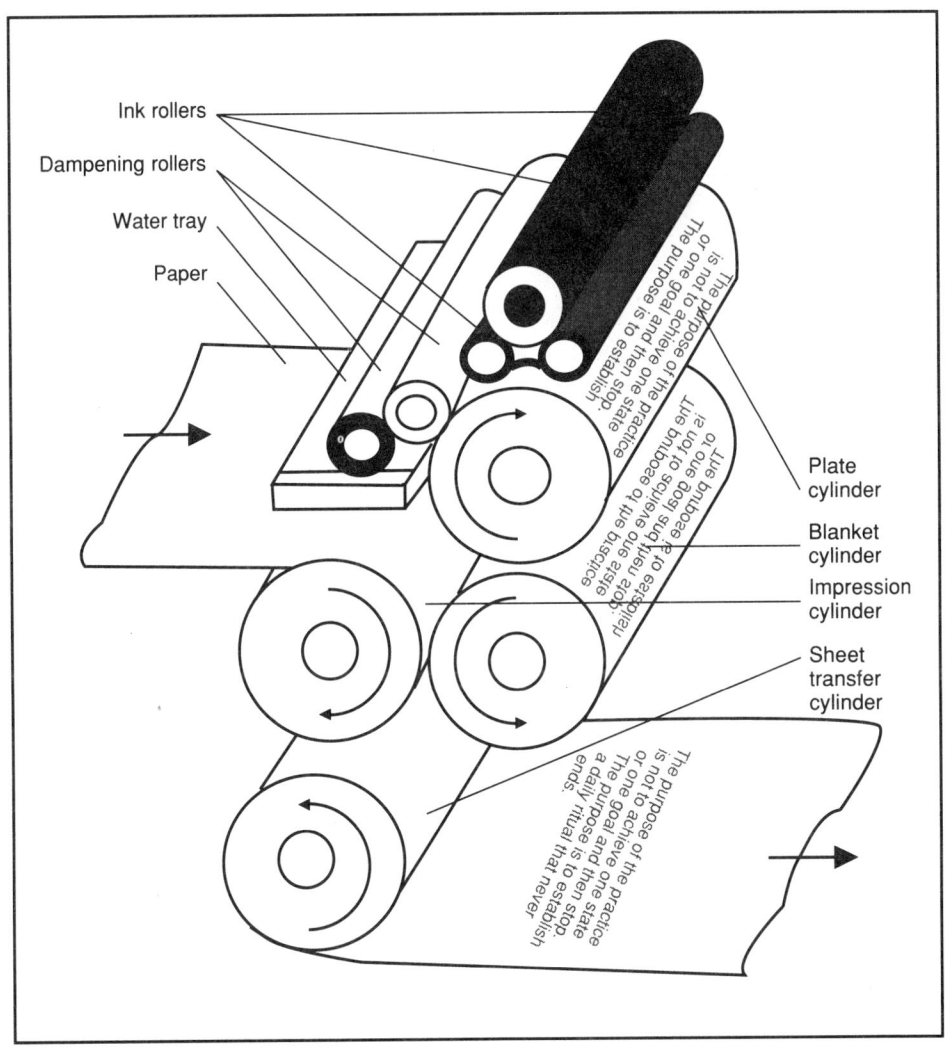

■ **Figure 10.13** Diagram of offset process.

In operation, the printing plate first comes into contact with dampening rollers, which wet the plate with a water-based solution. The water solution is accepted by the nonimage area and rejected by the image area. The ink, which is oil-based, is repelled by the water solution in the nonimage areas, and prints only the image area.

Once the plate is inked, it transfers the image to the rubber blanket, and the rubber blanket comes into contact with an impression cylinder, which presses it against the paper.

Gravure

Gravure printing is used for high-volume and high-quality printing, such as color magazines, museum catalogs, and art books. In gravure printing all image areas are made up of tiny dots (halftone dots) which are etched into the surface of the plate. The image area is made up of lots of little pits in the plate. The plate is inked, and then wiped clean, leaving ink only in the image area. An impression cylinder then presses the paper directly against the plate.

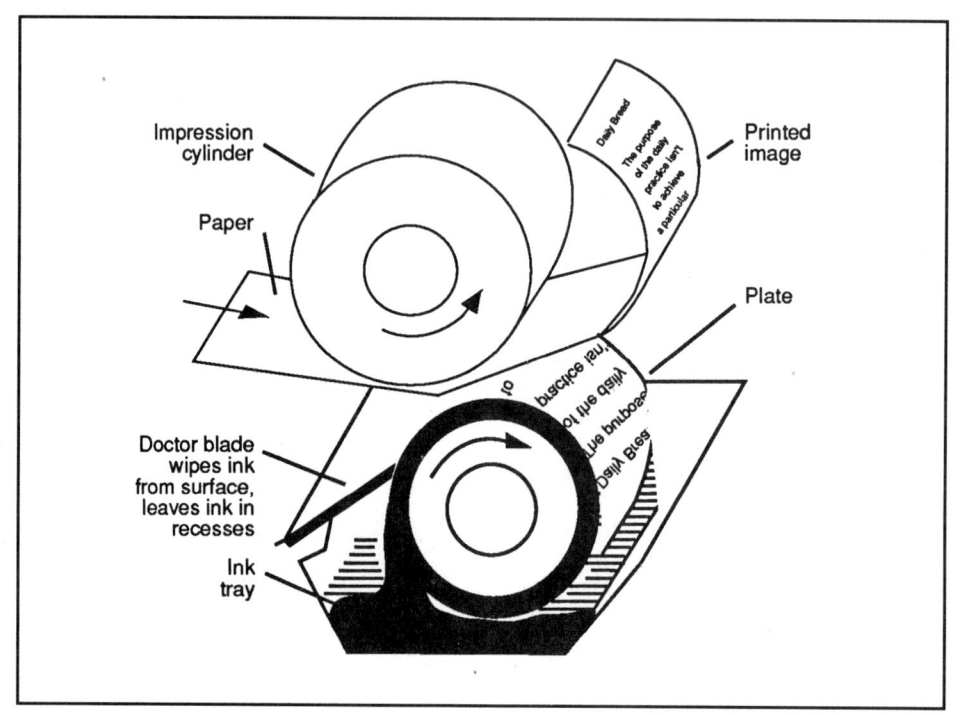

■ **Figure 10.14** Diagram of gravure process.

This method requires that everything, including type, be screened by the printer. In this case, however, the dots vary not only in diameter, but in depth as well. This allows the press to deposit varying densities of ink on the paper, and thus to reproduce a wider range of grays (tonal gradations) and richer blacks (deep pits that hold lots of ink) than with other printing methods.

Sheet-Fed vs. Web-Fed Presses

Printing presses also differ in whether they print precut sheets (sheet-fed) or continuous rolls of paper (web-fed).

■ **Figure 10.15** Sheet-fed Heidelberg press.

■ **Figure 10.16** Large Heidelberg web press.

Sheet-fed is appropriate for short- to medium-print runs, and are preferable for fine-registration, high-quality work. Sheet-fed press is required if you are printing on heavy paper stock or using special effects like embossing.

Web-fed presses are large, high-speed presses. Web presses are used to print on very light paper stocks, like newsprint, that cannot be handled in a sheet feeder. They are much more economical than sheet fed presses for long press runs, but they cannot provide a high level of color and registration precision. Running at such speeds, you can't stop web-presses to make the same kind of fine adjustments that you can on a sheet-fed press. When you design a publication for web printing, therefore, you want to keep it fairly simple and avoid elements such as crossovers, traps, and obvious color matching from page to page.

If you're going to print your newsletter on a web offset press, you should also be aware before designing your piece that this type of press, while faster and less expensive for some jobs, cannot provide the accuracy and color consistency of a sheet-fed press. You'll want to avoid design elements that could draw attention to discrepancies, such as colored bars at the tops of pages, and rules or other graphics elements that cross over facing page boundaries.

Similarly, you can plan your publication for most economical use of color if you know on what kind of printing press it's going to be run and how your printer will run it. For example, if you have an eight-page four-color brochure, on some presses it will be printed so that four pages are on one side of the sheet and the other four pages on the reverse. First one side will be printed, then the plates will be changed and the other side will be printed. This means that you can save money by printing four-color only on one side. Your printer can tell you which pages these will be (they will not be consecutive), and you can plan your design so that only those pages have four-color images.

You can take the same brochure, however, and print it on a different press using a different method, and it will cost you no more to print *all pages* in color. If the job is being printed on a large-enough press "work and turn" or "work and tumble," all eight pages will print on one side of the sheet, and then print in reverse order on the other side. This means that the same plates are used for both runs—and there is no extra charge for running color throughout.

INKS

There are different kinds of ink for the various printing processes. Offset inks, in general, must be fairly tacky and heavy so that they do not run or bleed. They must also be more concentrated in color than letterpress inks, which are more thickly deposited on the paper.

Within the category of offset inks, there are also special subcategories of inks that are appropriate for different types of jobs. For example, there are special rubproof inks for printing packaging. There are inks formulated to be absorbed easily into the rough, uncoated papers used for newspapers. It is usually up to the printer to make the appropriate selection based on these factors, and on your specifications.

There are really a wide variety of choices you can make as well, and not just only in regard to color. For example, in addition to the regular match inks, there are high-gloss inks, fluorescent inks, metallic inks, and opaque inks. You should discuss these options with your printer (he or she can tell you whether they will be appropriate for your job) and consider them carefully in relation to your design and your choice of paper.

For example, while most inks are transparent, you can also order some inks in opaque form. This would give you denser color for printing clearly on a dark background or a textured stock. Similarly, high-gloss inks can impart a striking, luxurious appearance to the work, but their effect will be lost unless they are printed on the correct type of paper. The glossiness of high-gloss inks is made possible by characteristics in their makeup that resist absorption into the paper and allow them to sit on the surface. Thus, you will enhance the effect by printing them on a coated, or cast-coated stock, papers that also resist absorption.

In addition to inks, many designers use varnishes, printed alone or over inks. Varnishes come in both gloss and dull, clear and tinted. Matte varnishes are often used across an entire page to give it a rich finish or to protect solid color areas (this is particularly advisable on covers). Gloss varnishes are used in the same way, and are also printed over particular parts of the page, such as pictures, heads, and rules. This is called spot varnishing. Tinted spot varnishes, full-color or screened, are often used by themselves to print large graphic elements, imparting a subtle beauty to page backgrounds or covers.

As with inks, the printer must create a separate set of films and plates for each varnish. The use of spot varnish also requires cutting mattes to isolate the elements that will be varnished.

PAPERS

In Chapters 7 and 8 we mentioned that there are different types of paper that you can use when printing your master pages out on a laser printer. There are other types of papers that are appropriate for the different kinds of presses. Offset paper, for example, must resist moisture since water is used in the printing process. Appropriate papers also resist "picking" (the flaking off of little bits of paper under the pull of the inked blanket), since the inks used in offset are more tacky than in other printing processes.

In addition to these general characteristics, there are five other key consideration for selecting papers: grain, bulk, opacity, weight, color, and finish.

Grain

Grain (the direction of the fibers in the paper) is not something you really have to worry about. The printer will select the appropriate grain paper for the press and for the type of fold. Papers cut and fold more easily along the grain rather than across the grain. Sometime the choice of final paper stock will affect the design of the publication. For example, as we mentioned in Chapter 3, if you are going to be printing on a textured paper stock, you will probably want to avoid very light italic faces in your design. The thin diagonal strokes of such faces may not print clearly on a textured stock. The color of the paper and the ink as well should be considered in relation to typeface readability and how they will enhance or detract from illustrations.

Bulk

Bulk (thickness) is the result of two factors: paper weight and finish. An 80 lb. paper, for example, with a rough textured finish, could have a bulk equal to a 100 lb. smooth-finish paper. By changing either one or both of these factors, you can create a very different feeling in your piece. If you're trying to create an impression of stolidity or elegance, you might want to maximize bulk. On the other hand, if you have a brochure that's long and packed with information, and you don't want readers to be too overwhelmed, you probably ought to minimize bulk. You also must consider bulk if you're planning to mail your publication. The difference between one paper and another can cost quite a bit in postage.

Opacity

Opacity (how much "show-through" there is from one side of a printed sheet to the other) is a result of paper weight and bulk. Heavier, bulkier papers have more fibers and thus are more opaque (Figure 10.17). Opacity is also affected by how much ink the paper absorbs, and that can result from finish as well. How much opacity you need depends on the kind of material you're going to be printing. If you have a lot of photographs or fairly dense line art, you will need a more opaque paper than if your publication is primarily text. When you're selecting papers, you can judge the opacity of samples by placing them over a printed page and comparing show-through.

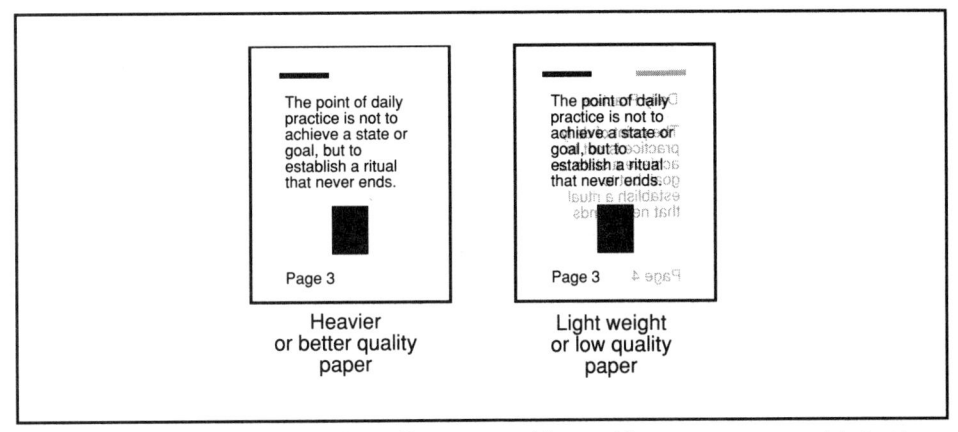

■ **Figure 10.17** Low- and high-quality papers with a test image on reverse side to show opacity.

These first three factors are things to consider as you look at paper samples and think about your design and how you're going to distribute and use your publication. They are, normally, not the characteristics that you would state when specifying a paper to your printer. In general, paper is specified by manufacturer's name, the name of the paper, and by weight, color, and finish. For example, you might specify a "Warren LOE Dull 70 lb. text, Warm White, gloss finish."

Weight

Weight (also known as "basis weight") is determined according to how much a ream (500 sheets) of standard-size papers weigh. Standard sizes of papers vary, however, depending on the paper type. For example, the kinds of papers you would normally use for the inside of a brochure or a book, called text-weight papers, have a standard sheet size of 25 inches by 38 inches. Cover-weight papers, on the other hand, have a standard sheet size of 20 inches by 26 inches. Thus, a 100 lb. text paper and a 56 lb. cover paper would actually weigh about the same.

Common paper weights for books are 50, 55, or 60 lb. text; and 80 lb. for jacket stock and 10 or 12 point cover stock. Brochures are 70, 80, and 90 lb. text; and 65, 80, or 100 lb. cover. A good combination is an 80 lb. text weight and a 100 lb. cover weight. If your design calls for a "self-cover" (the cover and the inside are printed together on the same paper), however, you will probably want to compromise by selecting a heavier text paper, perhaps using an 80 lb. cover stock throughout.

Color

Color choices are available in abundance in paper today. Most paper sample books will include a couple of dozen colors for each paper type. Be careful not to get carried away, however. Colored paper can impair readability. It's often most appropriate for covers (where it can greatly extend the visual interest of a one- or two-color job) or for special accent (such as in an annual report, where you want to set the narrative off from the financials). Remember that if you're going to mix papers, you must design your publication so that all pages that are going to be printed on the second paper are in the same signature (for example, the center four pages of an eight-page brochure). If you don't you'll be paying premium charges for hand-tipping (gluing) pages in.

In addition to papers with a wide range of hues, there are also a wide range of white papers. In one paper swatchbook alone, showing choices in a single brand from a single manufacturer, you can choose from: "Bright White," "Oyster White," "Plain White," "Ivory," "Warm White," and "Frost White." Your choice will affect not only the overall look and feeling of the piece, but how your illustrations print as well. Remember that your brightest highlights in a printed picture can be no brighter than the sheet of paper they're printed on.

Finish

Finish (the way the surface of the paper has been treated) is perhaps the most critical factor of all, since it provides the surface on which the ink is printed. Finish affects paper bulk and ink absorption. It affects the readability of type and the crispness and brilliance of illustrations.

There are two major categories of finishes: coated and uncoated.

Uncoated papers are good for text legibility and for line art reproduction. Newsprint is an uncoated stock with an especially high level of absorption. Better grades of uncoated stock include antique finish (rough, high bulk), eggshell (smoother), machine finish (smoother still), or English (smooth enough to print halftones, but now mostly replaced for that purpose by coated stock).

Rule of Thumb:

If you're publishing a newsletter and you're going to print it on a fairly low-grade paper, such as newsprint or even vellum, you'll want to avoid using photographs that have a lot of detail. Since the rough surface of such papers tends to absorb and spread ink, printed images will lack crisp definition and cannot hold detail.

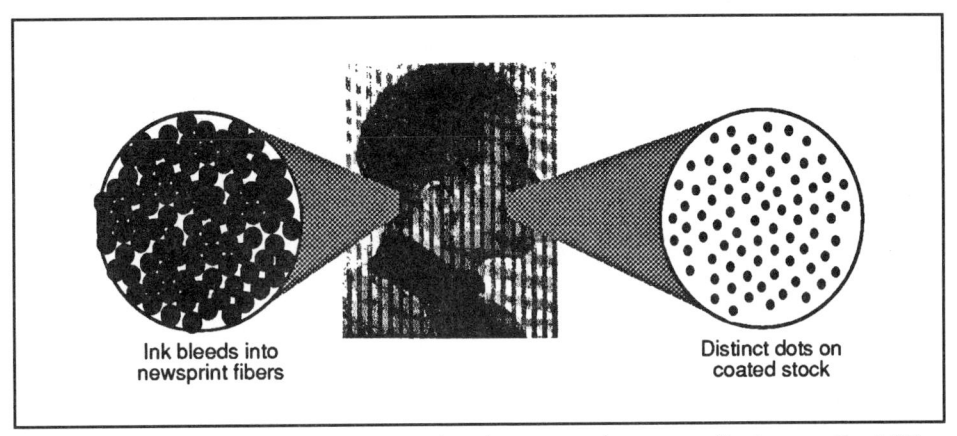

Ink bleeds into newsprint fibers

Distinct dots on coated stock

■ **Figure 10.18** Comparison of scan printed on newsprint vs. an offset paper like LOE.

Coated papers have a special clay coating that keeps the ink from coming in contact with the paper fibers and being absorbed into the paper. The more ink stays on top of the paper, the more brilliant the printed image. Thus, coated papers are almost always used for halftones and four-color process.

Finishes of coated papers can be gloss, dull, or matte. Dull finishes are easier on the eyes when reading type. Gloss finishes make pictures pop off the page. Matte finishes are a good compromise for publications that include lots of text and illustrations. Within these categories, there are numerous subcategories and variations, depending on how the coating and finishing were performed. Thus, you will hear of "conversion-coated," "film-coated," "cast-coated," and "blade-coated" papers among others. Each of these has different characteristics and is appropriate for different kinds of publications. Cast-coated papers are the highest gloss papers available, and the most expensive. It's not necessary to know all about papers (there are so many new papers being introduced these days that it is impossible to keep up with it anyway). It is necessary to ask your printer for samples, including printed samples if he has them.

Postpress Production

Once the sheets have been printed, they must dry before they can be folded, gathered into signatures, bound, and trimmed. (Web-fed jobs, however, are normally folded on-press.)

FOLDING

The printer may have his own folding and binding machines, or he may send the job to an adjunct shop. In addition to the standard folds of four-page, eight-page, and sixteen-page signatures, these machines are often capable of doing a wide range of specialty folds, such as accordion folds, gatefolds, and French folds. In general, the greater the number of folds and the more complex, the more expensive the job will be.

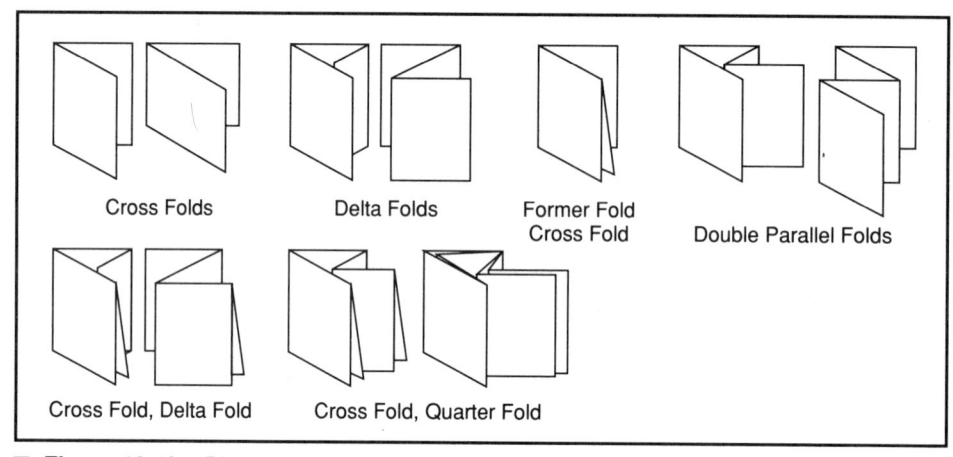

■ **Figure 10.19** Diagrams of fancy folds.

If you've used a heavyweight paper for your cover, or if your piece is folded against the grain, you will probably also want to have the fold scored. Scoring (creasing with a heavy weight) ensures a cleaner, more even fold.

EMBOSSING AND DIE-CUTTING

Embossing and *die-cutting* are special effects that are usually performed on a small (often hand-operated) letterpress after printing.

A die-cut is literally a piece of the brochure that is cut and removed or folded in a special way. Die-cuts are commonly used on brochure covers, direct mail pieces, and greeting cards and invitations.

■ **Figure 10.20**   Printed piece with die cut.

An emboss is a raised image, or relief, which is created by impressing the paper with a metal stamp. A blind emboss is a relief with no ink. A registered emboss is preprinted, and the emboss is positioned directly on top of it. Instead of an ink, you can also use a metallic foil in embossing. This makes the publication look expensive (and it is).

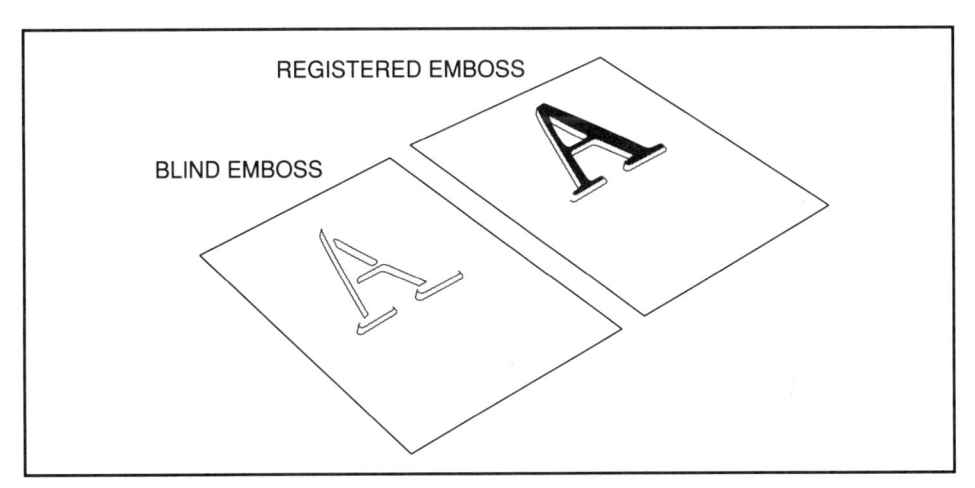

■ **Figure 10.21**   Printed pieces showing blind and registered embosses.

BINDING

Binding is usually the last step in the production process. The way a book is to be bound has to be taken into account from the very beginning, as it has implications for the design and particularly for the preparation of mechanicals.

Smythe-sewn means that the individual signatures are actually stitched together before being bound in a soft or hard cover (hardcover Smythe-sewn bindings are often called edition-bound or "casebound"). This is the most durable form of binding, and also the most expensive.

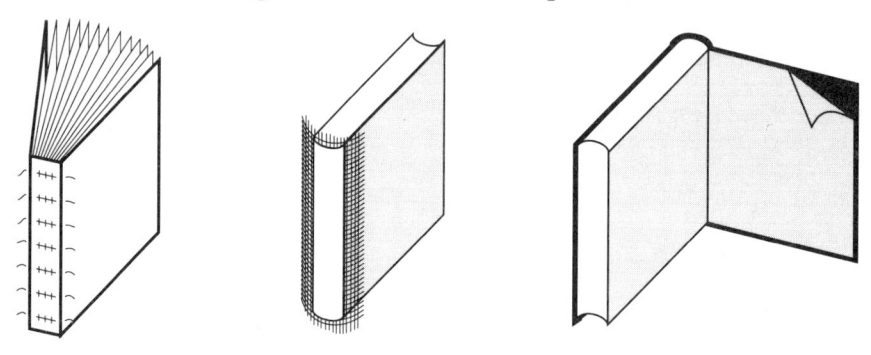

Figure 10.22 Diagram Smythe-sewn, picture of casebound book.

Perfect binding is the binding used in most paperback books. In perfect binding, the signatures are gathered and then trimmed crudely at the gutter. This leaves a rough surface onto which glue and then a gauzelike material are applied. A soft or hard cover is then applied on top, and the entire publication is trimmed smoothly on the other three sides.

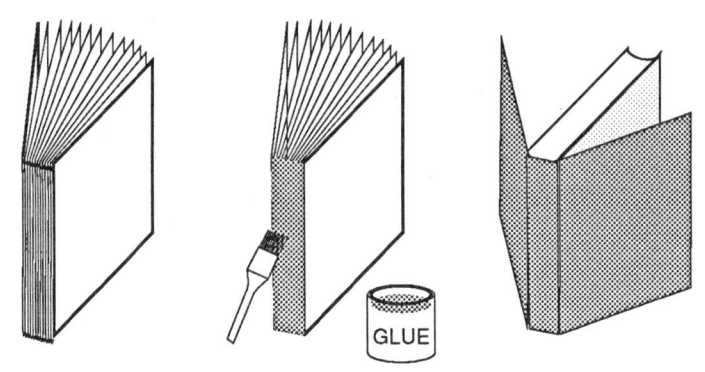

Figure 10.23 Diagram of perfect bound book.

This is an appropriate binding for medium-to-long documents such as textbooks, catalogs, and certain types of sales guides and product manuals (those that do not have to be updated constantly). Mechanicals for perfect bound publications should allow an extra 3/16 inch at the gutter.

Saddle-wire stitching is the type of binding seen most often on brochures. It is usually just a couple of heavy staples inserted at the spine of the book from the back to the center spread. It's the simplest, fastest, and least expensive binding method. It can only be used, however, for fairly thin publications. Unlike perfectbound and side-wired bindings (see below), however, saddle-stitched publications can lie open and flat, and are thus easier to handle and read.

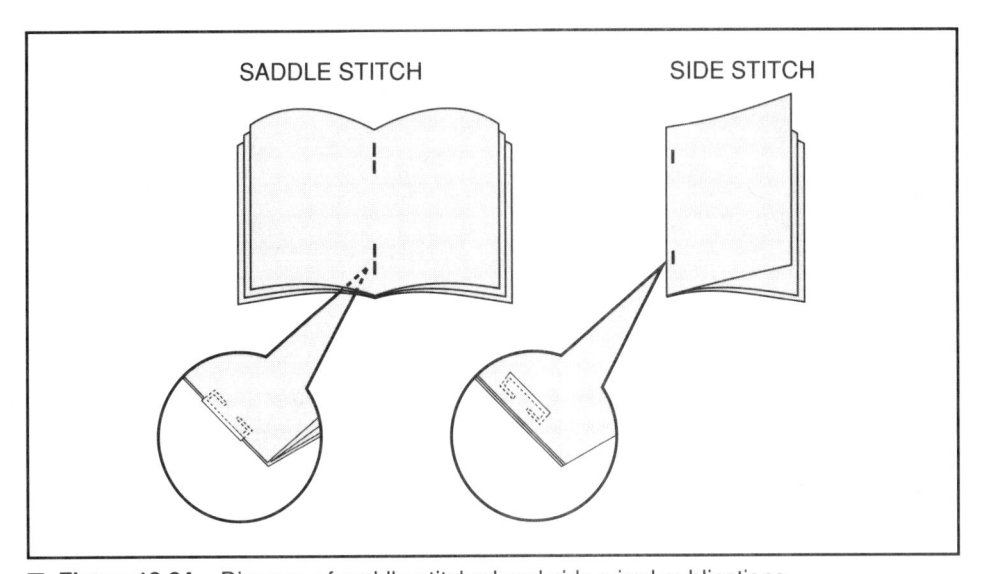

■ **Figure 10.24** Diagram of saddle-stitched and side-wired publications.

Side-wire stitching is the alternative method for more bulky publications. It too involves just a couple of staples, although these are much larger than in saddle-wire. The staples are inserted ¼ inch from the spine, beginning at the front cover and closing at the back cover. Heavy paper covers are usually glued on top. If you are preparing mechanicals for side-wire binding, you must leave a wide inside gutter so that the page-image area is not lost when the publication is opened.

Mechanical bindings are a general category of prefabricated bindings, such as ring, coil, and strip (velo). A looseleaf notebook, for example, usually has a three-ring mechanical binding.

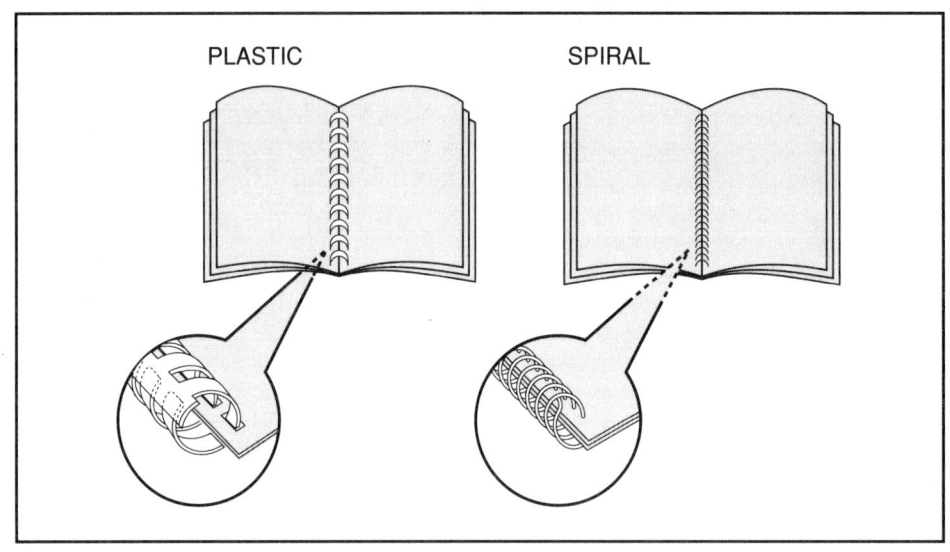

■ Figure 10.25 Pictures of mechanically bound publications.

Signatures that are going to be mechanically bound are gathered, trimmed, and usually, depending on the binding, drilled. Separate covers of heavy paper or plastic are drilled and attached in the same way.

The advantage of mechanical bindings (except strip binding) is that pages can lie flat when the book is open. This makes them ideal for manuals, cookbooks, and other publications that people need to refer to as they do other things. Also, mechanical bindings are relatively inexpensive for short runs—perfect binding and some of the other methods mentioned become less expensive in large quantities. Some mechanical bindings are also easily removed, making them suited to frequently revised publications.

If you are preparing mechanicals for this type of binding, you will need to leave some amount of extra space at the gutter. Check with your printer for how much is required by the particular method of mechanical binding you've selected.

Checking the Delivery

You've waited breathlessly. It seemed they would never come. But here they are. You're surrounded by boxes of your final publication at last. Do you start to give them out to everyone in the office? Do you discretely place one in the boss's in-basket? Do you send a few copies to your mother? Yes, but check them first.

The best way to check a delivery (unless your print run is so small that you can literally look at every copy) is to spot check each box. Look to make sure that bindings are straight and pages are even. Check for smears and scratches (which usually means the printer didn't allow press sheets to dry sufficiently before binding). Make sure that overall color and sharpness are up to at least the level you approved at the press run. You may find some slight variation in the darkness of the ink that occurs between different pages if the press must be reinked or readjusted manually throughout the print run, but be sure that the range of variation is acceptable.

Keep a count of how many you've looked at, and put any unsatisfactory copies aside. Don't be too worried if one box has a number of poor copies—it's when two or three boxes have poor copies that you want to look even more carefully. Depending on what percentage of the shipment has problems, you decide whether you're going to accept it or not.

What's reasonable to expect? First of all, you can't expect perfection. As we've said, printing is a process with many variables. Over the course of a print run, even with the most fastidious pressman, some parts of the run are simply going to be a little less perfect than others. You should probably expect somewhere around 5 percent of the copies to be unsatisfactory. Anything more than that merits a discussion with your printer.

If you do think the shipment is unacceptable, the printer will probably want to take it back and have his people check all the boxes, both to determine precisely the extent of the problem and to determine how much of the original run can be salvaged. Depending on what he finds out, he may offer to reprint the run free of charge, to offer you a discount, or to charge you for just the acceptable copies.

If you agree to this last alternative, you could actually end up with close to your original print run anyway. This is because you will often receive an overrun of 5 to 10 percent. With high-speed presses it is difficult to print a precise number of copies. Thus, in standard printing practice, the client agrees (sometimes this is contractual) to accept and pay for the overrun. If you prefer not to be charged for the extra copies, you may have to agree to accept the possibility of a 5 to 10 percent under-run.

Glossary

AA
Author's alteration: A change requested by the author, publisher, or other agent, after copy has been set. Any requested deviation from the copy that was originally submitted to the typesetter or printer.

Accent
(diacritical or critical) One of a variety of marks above, below, or through certain characters where the pronounciation characteristics need to be specially denoted. An accent may also be used to provide an assist in determining syllabic emphasis. Accents may be set as separate characters and stored separately on a front matrix, or may be integrated with the characters they accent.

Accessory
See desk accessory, peripheral device.

Acronym
A word formed from the initial letters of a name or phrase, such as ROM (from read-only memory), RAM (from random access memory), and WYSIWYG (from what-you-see-is-what-you-get).

Actual Size
A view of a page on the screen, scaled to approximately the same size it will print, depending on the characteristics of your screen display.

Agate
A measurement equivalent to ¼ inch. Also, the size of type often used in newspapers for classified ads, approximately 5.5 points. Fourteen lines of agate type equals one inch depth.

Aliasing
Undesirable jagged lines and edges in the image displayed on the screen. Improved by antialiasing algorithms.

Alignment
How text lines up on a page or in a column: align left (flush left, ragged right), align center, align right (flush right, ragged left), or justify (flush on both the left and right). The exact correspondence at the top or bottom of letters and characters of type font, or the setting of lines so that their ends appear even. Horizontal alignment is based on the baseline. Vertical alignment is based on the margins. Also, the positioning of lines on a printed page so that they are registered with type on adjacent or reverse pages.

Alphabet Length
The length of the alphabet, lowercase a through x, for any typeface. By comparing the length of these letters (when set normally in the same size) for different typefaces, one can evaluate comparative "mass". A typeface with a low alphabet length would set more characters in the same space than a typeface with a high alphabet length. This same relationship is also expressed as "characters per pica" (CPP)—the number of characters that fit in one pica. Sometimes alphabet length is expressed in the relative units of the typeseting machine. The comparative capability still exists. Character count is the average number of characters per line multiplied by the total lines. Characters Per Line = CPP x Line Length. See also Copy fitting.

Alphanumeric
(alphameric) Contraction of alphabetic and numeric. Pertaining to the characteristic of a character or group of characters that are either letters of the alphabet, numbers, or associated symbols. Special codes telling the typesetter or computer what to do are not alphanumeric.

Alternate characters
Multiple versions of the same letter in the font to allow a greater variety of letter combinations. Multiple versions of the same character are available to allow more creativity in headline setting. Most alternate characters are "swash" versions that over-or under-hang adjacent characters. See Swash character.

Apex
The top junction of two stems, such as at the point of the capital A or at the center of the capital W. The opposite of an apex—that is the bottom junction of two stems is the vortex.

Application program
A program written for some specific purpose, such as word processing, graphics, page composition, or telecommunication. Compare system program.

Application software
A collective term for application programs.

Arc
Any curved stroke other than a bowl. See figure under Letter element.

Archive
(1) The storage of files that are not needed currently but may be needed in the future, or the storage area that holds those files. (2) To create an archive or to move a file into an archive. (3) The characteristic of a file that is in an archive, or will be put into one soon, or has just been taken out. See also Back up.

Area composition
The system of preparing type for output in such a way that as many elements as possible are in place, thus reducing or eliminating pasteup. Area composition may achieve full page makeup, where no pasteup is needed at all.

Arm
A horizontal or diagonal stroke starting from the stem, as in the cap E or F. See figure under Letter element.

Ascender
The portion of a lowercase letter that rises above its main body. Technically, only three letters of the alphabet have ascenders: b, d, and h. Uppercase letters and the lowercase letters f, k, l, and t also reach the height of the ascenders. Line spacing or leading should be sufficient so that the ascenders of one line do not touch the descenders of another line. See figure under Font size. See also Descender.

Ascent line
A horizontal line that coincides with the tops of the tallest characters in a font. See figure under Font sizes. See also base line, descent line, x-height.

ASCII
Acronym for American Standard Code for Information Interchange, pronounced "ASK-ee." A code in which the numbers from 0 to 127 stand for text characters. The ASCII character includes the upper- and lower-case alphabet, numbers, special symbols, and control codes. The form in which text is stored when saved as "text only," an option available under the Save command for most databases, spreadsheets, and word processors. These files include all of the characters of the text itself (including tabs and carriage returns), but do not include non-ASCII codes used by some applications to indicate character and paragraph formats. One ASCII character can be stored in one byte of memory, i.e., ½ of a memory word in a 16-bit processor architecture or one full word in an 8-bit computer architecture.

Author's alterations
See AA.

Back up
(v) To make a spare copy of a disk or of a file on a disk. Backing up your files and disks ensures that you won't lose information if the original is lost or damaged. (n) A copy of a disk or of a file on a disk. Redundant equipment that may be used if the primary system or unit fails to operate.

Bad break
Term used to refer to line breaks that hyphenate words incorrectly or separate two words that need to stay together (such as "Mr. Smith"), and to page breaks and column breaks that result in widows or orphans. See Orphans/widows.

Banner
A large headline, especially one that extends across a full page.

Bar
An arm connected on both sides, as in the capital H. See figure under Letter element.

Base line
A horizontal line that coincides with the bottom of each character in a font, excluding descenders (tails on letters like "p"). The imaginary line on which characters appear to rest in a line of type. Some characters actually drop somewhat below for better visual base alignment.

Baud
A unit of data transmission speed the number of discrete signal state changes per second. Often, but not always, equivalent to bits per second. Compare bit rate.

Beak
The strokes at the ends of arms and serifs, such as in the letters E, F, G, T, and Z. See figure under Letter element.

Binary file
A file whose data is to be interpreted in binary form. Machine-language programs and pictures are stored in binary files. Compare Text file.

Bit
A contraction of binary digit. The smallest unit of information that a computer can hold. The value of a bit (1 or 0) represents a simple two-way choice, such as yes or no, on or off, positive or negative, something or nothing. There are eight bits in a byte. See also Binary system.

Bit map
A graphic image or text formed by a pattern of dots. Low-resolution images are sometimes called "paint-type" files, and they usually have a lower number of dots per inch (dpi) than high-resolution scans.

Bleed
Term used to describe a printed image that extends to the trimmed edge of the sheet or page.

Block
See Text block.

Blue lines
Term used to describe a preliminary test printing of a page to check the offset printer's plates. This test printing is done using a photochemical process (rather than printers' inks) that produces a blue image on white paper.

Blue pencil/blue line
Traditionally, a guide line that is drawn using a blue pencil or printed in light blue ink on the boards that are used for pasting up a page layout manually. The blue ink is sometimes called nonrepro blue because it will not be picked up by the camera when a page is photographed to make plates for offset printing. Most electronic page-composition products let you create nonprinting margins, column guides, and ruler guides on the screen to help you position text and graphics, but these lines will not appear when the page is printed out.

Board
(1) A sheet of heavy weight paper or card stock onto which typeset text and graphics are pasted manually. See also Blue pencil/blue line. (2) (printed circuit board) (memory board) A sheet of plastic laminate on which the interconnections of an electric circuit or a computer memory are printed or fixed.

Body
(1) The main section of a brochure, book, article, or other text material. (2) The size of type when considered from the top of the ascenders to the bottom of the descenders. See figure under Font size.

GLOSSARY

Body copy
The main part of the text of a publication, as distinguished from headings and captions. See also Body type.

Body type
The type (font) used for the body copy. Generally, fonts that are used for body copy, as distinguished from display type.

Boilerplate
A set of repetitive blocks of copy that may be picked up and included routinely without the need to recreate them each time. See also Template.

Bold
(boldface) A generic description of type that is heavier than the text type with which it is used.

Bowl
The strokes enclosing a counter. Counter refers to the space, where the term "bowl" refers to the lines enclosing the counter. A "complete" bowl is formed by curved strokes only, and a "modified" bowl has the stem forming one of the sides. A "loop" is a bowl that serves as a florish, as the descending part of some lowercase g characters. See figure under Letter element.

Broadside
A sheet of paper printed as one page is a broadside Fold it once and it is a folio (four pages), twice and it is a quarto- eight pages), three times and it is a octavo (16 pages), four times and it is a 16 MO (32 pages), five times and it is a 32 MO (64 pages).

Brochure
A folded pamphlet or small booklet.

Buffer
A "holding area" of the computer's memory where information can be stored by one program or device and then read at a different rate by another; for example, a print buffer. In editing functions, an area in memory where deleted (cut) or copied data is held. In some applications, this area is called the clipboard. See also type-ahead buffer.

Built-in fonts
Fonts built into the printer. Compare with Cartridge fonts and Downloadable fonts. See also Fonts.

Bullet
A common pi character usually used to draw attention to listed items.

Business Graphics
Graphic representation (such as in pie charts and bar graphs) of statistical or other business information.

Byte
A unit of information consisting of a fixed number of bits. One byte consists of a series of eight bits, and a byte can represent any value between 0 and 255. A byte is the smallest unit of processing in any computer architecture, and is frequently made equal to ½ or ¼ the number of bits in each word. The sequence represents an instruction, letter, number, punctuation mark, or other character. In typesetting systems, a byte often contains a single character or code. See also kilobyte, megabyte.

CAD/CAM
(Computer-Aided Design/Computer-Aided Manufacturing) A software application that supports the electronic creation or modification of the design of products or product components, to create highly accurate sketches, to calculate product specifications, and to perform similar functions.

Callout
The text used to point out and identify parts of an illustration. Also, headings that appear in a narrow margin next to the body copy. See also Pull-out quotes.

Camera-ready art
The complete pages of a publication assembled with text and graphics and ready for reproduction. Literally refers to the pages that are ready to be photographed as the first step in the process of making plates for offset printing. See also Mechanicals, Offset printing.

Cap
A contraction of capital, meaning an uppercase character. See also Drop cap.

Capitals
The letters A through Z, usually including the ampersand.

Cap Height
The height of a point size from the baseline to the top of the uppercase letter. See figure under Font size.

Cap Line
An imaginary line defining the height of the capital letters of a particular typeface. Caps can be higher or lower than ascending characters. Old (Roman) Style typefaces usually have caps shorter than the ascendors. See figure under Font size.

Caps and small caps
Text with letters that are normally lowercase set as uppercase letters that are smaller than the normal capitals in a font. The cap height is equal to or very slightly larger than the X height of the matching size. Small caps differ from caps in a smaller size by the width of the character stroke.

Captions
Descriptive text identifying photographs and illustrations. See also Callout.

Carriage return
An ASCII character that ordinarily causes a printer or display device to place the next character on the left margin, i.e., the end of one line and the beginning of the next. Also, a line break that you enter by pressing the carriage return (RETURN key) at the end of a line or a paragraph. Sometimes called a hard carriage return to distinguish it from the soft carriage returns that occur due to word wrap at the right margin or the right edge of a column.

Case
The condition of letters, either capital or noncapital (upper - or lowercase). Derived from the practice, in hand typesetting, of storing capital letters in a wooden case above the case with the noncapital letters. See also Supercase.

Catalog
(1) A list of all files stored on a disk. Sometimes called a directory. (2) In publishing, a printed list of products.

Cathode-ray tube (CRT)
An electronic device, such as a television picture tube, that produces images on a phosphor-coated screen. The phosphor coating emits light when struck by a focused beam of electrons. A common display device used with personal computers.

Central processing unit (CPU)
The "brain" of the computer; the microprocessor that performs the actual computations in machine language. See also Microprocessor.

Character
Any symbol that has a widely understood meaning and thus can convey information. Some characters-such as letters, numbers, and punctuation-can be displayed on the monitor screen and printed on a printer. Compare Control character.

Character keys
Keys on a computer keyboard-such as letters, numbers, symbols, punctuation marks-used to generate text or to format text; any key except Shift, Caps Lock, Command, Option, Control, and Escape.

Character pitch
A measurement used for typewritten text. The number of characters per inch printed along a horizontal line.

Character set
The entire set of characters that can be shown on a monitor or used to code computer instructions. In a printer, the entire set of characters that the printer is capable of printing. In typography, the entire set of characters that are part of a single font.

Character style
A set of stylistic variations, such as bold, italic, and underline. The empty set indicates plain text (no stylistic variations).

Character Printer
A printer that produces one character image at a time. Characters may be printed left to right on each line, or in alternating directions on alternate lines.

Check Copy
A proof copy of a publication, sent to the customer to assure that all printing and binding operations are correct. Also used as a master copy for the printer or binder.

Cicero
A unit of measure in the Didot point system equivalent to 4.55 millimeters (slightly larger than the pica); commonly used in Europe for measuring font size.

Clipboard
The holding place in the computer's memory for what you last cut or copied; a buffer area in memory. A holding place for temporarily storing the text or graphics. Information on the Clipboard can be inserted (pasted) into documents.

Clipping
See Cropping.

Collated
Printed in order, with the first page on top of the stack that comes out of the printer. An option under the Print command in many electronic publishing applications. Multiple copies are grouped into whole copies of the publication under this option.

Color separations
In offset printing, separate plates used to lay different colors of ink on a page printed in multiple colors, to reproduce the proportional amount of cyan, magenta, yellow, and black in the original.

Color sequencing
Changing the color of individual or groups of pixels in a raster display device.

Column inch
A measurement in which a newspaper or magazine column width is multiplied by vertical inches to calculate advertising rates. Sometimes used to estimate the amount of text that will fit an area (though counting characters is more common). See also Copy fitting.

Column rules
Vertical lines drawn between columns.

Command
An instruction that causes the computer to perform some action. A command can be typed from a keyboard, selected from a menu with a hand-held device (such as a mouse), or embedded in a program.

Comp
Traditionally, a designer's "comprehensive" sketch of a page design that shows the client what the final page will look like when it is printed. Usually a full-size likeness of the page, the comp is a few steps closer to the final than a "pencil rough" and can be composed using ink pens, pencils, color markers, color acetate, pressure-sensitive letters, and other tools available at art supply shops. Using desktop publishing applications on the Macintosh, a comp can look more like the finished product, with typeset text, ruled lines, and shaded boxes created in PageMaker directly, and the "comp" can be used as a starting point in building the final document.

Composition
The process of assembling characters, words, lines, and paragraphs, or of formatting typeset text into blocks or pages for reproduction by printing. Broadly speaking, composition is equivalent to typesetting.

Composition software
A program or set of programs designed for the purposes of composition, and generally including hyphenation and justification routines, correction and editing programs, and file management capability.

Compositor
A person who sets type by manual or mechanical means. The term is not generally used in computerized typesetting.

GLOSSARY

Computer graphics
That group of systems and programs that make or manipulate nontextual data like photographs, charts, or line drawings. Also, the layout of pages of material by means of interaction with a computer-generated picture of the material. Interaction takes place through use of a keyboard, light pen, track ball, or other controlling device. The changes appear at once on a video display as they are made by the operator.

Condensed type
A narrow typeface having proportionally less character width than a normal face of the same size. Although you can achieve this effect electronically through some graphics and typesetting programs by condensing characters from the normal font, usually condensed characters are individually designed as a separate font. Some applications use the term condensed to indicate tightened letter spacing, in which the words are condensed but the individual characters retain their normal width. Condensed typefaces are used where large amounts of copy must fit into a relatively small space(tabular composition being the most common area of usage). See also Kerning, Tracking.

Configuration
(1) The total combination of hardware components-central processing unit, video display device, keyboard, and peripheral devices-that make up a computer system. (2) The software settings that allow various hardware components of a computer system to communicate with each other.

Continued line
See Jump line.

Continuous-tone
An illustration or photograph—whether black-and-white or color—that consists of many shades between the lightest and the darkest tones, and which is not broken up into dots. Continuous-tone images usually need to be converted into dots—either by scanning or by half-toning—in order to be printed in ink or on a laser printer.

Contour
To set type in a shaped block; to set type so as to "wrap-around" or "run-around" an illustration or other nontext element on the page. Traditionally, it is accomplished via multiple line indents. A special sheet with pica and point graduations is used to calculate the value of the indents. The sheet is usually transparent and placed over the art or shape so that all indents can be established. Some page-layout applications can contour type automatically around irregular shapes. See Wraparound.

Contrast enhancement
In electronic image processing, various automated and semiautomated techniques that change the distribution of intensity levels in images by remote sensing.

Control character
A character or signal that modifies the meaning of the codes that follow it until another control character is used. It normally signifies that whatever follows is to be regarded as a command rather than data. See also Control key.

Control codes
A keyboard character, or sequence of characters, that initiates, stops, or modifies a particular function.

Control key
A general term for a key that controls the operation of other keys; for example, Caps Lock, Command, Control, Option, and Shift. When you hold down or engage a control key while pressing another key, the combination makes that other key behave differently. Also called a Modifier key.

Conversion service
A service bureau that converts data from one type of storage media to another, or from one type of hardware or software to another. The bureau provides access to the equipment that can handle a wide range of data formats. Desktop publishers have some degree of "conversion" capability built into word processors and page-composition applications.

Copy fitting
To determine the amount of copy (text) that will fit in a given area on a page or in a publication, using a specified font. Also, to make copy fit on a page by adjusting the line spacing, word spacing, and/or letter spacing.

Counter
The fully or partially enclosed portion of a letter, such as in the lowercase e, which has a full counter above and a partial counter below. Counter refers to the space, where the term bowl refers to the lines enclosing the counter. See figure under Letter element.

CPU
See Central processing unit.

Crop
To trim from the edges of a graphic, thereby removing part of it, to make the image fit a given space or to remove unnecessary parts of the image.

Crop marks
Lines printed on a page to indicate where the page will be trimmed when the final document is printed and bound. Most page-composition applications can print these marks if the page size is smaller than the paper size.

Crossbar
A horizontal stroke that crosses through the stem, such as in the lowercase t. See figure under Letter element.

Crotch
The inside of an apex or vortex. See figure under Letter element.

CRT
See Cathode-ray tube.

Cursor
A symbol displayed on the screen marking where the user's next action will take effect or where the next character typed from the keyboard will appear.

Cut
To remove something by selecting it and choosing the Cut command. What you cut is placed on the clipboard. See also Buffer.

Cyan
The subtractive primary color that appears blue-green and absorbs red light. Used as one ink in four-color printing. Also known as process blue.

Dashes
Ranging from the smallest to the largest, here are the dashes that are used in typography: Hyphen, En Dash, ¾ Em Dash, Em Dash, Rule line.

Data disk
A disk that contains your work-letters, budgets, pictures, and so on-in the form of files.

Data format
The form in which data is stored, manipulated, or transferred. Serial data transmitted and received typically has a data format of one start bit, five to eight data bits, an optional parity bit, and one or two stop bits.

Decimal tab
In tabular composition, vertical alignment on the decimal point.

Default
The initial setting of a value or option by the program. Used to describe the value of values, or mode that a computer will use in processing information when no other value or mode is specified by the operator or programmer. A preset response to a question or prompt. Default settings can usually be changed by the operator.

Delimiter
Separator. A code or character that is used specifically to indicate the start or end of a code, command, instruction, or string of data. A comma-delimited file contains data with elements separated by commas; a tab-delimited file separates individual data elements with tabs.

Density
(1) The degree of darkness of characters or images produced by a phototypesetter or other imaging device. (2) The amount of type per unit of line length. (3) A measurement of the amount of data that can be stored on a given surface of area of magnetic recording material.

Depth
The vertical measurement of a page, figure, table, or other block of material. See also Column inch.

Descender
The portion of a lowercase letter that hangs below the baseline. Five letters of the alphabet have descenders: g, j, p, q, and y. See figure under Letter element. See also Ascender, Baseline.

Descent line
A horizontal line that coincides with the bottoms of character descenders (such as the tail on a lower-case "p") extending farthest below the base line. See figure under Font size. See also Ascent line, Base height, Font size, and X-height.

Desktop publishing
The use of personal computers and software applications to produce camera-ready publications. A system providing you with the ability to produce publication-quality documents. Falls under the broader category of Electronic publishing.

Dialog box
A window or full-screen display in response to a command that calls for setting options.

Dialup
Pertaining to terminals and systems that have modems for accessing computers by dialing a special computer telephone number, as opposed to terminals that are directly wired to the computer.

Dictionary
In electronic typesetting, a list of words that are indicated with preferred or acceptable hyphenation points (hyphenation dictionary). Dictionaries may be used by the computer to determine correct hyphenation during the justification process, or correct spelling during an editorial process. See also Exception Dictionary.

Digital
A method of data storage and/or transmission wherein each code is given a unique combination of bits. Each bit generally indicates either the presence or absence of a condition (such as on-off, yes-no, true-false, open-closed). Contrast with Analog.

Digitize
To convert an image to a series of binary codes that can be stored in the computer. Digitizers include electronic drawing boards (tablets), flat-work scanners (for printed images and photographs), and video scanners (for storing images from a camera or a monitor). See Scanned image files.

Digitized character
A character shape that is specified as a series of numeric values in binary encoded form. The numbers can represent points (bit-maps) that must be exposed in order to create the character in light on a CRT or laser typesetter. They can also be a set of x/y coordinates connected by arcs or straight-line segments that define the outline of the character. A special computation called a dotfill algorithm then computes the points needed to create the character on the imaging device. See also Fonts, bit-map fonts, outline fonts.

Dingbats
Traditionally, ornamental characters like bullets, stars, and flowers used by printers to decorate a page or as special characters within the text. The laser font Zapf Dingbats includes many of these traditional symbols as well as some new ones. See also Pi characters.

Dipthong
A combination of two vowels into a single graphic and a single sound, as in ae or oe.

GLOSSARY

Direct entry phototypesetter
A phototypesetter whose keyboard is directly connected to the photographic unit. As the operator inputs data, the material is immediately produced on the output mechanism. There may be a buffer area to provide a delay or storage capability. No more than one keyboard, however, may have access to the output or storage mechanism.

Directory
A list of files contained in a computer's storage area, automatically created and maintained by the operating system. A file that contains a list of all the names and locations of other files stored on a disk. A pictorial, alphabetical, or chronological list of the contents of a folder or a disk. Also, an area reserved on the hard disk where a group of related files can be stored together. Each directory can have subdirectories. A directory is sometimes called a catalog.

Discretionary hyphen
A hyphen that you insert (in addition to the automatic hyphens that might have been inserted by automatic hyphenation) to identify where a word can be divided to fit text in the specified line length, if necessary. The hyphen shows on the screen and on the printed page only if it falls at the end of a line.

Disk
An information-storage medium consisting of a flat, circular, magnetic surface on which information can be recorded in the form of small magnetized spots, in a manner similar to the way sounds are recorded on tape. See Floppy disk, Hard disk.

Disk cartridge
A hard or rigid disk (disk pack) that may be removed from its drive and replaced by another disk.

Disk drive
The device that holds a disk, retrieves information from it, and saves information to it.

Disk head
The device mounted in a disk drive which is used to read or write information on the disk by reading or changing the magnetic fields.

Disk space
The amount of space available on a disk for storing or processing a document or an application.

Display
(1) A general term to describe what you see on the screen of your display device when you're using a computer; from the verb form, which means "to place into view." (2) Short for a display device.

Display type
Type used for headlines, titles, headings, advertisements, fliers, etc. Display type is usually a large point size (several sizes larger than body copy) and can be a decorative font.

DOS
Disk Operating System. Any number of widely used operating systems, so-called because a primary function they provide is the control of auxiliary storage in the form of disks.

Dot-matrix character
A pattern of dots that is used to form an image of a character in hard copy by means of electrostatic, ink jet, CRT, or laser printing. The character is stored in the computer as a series of dots, which are then arranged on a grid to form the character. The dot matrix may contain 5 horizontal and 7 vertical positions, or up to 300 positions in each direction for laser characters. The greater the number of dot positions, the higher the character resolution. Dot-matrix characters are the simplest form of digital type. See also Bit map type, Outline type.

Dot-matrix printer
A printer that creates text and graphics by pressing a matrix of pins through the ribbon onto the paper. These impact printers usually offer lower resolution (dots per inch) than non-impact laser printers, and are used for draft printouts only in publishing.

Dots per inch (dpi)
See Resolution.

Double sided
A publication that will be reproduced on both sides of a sheet of paper. The front side of a page is the odd-number side; the back side is the even-number side.

Download
To transmit data from one central computer to another device or to a remote terminal (downline-load).

Down time
(1) The time during which a computer or other device is not operational, usually implying that personnel or other devices are being kept idle to the detriment of production. (2) The time during which production does not occur, such as between the last shift of the day and the first shift of the next day.

DPI
See Dots per inch.

Draw-type files
See Object-oriented files.

Drive
See Disk drive.

Driver
A program that controls (drives) the operation of a device (such as a printer) or interface (such as a PostScript processor). The driver program interprets the computer data, providing the commands and signals required by the device or interface. The driver may output directly to the device or interface, or may provide papertape output which is then made ready by the device.

Drop cap
A single capital letter, larger than the standard text size, set into a block of text, with one or more lines indented to accommodate the cap. The top of the cap generally aligns with the top of the first line of text.

Drop-down menu
A list of commands that is displayed when you select a menu word. Usually menu titles appear on a "menu bar" along the top of the screen and the menued commands "drop down" in a listing below the titles when they are selected.

Dummy publication
Traditionally, a pencil mock-up of the pages of a publication, folded or stapled into a booklet, that the offset print shop uses to verify the correct sequence of pages and positioning of photographs. A dummy can range from a simple pencil "thumbnail" to a full-sized more detailed "rough" to a highly detailed and precise "comprehensive." See also Rough, Comp, Thumbnail, Template.

Duplex
Pertaining to a transmission where data may be received and transmitted. Half-duplex describes a system where transmission and reception may not be performed simultaneously, full-duplex a system where transmission and reception may be performed simultaneously.

Duplex fonts
Two fonts in a typesetter, each of which has identical escapement values for corresponding characters. A set of duplex fonts may use the same width table or card.

EAR
A short stroke, such as that extending from a lowercase g. See figure under Letter element.

EBCDIC
Extended Binary Coded Decimal Interchange Code. An eight-bit character code used primarily in IBM equipment. Each code represents one of 256 discrete alphanumeric or command characters. See also ASCII.

Edit
(1) To change or modify. To review copy and mark it for changes and/or corrections. In this context, edit refers to the function of a supervisory person performing editorial tasks on another's written material. (2) To modify and rearrange material according to a proofreader's recommendations. For example, to insert, remove, replace, or move text in a document. In this context, editing is generally done on an interactive terminal, which will display the contexts of an existing data file so that changes may be made before the file is restored.

Electronic mail
A message service using electronics and telecommunications to deliver hard or soft copy information. These may take the form of text-only messages or of images that include text in font form and graphic material.

Electronic publishing
(1) A very broad term for computerized technologies that combine in one system all or many of the processes leading to the creation of camera-ready mechanicals. These capabilities include text entry and editing; graphic-image acquisition, creation, and manipulation; typographic composition; automated page make-up and pagination, including the ability to merge text with graphics; and output hardware capable of merging both text and graphics into a camera-ready output image on film, paper, or plates. (2) The use of computers and electronic typesetters to typeset text and compose pages. Usually involves the use of electronic codes to identify fonts and positioning of text. Distinguished from letterpress and hot lead systems. See also Desktop publishing.

Electrostatic printer
A printer that uses electrostatic techniques to produce the final character image.

Ellipse
A regular-shaped oval. Distinguished from irregular ovals that are egg-shaped.

Ellipses
Series of three dots in text (...), used to indicate that some of the text has been deleted (usually from a quotation). An ellipsis also appears after every menu command that opens to a dialog box. See also Em leader.

Em
A unit of measure, a width of a space or a character, equal to the point size of the font (usually equal to the escapement value of the upper case M). A 12-point Em is 12 points wide, for example. Identifies the width of an Em dash or an Em space.

Em dash
A dash sitting approximately centered on the x-height of characters, one Em long, used to indicate a pause in the written material. The Em dash (and ¾ Em) are used to indicate missing material such as "Dr. — was the murderer" or for parenthetical remarks to show a break in thought or special emphasis, such as "Hello—he thought at the time—". Em dashes are also used to replace a colon, "Here's the list—." Em dashes may be open—with a word space on either side of it— or closed—with no space. The open style allows for more alternatives for endofline breaks although some newer systems will break at an Em dash if it occurs at the end of a line. The ¾ Em dash is just a slightly smaller Em dash and is used where the Em dash appears too wide for the typeface in use. Dashes should not be carried over to the beginning of the following line, if possible.

EM fraction
A standard fraction of uniform width (1 Em) using a diagonal divider and available for common fractions.

EM leader
Two dots, similar to periods, spaced evenly within the space of one Em. Used with an En leader to create ellipses in typeset material. See Ellipses.

EM space
A fixed amount of white space one Em wide (Em quad) (mutt).

Embedded codes
ASCII codes typed into a stream of text to identify type specifications. Usually called embedded codes to distinguish them from the invisible formatting codes created by some systems.

En
One half the width of an Em (usually equal to the escapement value of the uppercase N). Identifies the width of an En dash or an En space. A 12-point En is 6 points wide. See also Em.

En dash
A dash sitting approximately centered on the x-height of characters, one En long, used in compounded words. The En dash is used where the word "to" or "through" is represented, such as "Pages 19" or "January 13–19". It also connects two nouns of equal weight, such as "East–West" alliance. The En dash may also replace a colon. If you do not have an En dash, kern two hyphens together. The En dash should always be closed (no space on either side).

EN fraction
A standard of uniform width (1 En) using a horizontal divider. Also called case fraction, stack fraction.

EN leader
A dot, similar to a period, centered within the space of one En. Used with an Em leader to create ellipses in typeset material.

EN space
(En quad) (nut) A fixed amount of white space one En wide.

End of line
The point at which one line ends and another begins, either by operator command or by computer decision. In text, the end of a line can be indicated by a variety of codes to distinguish between hard carriage returns (end of paragraph), soft carriage returns (end of line), and overprint codes (no line feed). Indicated by EOL in some systems. Also Ctrl-M, Ctrl-N, Ctrl-P.

End pages
(1) The pages at the end of the tree-structured database which contain information. (2) Blank pages at the beginning or end of a book provided for proper imposition and attractive appearance.

Escapement
The mechanism responsible for the spacing before or between characters. Some typesetters flash (print) a character, then escape the width of that character; some typesetters escape the width of the next character, then flash (print) it. Only laser typesetters do not use the concept of escapement. They create characters a line at a time in small incremental sweeps rather than one character at a time like photo-flash and CRT setters.

Escapement value
The width of the character just set, or the next character, generally in relative units (which see), that the typesetter must escape in order that the next character (or preceding character) does not overlap. On most typewriters, the escapement value of each character is identical. On typesetters, the escapement value of each character is different, with an "I" having a smaller escapement value than an "M." Escapement value is a concept carried over from mechanical typesetting days. Most modern typesetters identify three segments in the character width. These are leading and trailing sidebearings (white space) and character body width.

Even parity
The transmission of data so that all codes having an odd number of one-bits have a bit added to make them have an even number of one-bits. The added bit is generally placed in the eight channel of an eight-level code. See Parity bit.

Exception dictionary
An electronic list of words that can be accessed by a text processing program for correct or preferred hyphenation points. The list is shorter than a full dictionary since it contains only those words that are exceptions to the normal rules for hyphenation (which can be applied using a system of hyphenation logorithms or formulas). See also Hyphenation.

Expanded
Pertaining to a typeface that has characters whose width is greater than their height would generally dictate. Expanded typefaces look "stretched" horizontally. Although you can achieve this effect electronically through some graphics and typesetting programs by expanding characters from the normal font, usually expanded characters are individually designed as a separate font. Some applications use the term expanded to indicate looser letter spacing, in which the words are expanded but the individual characters retain their normal width. Expanded faces are often used for heads, subheads and small blocks of ad copy. See also Kerning, Tracking.

Face
(1) The printing surface of metal type. (2) Another term for typeface.

Facing pages
In a double-sided publication, the two pages that face each other when the publication is open. Facing pages consist of an even-number page on the left and an odd-number page on the right.

Facsimile
(1) A printed, handwritten, or photographic image which is to be electronically transmitted. FAX. (2) A system for the electronic transmission of printed, handwritten, or photographic images.

Figure
(1) A single digit (0-9). (2) An illustration, diagram, chart, photograph, or other display material to be included within, but set apart from, text.

File
Any named, ordered collection of information stored on a disk. Application programs and operating systems on disks are examples of files. You make a file when you create text or graphics, give the material a name, and save it to disk; in this sense, synonymous with document.

File maintenance
The activity of keeping a file current by updating, adding, or deleting data. A general term for copying files, deleting files, and other chores involving updating the contents of disks.

File management
The activity of a computer in keeping track of what is happening to files, maintaining files, and allowing files to be edited. Also, a disciplined approach to organizing all of the files realted to a single company, department, or project; a set of standards for naming files and directories.

File server
A combination of controller software and a mass-storage device that allows computer users to share common files and applications through a network.

434 THE ELECTRONIC PUBLISHER

Filename
The name that identifies a file. The maximum character length of a filename and the rules for naming a file vary under different operating systems. Compare Pathname.

Film
Photosensitive material, generally on a transparent base, which receives character images, and may be chemically processed to expose those images. In phototypesetting, any photosensitive material, transparent or not, may be called film.

Film strip
A piece of specially treated film on which character images are arranged, and when light is flashed through it, the characters will be exposed on the receiving surface (film or paper) to produce typeset characters.

First-generation typesetter
A photocomposition typesetter using a film strip or other carrier of character images, wherein each character in turn is positioned before a light source, and light is flashed through the character image to produce a typeset character. The mechanics of the typesetter imitate those of a hot metal linecaster.

Fixed disk
A hard or rigid disk that is not removable from its drive.

Fixed space
A particular amount of white space, such as an Em, En, or thin space, which will not be "stretched" for justification purposes as will a spaceband. The most common widths are the Em (a square formed by the valve of the point size-a 9-point Em space will be 9-points wide no matter what the face), the En (half the Em) and the Thin (either ¼ or ⅓ of an Em). The Figure space would have the same width as the numerals 1–10 and the dollar sign, although the En may be used for this in some systems.

Floppy disk
A disk made of flexible plastic, as compared with a hard disk, which is made of metal. The term floppy is now usually applied only to disks with thin, flexible disk jackets, such as 8-inch and 5¼ -inch disks. There are three basic sizes: 8 inches (up to 360 KB capacity); 5¼" (up to 1.2 MB capacity); 3½" (up to 720 KB). With 3½-inch disks, the disk itself is flexible, but the jacket is made of hard plastic; thus, 3½-inch disks aren't particularly "floppy." See 5¼-inch disk, 3½-inch disk.

Flush
Aligned with, even with, coming to the same edge as. See Alignment.

Flush paragraph
A paragraph that has no beginning line indent.

Flush right (or right justified)
Text in which lines end at the same point on the right margin—opposite of ragged right or left justified. See also Alignment.

Flying spot scanner
A type of optical scanning mechanism that utilizes a CRT-generated beam of light to raster-scan a stationary document mounted on a flat-bed platen. See also Scanner, Digitize.

Folio
(1) Page number on a printed page, often accompanied by the name of the document or secton and date of publication. Running heads or feet may include folios. See also Header, Footer. (2) A broadside folded once to create a four-page publication. See Broadside.

Font
(1) One complete set of characters in the same face, style, and size, including all of the letters of the alphabet, punctuation, and symbols. For example 12-point Times Roman is a different font from 12-point Times Italic, 14-point Times Roman, or 12-point Helvetica. Screen fonts (bit-mapped fonts used to display text accurately on the screen) can differ slightly from the printer fonts (outline fonts used to describe fonts to the laser printer) because of the difference in resolution between screens and printers. (2) The specific physical device used to store the characters in a font, such as a film strip, grid, disk, or case (in metal type).

Font rectangle
The smallest rectangle enclosing all the character images in a font, if the images were all superimposed over the same character origin.

Font scaling
A feature that allows computers to create all sizes of a font from one size.

Font size
The size of a font of characters in points; equivalent to the distance between the ascent line of one line of text and the ascent line of the next line of single-spaced text. See also point size, base line, descent line, point, x-height.

Footer
One or more lines of text that appear at the bottom margin of a document. A footer appears on every page and can include text, pictures, page numbers, the date, and the time. Also called running footer or running foot. Compare Header.

Footnote
A reference or explanatory material used at the bottom of a page to comment on the material in the text. Footnotes and footnoted material are usually designated with matching symbols, such as asterisks, daggers, or numbers, so that the footnote may be referred to as the text is being read. Sometimes all the footnotes in a chapter are presented at the end of the chapter or at the end of the text.

Footnote callout
The symbol or number within text that directs the reader's attention to the appropriate footnote at the bottom of the page (or end of the chapter).

Footnoting capability
The ability of a computer pagination system to identify footnote callouts and footnotes and arrange pages so that footnotes automatically appear on the same pages as their referred text.

Format
(1)(n) The form in which information is organized or presented. (2) The general shape and appearance of a printed page, including page size, margins, character width and spacing, line spacing, and so on.

GLOSSARY

The basic design of a job to be typeset: its size, shape, typestyle, etc. Also, the character format (font) and paragraph format (alignment, spacing, and indentation). (3) In computerized typesetting, a series of codes that are to be used repetitively may be organized and stored as a "format" with a given name or number. When the operator wishes those previously stored codes to be used as if a keyboard explicitly, the format is "called" or invoked by its given name or number. (4) To add or determine the typesetting codes that will produce the desired results in typeset material. (5) (v) To set up a disk in the proper way to receive codes for a particular device. To divide a disk into tracks and sectors where information can be stored. Blank disks must be formatted before you can save information on them for the first time; synonymous with initialize.

Fourth-generation typesetter
A typesetter that uses a more advanced technology than third-generation (CRT) typesetters. The term has been used to refer to laser typesetters.

Fraction
A numeric symbol indicating a portion of a whole number. A fraction is made up of a numerator, a denominator, and a dividing line. Split fractions are fake fractions in which the numerator and denominator are formed from inferior and superior sized figures, each centered over the other, and divided by a horizontal rule. Piece fractions are En and Em fractions using only the denominators supplied. The numerators are created using special numerals, such as the superiors. See also Em fraction, En fraction.

Function code
See Embedded code, Control code, Control key.

G (Giga)
An abbreviation for one million units. One gigabyte of data is equal to 1,000 megabytes. See also M (Mega).

Galley
(1) In hot metal, a shallow tray used to assemble and hold slugs of metal type before it is cast into pages. (2) (Galley proof). A sheet of paper made by taking an impression of the type in a galley tray so it may be proofread. (3) A length of phototypeset or electronically output material used for proofing before positioning the material in final camera-ready form. (4) A series of phototypeset galleys on the same length of film or photosensitive paper, before the individual galleys are cut apart. (5) To break phototypeset material into prespecified lengths during the keyboarding or output process.

Generate
To produce a typeset galley or page, or the coded text that will go into the page, from a set of skeletal coding under the control of parameters.

Generic font
A screen representation of alphanumeric characters on a screen which may not reflect what the final printed characters will look like.

Ghosting
A procedure in which two images are combined together electronically. The images are given specific weight in relation to each other to create the effect.

Global search
A computer search through the entire file or job in order to locate and correct all occurences of the same characters (global search-and-replace) (global substitution).

Gothic
Pertaining to a plain, sans serif typeface with lines of unvarying thickness.

Gradation change
An adjustment of an electronic image, along a characteristic curve, in order to change such variables as highlights, midtone, shadow, minimum dot and maximum dot values.

Graph
(1) A pictorial representation of data. (2) An abbreviation of a paragraph.

Graphic
(1) A sign, symbol, illustration within the typeset material. (2) Pertaining to visual material or artistic representation.

Graphical primitives
A set of instruction codes transmitted to a terminal that defines basic graphics shapes such as circles, lines, etc.

Graphic arts
The field or technology encompassing typesetting, printing, telecommunications, publishing, advertising, and other related artistic/professional endeavors.

Graphics
(1) Information presented in the form of pictures or images. (2) The display of pictures or images on a computer's display screen. Compare Text.

Graphic terminal
A video terminal (graphics workstation) capable of displaying graphics.

Gravure
An intaglio printing technique where the image to be printed is etched into an image carrier (such as a roller), and transferred to the paper.

Gray balance
The proper amount of cyan, magenta, and yellow printing to produce a gray scale with no apparent dominant hue.

Gray scale
A strip of reflection gray steps ranging from white to black for analyzing printing characteristics. Densities of the steps are representative of densities found in the copy so it is placed at the side of the original during the photographic process. In imaging technology, the corresponding white-to-black range of steps as applicable to video technology.

Greek text
Traditionally, a block of text used to represent the positioning and point size of text in a designer's comp of a design. Standard "greek" text used by typesetters actually Latin: "Lorem ipsum dolor sit amet..." etc.

Greeking
The conversion of text to symbolic bars or boxes that show the position of the text on the screen but not the alphanumeric characters.

Grid
The underlying design plan for a page. In Page-Maker, the grid is composed of a series of non-printing horizontal and vertical lines—margins, column guides, and ruler guides—that intersect to form a "grid."

Gutter
The inside margins between the facing pages of a document. Sometimes this term is used to describe the space between columns. In some word processors, the gutter measure is actually entered as the difference between the inside margin and the outside margin measures.

H & J
Hyphenation and Justification. The practice of adjusting blocks of type so that they are both left and right aligned, with hyphenation occurring as appropriate, wordspaces adjusted for good fit, and overall appearance satisfactory. Often referred to simultaneously as H&J since justified text usually requires hyphenation to minimize "rivers" of white space within the columns. See also Hyphenation, Justification.

Hairline
The thinnest rule possible—generally 0.25 point. (Some laser printers do not support hairline rules.) See figure under Rules.

Halftone
The conversion of continuous-tone artwork (usually a photograph) into a pattern of dots or lines that look like gray tones when printed by the offset printing press.

Halftone screen
A screen with a grid pattern that is placed over a continuos tone image or photograph on the camera-ready boards, or over the film during its exposure in platemaking, to produce halftone dots.

Hanging indent
The first line of a paragraph when it extends to the left of the rest of the lines in the same paragraph. A hanging indent format can also be used to create headings that are set to the left of the body copy. See figure under Indentation.

Hard carriage return
See Carriage Return.

Hard copy
(1) Information printed on paper, as opposed to being stored on disk. A permanent visual record of the output of a computer or printer. Phototypeset material is not referred to as hard copy, but a printout of what will be typeset is hard copy. (2) (original copy) The material sent to a typesetter in typed or handwritten form, for conversion into typeset material.

Hard disk
Disk storage that is built into the computer or into a piece of hardware connected to the computer and sealed into a drive or cartridge. A hard disk can store very large amounts of information compared with floppy disk storage. Hard disks can be either fixed disks or removable disk cartridges.

Hard carriage return
See Carriage return.

Hardware
In computer terminology, the machinery that makes up a computer system. Compare Firmware, Software.

Head
(1) A display line or caption, usually set in a larger size or different font than accompanying text material. See Headline. (2) An electronic devide that reads or writes information from a magnetic surface. See Disk head.

Header
(1) An identifying line at the top margin of a printed document. A header is repeated on every page and can include text, pictures, page numbers, the date, and the time. Also called running header or running head. See also Footer and Folio. (2) As part of the data file format, the particular marker or designation that indicates the beginning of a file, or that refers to the file's location.

Headline
The title of an article in a newsletter, newspaper, or magazine.

Hierarchical filing system
A disk storage system in which files can be stored in separate directories, and directories can have subdirectories. See also Directory.

High-resolution graphics
The display of graphics on a screen as a six-color array of points, 280 columns wide and 192 rows high. When a text window is in use, the visible high-resolution graphics display is 280 by 160 points. See also Low-resolution graphics.

Hot type
A mechanical typesetting technology in which molten metal (hot metal) is used to produce lines of relief type characters as they are typed in on a keyboard. See also Linecaster.

Hot zone
See Hyphenation zone.

Hyphen
The hyphen is used for breaking words on syllables at the end of lines to allow even spacing in justification and for compound or connected words (mother-in-law).

Hyphenation
The practice of dividing words by leaving part of the word at the end of one line and continuing it on the next, with a hyphen at the end of the first part of the word. Hyphenation can be achieved in several ways: some programs let you insert "discretionary hyphens" manually (hyphens that are visible only when they fall at the end of a line); some programs insert hyphens automatically based on a dictionary of words; some programs use a logic formula to hyphenate words, based on precise rules for that language. Usually, dictionary hyphenation takes longer than logical hyphenation but is more accurate; hyphenation rules are often difficult to reduce to programming steps, hence the use of exception dictionaries. See also Dictionary, Exception dictionary.

GLOSSARY

Hyphenation zone
A sometimes adjustable area at the right-hand margin, controlling placement and hyphenation of the last word on a line of text.

Icon
A functional graphic representation of a tool, file, or command displayed on a screen.

Image
(1) The photographic master from which the character shape will be produced, such as a font disk. (2) The typeset character, or final picture that is produced by photographic means. (3) In data processing, an exact duplicate of an array of information, or data stored in or in transit to another storage medium.

Image area
The area of a page inside the margins where you put most of the text and graphics.

Impact printer
A printer that uses a physical mold for the character image, and impresses the image on the paper by striking a carbon or cloth ribbon against the paper with the character mold. The character masters may be on a daisy wheel, a metal band, a ball, or some other carrier.

Imposition
The positioning of pages before printing so that after printing, folding, and cutting, all pages will appear in the proper sequence.

Indentation
Positioning of the first line of a paragraph and/or the subsequent lines of a paragraph to the right of the left column guide (to create a left indent), or positioning the right margin of the paragraph to the left of the right column guide (to create a right indent) relative to the other text on the page. A delayed indent does not take effect until after a specified number of lines have been set. A hanging indent takes place on all but the first lines of each text block. A nested indent is measured from the margin of the last indent, rather than the absolute margin. A paragraph indent falls at the beginning of the first line of a paragraph. A runaround (runaround sue) indent takes place for a specified number of lines, usually to leave room for an illustration. A skewed indent is changed for each line, giving the margin a slanted appearance.

Index
(1) An ordered list of items used as a reference to determine the location of material in a file or document. (2) A symbol or number used to identify a particular value in a series of similar values.

Inferior
See Subscript.

Inhouse
Pertaining to a procedure or device within a company that services only that company (inplant) rather than outside customers.

Initial
Initial letters are sometimes used at the beginning of chapters or paragraphs. The first style, and historically the oldest, is the sunken or "drop cap" position. The second style is the raised or "stick up"

initial, and it rests on the base line of the first or subsequent line of text and rises above the top line of the text.

Initialize
(1) To set to an initial state or value in preparation for some computation. (2) To prepare a blank disk to receive information by organizing its surface into tracks and sectors; same as format.

Inkjet printer
A printer that uses finely directed sprays of ink to produce the chacracter image.

Insertion point
The place in a document where something will be added; it is usually represented by a blinking vertical bar on the screen.

Inside margin
The left margin of a right-hand (odd-number) page; the right margin of a left-hand (even-number) page. The inside margin is often wider than the opposite margin, to accommodate binding. See also Gutter.

Interword spacing
See Word spacing.

Invert
See Reverse.

Italic
Letters that slope toward the right, as distinguished from upright, or Roman, characters. Usually have more rounded corners and serifs. Typefaces whose original designs are somewhat slanted (such as Mergenthaler's Eras) are not italic. Some CRT typesetters produce pseudoitalic (oblique) versions of Roman fonts by skewing the digitized Roman character.

Jump line
Text at the end of the text of an article on a page in a newsletter, magazine, or newspaper, indicating on what page the article is continued. Also, the text at the top of a continued article, indicating where the article is continued from.

Justification
The process of composing and adjusting lines of type by adding space between the words and characters so that the lines are aligned on the left and right margins. Hyphenation may also occur. Photographic justification is the process of justifying a line by uniformly expanding all character and word space on the line. Vertical justification is the process of adding space between lines or paragraphs to achieve alignment of columns top and bottom.

Justified text
Text that is flush at both the left and right edges. See figure under Alignment.

K
Abbreviation for kilo, which is commonly used to mean 1,000. In computer terminology, however, K often refers to the number 1,024, and is used to specify the amount of storage available on a disk or in memory. Therefore, a system with 8K of memory has 8,192 bytes of storage capacity.

Kern
(1) To adjust the spacing between letters, usually to move them closer together. See Kerning. (2) The part of a letter that actually overhangs the body of the letter itself, such as the top curl of the lowercase f in a serif typeface.

Kerning
Amount of space between letters, especially certain combinations of letters that must be brought closer together than others in order to create visually consistent spacing among all letters. The uppercase letters AW may appear to have a wider gap between them than the letters MN, for example, unless there is a special kerning formula set up for the AW combination. See also Tracking.

Kerning pairs
In a computerized typesetting system, certain pairs of characters may be defined with specific kerning values. When type is set, kerning is automatically done between those specified pairs.

Keylining
A copy preparation technique used for some types of color separation wherein an artist outlines certain areas of artwork on a tissue overlay, with instructions to the printer or camera operator. Keylining can also show the placement, content, and approximate size of an illustration.

Ladder
Several consecutive hyphenated lines on a page, considered typograhically undesirable.

LAN
(See Local area network)

Landscape printing
The rotation of a page design to print text and graphics horizontally across the 11-inch width of the paper. See also Portrait printing.

LASER
An acronym for Light Amplification by Stimulated Emission of Radiation. A source of a single-colored, very narrow, coherent beam of light. Unlike most light, laser light may be focused very precisely with little dispersion. Lasers used in a wide variety of technologies including laser printers, phototypesetters and other output imaging devices, facsimile, and optical disks.

Laser platemaking
The use of lasers for scanning pasteups and/or exposing plates in the same or remote locations for printing.

Laser printer
A printer that uses a laser to xerographically generate the image to be reproduced. Laser printers are typically the most sophisticated printers, often capable of producing both character and graphics images via raster image processing technology, often rivaling typographic quality. They are the output devices usually associated with desktop publishing.

Laser printing
Term used to describe printing with one of the toner-based laser printers that are available for PCs. These printers use laser technology—light amplification by emission of radiation— to project an intense light beam with a very narrow band width ($1/300$ of an inch in 300-dot-per-inch printers) to create the charge on the printer drum that picks up the toner and transfers it to the paper. Some typesetters (such as the Linotronic 100 and 300) also use laser technology in conjunction with their photochemical processing, but these are usually referred to as phototypesetters rather than laser printers.

Layout
The process of arranging text and graphics on a page. Also, a sketch or plan for the page. Also, the final appearance of the page. In platemaking, a sheet indicating the settings for the step-and-repeat machine.

Layout grid
See Grid.

Leader
(1) A record, preceding a group of records, which provides preliminary information concerning the succeeding records. (2) The blank length of tape at the beginning of a reel of magnetic tape, or the uncoded length at the beginning of a length of paper tape.

Leaders
Dotted or dashed lines that can be defined for tab settings.

Leading
Pronounced "LED-ing;" the amount of blank vertical space between the descent line of one line of text and the ascent line of the next line of single-spaced text. The amount of vertical spacing, expressed in points, between the base lines of two lines of text. Historically, the insertion of thin strips of metal (made of a metal alloy that included some proportion of lead) between lines of cast type to add space between the lines and to make columns align vertically, and leading was measured by the thickness of the leading slug only. In modern typography, the vertical spacing between the baselines of two lines of text, and leading is measured as the sum of the point size plus the thickness of the leading. This is the line spacing setting in some applications. As an example of the terminology used in describing line spacing, 12-point Times with one point of leading would be considered "one-point leaded" type; or 12-point Times with 13-point leading, or 12 on 13 Times. The type specs are sometimes written as 12/13 Times. Reverse leading is the action of a phototypesetter in reversing the imaging film to cause the next line of type to print higher on the page than the previous line, or changing the leading in electronic page layout to achieve this effect.

Letter elements
The calligraphic design elements that comprise the identity of individual characters. (See also Serif) Apex: the top junction of two stems, such as at the point of the capital A or at the center of the capital W. Arc: any curved stroke other than a bowl. Arm: a horizontal or diagonal stroke starting from the stem, as in the cap E or F. Bar: an arm connected on both sides, as in the capital H. Beak: the strokes at the ends of arms and serifs, such as in the letters E , F , G , T , and Z. Bowl: the strokes enclosing a counter. Counter: the fully or partially enclosed

GLOSSARY

portion of a letter, such as in the lowercase e which has a full counter above and a partial counter below. Crossbar: a horizontal stroke that crosses through the stem, such as in the lowercase t. Crotch: the inside of an apex or vortex. Ear: a short stroke, such as that extending from a lowercase g. Loop: a bowl that serves as a flourish, as in the descending part of some lowercase g characters. Spine: the main curved arc section of the letter S. Stem: the main vertical stroke or strokes of a character. Tail: downward-sloping short stroke, ending free. Vortex: the bottom junction of two stems, such as in the letter W, having two vortex points.

Letter spacing
The space between letters in a word. Also, the practice of adding space between letters. See also Kerning, Tracking, Word spacing.

Ligatures
Character combinations that are often combined into special characters in a font. For example, some downloadable fonts come with the combinations "fi" and "fl" as special characters.

Line art
Illustrations composed of black and white only, with no shades of gray.

Line break
The end of a line of text that is created by automatic word wrap and hyphenation. See also Carriage return.

Linecaster
A hot metal typesetting device that assembles a line of character molds, then casts a piece of metal containing the whole line of character images. The metal slugs are then assembled into columns. (line casting machine) (Linotype).

Line length
The horizontal measure of a column or a line of text. The number of characters that fit in a line on the screen or on a page.

Line printer
A printer that produces an entire line of characters at once.

Line spacing
See Leading.

Local area network (LAN)
A collection of devices and communication channels that connect a group of computers and peripheral devices together so that they may communicate with each other. Typically, local area networks occupy a single building or office area.

Logo
A company trademark. A unique symbolic design that may include both imagery and type intended to represent or provide identification of a company or organization. Also, the banner on the front cover of a magazine or newsletter.

Loop
A bowl that serves as a flourish, as in the descending part of some lowercase g characters. See figure under Letter element.

Lower case
See Case.

Low-resolution graphics
The display of graphics on a display screen as a 16-color array of blocks, 40 columns wide and 48 rows high. For example, on a Macintosh when the text window is in use, the visible low-resolution graphics display is 40 by 40 plotting points-that is, 40 by 40 pixels. See also high-resolution graphics.

M (Mega)
Abbreviation for Mega, which is commonly used to mean one million. In computer terminology however, M refers to the number 1,048,576, and is used to specify the amount of storage available on a disk or in memory. A one megabyte disk can record 1,048,576 bytes of data.

Magenta
The subtractive primary color that appears blue-red and absorbs green light. Used as one ink in four-color printing. Also known as process red.

Magnetic ink character recognition
A technique in which character images are recognized by the pattern of the magnetic ink in which they are printed, rather than by reflected light, as in optical numbers on business checks, which was the first character recognition system in widespread use.

Main memory
The part of a computer's memory whose contents are directly accessible to the microprocessor; usually synonymous with random-access memory (RAM). Programs are loaded into main memory, where the computer keeps information while you're working. Sometimes simply called memory. See also Read-only memory, Read-write memory.

Mainframe computer
A central processing unit or computer that is larger and more powerful than a minicomputer or a personal computer (microcomputer). Frequently called mainframe for short.

Makeready
Copy or machine preparation of graphic material before production.

Makeup
The assembly of blocks of text into pages, whether by hand or by computer. See Layout.

Manuscript
The original written or typewritten copy of the author's text, from which type will be set.

Margin
(1) Traditionally, the distance from the edge of the page to the edge of the layout area of the page. The dotted (nonprinting) lines near the borders of the screen page that mark the margins of a page. Usually refers to the space between text and the edge of the page, as opposed to space between columns. (2) The position of the leftmost edge of the type image on the page.

Markup
The written specification (specs) indicating the particulars of typography and measurement, used as guidelines or instructions for implementation of the work. See also Specifications.

Massage
To process within a computer, especially in order to add line endings, page parameters, and positioning instructions. Text is said to be massaged between input and output.

Masthead
Section of newsletter or magazine giving its title and details of staff, ownership, advertising, subscription dates, etc.; sometimes used to describe the banner or wide title on the front cover of a magazine or the front of a newsletter or newspaper. See also Logo.

Matrix printer
A printer that produces character images made up of dots rather than lines and strokes.

Measurement systems
Depending on your application, you can work in inches, decimal inches, millimeters, picas and points, or ciceros.

Mechanical
Traditionally, the final pages or boards with pasted-up galleys of type and line art, sometimes with acetate or tissue overlays for color separations and notes to the offset printer. See also Board, Camera-ready art.

Memory
A hardware component of a computer system that can store information for later retrieval. The area inside the computer where information is stored temporarily while you are working (also called RAM or random access memory). The amount of memory a computer has directly affects its ability to perform complex functions. See Main memory, Random-access memory, Read-only memory, Read-write memory.

Menu
A list of choices presented by a program, from which you can select an action.

Microcomputer
A computer whose processor is a microprocessor. See also mainframe.

Mixing
The practice of putting more than one size typeface on a single line.

Mnemonic
An easily remembered or identifiable abbreviation for an instruction, routine, or format.

Modem
Short for modulator/demodulator. A peripheral device that links your computer to other computers and information services using the telephone lines.

Moiré pattern
A grid pattern (usually undesireable) that can result when two transparent dot-screen fill patterns are overlayed, or when a bit-map graphic with gray fill patterns is reduced or enlarged.

Monospace font
Any font in which all characters have the same width. (Mono means one.) For example, in a font used to show program listings, the letter M is the same width as the letter I. Thus, MMMMM is the same width as IIIII.

Mortise
(1) To kern hot metal type by removing pieces of metal from the "white space" areas of character molds so that two characters will fit together more closely. See Kern, Kerning. (2) A cut-out area for the insertion of art.

Mouse
A hand-controlled device used to direct the movements of a cursor on a display. The mouse controls a pointer on the screen whose movements correspond to those of the mouse. You use the pointer to select operations, to move data, and to draw with in graphics programs.

Multiplex
To simultaneously transmit two or more messages over the same communications channel to different receivers.

Multiprocessing
Petaining to the simultaneous execution of two or more programs or instruction sequences by a computer or network.

Multitasking
Describing a computer's ability to carry out two or more functions simultaneously.

Negative
A reverse image of a page, produced photographically on a clear sheet of film as an intermediate step in preparing plates from camera-ready mechanicals for offset printing.

Network
A collection of interconnected, individually controlled computers, together with the hardware and software used to connect them. A network allows users to share data and peripheral devices such as printers and storage media, to exchange electronic mail, and so on. See also Local area network.

Newspaper line
A standard copy measurement; a theoretical line of type 11 picas long, with about 30 characters to the line.

Nonbreaking space
A special character inserted between two words so they cannot be separated by a line break.

Numeric keypad
A calculator-style keypad, either built-in or a peripheral, which you can use to type numbers. The layout of numbers on the keypad makes it easier and faster to use than the regular keyboard. Some application programs designate the keys of a numeric keypad as special function keys.

Object-oriented files
"Draw-type" files that are a sequence of drawing commands (stored as mathematical formulas) which describe graphics that you would manually produce with a pencil, straightedge, and compass (such as mechanical drawings, schematics, charts, and ad graphics). Usually contrasted with "paint-type" files or bit-maps. See also Bit-maps.

Oblique
(pseudo-italic) The characteristic of a typeface that has been skewed from a digitized Roman character, thus looking like an italic typeface.

GLOSSARY   441

Octavo
A broadside folded 3 times to create a 16-page publication. See figure under Broadside.

Odd parity
The transmission of data so that all codes having an even number of one-bits have a bit added to make them have an odd number of one-bits. See Parity bit.

Offset
The inadvertent transfer of a still wet-ink image from one page to another directly after the printing process.

Offset printing
The type of printing done using a printing press to reproduce many copies of the original that is printed out on a laser printer. The press lays ink on a page based on the raised image on a plate that is created by photographing the camera-ready masters.

Operating system
A program that organizes the actions of the parts of the computer and its peripheral devices. See also DOS

Optical character recognition
(pattern recognition) A method of converting graphics symbols (particularly alphanumerics) to shapes. Until recently, material prepared for optical character recognition had to be typed in a specific format, and with a specific type element.

Optical character reader
(page reader) A device that is capable of converting graphics symbols to electronic signals.

Optical scanner
A device that uses light to scan and convert text, graphics, or other visual images into digitized data that can be read by a computer.

Orientation
The page position: tall or wide. Tall orientation means that when the text runs horizontally across the narrower width of the page, the columns run down the longer length of the page. Wide orientation means that the text runs horizontally across the wider width of the page.

Ornaments
Symbols or decorative elements. See Dingbats.

Orphans/Widows
The first or last line of a paragraph is called an orphan when it is separated from the rest of the paragraph by a page break. A heading separated from the body text that follows is also an orphan. The last line of a paragraph is called a widow, and it is an orphan when it is forced onto a new page by a page break and separated from the rest of the paragraph. The term widow is also used to describe bad line breaks that result in the last line of a paragraph having only one word, especially when it falls at the end of a column or page. Widows and orphans are generally considered bad page breaks (or column breaks) by most publishers. Some packages let you set up automatic controls for the minimum number of lines that can be separated by a page break.

Outline font
(1) A printer font in which each letter of the alphabet is stored as a complex mathematical formula, as distinguished from bit-map fonts that are stored as a pattern of dots. (2) A typeface with no guts. Outline faces are used in display work.

Output
(n) Information transferred from a computer to some external destination, such as the display screen, a disk drive, a printer, or a modem. Compare input.

Outside margin
The nonbound edge of a publication. In single-sided publications, this is the right margin. In double-sided publications, the outside margin is the right margin of a right-hand (odd-number) page; the left margin of a left-hand (even-number) page.

Overlay
A transparent acetate or tissue covering over a printed page, where color indications and other instructions to the offset printer are written. Also, an overhead transparency that is intended to be projected on top of another projection.

Overrun
The quantity of printed copies over and above the number ordered to be printed.

Overset
To exceed the stated line length. Type may occasionally be overset on purpose, to fit a small word or element onto a line where it would otherwise create a widow or a bad appearance.

Page
(1) One side of a sheet of paper. Both sides together are called a sheet or leaf. (2) A frame or screenful of data.

Page composition
See Composition.

Page description language
A program that allows rasterizing output devices such as laser printers and typesetters to output images that may include both graphics and text.

Page makeup
See Page layout.

Pagination
(1) The numbering of the pages of a book. (2) The process of performing page makeup through a computer program according to page parameters designated by the operator or by a database.

Paint program
Graphics software based on traditional techniques of drawing and painting, including color.

Paint-type file
See Bit-map.

Palette
The range of colors available for a video-based paint program.

Paper size
Each size of paper a printer can print on. Standard sizes are letter (8 ½ inches by 11 inches), legal (8 ½ inches by 14 inches), and European A4 (8.27 by 11.69) and B5 (6.93 by 9.84).

Paper tape
A medium once heavily used in typesetting and other computers consisting of lengths of paper ⅞ inch or 1 inch wide, with perforated holes representing bits.

Paragraphs
Units of English composition. In electronic media, copy blocks that fall between two hard carriage returns. Paragraphs are often further defined by an indent at the beginning of the first line and often delineated by a short line of characters at the end or additional line spacing. The short line at the end of a paragraph, if less than one-third the line length is called a widow. If a widow is carried to the top of a column or page, it is called an orphan. See Carriage return, Orphans/widows.

Parallel interface
A data transmission technique in which a group of binary digits (bits) are transferred simultaneously over multiple lines. Usually, eight bits that correspond to a character are transferred as a single operation. (Compare Serial interface)

Parity bait
A bit used for checking the accuracy of the other bits in a character or word during data transmission or processing (check bit). A method of verifying the accuracy of a transmitted bit pattern by examining the code to determine whether its value is odd or even.

Password
An identification number keyed by the operator and checked by the computer before the file or database may be accessed.

Paste
To place the contents of the clipboard-whatever was last cut or copied-at the insertion point.

Pasteup
See Mechanical.

Percent
The symbol representing percentage (%). When you do not have one, spell out "per cent" as two words. Italic would be preferable.

Peripheral device
A piece of hardware-such as a video monitor, disk drive, printer, or modem-used in conjunction with a computer and under the computer's control. Peripheral devices are often (but not necessarily) physically separate from the computer and connected to it by wires, cables, or some other form of interface. Such devices often require peripheral cards.

Photocomposition
See Phototypesetting.

Photodiode sensor array scanner
A type of scanner that employs a stationary configuration of tiny photodiodes arranged in a matrix that equals in width one lateral scan line of document. Typically used in flatbed scanners.

Photolettering
Referring to a variety of devices that produce display and headline type by photographic means, usually without computerized assistance.

Photomechanical
Pertaining to any reproduction process in which photography is employed in the creation of the image, including photoengraving, phototypesetting, photolithography, and others.

Phototypesetter
A device that sets type photographically, generally under the control of some degree of computerization. See also First-, Second-, Third-, and Fourth-generation typesetters.

Phototypesetting
A method of setting type photographically, by using optical or digital masters of character images, light sources, magnifying lenses, and photosensitive paper. This process is sometimes referred to as "cold type" to distinguish it from the older method of casting characters, lines or whole pages in lead (i.e., hot type).

Pi characters
Type characters not among the alphanumeric set, such as stars, bullets, daggers, and fractions. While every font has a few pi characters, some fonts, such as Zapf Dingbats, are composed entirely of pi characters. See Dingbats.

Pica
A unit of measure equal to approximately 1/6 of an inch, or 12 points.

Pixel
Short for picture element. A point on the graphics screen; the visual representation of a bit on the screen (white if the bit is 0, black if it's 1). The smallest unit on a computer screen display. Also a location in video memory that maps to a point on the graphics screen when the viewing window includes that location. See also Bit.

Platen
The rubber roller in a printer that provides support for the paper while the printhead prints on it.

Point
(1) Smallest unit of measure in typographic measurement. There are 12 points in a pica, 72 points in an inch. (2) In papermaking, a point is .001 inch when specifying book binding boards.

Point size
Standard unit of measure for type, measured roughly from the top of the ascenders to the bottom of the descenders in a line of type. See figure under Font size. However, because of variances in type design, the designated point size of a particular font might be somewhat different from the actual measurement. A point is the smallest unit of measure in typographic measurement. There are 12 points in a pica, 72 points in an inch. A point equals 1/12 pica, or 1/72 inch. See also Pica.

Port
A communications channel between a computer or other device, such as a terminal or a tape reader.

GLOSSARY

Portrait printing
The normal printing orientation for a page: horizontal text on an 8½-inch wide sheet of paper. See also Landscape printing.

PostScript
A page-description language developed by Adobe Systems, Inc., that is used by many different models of high-resolution printers and typesetters.

Prepress proofs
Sometimes called blue lines, these are proofs made using photographic techniques. See also Press proofs.

Press proofs
A test run of a color printing job through the printing press to check registration and color. See also Prepress proofs.

Primary colors
The elemental colors of either pigments or light. Red, green, and blue are additive primaries. White light is produced when red, green, and blue lights are added together. Cyan, magenta, and yellow are subtractive primaries. The inks used to print three color process or four color process with black.

Primitive
See graphical primitives.

Print area
The area of a piece of paper where a printer can reproduce text or graphics. The print area is usually smaller than the paper size.

Print queue
The files waiting to be sent to the printer by the spooler in the order they are received. See also Spooler.

Printer
A device that produces a copy on paper of the text or graphics you create using your computer. A character printer produces one character image at a time. Characters may be printed left to right on each line, or in alternating directions on alternate lines. An electrostatic or xerographic printer uses electrostatic techniques to produce the final character image. An impact printer uses a physical mold for the character image, and impresses the image on the paper by striking a carbon or cloth ribbon against the paper with the character mold. The character masters may be on a daisy wheel, a metal band, a ball, or some other carrier. An inkjet printer uses finely directed sprays of ink to produce the character image. A laser printer uses a laser to xerographically generate the image to be reproduced. Laser printers are typically the most sophisticated printers, often capable of producing both character and graphics images via raster image processing technology, often rivaling typographic quality. They are the output device usually associated with desktop publishing. A line printer produces an entire line of characters at once. A matrix printer produces character images made up of dots rather than lines and strokes. A proofing printer is used with a typesetting computer to produce proofs of file contents before actual typesetting is done. A thermal printer uses heat-sensitive paper to carry the character image. A wire printer forms characters by the selection of solenoid operated matrix wires, which print the selected characters by impact against a ribbon. See also Character printer, Daisy wheel printer, Dot-matrix printer, Laser printing.

Printer font
A bit-map or outline font that is installed in the printer or downloaded to the printer when a publication is printed. Usually distinguished from the screen font that is used to display the text on the computer screen. See also Font.

Printhead
The part of a printer that moves horizontally along the platen and performs the actual printing.

Printout
A record of the contents of a computer file produced by a printer, often on continuous form paper with perforations at each edge.

Program
(n) An application. A set of instructions describing actions for a computer to perform in order to accomplish some task, conforming to the rules and conventions of a particular programming language.
(v) To write a program.

Programming language
A set of symbols and associated rules or conventions for writing programs; for example, PostScript, BASIC, Logo, and Pascal are programming languages.

Proof
A copy of typeset material used for proofreading, corrections, and alterations.

Proofread
To read a preliminary printout of a page and check for spelling errors, alignment on the page, and other features that are not related to the technical accuracy of the content.

Proofing printer
A printer used with a typesetting computer to produce proofs of file contents before actual typesetting is done.

Proofs
See Prepress proofs, Press proofs, Blue lines.

Proportional font
Any font in which different characters have different widths; thus, the space taken up by words having the same number of letters varies. For example, in the typeface used here the letter M is wider than the letter I, so that MMMMM produces a wider string than IIIII. See monospace font.

Proportional spacing
The characteristic of a typeface wherein each letter has its own escapement value. Some typewriters and printers provide the elements that use proportional spacing, although the majority of these devices use only monospaced fonts.

Pull-out quote
Quotes extracted from a newsletter or magazine article and printed large in the column, often blocked off with ruled lines.

Punctuation
One of the first printers to break up text with punctuation was Aldus Manautius before 1500.

The period was the full stop at the end of a sentence and the slash / was used as a comma, to indicate a pause in reading.

Quad
(1) A piece of metal with no printing surface that is used to fill up a line of hot metal type, thus forcing the character images into place on the line. (2) To fill up a line of hot metal type with quads. (3) To enter a code in a computerized typesetter or typesetting system that will position a line of type to the left, right, or center. Today, both flush and quad are used interchangeably.

Quarto
A broadside folded twice to create an eight-page publication. See figure under Broadside.

Queue
A group of items arranged in a particular sequence, waiting to have some process performed.

Quote
Quote marks are opening and closing punctuation marks to indicate verbal statements or to define or emphasize certain words. Double quotes are normally used, with single quotes used within a double quote, as in "Doubles on the outside, 'singles' on the inside." The closed quote is an apostrophe.

Ragged-right
Text in which lines end at different points near the right margin—opposite of flush right or justified text. See figure under alignment.

RAM
See Random-access memory, Read-only, and Memory.

Random-access memory (RAM)
Memory in which information can be referred to in an arbitrary or random order. As an analogy, a book is a random-access storage device in that it can be opened and read at any point. RAM usually means the part of memory available for programs from a disk; the programs and other data are lost when the computer is turned off. A computer with 512K RAM has 512 kilobytes available to the user. (Technically, the read-only memory (ROM) is also random access, and what's called RAM should correctly be termed read-write memory.) Compare Read-only memory, Read-write memory.

Raster
The set of parallel horizontal scan lines that form a television or video display image. Each scan line is reproduced many times per second.

Raster scan
The generation of a beam of light or electrons according to a predetermined rather than a random pattern.

Raster image processor
(RIP) A device with associated software that prepares electronic image files for output on a raster image device such as a laser printer or typesetter.

Raw data
Data that has not been processed, reorganized, or manipulated.

Read-only memory (ROM)
Memory whose contents can be read, but not changed; used for storing firmware. Information is placed into read-only memory once, during manufacture; it then remains there permanently, even when the computer's power is turned off. Compare Random-access memory, Read-write memory.

Read-write head
That part of a disk drive that rotates the magnetized surface and either reads or writes magnetic memory onto the disk.

Record
In a database, a single related grouping of data items (such as a company name, address, telephone number).

Recto
The right-hand page of a book, opposite of verso.

Reference marks
Reference marks are used instead of superior figures, usually if there are only a few footnotes. The proper sequence is: Asterisk (Single) Dagger, Double Dagger, Paragraph Mark, Section Mark, Parallel Rules. If more are needed, the marks start at the beginning and are doubles. At that point you should have used superior numbers. Reference marks are placed after the text to be referenced. Usually there is no space before the reference mark, although some customers may prefer a thin space.

Refresh
(1) The generation of an image on a cathode tube with sufficient frequency that the image appears constant. The image must be refreshed rather than constant because the phosphor that displays the image will not hold that image for more than an instant. (2) To stabilize the data on a magnetic surface by reading it and rewriting it. This has the effect of refreshing the magnetic charge on the surface.

Registration
The accuracy with which images are combined or positioned, particularly in reference to multicolored printing where each color must be precisely aligned for the accurate reproduction of the original.

Registration mark
One of a number of small reference patterns placed on art work to aid in the registration process before or during printing.

Remote
Pertaining to communication with a device located at some distance from the central device, but connected in some way, with cables, wires, or telephone hookup.

Resolution
The number of dots per inch (dpi) used to represent an alphanumeric character or a graphics image. In vector displays, resolution is measured as lines per inch. In raster displays, resolution is expressed as the number of horizontal and vertical pixels that can be displayed. In hard copy output from photo or laser typesetters or printers, resolution is measured as lines per inch or dots per inch. High-resolution images look smoother and have more

GLOSSARY 445

dots per inch than low-resolution images. The resolution of images displayed on the screen is usually lower than that of the final laser printout. Laser printers print 300 dots per inch or more; phototypesetters print 1200 dots per inch or more.

Reverse
The opposite of the normal appearance of text or a graphic on the printed page. Normally, text and graphics are black on a white background—when reversed, they are white on a black background. This option is called invert on some systems.

Reverse leading
The action of a phototypesetter in reversing the imaging film to cause the next line of type to print higher on the page than the previous line, or changing the leading in electronic page layout to achieve this effect.

RGB
Red, green, blue. The additive color primaries. Used in reference to color computer graphics and video technology.

RGB monitor
A type of color monitor that receives separate signals for each color (red, green, and blue). See Composite video.

Right justified
See Flush right, Alignment.

Rigid disk
See hard disk.

River
The optical path of white space that sometimes occurs when word spaces in successive lines of type happen to end up immediately below each other for some distance. This accident is considered undesirable in typography, and may be correctd by moving words from one line to another to reposition the word spaces. See also Typographic Color.

ROM
See Read-only memory.

Roman
Upright text styles, as distinguished from italic. Sometimes used to refer to normal style on an application's menu as opposed to bold or italic.

Rotate
(1) In computer graphics, to turn all or part of a display image about an axis perpendicular to the display surface. (2) In three-dimensional graphics, to revolve all or part of a picture about any required axis.

Roughs
Traditionally, the preliminary page layouts done by the designer using pencil sketches to represent miniature page design ideas. See also Thumbnails.

RS-232 Port
A standard plug with 25 pins, used to connect computers and I/O devices.

Ruler
Rulers displayed on the screen that show measures against the page layout in inches, picas, or millimeters. In word processing, a graphic representation of a ruler on which you set the format for the document, such as right and left margins, line spacing, indentation, and tabs.

Rules or ruled lines
Black lines of various styles that can be drawn on a page and set to various thicknesses. When incorporated as part of a line of text, the rule line (often, but not always, aligning at the baseline) is used for horizontal ruling, including underlining. The problem with a line of rules is that the width of the rule may not divide evenly into the line length. Rules are commonly the Em width, the width of the point size. If the line length is an even number of picas, the 12 point rule (12 pts. wide) would go in evenly. If the line length is in half picas, the 6 point rule (6 pts. wide) would divide evenly. If there is other copy on the line, then there is only luck. Since the typesetting machine might put the excess space at the end, you should put a word space between the other copy and the start of the rule so the excess space has a place to go. This may not be so with newer digitized typesetters.

Runaround
See Text wrap.

Run-in
Referring to a heading or caption that does not stand apart from the text it heads, but acts as the first part of the text.

Running heads and feet
See Header and Footer.

Running text
A block of text in which the visual line endings have no relation to the context of the material, except coincidentally. Paragraphs, pages, and other narrative material are made up of running text.

Sans serif
Without serifs; serifs are fine lines that finish off the main strokes of a letter—like the little "feet" on the bottom of the horizontal strokes in the letter M in Garamond typeface. Type faces without serifs, such as Helvetica and Avant Garde. See also Serif.

Scale
(1) To determine the corect final size for an image that must be enlarged or reduced to fit an area. (2) To transform the size or shape of all or part of a display image by multiplying or dividing coordinate dimensions.

Scan
To examine or expose an image by means of moving a light beam or "flight spot." Scanning technology is used in optical character recognition, laser printing, ink-jet printing, and CRT typesetting, as well as in other areas.

Scanned-image files
Bit-map files created with hardware that digitizes images i.e., converts a two- or three-dimensional image to a collection of dots stored in the computer's memory or on disk.

Scanner
An electronic input device that converts analogue images, such as continuous-tone photographs, line art, or typographic copy into a digital data file that can be manipulated as an electronic display image.

Screen
(1) The display surface of a video terminal or cathode ray tube. See also Display screen. (2) Gray tone composed of a pattern of dots and usually identified as a percentage of black: a 100 percent screen is solid black; a 10 percent screen is light gray. The amount of dots per inch in the screen controls the degree of clarity in the image. The size of each dot within the screen controls the "darkness" of the area, and is referred to as the percentage of possible size of the dot. As a very simplistic explanation, in a 100-line screen, dots are arranged in a matrix of 100 diagonal lines within a square inch. Each dot may potentially be 1/100 of an inch in diameter. In a 100-line, 60 percent screen, each dot is 6/1000 of an inch in diameter within a 1/100 inch diameter of a white space. The dots themselves, however, are not exactly round. Screened paragraphs contain dots whose size varies according to the image at each point.

Screen font
See Font.

Script fonts
Type designed to look like handwriting or calligraphy, such as Zapf Chancery.

Search string
An identified sequence of characters that exists somewhere in a file, and which the operator has requested that the computer locate and display.

Second generation typesetter
A typesetter using a photomechanical technology, but which does not imitate a hot metal typesetter in its design. Second-generation typesetters are those that use rotating disks or film strips to carry master character images. Light is selectively flashed through the character image, focused through movable or interchangeable lenses, and received on photosensitive film or paper. Escaspement is provided by means of a moving mirror that alters the light path, or by moving the film or the font matrix.

Serif
Line crossing the main strokes of a letter. Typefaces that have serifs include Times, Courier, New Century Schoolbook, Bookman, and Palatino. See also Sans serif.

Set size
(1) The relative amount of space required for each character in a typeface (set width). The set size may be different than the point size; an expanded typeface in 9-point, for instance, may have the spacing requirements of a 12-point typeface, and would have a 12-point set size. By instructing the typesetter to expand or reduce the set width of a particular font, the density of the typeface may be altered. (2) In CRT typesetters, the actual width of a point size. When the set size is changed, the typesetter adjusts the digitized image to produce a condensed or expanded typeface, according to the point size in use and the set size requested. (3) The actual size, in points, of the Em space, which may be different than the point size.

Set width adjustment
The practice of reducing or expanding the set width (set size) to increase the white space between characters. Set width adjustment is regularly done in larger point sizes on phototypesetters to increase the readability of typeset material. Set width expansion is sometimes called reverse letterspacing. (white space adjustment) (overall kerning).

Side bearings
The amount of white space on either side of a character that separates it from the characters on either side.

Signature
In printing and binding, the name given to a printed sheet of (usually) 16 pages after it has been folded. Most books are made up of a series of signatures.

Simplex
A modem that either sends or receives information but cannot do both during one transmission.

Single-sided
A publication whose pages will be reproduced on one side of a sheet of paper.

Sink
The amount by which the first line on the page is dropped from the standard beginning of the page, as in chapter headings.

Size
(1) To make a graphic smaller or larger on a page. (2) A material that is applied or added to paper during its manufacture to change its ink or water absorbency. (3) See Font size.

Slug
(1) An identification line showing to which story a section of copy or typeset material belongs. Slugs are usually placed at the top corner of submitted copy and on the top line of galley. (2) A strip of metal produced by a hot metal typesetter, containing a line of character images.

Small caps
See Caps and Small caps.

Snap-to
The effect of various types of nonprinting guide lines—grid lines, margin guides, ruler guides, and column guides—that exert a "magnetic" pull on the cursor, text, or a graphic that comes close to the guides in some page layout and drawing programs. This feature is useful for accurately aligning text and graphics.

Soft carriage return
A line-feed/carriage return inserted and removed automatically by text processing software to create variable word wrap. See also Carriage return.

Software
A collective term for programs and the instructions that tell the computer what to do. Software is usually stored on disks. Compare Firmware, Hardware.

Solid
The characteristic of type that is set with a leading equal to the point size. Lines that are set solid have no leading, or interlinear spacing, added between lines. The space appearing between the lines is the space reserved in the typeface design for the ascenders and descenders.

Spaceband
The space between words that may be expanded in justification (word space). Derived from the name of a wedge-shaped device that is dropped between words on a hot metal typesetter, and which pushes the words apart to justify the line.

Spacing guides
Any device used to help standardize the spacing between text and graphics, or between headings and body copy, or between any elements on a page.

Specifications
Measurements, such as line space, line length, type size, and font number, which are necessary for typesetting. (specs).

Spine
The main curved arc section of the letter S. See figure under Letter element.

Spooler
An application that sends files to the printer. A spooler holds files in the print queue, and prints them in the order they were received. A spooler allows you to continue working on other files while a file prints.

Stat
A photographic copy of type or art in the same size or a different size than the original. (photostat).

Stem
The main vertical stroke or strokes of a character. See figure under Letter element.

Strike-on typesetting
A typesetting technology that produces character images by using a physical character image to strike through a carbon or cloth ribbon onto paper. See also cold type. (cold composition, cold type).

Style
A variation of a font, such as Roman, bold, italic, underline, shadow, or outline.

Style sheet
A collection of type specs and format definitions that can be saved and used in many different documents.

Subdirectory
A directory within a directory; a file containing the names and locations of other files.

Subscript
A letter or number printed lower than the baseline of the text that surrounds it. See also Superscript.

Supercase
In typesetting, a set of characters that are neither upper nor lowercase. Usually they are special symbols, and designated as supercase because they can be accessed by a special supershift code without changing typefaces.

Superior
See Superscript.

Superscript
A letter or number printed higher than the baseline of the text that surrounds it.

Swash characters
Alternate characters in display typefaces that usually over or underhang adjacent characters with curved flourishes.

Synchronous
(sync). Occurring concurrently, and with a regular or predictable time relationship. In transmission, referring to the ability of the sending and the receiving devices to run continuously at the same frequency.

Syntax
The rules that govern the sentence structure in a language, or the statement structure in a computer language.

System program
A program that makes the resources and capabilities of the computer available for general purposes, such as an operating system or a language translator. Compare Application program.

System software
The component of a computer system that supports application programs by managing system resources such as memory and I/O devices.

Tab
Short for tabulator; on typewriter keyboards, a key that allows you to set automatic stops (tab stops) or margins for columns, as in a table of figures.

Tab key
A key that, when pressed, generates the tab character. The key's action is to move the insertion point or cursor to the next tab marker, or, in a dialog box with more than one place to enter information, to the next rectangle. The Tab key thus works essentially like a typewriter tab key.

Tab marker
An icon on a text a ruler that marks the position to which the tab key will move the insertion point.

Tabular composition
Composition that involves setting multiple columns of copy, often numbers, in vertical alignment within each column.

Tail
A downward-sloping short stroke, ending free. See figure under Letter element.

Take
All or part of a typesetting job; that part of the copy that will be typeset at one time, as a galley.

Telecommunication
Transmitting information across varying distances, such as over telephone lines.

Teleprocessing
Computer operations carried out via long-distance communications network.

Template
A page-layout file containing only the layout grid, master pages, estimated number of pages, and boilerplate text and graphics for a periodical or book. Serves as the starting point for creating many similar documents, such as chapters of a book or

issues of a newsletter. Variable items—text and graphics that are not common to all chapters or issues—are added to the template document and saved under another name so the template document remains unchanged.

Terminal
The portion of a computer system through which you interact with the computer; namely, the display screen or monitor plus the keyboard, mouse, or other input device. Synonymous with console.

Text
(1) Information presented in the form of readable characters. (2) The body of type matter on a page, as opposed to headlines, callouts, or folios. (3) The display of characters on a display screen. Compare Graphics.

Text file
A file containing information expressed in text form and whose contents are interpreted as characters encoded using the ASCII format. Compare Binary file.

Text wrap
Automatic line breaks at the right edge of a column or at the right margin of a page. Also, the ability to wrap text around a graphic on a page layout. Some systems have an automatic text wrap feature that will shorten lines of text when a graphic is encountered. In other systems, you need to change the length of lines by changing column margins or by inserting hard carriage returns to shorten lines. See also Carriage return.

Text-only document
Text saved without any type specifications or other formatting. (See also ASCII).

Thermal printer
A printer that uses heat-sensitive paper to carry the character image.

Thin space
A small fixed space equal in width to the period or comma (usually about half of an En space).

Third-generation typesetter
A typesetter that forms the character image by means of a photographic or digital record of the character's shape, rather than using a physical character master. The character image is formed on the face of a cathode ray tube, and transferred to photosensitive material by means of fiber optics or a lens.

Thumbnail
A miniature copy or sketch of a page. See also Pencil rough.

Tight line
(1) A line of type in which type is fairly dense, with little or no word spacing or letter spacing. (2) A line of characters that will not fit the line measure. In hot metal typesetting, a tight line will not fit the vice jaws that carry the characters, and may cause the machine to jam.

Toggle switch
Used to describe cases in which the same command is invoked to turn a feature on and off.

Tones
The shades of a photograph or illustration printed as a series of dots. Each tone is a percentage of black. The smaller the percentage, the lighter the tone.

Track
The path along which information is recorded on a magnetic disk. A disk consists of a series of concentric tracks.

Tracking
A type of kerning whereby the spaces between letters in a word are expanded or condensed by a specified number of points or a percentage factor. Some applications offer tracking as Condensed and Expanded options, and others misname it under the kerning option. See also Kerning.

Translation table
A set of equations that typically performs search-and-replace routines on data.

Triplex
Referring to phototypesetting font masters that contain three fonts, each having the same escapement values for corresponding characters.

Turnaround
(1) The length of time required to produce a job or complete a function from time in to time out. (2) The time required to reverse the direction of transmission in half-duplex devices.

Turnkey
Pertaining to a product that is delivered complete with any special hardware or software required, ready to run, without special onsite programming.

Type-ahead buffer
A buffer that accepts and holds characters that are typed faster than the computer can process them.

Typeface
A single type family of one design of type in all sizes and styles. Times and Helvetica are two different typefaces, for instance. Each typeface has many fonts (i.e., sizes and styles). Sometimes the terms typeface and font are used interchangeably.

Typesetter
(1) Any device that produces type arranged on a page in an organized fashion. (2) A person who sets type.

Typestyle
A collection of various type families related by common characteristics. There are essentially four type styles: Roman, with serif or sans serif letters of varying stroke thickness; Italic, having varying slants to the character stroke; Gothic, being sans serif with character strokes of uniform thickness; and Script, having letters that join together imitating handwriting.

Typo
An abbreviation for typographical error. Any unintentional mistake on the part of the operator resulting in misspelling or misplacement of type.

GLOSSARY

Typographic Color
The "color" of a page of type refers to the overall shade of gray perceived by the eye, which might be interrupted by bad word or character spacing or uneven leading. "Typographic" color can only be accomplished by reviewing type after setting.

Typography
The art and practice of arranging type in pleasing ways by using combinations of fonts and layouts, and adjusting the type in such a way as to produce the most aesthetic result.

Uppercase
See Caps and Small caps.

Vector graphics
Any computer graphics technique that presents images as a series of lines on an X-Y axis. See Object-oriented graphics.

Vertical justification
The ability to adjust the length of a text block by adjusting the spacing between lines of text (leading) in fine increments in order to make columns and pages end at the same point.

Video display terminal
(display terminal). An operator station that includes a display screen as part of its hardware. VDTs at one time were called CRTs, until CRTs became widely used in character generation for typesetters.

Vortex
The bottom junction of two stems, such as in the letter W, having two vortex points. See figure under Letter element.

Web
A continuous roll of paper which is fed through a rotary printing press. Many web presses can accept more than one web at a time, and can fold, cut, and collate the finished product.

Weight
The relative thickness and/or blackness of type characters, as in boldface, lightface, demi, or medium.

White space
Empty space on a page, not used for text or graphics.

White space reduction
A standard component of typesetting software that is intended to produce visually uniform interletter spacing in all character sizes.

Widow
See Orphans/widows.

Window
(1) The area that displays information on a desktop; you view a document through a window. You can open or close a window, move it around on the desktop, and sometimes change its size, scroll through it, and edit its contents. (2) The portion of a collection of information (such as a document, picture, or worksheet) that is visible in a viewport on the display screen. Compare Viewport.

Wire printer
A printer that forms characters by the selection of solenoid operated matrix wires, which print the selected characters by impact against a ribbon.

Wordprocessing
The use of automated equipment to input, revise, and output data. The major characteristic of word processing is its use for the storage, manipulation, and retrieval of large quantities of text material. Word processing equipment varies in its capability to provide automatic page formatting. Output is sometimes on some type of printer.

Word processor
A type of application program designed to make writing and editing easier and faster.

Word space
(1) The space between words, which may be expanded for purposes of justification. (2) To adjust the spaces between words, making them larger than the minimum allowable size. See also Kerning, Letter spacing, Tracking.

Word wrap
The automatic adjustment of the number of words on a line of text to match the margin settings. The carriage returns that result from automatic word wrap are called soft carriage returns to distinguish them from the hard carriage returns that result when the Return key is pressed to force a new line. See also Text wrap, Carriage return.

Workstation
A basic physical unit of a system typically comprised of a display, keyboard, and media drives.

Wrap
See Text wrap and Word wrap.

Wraparound
The automatic continuation of text from the end of one line to the beginning of the next, so that you don't have to press the Return key at the end of each line as you type. See also Text wrap, Word wrap.

Write-protect
To prevent a storage medium from having data added or deleted, an example of which is the use of an adhesive tab placed over the square notch on the edge of a floppy disk.

WYSIWYG
Acronym for "What-You-See-Is-What-You-Get," pronounced "whizzy-wig." A term used to describe systems that display pages on the screen with text and graphics exactly as they will appear when printed. Some systems are more WYSIWYG than others in the accuracy of the display. The term is also used to describe word processing programs that display different fonts on the screen.

X coordinate
The horizontal location of data on a graph, CRT, or page layout, or the horizontal distance from a selected reference point.

Xerography
A printing or copying technology in which an image is transferred electronically, by either a lens or a laser scanner, to the electrically charged photoconductive surface of a drum. Dry ink with an opposite charge is applied to the surface of the drum, forming the image, which is then transferred to paper.

X-height
A distinguishing characteristic of a font. The height of a lowercase x in a given font; the height, measured from the base line, of the main portion of most lowercase letters in a font, excluding ascenders and descenders. The height of lowercase letters that do not have ascenders or descenders, such as "x," "a," and "c." Also called the body of the type. See figure under Font size. See also Ascent line, Base line, Descent line.

Xerographic printer
A printer that uses electrostatic techniques to produce the final character image.

X-ON/X-OFF
(CC1/DC3) A telecommunications system that allows the receiving computer to signal the sender to stop transmission momentarily. When the receiver is ready, another signal is sent to begin transmission again.

Y coordinate
The vertical location of data on a graph, CRT, or page layout, or the vertical distance from a selected reference point.

Yellow
The subtractive primary color that appears yellow and absorbs blue light. Used as one ink in four-color printing.

Index

A

AA, defined, 425
accents, 205-207, 425
accessory, defined, 425
acronym, defined, 425
actual size, defined, 425
ad profiles, 167-168
adding fonts, 82-83
additive color mixing, 385
additive primaries, 372, 384
ads, 171-174, 260-261
ads, 321
    positioning, 167-168
agate, defined, 425
aliasing, defined, 425
alignment, 107-108
    defined, 425
    commands, 176, 290
    graphics, 230
    labels, 231-233
    proofing for, 209
    snap-to, 289
    spacing guides, 158-160
    tabular, 99
all caps, 94, 184
    leading and kerning, 95
    use of, 95
Allied Linotronic, 84
alphabet length, defined, 425
alphanumeric, defined, 425
alternate characters, defined, 425
apex, defined, 425
Apple LaserWriter, 83-84
application program, defined, 425
application software, defined, 425
arc, defined, 425
archive files, 47, 268-269, 425

area composition, defined, 425
arm, defined, 426
artwork
    copyright, 57
    special handling, 327-339
ascender, 74, 426
ascent line, defined, 426
ASCII, defined, 426
author, role of, 26-27
author's alterations, defined, 426
author's guidelines, typing, 182-184

B

backup files, 268-269, 426
bad break, defined, 426
banner, defined, 426
bar, defined, 426
base line, 74, 426
    with large caps, 115
BAUD rate, 18, 426
beak, defined, 426
benefits of using templates, 144-146
bids, printing, 390-395
binary file, defined, 426
binder, role of, 33
binding, 46, 389-422, 420
bit, defined, 426
bit map, defined, 426
bit-mapped fonts, 80
bit-mapped graphics, 217-219
bit-mapped vs. object oriented graphics, 218
black areas, 321-322
bleed, 295, 347-348, 426
block, defined, 426
blocked ad format, 167
blue lines, defined, 426
blue pencil/blue line, defined, 426

boards, 325, 426
body, defined, 426
body copy
    defined, 427
    typefaces, 74-75
    size, 78
body text, 132
body type, defined, 427
boilerplates, 143-164, 427
    graphics, 244-250
bold
    defined, 427
    use of, 94
book faces, 100-101
book pages, 131
books, 259-260
borders, 134
bottom margin, 129-130
    ragged, 301
bowl, defined, 427
boxes, 104
broadside, defined, 427
brochures, 93, 171-174, 260-261, 427
budget
    production, 37
    equipment, 38
buffer, defined, 427
built-in printer fonts, 83-85, 427
bulk, paper, 414
bullets, 104, 427
business graphics, defined, 427
business reports, 259-260
    design, 169-171
butts, 365-368
byte, defined, 427

C

cache, font, 88
CAD/CAM, defined, 427
calligraphic faces, 102
callout, defined, 427
camera-ready art, defined, 427
camera-ready pages, 317-356
cameraman, role of, 32
cap, defined, 427
cap height, 74, 427
cap line, defined, 427
capitals, defined, 427
caps, 78, 94, 184
caps and small caps, 94
Caps and small caps, defined, 427
captions, 116, 132-133, 162-163, 227, 231-233, 296, 427
carriage returns, 183, 189-191, 427
cartridge fonts, 85
case, defined, 427
catalog, defined, 428
catalogues, 171, 260
cathode-ray tube (CRT), defined, 428
central processing unit (CPU), defined, 428
character
    defined, 428
    counts, 116-122
    formatting, 198-207
    keys, defined, 428
    pitch, defined, 428
    printer, defined, 428
    sets, 74, 428
    styles, defined, 428
characters
    symbols, 103-104
    typing, 184
charts, 174-176, 262-263
check copy, defined, 428
checklists
    production steps, 35-36
    author's, 41
ciceros, 276, 428
clipboard, 298, 428
clipping, defined, 428
coated paper, 417
codes
    characters, 205-207
    embedded, 202-203
    hidden, 203
    typesetting, 187-188
coding for text format, 198-207
collated copies, printing, 308, 428
color
    acetate, 386-387
    correction, 374-375

INDEX

images, 240
ink pens, 386-387
key, 362, 400
mixing, 372, 385
overlays, 386-387
pages, 299-300
paper, 416
printers, 216, 386-387
printing, 173, 357-388
process, 371-381
process vs. spot, 358-359
proofing, 381-386
proofs, 382
scanning, 377-378
separation, electronic, 377
separations, 361-363, 371-381, 428
separations, manual, 363
separations, sources, 375-379
sequencing, defined, 428
swatchbooks, 364-365
transparencies, 386-388
column guides, 149
column inch, defined, 428
column rules, defined, 428
columns, 279-286
number of, 127-129
comma-delimited data, 197
command, defined, 428
composition, defined, 428
composition software, defined, 428
compositor, defined, 428
computer graphics, defined, 429
computers, 10
condensed type, 111, 429
configuration, defined, 429
consistency, 125-126, 229
enforcement, 146
spacing guides, 158-160
contact film, 350
context coding, 204-205
continued line, defined, 429
continuous tone art, 327-339, 429
contour, defined, 429
contracts, 51-68
contrast enhancement, defined, 429
control character, defined, 429

control codes, defined, 429
control key, defined, 429
conversion service, defined, 429
conversion, text files, 188-189
copy casting, 116-122
copy editing, 42
copy editor, role of, 29
copy fitting, 300-305
copy fitting, 208, 429
copyright, 51-68
  agreements, 51-58, 65
  artwork, 57
  books, 53
  contributions, 56
  expired, 58-59
  inapplicable, 58-62
  infringement, 60-62
  periodicals, 55
  promotional materials, 56
  reports, 55
  statement, 52
  waived, 58-62
costs, printing, 326, 390-395
counter, 74, 429
Courier, use of, 99-100
CPU, defined, 429
credits, 51-68, 62-63
crop, defined, 429
crop marks, 272-273, 309, 429
cropping
  aids, 341
  graphics, 295
  marking for, 340-344
  special effects, 344-347
crossbar, defined, 429
crossover, 347-348
crotch, defined, 429
CRT, defined, 429
cursive typefaces, 74
cursor, defined, 429
custom grids, 152
cut, defined, 430
cyan, defined, 430

D

dashes, 189-191, 430
data conversion, 194-198
data disk, defined, 430
data formats, 194-198, 430
    coding, 204-205
database as source of text, 194-198
date and time, 269
decimal tab, defined, 430
decorative typefaces, 74, 103
defaults, 292, 430
    type specifications, 154
delimiter, defined, 430
density, defined, 430
depth, defined, 430
    of text, estimating, 116-122
descender, 74, 430
descent line, defined, 430
design, 9, 42-43
    alternatives, 140-141
    copyright, 60
    electronic methods, 136-142
    elements, 90-91, 123-177, 138-140
    ideas, series of, 140
    page layout, 123-177
    principles, 124-136
    principles, graphics, 225-229
    reports, 169-171
    specifications, 43
    specifications, example, 141
    templates, 143-164
    testing, 163-164
    typography, 89-116
designer, role of, 27-28
desktop publishing
    benefits, 2
    definition, 2, 430
    componemts, 2
    equipment, 8, 14-18
    examples, 1, 12-14
    fonts used in, 82-88
    software, 11, 253-255
    typefaces, 98
dialog box, defined, 430
dialup, defined, 430

dictionary, defined, 430
die-cuts, 418-419
digital, defined, 430
digital proofs, 383
digitize, defined, 430
digitized artwork, copyright, 57
digitized character, defined, 430
digitized images, 219-222
digitizers, 215
dingbats, 103-104, 430
dipthong, defined, 430
direct entry phototypesetter, defined, 431
direct-digital proofs, 383
directories, 171, 260
directory, disk, 431
discretionary hyphen, defined, 431
disk, defined, 431
disk cartridge, defined, 431
disk drive, defined, 431
disk file
    date, 269
    names, 243-244
    organization, 263-270
disk files
    archiving, 47
    text, 188-198
disk head, defined, 431
disk space, defined, 431
display, defined, 431
display ads, 171-174, 260-261, 321
display typefaces, 74-75, 103, 431
distribution, 47
DOS, defined, 431
dot-matrix character, defined, 431
dot-matrix printers, 215, 431
dots per inch, 7, 218-219, 431
    72 vs. 300, 221
    printing, 320
dots, flat tone, 349
dots, halftone, 320
double-sided documents, 277-279, 431
down time, defined, 431
download, defined, 431
downloadable fonts, 79, 85-87
    permanent vs. temporary, 307-308
    when to, 87

INDEX

dpi, see dots per inch
draw-type graphics, 222-224, 431
drive, defined, 431
driver, defined, 431
drop cap, defined, 431
drop out for graphic, 338
drop-down menu, defined, 431
dummy publication, defined, 432
dummy text, 119-120, 154-155
duotones, 368-369
duplex, defined, 432
duplex fonts, defined, 432
Dutch wrap, 168

E

EAR, defined, 432
EBCDIC, defined, 432
editing, 42, 432
    aids, electronic, 193-194
    to fit, 301
editor
    copy, 29
    managing, 25-26
    specifications, 30-31
electronic
    design aids, 136-142
    mail, defined, 432
    publishing, defined, 432
    templates, 143-164
electrostatic printer, defined, 432
ellipse, defined, 432
ellipses, defined, 432
Em, 432
    dashes, 184
    fraction, defined, 432
    leader, defined, 432
    space, defined, 432
embedded codes, 202-203, 432
embossing, 418-419
En, 432-433
    dashes, 184
    fraction, defined, 433
    leader, defined, 433
    space, defined, 433
Encapsulated PostScript graphics, 224-225
end of line, defined, 433

end pages, defined, 433
EPS format, graphics, 224-225
equipment, 8, 14-18
    capabilities, 136-138
    cost, 38
    graphics, 214-216
escapement, 433
estimates, printing charges, 392
even parity, defined, 433
exception dictionary, defined, 433
excerpts, copyright, 59
expanded type, 111, 433
expert reader, role of, 28-29
expired copyrights, 58-59

F

face, defined, 433
facing page designs, 152-153
facing pages, 129, 267, 271, 277-279, 287, 290, 433
facsimile, defined, 433
fair use, copyright, 59
figure, defined, 433
    captions, 132, 227, 231-233, 296
    labels, 116, 162-163, 227, 231-233
    numbering, 243-244
file
    date of, 269
    defined, 433
    maintenance, defined, 433
    management, defined, 433
    names, 243-244
    naming, 263
    organization, 263-270
    server, defined, 433
    size, optimum, 265-268
    size, scans, 336
filename, defined, 434
files
    archiving, 47
    backup, 268-269
fillers, 301
film, defined, 434
film strip, defined, 434
film-based proofs, 382
finish, paper, 416

first-generation typesetter, defined, 434
fitting copy, 300-305
fixed disk, defined, 434
fixed space, defined, 434
flat, printed, 404
flat-tone screens, 348-351
flat-toned screened color, 368
flats, 354-356
    printing, 396-399
floppy disk, defined, 434
flush, defined, 434
flyers, 171-174, 260-261
flying spot scanner, defined, 434
folding, 418
folds, 172, 261
folios, 134-135, 434
fonts
    adding, 82-83
    cache, 88
    cartridge, 85
    defined, 72-79, 434
    draft vs. final versions, 81
    downloadable, 85-87
    downloading, 307-308
    installed, 81, 83-87
    library, 269
    limitations, 86, 136-138
    limiting number of, 90
    list, 89-92
    number of, 135
    outline vs. bit-mapped, 80-81
    printing, 87-88
    rectangle, defined, 434
    scaling, defined, 434
    size, defined, 434
footer, 284, 434
    dummy, 156
    position, 134-135, 275
footnote, defined, 434
footnote callout, defined, 434
footnoting capability, defined, 434
for position only, 339
format, defined, 434
format text, when to, 199
formatting
    data, 194-198

text, 155
text, mail merge, 195
four-color process, 371-381
fourth-generation typesetter, defined, 435
fraction, defined, 435
function code, defined, 435

G

G (Giga), defined, 435
galley, defined, 435
ganged ad format, 167
ganging, 344
GANTT chart, 34
generate, defined, 435
generated codes, 204-205
generic font, defined, 435
genre, publication, 164-176
ghosting, defined, 435
global searches, 189-191, 435
glossary, electronic, 193
Gothic, defined, 435
gradation change, defined, 435
grain, paper, 414
graph, defined, 435
graphic
    defined, 435
    design principles, 225-229
    elements, 155
    terminal, defined, 435
    primitives, defined, 435
graphic arts, defined, 435
graphics, 45, 213-251, 435, see also figures
    applications, 13
    bit-mapped, 217-219
    capabilities, 137
    captions, 296
    color, 240
    cropping, 295
    equipment, 214-216
    for text, 294
    handling, 294-298
    importing, 293
    layered, 235
    marking for printer, 340-354
    paste up, 327-339
    printers, 215

INDEX 457

production techniques, 229-244
proofing, 250-251
repeating, 285
resolution, 218-219
sources of, 216-225
standing, 285
tablets, 214
templates, 162-163, 244-250
use of, 132
gravure, 402, 410-411, 435
gray backgrounds, caution, 228
gray balance, defined, 435
gray levels, number of, 334
gray scale, 215, 435
gray scale information, 219-222, 334
gray screens, 133-134, 262
gray shades, 236-237, 321-322
greek text, 119-120, 435
Greeking, defined, 436
grid systems, 127-129, 151-153, 279-286, 436
    graphics, 230, 249
    multiple, 170
    templates, 143-164
    variations, 165-166s, 289
guidelines, author's, 41
guides
    lettering, 245-246
    line weights, 245-246
    non-printing, 283
    spacing, 247-249
gutter, defined, 436

H

H & J, defined, 436
hairline
    caution, 228
    defined, 436
halftone, 327-339
    creating, 331-335
    defined, 436
    screen, defined, 436
    screened spot color, 368-369
    veloxes, 336-337
hanging indent, defined, 436
hard carriage return, defined, 436
hard copy, defined, 436

hard disk, defined, 436
    directories, 263
    storage, 15
hardware, defined, 436
head, defined, 436
header, 284
    defined, 436
    dummy, 156
    position, 134-135, 275
headline
    defined, 436
    kerning, 111-113
    size, 78
Helvetica
    alternatives to, 102
    history of, 101-102
Hewlett-Packard printers, 85
hierarchical filing system, defined, 436
high-resolution graphics, defined, 436
hot type, defined, 436
hot zone, defined, 436
hyphen, defined, 436
hyphenation, 108, 184, 193, 303, 436
    proofing for, 210
    zone, defined, 437

I

icon, defined, 437
ideas, copyright, 62
illustration, 45, 213-251, see also figures
illustrator, role of, 28
Illustrator, Adobe, 224-225
image, defined, 437
    combination, 238
    composition, 238
    placement, 344-347
    retouching, 237-239, 352-354
    scaling, 241-243
image area, 137-138, 322, 437
impact printer, defined, 437
imposition, 238, 396-399, 437
inches, 276
indentation, paragraph, 106-107
    defined, 437
    proofing for, 209
index, defined, 437

inferior, defined, 437
infringement, copyright, 60-62
inhouse, defined, 437
initial, defined, 437
initial caps, 110
initial letters, 114-116
initialize, defined, 437
inkjet printer, 216, 437
inks, 413
    affect on design, 94
insertion point, defined, 437
inside margin, defined, 437
installing fonts, 82-87
instructions to printer, 325, 340-354
instructions for template, 161-162
intellectual property, 51
interviews, copyright, 59
interword spacing, defined, 437
inventions, copyright, 62
invert, defined, 437
island format, 167
italics, defined, 437
    use of, 94

J

jump line, defined, 437
justification, 107-108, 303, 437
    vertical, 129-130, 302

K

K (Kilo), defined, 437
kern, defined, 438
kerning, 111-113
    and all caps, 95
    defined, 438
    methods of, 112-113
    pairs, defined, 438
    proofing for, 210
keyline mechanical, 325, 360, 366
keylining, defined, 438

L

labels, figure, 116, 162-163, 227, 231-233
ladder, defined, 438
LAN, defined, 438
landscape printing, defined, 438
large caps, 110, 114-116
LASER, defined, 438
    fonts, 80, 82-88
    paper, 321
    platemaking, defined, 438
    printers, 7, 17, 216, 438
    printing, defined, 438
laser-printed masters, 319-323
LaserWriter, 83-84, 137-138
layered graphics, 235
layout, defined, 438
layout artist, role of, 32
layout grid, defined, 438
leader, defined, 438
leaders, defined, 438
leading, 74, 108-110, 302, 438
    and all caps, 95
length of lines of text, 106-107
letter elements, defined, 438
letter shapes, 112
letter spacing, 76, 113, 304, 439
    proofing for, 210
lettering guides, 245-246
letterpress, 402, 408
ligatures, 113, 439
line art, 327-339, 439
line break, defined, 439
line conversion, 330
line count, estimating, 116-122
line length, 135
    defined, 439
    optimum, 106-107
line printer, defined, 439
line spacing, 108-110, 302, 439
line weight, 245-246
linecaster, defined, 439
lines, ruled, 133-134
Linotronic typesetter, 84, 137-138
list formats, 171, 260
lithography, 408-410

local area network (LAN), defined, 439
logo, defined, 439
loop, defined, 439
low-resolution graphics, defined, 439
lower case, defined, 439

M

M (Mega), defined, 439
magazine pages, 132
magazines, 255-258
    templates for, 164-169
magenta, defined, 439
magnetic ink character recognition, defined, 439
mail merge formats, 195
main memory, defined, 439
mainframe computer, defined, 439
makeready, defined, 439
makeup, defined, 439
manager, production, 29-30
managing editor, role of, 25-26
manual paste up, 298
manuals, 259-260
manuscript, defined, 439
    preparation, 182-184
margins, 127-129, 146-149, 271, 274-276, 322, 439
    bottom, 129-130
    changing, 184
    ragged, 131
marking an image for handling, 340-354
marking copy for format, 201
markup, defined, 439
massage, defined, 440
master pages, 156, 279-286
    originals, 317-356
masthead, defined, 440
match color, 369-370
matrix printer, defined, 440
measurement system, 150, 276, 440
mechanical bindings, 422
mechanical color separations, 376-377
mechanicals, 317-356, 323-326, 354, 440
memory, computer, 15, 440
menu, defined, 440
microcomputer, defined, 440
millimeters, 276

mirror-image facing page designs, 152-153, 170, 260
mixing, defined, 440
mnemonic, defined, 440
modem, 18, 440
moiré pattern, 371, 440
monitors, 16
    graphics, 214
monospaced type, 99-100, 440
mortise, defined, 440
mouse, 214, 440
multiplex, defined, 440
multiprocessing, defined, 440
multitasking, defined, 440

N

naming conventions, 243-244
negative, defined, 440
network, 18, 268, 440
newsletters, 255-258
    templates for, 164-169
newspaper line, defined, 440
newspaper pages, 132
nonbreaking space, defined, 440
nonproportional typefaces, 76
notation, proofing, 186
number of pages, 288
numbering figures, 243-244
numeric keypad, defined, 440

O

object-oriented graphics, 222-224, 440
oblique type, 79, 440
octavo, defined, 441
odd parity, defined, 441
offset
    defined, 441
    lithography, 408-410
    printer, 33
    printing, 9, 402, 407, 441
on-screen color proofing, 384
opacity, paper, 414
operating system, defined, 441
optical character readers, 185, 441
optical character recognition, defined, 441

optical scanner, defined, 441
organization, disk files, 263-270
orientation, 274, 441
ornaments, defined, 441
orphans/widows, defined, 441, see widows and orphans
outline font, 80, 441
outline type style, 78
output
    defined, 441
    devices, 17
    resolution, 332
outside margin, defined, 441
overhead transparencies, 96, 174-176, 262-263
    color, 386-388
overlays, 262
    acetate, 367
    color, 362
    defined, 441
    mechanical, 325
    tissue, 338, 360
overrun, defined, 441
overset, defined, 441

P

page, defined, 441
page composition, 5, 46, 253-313, 441
    individual, 286-300
    methods, 286-300
    software, 11
page comps, 139
page description language, defined, 441
page design, 123-177, 165
    grid, 127-129
page count estimate, 279
page layout, see page composition, paste up
page layout, see layout artist
page layout methods, 286-300
page length, 288
page limit, 279
page makeup, defined, 441
page numbers, 267
page orientation, 271, 274
page proofs, 399
page setup, 271
page size, 146, 272

    vs. paper size, 147, 272-273
    non-standard, 310-311
pages
    forced right, 290
    number of, 279, 288
    printing selectively, 308
pagination, defined, 441
paint program, defined, 441
paint-type graphics, 217-219, 441
palette, defined, 441
panel format, 167
Pantone color swatchbooks, 364-365
paper
    affect on design, 94
    for laser printing, 321
    orientation, 271, 274
    quality, 228, 415
    quality and halftones, 320
    size, 146, 272, 442
    size vs. page size, 147, 272-273
    sizes, standard, 272, 276
    stock, 320
    stock, coated, 417
    tape, defined, 442
    types, 414-417
paragraph
    format, 191-192
    formatting, 198-207
    spacing, 106-107
    spacing, proofing for, 209
paragraphs, defined, 442
parallel interface, defined, 442
paraphrasing, copyright, 59
parity bait, defined, 442
password, defined, 442
paste, defined, 442
paste up, 5, 317-356, 442
    manual, 298, 324, 340-354
pen, line weight, 245-246
percent, defined, 442
perfect binding, 420
periodicals, 255-258
peripheral device, defined, 442
permissions, 51-68
    to reprint, 62-63
PERT chart, 34

INDEX

photocomposition, defined, 442
photodiode sensor array scanner, defined, 442
photographer, role of, 28
photographic color separations, 377-378
photographic halftones, 337-339
photographs, copyright, 57
photolettering, defined, 442
photomechanical, defined, 442
phototypesetters, 216, 442
pi characters, defined, 442
PIC format graphics, 223
picas, 76, 276, 442
PICT format graphics, 223
pixel, defined, 442
platemaking, 401
platen, defined, 442
plates, types of, 402
plotters, 216, 359
PMS color swatchbooks, 364-365
point, 76, 442
point size, 74, 76, 442
   and line length, 135
   large, 96, 135
   small, 188
port, defined, 442
portrait printing, defined, 443
positioning graphics, 338
postpress production, 418-423
PostScript
   defined, 443
   fonts, 82-88
   graphics, 224-225
   interpreter as RIP, 332
   printer, 77
   typefaces, 98
prepress proofs, defined, 443
prepress systems, 240
presentation materials, 96, 174-176, 262-263
   color, 386-388
press proofs, 382, 443
press sheet, 405
presses
   color, 391
   sheet-fed vs. web-fed, 411-412
   types of, 169
price lists, 171, 260

primary colors, 372, 384, 443
primitive, defined, 443
principles
   of design, 124-136
   of typography, 92-97
print area, defined, 443
print queue, defined, 443
print spoolers, 312
printed flat, 404
printer, offset, 33
   role of, 33
printers, desktop, 4, 6, 17, 443
   fonts, 83-87, 443
   graphics, 215
   limitations, 137-138
   memory, 86
   PostScript, 77
   selecting, 154, 279
   types of, 305-306
printhead, defined, 443
printing, 46
   area, 137-138
   area, limits of, 322
   collated copies, 308
   costs, 390-395
   electronic, 305-312
   flats, 396-399
   fonts, 87-88
   offset, 9, 317-356, 389-422
   presses, types, 408-412
   process, 406-418
   resolution, 320
   sequence of pages, 308
   time, graphics, 233-234
printout, defined, 443
process color, 371-381
   as match color, 369-370
   vs. spot color, 358-359
process match color, 369-370
production manager, role of, 29-30
production process, mapped to this book, 49
production schedule, 34
production steps, 33-47
   list, 258
   listing, 161-162
production, graphics, 229-244

program, defined, 443
programming language, defined, 443
project definition, 36-38
proofing for color, 381-386
proofing printer, defined, 443
proofread, defined, 443
proofreader, role of, 30
proofreading, 184-185, 312
    checklist, 41
    graphics, 250-251
    marks, 185-187
    typeset text, 208-211
proofs
    defined, 443
    digital, 383
    film-based, 382
    page, 399
    press, 382
    printer, 399
    soft, 384
property, intellectual, 51
proportional
    font, defined, 443
    scaling, 241-243
    spacing, alignment, 99, 443
proportionally spaced typeface, 76
proposals, 36-38
    design, 169-171
public domain, 58-59
publication design, 123-177
publication elements, 138-140
publication types, 164-176, 255-263
publisher, role of, 24-25
publishing cycle, 23-49
pull quotes, 301, 443
punctuation, defined, 443
pyramid formats, 168

Q

quad, defined, 444
quality, printing, 326
quarto, defined, 444
queue, defined, 444
quote, defined, 444
quote marks, 189-191
quote sheet, printing, 394

quotes as fillers, 301
quotes, printing charges, 392

R

ragged bottom margin, 301
ragged-right text, 107-108, 444
RAM, defined, 444
random-access memory (RAM), defined, 444
raster, defined, 444
raster image processor, 332, 444
raster scan, defined, 444
raw data, defined, 444
read-only memory (ROM), defined, 444
read-write head, defined, 444
readers
    expert, 28-29
    proofing, 30, 184-185
record, defined, 444
recto, defined, 444
reduction
    methods, 237
    to improve quality, 237
reference aids, 134-135
reference marks, defined, 444
refresh, defined, 444
registration, 365-368, 444
    mark, defined, 444
remote, defined, 444
repeated elements, 156-157, 249
repeated steps, list, 288
reports, 259-260
    design, 169-171
reproduction, 9, 389-422, 406-418
resolution, 6, 444
    comparison, 142
    graphics, 218-219
    printing, 136-137, 221, 305-306, 320
    scanning, 221
    screen vs. output, 332
responsibilities, division of, 24-33
retouching, 237-239, 352-354
reverse, defined, 445
reverse leading, defined, 445
reverse order, printing, 308
reverse type, 78, 293
revision, cycles, 40

INDEX

RGB, defined, 445
RGB monitor, defined, 445
right justified, defined, 445
rigid disk, defined, 445
river, defined, 445
ROM, defined, 445
ROM fonts, 83
Roman, defined, 445
rotate, defined, 445
rough page layout, 139, 166, 445
RS-232 Port, defined, 445
rubylith, 338
ruled lines, 133-134, 245-246
ruler, defined, 445
ruler lines, number of, 191-192
ruler, on screen, 150, 245, 282
rules or ruled lines, defined, 445
run-in, defined, 445
runaround, 296, 445
running heads and feet, defined, 445
running text, defined, 445

S

saddle-wire stitching, 421
sans serif, defined, 445
    faces, use of, 101-102
    typeface, 75
scale, defined, 445
scaling
    images, 241-243
    marking for, 340-344
    systems, graphics, 250
    visually, 342
    wheel, 343
scan, defined, 445
scanned images, 219-222
    copyright, 57
    defined, 445
scanned text, 185
scanners, 16, 215, 445
schedule, 34
screen, defined, 446
    font, defined, 446
    lines per inch, 320
    resolution, 332
    textures, halftones, 330

screened process color, 369-370
screened spot color, 368
screening, manual, 351
screens, 142, 236-237, 262
    flat tone, 348-351
    gray, 133-134
    percentages, 350
script typefaces, 74, 103, 446
search string, defined, 446
second generation typesetter, defined, 446
selecting graphics, 294-298
separation proofs, 385
separations, see color separations
serif, 74
serif, defined, 446
serif typeface, 75
    use of, 100-101
set size, defined, 446
set width adjustment, defined, 446
shadow type, 78
sheet-fed presses, 411-412
side bearings, defined, 446
signature, defined, 446
silhouettes, 345-347
simplex, defined, 446
single-sided documents, 278, 446
sink, defined, 446
size
    defined, 446
    disk files, 265-268
    page, 272
    page vs. paper, 147
    type, 76-78
sizing images, 241-243
sketching page layouts, 165, 286-300
slides, 96, 174-176, 262-263
    as color masters, 379
    color artwork, 386-388
    proportions, 128
slug, defined, 446
small caps, 78, 94, 446
smoothing, graphics, 219
Smyth-sewn binding, 420
snap-to effect, 289, 446
soft carriage return, defined, 446
soft proofs, 384

software, 11
    capabilities, 136-138
    defined, 446
    graphics applications, 13
    page composition, 11, 253-255
    word processors, 12
solid, defined, 446
space fillers, 301
spaceband, defined, 447
spacing, 76, 230
    between lines, 108-110
    consistency, 125-126
    guides, 126, 158-160, 247-249, 447
    labels, 227
    letter, 304
    proofing for, 210
    word, 304
spatial continuity, 226-227
spec editor, role of, 30-31
special characters, 103-104, 205-207
special effects, images, 344-347
specifications, design, 43, 447
    graphics, 162-163
spelling checkers, 193
spine, defined, 447
spooler, defined, 447
spot color
    preparation, 359-370
    tints, 368
    vs. process color, 358-359
spreadsheet as source of text, 194-198
standards for text preparation, 182-184
stat, defined, 447
stem, defined, 447
steps
    list, 35-36, 258, 288
    mapped to book, 255
    production, 33-47
    repeating, 144-145
strike-on typesetting, defined, 447
stripping, 395-396
style of type, 78-79, 447
style sheet, author's, 182-184
style sheets, 155, 203-204, 447
subdirectory, defined, 447
subscript, defined, 447

subtractive color mixing, 385
subtractive primaries, 372
supercase, defined, 447
superior, defined, 447
superscript, defined, 447
swash characters, defined, 447
swatchbooks, 364-365
symbol typefaces, 103-104
symbols, 74
    coding for, 205-207
    repeated elements, 249
synchronous, defined, 447
syntax, defined, 447
system
    capabilities, 136-138
    date and time, 269
    program, defined, 447
    software, defined, 447

T

tab, 183, 189-191, 200, 447
    key, defined, 447
    marker, defined, 447
    settings, 191-192
    use of, 99
tables, 262-263
    tabular, 174-176
tablets, graphics, 214
tabloid pages, 132, 255-258, 272-273
    templates for, 164-169
tabular material, 99, 235, 447
tail, defined, 447
take, defined, 447
target printer, 154, 279
team, gathering, 38
telecommunication, 18, 188-189, 447
teleprocessing, defined, 447
template
    benefits, 144-146
    components, 146-161, 279-286
    defined, 447
    graphics, 162-163, 244-250
    page layout, 270-279
    pages, 279
    systems, 143-164
    testing, 163-164

INDEX

templates, number of, 160
    reports, 169-171
terminal, defined, 448
test printing, 306
testing, templates, 163-164
text
    as graphic logo, 294
    cleanup, 189-191
    copyfitting, 208
    defined, 448
    dropped out of background, 351
    elements, 155
    file, defined, 448
    file conversion, 188-189
    file size, 265-268
    formats, 155
    formatting, 188-198, 191-192, 198-207, 291
    formatting, mail merge, 195
    importing, 292
    length and leading, 121
    length, estimating, 116-122
    line length, 106-107
    preparation, 181-211, 188-198
    preparation, guidelines, 41
    processing, 42, 181-211
    typing, 291
    width, 149
    wrap, 296, 448
text-only formats, 196, 448
texture mapping, 239
thermal printer, defined, 448
thin space, defined, 448
third-generation typesetter, defined, 448
thumbnail, defined, 448
thumbnails, 165, 257-258, 287, 309
tight line, defined, 448
tiling, 272-273, 310-311
Times
    alternatives to, 100-101
    history of, 100
tinted type, 348-351
titles, kerning, 111-113
toggle switch, defined, 448
tones, defined, 448
track, defined, 448
tracking, defined, 448

trade secrets, 64
trademarks, 63
translation table, defined, 448
transparencies, 174-176
    color, 386-388
    overheads, 96
traps, 365-368
trim size, 146-148
triplex, defined, 448
turnaround, defined, 448
turnkey, defined, 448
type casting, 116-122
    reference book, 118-119
type gauge, 118-119
type quality, 88
type sample sheet, 92
type specification process, 89-116
    marked, 201
type-ahead buffer, defined, 448
typeface, 4, 74-76, 448
typefaces
    characteristics of, 97-104
    downloadable, 79
    mixing, 104-105
    names, 98
    number of, 77, 86, 92-93, 104-105, 135, 136-138
    selection of, 97-104
typeset masters, 319-323
typesetter, role of, 31
typesetter, 216, 448
typesetting, 8, 44-45
    codes, 187-188, 198-207, 202-203
    equipment, 17
    text, 198-207
typestyle, defined, 448
typewriter faces, 99-100
typing text, 181-211, 182-188, 291
    guidelines, 41
typo, defined, 448
typographic color, defined, 449
typographic design, 89-116
typography, 71-122, 449
    basic principles, 92-97
    terms defined, 72-82

U

underscores, use of, 94
unit of measure, 150, 283
uppercase, defined, 449

V

vector graphics, 222-224, 449
veloxes, 336-337
vertical justification, 129-130, 449
video display terminal, defined, 449
video images, copyright, 57
vortex, defined, 449

W

web, defined, 449
web press, 169, 411-412
weight, defined, 449
    of typeface, 76
    of paper, 415
well format, 167
white lines, caution, 228
white space, 130-132, 173, 449
    reduction, defined, 449
white type, 293
widow, defined, 449
widows and orphans, 210
window, defined, 449
wire printer, defined, 449
word counts, 116-122
word processing, 12, 42, 181-211, 200, 449

word space, defined, 449
word spacing, 304
    proofing for, 210
word wrap, 183, 449
work areas, 156-157
work made for hire, 54
    agreement, 66
workgroups, 18, 268
workstation, defined, 449
wrap, defined, 449
wraparound, defined, 449
wrapping text around graphics, 296
write-protect, defined, 449
writing, 39-40
WYSIWYG, 6, 176, 214, 449

X

X coordinate, defined, 449
x-height, 74, 450
X-ON/X-OFF, defined, 450
Xerographic printer, defined, 450
Xerography, defined, 450

Y

Y coordinate, defined, 450
yellow, defined, 450

Z

zero point, 151, 284